The
Media Studies Reader

The
Media Studies Reader

Edited by

Tim O'Sullivan

Reader in Media Education and Cultural Studies, School of Humanities, De Montfort University, Leicester, UK

and

Yvonne Jewkes

Associate lecturer in Media and Cultural Studies, Open University, UK

ARNOLD

A member of the Hodder Headline Group
LONDON • NEW YORK • SYDNEY • AUCKLAND

First published in Great Britain in 1997 by
Arnold, a member of the Hodder Headline Group
338 Euston Road, London NW1 3BH

Copublished in the United States of America by
Oxford University Press Inc.,
198 Madison Avenue, New York, NY 10016

British Library Cataloguing in Publication Data
A catalogue record for this book is available from the British Library

Library of Congress Cataloging-in-Publication Data
A catalog record for this book is available from the Library of Congress

ISBN 0 340 645474 (Pb)
ISBN 0 340 645261 (Hb)

2 3 4 5 6 7 8 9 10

Typeset by Saxon Graphics Ltd., Derby
Printed and bound in Great Britain by J. W. Arrowsmith Ltd, Bristol

Contents

Acknowledgements

The authors would like to thank Stephen Barnard, Pam Birley, Rinella Cere, Steve Chibnall, Simon Cross, Joyce Gardiner, Jane Hammond-Foster, Shaun Moores, Marcia Ricketts, Lesley Riddle, Judith Smith, Paul Wells, Terry Willits, David Wright and the copyright holders listed below.

ESTHER ADAMS: Selection from *Television and the North* by Esther Adams. Copyright © 1985 Esther Adams. Reprinted by permission of Department of Cultural Studies, University of Birmingham

MARTIN BARKER: Selection from 'The Lost World of Stereotypes' from *Comics: Ideology, Power and the Critics* by Martin Barker. Copyright © 1989 Martin Barker. Reprinted by permission of Manchester University Press

STEPHEN BARNARD: Selection from *On the Radio: Music Radio in Britain* by Stephen Barnard. Copyright © 1989 Stephen Barnard. Reprinted by permission of Open University Press

ROGER BOLTON: Selection from 'The Problems of Making Political Television: A Practitioner's Perspective' by Roger Bolton from *Communicating Politics* edited by P. Golding, G. Murdock, and P. Schlesinger. Copyright © 1986 Roger Bolton. Reprinted by permission of Pinter Publishers, 125 Strand, London, England

HADLEY CANTRIL: 'The Invasion from Mars' from *Readings in Social Psychology* edited by Newcomb, Hartley, *et al.*, published by Henry Holt & Co., New York, 1947, a summary from *The Invasion from Mars* by Hadley Cantril, Hazel Gaudet and Herta Herzog. Copyright © 1940/1968. Renewed by Princeton University Press. Reprinted by permission of Princeton University Press

IAN CONNELL and GEOFF HURD: 'Higher Education, Training and the Cultural Industries: A Working Partnership' by Ian Connell and Geoff Hurd. Copyright © 1988 Ian Connell and Geoff Hurd. Reprinted by permission of the Authors

JOHN CORNER: 'Media Studies and the "Knowledge Problem"' from *Screen* 36(2), Summer 1995. Copyright © 1995 John Corner. Reprinted by permission of Oxford University Press

MARJORIE FERGUSON: Selection from *Forever Feminine* by Marjorie Ferguson, published by Heinemann Educational Books, London. Copyright © 1983 Marjorie Ferguson. Reprinted by permission of the Author

PETER GOLDING: Selection from 'The Missing Dimensions' by Peter Golding from *Mass Media and Social Change* edited by E. Katz and T. Szecsko. Copyright © 1981 Peter Golding. Reprinted by permission of Sage Publications Ltd, London

A. GOODWIN: 'Riding with Ambulances: Television and Its Uses' by A. Goodwin from *Sight and Sound* 3(1). Copyright © 1993 A. Goodwin. Reprinted by permission of *Sight and Sound* magazine, London

ANN GRAY: Selection from *Video Playtime* by Ann Gray. Copyright © 1992 Ann Gray. Reprinted by permission of Routledge, London

ANNE KARPF: 'Crippling Images' in *Doctoring the Media* by Anne Karpf. Copyright © 1988 Anne Karpf. Reprinted by permission of Routledge, London

PETER KEIGHRON: 'Video Diaries: What's up Doc?' by Peter Keighron from *Sight and Sound* 3(10). Copyright © 1993 Peter Keighron. Reprinted by permission of *Sight and Sound* magazine, London

RICHARD KILBORN: Selection from *Television Soaps* by Richard Kilborn. Copyright © 1992 Richard Kilborn. Reprinted by permission of Batsford Ltd, London

JOHN LANGER: Selection from 'Television's "Personality System"' by John Langer from *Media, Culture and Society* 4, 1981. Copyright © 1981 John Langer. Reprinted by permission of Sage Publications Ltd, London.

JUSTIN LEWIS: Selection from 'The Power of Popular Television: The Case of *Cosby*' from *The Ideological Octopus: An Exploration of Television and its Audience* by Justin Lewis. Copyright © 1991 Justin Lewis. Reprinted by permission of Routledge Inc., New York

DAVID LYON: Selection from *The Information Society: Issues and Illusions* by David Lyon, published by Polity Press, Cambridge. Copyright © 1988 David Lyon. Reprinted by permission of Blackwell Publishers, Oxford

JOSHUA MEYROWITZ: Selection from *No Sense of Place: The Impact of Electronic Media on Social Behaviour* by Joshua Meyrowitz. Copyright © 1985 Joshua Meyrowitz. Reprinted by permission of Oxford University Press Inc.

SHAUN MOORES: Selection from *Interpreting Audiences* by Shaun Moores. Copyright © 1993 Shaun Moores. Reprinted by permission of Sage Publications Ltd, London

DAVID MORLEY: Selection from *Television, Audiences and Cultural Studies* by David Morley. Copyright © 1992 David Morley. Reprinted by permission of Routledge, London

GRAHAM MURDOCK: Selection from 'Communications and the Constitution of Modernity' by Graham Murdock from *Media, Culture and Society* 15, 1993. Copyright © 1993 Graham Murdock. Reprinted by permission of Sage Publications Ltd, London

GRAHAM MURDOCK and ROBIN MCCRON: Selection from 'The Television and Delinquency Debate' in *Screen Education* 30, 1979. Copyright © 1979 Graham Murdock and Robin McCron. Reprinted by permission of Screen, The John Logie Baird Centre, Glasgow

KEITH NEGUS: Selection from *Producing Pop: Culture and Conflict in the Popular Music Industry* by Keith Negus. Copyright © 1994 Keith Negus. Reprinted by permission of Arnold Publishers, London

HUGH O'DONNELL: 'Mapping the Mythical: A Geopolitics of National Sporting Stereotypes' by Hugh O'Donnell from *Discourse and Society* 5(3), 1994. Copyright © 1994 Hugh O'Donnell. Reprinted by permission of Sage Publications Ltd, London

TESSA PERKINS: Selection from 'Rethinking Stereotypes' by Tessa Perkins from *Ideology and Cultural Production* edited by Michele Barratt, *et al.* Copyright © 1979 Tessa Perkins. Reprinted by permission of Croom Helm, London

JULIAN PETLEY: 'In Defence of "Video Nasties"' by Julian Petley from *British Journalism Review* 5(3), 1994. Copyright © 1994 Julian Petley. Reprinted by permission of John Libbey Media, Luton

MARK PURSEHOUSE: Selection from 'Looking at *The Sun*: Into the Nineties with a Tabloid and its Readers' by Mark Pursehouse from *Cultural Studies from Birmingham* 1. Copyright © 1991 Mark Pursehouse. Reprinted by permission of Department of Cultural Studies, University of Birmingham

T. H. QUALTER: 'The Social Role of Advertising' from *Advertising and Democracy in the Mass Age* by T. H. Qualter. Copyright © 1991 T. H. Qualter. Reprinted by permission of Macmillan Ltd, London, and St Martin's Press Inc., New York

HOWARD RHEINGOLD: Selection from *The Virtual Community: Surfing the Internet* by Howard Rheingold, published by Minerva, London. Copyright © 1994 Howard Rheingold. Reprinted by permission of Reed Consumer Books Ltd, and Abner Stein Ltd, New York

PADDY SCANNELL: Selection from 'Public Service Broadcasting and Modern Public Life' by Paddy Scannell from *Media, Culture and Society* 11, 1989. Copyright © 1989 Paddy Scannell. Reprinted by permission of Sage Publications Ltd, London

HERBERT SCHILLER: Selection from 'Not Yet the Post-Imperialist Era' by Herbert Schiller from *Critical Studies in Mass Communication* 8, 1991. Copyright © 1991 Herbert Schiller. Reprinted by permission of *Critical Studies in Mass Communication*, The Speech Communication Association, Canada

NICK STEVENSON: Selection from 'Critical Perspectives within Audience Research' from *Understanding Media Cultures* by Nick Stevenson. Copyright © 1995 Nick Stevenson. Reprinted by permission of Sage Publications Ltd, London

DOMINIC STRINATI: 'Postmodernism and Popular Cultu'
Review 1(4), 1992. Copyright © 1992 Dominic Strinati. Re_ᵽ
mission of Philip Allen Publishers Ltd.

JOHN B. THOMPSON: 'Mass Communication and Modern Cɯ
Contribution to a Critical Theory of Ideology' from Sociology 22(3), 198ɕ
Reprinted by permission of Cambridge University Press

MICHAEL TRACEY: Selection from 'The Poisoned Chalice? International
Television and the Idea of Dominance' by Michael Tracey from Daedalus,
from the issue entitled The Moving Image, 114(4), Fall 1985. Copyright ©
1985 Michael Tracey. Reprinted by permission of Daedalus, Journal of the
American Academy of Arts and Sciences, Cambridge, USA

ANDREW TUDOR: Selection from 'On Alcohol and the Mystique of Media
Effects' by Andrew Tudor from Images of Alcoholism edited by J. Cook and
M. Lewington, published by British Film Institute, London. Copyright ©
1979 Andrew Tudor. Reprinted by permission of the Author

JANET WASKO: Selection from Hollywood in the Information Age by Janet
Wasko. Copyright © 1994 Janet Wasko. Reprinted by permission of Polity
Press, Cambridge, and University of Texas Press

SIMON WATNEY: Selection from 'Policing Desire: Pornography, Aids and
the Media' by Simon Watney. Copyright © 1989 Simon Watney. Reprinted
by permission of Cassell, London

RAYMOND WILLIAMS: Selection from Culture and Society 1780–1950 by
Raymond Williams. Copyright © 1961 Raymond Williams. Reprinted by
permission of Random House UK

Introduction

One of the defining characteristics of modern social and cultural life has involved living and learning to live in a culture of mediation. From the late nineteenth century onwards, Western and other cultures have become increasingly reliant upon and saturated with forms of mass communicated information and entertainment. The rise of the popular press and publishing industries, the expansion of film, radio, advertising and television have transformed and extended the experience of everyday life and redefined crucial aspects of the relationships between the public and the private spheres. In the process, our senses of identity – who we think we are – and of immediate situation – where we think we are – have become powerfully linked with forms of culture which are mediated from beyond the geographical and temporal confines of the everyday and the personal. As one writer has recently argued, the *mediascapes* of modern life have become increasingly global in their operation and character.[1]

The 'mass' media (and, as Raymond Williams cautioned more than 30 years ago, it is important to use the prefix 'mass' with care[2]) have not only expanded and developed as a prerequisite for modernity, but have also gained an equivocal reputation and been defined as problems for modern times. They have recurrently sparked debates which have centred on three, often linked, levels of concern: first, the power and influence of the media as *public* institutions charged with the responsibilities of making sense of the world for their audiences, readers and viewers; second, the assumed or claimed impact of forms of media consumption and reception on the *private* sphere; third, a particular focus on the media's role in the production and politics of forms of *popular* culture and their claimed consequences. From their early days, modern media have been regarded with suspicion and have themselves become the central figures in a series of cyclical moral panics about what has been perceived as their increasingly pervasive and intrusive presence.

The structure of much modern popular debate about the media was established in the early part of the twentieth century when they seemed to encapsulate perfectly aspects of the 'mass society' which was perceived to be emerging as the condition of modern times. On the one hand, especially in the forms of film and broadcasting propaganda, the new media seemed capable of mass manipulation, of exercising new sorts of power and control over vulnerable, atomised populations, uprooted and estranged from their traditional communities and ways of life. On the other, the appearance and the success of new, twentieth century, 'mass' mediated cultural forms was also taken by critics to indicate a profound challenge to cultural values, as the popular was perceived to threaten established definitions and boundaries of 'the good', 'the civilised' and 'the cultured' in a number of ways. At the heart of these and related concerns lies a view of the modern media as powerful institutions which have become increasingly technologised and which are capable of direct 'effects' on their audiences and users. Isolated acts and general levels of violence, criminality, promiscuity and many other negative social developments have been recurrently and frequently attributed to the media. The tendency to isolate the media from their social and commercial contexts and to cast 'them' as causal agencies has implicitly underpinned a great deal of modern thought, speculation and popular debate.

More recent postmodern accounts of the media have sought to break out of these ways of thinking, emphasising the overwhelming centrality of modern communication systems and technologies and proclaiming the triumph of the mediated and the simulated, of the relative over the absolute. In such a scenario, the media emerge as part cause, part symptom of the postmodern condition.

If the media have been defined as a problematic focus for a range of political and cultural commentators in this century, they have also endured a troubled relationship with formal education. The questions of how, why and whether to include the media as objects within educational curricula have resulted in a number of educational responses, largely in the postwar period. Often these have oscillated between arguments about making available certain kinds of critical awareness of the media, and an emphasis upon teaching and learning about participation and practice in the production of media output. The first of these positions stresses the necessity for a kind of informed and *critical media literacy*, in touch with (post)modern times and enabling full and critical participation in contemporary media culture. Stuart Hall, for instance, has stated this case forcefully on a number of occasions, arguing that Media and Cultural Studies are profoundly logical subjects for study given the expanding nature of contemporary media and cultural industries and their centrality within social and political process. Given this state of affairs, the subjects provide 'what you need to know' in order to live in the postmodern world. The second type of response advances a slightly different case which has foregrounded forms of media education for practice – for practical involvement, vocational preparation and creative relevance. The history of media education and of the fairly recent development of Media Studies as a defined subject area has developed around and between these two poles. In recent years, however, the expansion of educational provision in Media Studies and related subjects, including Cultural and Communication Studies, has itself become an object of media attention, especially in Britain.

Much of this has simply and depressingly replayed older elitist or profoundly anti-intellectual anxieties about the place, position and value of the study of popular forms which have accompanied Media Studies from its earliest days. Attempts to take popular culture seriously have always encountered resistance, a dismissive 'bias' against the idea that they could constitute a valid subject for enquiry in their own right as opposed to within the narrow confines of particular definitions of vocational relevance. However, much of the recent wave of this criticism has undoubtedly been prompted, if not reignited, by the sheer and rapid growth in the numbers of students applying for, studying on and graduating from such courses.

It is for these students, those on 'A' level or undergraduate courses in Media Studies and other related areas, that this reader has been designed. Its principal aim is to introduce the key dimensions and debates which characterise the field and act as a springboard for further study. What follows is the result of a series of often difficult and demanding choices. We have organised the readings into five main sections. Underlying this organisation is a thematic sequence which commences with some broad, contextualising extracts which foreground the relationships between 'The Media and Modern Life'. This is followed by sections on 'Stereotypes and Representations', 'Audiences and Reception', 'Producers and Production' and finally 'Global Media and New Media'. While we have used this sequence to organise the readings, interest or other factors may lead you to use them out of their sequential order. Each section is prefaced with a short introductory overview, each reading is also contextualised and accompanied by a series of questions, designed to provide a basis for discussion or reflection, and these are in turn complemented by suggestions for further reading.

If you have any comments or suggestions about the reader, please contact us via the publishers.

Tim O'Sullivan, Yvonne Jewkes
October 1996

Notes

1. A. Appadurai, 'Disjuncture and Difference in the Global Cultural Economy', *Theory, Culture and Society*, 7 (1990), pp. 295–310. See also for recent useful discussion J.B. Thompson, *The Media and Modernity* (Cambridge, Polity Press, 1996).
2. See Section 1, Reading 2.

Section 1

The Media and Modern Life

The six readings which follow consider the modern, especially postwar, growth and development of electronic media. In various ways, the readings assess how radio, television and the emerging new media technologies fit into the economic, political and cultural systems of modern life in both its public and private spheres. In doing so, they offer a fairly cohesive definition of 'modernity' and demonstrate how media institutions and products have been implicated in the ideological structures and struggles which, over the last 50 years have accompanied countless scientific and technological innovations, unprecedented political upheaval across the globe and a shift, in Western societies, from industrialisation and manufacturing-based economies to a widespread growth in leisure and consumerism.

The first reading, by **Hadley Cantril**, concerns public reaction to the famous 1938 radio drama based on H. G. Wells' *War of the Worlds*, which was accordant with 'mass society' theories and beliefs about the potentially harmful effects of the media at that particularly turbulent period in history. The subsequent readings by **Raymond Williams** and **John B. Thompson** explore further the notion of 'mass' – mass media, mass communication and so on – and analyse the development of media as important ideological agencies in the face of competing social and political forces. **Joshua Meyrowitz** (reading 4) extends the discussion of the increasingly important role that media and communications have come to play in public and in private, and focuses attention on the ways in which the realms of subjective, everyday experience are expanded and mediated by modern communication systems. One of the main tenets of **Graham Murdock's** argument (reading 5) is that a central concern in the study of media and communications systems must, as a result, involve an understanding of their relations to power and politics. Finally **Paddy Scannell** focuses attention on the role of broadcasting in shaping national cultures and constructing and mediating a sense of national life. His concern lies in understanding the centrality of forms of public broadcasting, as embodied in institutions such as the BBC, and their contributions to modern, democratic forms of social life.

These introductory readings also pose important questions about the nature of culture in modern society, the representation by media of social groups and the development of education – including the rise of Media Studies as a subject for academic study – all of which form a focus for discussion in later extracts. Thus, Section 1 introduces many of the principal discourses, debates and theoretical concerns which have characterised the study of the media in the modern era and as such provides a useful starting point for many of the key concepts and arguments that are picked up and explored in subsequent sections of the book.

1

The Invasion from Mars
Hadley Cantril

Originally published as *The invasion from Mars: a study in the psychology of panic*, with H. Gaudet and H. Herzog. (Princeton University Press 1940). This edited selection is taken from a short summary of the full study, in W. Schramm and D. F. Roberts (eds.), *The processes and effects of mass communication* (University of Illinois Press 1954)

Based on an early combination of an extraordinary 'media event' and its detailed study which occurred in America just prior to the Second World War, this first reading has become a 'classic' reference and metaphor for much thinking about the media in the modern period. It focuses on public reaction to a radio drama adaptation of H. G. Wells' *War of the Worlds* broadcast to American audiences on Hallowe'en Night in October 1938. A great many listeners reacted to the play as if it were a *real* report of invading creatures from Mars, radio fiction was understood as radio fact and panic outbreaks ensued on a significant scale. The event encapsulates the popularly held view of the widespread intrusive and *persuasive power* of the modern media to cause and trigger mass outbreaks of usually negative social consequence and psychological effect. Like the invading Martians with their ray guns and poisonous gases, the media have often been perceived as alien invaders, dangerous and life-threatening in their impact on established forms of social and cultural life.

What follows is an extract which deals with some of the reports of people who misperceived the fictional performance and the recorded versions of their various and alarmed responses. On the face of it, the story of 'the invasion from Mars' would seem to embody the crude *hypodermic syringe model* of media effects, namely a singular, immediate and dramatic effect – in this case, mass panic – caused by the broadcast. In fact, as the research by Cantril and his associates demonstrates, explaining the reactions to the broadcast involves consideration of a complex series of social, political and psychological factors. It was the life-like quality of the broadcast, interacting with the social and cultural situation of some listeners in late 1930s America, which brought about the scare.

On the evening of October 30, 1938, thousands of Americans became panic-stricken by a broadcast purported to describe an invasion of Martians which threatened our whole civilization. Probably never before have so many people in all walks of life and in all parts of the country become so suddenly and so intensely disturbed as they did on this night.

Such rare occurrences provide opportunities for the social scientist to study mass behavior. They must be exploited when they come. Although the social scientist unfortunately cannot usually predict such situations and have his tools of investigation ready to analyze the phenomenon while it is still on the wing, he can begin his work before the effects of the crisis are over and memories are blurred. The situation created by the broadcast was one which shows us how the common man reacts in a time of stress and strain. It gives us insights into his intelligence, his anxieties, and his needs, which we could never get by tests or strictly experimental studies. The panic situation we have investigated had all the flavor of everyday life and, at the same time, provided a semi-experimental condition for research. In spite of the unique conditions giving rise to this particular panic, the writer has attempted to indicate throughout the study the pattern of the circumstances which, from a psychological point of view, might make this the prototype of any panic.

The fact that this panic was created as a result of a radio broadcast is today no mere circumstance. The importance of radio's role in current national and international affairs is too well known to be recounted here. By its very nature radio is the medium par excellence for informing all segments of a population of current happenings, for arousing in them a common sense of fear or joy; and for exciting them to similar reactions directed toward a single objective.

Because the social phenomenon in question was so complex, several methods were employed to seek out different answers and to compare results obtained by one method with those obtained by another. Much of our information was derived from detailed interviews of 135 persons. Over 100 of these persons were selected because they were known to have been upset by the broadcast.

Long before the broadcast had ended, people all over the United States were praying, crying, fleeing frantically to escape death from the Martians. Some ran to rescue loved ones. Others telephoned farewells or warnings, hurried to inform neighbors, sought information from newspapers or radio stations, summoned ambulances and police cars. At least six million people heard the broadcast. At least a million of them were frightened or disturbed.

For weeks after the broadcast, newspapers carried human-interest stories relating the shock and terror of local citizens. Men and women throughout the country could have described their feelings and reactions on that fateful evening. Our own interviewers and correspondents gathered hundreds of accounts. A few of these selected almost at random will give us a glimpse of the excitement. Let the people speak for themselves.

'I knew it was something terrible and I was frightened,' said Mrs. Ferguson, a northern New Jersey housewife, to the inquiring interviewer. 'But I didn't know just what it was. I couldn't make myself believe it was the end of the world. I've always heard that when the world would come to an end, it would come so fast nobody would know – so why should God get in touch with this announcer? When they told us what road to take and get up over the hills and the children began to cry, the family decided to go out. We took blankets and my grand-daughter wanted to take the cat and the canary. We were outside the garage when the neighbor's boy came back and told us it was a play.'

[...]

Archie Burbank, a filling station operator in Newark, described his reactions. 'My girl friend and I stayed in the car for a while, just driving around. Then we followed the lead of a friend. All of us ran into a grocery store and asked the man if we could go into his cellar. He said, "What's the matter? Are you trying to ruin my business?" So he chased us out. A crowd collected. We rushed to an apartment house and asked the man in the apartment to let us in his cellar. He said, "I don't have any cellar! Get away!" Then people started to rush out of the apartment house all undressed. We got into the car and listened some more. Suddenly, the announcer was gassed, the station went dead so we tried another station but nothing would come on. Then we went to a gas station and filled up our tank in preparation for just riding as far as we could. The gas station man didn't know anything about it. Then one friend, male, decided he would call up the *Newark Evening News*. He found out it was a play. We listened to the rest of the play and then went dancing.'

Mrs. Joslin, who lives in a poor section of a large eastern city and whose husband is a day laborer, said, 'I was terribly frightened. I wanted to pack and take my child in my arms, gather up my friends, and get in the car and just go north as far as we could. But what I did was just set by one window, prayin', listenin', and scared stiff and my husband by the other snifflin' and lookin' out to see if people were runnin'. Then when the announcer said "evacuate the city," I ran and called my boarder and started with my child to rush down the stairs, not waitin' to ketch my hat or anything. When I got to the foot of the stairs I just couldn't get out, I don't know why. Meantime my husband he tried other stations and found them still runnin'. He couldn't smell any gas or see people runnin', so he called me back and told me it was just a play. So I set down, still ready to go at any minute till I heard Orson Welles say, "Folks, I hope we ain't alarmed you. This is just a play!" Then, I just set!'

If we are to explain the reaction, then, we must answer two basic questions: Why did this broadcast frighten some people when other fantastic broadcasts do not? And why did this broadcast frighten some people but not others? An answer to the first question must be sought in the characteristics of this particular program which aroused false standards of judgment in so many listeners.

No one reading the script can deny that the broadcast was so realistic for the first few minutes that it was almost credible to even relatively sophisticated and well-informed listeners. The sheer dramatic excellence of the broadcast must not be overlooked. This unusual realism of the performance may be attributed to the fact that the early parts of the broadcast fell within the existing standards of judgment of the listeners.

A large proportion of listeners, particularly those in the lower income and educational brackets, have grown to rely more on the radio than on the newspapers for their news. Almost all of the listeners, who had been frightened and who were interviewed, mentioned somewhere during the course of their retrospections the confidence they had in radio and their expectation that it would be used for such important announcements. A few of their comments indicate their attitudes:

'We have so much *faith in broadcasting*. In a crisis it has to reach all people. That's what radio is here for.'

'The announcer would not say if it was not true. *They always quote if something is a play*.'

As in many situations where events and ideas are so complicated or far removed from one's own immediate everyday experience that only the expert can really understand them, here, too, the layman was forced to rely on the expert for his interpretation.

The logical 'expert' in this instance was the astronomer. Those mentioned (all fictitious) were Professor Farrell of the Mount Jennings Observatory of Chicago, Professor Pierson of the Princeton Observatory, Professor Morse of MacMillan University in Toronto, Professor Indellkoffer of the California Astronomical Society and 'astronomers and scientific bodies' in England, France, and Germany. Professor Richard Pierson (Orson Welles) was the chief character in the drama.

When the situation called for organized defense and action the expert was once more brought in. General Montgomery Smith, commander of the state militia at Trenton, Mr. Harry McDonald, vice-president of the Red Cross, Captain Lansing of the Signal Corps, and finally the Secretary of the Interior described the situation, gave orders for evacuation and attack, or urged every man to do his duty.

This dramatic technique had its effect.

'I believed the broadcast *as soon as I heard the professor from Princeton* and the officials in Washington.'

'I knew it was an awfully dangerous situation *when all those military men were there and the Secretary of State spoke*.'

The realistic nature of the broadcast was further enhanced by descriptions of particular occurrences that listeners could readily imagine. Liberal use was made of the colloquial expressions to be expected on such an occasion. The gas was 'a sort of yellowish-green'; the cop warned, 'One side, there. Keep back, I tell you'; a voice shouts, 'The darn thing's unscrewing.' An example of the specificity of detail is the announcement of Brigadier General Montgomery Smith: 'I have been requested by the Governor of New Jersey to place the counties of Mercer and Middlesex as far west as Princeton, and east to Jamesburg, under martial law. No one will be permitted to enter this area except by special pass issued by state or military authorities. Four companies of state militia are proceeding from Trenton to Grovers Mill and will aid in the evacuation of homes within the range of military operations.'

The events reported proceeded from the relatively credible to the highly incredible. The first announcements were more or less believable, although unusual to be sure. First there is an 'atmospheric disturbance,' then 'explosions of incandescent gas.' A scientist then reports that his seismograph has registered a shock of earthquake intensity. This is followed by the discovery of a meteorite that has splintered nearby trees in its fall. So far so good.

But as the less credible bits of the story begin to enter, the clever dramatist also indicates that he, too, has difficulty in believing what he sees. When we learn that the object is no meteorite but a metal casing, we are also told that the whole picture is 'a strange scene like something out of a modern Arabian Nights,' 'fantastic,' that the 'more daring souls are venturing near.' Before we are informed that the end of the casing is beginning to unscrew, we experience the announcer's own astonishment: 'Ladies and gentlemen, this is terrific!' When the top is off he says, 'This is the most terrifying thing I have ever witnessed.... This is the most extraordinary experience. I can't find words....'

The bewilderment of the listener is shared by the eye-witness. When the scientist is himself puzzled, the layman recognizes the extraordinary intelligence of the strange creatures. No explanation of the event can be provided. The resignation and hopelessness of the Secretary of the Interior, counseling us to 'place our faith in God,' provides no effective guide for action.

In spite of the realism of the broadcast, it would seem highly unlikely that any listener would take it seriously had he heard the announcements that were clearly made at the beginning of the hour. He might then have been excited, even frightened. But it would be an excitement based on the dramatic realism of the program. There would not be the intense feeling of personal involvement. He would know that the events were happening 'out there' in the studio, not 'right here' in his own state or his own county. In one instance a 'correct' (aesthetically detached or dramatic) standard of judgment would be used by the listener to interpret events, in another instance a 'false' (realistic or news) standard of judgment would be employed. Tuning in late was a very essential condition for the arousal of a false standard of judgment. To be sure, many people recognized the broadcast as a play even though they tuned in late. It is important to raise and to answer the question of how anyone who tuned in at the beginning could have mistaken the clearly introduced play for a news broadcast. Analysis of these cases reveals two main reasons why such a misinterpretation arose. In the first place, many people who tuned in to hear a play by the Mercury Theatre thought the regular dramatic program had been interrupted to give special news bulletins. The technique was not a new one after their experience with radio reporting of the war crisis in September, 1938. The other major reason for the misunderstanding is the widespread habit of not paying attention to the first announcements of a program. Some people do not listen attentively to their radios until they are aware that something of particular interest is being broadcast.

Tuning in late was very decisive in determining whether or not the listener would follow the program as a play or as a news report. For the story of the Martian invasion was so realistic that misinterpretation was apt to arise without proper warning signals.

In spite of the fact that many persons tuned in late to hear this very realistic broadcast, by no means all of them believed it was news. And not all of those who thought the invasion was upon them behaved the same way in the face of danger. Before we can understand the reasons for the varying behavior, the reactions must be arranged in some significant grouping. Otherwise no fruitful conceptualization is possible.

Classifying the listeners

1. Those who checked the internal evidence of the broadcast

The persons in this category were those who did not remain frightened throughout the whole broadcast because they were able to discern that the program was fictitious. Some realized that the reports must be false because they sounded so much like certain fiction literature they were accustomed to.

'At first I was very interested in the fall of the meteor. It isn't often that they find a big one just when it falls. But *when it started to unscrew and monsters came out, I said to myself, "They've taken one of those Amazing Stories and are acting it out."* It just couldn't be real. It was just like some of the stories I read in *Amazing Stories* but it was even more exciting.'

2. Those who checked the broadcast against other information and learned that it was a play

These listeners tried to orient themselves for the same reasons as those in the first group – they were suspicious of the 'news' they were getting. Some simply thought the reports were too fantastic to believe; others detected the incredible speeds revealed; while a few listeners checked the program just because it seemed the reasonable thing to do. Their method of verifying their hunches was to compare the news on the program to some other information.

'I tuned in and heard that a meteor had fallen. Then when they talked about monsters, I thought something was wrong. *So I looked in the newspaper* to see what program was supposed to be on and discovered it was only a play.'

3. Those who tried to check the program against other information but who, for various reasons, continued to believe the broadcast was an authentic news report

Two characteristic differences separated the people in this group from those who made successful checks. In the first place, it was difficult to determine from the interviews just why these people wanted to check anyway. They did not seem to be seeking evidence to test the authenticity of the reports. They appeared, rather, to be frightened souls trying to find out whether or not they were yet in any personal danger. In the second place, the type of checking behavior they used was singularly ineffective and unreliable. The most frequent method employed by almost two-thirds of this group was to look out the window or go outdoors. Several of them telephoned their friends or ran to consult their neighbors.

There are several reasons why the checks made by these persons were ineffectual. For some of them, the new information obtained only verified the interpretation which their already fixed standard of judgment provided.

'I looked out of the window and everything looked the same as usual *so I thought it hadn't reached our section yet.*'

'We looked out of the window and Wyoming Avenue was black with cars. *People were rushing away, I figured.*'

'No cars came down my street. "Traffic is jammed on account of the roads being destroyed," I thought.'

4. Those who made no attempt to check the broadcast or the event

It is usually more difficult to discover why a person did *not* do something than why he did. Consequently it is more difficult for us to explain why people in this group did not attempt to verify the news or look for signs of the Martians in their vicinity than it was to determine why those who attempted unsuccessful checks displayed their aimless behavior. Over half of the people in this group were so frightened that they either stopped listening, ran around in a frenzy, or exhibited behavior that can only be described as paralyzed.

Some of them reported that they were so frightened they never thought of checking.

'We were so intent upon listening that we didn't have enough sense to try other hook-ups—*we were just so frightened.*'

Others adopted an attitude of complete resignation. For them any attempt to check up, like any other behavior, appeared senseless.

'I was writing a history theme. The girl from upstairs came and made me go up to her place. Everybody was so excited I felt as if I was going crazy and kept on saying, "What can we do, *what difference does it make* whether we die sooner or later?" We were holding each other. Everything seemed unimportant in the face of death. I was afraid to die, just kept on listening.'

Some felt that in view of the crisis situation, action was demanded. A few prepared immediately for their escape or for death.

'I couldn't stand it so I turned it off. I don't remember when, but everything was coming closer. My husband wanted to put it back on but I told him *we'd better do something instead of just listen*, so we started to pack.'

Some listeners interpreted the situation in such a way that they were not interested in making a check-up. In a few instances the individual tuned in so late that he missed the most incredible parts of the program and was only aware of the fact that some kind of conflict was being waged.

'I was in my drugstore and my brother phoned and said, "Turn the radio on, a meteor has just fallen." We did and heard gas was coming up South Street. There were a few customers and *we all began wondering where it could come from.* I was worried about the gas, it was spreading so rapidly but I was puzzled as to what was actually happening, when I heard airplanes I thought another country was attacking us.'

Why the panic?

A variety of influences and conditions are related to the panic resulting from this particular broadcast. We have found no single observable variable consistently related to the reaction, although a lack of critical ability seemed particularly conducive to fear in a large proportion of the population. Personality characteristics made some people especially susceptible to belief and fright; the influence of others in the immediate environment caused a few listeners to react inappropriately. The psychological pattern revealed by these and other influences must be shown if we are to understand the situation as a whole and not have to resort exclusively to the understanding of single, isolated cases.

Why the suggestion was or was not believed

What is most inconceivable and therefore especially interesting psychologically is why so many people did not do something to verify the information they were receiving from their loudspeakers. The failure to do this accounts for the persistence of the fright. To understand any panic – whether the cause is a legitimate one or not – it is necessary to see precisely what happens to an individual's mental processes that prevents him from making an adequate check-up.

The persons who were frightened by the broadcast were, for this occasion at least, highly suggestible, that is, they believed what they heard without making sufficient checks to prove to themselves that the broadcast was only a story. Those who were not frightened and those who believed the broadcast for only a short time were not suggestible – they were able to display what psychologists once called a 'critical faculty.' The problem is, then, to determine why some people are suggestible, or to state the problem differently, why some people lack critical ability.

There are essentially four psychological conditions that create in an individual the particular state of mind we know as suggestibility. All these may be described in terms of the concept of standard of judgment.

In the first place, individuals may refer a given stimulus to a standard or to several standards of judgment which they think are relevant for interpretation. The mental context into which the stimulus enters in this case is of such a character that it is welcomed as thoroughly consistent and without contradiction. A person with standards of judgment that enable him to 'place' or 'give meaning to' a stimulus in an almost automatic way finds nothing incongruous about such acceptance; his standards have led him to 'expect' the possibility of such an occurrence.

We have found that many of the persons who did not even try to check the broadcast had preexisting mental sets that made the stimulus so understandable to them that they immediately accepted it as true. Highly religious people who believed that God willed and controlled the destinies of man were already furnished with a particular standard of judgment that would make an invasion of our planet and a destruction of its members merely an 'act of God.' This was particularly true if the religious frame of reference was of the eschatological variety providing the individual with definite attitudes or beliefs regarding the end of the world. Other people we found had been so influenced by the recent war scare that they believed an attack by a foreign power was imminent and an invasion – whether it was due to the Japanese, Hitler, or Martians – was not unlikely. Some persons had built up such fanciful notions of the possibilities of science that they could easily believe the powers of strange superscientists were being turned against them, perhaps merely for experimental purposes.

Whatever the cause for the genesis of the standards of judgment providing ready acceptance of the event, the fact remains that many persons already possessed a context within which they immediately placed the stimulus. None of their other existing standards of judgment was sufficiently relevant to engender disbelief. We found this to be particularly true of persons whose lack of opportunities or abilities to acquire information or training had insufficiently fortified them with pertinent standards of judgment that would make the interpretation of the broadcast as a play seem plausible. More highly educated people, we found, were better able to relate a given event to a standard of judgment they *knew* was an *appropriate* referent. In such instances, the knowledge itself was used as a standard of judgment to discount the information received in the broadcast. These listeners, then, had the ability to refer to relevant standards of judgment which they could rely on for checking purposes and therefore had no need of further orientation.

A second condition of suggestibility exists when an individual is not sure of the interpretation he should place on a given stimulus and when he lacks adequate standards of judgment to make a reliable check on his interpretation. In this situation the individual attempts to check on his information but fails for one of three reasons. (1) He may check his original information against unreliable data which may themselves be affected by the situation he is checking. We found that persons who checked unsuccessfully tended to check against information obtained from friends or neighbors. Obviously, such people were apt themselves to be tinged with doubt and hesitation which would only confirm early suspicions. (2) A person may rationalize his checking information according to the original hypothesis he is checking and which he thinks he has only tentatively accepted. Many listeners made hasty mental or behavioral checks but the false standard of judgment they had already accepted was so pervasive that their check-ups were rationalized as confirmatory evidence. For example, one woman said that the announcer's charred body was found too quickly but she 'figured the announcer was excited and had made a mistake.' A man noticed the incredible speeds but thought 'they were relaying reports or something.' Others turned to different stations but thought the broadcasters were deliberately trying to calm the people. A woman looked out of her window and saw a greenish eerie light which she thought was from the Martians. (3) In contrast to those who believe almost any check they make are the people who earnestly try to verify their information but do not have sufficiently well-grounded standards of judgment to determine whether or not their new sources of information are reliable.

A third and perhaps more general condition of suggestibility exists when an individual is confronted with a stimulus which he must interpret or which he would like to interpret and when *none* of his existing standards of judgment is adequate to the task. On such occasions the individual's mental context is unstructured, the stimulus does not fit any of his established categories and he seeks a standard that will suffice him. The less structured his mental context, the fewer meanings he is able to call forth, the less able will he be to understand the relationship between himself and the stimulus, and the greater will become his anxiety. And the more desperate his need for interpretation, the more likely will he be to accept the first interpretation given him. Many conditions existed to create in the individuals who listened to the invasion from Mars a chaotic mental universe that contained no stable standards of judgment by means of which the strange event reported could be evaluated. A lack of information and formal educational training had left many persons without any generalized standards of judgment applicable to this novel situation. And even if they did have a few such standards these were vague and tenuously held because they had not proved sufficient in the past to interpret other phenomena. This was especially true of those persons who had been most adversely affected by the conditions of the times.

The prolonged economic unrest and the consequent insecurity felt by many of the listeners was another cause for bewilderment. The depression had already lasted nearly ten years. People were still out of work. Why didn't somebody do something about it? Why didn't the experts find a solution? What was the cause of it anyway? Again, what would happen, no one could tell. Again, a mysterious invasion fitted the pattern of the mysterious events of the decade. The lack of a sophisticated, relatively stable economic or political frame of reference created in many persons a psychological disequilibrium which made them seek a standard of judgment for this particular event. It was another phenomenon in the outside world beyond their control and comprehension. Other people possessed certain economic security and social status but wondered how long this would last with 'things in such a turmoil.' They, too, sought a stable interpretation, one that would at least give this new occurrence meaning. The war scare had left many persons in a state of complete bewilderment. They did not know what the trouble was all about or why the United States should be so concerned. The complex ideological, class, and national antagonisms responsible for the crises were by no means fully comprehended. The situation was painfully serious and distressingly confused. What would happen, nobody could foresee. The Martian invasion was just another event reported over the radio. It was even more personally dangerous and no more enigmatic. No existing standards were available to judge its meaning or significance. But there was quick need for judgment, and it was provided by the announcers, scientists, and authorities.

Persons with higher education, on the other hand, we found had acquired more generalized standards of judgment which they could put their faith in. The result was that many of them 'knew' that the phenomenal speeds with which the announcers and soldiers moved was impossible even in this day and age. The greater the possibility of checking against a variety of reliable standards of judgment, the less suggestible will a person be. We found that some persons who in more normal circumstances might have had critical ability were so overwhelmed by their particular listening situation that their better judgment was suspended. This indicates that a highly consistent structuration of the external stimulus world may, at times, be experienced with sufficient intensity because of its personal implications to inhibit the operation of usually applicable internal structurations or standards of judgment. Other persons who may normally have exhibited critical ability were unable to do so in this situation because their own emotional insecurities and anxieties made them susceptible to suggestion when confronted with a personally dangerous circumstance. In such instances, the behavioral consequence is the same as for a person who has no standards of judgment to begin with, but the psychological processes underlying the behavior are different.

A fourth condition of suggestibility results when an individual not only lacks standards of judgment by means of which he may orient himself, but lacks even the realization that any interpretations are possible other than the one originally presented. He accepts as truth whatever he hears or reads without even thinking to compare it to other information.

Why such extreme behavior?

Granted that some people believed the broadcast to be true, why did they become so hysterical? Why did they pray, telephone relatives, drive at dangerous speeds, cry, awaken sleeping children, and flee? Of all the possible modes of reaction they may have followed, why did these particular patterns emerge? The obvious answer is that this was a serious affair. As in all other panics, the individual believed his well-being, his safety, or his life was at stake. The situation was a real threat to him. Just what constitutes a personal threat to an individual must be briefly examined.

When an individual believes that a situation threatens him he means that it threatens not only his physical self but all of those things and people which he somehow regards as a part of him. This ego of an individual is essentially composed of the many social and personal values *he* has accepted. *He* feels threatened if his investments are threatened, *he* feels insulted if his children or parents are insulted, *he* feels elated if his alma mater wins the sectional football cup. The particular pattern of values that have been introcepted by an individual will give him, then, a particular ego. For some individuals this is expanded to include broad ideals and ambitions. *They* will be disturbed if a particular race is persecuted in a distant country because that persecution runs counter to their ideal of human justice and democracy; *they* will be flattered if someone admires an idea of theirs or a painting they have completed.

A panic occurs when some highly cherished, rather commonly accepted value is threatened and when no certain elimination of the threat is in sight. The individual feels that he will be ruined, physically, financially, or socially. The invasion of the Martians was a direct threat to life, to other lives that one loved, as well as to all other cherished values. The Martians were destroying practically everything. The situation was, then, indeed a serious affair. Frustration resulted when no directed behavior seemed possible. One was faced with the alternative of resigning oneself and all of one's values to complete annihilation, or of making a desperate effort to escape from the field of danger, or of appealing to some higher power or stronger person whom one vaguely thought could destroy the oncoming enemy.

If one assumed that destruction was inevitable, then certain limited behavior was possible: one could cry, make peace with one's Maker, gather one's loved ones around and perish. If one attempted escape, one could run to the house of friends, speed away in a car or train, or hide in some gas-proof, bomb-proof, out-of-the-way shelter. If one still believed that something or someone might repulse the enemy, one could appeal to God or seek protection from those who had protected one in the past. Objectively, none of these modes of behavior was a direct attack on the problem at hand; nothing was done to remove the cause of the crisis. The behavior in a panic is characteristically undirected and, from the point of view of the situation at hand, functionally useless.

Questions

1 The study deals with radio in pre-television America. Nowadays, radio is seldom seen as a 'dangerous medium' but the study has parallels with concerns and scares made in the context of modern media. Can you think of any recent examples of 'panic' or alleged effect which could be considered in this context? How have media audiences changed from 1938 to the present day?

2 The study notes the ways in which people in modern times have increasingly come to rely or depend upon mediated information – especially in the form of news – for the authentic 'truth' of the world and events occurring outside direct, first-hand experience. What do you see as the key issues at stake in debating this relationship nearly 50 years after the study was conducted?

Further reading

Glover, D. 1984: *The sociology of the mass media*. Ormskirk: Causeway Press.
McQuail, D. 1977: The influence and effects of mass media. In Curran, J., Gurevitch, M. and Woollacott, J. (eds.), *Mass communication and society*. London: Edward Arnold.

McQuail, D. 1994: *Mass communication theory: an introduction*. London: Sage.

Merton, R. 1946: *Mass persuasion*. New York: Free Press.

Tudor, A. 1979: On alcohol and the mystique of media effects. In Cook, J. and Lewington, M. (eds.), *Images of alcoholism*. London: BFI. (See Section 3, reading 1.)

Recordings of the original broadcast are available on cassette and CD: e.g. Golden Age Radio, vol. 1, Metacom, ISBN 0–88676–569–2.

2

Mass and Masses
Raymond Williams

From *Culture and society 1780–1950* (Penguin 1961)

Williams is rightly regarded as one of the significant, if not founding voices of modern cultural and media studies. Subsequent to his death in 1988, his contribution and reputation are being given due recognition and assessment. This reading is taken from the conclusion to one of his earliest studies, which was completed in 1956. The overall project, put into motion in this study, was the development and elaboration of a new and general theory of culture. In *Culture and society*, Williams seeks to map out and trace key historical moments and themes concerning the ways in which the idea of culture has come to be understood in modern Britain. The analysis is grounded in the study of shifts in the meanings of key words – democracy, art, industry, etc. – and a commentary on key writers and thinkers – such as Robert Owen, Samuel Coleridge, George Orwell – taken to be indicative of allied forms of historical transition.

From looking backwards at the historical past, Williams turns, in the final phase of the book, to consider the more recent present. In his assessment of the first half of the twentieth century, he draws attention to and challenges conventional understanding associated with the idea of 'mass', so fundamental to thinking about modern *mass* culture, forms of *mass* production and *mass* consumption. In a period – 40 years after the publication of *Culture and society* – when the ideas of mass society, mass media and mass communication are being contradicted by the forces of cultural fragmentation and proliferation, the notion of 'mass' still continues to exert considerable power. This extract seeks to contextualise the ideas lurking behind the prefix 'mass', to render it uncomfortable and unstable, and to challenge its utility or value in modern debate.

We now regularly use both the idea of the 'masses', and the consequent ideas of 'mass-civilization', 'mass-democracy', 'mass-communication' and others. Here, I think, lies a central and very difficult issue which more than any other needs revision.

Masses was a new word for mob, and it is a very significant word. It seems probable that three social tendencies joined to confirm its meaning. First, there was the concentration of population in the industrial towns, a physical massing of persons which the great increase in total population accentuated, and which has continued with continuing urbanization. Second, there was the concentration of workers into factories: again, a physical massing, made necessary by machine production; also, a social massing, in the work-relations made necessary by the development of large-scale collective production. Third, there was the consequent development of an organized and self-organizing working class: a social and political massing. The masses, in practice, have been any of these particular aggregates, and because the tendencies have been interrelated, it has been possible to use the term with a certain unity. And then, on the basis of each tendency, the derived ideas have arisen: from urbanization, the mass meeting; from the factory, in part in relation to the workers, but mainly in relation to the things made, mass-production; from the working class, mass-action. Yet, masses was a new word for mob, and the traditional characteristics of the mob were retained in its significance: gullibility, fickleness, herd-prejudice, lowness of taste and habit. The masses, on this evidence, formed the perpetual threat to culture. Mass-thinking, mass-suggestion, mass-prejudice would threaten to swamp considered individual thinking and feeling. Even democracy, which had both a classical and a liberal reputation, would lose its savour in becoming mass-democracy.

Now mass-democracy, to take the latest example, can be either an observation or a prejudice; sometimes, indeed, it is both. As an observation, the term draws attention to certain problems of a modern democratic society which could not have been foreseen by its early partisans. The existence of immensely powerful media of mass-communication is at the heart of these problems, for through these public opinion has been observably moulded and directed, often by questionable means, often for questionable ends. I shall discuss this issue separately, in relation to the new means of communication.

But the term mass-democracy is also, evidently, a prejudice. Democracy, as in England we have interpreted it, is majority rule. The means to this, in representation and freedom of expression, are generally approved. But, with universal suffrage, majority rule will, if we believe in the existence of the masses, be mass-rule. Further, if the masses are, essentially, the mob, democracy will be mob-rule. This will hardly be good government, or a good society; it will, rather, be the rule of lowness or mediocrity. At this point, which it is evidently very satisfying to some thinkers to reach, it is necessary to ask again: who are the masses? In practice, in our society and in this context, they can hardly be other than the working people. But if this is so, it is clear that what is in question is not only gullibility, fickleness, herd-prejudice, or lowness of taste and habit. It is also, from the open record, the declared intention of the working people to alter society, in many of its aspects, in ways which those to whom the franchise was formerly restricted deeply disapprove. It seems to me, when this is considered, that what is being questioned is not mass-democracy, but democracy. If a majority can be achieved in favour of these changes, the democratic criterion is satisfied. But if you disapprove of the changes you can, it seems, avoid open opposition to democracy as such by inventing a new category, mass-democracy, which is not such a good thing at all. The submerged opposite is class-democracy, where democracy will merely describe the processes by which a ruling class conducts its business of ruling. Yet democracy, as interpreted in England in this century, does not mean this. So, if change reaches the point where it deeply hurts and cannot be accepted, either democracy must be denied or refuge taken in a new term of opprobrium. It is clear that this confusion of the issue cannot be tolerated. Masses = majority cannot be glibly equated with masses = mob.

A difficulty arises here with the whole concept of masses. Here, most urgently, we have to return the meanings to experience. Our normal public conception of an individual person, for example, is 'the man in the street'. But nobody feels himself to be only the man in the street; we all know much more about ourselves than that. The man in the street is a collective image, but we know, all the time, our own difference from him. It is the same with 'the public', which includes us, but yet is not us. 'Masses' is a little more complicated, yet similar. I do not think of my relatives, friends, neighbours, colleagues, acquaintances, as masses; we none of us can or do. The masses are always the others, whom we don't know, and can't know. Yet now, in our kind of society, we see these others regularly, in their myriad variations; stand, physically, beside them. They are here, and we are here with them. And that we are with them is of course the whole point. To other people, we also are masses. Masses are other people.

There are in fact no masses; there are only ways of seeing people as masses. In an urban industrial society there are many opportunities for such ways of seeing. The point is not to reiterate the objective conditions but to consider, personally and collectively, what these have done to our thinking. The fact is, surely, that a way of seeing other people which has become characteristic of our kind of society, has been capitalized for the purposes of political or cultural exploitation. What we see, neutrally, is other people, many others, people unknown to us. In practice, we mass them, and interpret them, according to some convenient formula. Within its terms, the formula will hold. Yet it is the formula, not the mass, which it is our real business to examine. It may help us to do this if we remember that we ourselves are all the time being massed by others. To the degree that we find the formula inadequate for ourselves, we can wish to extend to others the courtesy of acknowledging the unknown.

I have mentioned the political formula by means of which it seems possible to convert the majority of one's fellow human beings into masses, and thence into something to be hated or feared. I wish now to examine another formula, which underlies the idea of mass-communication.

Mass-communication

The new means of communication represent a major technical advance. The oldest, and still the most important, is printing, which has itself passed through major technical changes, in particular the coming of the steam-driven machine press in 1811, and the development of ever faster cylinder and rotary presses from 1815. The major advances in transport, by road, rail, sea, and air, themselves greatly affected printing: at once in the collection of news and in the wide and quick distribution of the printed product. The development of the cable, telegraph, and telephone services even more remarkably facilitated the collection of news. Then, as new media, came sound broadcasting, the cinema, and television.

We need to look again at these familiar factual elements if we are to be able adequately to review the idea of 'mass-communication' which is their product. In sum, these changes have given us more and normally cheaper books, magazines, and newspapers; more bills and posters; broadcasting and television programmes; various kinds of film. It would be difficult, I think, to express a simple and definite judgement of value about all these very varied products, yet they are all things that need to be valued. My question is whether the idea of 'mass-communication' is a useful formula for this.

Two preliminary points are evident: first, that there is a general tendency to confuse the techniques themselves with the uses to which, in a given society, they have been put; second, that, in considering these uses, our argument is commonly selective, at times to an extreme degree.

The techniques, in my view, are at worst neutral. The only substantial objection that is made to them is that they are relatively impersonal, by comparison with older techniques serving the same ends. Where the theatre presented actors, the cinema presents the photographs of actors. Where the meeting presented a man speaking, the wireless presents a voice, or television a voice and a photograph. Points of this kind are relevant, but need to be carefully made. It is not relevant to contrast an evening spent watching television with an evening spent in conversation, although this is often done. There is, I believe, no form of social activity which the use of these techniques has replaced. At most, by adding alternatives, they have allowed altered emphases in the time given to particular activities. But these alterations are obviously conditioned, not only by the techniques, but mainly by the whole circumstances of the common life. The point about impersonality often carries a ludicrous rider. It is supposed, for instance, that it is an objection to listening to wireless talks or discussions that the listener cannot answer the speakers back. But the situation is that of almost any reader; printing, after all, was the first great impersonal medium. It is as easy to send an answer to a broadcast speaker or a newspaper editor as to send one to a contemporary author; both are very much easier than to try to answer Aristotle, Burke, or Marx. We fail to realize, in this matter, that much of what we call communication is, necessarily, no more in itself than transmission: that is to say, a one-way sending. Reception and response, which complete communication, depend on other factors than the techniques.

What can be observed as a fact about the development of these techniques is a steady growth of what I propose to call *multiple transmission*. The printed book is the first great model of this, and the other techniques have followed. The new factor, in our society, is an expansion of the potential audience for such transmissions, so great as to present new kinds of problem. Yet it is clear that it is not to this expansion that we can properly object, at least without committing ourselves to some rather extraordinary politics. The expansion of the audience is due to two factors: first, the growth of general education, which has accompanied the growth of democracy; second, the technical improvements themselves. It is interesting, in the light of the earlier discussion of 'masses', that this expansion should have been interpreted by the phrase 'mass-communication'.

A speaker or writer, addressing a limited audience, is often able to get to know this audience well enough to feel a directly personal relationship with them which can affect his mode of address. Once this audience has been expanded, as with everything from books to televised parlour-games it has been expanded, this is clearly impossible. It would be rash, however, to assume that this is necessarily to his and the audience's disadvantage. Certain types of address, notably serious art, argument, and exposition, seem indeed to be distinguished by a quality of impersonality which enables them frequently to survive their immediate occasion. How far this ultimate impersonality may be dependent on a close immediate relationship is in fact very difficult to assess. But it is always unlikely that any such speaker or writer will use, as a model for communication, any concept so crude as 'masses'. The idea of mass-communication, it would seem, depends very much more on the intention of the speaker or writer, than on the particular technique employed.

A speaker or writer who knows, at the time of his address, that it will reach almost immediately several million persons, is faced with an obviously difficult problem of interpretation. Yet, whatever the difficulty, a good speaker or writer will be conscious of his immediate responsibility to the matter being communicated. He cannot, indeed, feel otherwise, if he is conscious of himself as the source of a particular transmission. His task is the adequate expression of this source, whether it be of feeling, opinion, or information. He will use for this expression the common language, to the limit of his particular skill. That this expression is then given multiple transmission is a next stage, of which he may well be conscious, but which cannot, of its nature, affect the source. The difficulties of expressing this source – difficulties of common experience, convention, and language – are certainly always his concern. But the source cannot in any event be denied, or he denies himself.

Now if, on this perennial problem of communication, we impose the idea of masses, we radically alter the position. The conception of persons as masses springs, not from an inability to know them, but from an interpretation of them according to a formula. Here the question of the intention of the transmission makes its decisive return. Our formula can be that of the rational being speaking our language. It can be that of the interested being sharing our common experience. Or – and it is here that 'masses' will operate – it can be that of the mob: gullible, fickle, herd-like, low in taste and habit. The formula, in fact, will proceed from our intention. If our purpose is art, education, the giving of information or opinion, our interpretation will be in terms of the rational and interested being. If, on the other hand, our purpose is manipulation – the persuasion of a large number of people to act, feel, think, know, in certain ways – the convenient formula will be that of the masses.

There is an important distinction to be drawn here between source and agent. A man offering an opinion, a proposal, a feeling, of course normally desires that other persons will accept this, and act or feel in the ways that he defines. Yet such a man may be properly described as a source, in distinction from an agent, whose characteristic is that his expression is subordinated to an undeclared intention. He is an agent, and not a source, because the intention lies elsewhere. In social terms, the agent will normally in fact be a subordinate – of a government, a commercial firm, a newspaper proprietor. Agency, in the simple sense, is necessary in any complex administration. But it is always dangerous unless its function and intention are not only openly declared but commonly approved and controlled. If this is so, the agent becomes a collective source, and he will observe the standards of such expression if what he is required to transmit is such that he can wholly acknowledge and accept it – re-create it in his own person. Where he cannot thus accept it for himself, but allows himself to be persuaded that it is in a fit form for others – presumably inferiors – and that it is his business merely to see that it reaches them effectively, then he is in the bad sense an agent, and what he is doing is inferior to that done by the poorest kind of source. Any practical denial of the relation between conviction and communication, between experience and expression, is morally damaging alike to the individual and to the common language.

Yet it is certainly true, in our society, that many men, many of them intelligent, accept, whether in good or bad faith, so dubious a role and activity. The acceptance in bad faith is a matter for the law, although we have not yet gone very far in working out this necessary common control. The acceptance in good faith, on the other hand, is a matter of culture. It would clearly not be possible unless it appeared to be ratified by a conception of society which relegates the majority of its members to mob-status. The idea of the masses is an expression of this conception, and the idea of mass-communication a comment on its functioning. This is the real danger to democracy, not the existence of effective and powerful means of multiple transmission. It is less a product of democracy than its denial, springing from that half-world of feeling in which we are invited to have our being. Where the principle of democracy is accepted, and yet its full and active practice feared, the mind is lulled into an acquiescence, which is yet not so complete that a fitful conscience, a defensive irony, cannot visit it. 'Democracy would be all right,' we can come to say, 'it is indeed what we personally would prefer, if it were not for the actual people. So, in a good cause if we can find it, in some other if we can not, we will try to get by at a level of communication which our experience and training tell us is inferior. Since the people are as they are, the thing will do.' But it is as well to face the fact that what we are really doing, in such a case, is to cheapen our own experience and to adulterate the common language.

Mass-observation

Yet the people are as they are, the objection is returned. Of course the masses are only other people, yet most other people are, on the evidence, a mob. In principle, we would wish it not to be so; in practice, the evidence is clear.

This is the negative side of the idea of mass-communication. Its evidence is collected under the title of mass-culture, or popular culture. It is important evidence, and much of it is incontrovertible. There remains, however, the question of its interpretation. I have said that our arguments on this matter are normally selective, often to an extreme degree. I will try now to illustrate this.

We are faced with the fact that there is now a great deal of bad art, bad entertainment, bad journalism, bad advertisement, bad argument. We are not likely to be diverted from this conclusion by the usual diversionary arguments. Much that we judge to be bad is known to be bad by its producers. Ask any journalist, or any copywriter, if he will now accept that famous definition: 'written by morons for morons'. Will he not reply that in fact it is written by skilled and intelligent people for a public that hasn't the time, or hasn't the education, or hasn't, let's face it, the intelligence, to read anything more complete, anything more careful, anything nearer the known canons of exposition or argument? Had we not better say, for simplicity, anything good? Good and bad are hard words, and we can, of course, find easier ones. The strip newspaper, the beer advertisement, the detective novel – it is not exactly that they are good, but they are good of their (possibly bad) kind; they have the merits at least of being bright, attractive, popular. Yet, clearly, the strip newspaper has to be compared with other kinds of newspaper; the beer advertisement with other kinds of description of a product; the detective novel with other novels. By these standards – not by reference to some ideal quality, but by reference to the best things that men exercising this faculty have done or are doing – we are not likely to doubt that a great deal of what is now produced, and widely sold, is mediocre or bad.

But this is said to be popular culture. The description has a ready-made historical thesis. After the Education Act of 1870, a new mass-public came into being, literate but untrained in reading, low in taste and habit. The mass-culture followed as a matter of course. I think always, when I hear this thesis, of an earlier one, from the second half of the eighteenth century. Then, the decisive date was between 1730 and 1740, and what had emerged, with the advance of the middle classes to prosperity, was a new middle-class reading public. The immediate result was that vulgar phenomenon, the novel. As a matter of fact there is in both theses a considerable element of truth. If the former is not now so commonly mentioned, it is only because it would be indiscreet, in a situation where 'good' and 'middle class' are equivalent terms. And of course we can properly see the earlier situation in its true perspective. We can see that what the rise of the middle classes produced was not only the novel but many other things good and bad. Further, now that the bad novels are all out of print, and the good ones are among our classics, we see that the novel itself, while certainly a phenomenon, cannot be lightly dismissed as vulgar. Of the situation after 1870 we are not able to speak so clearly. For one thing, since the emergence as a whole still divides us, we can resent the cultural situation for political reasons and not realize this. For another, since the period has not fallen into settled history, we can be much more subjective in our selection of evidence.

1870 is in fact very questionable as a decisive date. There had been widespread literacy much earlier than this, the bad popular press is in fact also earlier. The result of the new educational provision was in part an actual increase in literacy, in part an evening-up between the fortunate places and the unfortunate. The increase is certainly large enough to be important, but it was no kind of sudden opening of the flood-gates. In itself, it is far from enough to account for the institution of the now characteristic features of popular culture.

Further, we need to remember that the new institutions were not produced by the working people themselves. They were, rather, produced for them by others, often (as most notably with the cheap newspaper and commercial advertisement on a large scale) for conscious political or commercial advantage. Such things in this sphere as the working people produced for themselves (radical newspapers, political pamphlets and publicity, trade-union banners and designs) were, if by no means always good, at least quite different in important respects. Again, it is wrong to see the new institutions as catering only for the new class. The new types of newspaper and advertisement were and are much more widely received. If the masses are to be defined as those for whom these institutions now cater, and by whom they are now received with apparent satisfaction, then the masses extend far beyond the categories of, say, the manual workers, or those whose education has been restricted to an elementary stage. I make this point because 'masses = working and lower-middle class' is so commonly confused with 'masses = mob'. The mob, if there is one, is at almost everyone's elbow; it may, indeed, be even nearer than that.

And if this is so of the new newspapers and advertisements, it is even more true of the other bad work which has been noted, in the novel, in the theatre, in the cinema, in the wireless and television programmes. If, in this kind of entertainment, there has been a continual decline of standards, then it is not from 1870 that we shall date this, but at least from 1740. As a matter of fact, I see little evidence why the backward dating should stop there, but then I am not so sure about the continual decline in standards. The multiplication of transmission, and the discovery of powerful media, seem to me mainly to have emphasized and made more evident certain long-standing tastes and means of satisfying them. I shall return to this point when I have made a further observation about our practices of selection.

In the matter of selection, there are two main points. First, it is clear that in an anxiety to prove their case, which is indeed an important one if the badness is not to go unchallenged, the contemporary historians of popular culture have tended to concentrate on what is bad and to neglect what is good. If there are many bad books, there are also an important number of good books, and these, like the bad books, circulate much more widely than in any previous period. If the readers of bad newspapers have increased in number, so have the readers of better newspapers and periodicals, so have the users of public libraries, so have students in all kinds of formal and informal adult education. The audiences for serious music, opera, and ballet have increased, in some cases to a remarkable degree. Attendances at museums and exhibitions have, in general, steadily risen. A significant proportion of what is seen in the cinemas, and of what is heard on the wireless, is work of merit. In every case, certainly, the proportions are less than we could desire, but they are not negligible.

Secondly, it is important to remember that, in judging a culture, it is not enough to concentrate on habits which coincide with those of the observer. To the highly literate observer there is always a temptation to assume that reading plays as large a part in the lives of most people as it does in his own. But if he compares his own kind of reading with the reading-matter that is most widely distributed, he is not really comparing levels of culture. He is, in fact, comparing what is produced for people to whom reading is a major activity with that produced for people to whom it is, at best, minor. To the degree that he acquires a substantial proportion of his ideas and feelings from what he reads he will assume, again wrongly, that the ideas and feelings of the majority will be similarly conditioned. But, for good or ill, the majority of people do not yet give reading this importance in their lives; their ideas and feelings are, to a large extent, still moulded by a wider and more complex pattern of social and family life. There is an evident danger of delusion, to the highly literate person, if he supposes that he can judge the quality of general living by primary reference to the reading artifacts. He will, in particular, be driven to this delusion if he retains, even in its most benevolent form, the concept of the majority of other people as 'masses', whom he observes as a kind of block. The error resembles that of the narrow reformer who supposes that farm labourers and village craftsmen were once uneducated, merely because they could not read. Many highly educated people have, in fact, been so driven in on their reading, as a stabilizing habit, that they fail to notice that there are other forms of skilled, intelligent, creative activity: not only the cognate forms of theatre, concert, and picture-gallery; but a whole range of general skills, from gardening, metalwork, and carpentry to active politics. The contempt for many of these activities, which is always latent in the highly literate, is a mark of the observers' limits, not those of the activities themselves. Neglect of the extraordinary popularity of many of these activities, as evidence of the quality of living in contemporary society, is the result of partisan selection for the reasons given.

This point comes to be of particular importance when we remember that the general tendency of modern development has been to bring many more levels of culture within the general context of literacy than was ever previously the case. A number of tastes which would formerly have been gratified in pre-literate and therefore largely unrecorded ways are now catered for and even fostered in print. Or, to put it in another way, the historical counterpart of a modern popular newspaper, in its informing function, is not an earlier minority newspaper, but that complex of rumour and travellers' tales which then served the majority with news of a kind. This is not to surrender the finest literacy we have, which at all times offers a standard for the newly literate functions. But, equally, to look at the matter in this way helps us to keep a just sense of proportion.

Questions

1   The extract traces a number of meanings which have historically developed and condensed around the word 'mass'. According to Williams, what are the principal ideas and values that have been associated with the term?

2   Is the idea or spectre of 'the mass' still a popular way of thinking about aspects of modern life and experience? List a number of terms which are commonly prefixed with 'mass' and think about their common or distinctive features. What judgements are implied by the term?

3   How are the notions of mass media and mass communication implicated in such debates, judgements and values? Can you think of any recent relevant examples? Does it make sense to talk of a mass medium or of the mass media? What are the alternatives?

Further reading

Eldridge, J. and Eldridge, L. 1994: *Raymond Williams: making connections*. London: Routledge.

Gray, A. and McGuigan, J. (eds.) 1993: *Studying culture: an introductory reader*. London: Edward Arnold.

Inglis, F. 1995: *Raymond Williams*. London: Routledge.

LeMahieu, D. H. 1986: *A culture for democracy*. Oxford: Oxford University Press.

Lury, C. 1992: Popular culture and the mass media. In Bocock, R. and Thompson, K. (eds.), *Social and cultural forms of modernity*. Cambridge: Polity.

McGuigan, J. 1992: *Cultural populism*. London: Routledge.

Williams, R. 1974/1990: *Television: technology and cultural form*. London: Fontana.

Williams, R. 1976: *Keywords: a vocabulary of culture and society*. London: Fontana.

3

Mass Communication and Modern Culture
John B. Thompson

From *Sociology* 22(3), 359–83 (1988)

In this reading, Thompson initially focuses on the impact of systems of mass communication on modern cultural life and experience. His overall aim in the original article was to argue for the centrality of the study of the media and modern culture in a fully developed sociological understanding of modernity and modern conditions. Fundamental to his approach is a view of the modern media as key *ideological* agencies in modern society, powerfully implicated in the production and circulation of symbols, images, values and ideas.

The extract commences with some ideas about the place and presence of the media in modern times, then proceeds to the central question concerning the relationship between social and historical development *in general*, and the expansion of the institutions and systems capable of mass cultural transmission, the 'mass' media. Thompson suggests that the growth of 'mass communication' in the modern period has seen several distinctive and important developments which distinguish it from face-to-face, direct forms of interpersonal communication. Finally, the extract outlines three aspects or components of mass communication, which provide a useful and applicable 'map' with which to chart and develop approaches to studying the media.

Few people would deny that the nature of cultural experience in modern societies has been profoundly affected by the development of mass communication. Books, magazines and newspapers, radio, television and cinema, records, tapes and videos: these and other forms of mass communication occupy a central role in our lives, providing us with a continuous flow of information and entertainment. Newspapers, radio and television are major sources of information, ideas and images concerning events which take place beyond our immediate social milieu. The figures who feature in films and programmes become common points of reference in a culture which extends far beyond the sphere of social interaction, while films, programmes and other products form a tissue of shared experience and collective memory. Even those forms of entertainment which have existed for many centuries, such as popular music and sports, are today inseparable from the media of mass communication. Pop music, competitive sports and other activities are today sustained by the media industries, which are involved not merely in the transmission of pre-existing cultural forms but in their creation and reproduction.

[...]

The modalities of cultural transmission in modern societies have been profoundly affected by the development of institutions of mass communication. The development of these institutions – of newspapers, book publishers, broadcasting organizations, etc. – marked the emergence of new forms of information diffusion and cultural transmission. The production and circulation of meaningful objects and expressions became increasingly mediated by industrial organizations concerned with the commodification of symbolic goods. Prior to the development of the popular press and broadcasting, most cultural forms and processes were produced and reproduced through oral language and face-to-face interaction. While systems of writing have probably existed since the third millennium B.C., the practice of reading and writing has, for most of the 5,000 years since then, been restricted to a small minority of the population. It seems likely that writing was originally linked to the task of recording information relevant to trade and administration; it was thus a means whereby power could be exercised by individuals engaged in commerce and political rule.[1] With the development of the printing industry in Europe in the fifteenth and sixteenth centuries, the capacity to produce multiple copies of texts and documents was rapidly increased. It is estimated that in 1580 as many as 150 book titles were published in England, compared to only 13 titles in 1510.[2] The development of the newspaper industry in the eighteenth and nineteenth centuries significantly extended the availability of the written word. The first daily newspaper in England, the *Courant*, appeared in 1702; the first Sunday newspaper, the *Sunday Monitor*, appeared in 1779. By 1850 the estimated total circulation of the daily newspapers was around 60,000, while the estimated total circulation of the Sunday newspapers was around 275,000. As the levels of illiteracy declined in England and elsewhere in Europe during the second half of the nineteenth century, the circulation of daily and Sunday newspapers steadily increased. By the end of the nineteenth century the leading daily paper in England, the *Daily Telegraph*, had a circulation of around 300,000 and the leading Sunday paper, *Lloyd's Weekly News*, reached a circulation of one million.

The growth of the mass circulation newspapers continued into the twentieth century, although this trend has tapered off in recent years. By 1947 the circulation of Sunday papers in Britain was 28.3 million and the circulation of national morning papers was 15.6 million. After 1950, however, the circulation of Sunday papers and national morning papers began to decline; the circulation of the morning papers fell from a peak of nearly 17 million in 1950 to just over 14 million in 1975. The decline in newspaper circulation coincided with the growth of television as a medium of mass communication. Although experiments with television took place in the late 1920s and throughout the 1930s, it was not until after the Second World War that it became a major medium.[3] Television broadcasting in Britain was controlled initially by the British Broadcasting Corporation, but in 1954 the BBC's monopoly was broken by the establishment of the commercial television channel ITV. The 1950s and 1960s witnessed a massive and rapid growth in the size of the television audience. The number of television licences in Britain increased from 3 million in 1954 to 15 million in 1968. In 1950 only 10% of homes had TV sets, whereas in 1963 they could be found in 90% of homes (Golding 1974:35). Today television viewing accounts for a substantial part of people's time. The average amount of time spent watching television in Britain in early 1984 was 22 hours per week among men and more than 25 hours among women: this is nearly 60% of the average amount of time spent at work. The amount of time spent watching television is even higher for the elderly, averaging around 30 hours per week for those aged 65 and over (*Social Trends* 1985:150).

Although these figures relate to Britain, they are indicative of trends characteristic of many modern industrial societies.[4] Cultural forms in modern societies are increasingly mediated by the mechanisms and institutions of mass communication. These have emerged in a relatively short period of time, and are currently undergoing further significant changes as a result of the deployment of new technologies, such as those involving cable and satellite transmission.[5] In a period of less than 200 years the conditions under which individuals acquire information about the world, derive entertainment and participate in public life have changed dramatically. For many people in industrial societies today, the products and institutions of the mass media – newspapers, books, magazines, radio, cinema, television – are a principal source of information and entertainment. Hence much of the information and entertainment which we receive and consume is a *product* of specific institutions, a product which is the outcome of the mechanisms and criteria characteristic of these institutions. These mechanisms and criteria operate as filters for the selection, production and diffusion of items of information and entertainment; they help to establish what may be described as the *selective reproduction of cultural forms*. In creating media products, the personnel of media institutions draw upon everyday forms of culture and communication, incorporating these forms into media products and thereby reproducing, in a selective and creative way, the cultural forms of everyday life. Selectivity and creativity: the operation of media institutions involves both a *selective extraction* from the contents of everyday forms of culture and communication and a *creative extension* of these forms. It involves both production and reproduction, both repetition and creativity. In these two respects the cultural forms of modern society are mediated by the mechanisms and institutions of mass communication.

In speaking of 'mass communication', we are presupposing a very special sense of the term 'communication'. In general the term communication refers to the transmission of meaningful messages. These messages are often expressed in language, but they may also be conveyed by images, gestures or other symbols used in accordance with shared rules or codes. A great deal of communication in everyday life takes place in the context of face-to-face social interaction: messages are conveyed to an individual or individuals who are physically present, and whose responses provide the person conveying the message with an immediate and continuous source of feedback. In the case of mass communication, however, the nature of the communicative process is quite different. Let me highlight four important differences. In the first place, while messages in mass communication are produced for an audience, the individuals who comprise the audience are not physically present at the place of production and transmission or diffusion of the message; mass communication involves what we may describe as an *instituted break between production and reception*. Hence the personnel involved in the production and transmission or diffusion of the message are deprived of the immediate and continuous sources of feedback characteristic of face-to-face interaction. The communicative process in mass communication is marked by a distinctive form of *indeterminacy*, since the message must be produced and transmitted or diffused in the absence of direct and continuous monitoring of audience response. The personnel involved in mass communication employ a variety of strategies to cope with this (cf. McQuail (1969), Burns (1969)). They draw upon past experience and use it as a guide to likely future outcomes; they employ well-tried formulae which have a predictable audience appeal; they make occasional but highly selective use of audience monitoring devices, such as the information provided by market research or by the routine monitoring of audience size and response. These and other strategies are institutional mechanisms which enable them to reduce indeterminacy in a way that concurs with the aims of the institutions of mass communication.

A second difference between mass communication and the exchange of messages in everyday life concerns the nature of the *technical* means of mass communication. In contrast to everyday interaction, where the exchange of messages typically occurs as a transient verbal utterance or visual display, the messages are inscribed in texts or encoded in some other material medium such as film, tape, records or discs. These and other *information storage mechanisms* affect the nature of the message itself and endow it with a permanence which the utterances exchanged in everyday interaction do not have. They affect the nature of the message in the sense that they determine what can and cannot be recorded and transmitted in the medium concerned. In this respect there are significant differences between the various media which demand systematic and detailed analysis. The kinds of messages that are recorded in written texts such as books or newspapers, for example, are quite different from the messages recorded on film and transmitted on television, in so far as the latter consist of complex audio-visual constructs in which language is spoken in accordance with the grammar and conventions of everyday speech, and in which the temporal flow of the message is intrinsic to it. The recording of messages in the various media of mass communication also endows them with a permanence which extends beyond the moment of recording. The messages are stored in a medium which persists; they thereby acquire a temporality quite different from that characteristic of utterances in face-to-face interaction: they are extended in time, temporalized, historicized. Indeed, they become *part of* history, in the double sense of belonging to the past as well as the present and of constituting some of the resources through which the past is reconstructed and understood. The messages conveyed by the mass media form part of the tissue of tradition in modern societies and the legacy through which our historical memories are formed.

A third characteristic of mass communication which distinguishes it from the communicative process in everyday social interaction is that the messages in mass communication are generally *commodified*, that is, constituted as objects which are exchanged in a market. Mass communication may be regarded as *the institutionalized production and diffusion of symbolic goods via the transmission and storage of information/communication*. Media messages are incorporated into products which are sold, or which are used to facilitate the sale of other goods; hence calculations concerning the marketability of the product shape the character and content of the message produced. In the newspaper industry, for example, changes in the format and content of newspapers are often linked to strategies aimed at maintaining or increasing circulation. In the film industry and in broadcasting, marketing considerations also play an important role; one indication of this is the growing tendency to produce films and programmes for an international audience, so that they can be distributed in a global market. The commodification of messages is facilitated by the fact that they are *reproducible*, that is, fixed in a medium which enables them to be produced in multiple copies for sale and distribution. The mode of reproduction varies significantly from one medium to another. In each case, however, media institutions commonly seek to control the mode of reproduction, since it is a major source of the revenue derived from their products. The capacity to control the mode of reproduction has been threatened in recent years by the development of new technologies, such as tape recording, video recording and photocopying, which enable messages to be accurately and cheaply reproduced. Thus the property which facilitates the commodification of media messages is also the property which enables that process to be undercut. In this respect, the mechanisms and institutions of mass communication are embedded in a broader social field characterized by asymmetrical relations of power and ongoing struggles for access to, or for the preservation of, scarce resources.

A fourth distinctive characteristic of mass communication concerns the availability of the messages, that is, the fact that the messages are potentially available to an extended audience which is altogether different from the interlocutors of a face-to-face interaction. The fixation and transmission or diffusion of media messages extends their availability in time and space, enabling them to endure and to reach a large number of spatially dispersed recipients. But the fact that they are potentially available to an extended audience does not mean that they are actually available in an unrestricted fashion; on the contrary, their circulation is *restricted and regulated in a variety of ways*. It is restricted by commercial considerations, for example, in the sense that the institutions which produce them may also seek to control their diffusion in order to secure their financial return. The circulation of media messages may also be restricted by state institutions. Since the early development of the media industries in the seventeenth and eighteenth centuries, state institutions have sought to exercise some control over the circulation of media messages. The state has employed various mechanisms, from the early stamp duties on newspapers to the current regulating bodies which monitor broadcasting, to restrict the availability of messages. There are many reasons why, in differing circumstances, state officials may act to restrict availability. One reason which may be of particular importance is that the diffusion of messages may be regarded as a threat to the capacity of the state to exercise power on the basis of restricted access to information. Another reason is that certain kinds of messages may be thought to endanger the capacity of the state, or of particular governments or officials, to secure sufficient public support for the effective implementation of decisions and policies. It is thus the very availability of media messages – that is, their capacity to circulate among an extended audience – that may induce state officials to restrict their circulation. The relations between media institutions and the state are fraught with tension and potential conflict, as is amply illustrated in Britain by a variety of controversies involving the government, the political parties and the BBC, from the General Strike of 1926 to the present day.[6]

The capacity of media messages to circulate among an extended audience is one of the characteristics in virtue of which we commonly speak of *mass* communication: it is communication for a mass audience, for the masses. But the term 'mass' may be misleading on this context. For this term connotes not only a large quantity but also an indefinite shape, an inert, undifferentiated heap. However the messages transmitted by the mass media are received by specific individuals situated in definite social-historical contexts. These individuals attend to media messages with varying degrees of concentration, actively interpret and make sense of these messages and relate them to other aspects of their lives. This ongoing appropriation of media messages is an inherently critical and socially differentiated process. It is inherently critical in so far as the appropriation of media messages is a process of creative interpretation in which individuals actively construct sense and plot, actively approve or disapprove of what is said and done, and thereby assimilate media messages into their own social-historical context, transforming these messages in the very process of assimilation. The appropriation of media messages is also a socially differentiated process in the sense that the individuals who make up the audience are differentiated in terms of specific social attributes such as class, gender and age. Media messages are received by individuals who are situated in socially structured contexts. It cannot be assumed that these messages will be appropriated in the same way by different individuals in different contexts. On the contrary, it may be the case that there are systematic variations in their appropriation of media messages, variations which are linked to socially structured differences within the audience.

[...]

Analysing mass communication

In this final section I wish to show how the approach developed above can be employed in the study of mass communication. In doing so I do not want to suggest that the many other methods which have been used in the history of media research are without interest. On the contrary, some of these methods are of great value and form an integral part of the approach that I shall sketch. The distinctiveness of this approach nevertheless stems from the concern to analyse mass communication *as a cultural phenomenon*, that is, to study mass communication in terms of the historically specific and socially structured forms and processes within which, and by means of which, symbolic forms are produced, transmitted and received. Hence we shall not lose sight of the fact that we are dealing with meaningful objects and expressions which call for interpretation, while at the same time recognizing that the production and transmission of these objects and expressions are socially situated and institutionally mediated processes. The distinctiveness of this approach also stems from the concern to specify the ways in which the objects and expressions of mass communication may be studied as *ideological*. I shall try to show that the latter concern requires us to pay particular attention to the complex problems raised by the reception and appropriation of media messages by socially differentiated individuals and groups.

Let me begin by distinguishing between three aspects of mass communication. These aspects are closely interconnected in the process of producing and transmitting media messages, but by distinguishing between them we can delineate three object domains of analysis. The first aspect is the process of production and diffusion, that is, the process of producing the material of mass communication and transmitting or distributing it via channels of selective diffusion. This process is situated within specific social-historical circumstances and generally involves particular institutional arrangements. The second aspect is the construction of the media message. The material transmitted by mass communication is a product which is structured in various ways: it is a complex symbolic construction which displays an articulated structure. The third aspect of mass communication is the reception and appropriation of media messages. These messages are received by individuals, and groups of individuals, who are situated within specific social-historical circumstances, and who employ the resources available to them in order to make sense of the messages received and to incorporate them into their everyday lives.

Consider first the analysis of the production and diffusion of television programmes. Such analysis is concerned above all with what I described earlier as social-historical analysis, that is, with the study of the social-historical and institutional context within which, and by means of which, programmes are produced and transmitted. This context consists of, among other things, these characteristics: the institutional organization of producers and of transmission networks; patterns of ownership and control within broadcasting institutions; the relations between broadcasting institutions and state organizations responsible for monitoring output; the techniques and technologies employed in production and transmission; the routine and practical procedures followed by television personnel; the aims of producers and programmers and their expectations of audience response; and so on. Some of these characteristics can be examined by means of empirical, including documentary, research. Others, such as the routine and practical procedures followed by television personnel or their aims and expectations, can be elucidated only by employing a more contextual, interpretative approach. Suppose we wanted to analyse, for example, the processes involved in the production of a particular television programme. In addition to examining the overall institutional context within which the programme is produced, including the various decision-making processes and the allocation of resources, we would want to analyse in detail the processes of script-writing, casting, filming, editing and scheduling.[7] We would want to examine the routine procedures followed in the design and actualization of the programme, as well as the special competencies and criteria employed. We would want to consider variations between different kinds of programme – for example, the extent to which, in different kinds of programme, pre-scripted material is supplemented by impromptu performances and modified in the very process of actualization. This kind of research would help to illuminate the rules, procedures and assumptions implicit in the production process, including assumptions about the audience and its needs, interests and abilities. These rules, procedures and assumptions are part of the social conditions and codes which media personnel draw upon and implement in producing particular programmes. Together with other aspects of the institutional context, these conditions and codes both facilitate and circumscribe the production process, thereby enabling the media message to be produced as a meaningful symbolic construction.

The second aspect of mass communication is the construction of the media message. When we focus on its construction and analyse its characteristics, we give priority to what I described earlier as formal or discursive analysis; that is, we analyse it primarily as a complex symbolic construction which displays an articulated structure. Among the structural features that we may highlight in the analysis of television are: the syntax, style and tone of the language employed; the juxtaposition of word and image; the angles, colours and sequences of the imagery used; the structure of the narrative or argument; the extent to which the narrative or argumentative structure allows for sub-plots, digression or dissent; the use of specific devices such as flashbacks and voice-overs; the ways in which tension is combined with features such as humour, sexuality and violence; the interconnections between particular programmes which form part of a finite or open-ended sequence; and so on. These and other structural features of television messages can be analysed by a variety of techniques, from different forms of content analysis to various kinds of semi-otic, narrative and discourse analysis.[8] It is important to emphasize, however, that the analysis of the internal structural features of media products is limited in certain respects. It is limited, in the first place, in so far as it abstracts from the process of production and diffusion. Hence it does not take account of the social and institutional conditions within which, and by means of which, media messages are produced and transmitted. The analysis of the internal structural features of media products is also limited in so far as it abstracts from the reception and appropriation of media messages. Hence it does not take account of the sense which these messages have for the individuals who watch them, hear them, read them, nor of the ways in which these individuals interpret media messages, accept them, reject them and incorporate them into their lives.

The reception and appropriation of media messages is the third aspect of mass communication which defines a domain of analysis. A great deal of research has been done, and continues to be done, on the reception of media messages and on the size and nature of audience response. Researchers have sought to study, for example, the short-term and long-term effects of media messages, the ways in which audiences use the media and the gratifications which they derive from them.[9] But these approaches, however interesting they may be, pay insufficient attention to the ways in which different individuals and groups actively make sense of media messages and integrate them into other aspects of their lives. The different phases of the depth-hermeneutical procedure can be used to explore what we may describe as the *modes of reception* of media messages. Thus in the study of television we must examine, by means of social-historical analysis, the specific circumstances and the socially differentiated conditions within which individuals receive television messages. The specific circumstances: in what contexts, with what company, with what degree of attention, consistency and commentary, do individuals watch programmes, or series of programmes, of differing kinds? The socially differentiated conditions: in what ways does the reception of media messages vary according to considerations such as class, gender, age, ethnic background and the country of the recipient? The latter question can be pursued by care-fully designed research which uses structured interviews to explore how dif-ferent individuals, and different groups of individuals, make sense of particular programmes.[10] These interviews yield recipient texts which can in turn by analysed in various ways, for example by methods of formal or discur-sive analysis. The features of one recipient text can be compared and contrast-ed with those of others and together they can be considered in relation to the construction of the media message itself. The formal or discursive analysis of these texts does not displace the need for the creative interpretation of media messages and recipient responses. Drawing upon the formal analysis of struc-tural features and the social-historical analysis of the conditions of produc-tion/diffusion and reception/appropriation, the process of interpretation seeks to explicate what is said and not said, asserted and implied, represented and obscured, in media messages and recipient texts. It seeks to unfold the possible meanings of media messages, and it seeks to show how recipients make sense of these and incorporate them into their lives. As an interpretation, this process necessarily builds upon, and potentially intervenes in, the everyday activities of the subjects who make up the social world.

Against the background of this general approach to the study of mass communication, we can reconsider what is involved in the analysis of ideology. Earlier attempts to analyse the ideological character of the mass media have tended to focus on the production or the construction of the media message. Thus the early critical theorists and authors influenced by them tended to subsume the mass media within a general analysis of the 'culture industry', arguing that the imperatives of capitalist production result in standardized and repetitive products which leave no room for critical reflection (see especially Horkheimer and Adorno (1972)). These theorists tend to assume that the products of the culture industry effectively numb the minds of the masses, deceiving them, captivating them and absorbing them into a system which is thereby reproduced. While critical theorists are right to call attention to the developmental characteristics of the culture industries, their assumption concerning the effects of cultural products is a supposition without support: it lacks clear and convincing documentation. Other attempts to analyse the ideological character of the mass media have suffered from similar limitations. The work conducted within a broadly 'structuralist' or 'semiotic' approach has shed light on the structural features of media messages. But by focusing on the construction of the message, such work generally fails to examine how messages are produced and received in specific social-historical circumstances.[11] Hence when this work employs the concept of ideology, it often does so in a vague and general way. It often takes for granted a social-historical analysis of the institutions and divisions in modern societies, although it does not provide an explicit statement and defence of this analysis. It often analyses ideology in terms of the structural features of the message itself, without examining the ways in which messages are interpreted by the individuals upon whom this ideology is supposed to take hold. The work conducted within a structuralist or semiotic approach is therefore of limited value, for it pays insufficient attention to the specific social and institutional conditions within which, and by virtue of which, media messages may be ideological.

The limitations of earlier work can be avoided by situating the analysis of the ideological character of the mass media within a more general approach to the study of mass communication. This approach enables us to see that the three distinct aspects – production/diffusion, construction and reception/appropriation – are all essential ingredients in the analysis of its ideological character. The study of production and diffusion is an essential ingredient because it elucidates the institutions and social relations which enable media messages to be produced and transmitted. Since these are the outcome of specific production processes and are circulated via channels of selective diffusion, the study of these processes and channels may shed light on the construction and availability of media messages. The study of the construction of media messages is an essential ingredient because it examines the structural features by virtue of which they are complex symbolic phenomena, capable of mobilizing meaning. By examining structural features such as the syntax and style of the language employed, or the structure of the narrative or argument, this kind of analysis brings out the constitutive characteristics of the message, that is, the characteristics with which the message is constructed as meaningful. The study of the reception/appropriation of media messages is an essential ingredient because it considers both the social-historical conditions within which messages are received by individuals, and the ways in which these individuals make sense of the messages and incorporate them into their lives. It considers how the meaning mobilized by media messages is taken up by the individuals who receive them; hence it examines the ways in which these messages are effective within the social relations in which the individual recipients are enmeshed.

If we adopt this general approach to the analysis of the ideological character of the mass media, then we can see that many of the crucial questions concern the relations between the production/diffusion and construction of media messages, on the one hand, and their reception/appropriation by individuals situated within specific social-historical conditions, on the other. It is within this semantic space that the meaning mobilized by media messages becomes (or does not become) effective in the social world, serves (or does not serve) to sustain relations of domination. The interpretation of ideology in the mass media cannot be based solely on the analysis of the production and construction of messages: it must also be based on an analysis of the conditions and characteristics of reception. Thus one of the tasks confronting the interpretation of ideology in the mass media is that of relating the production/diffusion and construction of media messages, on the one hand, to the production and construction of recipient texts, on the other. In this way the process of interpretation can begin to explicate the connections between the mobilization of meaning in media messages and the relations of domination which this meaning serves to sustain. What these relations of domination are, and whether this meaning serves to sustain or to subvert them, to reinforce or to undermine them, are questions which can be answered only by linking the production/diffusion and construction of media messages to the ways in which they are received and interpreted by individuals situated within specific social-historical contexts.

[...]

By attending to the complex ways in which media messages are received and interpreted, we can begin to examine how the meaning mobilized by them is transformed in the process of reception, is appropriated by individuals situated in the structured contexts of everyday life and serves therein to sustain or disrupt relations of domination. We can thus open the way for a dynamic, critical approach to the analysis of ideology in the mass media. While taking account of the production/diffusion and construction of media messages, this approach does not remain at the level of analysing their structural features but seeks to relate these features to the ways in which messages are understood by, and the sense which the reception of these messages has for, individuals situated in specific social contexts. The analysis of ideology in the mass media thus bears a potentially critical relation, not only to the construction of meaning in media messages, but also to the interpretation of messages by recipients and to the relations of domination which characterize the contexts within which these messages are received. To analyse ideology in the mass media is to offer an interpretation which may intervene, which may serve as a resource for critical reflection among the very individuals who receive and interpret media messages as a routine part of their everyday lives. It may enable the subjects who make up the social world to reflect critically on their understanding of media messages and on the structured social relations of which they are part.

Notes

1. The origins of writing, and its relation to administrative activities and the exercise of power, are examined in Gelb (1952), Innis (1950), Goody (1977), Giddens (1985).
2. For more detailed accounts of the development of the printing and newspaper industries in England and elsewhere in Europe see Steinberg (1974), Williams (1961), Olson (1966), Collins (1959), Boyce, Curran and Wingate (1978), Curran and Seaton (1985).
3. Detailed discussions of the development of broadcasting in Britain may be found in Briggs (1961–), Burns (1977), Curran and Seaton (1985), Tunstall (1983).
4. The development of broadcasting in the United States is documented by Head (1976). For a discussion of the development of the media industries in France see Flichy (1980).
5. Some aspects of new communications technologies and their consequences are discussed in Chayes *et al.* (1973), Galloway (1972), Mattelart (1979), Ferguson (1986).
6. Among recent controversies are those stemming from criticisms of the BBC by the Chairman of the Conservative Party for the BBC's allegedly biased coverage of the American bombing of Libya, and from a raid by Special Branch officers on the BBC's offices in Glasgow in order to seize material relating to the 'Secret Society' series of programmes.
7. There are numerous studies of the production of television programmes which are pertinent here. Many are concerned with the production of news; see, for example, Golding and Elliott (1979), Schlesinger (1978), Tuchman (1978).
8. The relevant literature is extensive. For a small selection see Rosengren (1981), Schlesinger, Murdock and Elliott (1983), Davis and Walton (1983), Rowland and Watkins (1985).
9. For a selection of relevant literature see Halloran (1970), Seymour-Ure (1973), Gerbner and Gross (1976), Blumler and Katz (1974).
10. Interesting attempts to pursue this line of reflection may be found in Piepe, Emerson and Lannon (1975), Morley (1980, 1986), Hodge and Tripp (1986), Liebes and Katz (1986).

11. This limitation is evident, for example, in the otherwise illuminating work of Williamson (1978).

References

Blumler, Jay G. and Katz, Elihu (eds.) 1974: *The uses of mass communications: current perspectives on gratifications research*. London and Beverly Hills: Sage.

Boyce, George, Curran, James and Wingate, Pauline (eds.) 1978: *Newspaper history: from the seventeenth century to the present day*. London: Constable.

Briggs, Asa 1961–: *The history of broadcasting in the United Kingdom*, 4 vols. London: Oxford University Press.

Burns, Tom 1969: Public service and private world. In Halmos, Paul (ed.), *The sociology of mass-media communicators. The Sociological Review Monograph* 13, 53–73.

Burns, Tom 1977: *The BBC: public institution and private world*. London: Macmillan.

Chayes, Abram, *et al.* 1973: *Satellite broadcasting*. London: Oxford University Press.

Collins, Irene 1959: *The government and the newspaper press in France 1814–1881*. London: Oxford University Press.

Curran, James and Seaton, Jean 1985: *Power without responsibility: the press and broadcasting in Britain*, 2nd edn. London: Methuen.

Davis, Howard and Walton, Paul (eds.) 1983: *Language, image, media*. Oxford: Basil Blackwell.

Ferguson, Marjorie (ed.) 1986: *New communication technologies and the public interest: comparative perspectives on policy and research*. London and Beverly Hills: Sage.

Flichy, Patrice 1980: *Les Industries de l'imaginaire: pour une analyse économique des media*. Grenoble: Presses universitaires de Grenoble.

Galloway, Jonathan, F. 1972: *The politics and technology of satellite communications*. Lexington, Mass.: D. C. Heath.

Gelb, I. J. 1952: *A study of writing: the foundations of grammatology*. London: Routledge & Kegan Paul.

Gerbner, George and Gross, Larry P. 1976: Living with television: the violence profile. *Journal of Communication* 261, 173–99.

Giddens, Anthony 1985: *The nation-state and violence*. Cambridge: Polity Press.

Golding, Peter 1974: *The mass media*. Harlow, Essex: Longman.

Golding, Peter and Elliott, Philip 1979: *Making the news*. London: Longman.

Goody, Jack 1977: *The domestication of the savage mind*. Cambridge: Cambridge University Press.

Halloran, James (ed.) 1970: *The effects of television*. London: Panther.

Head, Sidney, W. 1976: *Broadcasting in America: a survey of television and radio*. Boston, Mass.: Houghton Mifflin.

Hodge, Robert and Tripp, David 1986: *Children and television: a semiotic approach*. Cambridge: Polity Press.

Horkheimer, Max and Adorno, Theodor W. 1972: The culture industry: enlightenment as mass deception. In their *Dialectic of enlightenment*, tr. John Cumming. New York: The Seabury Press, 120–67.

Innis, Harold A. 1950: *Empire and communications*. Oxford: Oxford University Press.

Liebes, Tamar and Katz, Elihu 1986: Patterns of involvement in television fiction: a comparative analysis. *European Journal of Communication* 1, 151–71.

Mattelart, Armand 1979: *Multinational corporations and the control of culture: the ideological apparatuses of imperialism*, tr. Michael Chanan. Brighton, Sussex: Harvester.

McQuail, Denis 1969: Uncertainty about the audience and the organization of mass communication. In Halmos, Paul (ed.), *The sociology of mass-media communicators*.

The Sociological Review Monograph 13, 75–84.

Morley, David 1980: *The 'nationwide' audience: structure and decoding*. London: British Film Institute.

Morley, David 1986: *Family television: cultural power and domestic leisure*. London: Comedia.

Olson, Kenneth, E. 1966: *The history makers: the press of Europe from its beginnings through 1965*. Baton Rouge: Louisiana State University Press.

Piepe, Anthony, Emerson, Miles and Lannon, Judy 1975: *Television and the working class*. Westmead, Farnborough, Hants: Saxon House.

Rosengren, Karl Erik (ed.) 1981: *Advances in content analysis*. London and Beverly Hills: Sage.

Rowland, Willard D. and Watkins, Bruce (eds.) 1985: *Interpreting television: current research perspectives*. London and Beverly Hills: Sage.

Schlesinger, Philip 1978: *Putting 'reality' together: BBC news*. London: Constable.

Schlesinger, Philip, Murdock, Graham and Elliott, Philip 1983: *Televising 'terrorism': political violence in popular culture*. London: Comedia.

Seymour-Ure, Colin. 1973: *The political impact of mass media*. London: Constable.

Social Trends 15. 1985. London: HMSO.

Steinberg, S. H. 1974: *Five hundred years of printing*. Harmondsworth, Middlesex: Penguin.

Tuchman, Gaye 1978: *Making news: a study in the construction of reality*. New York: The Free Press.

Tunstall, Jeremy 1983: *The media in Britain*. London: Constable.

Williams, Raymond 1961: *The long revolution*. Harmondsworth, Middlesex: Penguin.

Williamson, Judith 1978: *Decoding advertisements: ideology and meaning in advertising*. London: Marion Boyars.

Questions

1   How are modern systems of mass communication distinguished, in the extract, from earlier forms of direct, interpersonal communication?

2   Apply the three aspects of mass communication which Thompson outlines, to the study of a medium other than television.

3   Discuss the development of 'new' forms of mass communication or 'new' media (the internet, satellite and cable broadcasting, etc.) in the light of ideas and arguments put forward in the extract.

Further reading

Curran, J. and Gurevitch, M. (eds.) 1996: *Mass media and society*, 2nd edn. London: Edward Arnold.

McQuail, D. 1994: *Mass communication theory: an introduction*. London: Sage.

O'Sullivan, T., Dutton, B. and Rayner, P. 1994: *Studying the media: an introduction*. London: Edward Arnold.

Thompson, J. B. 1990: *Ideology and modern culture*. Cambridge: Polity Press.

Thompson, J. B. 1995: *The media and modernity*. Cambridge: Polity Press.

4

The Separation of Social Space from Physical Place
Joshua Meyrowitz

From No sense of place: the impact of electronic media on social behaviour (Oxford University Press 1985)

The central theme in this reading, as the title implies, is the analysis of how modern communication systems have had significant consequences for social experience and identity. In this part of his discussion, Meyrowitz develops a key issue which has preoccupied a number of writers and researchers, notably for instance the work of Marshall McLuhan in the 1960s. The extract extends one of the key points made by Thompson in the previous reading concerning the ways in which mass communication systems have both extended and expanded forms of communication across time and space. If, as in pre-industrial cultures, the physical boundaries and horizons of one's place and location once limited and anchored experience and identity, under conditions of modernity this is no longer the case. Increasingly, modern social life, especially in the 'electronic age', has meant living not only in a culture of physical situation but also in the world of *mediated* culture – mediated into the situation by means of film, radio, television screen and computer terminal. Meyrowitz suggests that the emergence of these and other communication technologies have effected revolutionary changes in modern consciousness and experience. The landscapes of immediate environment and location coexist and are shot through with other worlds – mediascapes – from 'outer space'.

Being 'alone' in a given place once meant that one was out of range of others' scrutiny. For people to experience each other directly, they had to travel through space, stay through time, and be admitted through the entrances of rooms and buildings. And these rules of physical place pertained to tents and palaces alike.

Although oral and print cultures differ greatly, the bond between physical place and social place was common to both of them. Print, like all new media, changed the patterns of information flow *to* and *from* places. As a result, it also changed the relative status and power of those in different places. Changes in media in the past have always affected the relationship *among* places. They have affected the information that people *bring* to places and the information that people have *in* given places. But the relationship between place and social situation was still quite strong. Electronic media go one step further: They lead to a nearly total dissociation of physical place and social 'place.' When we communicate through telephone, radio, television, or computer, where we are physically no longer determines where and who we are socially.

Physical passage and social passage

The relationship between physical place and social situation still seems so natural that we continue to confuse physical places with the behaviors that go on in them. The words 'school' and 'home,' for example, are used to refer both to physical buildings and to certain types of social interaction and behavior.

Before electronic media, there was ample reason to overlook the difference between physical places and social situations. Places defined most social information-systems. A given place-situation was spatially and temporally removed from other place-situations. It took time to travel from situation to situation, and distance was a measure of social insulation and isolation. Since rooms and buildings can be entered only through set doorways, people once could be included in and excluded from situations in clearly observable and predictable ways. Electronic media, however, make significant inroads into the situations once defined by physical location.

Communication and travel were once synonymous. Our country's communication channels were once roads, waterways, and railroads. In the 1830s, the fastest means of communication in the United States was the Pony Express. It took ten and a half days to communicate a message from Missouri to California.[1] The invention of the telegraph caused the first break between information movement and physical movement. For the first time, complex messages could move more quickly than a messenger could carry them.[2] With the invention and use of the telegraph, the informational differences between different places began to erode.

Just as students today are less anxious about attending a faraway college when home is only a phone call away, so did the telegraph greatly aid in the settlement of the Western frontier. The telegraph brought East and West [coasts of the USA] closer together informationally. Physical distance as a social barrier began to be bypassed through the shortening of communication 'distance.' The mutual monitoring of East and West made the country seem smaller and other places and people closer.

Movement from situation to situation and from social status to social status once involved movement from place to place. A place defined a distinct situation because its boundaries limited perception and interaction. Like all electronic media, the telegraph not only defies limits formerly set by distance, but also bypasses the social rite of 'passage,' that is, the act of moving both physically and socially from one 'position' to another.

If people are to behave very differently in different social situations, some clear form of movement from one situation to the next is needed. If a celebration and a memorial service take place in the same place and time, there can be no distinct behaviors for each situation. Entrances and the rites associated with them, whether formal (carrying a bride over the threshold) or informal ('Please knock before you enter my room'), have traditionally allowed for orderly transitions from situation to situation and from behavior pattern to behavior pattern.

The boundaries marked by walls, doors, and barbed wire, and enforced by laws, guards, and trained dogs, continue to define situations by including and excluding participants. But today such boundaries function to define social situations only to the extent that information can still be restricted by restricting physical access. And while much social information is still accessible only by going to a certain place or by meeting people face-to-face, the once consonant relationship between access to information and access to places has been greatly weakened by recent changes in communication media.

The messages in all early media – stone, clay, papyrus, parchment, and paper – have physical volume and weight. When they are heavy or unmovable, people have to go to a specific place to experience them. Even when they are portable, however, they still have to be physically transported from place to place, and they move with the people who possess them. They have to be carried into places, stored in places, and carried out of places. These media, like the people who carry them, are subject to the restraints of social and physical passage.

Electronic messages, however, do not make social entrances; they steal into places like thieves in the night. The 'guests' received by a child through electronic media no longer can be stopped at the door to be approved of by the masters of the house. Once a telephone, radio, or television is in the home, spatial isolation and guarding of entrances have no effect on information flow. Electronic messages seep through walls and leap across great distances. Indeed, were we not so accustomed to television and radio and telephone messages invading our homes, they might be the recurring subjects of nightmares and horror films. Whether the effects of such media on our society are good, bad, or neutral, the reprocessing of our physical and social environment is revolutionary.

As a result of electronically mediated interactions, the definition of situations and of behaviors is no longer determined by physical location. To be physically alone with someone is no longer necessarily to be socially alone with them. When there are other people 'there' on the telephone, or radio, or television, intimate encounters are changed.

By altering the informational characteristics of place, electronic media reshape social situations and social identities. The social meaning of a 'prison,' for example, has been changed as a result of electronic media of communication. Prisons were once more than places of physical incarceration; they were places of informational isolation as well. A prisoner was not only limited in movement but also 'ex-communicated' from society. The placement of prisoners in a secure, isolated *location* once led to both physical and informational separation from society. Today, however, many prisoners share with the larger society the privileges of radio, television, and telephone.[3] Whether this is good or bad is difficult to say, but it is different.

Prisoners' access to the world changes the social environment of both those inside and outside prison. Those outside prison cannot use television as a 'private' forum in which to discuss problems of crime and crime prevention, and prisoners can 'enter' society through the wires of the telephone. One survey of 208 inmates indicated that nine out of ten prisoners had 'learned new tricks and improved their criminal expertise by watching crime programs.'[4] Special publications such as *The Prisoner's Yellow Pages* have been prepared to help prisoners contact law libraries, counselling services, and employment agencies.[5]

For better or worse, those prisoners with access to electronic media are no longer completely segregated from society. The use of electronic media has led to a redefinition of the nature of 'imprisonment' and to a de facto revision of the prison classification system: The communication variables of 'high information' prisons versus 'low information' prisons now have been added to the physical variables of 'high security' and 'low security.'

The example of prisons may be extreme, but the impact of electronic media on prisoners is paralleled by the effects of electronic media on children, women, the poor, the disabled, and other groups whose social place was once shaped, at least in part, by physical isolation from the larger world.

Electronic media bring information and experience to everyplace from everyplace. State funerals, wars, hostage crises, and space flights are dramas that can be played on the stage of anyone's living room. And the characters in these dramas are experienced almost as if they were sitting on the living room sofa.

Communicating through electronic media is certainly not equivalent to traveling from place to place and interacting with others in live encounters, but the information transmitted by electronic media is much more similar to face-to-face interaction than is the information conveyed by books or letters. And 'relationships' with others through electronic media are accessible to virtually everyone without regard to physical location and social 'position.'

Media 'friends'

Electronic media's encroachment on place is suggested in one of the clichés of the broadcasting industry: 'This show is brought to you *live* from ...' Once, physical presence was necessary for the experience of a 'live,' ongoing event. You 'had to be there' to experience an informal and intimate interaction. Place once defined a very special category of communication. Electronic media, however, have changed the relative significance of live and mediated encounters. Through electronic media of communication, social performers now 'go' where they would not or could not travel, and audiences are now 'present' at distant events.

What sort of relationship is formed between people who experience each other only through electronic media? In a perceptive article on media written in the 1950s, Donald Horton and R. Richard Wohl suggest that even when the communication is unidirectional, such as in radio and television, a special relationship develops that did not and could not exist in print media. What is unusual about the new mass media, they suggest, is that they offer the illusion of face-to-face interaction with performers and political figures. 'The conditions of response to the performer are analogous to those in a primary group. The most remote and illustrious men are met *as if* they were in the circle of one's peers.'[6]

Horton and Wohl suggest that the new media lead to a new type of relationship which they call 'para-social interaction.' They argue that although the relationship is mediated, it psychologically resembles face-to-face interaction. Viewers come to feel they 'know' the people they 'meet' on television in the same way they know their friends and associates. In fact, many viewers begin to believe that they know and understand a performer better than all the other viewers do. Paradoxically, the para-social performer is able to establish 'intimacy with millions.'

Horton and Wohl's framework explains the popularity of talk show hosts such as Jack Paar, Johnny Carson, and Dick Cavett. These are people, according to Horton and Wohl, who have no traditional performance skill; they are not singers, musicians, actors, or even professional-quality comedians. The content of their 'performance' is mostly small talk and running gags. Yet they are likeable and interesting in the same way that a close friend is likeable and interesting. The viewer can rely on them to be 'themselves.' As Horton and Wohl suggest, the pure para-social performer is simply 'known for being known.' Within this framework, it makes sense that stories about Johnny Carson's threats to resign from the 'Tonight' show, his arrest for suspicion of drunk driving, and his divorce settlement have been reported on the network news and in front page headlines.

Even performers with traditional skills often exploit the intimacy of the new media (or find that they cannot avoid it). As a result of close personal observation, many athletes, musicians, journalists, and politicians are now judged not only on the basis of their 'talent' but also on the basis of their personalities. The para-social framework may explain why many singing stars turn to more and more personal lyrics and themes as their careers develop and why public officials often add more private information to their public speeches as they become more widely known. The theory can also be extended to actors playing fictional roles. For many viewers, soap opera and other television characters are real people to whom they can turn for inspiration and advice. During his first five years on network television, the fictional 'Dr. Marcus Welby' received a quarter of a million letters, most requesting medical advice.[7]

Horton and Wohl do not link their framework to an analysis of the impact of electronic media on physical place, but they do offer observations that support such an analysis. They note, for example, that the para-social relationship has its greatest impact on the 'socially isolated, the socially inept, the aged and invalid, the timid and rejected.'[8] Because electronic media provide the types of interaction and experience which were once restricted to intimate live encounters, it makes sense that they would have their greatest effect on those who are physically or psychologically removed from everyday social interaction. (One researcher has found that the strength of the para-social relationship increases with the viewer's age, that many elderly people think of newscasters as their friends, and that some older viewers 'interact' with newscasters by responding to them verbally.') Even among 'average' people, the para-social relationship takes its place among daily live interactions with friends, family, and associates. Indeed, 'real' friends often discuss the antics of their para-social friends.

The para-social framework is extremely useful in analyzing many phenomena not specifically discussed by Horton and Wohl. The framework explains, for example, why it is that when a 'media friend' such as Elvis Presley, John Kennedy, or John Lennon dies or is killed, millions of people may experience a sense of loss as great as (and sometimes greater than) the feelings of loss accompanying the death of a relative or friend. Even an awareness of the para-social mechanism is not enough to permit escape from its 'magic'; the death of John Lennon, for example, was strangely painful to me and my university colleagues who had 'known' him and grown up 'with' him. Sociologist Candice Leonard has suggested that such mediated relationships lead to a 'new genre of human grief.'[10]

Unlike the loss of a real friend or relative, the death of a media friend does not provide traditional rituals or clear ways to comfort the bereaved. Indeed, the mourning for a para-social friend is filled with paradox and helplessness. Attempts to comfort the dead person's family with words or flowers are intrusions by strangers. And intensely felt personal grief is simultaneously strengthened and weakened by the extent to which it is shared with the crowd. In order to banish the demons of grief and helplessness, therefore, thousands of people take to the streets or hold vigils near the para-social friend's home or place of death.

Ironically, but appropriately, the media provide the most ritualized channels of mourning. Radio and television present specials and retrospectives. And many people use the telephone to contact real friends who shared the intimacy with the para-social friend. But the final irony is that, in some ways, the para-social performer does not die. For the *only* means through which most people came to know him or her – records, films, and videotape – are still available. The relationship is frozen, rather than destroyed. In part, it is the potential and hope for increased intimacy that dies, and the never to be face-to-face consummation of the relationship that is mourned.

The para-social relationship has also led to a new form of murder and a new type of murder motive. Police generally distinguish between two types of murders: those committed by a person who knows the victim, and those committed by a stranger. Yet, there is now a third category: the para-social murder. While the media and police noted that John Lennon's murderer was a 'complete stranger' – meaning that the two had never physically met – they overlooked the powerful para-social ties between them. Mark David

Chapman knew John Lennon so well that for a time he thought he *was* John Lennon.[11] A similarly bizarre relationship existed between would-be presidential assassin John Hinckley and actress Jodie Foster. Hinckley committed his 'historic act' in order to cement a 'personal' relationship with Foster.[12]

In both love and hate, normal and bizarre, the para-social relationship is a new form of interaction. It has some of the traditional characteristics of both live encounters and communication through books, but it is, in fact, neither.

In formulating the notion of para-social interaction, Horton and Wohl point to the differences between 'old' and 'new' media. But they overlook the overall evolutionary trend, even within each type of medium, toward a shrinking of the differences between live and mediated encounters. Writing systems have evolved toward greater replication of spoken sounds (from hieroglyphs to the phonetic alphabet) and photography and electronic media have evolved toward fuller representations of face-to-face sensory experiences.

Media theorist Paul Levinson has detailed the long-term evolutionary course of media.[13] He argues that the trend is toward fuller replication of the means of communication that existed *before* media and technology. Levinson's theory gives substance to our intuitive sense that one form of a medium is 'better' than another. The addition of voice to the telegraph, or sound to silent movies, or color to television, he suggests, is perceived as an 'improvement' simply because the medium becomes less like a medium and more like life.

Levinson uses his theoretical framework to reject the criticism of many social theorists who suggest that media are distorting the human condition by taking us further and further away from 'reality.' Levinson argues, in contrast, that human beings use media to recreate as 'natural' and as 'human' a means of communicating as possible, while at the same time overcoming pre-technological limitations to communication (lack of permanent records, impossibility of speaking or seeing across vast distances, impossibility of being in two places at once, and so on).

Levinson's fascinating description of media history shows how an early form of a medium first gives up aspects of the 'real world' in order to overcome a spatial or temporal limitation and how later forms of the medium then recapture aspects of natural communication. The telegraph, for example, gave up speech in order to travel quickly across the continent and globe; but then the telegraph evolved into the telephone which regained the human voice.

A major problem with Levinson's framework, however, is that he completely overlooks the ways in which the original spatial and temporal 'limits' help to define the nature of social interaction. In suggesting that media recreate reality, Levinson defines 'reality' in terms of sensory functions of communication – seeing, hearing, speaking. He ignores the ways in which the substance of human interaction changes when the barriers among situations are removed.

The theories of Levinson and of Horton and Wohl are helpful here because they suggest that face-to-face interaction is no longer the only determinant of personal and intimate interaction. The evolution of media has begun to cloud the differences between stranger and friend and to weaken the distinction between people who are 'here' and people who are 'somewhere else.' These frameworks suggest that electronic media are unique in that they mask the differences between direct and indirect communication. What is missing from these theories, however, is an appreciation of how much social behavior changes when people are able to communicate 'as if' they were in the same place when they are, in fact, in different places.

[...]

Time and space 'saturation'

With its natural insulation, physical place was once the prime determinant of the definition of a situation. The spatial and temporal isolation of a physical location allowed for *one* definition of the situation to 'saturate' the time/space frame. Goffman discusses 'saturation' as a characteristic of Anglo-American societies where social performances tend to be given indoors and where 'the impression and understanding fostered by the performance will tend to saturate the region and time span, so that any individual located in this space-time manifold will be in a position to observe the performance and be guided by the definition of the situation which the performance fosters.'[14]

Any medium can pull a person out of the definition of the situation. Print media and electronic media, however, differ in their impact on the definitions of situations and on the relationship between situations and places.

Print media tend to create new, totally absorbing definitions. Reading is best done alone, in a quiet place, and to the exclusion of other activities. Indeed, special places are designated for reading. These places are designed to separate people, often into single-person cubicles. A reader, of course, is 'connected' with other people by reading what they have written or what has been written about them, but the reader tends to be removed from those physically present. (Indeed, even when someone hands you a greeting card, you must ignore them for a moment in order to read it.) In this sense, reading is 'anti-social'; it isolates the reader from live interactions. Reading is linear and absorbing. It is difficult to walk, talk, eat, exercise, make love, or drive an automobile while reading. Yet most of these activities are possible while watching television, and all are possible while listening to the radio.

In these ways, electronic media invade places, yet do not 'occupy' them in the way that other media such as books do. Television not only changes the definition of the situation in places, but it does so in an unstable and inconsistent manner.

[...]

Electronic media destroy the specialness of place and time. Television, radio, and telephone turn once private places into more public ones by making them more accessible to the outside world. And car stereos, wristwatch televisions, and personal sound systems such as the Sony 'Walkman' make public spaces private. Through such media, what is happening almost any-where can be happening wherever we are. Yet when we are everywhere, we are also no place in particular.

'Home is wherever there's a telephone,' says one telephone company ad. This analysis suggests, as well, that 'anywhere there's a telephone is no longer the same home.' Those entering many places no longer find them information-ally special. Places visited for the first time now look familiar if they (or places like them) have already been seen on television. And places that were once very different are now more similar because nearly every place has a television set, radio, and telephone. With electronic media, most places – from the child's room to the priest's home to the prisoner's cell – now have a strong common denominator. Those aspects of group identity, socialization, and hierarchy that were once dependent on particular physical locations and the special experi-ences available in them have been altered by electronic media.

Notes

1. Settel, 1967, p. 17.
2. One exception to this was the system of semaphore tower stations designed by Claude Chappe about fifty years before Morse's telegraph. The 'arms' were set in different positions to signify different letters. The system was adopted by the French government. But the semaphore was only a crude forerunner of the telegraph. The transmission of semaphore messages still depended on 'ordinary' sensory perception (the arms were large enough to be visible five miles away at the next relay station). No messages could be sent during bad weather or at night. And such a system must have been relatively difficult to construct and operate and impossible to duplicate in as many locations as the telegraph and other electronic media would later service. See Settel, 1967, p. 15 for a brief discussion of semaphores.
3. Access to media in prisons varies from state to state and from prison to prison, and, apparently, there have been no comprehensive surveys of media access in correction-al institutions. Available sources of information, however, indicate that there has been substantial access to media among most prisoners since the late 1960s. Charlotte A. Nesbitt, of the American Correctional Association notes that 'in most jails and prisons, prisoners do have access to telephones, radios, and television' (per-sonal correspondence, June 1983). A survey conducted in 1979 by the Criminal Justice Information Service (operated by the Contact organization) indicates that all states except Ohio allow prisoners to make telephone calls and that approximately fifty percent of the states allow inmates to receive calls ('Your Number, Please,' 1979). The Director of the Federal Prison System, Norman A. Carlson, reports that federal prisons do not allow personal television sets, but that each housing unit with-in each prison generally has at least one television set and that a majority vote among prisoners determines program selection (personal correspondence, June 1983). Many state prisons do allow personal television sets, radios, tape players, and stereos in prisoners cells (Donna Hunzeker, Director, Information Services, Contact Inc., per-sonal correspondence, June 1983).
4. Hendrick, 1977, p. 5.
5. Board of Institutional Ministry, 1978.
6. Horton and Wohl, 1956, p. 215.
7. Gross and Jeffries-Fox, 1978, p. 247.

8. Horton and Wohl, 1956, p. 223.
9. Levy, 1979.
10. Candice Leonard, personal communication, December 1980.
11. Mathews *et al.*, 1980. Like Lennon, Chapman played the guitar and married a Japanese woman. Chapman had also taped Lennon's name over his own on his workplace identification tag.
12. Hinckley's last love letter, 1981.
13. Levinson, 1979.
14. Goffman, 1959, p. 106.

References

Board of Institutional Ministry 1978: *The prisoners yellow pages*. Los Angeles: Universal Press.

Goffman, E. 1959: *The presentation of self in everyday life*. New York: Anchor.

Gross, L. and Jeffries-Fox, S. 1978: What do you want to be when you grow up, little girl? In Tuchman, G. (ed.), *Hearth and home: images of women in the mass media*. New York: Oxford University Press.

Hendrick, G. H. 1977: When television is a school for criminals. *TV Guide*, 29 January, 4–10.

Hinkley's last love letter 1981. *Newsweek*, 13 April, 35.

Horton, D. and Wohl, R. 1956: Mass communication and para-social interaction: observations on intimacy at a distance. *Psychiatry* 19, 215–29.

Levinson, P. 1979: *Human replay: a theory of the evolution of media*. Diss: New York University.

Levy, M. 1979: Watching TV news as para-social interaction. *Journal of Broadcasting* 23, 69–80.

Mathews, T. *et al.* 1980: Lennon's alter ego. *Newsweek*, 22 December, 34–5.

Settel, I. 1967: *A pictorial history of radio*. New York: Grosset & Dunlap.

Questions

1   Briefly summarise the key ideas covered in the extract, substituting some of your own examples for those discussed by Meyrowitz. What do you understand by *para-social interaction*? How have electronic media had implications for the public sphere and for private spaces and situations?

2   In a celebrated and much quoted metaphor, Marshall McLuhan once argued that modern media systems had the potential to establish a *'global village'*, networks of communication capable of shrinking the world, or at least of bringing it to us. What are the arguments and issues posed by this idea? How much of your own everyday media consumption takes you out of the immediate confines of space and time?

3   Underlying some of the assumptions made in the extract is a strong emphasis on electronic communication technologies as key factors in explaining historical and cultural change. Refer to any current or historical media technologies and assess the degree to which the technologies, considered in isolation, can be accepted as the most significant factors in understanding processes of social change.

Further reading

Carey, J.W. 1989: *Communication as culture: essays on media and society.* St Albans: Paladin.

Carpenter, E. 1976: *Oh, what a blow that phantom gave me!* St Albans: Paladin.

Ferguson, M. 1991: Marshall McLuhan re-visited: 1960s zeitgeist victim or pioneer postmodernist? *Media, Culture and Society* 13, 71–90.

Giddens, A. 1991: *Modernity and self-identity.* Cambridge: Polity Press.

Jensen, J. 1990: *Redeeming modernity.* London: Sage.

McLuhan, M. 1964: *Understanding media.* London: Routledge & Kegan Paul.

Morley, D. 1992: Where the global meets the local: notes from the sitting-room. In *Television, audiences and cultural studies.* London: Routledge. (See Section 5, reading 3.)

Stevenson, N. 1995: *Understanding media cultures.* London: Sage.

5

Communications and the Constitution of Modernity
Graham Murdock

From *Media, Culture and Society* 15, 521–39 (1993)

This extract continues the interrogation of the rise of modern social and cultural conditions and the centrality of increasingly large-scale networks and systems of mass communication in that process. In this essay, Murdock aims to counter and qualify some of the themes in recent postmodern writing by restating the need for forms of analysis and research which are both historically informed and take into account the central dynamics of modern communications systems. In understanding modern times, he argues, the organisation of media and communications systems have come to play an increasingly important role in shaping and constituting both institutional and everyday levels of culture and interaction.

The extract provides an account of the relationships between opposing versions of the modern consumer versus the modern citizen, as they have been mobilised in and underpinned media development in the twentieth century. It also serves to develop some key themes introduced in earlier readings in this section, concerning the impact of mass communications on the public and private spheres of contemporary culture and social life.

Approaching modernity

We can define modernity in its most general sense as that complex of processes that detached societies from the economic, social and cultural formations we now characterize as 'ancient' or 'traditional', and constructed the formations we have come to see as defining the distinctiveness of the contemporary world. These processes include: the rise of capitalism as the dominant mode of economic organization, the development of the nation-state as the modal unit of political administration and action, the ending of religious monopolies over thought and knowledge and the emergence of a more fragmented and contested cultural field, in which contending discourses struggle for public visibility and authority.

Several features of this definition are worth underlining. First, it insists that modernity is best seen as a set of dynamics rather than as a condition, a continual process of becoming rather than an accomplished state of being. The centrality of movement and mobility struck commentators with increasing force in the early decades of the nineteenth century as they witnessed modernity's coming of age. For Jane Austen in *Persuasion*, to be modern was to embrace a 'state of alteration'. For Charles Baudelaire, a little later, it was an altogether more vertiginous experience dominated by the 'ephemeral, fugitive and contingent'. While for Marx, in that much quoted passage in the *Communist Manifesto*, it was a wholesale process of 'creative destruction', in which the dynamics of capitalism swept away 'all fixed, fast-frozen relations' and ushered in an era of 'uninterrupted disturbance' and 'everlasting uncertainty'. This experience was, from the outset, a source of profound ambivalence, whereby hopes for progress and a better future were soured by the recognition of novel risks and new sources of servitude. Consequently, as Berman has reminded us, to be modern is to 'find ourselves in an environment that promises us adventure, power, joy, growth, transformation of ourselves and the world – and at the same time, that threatens to destroy everything we have, everything we know, everything we are' (Berman, 1983: 39).

[...]

One of the central tensions in modern experience centres on the competition between the identities of consumer and citizen. The development of the modern nation-state can be read, in part, as a history of attempts to manage mass participation in the political process. These efforts have been dominated by two opposed rhetorical figures. On the one side stood the crowd, emotional, seduced by dramatic images, acting in concert, bargaining by riot and demonstration. On the other side stood the citizen, rational, open to sequential argument, making considered personal choices and registering preferences soberly, in the solitude of the voting booth. Official discourse has, not surprisingly, devoted itself to advancing the responsibilities of citizenship and denigrating the seductions of the crowd. The figure of the consumer, however, presents considerable problems for this enterprise, for two reasons. First, the consumer system offers personal solutions to public difficulties. It promises that it is possible to purchase peace of mind and well-being by buying a suitable commodity. In so doing, it cuts across the appeals to the public good that underpin the rhetorics of citizenship. Secondly, as early observers were quick to see, consumer markets could be viewed as 'psychological crowds' in the sense that the vagaries of fashion and the advent of crazes also required immersion in the warm bath of collective action.

This perceived tension between the ideal citizen and the prototypical modern consumer mapped itself on to the institutional struggles between the systems of representation mobilized within the sphere of legitimated 'politics' (organized around party competition and pressure group lobbying) and the systems being developed within the emerging mass consumer system and the commercial cultural industries. These tensions emerge particularly clearly within the history of public broadcasting as it struggles to accommodate itself to the controlling impetus of the state and the requirements of mass democracy within a popular cultural field dominated by commercialized entertainment. From this perspective, what Bauman characterizes as a distinctively postmodern problem of representation is more usefully seen as an intensification of contradictions that have been unfolding since the early years of the century, when the state, the party system, the mass consumer system and the modern popular media, began to coalesce into something like their present forms. The present crisis of representation is precisely a crisis in the relationship between the discourses of the major parties (particularly on the Left) and the available institutions of public communications. These discourses are losing their purchase on public attention and support and are subject to challenge from counter-discourses rooted in racism, nationalism, fundamentalism and the new social movements. This fragmentation of the field of 'political' discourse creates an acute crisis for a public broadcasting system organized around the institutions and rhetorics of the major parties. At the same time, the accelerating privatization of the cultural field and the proliferation of new distribution channels alter the terms of public broadcasting's relation to commercialized popular culture and the consumer system. Competition for core productive resources, creative labour, intellectual property rights and audience time and allegiance intensifies. One response is to redefine the rights of citizenship as coterminous with the rights of consumers. As a result, public institutions begin to talk of the constituencies they serve as clients or customers. To understand these shifts, however, we need to see them as a further extension of the process of commodification that lies at the heart of modernity's political economy.

[...]

The rise of modern communications is inextricably bound up with the onward march of commodification. More and more areas of communicative activity become commodified. Cultural artefacts are increasingly made under conditions of wage labour for sale in the market. Newspaper readerships and audiences for commercial broadcasting become constituted as commodities for sale to advertisers. Ideas and expressions of all kinds become intellectual properties, protected by the walls and ditches of copyright law. What theorists of postmodern culture celebrate as intertextuality and playful pastiche, corporate lawyers prosecute as theft. When a British artist can be brought before the court for including 'unauthorized' images of the children's storybook character, Noddy, in a painting, it is difficult not to see cultural capitalism redrawing the boundaries of permissible quotation in its favour.

The process of commodification is also central to understanding the reorganization of what we can call the central coordinates of modernity – the new structures of time and space. Prompted by developments in human geography and elsewhere, questions about the role of time and space in constituting social order have recently received renewed attention from social theorists. Here again, Giddens has been in the vanguard. For him, explicating 'how the limitations of individual "presence" are transcended by the "stretching" of social relations across time and space' is *the* 'fundamental question of social theory' (Giddens, 1984: 38). He certainly sees this process as central to modernity, arguing that 'The dynamism of modernity derives from the separation of time and space and their recombination' (Giddens, 1990: 16–17).

The first of these movements, separation, has proved to be highly problematic for conceptualization, particularly in relation to space. Modern thought has tended to associate time with mobility and change and space with stasis and rootedness. And as Massey has pointed out, this dualistic thinking has prevented us from viewing space more productively, 'as a moment in the intersection of configured social relations' which have an existence through time (Massey, 1992: 80). This is easier to see in relation to 'pre-modern' societies since social activities generally required people to come together in a particular place at an agreed time. Buyers and sellers had to meet and bargain in the marketplace. Priests and believers performed rituals at special times in sacred sites set apart from mundane space. Storytellers and performers addressed physical audiences. Under conditions of modernity, however, a wide range of social relations can be sustained without co-presence. Space becomes detached from place. Markets become networks rather than spaces for encounters. Audiences become interpretive communities rather than physical congregations.

These new 'distanced' relations depend in turn on what Giddens calls 'disembedding' mechanisms, which 'lift out social activity from localised contexts, reorganising social relations across large time-space distances' (1990: 53). Money is one such mechanism, the modern media of communication are another. In combination they present a powerful transformative force. Goods can be ordered and delivered by mail. Deals can be done by letter and paper money. Tellers of tales can reach unseen audiences through printed texts which readers can then peruse at a time to suit them.

This increasing detachment of experience from specific times and places is accompanied by a second and, in many ways, contradictory movement towards standardization, based on the imposition of measures that are abstract, uniform and invariant. The standardization of calendars, coupled with the ascendency of clock time and the construction of a global grid of time zones (measured in degrees east or west of the Greenwich meridian) displaces other ways of marking the passage of time, relegating them to subordinate or localized positions. These include diurnal movements from light to dark, seasonal cycles, body rhythms, and liturgical intervals between feasts and fasts. Similarly, standard units of distance and territorial measurement incorporate space into a single regime of measurement.

Communications and modernity

What, then, can we say in general terms about the relations between communications and the formations of modernity? What lines of enquiry suggest themselves for future work? Several candidates have already presented themselves. By way of a conclusion, I want to offer a more synoptic account of where we might go from here.

We first need to reject all forms of technological determinism and media centrism. The history of communications is not a history of machines but a history of the way new media help to reconfigure systems of power and networks of social relations. In order to understand this process we must avoid instrumentalism. Communications technologies are certainly produced within particular centres of power and deployed with particular purposes in mind but, once in play, they often have unintended and contradictory consequences. They are, therefore, more usefully viewed not as technologies of control or of freedom, but as the site of continual struggles over interpretation and use. At the heart of these struggles, lies the shifting boundary between the public and private spheres. Tracing these movements provides a productive place to begin an investigation of the role of communications and the constitution of modernity.

It has become increasingly evident in the last few years that the metaphor of the text and the reader no longer captures the complexity of the people's relationship to communication systems. This has prompted researchers to develop alternative models based around notions of consumption and use. This line of enquiry has been pursued most vigorously in relation to the new domestic technologies of communication, particularly the video recorder, home computers and the telephone, which up until recently had been more or less passed over by communications research. This work challenges the conventional line that research has drawn between public and private media and obliges us to rethink our approach to the relations between communications and sociability.

These relations work in at least three dimensions. First, and perhaps most obviously, modern communicative facilities allow for the extension of intimacy. A man carries the photo of his wife in his wallet. A woman talks on the telephone to a close friend now living in another city. Secondly, they produce new forms of sociability and offer new pretexts for solitude and social withdrawal. Friends gather round the television screen to celebrate periodic rituals: the Cup Final, the Super Bowl, a Royal Wedding. More mundanely, media are incorporated into domestic routines marking off segments of the day and periods of gregariousness. They also provide new sites for separation and autonomy. A child withdraws to the bedroom to play a computer game. A mother takes time off from tending to her family's needs by reading a romantic novel. Thirdly, and more complexly, modern media produce new forms of parasocial interaction, in which people enjoy intimate relations with people they may never meet or talk to in person. A university student leaves a message on a computer bulletin board inviting replies. A listener calls a disc jockey at a radio station to ask for a favourite song to be played. An elderly, housebound lady follows the trials and tribulations of the characters in her favourite soap opera as though they were an extension of her own extended family. A dedicated fan searches out every film featuring their favourite star and avidly collects photographs and memorabilia. A politician's personal misdemeanours are paraded in the popular press, eroding the line between front- and backstage areas, public persona and private life.

These complex reconfigurations of the public and private domains are linked in turn to the ways that communications systems help to reconstitute space/time relations. One of the major social 'effects' of broadcasting has been to reinforce the hegemony of standard time. From Lord Reith's early celebration of the BBC's ability to carry the chimes of Big Ben into every home in the land, to the present ubiquity of time checks, broadcasting has helped to cement a standardized regime of time. But it has also helped to reconfigure personal time and its links to historical memory. As a mode of storage, it has constructed an unparalleled archive of personal, vernacular testimonies, professional performances and pronouncements by experts and public figures. This dense network of oral threads is now woven into the texture of popular memory, providing social markers for measuring the passage of personal time, and potent resources for the construction of new forms of reminiscence and nostalgia. Together with old films, past hit records and selected photographs, broadcast archives furnish the major means of connecting autobiography to history.

A parallel process is at work in the domain of space. It is not simply that modern communications systems are the basic precondition for modernity's characteristic separation of space from place, together with the displacement of locations by networks and the creation of new forms of social relations combining intimacy and distance. New communications facilities also generate entirely new forms of space. What is now called 'dataspace', for example, is the latest outcome of a long process through which measures of exchange value have become progressively less tangible. As the economic dynamics of modernity unfolded so gold coinage gave way to printed notes backed by gold, which in turn gave way to 'pure' paper money, which is then translated into computer records so that the money in my bank account exists now

> only as an object in the dataspace, located in the section defined by my bank's computers. While it has a physical representation as a pattern of magnetisation on a disc, its 'reality' is in the computer-defined domain of the dataspace. (Thompson, 1993: 17)

This example is a good instance of a general problem in our current approach to the development of modern communications. Discussions of 'dataspace' would not find their way into many accounts because they are seen to be about 'private' communications networks and, therefore, not relevant to the history of 'public' communications. A number of commentators have recognized that this simplistic division is unhelpful in relation to the new communications technologies, where networks such as bulletin boards straddle both domains. But they have failed to understand that it is equally unproductive for earlier periods. Against this we need to see the boundary separating public and private as continually contested, and to explore the shifting, and sometimes surprising, interactions between them.

Modern warfare is an instructive case in point. Most histories focus on the development of weapon systems, but it is arguable that the development of command control and communications systems is more important. These provide the basic preconditions for the effective coordination of troops and supplies across extensive theatres of conflict. They also shift the relationship between action and consequence. By facilitating the progressive detachment of aggression from its target, as in high-altitude bombing raids or long-distance artillery, communications systems reconfigure the moral calculus of conflict, producing images of the recent Gulf War in which video footage shot from the cockpit purported to show 'clean' surgical strikes on military targets. These images, originated in the privileged and restricted domain of internal military communication, were released into the public domain as part of a propaganda offensive. Only when counter images, taken on the ground, began to appear in the public domain did it become evident that the declared intentions had gone badly wrong, causing extensive civilian casualties. This slippage points to the increasing problems of maintaining an effective system of official controls over communication in an era of proliferating image making. Images carefully crafted for public consumption are counterposed against 'unauthorized' and vernacular images of public functionaries and their actions.

The contemporary crisis of representation is in part a crisis of control. A number of writers have stressed the central role of reflexivity in the constitution of modernity, the fact that 'modernity transforms the web of institutions' and that 'reflexivity is the measure and medium of this transformation' (Beck, 1992: 164). Communications systems play a central role in this process, since they are the main means through which information and debate about past plans and actions can be stored and retrieved. Control over access to the means of critical reflection is therefore of considerable significance. Recent commentaries on this issue have emphasized the central role of experts and expert systems in regulating reflexivity and addressing the issue of risk. What people know depends on what they are told and by whom. What they believe depends on who they trust. In the contest for minds and hearts under modernity, the claims of expertise have been continually pitched against the testimony of experience. This is particularly evident in certain forms of news and documentary expression, where the ethos of radical populism, with its deep-rooted distrust of officialdom in all its forms, has been anchored by the celebration of eye-witness accounts and grounded experience, whether provided by journalists or participants. As we noted earlier, however, the question of representation involves issues of cultural form as well as of social delegation. Here we need to explore, much more fully than we have done so far, the shifting relation between language and imagery in popular representation. The development of lithography and, later, of photo-journalism and the silent cinema, changed the terms of this relation, creating new collisions between the sequential arguments carried by language and the proliferating connotations detonated by the accompanying imagery. Claims to plausibility and authority came to depend as much on what speakers or writers looked like as on what they said. In approaching this problem, there is little to be gained from lamenting the loss of some imagined era of 'pure' discourse and complaining about the inability of commercial television or the tabloid press to stage rational debates. Instead, we need to investigate the complex interplay between formations of discourse and formations of visual representation as it has unfolded under modernity, and to trace its consequences for the constitution of public knowledge and belief.

As argued earlier, part of this history centres on the competing identities and vocabularies of motive offered by the rhetorics of consumption and citizenship. Bauman speaks for many recent writers when he argues that whereas 'classical' modernity was organized around production, postmodernity (or, as I prefer, high modernity) is oriented to consumption and that 'consumer choice has been entrenched as the point at which systematic reproduction, social integration and individual life world are coordinated and harmonized' (Bauman, 1992: 52). Once again, the shifting relations between the public and private spheres, understood in this instance as the progressive commercialization and commodification of public culture, is central to an adequate analysis. But Bauman is perhaps overly eager to claim a *fait accompli*. The consumer system is undoubtably central to late modernity, as both an institutional and cultural formation and as an organizing principle of everyday life. And the commercial communications system has certainly played a pivotal role in bringing this about, by providing the main site for the advertising and publicity that promotes the system and by offering an enticing array of consumer options in its own right. But its forward march has not gone uncontested. It has to contend with the still powerful rhetorics offered by the imagined community of the nation and with proliferating claims to social representation and social justice. In the end, arguments about unequal life chances cannot be entirely satisfied by the offer of an open choice of life styles in the marketplace. The history of the struggle between the discourses and dynamics of citizenship, consumerism and social division, is one we need to trace as a matter of urgency if we are to address the present crisis of representation in all its ramifications.

References

Bauman, Zygmunt 1992: *Intimations of postmodernity*. London: Routledge.
Beck, Ulrich 1992: How modern is modern society? *Theory, Culture and Society* 9(2), 163–9.

Berman, Marshal 1983: *All that is solid melts into air.* London: Verso.
Giddens, Anthony 1984: *The constitution of society.* Oxford: Polity Press.
Giddens, Anthony 1990: *The consequences of modernity.* Oxford: Polity Press.
Massey, Doreen 1992: Politics and space-time. *New Left Review* 196 (Nov./Dec.),
    65–84.
Thompson, Bill 1993: Tapping into a new universe. *Guardian* 18 February, 17.

Questions

1   Summarise and review the definition of modernity offered in the extract. What does Murdock suggest about the relations between communications and the formations of modernity?
2   How have the notions and identities of 'consumer' and 'citizen' been influential in the development of modern conditions and modern media systems?
3   How have recent advances in communications reshaped or reconfigured public and private domains? Develop some of these ideas with reference to examples of your own.

Further reading

Curran, J. and Gurevitch, M. (eds.) 1991: *Mass media and society.* London: Edward
    Arnold.
Dahlgren, P. 1995: *Television and the public sphere: citizenship, democracy and the
    media.* London: Sage.
Kellner, D. 1995: *Media culture.* London: Routledge.
McRobbie, A. 1994: *Postmodernism and cultural studies.* London: Routledge.
Stevenson, N. 1995: *Understanding media cultures: social theory and mass communi-
    cation.* London: Sage. (See Section 3, reading 7.).
Thompson, J.B. 1996: *The media and modernity.* Cambridge: Polity Press.

6

Public Service Broadcasting and Modern Public Life
Paddy Scannell

From *Media, Culture and Society* 11, 135–66 (1989)

In their differing ways the last three readings have suggested that the nature, scale and shape of twentieth-century experience has been profoundly transformed, extended and constituted by the expansion of mass communication systems. In this final reading of Section 1, Scannell focuses on the consequences of the development of broadcasting, both radio and television. In particular he is concerned to evaluate the historical contributions made to modern democratic cultures by the institutional practices and consequences of public service broadcasting.

In Britain and many other modern nation states, public service forms of broadcasting have entailed the organisation of radio and television services primarily as public utilities and resources, rather than as profitable commodities. This emphasis has encompassed their organisation and control as national cultural institutions owned, regulated and run in the public interest and dedicated to the public provision of information and entertainment. In these terms, broadcasters have been obliged to serve the public in various ways rather than simply to follow the dictates of commercial markets. The history of the development of broadcasting systems in many nation states from the 1920s onwards has been profoundly influenced by the values and discourses of public service, either in the form of publicly owned state monopolies (for example, the BBC, pre-1955) or more recently as a significant public element within mixed systems which allow for competition between commercial and public variants of radio and TV.

The ethos of public service broadcasting and the practices associated with it have changed considerably since earlier decades of the century. Scannell's historical assessment – and what follows is again only an extract from the whole essay – needs to be set in the context of two particular issues. First, the accelerating demise of the public service ideal which has occurred particularly as a result of the policies of deregulation in the British broadcast sector in the last 20 years and the expansion of new commercial and technological forms of media to challenge the previous dominance of public service media. Second, Scannell is concerned to argue for a more positive reassessment of the achievements and values of public service broadcasting than has generally been accorded. In particular he takes issue with what he sees as the rather one-dimensional critiques of public service broadcasting which have condemned it for its elitism and ideological bias. From his point of view, public service radio and television have enabled genuinely new forms of communicative relationships to emerge in an expanded, modern and democratic public sphere. This leads him to argue for the centrality of *communicative entitlements* or *communicative rights*, which he sees as enshrined in and guaranteed by public service provision and worthy of retaining into the twenty-first century.

> We defend public services as if they existed only for the poor when in fact their rationale is to create common conditions of life for all classes.
>
> (Michael Ignatieff, *Guardian*, 4 April 1988)

If broadcasting today is defensible as a public service it can only be as a service to the public. And yet what the word *public* means in the context of broadcasting remains remarkably underexamined in debates about the social role of radio and television now and in the future. When the Peacock Committee turned to the broadcasters for their interpretations of public service they remained unenlightened. 'We had some difficulty', their Report observed, 'in obtaining an operational definition from broadcasters', and it criticized the BBC particularly for being too vague or for claiming too much (Peacock, 1986: 130). If the broadcasters are confused, so too are politicians and academics. The former have always treated radio and television in terms of their immediate interests. The whole history of the relationship between broadcasting and the world of politics is one of manipulation and pressures (overt and covert) exerted on broadcast news and discussion by politicians, parties and governments (Scannell, 1984). As for academics in this country, from F. R. Leavis through Richard Hoggart to Stuart Hall, the dominant educational ideology has been that the media are manipulative, audiences are beguiled against their better interests and the benevolent, disinterested role of education is to teach critical awareness of how these manipulations take place 'behind men's backs'.

In this article I wish to revalue broadcasting's social role against its devaluation in arguments that regard it primarily as a form of social control, or of cultural standardization or of ideological (mis)representation. To the contrary, I wish to argue for broadcasting in its present form, as a public good that has unobtrusively contributed to the democratization of everyday life, in public and private contexts, from its beginning through to today. I do not see how there can be any reasonable case for the present system other than along such lines. I will attempt to defend this proposition first by developing an account of broadcasting as a public good and then considering the wider implications of this account in relation to possible objections and criticisms. In doing this I have in mind the work of Jurgen Habermas, whose concepts of the public sphere, and of communicative rationality, have helped to clarify my understanding of broadcasting. Again, I will not initially attempt a commentary on Habermas's theoretical concerns other than to note here that, although I do not accept the particular theoretical lines of enquiry he pursues, the issues he addresses and the problems he poses seem to me to be fundamental for the study of modern societies and the contributory role of modern media.

Two things I do take from Habermas that underlie what follows: a historical approach to the formation of broadcasting's public sphere (cf. Garnham, 1986, for a recent discussion of the concept), and a concern with the rational character of communication in everyday actual contexts. I will offer a brief, historical account of the development of broadcasting in this country which focuses on it as a *public* service in two related ways: first, in terms of a content – programme output – which constitutes a new kind of public life through the relaying and creation of real-world events and occasions that are public in a minimal sense, viz. open and accessible to the public. Two kinds of such events are taken into account; on the one hand those that are external to broadcasting but which broadcasting redistributes, from their own locations, to its audiences (a coronation, a football match) and, on the other hand, those that are internal to broadcasting which it has created for its audiences in its studios (a political interview, a chat show, a game show). The continuing interplay of such events, outside and inside the studios, make up what I will refer to as the public life of broadcasting. My second, related concern is with the audiences, the new kind of *general* public, on whose behalf this public life is routinely accessed and produced.

I have argued elsewhere that there were two essential characteristics that have remained, from the beginning through to the present, as constitutive of public service broadcasting: the provision of a service of *mixed* programmes on *national* channels available to all (Scannell, 1989). The principle of universal availability has technical and economic components. The full establishment of broadcasting presupposes a society that has, for the great majority, risen above the level of necessity. To enjoy the services of broadcasting people need at the least a marginal surplus of disposable time and income. In Britain before the war radio sets were not cheap, and represented a major item of expenditure in households with only pennies to spare each week. Nevertheless, 75 percent of households had a radio set by 1939, and today when 100 percent of households have radios it is common for household members to have their own sets; 98 percent of households presently have at least one television set. Thus as commodities radio and TV sets (as distinct from video display units) have become things that every household possesses.

At the same time the broadcasting authorities (BBC and IBA) have seen it as a fundamental part of their commitment to public service to make their programmes, as far as is technically possible, available to anyone with a receiving apparatus anywhere in the United Kingdom. The BBC's television services now reach 99.1 percent of the population. To reach that extra one-tenth of 1 percent, 65 new transmitting stations were added to the distribution system (Peacock, 1986: 130n). Such an investment is the mark of public service broadcasting's disregard of strictly commercial considerations in relation to its audiences. Where those are primary, broadcasters will deliver a service only to the most profitable markets – which lie in densely populated urban areas that can deliver large audiences without difficulties. The markets for cable services are likely to prove even more selective. The affluent areas of major towns and cities will be wired up, while the poorer areas will be neglected. More sparsely populated, remoter regions will be ignored entirely.

If the universal distribution of its services is one basic marker of a broadcasting service constituted as a public good, the other is the supply of mixed programme services to its nationwide audiences, i.e. a wide range of different kinds of programmes delivered on a single channel. The mix today is familiar in the output of the four national television channels at present available to all in the UK: news, current affairs, and topical magazine programmes; chat shows, game shows and quizzes; drama of all kinds from soap operas and situation comedies to police series and single-authored plays; documentaries on a wide range of topics – social issues, history, science, wildlife; religious programmes; children's programmes; music from the current top forty to the classics, opera and ballet; a wide and varying supply of sporting events that includes all the major sports and many new ones (to television, that is) such as American football, basketball, badminton and indoor bowling.

All this is deeply known and taken for granted, bedded down into the very fabric of daily life for all of us. In the sum of its parts broadcasting has brought into being a culture in common to whole populations and a shared public life of a quite new kind. It exists as such today in national television services but not in radio. The original Reithian concept of mixed programming was embodied in the pre-war National Programme (Scannell and Cardiff, 1982). After the war a three-tiered radio service was introduced – the Light, the Home and the Third Programmes – which stratified audiences into three broad cultural taste publics, lowbrow, middlebrow and highbrow. Reith, who had long since left the BBC, rightly saw this as a fundamental betrayal of his founding concept of public service broadcasting. The worm in the promising bud of his vision for radio was music. For obvious reasons music has always constituted the bulk of output on radio, but it was impossible – in the long run – to provide a general musical service on a single national channel because there is not, and never has been, a common musical culture (Scannell, 1981). Music consists of different taste publics defined as much in terms of what they loathe as what they like. This is especially so in relation to 'serious' music and the avant-garde for whom the idea of music for all, and of all music as of equal value, is anathema. Thus, the history of radio, viewed in the long term, can be seen as its gradual fragmentation into different musical taste publics (Radios 1, 2 and 3) with talk bracketed out into specific talk channels (Radio 4).

This development, which took place earlier in the United States under harsher economic pressures, is not explicable simply in economic terms. But it is economic and political pressures for deregulation today that threaten to fragment television into multiple-channel options provided by cable and satellite services owned by media entrepreneurs and conglomerates. Such services will consist either of low-cost repeats of popular Anglo-American television programmes and features films, or of generic programming in which all the material in a particular channel is of the same kind. This later development is at present most advanced in American cable services – Home Box Office (newly released films), MTV (music videos), CNN (Cable Network News) along with pay-per-view channels that offer mainly sporting fixtures.

Generic programming fragments the general public that is still constituted in today's four national UK television channels into particular taste publics whom advertisers are increasingly keen to target. In so doing it destroys the principle of equality of access for all to entertainment, informational and cultural resources in a common public domain. The Peacock Report has redefined broadcasting as a private commodity rather than a public good, replacing the general interest by individual interests. Individual consumers, in the media universe of the next century, as envisaged by Peacock, will choose what they want and pay for what they get. But consumers are not all equal in their purchasing power. The privatization of information, culture and entertainment may well create a two-tiered society of those who are rich and poor in such resources. Such a development would undercut the fundamentally democratic principles upon which public service broadcasting rests.

It is important to see that that service, as we know it today, rests upon a right of access, asserted by the broadcasters on behalf of their audiences, to a wide range of political, religious, social, cultural, sporting events and to entertainments that previously were available only to small, self-selecting and more or less privileged particular publics. What was *public* life before broadcasting? In a general sense there were certain kinds of buildings and spaces in which people could meet, outside their homes, for relaxation, pleasure or self-improvement; public parks and libraries and public houses. More specifically there were public events that took place in particular places for particular publics. Thus, attendance at church, a theatre, a concert or variety hall, a cinema, a football match, a public lecture, a political rally, a civic or state ceremony, would seem to constitute the main kinds of events that were, by definition, public – that is, open to anyone who could get there and afford (where necessary) the price of entry.

In the 1920s the broadcasters had a sharp struggle to establish the right of the microphone to relay such events beyond their immediate location and audience to the fast-growing listening public. Concert and variety impresarios feared a fall-off at the box office, the Football Association worried about declining gates and the churches foresaw diminishing congregations. Such initial fears were, in most cases, quite quickly overcome. More patient and persistent diplomacy was required before the authorities would allow the microphone to relay major state ceremonies, especially those involving royalty. One important kind of access that the BBC pressed for very early on was the right to transmit, on a daily basis, the proceedings of the House of Commons. This was rejected by Baldwin in 1926 and was not allowed (for radio) until fifty years later. Only now, on an experimental basis, has permission been granted for the television cameras to enter the lower House.

Thus the particular publics who hitherto had enjoyed privileged access to such events now had grafted onto them a *general* public constituted in and by the general nature of the mixed programme service and its general, unrestricted availability. The fundamentally democratic thrust of broadcasting lay in the new kind of access to virtually the whole spectrum of public life that radio first, and later television, made available to all. By placing political, religious, civic, cultural events and entertainments in a common domain, public life was equalized in a way that had never before been possible. Moreover whereas previously such events had been quite discrete and separate, they took on new meanings as they came in contact with each other in common national broadcast channels.

Consider the FA Cup Final, the Grand National or Wimbledon. All these existed before broadcasting, but whereas previously they existed only for their particular sporting publics they became through radio and television, something more. Millions now heard or saw them who had little direct interest in the sports themselves. The events became, and have remained, punctual moments in a shared national life. Broadcasting created, in effect, a new national calendar of public events. Unobtrusively threaded through the continuing daily output was the cyclical reproduction, year in year out, of an orderly and regular progression of festivities, celebrations and remembrances that marked the unfolding of the broadcast year. The calendar not only orga-nizes and coordinates social life, but gives it a renewable content, anticipatory pleasures, a horizon of expectations. The BBC calendar became the expressive register of a common, corporate public life that persists to this day.

Thus far I have considered a range of public events that existed before broad-casting, and which radio and television redistributed to far wider audiences than they had ever hitherto possessed. One consequence was that many of the performers in those events achieved, through broadcasting, fame on an unprecedented scale. Today the faces of royalty, of leading politicians, church-men, entertainers and sportsmen and women circulate on a global scale. Broadcasting has created a public world of public persons who are routinely made available to whole populations. But at the same time it has brought pri-vate persons into the public domain, thereby extending and enriching its char-acter. Private life has been profoundly resocialized by radio and television. They have brought into the public domain the experiences and pleasures of the majority in ways that had been denied in the dominant traditions of litera-ture and the arts. Raymond Williams has drawn attention to the gradual broadening of the basis of representation in literature and drama since the six-teenth century. In Shakespeare's day only those of gentle blood were suitable subjects for tragedy or romance. Rude mechanicals were fit subjects only for knockabout farce. Since then, art and literature have increasingly dealt with the uneventful lives of the middling classes. By the end of the last century, working people had become subjects for art and literature, but usually as objects of compassion or as social problems, and always as described by middle-class authors for middle-class readers.

Broadcasting, because its service was addressed to the whole society, gradu-ally came to represent the whole of society in its programmes. I do not wish to imply that this was simply or easily achieved then or now. Nor do I under-estimate the difficulties of middle-class, white, male institutions in adequately representing those who are other than themselves. Nevertheless, it is impor-tant to acknowledge the ways in which radio and television have given voices to the voiceless and faces to the faceless, creating new communicative entitle-ments for excluded social groups. We are now familiar with documentary pro-grammes on major social issues such as housing, unemployment or poverty, in which people who live in such conditions describe what they are like. Such techniques had actually to be discovered and when, before the war, listeners heard for the very first time an eye-witness account of slum conditions in Tyneside, or the unemployed themselves in 1934 describing how they tried to make ends meet on the dole, they created a sensation (Scannell, 1980).

The deceptively simple techniques of broadcast documentary programmes have given rise to much debate, and their surface naturalism has been criticized for occluding the possibility of exposing the causes that lie behind the personal testimonies of those that speak in them (Garnham, 1972). There are indeed limitations to these methods, to which I will return, but here I wish to note that, at the very least in enabling people to speak for themselves, the broadcasting institutions acknowledge their ability and their right to do so, as well as their right to be heard. All the techniques of documentary are designed to foreground the testimony of the speakers, to let them speak spontaneously and naturally, and to minimize the interventions and presence or the institutions of broadcasting. In the hierarchy of voices that speak in documentaries, the voices of ordinary persons, speaking as persons, tend to have a privileged status over the voices of experts, officials and commentators. Documentary techniques are grounded in consideration and respect for their subjects and their experiences.

But broadcasting has done a great deal more than to present ordinary people in programmes dealing with social issues and problems. It has discovered the pleasures of ordinariness, creating entertainment out of nothing more than ordinary people talking about themselves, playing games or doing silly things in front of live studio audiences. *That's Life!* such programmes say, and Esther Rantzen celebrates it. The first programme series to celebrate ordinary life and experience was *Harry Hopeful*, produced in the BBC's Manchester studio before the war for a northern working-class audience (Bridson, 1972: Scannell, 1986). This was the first time ordinary people came to the microphone to talk about themselves and their lives, to sing a song or recite a dialect poem, or perform a knockabout double-act with Harry Hopeful before a live studio audience of relatives, friends and neighbours. The show was the first to take ordinary people and their ordinary experience and transform them into a public, shareable and enjoyable event. The sound of the studio audience singing, laughing and applauding powerfully enhanced the effect of public and communicable pleasures which the programmes generated. In multiple ways this principle has since been extended in radio and television: the essential components are a studio, a host or compère, ordinary people as performers and a live, studio audience. *Have A Go!, Jim'll Fix It, The Generation Game* and *Blind Date* are all in the tradition that invites ordinary people into the public domain for shared laughter and enjoyment.

Broadcasting, then, brings public life into private life, and private life into public life, for pleasure and enjoyment as much as for information and education. The many voices that speak in this domain – the broadcasters themselves, public persons and private people – amount to a universe of discourse. The totality of output of mixed programmes in nationally networked channels adds up to a complete world. The repertoire appears exhaustive, and what lies outside its catchment – what is not broadcast – is not part of the 'normal' range of the needs and interests of the audience as expressed in the sum of its contents. To make this point is to underline the importance of trying to think of broadcast output as a totality, and always to register what it excludes as well as what it includes. The crucially sensitive 'boundary' topics for broadcasting have been political and moral: the state intervening to regulate the former and public opinion influencing the scope of the latter. Although today there are constraints on politics, sex and violence in terms of what can be said and shown, and how it can be said and shown, there is no doubt that broadcasting has in the sixty years of its life enormously extended the range of what can be talked about in its public domain.

[...]

One objection to this account might be that the audiences of radio and television are not genuine publics, and that it is a pseudo-public life that is constituted in broadcasting. Listeners and viewers watch and listen – it is said – as atomized, fragmented, isolated individuals, not as participant members accessible to each other in the moment of participation. Moreover there is no interaction between events and audiences; no *feedback*. Broadcasting is a one-way system of transmission, with no possibility of interaction that is the basis of any properly communicative situation. Here the metaphysics of presence reasserts itself again with the jargon of authenticity in support. Consider first the position of the 'authentic' publics in most public contexts: the audience at a concert or the theatre or a public lecture, the congregation in a church, the spectators at a sporting event, the members of a political meeting. In most of these cases, though the audiences are in each other's presence they are not communicatively present to each other. Indeed it would be quite mischievous to attempt to strike up a conversation with the person beside one in the pew, or during the lecture, the performance, the speech by the party leader. Such an effort at communication would violate the situational proprieties. On the other hand, it seems normal and natural while watching television – often with other people in the room – for there to be simultaneous comment and chat about the same event being watched 'in private'.

The reality is that the self-selecting publics in most public events accept – voluntarily and willingly as the price of admission and of being there – a whole range of quite unusual bodily and behavioural constraints: to kneel and stand in church, to applaud on cue at the rally or concert, to take notes at the lecture, and at all events to be silent and motionless for the most part. In most public events the nature of the communication is a one-way affair: there are the performers who perform and give voice and there are the live audiences to receive the performance and appreciate it. What live public events have is undoubtedly the 'aura' of presence, but aura is as low in communicative properties as it is high in ritual characteristics.

If the aura of presence glows more faintly for absent broadcast audiences they have far greater freedom in their behaviour while watching and listening. They can walk out on the event (a peculiarly difficult thing to do in church, for instance, or during a concert or play) and come back again, they can switch to some other channel, they can freely express their opinions about the merits or shortcomings of performer(s) and performance. In short, the absent listeners and viewers – the pseudo-public – have much wider behavioural and communicative options than the real and present publics whose behaviour is structured in deference to the event. Indeed, by virtue of not being present, absent viewers and listeners are not in thrall to the aura of the event and are thereby better able to see through the façade of rhetoric designed to rally the faithful and excoriate the faithless.

The force of this argument is to suggest that the circumstances of the absent listening and viewing public create participation without involvement. Where the live audience is committed to the event viewers and listeners may take a non-committal stance. It is not that the event is more real and meaningful for the live audience, less real and meaningful for listeners and viewers; rather there are different realities with different effects. The public life of broadcasting does not stand in a secondary and supplementary relationship to a prior and privileged public life based on presence. It has rather created new contexts, realities and meanings.

But, it might still be objected, the audience still remains fragmented, isolated and atomized – trapped in the sphere of privacy. This is to view individuals as figures in a Lowry landscape, with no social life or contact with others. But empirical research points to the manifold ways in which the output of radio and television today serve as topical and relational resources in mundane social encounters and conversations (Morley, 1986, for instance). Precisely because the public life of broadcasting is accessible to all, it is there to be talked about by all. Everyone is entitled to have views and opinions about what they hear and see. This is not the case with most other cultural resources.

[...]

Thus broadcasting, unobtrusively but no less remarkably, resocializes private life. Certain kinds of programme – soap operas, pre-eminently – are little ritual social events in which families or groups of friends watch together and talk about the programme before, during and after. Gossip is the life-blood of soap operas, as it is of ordinary daily life – 'The living breath of events', as Patricia Meyer Spacks calls it, quoting Faulkner (Spacks, 1986). Gossip in broadcasting, gossip about broadcasting in the tabloid press and in ordinary conversation – this is the very stuff of broadcasting's interconnection with so-called private life or, as I prefer, ordinary daily life. It points up the quality and character of its communicative ethos. If it seems both ordinary and trivial it is also relaxed and sociable, shareable and accessible, non-exclusive, equally talkable about in principle and in practice by everyone.

[...]

I have used the term 'communicative entitlement' several times in this article, and it needs clarification. Communicative entitlements presuppose communicative rights. Communicative rights (the right to speak freely, for instance) are enshrined in the written constitutions of some countries, but not in Britain. A minimal notion of guaranteed communicative rights in a precondition of forms of democratic life in public and private. If one party (the state, the police, teachers, parents, husbands) refuse to be answerable for their conduct to the other party (the electorate, suspects, pupils, children, wives), not only is this unreasonable – it denies a communicative entitlement and nullifies a right. Communicative entitlements can be claimed and asserted, within a presupposed framework of communicative rights. Rights of free assembly, to speak freely and (more often overlooked) to listen, contribute to creating formal, minimal guarantees for certain forms of public political and religious life. They seed the possible growth of wider and more pervasive claims from those denied a hearing in manifold public and private contexts, that they should be listened to: i.e. that they should be treated seriously. As equals.

I believe that broadcasting has enhanced the reasonable character and conduct of twentieth-century life by augmenting claims to communicative entitlements. It does this, as I have tried to show, through asserting a right of access to public life; through extending its universe of discourse and entitling previously excluded voices to be heard: through questioning those in power, on behalf of viewers and listeners, and trying to get them to answer. More generally, I have suggested, the fact that the broadcasters do not control the communicative context means that they must take into account the conditions of reception for their utterances. As such they have learned to treat the communicative process not simply as the transmission of a content, but a relational process in which how things are said is as important as what is said. All this has, I think, contributed to new, interactive relationships between public and private life which have helped to normalize the former and to socialize the latter.

In saying this I am not trying to idealize the present system, whose reasonable/rational character is contained within the framework and limitations of mass democratic politics which work, in many ways, to sustain the power of institutional public life over mundane, private life.

[...]

Broadcasting still operates within a particular definition of democracy established back in 1918 by the Representation of the People Act. The limits of representative democracy and of broadcasting's representative public service role within it are essentially the same; power accrues to the representatives, not those whom they represent. More participatory forms of politics and broadcasting are required if people are to play an active part in public life and decision-making, thereby exercising greater control over their own individual and social life. As far as broadcasting goes what is needed are many more properly local radio stations (dozens of stations in London, for instance) and more regional television networks to strengthen rather than vitiate the diversity of identities of place. Moreover, public access and participation in programmes, programming and programme making should be a key feature of decentralized radio and television services.

Such services should enhance but not displace the present system of public service broadcasting in this country and its commitment to properly public, social values. In my view equal access for all to a wide and varied range of common informational, entertainment and cultural services, carried on channels that can be received throughout the country, should be thought of as an important citizenship right in mass democratic societies. It is a crucial means – perhaps the only means at present – whereby common knowledges and pleasures in a shared public life are maintained as a social good for the whole population. As such it should be defended against its enemies.

References

Bridson, D. G. 1972: *Prospero and Ariel*. London: Gollancz.

Garnham, N. 1972: The politics of TV naturalism. *Screen*, Summer.

Garnham, N. 1986: The media and the public sphere. In Golding, P., Murdock G. and Schlesinge P. (eds.), *Communicating politics*. Leicester: University of Leicester Press.

Morley, D. 1986: *Family television: cultural power and domestic leisure*. London: Comedia.

[Peacock Report] 1986: *Report of the Committee on Financing the BBC*, Cmnd. 9284. London: HMSO.

Scannell, P. 1980: Broadcasting and the politics of unemployment, 1930–1935. *Media, Culture and Society* 2(1).

Scannell, P. 1981: Music for the multitude? The dilemmas of the BBC's music policy, 1923–1946. *Media, Culture and Society* 3(3)1, 243–60.

Scannell, P. 1984: 'A conspiracy of silence': the state, the BBC and public opinion in the formative years of British broadcasting. In McLennan G., *et al.* (eds.), *State and society in contemporary Britain*. Cambridge: Polity Press.

Scannell, P. 1986: The stuff of radio: developments in radio features and documentaries before the war. In Corner, J. (ed.), *Documentary and the mass media*. London: Edward Arnold.

Scannell, P. 1989: Public service broadcasting: history of a concept. In Goodwin, A. and Whannel, G. (eds.), *Understanding television*. London: Routledge.

Scannell, P. and Cardiff, D. 1982: Serving the nation: public service broadcasting before the war. In Waites, B., *et al.* (eds.), *Popular culture past and present*. London: Croom Helm.

Spacks, P.M. 1986: *Gossip*. Chicago/London: University of Chicago Press.

Questions

1   Summarise the arguments advanced in favour of public service broadcasting. According to Scannell, what contributions have public service broadcasters made to modern social and cultural life?

2   In his conclusion, Scannell argues that public service broadcasting should be defended against 'its enemies'. Who, or what, are these enemies in the 1990s, and what do they stand for? What arguments have been proposed *against* the continuation of public service broadcasting, and by whom, over the last decade?

3   Assess the likely future of public service broadcasting in the 1990s and beyond. How, in your view, should public service provision be funded and distinguished from commercial media provision? To what extent have cable and satellite forms of broadcasting irrevocably eroded public service provision?

Further reading

Blumler, J. (ed.) 1992: *Television and the public interest*. London: Sage.

Corner, J. 1995: *Television form and public address*. London: Edward Arnold.

Dahlgren, P. 1995: *Television and the public sphere: citizenship, democracy and the media*. London: Sage.

Garnham, N. 1986: The media and the public sphere. In Golding P., Murdock, G. and Schlesinge, P. (eds), *Communicating politics*. Leicester: University of Leicester Press.

Hood, S.(ed.) 1994: *Behind the screens: the structure of British television in the nineties*. London: Lawrence & Wishart.

Kellner, D. 1990: *Television and the crisis of democracy*. London: Sage.

Livingstone, S. and Lunt, P. 1994: *Talk on television: audience participation and public debate*. London: Routledge.

O'Malley, T. 1994: *Closedown? The BBC and government broadcasting policy 1979–92*. London: Pluto Press.

Stereotypes and Representations

In recent years, the media have frequently been criticised for representing social groups in a *stereotypical* fashion: that is, in a generalised, partial and selective way, where certain easily identifiable, and often negative, traits are used to define an entire group. This second section consists of ten readings which consider the relationship between representations and identities and aim to demonstrate the kinds of media representations which are both typical and stereotypical. Representations of social identities (genders, classes, races, nationalities, able-bodiedness etc.) are common to all media texts, and their critique and analysis has dominated Media and Cultural Studies in the postwar era. This explains, in part, why this section is the longest in the reader, but we have still been unable to include extracts on *all* aspects of representation and you may wish to consider others: for example, media representations of nature and the environment or stereotypes associated with environmental activists, teenagers or the elderly.

Media producers have often defended the use of stereotypes as a means of transmitting a lot of complex information in a familiar 'shorthand' and easily recognisable way. The section opens, however, with two articles which call into question the whole notion of stereotype. In the first, **Tessa Perkins** challenges conventional assumptions about their nature and purpose, and her reassessment identifies a number of limitations in the way that stereotypes have traditionally been defined and thought to operate. **Martin Barker** then goes further, claiming that the concept of stereotypes is based on entirely contradictory premises and is a 'useless tool' for the social scientist. But the fact that media texts frequently rely on stereotypical images to achieve audience recognition ensures that such representations of social identity continue to be one of the most researched and written-about areas in media education.

In spite of Barker's critique, there is some agreement that stereotypes have an ideological function in that they are a means of categorising social groups and evaluating their significance and status compared to others in a society or cultural group. When considering dimensions of social stratification such as race, class, gender and able-bodiedness, stereotypical representations take on a particular importance in assessing the dominant social group's treatment of others, particularly in the promotion and perpetuation of discrimination. This is illustrated through a diverse range of case studies starting with a piece by **Justin Lewis** (reading 9) which considers the representation of black people on British and American television and the particular ideological significance of *The Cosby Show*. Among the other readings in this section are those by **Anne Karpf** (reading 12) which examines the whole range of images of the disabled in the media, **Marjorie**

Ferguson (reading 14) who considers the role of women in postwar Britain as portrayed by women's magazines and **Terence Qualter** (reading 15) who addresses the specific issue of stereotypical images of race, class and gender in advertising.

In between these analyses of the most fundamental and commonly addressed dimensions of social stratification, we have included a number of readings which extend the debate and consider less widely researched components of mediated social identity, including one from **Simon Watney** (reading 13) which considers how accurate it is to describe the representation of people with AIDS as a 'moral panic', particularly at the height of sometimes controversial media coverage in the mid-1980s.

The section ends with a reading from an article by **John Langer** which shifts attention from representations of social groups to the way in which the media construct and mediate the identities of individuals on film and in television, investing them with particular 'star' qualities and personalities. In so doing, he reminds us that in spite of the media's tendency to categorise and stereotype us in terms of our nationality, race and so on, when it comes to our sense of self-identity many of us still look to screen icons and personalities as influential models.

7

Rethinking Stereotypes
Tessa Perkins

From M. Barratt, P. Corrigan, A. Kuhn and J. Wolff (eds.), *Ideology and cultural production* (Croom Helm British Sociological Association 1979)

To open this section on stereotypes and representations, Perkins identifies a number of shortcomings in the way that stereotypes are normally thought to operate. While acknowledging that they need to be simplistic and immediately identifiable and to contain implicit reference to a consensus about social relations, she asserts that some of the most fundamental assumptions on which stereotypes are based are, at the very least, highly questionable. For example, central to the notion of stereotypes, as understood by Walter Lippmann, who first introduced the concept in 1922, and the generations of media students, teachers and researchers who have followed him, is that they are: simple, erroneous, second-hand and resistant to modification. Perkins disputes all but the first of these assumptions (even this, she says, is inaccurate to the extent that stereotypes are both simple *and* complex), and she goes on to explain how many of our other ideas about the form that stereotypes take should be reassessed: for example, that stereotypes *have* to be negative, inaccurate and about oppressed or powerless groups.

Central to Perkins' understanding of stereotypes is that they are ideological concepts; they select personality traits, mental, sexual or personal, that have particular ideological significance. The form taken by stereotypes in a capitalist society will depend on the recipient group's structural position, and when applied to most categories their perceived mental abilities will be of greatest significance (hence the primary characteristic of the 'dumb blonde' is that she is of low intelligence, and assumptions about her personality and sexuality are secondary).

I should like first to focus on what seem to me to be dominant and often misleading assumptions about the nature of stereotypes, and which ... often prevent us from making theoretical statements about how stereotypes function ideologically.

According to these assumptions stereotypes are: (1) always erroneous in content; (2) pejorative concepts; (3) about groups with whom we have little/no social contact; by implication therefore, are not held about one's own group; (4) about minority groups (or about oppressed groups); (5) simple; (6) rigid and do not change; (7) not structurally reinforced. It is also assumed that (8) the existence of contradictory stereotypes is evidence that they are erroneous, but of nothing else; (9) people either 'hold' stereotypes of a group (believe them to be true) or do not; (10) because someone holds a stereotype of a group, his/her behaviour towards a member of that group can be predicted.

Although there is no discussion here of the last assumption, it is included because it refers to an area of considerable importance and complexity which has had to remain outside the scope of this paper. The ways in which we 'use' stereotypes of our own group to control relationships, and even to manipulate our oppressors, is one example of the importance of 'behaviour' and stereotypes.

The concept of 'stereotype' was first introduced into the social sciences by Lippmann in 1922 (see Harding, 1968), and his version remains the most widely accepted by social scientists and laymen alike. It includes most of the above assumptions. If a concept is referred to as a stereotype, then the implication is that it is simple rather than complex or differentiated; erroneous rather than accurate; secondhand, rather than from direct experience; and resistant to modification by new experience (Harding, 1968). I wish to argue that while stereotypes do take this form on occasion, it is only the first of these characteristics that can be considered a part of the definition of 'stereotype', and even here I have reservations.

In so far as all typifications are *simplifications* since they select common features and exclude differences, then all typifications are undifferentiated (and in that sense they are also erroneous). Is it then simply a matter of degree? Should we conceptualise stereotypes as being at one end of a continuum, such that they select fewer characteristics (thereby excluding more)? This seems to be the case if we think of such stereotypes as 'dumb blonde' or 'happy-go-lucky negro'. Furthermore, this is the criterion used in empirical research to decide whether or not a stereotype exists. However, this 'simplicity' is in two senses deceptive: firstly, it may in *some* cases be better described as abstractness. That is to say that some stereotypes operate on a higher level of generalisation than other typifications; to refer 'correctly' to someone as a 'dumb blonde', and to understand what is meant by that implies a great deal more than hair colour and intelligence. It refers immediately to *her* sex, which refers to her status in society, her relationship to men, her inability to behave or think rationally, and so on. In short, it implies knowledge of a complex social structure (in this way stereotypes are like symbols). So it is misleading to say stereotypes are simple *rather than* complex. They are simple and complex. Secondly, the description of stereotypes as simple rather than *differentiated* is similarly deceptive. The fact that there is a higher consensus (uniformity) about the adjectives which describe the characteristics of some groups, than there is about those which describe other groups, may tell us a lot about the social situation of the group being described, and does not necessarily imply prejudice or distortion. It may be the case that members of this group can 'legitimately' be characterised by three or four attributes. We cannot assume that there is an ideal number of adjectives by which to describe a group.

This is not to say that simplicity, complexity and differentiation are entirely irrelevant to the definition of stereotypes, but that they can be, and have been, misleading. Nevertheless these terms do identify the area in which we must look for differences between stereotypes and other typifications. For example it seems that differentiation of stereotypes is often accommodated by alternative stereotypes – 'dumb blonde'/'cunning minx' – rather than by an expansion of the stereotype. I will return to these questions later.

The implication that stereotypes are *'erroneous rather than accurate'* is widely accepted as part of the definition of stereotypes; inaccuracy in this context implying a false account of objective reality – blondes are not dumb, negroes are not happy-go-lucky. There are two main objections to this. Firstly, a lot of empirical research into, for example racial stereotypes, has led some theorists to oppose 'inaccuracy' with a 'kernel of truth' hypothesis. Secondly, if we claim that stereotypes are erroneous, then their potential ideological role is considerably reduced. If there were really no positive correlation between the content (perceived attributes) of a stereotype and the characteristics (actual attributes) of the group concerned, it would be tantamount to arguing *either* that the social (that is, commonly accepted) definitions of you have no effect on you, in which case it would be very difficult to see how ideology or socialisation works at all; or, that stereotypes do not represent social definitions and are sociologically insignificant since they are manifestations of pathological behaviour and thus mainly the concern of psychologists; or that they affect only your behaviour but not your 'true self', thus implying a divorce between behaviour and self

[...]

The claim that stereotypes are *'secondhand rather than from direct experience'* is similar to Klapp's (1962) distinction between stereotypes (as referring to things outside one's social world) and social types (referring to things with which one is familiar). Intuitively this seems valid. However, the consequences of accepting this distinction are unacceptable. This would rule out stereotypes of men and women, at the very least, since we all have direct experience of the opposite sex. Also it rules out stereotypes of one's own group, and hence the argument that stereotypes about one's group influence one's definition of oneself, and conversely, it ignores the influence of stereotypes on people's behaviour towards members of other groups. For example a teacher's stereotype of working-class children may affect the teacher's expectations of the child (and thus the child itself). So the potential role of stereotypes in socialisation, and thus in ideology, is once again reduced to a very secondary one. Secondhandness is anyway characteristic of the vast majority of our concepts and cannot therefore be used to distinguish between stereotypes and other concepts.

Is it then *'resistance to modification by new experience'* that is the key factor? The assumption here is that, normally, contact with the group in question would change the concept to bring it into line with reality, but that new experience will not modify a stereotype. Disregarding the fact that the assumption of inaccuracy is built into the notion of resistance, the main implication is that in contrast to other concepts, stereotypes are especially resistant (or rigid). This receives support from research into 'erroneous' and highly pejorative stereotypes which serve important psychological functions (for those holding

the stereotypes) and which cannot be given up without traumatic consequences. But such stereotypes are a special case. Most concepts are resistant in
the sense that they require more than one deviant case to change the concept.
In order to assess whether stereotypes are particularly rigid, we need to study
the conditions under which concepts change, how much information is necessary, how important the continued existence of confirmatory information is,
and how important the stereotype's conceptual status is (how much else would
have to change). This must surely be essential to our understanding of ideology. We cannot simply assert that stereotypes are rigid. We must look at the
social relationships to which they refer, and at their conceptual status, and ask
under what conditions are stereotypes more or less resistant to modification.
This is not to deny that stereotypes are very 'strong' concepts, and this may be
a distinguishing feature. The strength of a stereotype results from a combination of three factors: its 'simplicity'; its immediate recognisability (which
makes its communicative role very important), and its implicit reference to an
assumed consensus about some attribute or complex social relationships.
Stereotypes are in this respect prototypes of 'shared cultural meanings'. They
are nothing if not social. It is because of these characteristics that they are so
useful in socialisation – which in turn adds to their relative strength.

In trying to broaden the definition of stereotype ... there is a risk that it will
simply become indistinguishable from 'role'. According to sociological tradition, a role is a 'set of expectations and obligations to act in certain ways in
certain settings'. The child, in being taught the behaviour appropriate to
his/her (or others') status (role expectations) is also taught something more, a
more general lesson: that is, that group membership is important and
extremely significant; in a sense it 'determines' behaviour – different groups
behave differently and have different characteristics, different rights and
duties and consequently groups are related to each other in different, structured, ways – some deserve more respect than others and so on. (Schools may
now be particularly important in reinforcing and elaborating on this learning
of group identity and significance. Universal, compulsory education may have
played an important part in diminishing the influence of the trend to person-
alised socialisation in the family.)

To learn how to behave, then, involves learning to recognise (and then evaluate) people as members of groups – that is to apply group concepts to social
as well as to physical phenomena. The definition of oneself, and others, as a
member of a group is absolutely essential to the ideological effectiveness of
stereotypes. To learn about groups is to learn about status. Roles describe the
dynamic aspect of status.

What then is the relationship between role, status and stereotype? *Status*
refers to a position in society which entails a certain set of rights and duties.
Role refers to the performance of those rights and duties, it is relational.
Stereotype refers to both role and status at the same time, and the reference is

perhaps always predominantly evaluative. (Adjectives are most important, and are often combined with or reduced to value-laden nouns – dumb blonde, bum, nigger. But stereotypes are not always so succinct.) Stereotypes do not necessarily exist about all statuses. There is not a stereotype of a typist or a cardboard-box maker. There may be an 'image' of the sort of person that is likely to be a typist, but it is very much more fluid, generalised and descriptive than a stereotype is and may be entirely personal. I should acknowledge here that I am still not sure about how to identify the boundaries of stereotypes. I will make two points to clarify the matter. Firstly, it may be that there is not a 'national' stereotype of a typist, but that there is a localised one – that is to say that those who come into close or frequent contact with a group of typists do hold a stereotype of typists. It is possible that to this extent all statuses do give rise to local stereotypes. I should add to this that of course there are at least two stereotypes which include typists – namely the stereotype of women in general, which, combined with a class stereotype, defines the parameters of a general definition of a typist. But this is of a different order to, say, the prostitute or 'career woman' stereotype. Secondly, the boundaries of stereotypes are ultimately, I think, indefinable. What one can say, however, is that some stereotypes are much more 'highly defined' than others. The degree of definition reflects the degree of consensus that a stereotype exists, which does not mean to say that the stereotype is 'accurate'. I can illustrate this best by an example – I was discussing with a few people the 'mother's boy' stereotype, and we all agreed about its content. I then asked about 'father's girl'; this produced three different interpretations – all of which were semi-convincing, but none of which seemed definitive. Similarly with 'happy-go-lucky negro' as against 'teacher'. I would say then that the first one in each pair is a much more highly defined stereotype, and that the latter is relatively weak. But in both cases, the latter still constitutes a stereotype in a way that cardboard-box maker does not. We can introduce an arbitrary cut-off point – 50 per cent agreement and more is a stereotype; and indeed to do so is valid. But that fails to include the evaluative dimension which seems to distinguish stereotypes most clearly from roles.

Roles and statuses are also of course, intrinsically evaluative concepts. But the nature of, and the presentness of, the evaluation is different. A stereotype brings to the surface and makes explicit and central what is concealed in the concept of status or role. With a status or role we are commonly enjoined (by sociology textbooks) to look beneath them to discover the norms and values they supposedly 'rest on'; with a stereotype we must look beneath the evaluation to see the complex social relationships that are being referred to. This does not mean that stereotypes are simple *reflections* of social values; to suggest so would be to oversimplify the case. Stereotypes are selections and arrangements of particular values and their relevance to specific roles.

[...]

There is such a strong – if understandable – tendency to define stereotypes as pejorative that pejorativeness has become almost built into the meaning of the word 'stereotype'. 'Pejorative' implies a point of view, and there is a danger that if we build into the word 'stereotype' the assumption that they are pejorative concepts, we will unthinkingly be involved in adopting the point of view from which certain characteristics are seen to be 'bad', rather than asking (when appropriate) *why* are these characteristics 'bad.' (This happened of course in the early days of the women's movement.) I would argue anyway that there are stereotypes of all structurally central groups – class, race, gender, age. There is a male (he-man) stereotype, a WASP stereotype, a heterosexual stereotype, an upper class (leader) stereotype. These stereotypes are important because other stereotypes are partially defined in terms of, or in opposition to, them. The happy-go-lucky negro attains at least some of its meaning and force from its opposition to the 'puritan' characteristics (sombre and responsible) of the WASP. Positive stereotypes are an important part of the ideology and are important in the socialisation of both dominant and oppressed groups. In order to focus attention on the ideological nature of stereotypes it might be much more useful to talk of pejorative stereotypes and laudatory stereotypes, rather than to conceal the 'pejorativeness' in the meaning of the term.

It should now be clear that it is necessary to find a definition of stereotypes which neither includes nor excludes the assumptions just discussed – erroneousness, rigidity and so on. What is evident is that the various disputes have in fact identified the various forms taken by stereotypes. Lippmann's four characteristics describe one form of stereotype. What I want to suggest is that the nature and form of stereotypes vary, that this variation may not be arbitrary but may be related to the ideological or aesthetic functions of the stereotypes and/or to the structural position of the stereotyped group. We need to define 'stereotype' in a sufficiently open way so as to allow for the various forms it takes and yet try to isolate its distinctive characteristics. I would suggest that the following characteristics are essential parts of stereotypes:

A stereotype is:
(a) *A group concept*: It describes a group. Personality traits (broadly defined) predominate.
(b) *It is held by a group*: There is a very considerable uniformity about its content. Cannot have a 'private' stereotype.
(c) *Reflects an 'inferior judgemental process'*: (But not therefore leading necessarily to an inaccurate conclusion.) Stereotypes short-circuit or block capacity for objective and analytic judgements in favour of well-worn catch-all reactions (Fishman, 1956). To some extent all concepts do this – stereotypes do it to a much greater extent.
(d) (b) and (c) give rise to *simple structure* (mentioned earlier) which frequently conceals complexity (see (e)).
(e) High probability that social stereotypes will be *predominantly evaluative*.
(f) *A concept* – and like other concepts it is a selective, cognitive organising system, and a feature of human thought (Vinacke, 1957).

Two other points need to be made about stereotypes. Firstly, stereotypes can be 'held' in two ways. They can be 'held' in the sense that they are 'believed in'. And they can be 'held' in the sense that we know that a stereotype exists about a particular group and what its content is, even though we don't necessarily believe it. However, the division between these two is not always clear. It is not merely a question of either believing or not believing, but also of the strength and consistency of the belief. The nature of stereotypes is such that most people do hold them in the sense of knowing about them, just as they know the basic tenets of Christian belief; that is they are widely *distributed*. This wide distribution makes them readily available for use in interpreting the world, if the occasion demands, just as God may be invoked by semi-believers/semi-agnostics. The political (and ideological) importance of the wide distribution of stereotypes is that they can be, and are, appealed to at certain times. The current racist revival relies on people's knowledge of stereotypes, in the same way as a religious revival appeals to people's background of Christian knowledge with its explanatory potential and emotional content.

Secondly, stereotypes have what I refer to as a 'flexible range'. Essentially the same stereotype ('irrational woman') can be presented very starkly and blatantly or relatively complexly and 'realistically'. Cartoonists or comedians often appeal to the most stark (and exaggerated) version of a stereotype. Aesthetic disputes about whether or not a certain character in a film is a 'stereotype' may concern a relatively complex and 'realistic' version of a stereotype. This flexibility is undoubtedly important in maintaining credibility and communicability.

The form taken by stereotypes varies and some of this variation can be explained in terms of the group's structural position. Not all stereotypes perform identical ideological functions, nor are they related to 'objective reality' in the same way. Indeed they could not be. As will be seen later, stereotypes develop in various situations and cope with different sorts of problems. All I can do here is to outline one way of categorising stereotypes, and suggest reasons for, and consequences of, a couple of variations.

There are stereotypes about:
1. *Major Structural Groups*: colour (black/white); gender (male-female); class (upper/middle/working); age (child/young/adult/old). (Can make jokes about MS groups to mass audience.) *Everybody* is a member of *each* group.
2. *Structurally Significant and Salient Groups*: ethnic groups (Jews/Scots); artists and scientists; mothers-in-law; adolescents in the 1950s. (Comedians' topical jokes mainly from this group.)
3. *Isolated Groups*: social and/or geographic isolation. Gays; American Indians; students in the past; gypsies. (Can't make jokes about this group to mass audience unless it also belongs to another category – probably to *pariah*.)

4. *Pariah Groups*: gays; blacks; Communists in USA?; junkies? (Can make jokes to mass audience – but *may* be 'bad taste' to do so.) Groups here will also belong to another group (1–3).

5. *Opponent Groups*: upper-class twit; male chauvinist pig; reds; fascists. (Can *sometimes* make jokes to mass audience.) These contrast to others in so far as they are often developed by protesting, deviant or oppressed groups, about their opponents. They can be subdivided into: *counter stereotypes* – e.g. male chauvinist pig – which form part of a counter-ideology and are sufficiently developed to be about a particular group (status and role); and *blanket stereotypes* – which refer to all non-believers – all non-Marxists are fascists; all non-fascists are reds. *Counters* originate from a critical attempt at reinterpretation or re-evaluation (pejorative rather than laudatory) of a dominant group. *Blankets* reinforce group solidarity by claiming a monopoly on knowledge of the 'truth' and grouping all rival claims to 'truth' as equally irrelevant and invalid.

6. *Socially/Ideologically Insignificant Groups:* milkmen: redheads.

Accuracy – the central problem?

I have already dealt in passing with many of the issues which are related to accuracy. I have said that stereotypes are often 'valid'; that they are often effective in so far as people define themselves in terms of the stereotypes about them; that they are structurally reinforced; that they refer to role performances, and so on. However, having said all this there are important senses in which stereotypes are inaccurate or false. Here I refer to my earlier claim that stereotypes are similar to ideology in that they are both (apparently) true and (really) false at the same time. I will discuss this in the context of differences between stereotypes of dominant and oppressed groups. Two main points about their falsity are to be made: Firstly, stereotypes present interpretations of groups which conceal the 'real' cause of the group's attributes and confirm the legitimacy of the group's oppressed position. Secondly, stereotypes are selective descriptions of particularly significant or problematic areas and to that extent they are exaggerations.

Stereotypes are evaluative concepts about status and role and as such are central to interpreting and evaluating social groups, including one's own. Definition of oneself as a member of a group is essential to the socialisation process, and an important element of social control. Oppressed groups pose particular problems of control and definition. The fact that group membership is a much more salient part of the self-definition of oppressed groups than is membership of high status groups to them, reflects these problems (Holter, 1970, p. 210). This saliency is the effect of the contradiction and is a mechanism of social control. Because one's membership of a group is always present, so too is the stereotype of oneself and so too therefore, is a self-derogatory concept – to be socialised is to be self-oppressed. (Effectiveness of the ideology relies on this as does its 'legitimacy'.) But to have adopted this concept will have involved adopting contradictory value orientations as well, which means that the self-definition (self-oppression) is always vulnerable and needs constant reinforcing. Furthermore, the consciousness of oneself as a member of a particular group, which is essential to social control, is also potentially threatening. The continued and persistent class-consciousness of an often apparently a-political and apathetic working class, the feminine consciousness of 'unliberated' and repressed women, are evidence of this consciousness of group membership.

Stereotypes are particulary strong, I have argued, when they have to operate as conceptual (cognitive) resolutions of such contradictions. It is this resolution that is the real location of their inaccuracy. Stereotypes were described earlier as being descriptions of an effect (consciousness) which was then evaluated and inverted, so it becomes a cause, which then explains the differentiation of which it is actually a description. This process (similar in structure to alienation) is typical of ideology. The inversion of effect into cause is the primary means of conceptually resolving the contradiction involved, for example, in the socialisation of oppressed groups. However, it can become a cause only because it makes ideological sense. The content of stereotypes is not arbitrary (nor are they interchangeable). Stereotypes are selective descriptions – they select those features which have particular ideological significance. Hence, remarkably few stereotypes refer to such qualities as kindness, compassion, integrity – or even honesty (nor their opposites). Personality traits can be subdivided into: mental, sexual and personal. However it is the mental attributes which are definitive and which seem to 'dictate' the rest of the content. Other attributes become linked to mental characteristics in a non-reciprocal way. Dumb does not imply dirty; 'dirty' as a social description does imply 'stupidity'. The reason mental characteristics are dominant is that they are ideologically the most significant (and therefore convincing). Briefly, economic differentiation is the most important differentiation. The ideological criterion for economic differentiation in our capitalist society is primarily intelligence; and only secondly 'contribution' to the society and possession of skills which are necessary but 'supposedly' scarce (for example, decision-making, responsibility, leadership qualities). The most important and the *common* feature of the stereotypes of the major structural groups relates to their mental abilities. In each case the oppressed group is characterised as innately less intelligent. It is particularly important for our ideology that attributes should be conceived of as being innate characteristics either of human nature in general (competitiveness) or of women/men/blacks in particular, since this supports the belief that they are not the effect of the socio-economic system (and the order of things appears to be inevitable – the survival of the fittest and may the best man win). The fact that stereotypes do so often present attributes as if they were 'natural' is not a feature of stereotyping *per se*, so much as an indication that they are ideological concepts. The existence of endless research programmes into innate differences and the publicity their results receive, supports the legitimacy of stereotypes (regardless of the actual results) and of the ideological claim that social differentiation arises from innate differences. The notion that we can (do) have any control over social relationships is absent, and its absence confirms its irrelevance. This problem of course has considerable political importance to oppressed groups, and they need to question the efficacy of involving themselves in disputes about innate differences – there is no easy answer, I might add!

What then are the main differences between stereotypes of oppressed and of dominant groups? Stereotypes of oppressed groups are stronger and sometimes more numerous, and more 'present' in the consciousness (and self-definition) of the oppressed group. They will also be more present in the consciousness of the dominant group. A member of an oppressed group will, by definition, have limited access to the 'goods' of society, and the stereotype will confirm this limited access (and its legitimacy) but should not be seen as causing it.

Stereotypes of dominant groups will also confirm the boundaries of their own legitimate activity (as will the stereotypes of oppressed groups, of which dominant groups may be more conscious than their own stereotypes). It is *as* important for them to adopt the value structure and to confirm that the goods of society are 'good' as it is for others to continue to see them as good (if unattainable). (Good here refers to anything defined as socially desirable, not just material goods, for example going *out* to work rather than doing housework.) Men who choose (prefer) to stay at home to look after the children while their wives go out to work, challenge the value structure. And a challenge from a dominant group is potentially more threatening (if much less likely) than one from a subordinate group. (The content of gay stereotypes might deserve analysis in this light.) In that respect, a male/white/upper class stereotype is *more* limiting. A challenge from a subordinate group can often be interpreted as a confirmation of the value structure. Stereotypes of oppressed groups will be pejorative, but their pejorativeness is complex and often concealed. Stereotypes of pariah groups may be unambiguously pejorative, but the pejorativeness of female stereotypes is concealed since they must resolve the specific contradictions of women's position. Hence the stereotype presents female characteristics as desirable, for women, and masculine characteristics as undesirable. So the negative female stereotypes 'cunning minx', 'bluestocking', 'career woman' (or the lesbian ones) are stereotypes that essentially acknowledge that women may be intelligent (or aggressive) but define that intelligence as, in *their* case, undesirable (and 'unnatural'). These three stereotypes also reflect another aspect of female stereotypes which *is* more limiting than others – that is, a great many alternative stereotypes have been generated to accommodate this particularly difficult group. The 'bluestocking' or 'career woman' stereotype accommodates women in these categories by excluding them from being sexual beings or mothers. Male stereotypes are rarely so specific.

References

Fishman, J. 1956: An examination of the process of social stereotyping. *Journal of Social Psychology* 43.

Harding, J. 1968: Stereotypes. *International Encyclopaedia of the Social Sciences*.

Holter, H. 1970: *Sex roles and social structure*. Oslo: Universiteits forlaget.

Klapp, O. E. 1962: *Heroes, villains and fools*. Englewood Cliffs, NJ: Prentice-Hall.

Vinacke, W. E. 1957: Stereotypes as social concepts. *Journal of Social Psychology* 46.

Questions

1 Summarise the main arguments that Perkins puts forward regarding our traditional thinking about stereotypes. Among her assertions is that stereotypes are not necessarily erroneous, negative, about groups other than one's own, about minority or oppressed groups, and rigid or unchanging. What examples can you think of that would contradict this traditional view of stereotypes and support Perkins' analysis?

2 What representations from media material can you find which might be considered to be stereotypical? In which forms and genres are they most commonly found?

3 How do stereotypes change historically? Discuss and assess the emergence of any new stereotypes in the 1980s and '90s.

Further reading

Burton, G. 1990: *More than meets the eye*. London: Edward Arnold.

Cumberbatch, G., et al. 1990: *Television advertising and sex role stereotyping*. London: Broadcasting Standards Council.

Dyer, R. 1979: The role of stereotypes. In Cook, J. and Lewington, M. (eds.), *Images of alcoholism*. London: BFI.

Lippmann, W. 1922: *Public opinion*. New York: Harcourt Brace.

O'Sullivan, T., Dutton, B. and Rayner, P. 1994: *Studying the media*. London: Edward Arnold.

Pickering, M. 1995: The politics and psychology of stereotyping. *Media, Culture and Society* 17.

Seiter, E. 1986: Stereotypes and the media: a re-evaluation. *Journal of Communication* 36(2).

Tolson, A. 1996: *Mediations*. London: Edward Arnold.

8

The Lost World of Stereotypes
Martin Barker

From *Comics: ideology, power and the critics* (Manchester University Press 1989)

Barker goes even further than Perkins in his criticism of stereotypes, dismissing the whole concept as a 'useless tool for investigating media texts'. It is the fact that stereotypes are, on the one hand, condemned for being both inaccurate and misleading and yet, on the other, have to appear 'natural' and normal in order to gain audience recognition and fit in with consensual views of the world that causes him to be so critical of the concept.

His other main reason for viewing stereotypes as being of limited use, which he discusses at length earlier in the book, is that the implication behind much of the criticism that is levelled at the concept by those teaching Media Studies is that it is wrong to 'label' people and lump them together into easily identifiable groups. He argues that social psychologists have recognised that categorisation is a fundamental cognitive process that humans employ in order to help them make sense of their individual lives and give them a feeling of group identity. In fact he goes so far as to accuse those who write about stereotypes in the media of having set up a small industry around a theory which he considers to be of little or no use.

The trouble with 'stereotypes'

The search for 'stereotypes' in the media has become a small industry in its own right. The literature is now so large that it is pointless discussing just one or two. I want, instead, to draw out the main problems I see in its use. There are many, and I cannot deal with them all. Let the following be indications, and invitations to others to take the arguments further.

1. There are real problems with 'stereotyping' theory's demands that the media etc should 'reflect' society. In a society where, for example, black people are disproportionately kept in low-paid jobs and on the dole, or sent to prison, to have this simply 'reflected' in the media would cause outrage. Hence the demand shifts to one that these things should only be shown if they are explained in acceptable ways. I do not want to quarrel with this – only to make clear that thereby 'stereotype' has disappeared as a criterion.

But this isn't just a pragmatic problem. It creates two incompatible yet coexisting demands, as Steve Neale has noted.[1] On the one hand, a regularity may be dubbed a 'stereotype' if it shows a deviation from the 'real world'. So, a great deal of media representation of women is condemned for reinforcing the (false) stereotype that women want sex at any time. Or again, the proportion of black or women characters in the media is greatly out of line with their proportion in the population (or relevant subsection thereof). These are stereotypes as falsehoods, distortions of the world. On the other hand, something may be dubbed a 'stereotype' for the opposite reason, that it is so very like the world outside. Here, a good deal of media representation is condemned for showing women in the home, providing services to men – though of course it is in fact true that very many do. Or again, black people are overwhelmingly shown living in poor conditions, in ghetto areas; books etc have been condemned for showing this even though it is (regrettably) the case. These are stereotypes, this time, as self-fulfilling prophecies.

It ought to be clear that these two are sharply at odds with each other.[2] They would have to work on us in different ways, to be influential. The first has to block our perceiving the world as it really is; the second has to stop us seeing anything but the world as it is. This conflict is important, not just an inconsistency. More importantly, if we look behind the conflict, we may find out how it is (silently) resolved, and therefore has largely gone by unnoticed. This needs an understanding of the other main problems with the concept.

2. There is a hidden agenda in here, that it is wrong to present people as 'representatives of categories'. This is a point Richard Dyer makes very effectively. Discussing 'stereotypes' of gays in films, he points out how important it is to the possibilities of collective self-defence that there should be positive group-images.[3] Ellen Seiter takes this a stage further, suggesting that the hidden agenda on images of women is the 'bourgeois career individual', which is every bit as ideological as 'hearth and home' images.[4] The problem arises because the 'stereotyping' tradition grumbles, not about the particular content of a certain category, but about the fact of categorising at all. It is only this that renders that disagreement invisible.

3. Part of that agenda also is a peculiar theorisation of 'influence' which, ironically, in the end does away with the very notions of social power that first stimulated the enquiries. If it has a method, 'stereotyping' depends on content-analysis. The more widespread an image and the more often we encounter it, the argument runs, the greater the likely influence. Otherwise, why worry about frequency of appearance? This very passive view of audiences is a problem in itself. But as R. W. Connell has pointed out in another context, it has the curious effect of doing away with any reference to power.[5] Recall O'Connell's problem with the *Beano*. It was that girls are under-represented as characters. Suppose we put that right. Still missing from these comics would be any representation of the typical relations between boys and girls. Dealing with that in story-form is a quite different problem from 'getting the balance right'. For 'stereotype' theory, it would seem that girls learn their self-images only from the proportionate appearance of the sexes, not from how they relate to each other. The power of men over women has no place in 'stereotyping' theory.

4. There is an unsatisfactory account of how we form categories and use them. It would seem that categories just 'assemble' out of the balance of influences on us; and then – unless something positively interferes, like a good radical pointing out the error of our ways – we use them mechanically. There

are a wealth of visual metaphors in this kind of talk: 'images', 'representations', 'pictures in our heads', 'distorting our perceptions of the world'.[6] There is nothing wrong per se with using metaphorical talk. But it has two results here, which again help resolve that hidden inconsistency I pointed to earlier. These 'images' stand between us and the world. They mediate between us and the world, and stop us 'seeing the reality'. They are like sheets of glass which refract the light and make us see things awry. We can't easily see past them. So, when one distorts the world (stereotype as falsehood), it prevents us seeing clearly. But how does that explain the other kind, the too accurate stereotype? Only because these 'images' are seen as storehouses of the past. The power of the visual metaphor is to suggest staticness, trapping us in the past. This is the reason for the obsessive use of words like 'traditional', 'age-old' and 'outdated' in such work. Take as representative the following quotation: 'After all these years of battering on for a new deal for women, struggling with Equal Opportunities, Equal Pay, anti-sex discrimination, equal school curicula, striving to release young girls from the stultifying role stereotypes of the past, magazines like these [teenage romance comics] are actually travelling fast in the opposite direction.'[7] This kind of talk has long struck me as strange. The implication clearly is that 'stereotypes' have no relevance to the present, and might well have declined but for their continued media presentation. But also it is implied that stereotypes draw their power from ideas and images of the past; they are not creations in the present, fought for and made convincing to us, but residues of already-existing powers which dull and stultify us, trapping us back into those power-relations. I want to suggest that this is yet another component of the peculiar issue of 'time' in theories of ideology. Once again, ideology is seen as a force from the past, barring our access to a future.

5. The resultant politics are inevitably elitist, in two ways. First, 'stereotypers' still share Lippmann's assumptions which, from the start, were infected with elitist politics.[8] They never shed that infection. 'Stereotypes' exist within a pattern of oppositions:

Stereotype	*Non-stereotypes*
Pre-cognitive	Cognitive
Fixing the past	Pointing to the future
Typical site: the mass media	Typical site: 'education'

Inevitably we, the ones who have 'seen past them', must play a role in educating and saving others. They need our cognitive protection against these non-cognitive influences.

And just as inevitably, the question hangs in the air, why some individuals and groups are more prone to being influenced than others. This brings with it a class dimension. A variety of studies have shown that working class people are more prone to categorical thinking, than 'educated' middle class people.[9] According to the logic of the stereotyping approach, this must show the inferiority of their thinking. I reject that. To understand why, consider one 'stereotype' already mentioned by Cauthen *et al.*: 'fascism' and the 'fascist'.[10] Suppose we did decide to call our 'attitude to fascism' a stereotype: what might be in it? We might list 'intolerant', 'prejudiced', 'authoritarian', and 'violent'. Now there are quite a few individuals whose views I regard as fascist who are not personally violent. Does that mean that my 'stereotype' of fascism and fascists as 'violent' is a distortion? At the very best, it would be an exaggeration.

I want to dispute that hard, for reasons that to me do more damage than all other criticisms of 'stereotype'. Part of my conception of fascism concerns its tendencies as an organised political force. I would want to argue that fascism is not just a sum-total of its individual adherents' behaviours. It is a political movement, built round ideas about 'race', conspiracy theories and so on, whose inherent logic leads to class and racial violence. To define my view as a 'stereotype' involves turning fascism into an *aggregate of individual*; then my 'image' of them is more or less accurate inasmuch as it relates to those individuals. Against this, my conceptualisation of fascism involves treating it as a socially-organised phenomenon, in which individuals are not simply aggregated (with all their particular likenesses and unlikenesses, personal violence or otherwise). They are being mobilised for a socio-political movement; it is the potential of that movement I am assessing in calling fascism 'violent'. I am assessing its future, not just summarising its past.

'Stereotyping' dissolves all sense of social organisation. In protesting against category-inclusions, it dissolves all categories. What kinds of characteristic are seen by 'stereotypers' as the most likely to appear within our 'stereotypes'? They are almost always *individual physical or personality traits*. For example psychologists will ask us if we regard Jews as 'shrewd', 'clannish', 'greedy' etc – all individual personality traits. But how, within such a model, could we encompass the repeated fascist claim that Jews are mounting a world conspiracy, or that mixing their blood with ours will lead to racial degeneration? The whole 'stereotyping' edifice depends on hostility to thinking in group-terms.

Once dismiss that assumption, and the politics no longer flow from it. It is then open to me to argue that working class people are in general *more accurately* aware that the social world is really divided into categories. If they have a 'stereotype' of managers, or employers, as 'exploitative', 'greedy', 'selfish' etc, that is not a false generalisation. It is an accurate summary of their experience of the inherent tendencies that arise from occupying a concrete social position. It is not a statement about the personality of an individual, but a claim about what follows from occupying a definite position in a class society.[11]

My conclusion is that the concept of a 'stereotype' is useless as a tool for investigation of media texts. It is dangerous on both epistemological and political grounds.[12] Its view of influence and learning is empiricist and individualistic, and leads to the anti-democratic politics which Lippmann first set into it. Finally, it leads to an arbitrary reading of texts which tells us only about the worries of the analyst.

Notes

1. Steve Neale, 'The Same Old Story – Stereotypes and Difference', *Screen*, 1980.
2. Compare, for example, the following both taken from Judith Stinton (ed), *Racism and Sexism in Children's Literature* (London, Writers and Readers, 1979): 'These caricatures [of the Chinese] are part and parcel of the perception of Asians and their descendants as subhuman creatures, a perception which led members of the white community to persecute, ridicule, exploit and ostracise Chinese Americans.' (p. 81) 'For instance in Puerto Rican books, the minority child is repeatedly shown as living in a ghetto. The continual suggestion that this is the norm must surely help to make it so, when really these conditions are inherited rather than inherent.' (p. 4) In the first case, the stereotype (or caricatured perception) is seen as a distortion – and therefore powerful; in the second, the stereotype (or 'repeated showing') is seen as *too true* – and therefore powerful.
3. Richard Dyer, 'Stereotyping', in his (ed.) *Gays in Film* (London, BFI, 1977), pp. 27–39.
4. Ellen Seiter, 'Stereotypes and the Media: A Re-evaluation', *Journal of Communication*, Spring 1986, pp. 14–26. See also T. E. Perkins, 'Rethinking Stereotypes', in Michele Barrett, *et al.*, eds., *Ideology and Cultural Production* (London, Croom Helm, 1979).
5. See R. W. Connell, 'Theorising Gender', *Sociology*, 19:2 (1985), pp. 260–72.
6. See David Bloor, *Knowledge and Social Imagery* (London, Routledge & Kegan Paul, 1976), for a useful discussion of the problem of visual metaphors in thinking about ideology.
7. Polly Toynbee, *Guardian*, 30 October 1978.
8. It is indeed strange that Seiter, whose article is by far the most comprehensive critique of 'stereotyping' research I have come across, should end by positively recommending a return to Lippmann's formulations. In her article, Seiter in fact raises many of the objections which I have covered in this Chapter. Yet she ends by suggesting that the problems have arisen because theorists have moved too far from Lippmann. I cannot here review her arguments in detail, to show why I think she is mistaken.
9. See, for example, H. H. Hyman and P. B. Sheatsley, 'The Authoritarian Personality: A Methodological Critique', in R. Christie and M. Jahoda, eds., *Studies in the Scope and Method of the Authoritarian Personality* (Glencoe, Free Press, 1954).
10. N. Cauthen, I. Robinson and H. Krauss, 'Stereotypes – A Review of the Literature 1926–68', *Journal of Social Psychology*, 84.
11. It does not, of course, follow from this that there cannot be miscategorisations. An example of such ideological miscategorisation would be that now the problem is transformed to the specific nature of the categories, from one in which it is the sheer tendency to categorise.
12. A recent article by Susan Condor expresses many of the same reservations as I have done about 'stereotype' research, though her target is specifically their use in 'race-research'. She goes so far as to suggest that the categories of such research can unwittingly assist the very racism it wants to study. See her '"Race stereotypes", and racist discourse', *Text*, 8:1–2, pp. 69–90.

Further reading

See 'Further Reading' section in the previous reading.

Questions

1 Summarise the main points in Barker's argument using some of your own examples.
2 Can you think of some stereotypical representations which bear out Barker's objection to them as being accurate enough to gain immediate audience recognition yet misleading or false?
3 In your view, does the concept 'stereotype' have any useful contribution to make to Media Studies?

9

The Power of Popular Television: The Case of *Cosby*
Justin Lewis

From *The ideological octopus: an exploration of television and its audience* (Routledge 1991)

The first two readings in this section focused on the debates associated with the concept of 'stereotype' and its ideological processes: the social classification of particular groups and people as often highly simplified and generalised signs. A key theme in the development of Media and Cultural Studies in the post-1960 period has been the analysis of media images of race and ethnicity, and the part that such imagery might play in *naturalising*, reproducing and shaping forms of cultural difference. In the mid-1990s, with the images and issues relating to the Rodney King and O. J. Simpson trials in the United States, and to continuing tensions in many British inner cities, the politics of race – and of racism – remain significant areas for study and research. Have things changed at all in the last 30 years, in the forms of media representation which characterise images of black people and ethnic identities in popular culture?

The following extract is taken from a study of television audiences in Britain and the United States. In it, Lewis evaluates the case for and the case against *The Cosby Show*, a popular American situation comedy first broadcast in the US in the mid-1980s and widely exported since. His assessment usefully draws on a range of sources: academic writers, researchers, critical reviewers and cultural commentators, in addition to the records of his own audience interviews and research.

Reviewing The Cosby Show

The Cosby Show does not need much introduction. For those readers who have managed to avoid this extraordinarily successful TV show, let me congratulate you for your singularity and offer this brief synopsis.

The Cosby Show is a half-hour situation comedy about an upper middle-class black family, the Huxtables. Cliff Huxtable (played by Bill Cosby) is a gynecologist and obstetrician, and his wife Claire is a lawyer. They have four daughters and a son, and, as the series has grown older, they have acquired in-laws and grandchildren. The show focuses on the Huxtables' attractive New York brownstone home, which provides the set for an endless series of comic domestic dramas. There is little, thus far, to distinguish this television fiction from many others: we are used to a TV world populated by attractive professionals and their good-looking offspring. What makes the show unusual is its popularity, its critical acclaim, and the fact that all its leading characters are black.

These distinctive features have made *The Cosby Show* the subject of much speculation and discussion. At the heart of many of these discussions lies an apparent contradiction. Here we have a country that is still emerging from a deeply racist history, a society in which white people have treated (and continue to treat) black people with contempt, suspicion and a profoundly ignorant sense of superiority. And yet the most popular TV show in the U.S. over the last decade, among black and white people alike, is not only about a black family, but one portrayed without any of the demeaning stereotypes that have characterized images of black people in mainstream popular culture. Commentators have been provoked to try and resolve this apparent curiosity and, in so doing, to muse upon the show's social significance.

The most prevalent critical reaction, particularly during the first few years of the show, was to applaud Bill Cosby's creation as not only a witty and thoughtful sitcom, but an enlightened step forward in race relations. After decades of negative or degrading media images (see, for example, Hartsough, 1989), the Huxtable family presented black characters that black and white audiences could relate to. The celebratory tone of many reviews contained genuine hopes about what such a cultural intervention might achieve in dispelling racial prejudices in the United States.

The history of critical response to popular culture often follows a similar pattern: elaborate praise becomes an increasingly difficult burden to bear, and euphoria is almost invariably followed by a cynical backlash. *The Cosby Show*, for good or ill, is no exception to this rule. Critics have subsequently accused the show of presenting a misleadingly cozy picture, a sugar-candy world unfettered by racism, crime, economic deprivation and hardship. Some have argued that the Huxtables' charmed life is so alien to the experience of most black people that they are no longer 'black' at all, but, as Henry Lewis Gates puts it, 'in most respects, just like white people' (Gates, 1989). Gates has also argued that these 'positive images' can be counter-productive, since they suggest to the world the myth of the American dream, a just world where anyone can make it, and where racial barriers no longer exist:

> As long as *all* blacks were represented in demeaning or peripheral roles, it was possible to believe that American racism was, as it were, indiscriminate. The

social vision of 'Cosby,' however, reflecting the miniscule integration of blacks into the upper middle-class, reassuringly throws the blame for black poverty back onto the impoverished. (Gates, 1989)

At the risk of simplifying critical opinion, most analyses of *Cosby* fall broadly into one of two camps: the show is seen as either socially progressive or as an apology for a racist system that disadvantages most black people. Both views carry with them assumptions about media effects – the debate concerns the nature of this effect. This, in turn, raises questions about the meaning of the show for black and white audiences. The study presented in this chapter will I hope, begin to clarify some of these questions.

Cosby: the case against

Few would argue that *The Cosby Show* presents a typical or realistic view of the lives of black Americans. The Huxtable family, like their creator, have attained a level of wealth, comfort and success shared by only a tiny minority of black people in the United States. The period which produced *Cosby* also produced a deterioration in the social conditions of most black Americans (see Downing, 1988).

The success of *The Cosby Show* has, according to Gates, led to a curious divergence between media images and social realities. Bill Cosby has broken the mold of black media stereotypes and opened up our TV screens to a host of black performers:

> This is the 'Cosby' decade. The show's unprecedented success in depicting the lives of affluent blacks has exercised a profound influence on television in the last half of the 80s ... 'Cosby's' success has led to the flow of TV sitcoms that feature the black middle class, each of which takes its lead from the 'Cosby' show. (Gates, 1989)

And yet, outside the television world, there are a plethora of social statistics to demonstrate that many of the advances made by black Americans in the 1960s and 1970s are being reversed in the 1980s and 1990s, so that, as Gates puts it, there is very little connection between the social status of black Americans and the fabricated images of black people that Americans consume every day.

The gulf between television and the world outside is propounded by the Huxtables' charmed lives, a utopian familial harmony that has caused some critics to wince in disbelief. Mark Cripin Miller's description is characteristically derisive:

> And then there is the cuddliest and most beloved of TV Dads: Bill Cosby, who, as Dr. Heathcliff Huxtable, lives in perfect peace, and in a perfect brownstone, with his big happy family, and never has to raise his hand or fist, but retains the absolute devotion of his wife and kids just by making lots of goofy faces. (Miller, 1986, p. 206)

The problem that Gates and Miller are identifying is not simply that the show is an unrealistic portrayal of black family life – few sitcoms, after all, make any claim to represent social reality – but that the Huxtables sustain the harmful myth of social mobility.

The Huxtable family appear to have glided effortlessly into the upper eche-lons of American society. The show never offers us the slightest glimpse of the economic disadvantages and deep-rooted discrimination that prevent most black Americans from reaching their potential. Michael Dyson, in an other-wise positive assessment of the show, comments that

> it is perhaps this lack of acknowledgement of the underside of the American Dream that is the most unfortunate feature of the Huxtable opulence. Cosby defends against linking the authenticity of the Huxtable representation of black life to the apparently contradictory luxury the family lives in when he says: 'To say that they are not black enough is a denial of the American dream and the American way of life. My point is that this is an American family – an *American* family – and if you want to live like they do, and you're willing to work, the opportunity is there.' (Dyson, 1989, p. 30)

But, as Dyson suggests, this is a cruel distortion: 'Such a statement leads us to believe that Cosby is unaware that there are millions of people, the so-called working poor, who work hard but nevertheless fall beneath the poverty level.' And yet, writes Dyson, 'surely Cosby knows better than this.'

Whatever Bill Cosby's intention, some critics argue that the end result is extremely damaging. The Huxtables ultimately sustain the idea that 'anyone can make it,' the comforting assertion of the American dream; a myth that sustains a conservative political ideology that is blind to the inequalities that hinder those born on mean streets and pamper those born on easy street. As Miller puts it:

> Cliff's blackness serves an affirmative purpose within the ad that is *The Cosby Show*. At the center of this ample tableau, Cliff is himself an ad, implicitly pro-claiming the fairness of the American system: 'Look!' he shows us. 'Even I can have all this!' (Miller, 1986, p. 210)

This mythology is made all the more powerful, Miller argues, by the close identification between Cliff Huxtable and Bill Cosby. Behind the fictional doctor lies a man whose real life is *also* a success story: fact and fiction coa-lesce to confirm the 'truth' they embody.

Herein, the critics argue, lies the popularity of the show in the United States. The show may appear to herald a new dawn of racial tolerance, a world where white people accept black people into their living rooms as equals. This appearance, according to Miller, hides the more subtle fears of white viewers, to whom black people are still seen as a threat. Cliff, or Bill Cosby, is attractive to white viewers because, as Miller puts it, he represents 'a threat contained,' offering

> deep solace to a white public terrified that one day blacks might come with guns to steal the copperware, the juicer, the microwave, the VCR, even the TV itself;

at a time when

> American whites need such reassurance because they are now further removed
> than ever, both spatially and psychologically, from the masses of the black poor.
> (Miller, 1986, pp. 213–4)

The thrust of this argument, despite Miller's hyperbole, may provide us
with an insight into the ideological state of white people in the contemporary
United States. *The Cosby Show* is not simply a source of gentle reassurance, it
flatters to deceive. The U.S. is still emerging from a system of apartheid. Even
if legal and political inequalities are finally disappearing, economic barriers
remain. In an age when most white people have moved beyond the crudities
of an overt and naked racism, there is a heavy burden of guilt for all concerned. *The Cosby Show* provides his white audiences with relief not only
from fear, but from responsibility.

How far this account of the show's appeal explains its popularity and significance remains to be seen. Suffice to say, at this point, that whatever the audience study reveals about this argument, it moves us well beyond the parameters
of traditional TV audience research. It is impossible to design an audience
study that, in a simple and straightforward sense, measures the effect of the
show on attitudes toward race. An exploration of the show's influence forces
us to delve more deeply into the complex interaction between the program and
the viewer, and thereby into the delicate ideological suppositions that inform
the points where they meet, where they create meaning and pleasure.

There are, in the meantime, other things to consider before we can fully
appreciate the depth of audience responses to *The Cosby Show*. We have, after
all, only covered the more pessimistic aspects of the critical terrain.

Cosby: the case for

If we are to engage in a battle over the nature of what gets shown on prime-
time TV in the United States, we should be well versed in the art of the possible. Any attempt to change the form or content of mainstream television will
come up against two powerful bastions of conservatism: the profit-oriented
predilections of network and advertising executives, and the well-trained
expectations and tastes of TV audiences. We can create innovative programming ideas until we are blue in the face, but if the networks, advertisers or
viewers don't respond, then we are wasting our time.

The Cosby Show's focus on a black family and its departure from an accepted assortment of racial stereotypes did not make it an obvious candidate for
primetime. ABC turned the series proposal down, and, were it not for Bill
Cosby's track record (including, significantly, his ability to sell products on
TV commercials), it would probably never have made it on the air. To attack
the show because it panders to the needs of a mainstream white audience is to
attack its life-blood: the U.S. has a television culture where audience ratings

decide whether you live or die. This bottom line gives a television program very little room for maneuver. To have confronted the audience with the uncomfortable realities of racism would have been commercial suicide.

John Downing argues that any evaluation of the show must take account of this conservative cultural climate, and that despite its limitations; 'to be as good as it is *and* to have gotten past these barriers is a major achievement in itself' (Downing, 1988, p. 68). Ultimately, Downing acknowledges, the show does let 'racism off the hook': it is, nevertheless, a considerable step forward in the history of media representation. There is, Downing argues, 'an abundance of black culture presented in the series, expressed without fanfare, but with constant dignity' (*ibid.*, p. 61). The show celebrates black artists, from Ellis Wilson to Stevie Wonder, while political figures like Martin Luther King, or events like the civil rights march on Washington have been interwoven, albeit ever so gently, into the story-line.

The naming of the Huxtables' first grandchildren is a typical example of *The Cosby Show* style. Their eldest daughter, Sondra, decides to call her twins Nelson and Winnie. The episode that deals with this decision highlights the issue of naming, but makes no comment on its overt political connotations. The reference to the Mandelas is made quietly and unobtrusively, relying upon the audience's ability to catch the political ramifications of the statement.

If the subtlety of this approach is a virtue, it is one borne of necessity. During the show's second season, NBC tried to have the anti-apartheid sign on Theo's bedroom door removed. Bill Cosby, with the newly found clout of ratings success behind him, stood his ground and fought successfully to keep it there. What is interesting about this story is not only Cosby's triumph (would the network have capitulated to a show with a few less ratings points?), but the almost pathological fear of certain kinds of political discourse by those in charge of television entertainment. The fuss was made about a sign expressing a sentiment that is, outside the comparatively small 'market' of white South Africa, *supposed* to be fairly uncontroversial. The sign made no intrusion into the plot, and many viewers would probably not even notice its presence. The network's desire to remove such a meek symbol of black resistance from the airwaves demonstrates what progressive voices on primetime TV are up against.

The seriousness with which *The Cosby Show* approaches the issue of cultural representation has put it on a pedestal and exposed it to critical scrutiny. As Bill Cosby and program consultant Alvin Poussaint have pointed out, few other sitcoms are attacked for their failure to deal with issues of racism. This is, Poussaint has argued, a particularly unfair strain to put upon a situation comedy. Writing in *Ebony*, Poussaint points out that

> audiences tune in to be entertained, not to be confronted with social problems. Critical social disorders, like racism, violence, and drug abuse, rarely lend themselves to comic treatment; trying to deal with them on a sitcom could trivialize issues that deserve serious, thoughtful treatment. (Poussaint, 1988)

The limits of *The Cosby Show* are, according to Poussaint, the limits of the genre. This is a point, indeed, acknowledged by some critics. Gates, in an otherwise fairly critical piece, accepts that the very structure of a sitcom 'militates against its use as an agent of social change' (Gates, 1989).

Despite these constraints, what *Cosby* has confronted, many have argued, is the deep-rooted racism of white Americans who find it difficult to accept racial equality. Dyson, for example, has suggested that one of 'the most useful aspects of Cosby's dismantling of racial mythology and stereotyping is that it has permitted America to view black folk as human beings' (Dyson, 1989, p. 29). Here, at last, are media representations of successful and attractive black people who white people can respect, admire and even identify with.

It could be argued that references to discrimination and black struggle would, in this sense, be counter-productive, alienating substantial sections of the white audience and making identification with the Huxtables more difficult. We should also be aware of the particular nature of the television world. The Huxtables' class position may be unusual (for black *and* white people) in real life, but to be an affluent, attractive professional on television is to be 'normal.' There are, of course, assumptions about the audience embedded in this argument, just as there are in the arguments of those who are critical of the absence of a discourse of racial discrimination.

Some of the more positive evaluations of the show have made the interesting point that the discourse of discrimination that does find its way into the script is not racism but sexism. The show frequently uses humor to expose the inadequacy of the sexist or machismo attitudes of some members of its male cast. Some characters, like son-in-law Elvin or Rudi's friend Kenny (who spouts forth the sexist platitudes of his big brother), are deliberately set up to be undermined. While it is the characters of Claire and her daughters who take the lead in these instances, they are usually supported by the figure of Cliff, who has traveled some way beyond the sexist stereotypes so common in TV sitcoms.

It is unusual to find strong male characters in sitcoms who support a feminist stance taken by female characters. The male in a sitcom who adopts such a position invariably still runs the risk of ridicule. Downing suggests that, while *The Cosby Show*'s challenge to patriarchy has its limitations, Cliff's involvement in these comic episodes plays an important role in legitimating the show's feminist sentiments: 'His condemnation of everyday sexism perhaps communicates itself all the more powerfully to male viewers precisely because he cannot be written off as a henpecked wimp' (Downing, 1989, p. 60).

Downing's defense of *The Cosby Show* is not apologetic: it is a reminder that, however we judge it, the show is, in many respects, one of the more progressive forces in popular culture to emerge from the United States in recent years. This may not be saying very much – we are, after all, talking about a televisual history steeped in sexist and racist images – but it is worth remembering before we embark on a journey through the North American audience. Even if the audience study manifests many of the critic's worst fears, there are countless other television messages whose ideological consequences are almost too oppressive or frightening to even contemplate.

[...]

Decoding race

It is sometimes easy to forget that race and racial difference involve a great deal more than categories of physiognomy and skin pigmentation. The differences between a black person and a white person in the United States are deeply rooted in their distinct and separate histories, histories encapsulating a host of material and cultural distinctions that render the experience of being white quite different from the experience of being black. Race, in other words, is a social as well as a physical construction.

Racial discrimination, throughout its infamous history, has usually been predicated on a series of perceived symbolic links between skin color and culture. To colonialists, slave owners and promoters of apartheid, this meant a straightforward denunciation of black culture as uncivilized, inferior or threatening. Despite their manifest crudity, these racist attitudes have never been as simple or homogeneous as they sometimes appear. From colonialism onward, the racist discourses infusing white societies have borne contradictory assumptions about the relation between nature and nurture: black people have been seen as simultaneously within the reaches of white society *and* beyond it. The black person's soul was therefore treated as, on the one hand, a changeable commodity, open to the influences of missionary zeal, and, on the other hand, as the heart of darkness, inherently irredeemable.

Once placed in the industrial 'melting pots' of the late twentieth century, the struggles and achievements of black people in an oppressive white world have disentangled the fixity of many of the associations between race and culture. The ability of some black people, against the odds, to succeed in a predominantly white environment, has made notions of biological determinism decidedly less fashionable. While such notions have certainly not disappeared, they are now less common currency than ideas that flirt with the principle of racial equality. This does not mean the end of racism; far from it: as an instrument of repression, racism now takes more subtle forms.

In most Western countries, most particularly in the United States, the idea that white people and black people are irrevocably tied to discrete cultures has been seriously compromised by the promise of social mobility: the idea that anyone, regardless of race, creed or class, can make it. These compromises are now enshrined within legal structures that, while they do not guarantee racial equality, at least give the idea of equal rights a certain amount of credibility. Bill Cosby, whether as himself or as Dr. Heathcliff Huxtable, is easily assimilated into this ideology. He is, Miller argues, visible 'proof' of the meritocratic mythology that fuels the American Dream, a black person who has achieved success beyond the confines of a racially defined culture.

Racism is, however, a capricious creature, and it has adapted to this discursive climate by absorbing a number of contradictions. The history of racism is now embedded in an iniquitous capitalist system, where economic rather than racial laws ensure widespread racial segregation and disadvantage. This, in turn, encourages white people to believe in an imagined cultural superiority, while simultaneously giving credence to the idea that we are what we become, that culture is not God-given but a social construction.

The Cosby Show is, as I have suggested, both a singular and an ambiguous intervention into this complex ideological terrain.

[...]

Most forms of ambiguity are seldom tolerated in popular culture.

[...]

If we have learnt anything about *The Cosby Show*'s success thus far, it is that it is built on layers of ambiguity. The Huxtable family's straightforward appearance conceals a long and varied cast of characters: to some they are black, to others they are not; in one moment they are privileged, in another they are average. Ambiguity is least likely to be found (although it can be found then too) when *The Cosby Show* declares itself, ever so gently, on the issue of sexism. On the issues of race and class it remains very quiet, and throws open the doors to multiple meanings.

I have tried to chart the ideological effects of these ambiguities, to place them within the broader ideological contexts where meanings take on significance. What has become clear along the way, I hope, is that we can neither deride the show as reactionary nor praise it as progressive without suppressing some of its ambiguities. To many white people it informs a discourse of racial tolerance, a liberal acceptance of black people as equals. To its African American audience, and even some white viewers, it is a jewel in a pale and insipid sea of whiteness, an assertion of black cultural pride that confounds traditional media stereotypes.

At the same time, it panders to the limits of white liberalism, allowing white audiences the sanctimonious pleasure of viewing the world through rose-tinted spectacles, as *Harper's Magazine* puts it:

> The success of this handsome, affluent black family points to the fair-mindedness of whites who, out of their essential goodness, changed society so that black families like the Huxtables could succeed. Whites can watch *The Cosby Show* and feel complimented on a job well done.... On Thursday nights, Cosby, like a priest, absolves his white viewers, forgives and forgets the sins of the past. (*Harper's Magazine*, 1988, p. 50)

In so doing, it flatters to deceive, and adds credence to discourses that work only to sustain a system of racial inequality.

Could *The Cosby Show* be different? What would happen if it took on racism in the way it has taken on sexism? The ideological room for maneuver is, unfortunately, very small. In the age of the remote control device, an audience's tolerance for images that disturb them is limited: to tamper too much with the delicate semiology of *The Cosby Show* risks losing precisely the viewers who have the most to learn. There is, nevertheless, a little space in which to move forward, but it means treading very carefully and very softly.

References

Downing, J. 1988: *The Cosby Show* and American racial discourse. In Smitherman-Donaldson, G. and Van Djik, T. (eds.), *Disclosure and discrimination*. Detroit: Wayne State University Press.

Dyson, M. 1989: Bill Cosby and the politics of race. *Zeta*, September.

Gates, H. L. 1989: TV's black world turns – but stays unreal. *New York Times*, 12 November.

Hartsough, D. 1989: *The Cosby Show* in historical context explaining its appeal to middle-class black women. Paper Presented to the Ohio State University Film Conference.

Miller, M. C. 1986: Deride and conquer. In Gitlin, T. (ed.), *Watching television*. New York: Pantheon.

Poussaint, A. 1988: The Huxtables: fact or fantasy. *Ebony*, October.

Questions

1 Summarise the cases for and against *The Cosby Show* as outlined by Lewis in the extract. Are there, in your view, any issues which are not effectively discussed, or which deserve to be given further consideration?

2 Select a range of examples of images and coverage of black people and groups from different media – film, television, newspapers, magazines and advertisements. Discuss and assess them in the light of Lewis's arguments and the ideas and debates about stereotyping.

3 How are other ethnic and group identities and differences constructed and treated in media output?

Further reading

Bogle, D. 1994: *Toms, coons, mulattoes, mammies and bucks: an interpretive of blacks in American films*, 3rd revised edn. Oxford: Roundhouse Publishing.

Daniels, T. and Gerson, J. (eds.) 1989: *The colour black: black images in British television*. London: BFI.

Dines, G. and Humez, J. 1994: *Gender, race and class in media*. London: Sage.

Gillespie, M. 1995: *Television, ethnicity and cultural change*. London: Routledge.

Hartmann, P. and Husband, C. 1974: *Racism and the mass media: a study of the role of the mass media in the formation of white beliefs and attitudes in Britain*. London: Davis-Poynter.

Jhally, S. and Lewis, J. 1992: *Enlightened racism: Audiences, The Cosby Show and the myth of the American dream*. Boulder, Cob., and Oxford: Westview Press.

Pines, J. (ed.) 1992: *Black and white in colour: black people in British television since 1936*. London: BFI.

Ross, K. 1996: *Black and white media: black images in popular film and television*. London: Routledge.

Searle, C. 1989: *Your daily dose: racism and The Sun*. London: Campaign for Press and Broadcasting Freedom.

10

Mapping the Mythical: A Geopolitics of National Sporting Stereotypes
Hugh O'Donnell

From *Discourse and Society* 5(3), 345–80 (1994)

Continuing the theme of stereotyping and how group identities are constructed, this extract by O'Donnell examines the common stereotypes associated with nationality and national character. The article shows how sports reporting best exemplifies the way in which positive and negative components of stereotypes can exist side by side and, although confined to this area of media output, the extract opens a wider discursive debate around racist and xenophobic ideologies. Sports coverage, like many other media forms, exists and operates within a specific value system based on its economic and political positioning, and the fact that its discourse reflects those who have control over those systems is of no surprise. But for many commentators it is the combination of ritualism, drama and level of emotional involvement on the part of the audience which encourages and sustains the conferring of negative social identities and allows for the construction of a single trait (whether it be, for example, 'coolness under pressure' or 'undisciplined creativity') to epitomise an entire nation. O'Donnell demonstrates, through a content analysis of 53 publications from 15 different European countries, that specific stereotypes are not confined to individual countries but are almost entirely uniform both within and across national boundaries.

The Scandinavians When Jesper Parnevik won the Scottish Open Golf Championship in July 1993, Scotland's best-selling quality Sunday newspaper, *Scotland on Sunday*, spoke of 'his cool frame of mind, even by Swedish standards' (11 July 1993). A week later, in an article analysing the rise to prominence of Swedish golfers in general, the same newspaper pointed out that Swedish coaching was all about 'the mind, the temperament', adding: 'Everything in their sporting culture seems to hinge on the cerebral dimension' (18 July 1993).

The passages quoted illustrate two essential elements of a now well-established stereotype of Scandinavianness/Swedishness in the (non-Scandinavian) European media: coolness and clinical rationality. This stereotype has a long history both in and outside sport. It was a fundamental part of media presentations of the great Swedish tennis player of the 1970s, Björn Borg – often referred to as an 'iceberg', or even as 'Ice Borg' – and has surfaced again in relation to the current Swedish tennis star Stefan Edberg. Thus, commenting on the 1991 Wimbledon tournament, the Spanish daily *El Mundo* (3 July 1991) described him as 'cold and concentrated'. Germany's best-selling daily newspaper *Bild* (6

July 1991) referred to him as 'the Swedish ice block Stefan Edberg', and, when he lost the semi-final to Michael Stich, Scotland's best-selling quality daily, the *Glasgow Herald* (6 July 1991), said of him: 'It was almost as though the ice-cool temperament was melting away in the afternoon heat.'

As with all the stereotypes studied in this article, the Swedish stereotype also has an 'underside' which involves clearly negative judgements made against an implied but seldom stated norm. The downside of Scandinavianness is taciturnity, a lack of dynamism, even an absence of emotion. Thus, in its coverage of the 1990 Wimbledon tournament, the then Soviet Union's best selling sports daily, *Sovetsky Sport* (8 July 1990), having described Edberg as a 'Swedish iceberg', added that he was 'taciturn, as befits a Scandinavian'. This can lead to suggestions of a tendency to be boring: 'The 25-year old Swede tends to be ignored by the media ... which is not too surprising given his monotone voice and short, simple answers. There is always the danger of falling over sound asleep', wrote the *Glasgow Herald* (5 July 1991). The Belgian French-language daily *La Libre Belgique* (3 July 1991) agreed that Edberg was 'never very interesting'.

Swedish reporters are, of course, aware of this stereotype. Thus, at the beginning of the 1992 European Football Championship in Sweden (Euro '92) the Gothenburg daily *iDAG* (12 June 1992) wrote: 'Nordic cool has been shown at regular intervals in top-level sport. With tennis's Ice-Borg or Ice-Björn[1] as the absolutely classic example', also pointing out that the Eurosport commentator had described the Swedish football player Patrick Anderson as 'ice cool Anderson'. However, this stereotype is not in the main used by Swedes themselves....

Nordicness can occasionally be acquired by the inhabitants of other countries if the conditions of coolness and/or clinical rationality can be met. Thus when the 1992 Seville World Fair (Expo '92) proved to be a triumph of organization admired throughout the world, the Spanish weekly magazine *Cambio 16* (10 August 1992) suggested that 'the Seville Expo seems more Nordic than Southern and slapdash'. And when the Spanish athlete Fermin Cacho won the gold medal in the 1500 metres in the Barcelona Olympics, the Spanish sports daily *El Mundo Deportivo* (9 August 1992) described his performance as 'cold, calculating, more Nordic than Iberian'.

The Germans. When European sports journalists refer to Germany, the dominant stereotype of national character combines the idea of strong mental control with discipline, efficiency, reliability and hard work: the central elements of what Spain's best-selling daily *El Pais* (3 November 1993) calls 'the German legend'. This stereotype is found throughout the European media, and is at times reflected in the German press itself. Thus, talking of the German football team's national coach during Euro '92, the German weekly magazine *Stern* (25 June 1992) wrote: 'Discipline, order, punctuality – national trainer Berti Vogts leads his team in the tried and tested Teutonic tradition.'

In the terms of this stereotype, the Germans have, above all, the right mental 'attitude': a confidence in their ability to get the job done, and total commitment to the task in hand. In 1992, as Germany overcame Sweden 3–2 in the semi-final of Euro '92, the Norwegian tabloid *Dagbladet* (22 June 1992) wrote: 'Their attitude is the Germans' strongest weapon. A winning instinct and self-confidence their greatest quality.' The Norwegian quality daily *Aftenposten* (26 June 1992) agreed, supplying an anecdote to support its point of view: 'German self-confidence in football knows no bounds. The Germans were the only team to book their hotel rooms in Gothenburg for the European Championship final in advance.'

During the 1990 World Cup (Italia '90) the leading Swedish quality daily *Dagens Nyheter* (16 June 1990) described the German football team as a 'machine team', a phrase which would reappear verbatim in the Swedish tabloid *Aftonbladet's* coverage of Euro '92 (21 June 1992). The notion of mechanical efficiency accompanies German sportsmen and sportswomen across a range of sports. During Wimbledon 1991 the *Glasgow Herald* described German women's champion Steffi Graf as being 'in perfect working order' (7 June 1991). And as Denmark defeated Germany 2–0 in the final of Euro '92, the Norwegian tabloid *VG* (27 June 1992) wrote of the Danish fight 'against German machines which refused to give up'.

The notion of efficiency is also always explicit in relation to the Germans: 'the Becker serve is a triumph of natural genetics and Germanic efficiency', wrote the English *Observer* (23 June 1991); the Catalan daily *Diari de Barcelona*, speaking of Steffi Graf's performance in the final, referred to 'the characteristic reliability of the German'; and the *Glasgow Herald* (6 July 1991) left nothing to the imagination: speaking of the same player, it wrote: 'there is perhaps only one player at the championships whose game is reminiscent of mechanical efficiency'. And this notion is not restricted to journalistic discourse. In his book on the 'corporate image' of Germany, David Head (1992: 2) refers to the 'almost machine-like efficiency' of Steffi Graf.

Germanness can also be acquired momentarily by other nationals. During Euro '92, much was made of Sweden's supposedly 'disciplined' approach to the game. Commenting on this, *Aftonbladet* (24 July 1992) wrote: 'The Swedes are often called Scandinavia's Germans, and perhaps there is something in that.' A few days later, Norway's *Dagbladet* (27 July 1992) would also describe the Swedes as 'Scandinavia's Germans'. *Stern* (25 June 1992) likewise referred to an Italian referee who was 'famous in Italy for his Prussian hardness'.

The British. In the dominant British (principally English) stereotype, continental cerebrations are dismissed as 'airy-fairy' in favour of what Nairn (1988: 92) describes as 'an indispensable national aversion to theory'. Instead the accent is on a would-be 'realistic', pragmatic, no-nonsense approach. The values against which sports journalists judge British teams and sportspersons in general are work-rate, commitment, courage, giving it their all, fighting back in the face of adversity.

The strength and range of this stereotype of Britishness/Englishness was abundantly clear during Italia '90. Thus, when England defeated Cameroon, Franz Beckenbauer, the then German manager, suggested that 'the great strength of the English is that they never give up' (quoted in the Austrian tabloid *Kronen Zeitung*, 3 July 1990). English manager Bobby Robson agreed: 'our fighting spirit won through' (quoted in the Austrian tabloid *Kurier*, 3 July 1990). This stereotype accompanies British (especially English) footballers wherever they go. When England were defeated 2–1 by Sweden during Euro '92, the Swedish tabloid *Expressen* (18 June 1992) wrote: 'The English, as the English always do, fought nobly to the last. They are hard and tough.' And when Sporting Lisbon defeated Newcastle United 5–3 later that year, the leading Portuguese sports daily, *A Bola*, exclaimed (10 August 1992): 'Goodness gracious, how different the football played in England is!', going on to describe it as 'full of running, full of sweat, full of fight'.

Scotland occasionally shares in this stereotype: *Dagens Nyheter* (16 June 1990) quoted the then Scottish manager Andy Roxburgh as saying: 'We always play best when we have our backs to the wall.' And a Scottish defeat by Italy in 1993 prompted France's leading sports daily, *L'Équipe* (14 October 1993), to say: 'the Scots ... do not know the meaning of the words giving up'.

The French. In terms of stereotype of national character, France proves to be a site of discursive complexity. While lacking the dour discipline of the Germans and the fighting spirit of the British, the French are presented as essentially reasonable and indeed 'civilized'. At the same time they enjoy some of the inspirational qualities of the Latins, but without toppling over into irrational and irresponsible behaviour. The dominant stereotype is best represented by terms such as 'flamboyance', 'flair', 'inspiration', 'charm', even 'style'.

The French football team was absent from Italia '90, and its performance during Euro '92 was dismal. However, even disappointing French performances are explained by the lack of what are seen as their 'natural' characteristics. Thus, as France and England produced a lacklustre 0–0 draw during Euro '92, the *Herald*[2] (15 June 1992) expressed the wish that the French might still 'show a wee glimpse of the joie de vivre which ought to be their lot', while the English *Daily Telegraph* of the same day suggested that 'there was no romance in their gifted souls'. 'Where has French charm gone?', wrote the quality Swedish daily *Svenska Dagbladet* of 17 June 1992, while *Stern*, talking of the French national coach, suggested that 'even in defeat Michel Platini displays a melancholy charm' (25 June 1992).

This stereotype emerges regularly in media coverage of the Wimbledon tournament, particularly in relation to the French tennis player Henri Leconte. Thus, during the 1991 Wimbledon championship, *El Mundo Deportivo* (29 June 1991) described him as 'tremendously inspired'. This stereotype predominates above all in the British/English media. Thus, as Leconte played against (and eventually lost to) Boris Becker during the 1993 championship, the BBC commentators suggested that he was one of the three greatest tennis players of all time as far as 'artistry' was concerned, pointing also to his 'Gallic charm'. We may, of course, agree that Leconte is a skilful and stylish player, but the supposed 'Frenchness' of his style of play derives not from his play itself, but from the stereotype. This point, and the association of the stereotype with English audiences, was acknowledged, somewhat sardonically, by *L'Équipe magazine* (August 1991) when it wrote: 'England has a real weak spot for Leconte. "Dear Henry" [in English], so flamboyant and so unpredictable, so French, what!'

The Southern Europeans. In sports reporting on Mediterranean countries, the dominant stereotype is clearly that of the temperamental Latin, a stereotype which also extends to South America. This is one of the most deep-rooted stereotypes in northern European culture, its main elements being passion, hot temper, frivolity, sensuality, even hedonism.

This stereotype finds one of its most widespread expressions in reporting on football. The absence of Mediterranean teams during Euro '92 meant that, in footballing terms at least, it was in the reporting of Italia '90 that such stereotyping achieved its greatest expression, its main European bearers being the Italians. Thus the then Soviet daily *Pravda* (21 June 1990) assured its readers that 'the Italian team ... reflected the explosive nature of its people'. The ultimate symbol of fiery Italianness during Italia '90 was to be Vesuvius, representing the allegedly volcanic nature of the Italian temperament. When Italy was eliminated by Argentina in the semi-final, *Bild* (4 July 1990) wrote: 'Vesuvius, Naples and all of Italy weeps'. 'The Italians ... went to Naples and at the edge of Vesuvius were burned by the molten lava', added the Basque daily *Deia* (4 July 1990).

As the 1994 World Cup approaches, the Italians are again expected to bring emotion into football. Interviewed by the Barcelona daily *La Vanguardia* (28 November 1993), Alan Rothenburg, chairman of the USA World Cup Organizing Committee, pointed out: 'Few countries personify all the emotions of football, and Italy heads that list.'

The South Americans. The 'fieriness' of the Latins carries with it notions of unpredictable, even uncontrolled creativity. For all its entertainment value, however, this creativity – which is often described as 'magic', particularly in the case of Latin Americans – is viewed unfavourably if it does not bring results. Thus, when AC Milan defeated PSV Eindhoven in the Champions' League in 1992, PSV's Brazilian player Romário de Souza Faria (commonly known simply as Romario) had, according to the Flemish-language Belgian daily *Gazet van Antwerpen* (10 December 1992), 'conjured up a few magic tricks out of his Brazilian shuffle, but lacked any sense of efficiency'.

It is in relation to South America in particular that the ultimately damaging effect of such stereotypes comes most fully into view. Their inherent ambivalence, on the one hand, facilitates their routine reproduction, since their positive side allows their inclusion in areas of journalistic production where any suggestion of direct prejudice would be discouraged and perhaps even censored. But their negative underside – seldom expressed directly though always present in a submerged mode – is an indissociable part of the stereotype and is triggered by implication when any element of the stereotype is used. In this way apparently inoffensive characterizations contribute to the maintenance and reproduction of prejudice in a powerful but elusive form.

If flair and creativity are the positive pole of the Southern stereotype, its negative pole brings together notions of indiscipline, irrationality and recklessness. In the case of the Latin Americans, 'temperament' usually deteriorates into supercharged emotions and complete irresponsibility. Thus the Soviet daily *Izvestia* (26 June 1990) reported of the Brazilians:

> Suffice it to say that on those days when there are matches in which the national team is taking part the number of heart attacks doubles.... In the waiting room of a hospital in São Paulo a female patient died of a stroke – all the medical staff were enthusiastically watching the match between Scotland and Costa Rica. And while Maradona joyously waved the green–yellow strip of his defeated Brazilian opponent above his head, fourteen criminals managed to escape from the grounds of a prison also in São Paulo, taking advantage of the inconsolable grief of the guards. No-one was particularly surprised: it's football ...

Beneath its superficial humour, this report tells of social acquiescence in collective professional negligence. Beyond that still, stories of South American fans committing suicide following the defeat of their team, or even of war being declared as a result of football matches between Latin American countries (Goldlust, 1987: 118), are part of the popular folklore of footballing Europe.

A further element of the stereotype found particularly in relation to South American footballers is the figure of the 'Latin lover': one of the most enduring clichés of northern European culture, going back at least as far as the literary figures of Don Juan and Casanova. The Argentinian footballer Diego Maradona frequently triggered the activation of this element of the stereotype in the European press. For example, during its coverage of Italia '90, *Bild* (25 June 1990) – itself quoting the French Sunday newspaper *France Dimanche* – carried an article on his love life entitled 'Diego: Love in the Aeroplane, in the Taxi and in the Stadium', giving details of some of his apparently 600 'conquests'. And on 5 December 1993 the leading Swiss German-language daily, *Blick*, carried in its sports section a report on how the Columbian footballer Faustino Asprilla (who plays for Parma in Italy) had left his wife and child for German-Italian porn-star Petra Scharbach. The article points out, crucially, how this infatuation has affected the player's work rate: 'Asprilla, bewitched by the porn star, has not scored any goals since 27 October.'

The Africans. During Italia '90, an unexpectedly exogenous recipient of at least parts of the Latin stereotype was to emerge: the Cameroonians. Indeed, with the early exit of Brazil from the competition, they came to be presented as 'the Brazilians of Africa' (*El País*, 13 June 1990), displaying, according to the German weekly *Sport-Bild*, 'Brazilian artistry' (20 June 1990). Their links with the Latin stereotype are immediately apparent, though the details of the stereotype are visibly more extreme. Thus, they are seen as sharing the 'magic' of the Latins – for the *Hannoversche Allgemeine Zeitung* (9 June 1992) they were 'football magicians', for *Bild* (16 June 1992) 'the magicians from Africa' – but in this case it is, in the words of the Italian daily *Corriere della Sera* (15 June 1992), 'black magic', suggesting even more unenlightened forms of religiosity than those conventionally associated with Latins.

Another feature of the Latin stereotype which they share is 'temperament', but again its expression externalizes elements of the stereotype which are often left unsaid. Thus, not only did the *Hannoversche Allgemeine Zeitung* (29 June 1990) describe the Cameroonians as personifying 'African temperament' (which it contrasted with the 'Siberian chill' of their Soviet trainer!) and as being themselves 'bundles of temperament', but *L'Équipe* (25 June 1990) even described their football as a 'victory for the irrational'. The contradiction with industrious Britons, disciplined Germans and cool and rational Swedes could not be more obvious.

Language and power: a discursive network

Discourse and media institutions

That 'news implicitly promotes the dominant beliefs and opinions of elite groups in society' (Van Dijk, 1988: 83) is, as a general rule (albeit with a variety of arguable exceptions), surely unsurprising. The news industry is, from an economic point of view, just one other industry within advanced industrial societies, and is as an institution – whatever the views of individual journalists – saturated with the values of those who have effective control over the economic and political system within which it operates. In many cases nation-building projects of one kind or another – formal or informal, official or unofficial – are a major element in the furtherance of these elite interests. The role of the media, and in particular the crucial role which sports reporting can often play in such projects, has been well documented (see Blain et al., 1993). Indeed, one of the commonest features of sports reporting is the metonym whereby the nation is presented as a single sentient being (Blain et al., 1993: 80–2).

This feature of sports reporting, also, could scarcely be otherwise. Modern sport provides an international arena in which symbolic national confrontations are played out at times before audiences of hundreds of millions. Sport is now also deeply commercialized, and, as just another form of commercial enterprise, it functions on an international level as a site in which advanced countries can and must act out their preferred myths through self-and other-stereotypes, and celebrate those qualities which, in their own eyes, make them more modern, more advanced, in short *superior*. Social identity theory provides a useful theoretical model for explaining such macro-behaviour. As Abrams and Hogg point out:

> Within a particular intergroup relationship, it is often the case that one group has more resources, power, status and prestige. More powerful groups generally seek to maintain the *status quo*, promulgating their own system of values and ideology. Membership of subordinate groups may potentially confer negative social identity, especially if the dominant group's values are accepted. (1990: 4)

This process routinely involves downgrading other national groups. The salience of widely disseminated schematic discursive models such as stereotypes in this process is encouraged not only by the ritualistic framework of the sporting confrontations, but also by both the demotic nature of much sports reporting and the pressure to produce dramatic reportage under which sports journalists work (Goldlust, 1987: 94): these circumstances combine to enhance the use-value of totemic reductionism, packing pre-formed and easily absorbed narratives into off-the-shelf formulations. And since sport – following Norbert Elias's theory of the 'civilizing process' (Elias and Dunning, 1993: 63–90) – continues to constitute an area of social activity in which overt emotional engagement remains publicly acceptable in ways in which this would be unthinkable in other contexts (at least in western societies), the sports section of a newspaper is one in which a level of national sentiment and a corresponding density of highly charged national stereotypes are to be found which it is difficult (at least under peace-time conditions) to imagine elsewhere.

One of the most notable features of the stereotypes documented in this study, however, is their astonishing uniformity both within and across national boundaries. The quotations ... come from 53 publications ranging from tabloids to quality broadsheets (with their corresponding socially segmented audiences); from specialist sports newspapers with daily readerships of over one million to generalist weekly magazines; from publications embracing all shades of political opinion to those which (at least officially) embrace none; and geographically they are to be found throughout western Europe and also in the former Soviet Union. There are differences of tone, of course. The British tabloids, in particular, tend to be more aggressive than their continental European counterparts, most notably in their presentations of German stereotypes (Blain et al., 1993: 146–9). Nonetheless, the almost seamless uniformity of these stereotypes is remarkable. This impressively homogeneous diaspora testifies both to their power and to their age. Though they operate primarily on the local level – specifically at the point of reproduction – and in the furtherance of local interests, and are therefore subject to an array of local variables, their reach is, in a sense, geopolitical.

Notes

1. As well as being a name, the word 'björn' in Swedish also means 'bear': 'Is Björn' ('Ice-Björn') is pronounced identically to 'isbjörn', which means 'polar bear'.
2. The *Glasgow Herald* changed its name to the *Herald* on 3 February 1992.

References

Abrams, D. and Hogg, M. A. 1990: An introduction to the social identity approach. In Abrams, D. and Hogg, M. A. (eds.), *Social identity theory*. Hemel Hempstead: Harvester Wheatsheaf.

Blain, N., Boyle, R. and O'Donnell, H. 1993: *Sport and national identity in the European media*. Leicester: Leicester University Press.

Elias, N. and Dunning, E. 1993: *Quest for excitement: sport and leisure in the civilizing process*. Oxford: Blackwell.

Goldlust, J. 1987: *Playing for keeps: sport, media and society*. Melbourne: Longman Cheshire.

Head, D. 1992: *Made in Germany: the corporate identity of a nation*. London: Hodder & Stoughton.

Nairn, T. 1988: *The enchanted glass: the Britain and its monarchy*. London: Hutchinson Radius.

Van Djik, T. A. 1988: *News as discourse*. Hillsdale, NJ: Erlbaum.

Questions

1 Summarise the key ideas put forward in this extract. What examples can you find in recent national newspapers or broadcasts which support O'Donnell's view that sports coverage tends to deliver a series of 'highly charged national stereotypes'?

2 Why are stereotypical representations perhaps more likely to proliferate in sports reporting and be deemed more acceptable than is imaginable in other aspects of media output?

Further reading

Blain, N., Boyle, R. and O'Donnell, H. 1993: *Sport and national identity in the European media*. Leicester: Leicester University Press.

Hargreaves, J. A. (ed.) 1982: *Sport, culture and ideology*. London: Routledge.

Lapchick, R. E. and Benedict, J. R. (eds.) 1995: *Sport in society*. London: Sage.

Nowell-Smith, G. 1978: Television–football–the world, *Screen* 19(4), 45–59.

Real, M. 1990: Sport and the spectacle. In Downing, J., Mohammadi, A. and Sreberny-Mohammadi, A., *Questioning the media: a critical introduction*. London: Sage.

Whannel, G. 1992: *Fields in vision: television sport and cultural transformation*. London: Routledge.

11

Approaches to 'the North': Common Myths and Assumptions
Esther Adams

From *Television and 'the North'* (Centre for Contemporary Cultural Studies, University of Birmingham 1985).

In this short extract chosen from a detailed and diverse analysis of media representations of the north of England, Adams addresses a series of common myths and assumptions held by those *with* experience of northern England and those without. Her study is based on observation, interpersonal contact with people who live and work in the area and her own personal experience. Unlike other aspects of media representation, the construction of regional identities and differences remains a relatively under-researched area and has only recently begun to be addressed systematically. Adams' paper was written in the early 1980s, and so the examples that she goes on to use from genres such as soap opera and sit-com are now dated and the characters and story-lines would be largely unfamiliar to a modern audience. The general themes associated with northern (particularly northern working-class) culture may, however, be all too familiar. The stereotype of the northern woman being outwardly friendly but then 'gossiping behind your back' still abounds in soaps such as *Coronation Street* and *Brookside*, and the notion of the rural north being backward and quaintly eccentric is central to the characterisation in serials such as *Last of the Summer Wine*.

With or without actual experience of the area and its people, we all possess beliefs and assumptions about the North and Northerners, a considerable influence on such conceptions being the media. There is a famous starting-point in Orwell's work:

> ... There exists in England a curious cult of Northernness, a sort of Northern snobbishness ... The Northerner has 'grit,' he is grim, 'dour,' plucky, warm-hearted and democratic; the Southerner is snobbish, effeminate and lazy – that at any rate is the theory ... it was the industrialisation of the North that gave the North–South antithesis its peculiar slant.... the Northern business man is no longer prosperous. But traditions are not killed by facts, and the tradition of Northern 'grit' lingers. It is still dimly felt that a Northerner will 'get on,'.... that, really, is at the bottom of his bumptiousness.... When I first went to Yorkshire some years ago, I imagined that I was going to a country of boors.... But the Lancashire and Yorkshire miners treated me with a kindness and courtesy that were even embarrassing; for if there is one type of man to whom I do feel myself inferior, it is a coal-miner.... There is nevertheless a real difference between North and South, ... with no petty gentry to set the pace, the bourgeoisification of the working class, though it is taking place in the North, is taking place more slowly. All the Northern accents, for instance, persist strongly....[1]

But with post-war television there has been a set of further developments. In an attempt to relate beliefs, media representations and 'lived culture', a useful introduction is an outline of some more common myths and beliefs about the North, and, through more detailed studies of the media presentations, to see how strongly such notions are mobilised and given form, before entering into a wider discussion of their implications.

(i) *Northerners as Friendly/Unfriendly* The former view is often reinforced by accounts of hospitality, the willingness of people to talk to newcomers and virtual strangers, to offer help and be ready with advice or to give directions. Whether this is, as a characteristic, more true of the North, is debatable (similar 'friendly' traits can be observed in areas of the West Country and East Anglia) hence possibly showing that such characteristics of behaviour are more readily found in country and rural areas in general. The opposite view is, however, equally potent: that Northerners are reserved and withdrawn, almost hostile to 'intruders' into the community, being wary of anyone who talks differently, and requiring the newcomer to undergo a period of 'apprenticeship' before acceptance. Both traits can also be encountered operating simultaneously through marked patterns of *hospitality* and *hostility* (offers of help extended yet 'talking behind your back' in the next instant). Such behaviour is not only complex but puzzling, especially to those from more singular urbanised areas.

(ii) *The North as Ugly/Beautiful* Images abound of the North as heavily industrial, dirty, smoky, grey, and comprised of endless rows of terraced back to back houses which would have been demolished as slums long ago in any other part of the country. It is an image of the nineteenth century novel, of D. H. Lawrence, of L. S. Lowry prints and *When the Boat Comes In*: a vision of hangover from the (industrial) past.

> But the North is not entirely an invention of the last century; it has its dales and moors, its sheep and castles.[2]

It is these latter aspects of Northern landscape which become transformed into the pastoral image, the rural/rustic ideal. In such a land of fells, lakes, valleys, rivers and moors, a haven can be found from the town/city – a land of beauty, wonder, charm, and the poetry books of Wordsworth, Shelley, Keats, and Coleridge. It forms an antidote to the style and pace of urban existence, a place of retreat and escape: a place where the soul can be 'freed' from sociocultural constraints, and reborn into its 'natural' state.

> No living soul with poetry in his heart can fail to express himself among the wonderful surroundings one sees in the Lake District.[3]

Rather than being a place where people live, it is a place where people go to 'wax lyrical'.

(iii) *The North as Segregated/as Backwater* One form of this view is akin to the slum/country dichotomy where the land would seem to be divided between the poorer areas of the workers (the mining villages) and the open estates or acres of land belonging to individual farmers/landowners. Similarly geographical features separate towns and communities, some often isolated by mountains, rivers or valleys with the jugular of the M.6 being the 'lifeline' to the rest of 'civilisation'. New styles and fashions are believed to be slow to catch on, there is a tendency for more conservative ways of dress and thinking to prevail, and a wary scepticism of new trends and labour saving devices. It appears somewhat incredible that areas exist which still have to be connected to electricity supplies.

(iv) *Northerners as Quaint, Old-Fashioned and Superstitious* Ruralness and backwardness would seem to go hand in hand, adding to the quaint charm of the area.

> The people who have been born in the Lake District or in the Border country are naturally more superstitious and more inclined to believe in fairies, giants, wicked spells, curses and enchantments than, perhaps, people from any other part of the country. Nature in itself is mysterious and magical, the folk who live near enough to nature can believe almost anything.[4]

Because the area itself has been mythologised so must its people be differentiated from the rest – not necessarily special, merely quaint.

(v) *Northerners as Talkative* Gossiping, telling stories, monologues of the 'good old days' and willingness to have a 'good crack' with anyone are an integral part of Northern life and being 'sociable'. Hence such characteristics have become trademarks of the average Northerner, habits easily recognised, and easy (for actors and scriptwriters) to convey.

(vi) *Northerners as 'Salt of the Earth'* Again they are often seen as good for a laugh (n.b. their great use in comedy especially to represent low-life characters) being good, honest, no-messing ordinary folk, a bit basic perhaps, but on the whole 'all right'.

> ... rough and unpolished perhaps, but diamonds nevertheless; ragged but of sterling worth, not refined, not intellectual, but with both feet firmly on the ground – capable of a good belly laugh, charitable and forthright ... possessed of a racy and salty speech, touched with wit, but always with its hard grain of common sense.[5]

Notes

1. G. Orwell *The road to Wigan Pier* (Harmondsworth, Penguin, 1962), pp. 142–6.
2. M. Wolfers, 'The North: a study in class, community and custom', in R. Mabey ed., *Class: a symposium* (London, Blond, 1967), p. 146.
3. G. Findler, *Legends of the Lake Counties* (Clapham, Dalesman Press, 1967), p. 7.
4. Findler, *Legends of the Lake Counties*, p. 9.
5. R. Hoggart, *The uses of literacy* (London, Chatto & Windus, 1957), p. 15.

Questions

1   What examples can you think of from a range of media texts — film, television, advertising, news reports, comedies etc. — which rely on stereotypical constructions of regional difference? How is your own region represented?

2   How do British *soaps*, in particular, perpetuate some of the 'myths' of 'northern-ness' to which Adams is referring? To what extent can soaps such as *Coronation Street* or *Emmerdale*, for example, be said to be dealing in 'true-life' representations of people living in specific regional communities, and to what extent are they promoting false images of the north based on stereotypical representations and nostalgic yearnings for the past?

3   Adams uses the terms 'northern' and 'working-class' almost synonymously and when this paper was written there existed no soap operas set in the south of England and only one, *Crossroads*, set in the Midlands, but bearing little relation or reference to that area. Has the more recent *EastEnders*, which also concerns itself largely with the lives of working-class people, constructed its characters in any less of a stereotypical manner than its northern counterparts, or does it put forward equally limited and traditional views of Londoners?

Further reading

Brunsdon, C. and Morley, D. 1978: *Everyday television: 'Nationwide'*. London: BFI.

Carter, E., Donald, J. and Squires, J. (eds.) 1993: *Space and place: theories of identity and location*. London: Lawrence & Wishart.

Dodd, K. and Dodd, P. 1992: From the East End to *EastEnders*: representations of the working class, 1890–1990. In Strinati, D. and Wagg, S., *Come on down: popular media culture in post-war Britain*. London: Routledge.

Griffiths, A. 1993: Pobol y Cwm: the construction of national and cultural identity in a Welsh language soap opera. In Drummond, P., Peterson, R. and Willis, J. (eds.), *National identity and Europe*. London: BFI.

Massey, D. 1994: *Space, place and gender*. Cambridge: Polity Press.

McArthur, C. 1982: *Scotch reels: Scotland in cinema and television*. London: BFI.

Osmond, J. 1988: *The divided kingdom*. London: Constable.

Rutherford, J. 1990: *Identity: community, culture, difference*. London: Lawrence & Wishart.

Shields, R. 1991. *Places on the margin*. London: Routledge.

12

Crippling Images
Anne Karpf

From *Doctoring the media: the reporting of health and medicine* (Routledge 1988)

As we have seen from the previous readings in this section, one of the most common features of stereotypes refers to the social positioning and perceived mental abilities of the stereotyped group. This form of categorisation confirms the seemingly 'natural' position of oppressed or pariah groups in society and further contributes to, and perpetuates, the isolation and discrimination which they face.

Karpf looks at how representations of illness and disability affect our perceptions of both the medical profession and those who are being treated within it. She claims that the media are predominantly interested in 'miracle' cure stories rather than items about ordinary people with disabilities, and one of the few areas of television where images of the disabled are routinely shown is that of telethons, where children are most frequently used (and in her view exploited) to persuade people to part with money. Such charity events are accused of perpetuating the most damaging stereotypes of disability, creating images of dependency and humiliation which outweigh the financial gains and serve the interests of the able-bodied better than those of the disabled.

One of Karpf's most vehement accusations against the media, is that they commit 'sins of omission' although, arguably, since her book was written in 1988, representations of disability have become more commonplace in mainstream media output. The introduction of a baby with Down's Syndrome in *Brookside* and the paralysis of Angel in *Home and Away* are two examples from contemporary soaps that spring to mind (albeit that in the latter case the character made an unexpected full recovery after only a few weeks of physiotherapy, despite predictions from her doctor that she could remain in a wheelchair for the rest of her life). Films such as *My Left Foot, The Piano, Children of a Lesser God, Born on the Fourth of July* and *Rain Man* all featured characters with disabilities, and there are many other examples.

Disabled by whom?

The images of disability on the big and small screens are mainly medical and seemingly natural, uncontroversial and unchangeable. In the medical approach, disability results either from a cruel accident of nature (a genetic gaffe) or from Fate (causing riding accidents, sporting mishaps or car crashes). People with disabilities are courageous or long-suffering; we're invited to praise or pity them. They're applauded in 'aren't they wonderful' stories for triumphing over their disability, and for performing tasks as proficiently as the able-bodied (or even better). A blind woman climbs Everest,[1] a deaf woman is an award-winning professional percussionist.[2] Medicine offers them the possibility of a cure, or helps them function more 'normally' by supplying increasingly sophisticated technological aids, and charity is its sidekick, raising money and hope. The medical approach also encourages the take-up of prenatal screening and rubella immunisation to prevent handicap.[3] Programmes using the medical approach are usually presented and produced by able-bodied people, for the medical approach speaks to the able-bodied (and shows disability as seen by them); 'the disabled' are its objects.

The consumer approach, by contrast, addresses people with disabilities themselves, or their carers. Consumer programmes, often aimed at people with a specific disability like visual handicap or deafness, offer information about goods, services, and welfare benefits, reviewing new aids and equipment, and tackling problems such as access. They're strong advocates of self-help, acting (on air and off) as a clearing-house for self-help groups and charitable organisations. They're often presented by people with disabilities and are broadcast either in afternoon magazine programmes or the 'ghetto' weekend morning slots reserved for minorities and education programmes.

The look-after-yourself programme, when it looks at disability, speaks of its prevention. It proposes personal ways of maintaining health and avoiding disabling conditions, for instance through preconceptual care.[4] It offers advice, given or endorsed by doctors, aimed at the able-bodied.

In the environmental approach, disabled isn't a noun or adjective, it's a verb. People are disabled by the society they live in: social institutions and practices disable them more than their physical or mental handicap. The environmental approach explicitly challenges the medical approach, rejecting the notion of handicap as a 'natural' condition or a medical fact of life inevitably bringing other problems. 'If a person in a wheelchair is unable to take an office job because there are steps up to an office building, are we to assume that the fault lies with the wheelchair user for not being able to climb steps? I would say the fault lies in the architecture.'[5] Similarly, the absence of sign language interpreters at public meetings or events denies deaf people access to the hearing world. In the environmental approach, attention is shifted from people with disabilities to the wider culture: the problem is no longer the disability, but rather the failure of the able-bodied community to accommodate it. Social interaction, rather than an intrinsic physical condition, is to blame. In the environmental approach, people with disabilities aren't spoken for by others: they speak for themselves.

Braving the media

The past two decades' quiet revolution by people with disabilities has gone largely unrecorded by the media. Able-bodied broadcasters are still (and increasingly) enthralled by the dominant medical approach. 'Cure' stories are favourites, like 'the miracle of the man who got his sight back after 36 years',[6] or the sick child whose leg was amputated, and her heel reattached as a knee fixed to an artificial leg. The disability movement argues that:

we celebrate deaf people, but they celebrate people who aren't deaf any more. They love stories about children who have been given marvellous new hearing aids, deaf people who've learnt to play instruments.... The emphasis is always on becoming as much like hearing people as possible.[7]

Courage is their defining characteristic. Children with disabilities must always be smiling, since 'a happy child seems to be the only acceptable image of disability'.[8] They achieve Douglas Bader feats of fortitude, as if individual acts of heroism represented the solution to their daily problems and disability was only an individual and psychological challenge, not also a practical and collective one. Exceptional disabled people are particularly popular, notching up achievements impossible or irrelevant to most people with disabilities – hence the blind mountain-climber or runner – even though the average British blind person is elderly, female, and usually hard up.[9]

This kind of coverage was especially prevalent in the International Year of Disabled People (1981), when 'children received bravery awards for lying in bed and undergoing operations. A thalidomide "heroine" made headlines for passing her driving test. Television news showed a compulsive tendency to film us struggling to make a cup of tea with an able-bodied commentary over-laid.'[10] Television often uses these images for its leave'em-happy final news story, usually occasioned by a visit from Royalty.

Telethons: child appeal

Telethons, fund-raising television marathons, are the annual opportunity for celebrities and audiences to have fun while doing good. Simultaneously glitzy and worthy, they're usually 12- or 24-hour affairs, with celebrities dropping into the studio to chat or perform, and filmed inserts of charities needing money or showing what past recipients did with theirs. Viewers and listeners phone in to pledge donations and the presenters, regularly announcing the total to date, exhort the audience to the finishing-line – the target sum.

Telethons demand enormous organisation – one used 650 telephones staffed by British Telecom telephonists. The BBC telethon 'Children in Need' ropes in every BBC local and national radio station, as well as the BBC TV networks. And the 1985 Thames Telethon completely displaced the station's regular schedules for twenty-four hours. Telethons originated in the United States, where the best known is comedian Jerry Lewis' Labor Day telethon, which has raised large sums for muscular dystrophy charities for nineteen years. When the BBC borrowed the idea in 1980 they decided that the British public wouldn't stomach the full American revelry, with its unrestrainedly heart-tugging appeals in a 24-hour non-stop variety show. The BBC version is a more muted affair, aiming to reach the (smaller, local) chari-ties the other appeals don't reach. Its recipients are children with mental or physical handicaps (who get some 40 per cent of the grants), or those with behaviour disorders in care, hospital, or living in under-resourced or stressful places. The sums raised by telethons are sizeable. Between them in 1985, the BBC and Thames TV telethons raised over £5 million, and in 1985/6 British commercial radio stations raised over £2.6 million in cash for charity through events like a Walkathon (a 25-mile charity walk).

But although the receiving organisations are understandably pleased to have the money, telethons have been roundly indicted by American disability activists for perpetuating damaging stereotypes of disability which outweigh the financial gains. While acknowledging both organisers' and donors' good intentions, they argue that they arouse 'there, but for the grace of God' feelings in their audience which oppress people with disabilities.

> In order to get their money, they have to humiliate me ... to me, a wheelchair is a solution, not a sentence. Because I use a wheelchair, I am able to do many things I otherwise could not. I am not 'confined to a wheelchair'. I don't 'face a life without meaning', and I'm not a 'poor, unfortunate cripple who needs your help.'[11]

Although British telethons are more subtle, their images usually more positive and optimistic, the British disability movement too deplores:

> fund-raising at a distance ... the twentieth-century version of the beggar in the streets. Even the begging bowls are no longer in our own hands.... [It] gives people a sense of doing something for us without bringing them into contact with us.[12]

Most British telethons focus almost exclusively on children, since cute youngsters undoubtedly head the hierarchy of tele-appeal, with less cute oldsters at the bottom. There's a total mismatch between the age of those people with disabilities who appear on telethons (and TV in general), and the age of the majority of people with disabilities in the general population. Moreover, although the BBC's rules specifically forbid them giving grants to relieve a statutory body of its responsibilities, disadvantaged groups are especially disadvantaged at a time of cuts, and telethons (since they rarely collect for luxuries) can't help but contribute to the idea that it's the job of private organisations and not the state to provide or collect essential funds. They also reinforce an image of people with disabilities as dependent on charity. Even where telethons increase the visibility of people with disabilities, their one-off occurrence inevitably smacks of tokenism.

For whose benefit are telethons organised? It's not always clear. Parts of the 1985 Thames Telethon were commercially sponsored, causing one TV critic to observe that

> no shove ha-penny contest went unsponsored. This made for wall-to-wall advertising and a steady line of executives crossing the stage like ants, each carrying a large cardboard cheque. 'Give a big hand to the chairman of Burtons' ... 'Sponsored by those lovely folk from Panasonic.'[13]

Commercial companies gain a whiff of worthiness and all are beyond reproach when the vulgarity's for charity. Since telethons make the able-bodied feel bountiful (and many would be affronted to hear that people with disabilities feel oppressed by their pity), telethons may really be for the able-bodied. As the Controller of BBC 1, who authorised the first British telethon said, 'It makes me feel warm.'[14]

Medico-charitable broadcasting has a long history. President Roosevelt, paralysed from polio in 1921, enlisted popular entertainers such as Eddie Cantor to raise funds for polio treatment and research via network radio on his birthday each year. But at the same time, Roosevelt resolved never to appear helpless, dependent, or defeated by polio, and so wouldn't allow himself to be photographed in a wheelchair. The press and media generally co-operated. Roosevelt, while he tried to improve conditions for people with polio, couldn't allow himself to identify with them for fear of damaging his robust political image, and many Americans never knew, or forgot, that their President couldn't walk unaided.

Could telethons be different? In 1979 United Cerebral Palsy (UCP), an American organisation known for it's 'look, we're walking' telethons, decided to change them. They wrote up the speeches the celebrities were supposed to make, asked people with disabilities to monitor the telethon, and set out guidelines stressing that telethons should show both adults and children and should reflect the degrees of disability typical among people with cerebral palsy. Celebrities were to be thoroughly informed about the condition and use appropriate terminology, avoiding terms like victim, poor, crippled, unfortunate, tragedy and other words arousing pity rather than respect. They were also to avoid asking viewers to give out of thankfulness that their own children were born healthy, and UCP outlawed images which placed undue emphasis on people with cerebral palsy walking and talking, leading to unrealistic public expectations and damaging the self-image of people with cerebral palsy who would never be able to do either. They also wanted to draw attention to the organisation's advocacy role in helping people with disabilities realise their own desires and needs, like gaining access to public education, barrier-free buildings and transport, housing, and jobs.

When people with disabilities monitored the telethon, they found it a significant but limited improvement. Though the main issues emerged, 'the celebrities are tuned to seize on the theatrics of the moment. Given national television exposure, they are not going to be held to tight, pre-drafted scripts. So when they see a moment of possible drama, they seize it.'[15]

Screened out

Sins of omission are perhaps even more significant in media coverage of disability than sins of commission. People with disabilities and the issues affecting them are largely invisible on radio and television. A common format is to have a discussion between someone who works *with* people with disabilities, and the mother *of* a person with a disability, speaking on their behalf, but not disabled people themselves. And people with disabilities are rarely invited to participate in media discussions about abortion, prenatal screening, or the switching-off of life-support systems for people with severe handicaps.

The vast majority of people with disabilities are socially and economically disadvantaged, yet TV and radio news programmes rarely report on the implications for them of events like health cutbacks or inflation, and though motorists, drinkers, and smokers are routinely interviewed after the Budget for their reactions to price rises, people with disabilities are never asked for their reactions to benefit freezes. People with disabilities are the largest section of the unemployed, yet they're never referred to in media coverage of unemployment.[16] Indeed, they rarely figure in mainstream programmes at all, and when they do it's usually *because* of their disability. Broadcasters and news journalists seem to assume that their audience is able-bodied, even though a significant proportion of them must have a disability since about one in five people in Britain have a severe disability.

[...]

Disabling drama

Fictional programmes distort disability just as consistently as non-fictional. A study of American prime-time TV shows found that none of the disabled characters were over sixty-five, and 40 per cent of them were children. They were mainly working class, excluded from important family roles, living generally in schools and institutions. Two-thirds were single, almost half were recipients of some kind of verbal or physical abuse, most were regarded as objects of pity and care and experienced a miracle cure at the end of the programme.[17] Another study of American prime-time commercial television found handicapped characters seldom appearing in incidental roles: in 85 half-hour slots, not one was visible in groups of shoppers, spectators, jurors, customers or workers. When people with disabilities were positively characterised, their handicap was central to the plot (and, by implication, to their lives): they struggled valiantly with conditions like blindness, but were never an astute college professor who happened to be blind, or the capable lawyer in a wheelchair. They were also often stigmatised as baddies, evil characters representing a threat to society in the tradition of Long John Silver or *Peter Pan*'s Captain Hook.[18]

In 1986 the British group Fairplay, campaigning for accurate media representation of the number and nature of people with disabilities, wrote to the producers of the soap operas 'Brookside' and 'EastEnders' to encourage them to introduce a disabled character. 'EastEnders' didn't. 'Brookside' wrote in a deaf character, and was the first British soap to do so, though she seemed to have uncanny ability to hear without the other characters making any concessions to her deafness.

On the big screen, disabled characters are frequently misshapen monsters and baddies. From the disfigured murderer of *The Phantom of the Opera* (1925) to the dwarf killer of Nicholas Roeg's *Don't Look Now* (1973), people with disabilities have been depicted as grotesques; outlawed from able-bodied society (Dustin Hoffman's lame, pitiable low-life conman, Ratso, in John

Schlesinger's 1969 *Midnight Cowboy*); fixated on beautiful but unattainable women (Charles Laughton as *The Hunchback of Notre Dame*, 1939), and impelled to destroy what they can't join or have. Gnarled bodies often signify gnarled minds (Shakespeare's Richard III has a lot to answer for). At the other end of the spectrum is *Reach for the Sky*, the most popular film in Britain in 1956 and one of the most emblematic films ever made about disability, in which Kenneth More played Douglas Bader, the legless wartime aviator with the tenacious spirit. *Reach for the Sky* 'hangs like an albatross round the neck of every person in this country who's been conditioned to believe that it would take unadulterated heroism to cope with their disability'.[19]

Another recurring figure in films about disability is 'the able-bodied miracle worker from whom the central character draws the strength to persevere and learn to live a normal life'.[20] Women are often disabled in films to allow men to cure them (such as Rock Hudson in Douglas Sirk's 1954 melodrama *Magnificent Obsession*, who becomes a doctor to cure Jane Wyman's blindness for which he feels responsible). Thrillers like the 1967 *Wait Until Dark* include blind women (the ultimate victim), or they heighten the tension by using deaf women ('the last word in "dumb blond"'[21]).

Well-intentioned movies are even worse. The praised 1980 film *The Elephant Man* was based on the true story of Joseph Merrick, a Victorian man with a misshapen head, displayed as a fairground freak until rescued by a philanthropic surgeon who takes him to the London Hospital, where he's accepted by some of the aristocracy who recognise his inner gentility. The film was moving and seemed progressive: Merrick advanced from being exhibited to being admired as a sensitive individual. Yet once again, a kindly, able-bodied person provided the key to his improved fortune, while Merrick himself, unfailingly dignified and strikingly free of anger and despair, seemed wholly unbrutalised by his experiences.[22] His attempt to sleep in a 'normal' position finally killed him.

Less equal than others

Employment is the nub of the problem. As long as media images of disability continue to be shaped by able-bodied people, and intended for an able-bodied audience, the stereotypes will flow. The employment of people with disabilities in broadcasting and their media image are inextricably linked. When in 1986 Fairplay organised a survey of British TV companies, it found that, although most had equal opportunity policies, very few had a programme to implement them. What's more, they often cast able-bodied actors as disabled characters, producing unconvincing portrayals which the disability movement likens to those of blacked-up white actors in the past.

The effects of this exclusion from broadcasting on and off-screen are hard to determine. Certainly, people with disabilities are excluded from many other cultural institutions, and their daily experiences and material circumstances are as

oppressive as any images. Moreover, the media rarely originate ways of thinking, and stereotypes of disability are as current in the broader culture as on television and film. Yet if the media have the power to reinforce, and their
systematic fixations and omissions help fortify or diminish groups' claims of legitimacy, then the media coverage of people with disability must surely play a
part in disenfranchising them. They themselves argue that broadcasting and films
have helped reinforce negative attitudes towards them, and have failed to challenge stereotypes, dissipate fear and discomfort, or provide images of interaction
between people with and without disabilities. At the same time, handicapped
people themselves and their families aren't being exposed to images of handicapped adults living productive, comfortable lives in the mainstream of society.[23]

Broad cast

There has always been a small batch of films and programmes challenging the
dominant approach to disability. The cinema furnished the earliest examples
with its dramas about maimed returning war heroes, like William Wyler's
1946 *The Best Years of Our Lives*. A hugely successful sensitive rehabilitation
movie, it showed a sailor who lost both his hands in the war (played by
Harold Russell who himself had lost his hands in war training) withdrawing
from the community until he was slowly coaxed back. Though some saw the
ending as a cop-out (he adjusts to his new situation through the love of a fine
woman), and others complained of a prying camera, lingering on his steel
claws picking up cigarettes, the film raised public consciousness about the
consequences of war-created disability.

Fred Zinnemann's 1950 film *The Men*, in which Marlon Brando made his
screen debut as a soldier paralysed by the war, went much further. Set almost
entirely in a hospital (the cast including forty-five real disabled war veterans),
it portrayed Brando's problems in adapting to his disability and his fellow
paraplegics' attempts to staunch his self-pity. Wholly unsaccharine in
approach, it showed 'vets' dying and depressed, the problems caused by trying
to adhere to able-bodied norms (Brando's obsessive attempt to be married
standing up ends in failure), and the easy, oppressive pity of the able-bodied
('we make other people feel uncomfortable ... we remind them that their bodies can be broken just like that, and they don't like it').

The Men broke a taboo by talking about disability and sex, but *Coming
Home*, Hal Ashby's 1978 film about the effect of the Vietnam War on three
people, was a sexually explicit (some thought voyeuristic), powerful presentation of disability. It showed a Vietnam 'vet', paralysed from the waist down,
falling in love with the wife of a hawkish Marine Captain brutalised by his
experience in Vietnam, and implicitly questioned which of the two men was
the real cripple. Once again, it portrayed people with disabilities as angry,
rejecting pity and charity, and physically active,[24] with all of them (except for
Jon Voight in the main role) played by real disabled Vietnam veterans. And

this time the man in the wheelchair got the woman. The film ended with the hero rechannelling his anger from self-destructively inwards to constructively outwards, by becoming politically active.

But latterly, American prime-time television has been leading the way in new presentations of disability. 'Cagney and Lacey' has been innovative, and in the show's 1986 season Cagney had a relationship with a man in a wheelchair, which drew an enthusiastic audience response. 'Dallas', too, included a deaf child; 'Hill Street Blues' has had disabled characters and themes; and the Public Broadcasting System (PBS) has introduced people with disabilities into children's programmes such as 'Mister Rogers', 'Zoom', and 'Sesame Street'. American TV commercials are also changing: a man in a wheelchair is unremarkably included in a group sporting 501 Levi jeans, a schmaltzy romantic couple use sign language (plus subtitles) to decide to go and eat at McDonalds,[25] and the blind man in a wheelchair is an IBM systems analyst.

By contrast, Britain is poorly served. There isn't a single British TV commercial which includes people with disabilities, and aside from 'The Singing Detective' – Dennis Potter's outstandingly authentic series about a man immobilised by arthritis, the skin condition psoriasis, and the attitudes of hospital staff – only the soap opera 'Crossroads' has made significant attempts to introduce disabled characters. As well as a character involved in a disabling road accident who subsequently used a wheelchair, and an educationally subnormal young man, the show in 1983 included a running story about mental handicap using a real Down's Syndrome child.[26]

[...]

People with disabilities are campaigning to end the apartheid of disability in the media (and beyond). They want disabled people integrated into all kinds of programmes....

People with disabilities want to speak for themselves.

Notes

1. BBC Radio 4, 'Woman's Hour' (7 January 1986).
2. BBC Radio 4, 'The Glennie Determination' (7 January 1986), and BBC 1, 'Wogan' (24 January 1986).
3. The medical approach often grossly inflates the proportion of congenital abnormalities, detectable by prenatal screening. In reality, most people acquire disabilities later in life, as the result of an accident or chronic illness like a stroke, where prenatal screening is irrelevant.
4. The spread of the look-after-yourself approach and its emphasis on the perfectability of the body has created a climate in which disability is even more deviant.
5. Allan T. Sutherland, *Disabled We Stand* (London, Souvenir Press, 1981), p. 15.
6. BBC TV, 'Six O'Clock News' (14 July 1986).
7. Maggie Woolley interviewed by Julienne Dickey, 'Deafness and the Media', *Women's Media Action Bulletin*, 19 (January 1983), p. 3.
8. Keith Armstrong and Wendy Moore, 'Shut Out by the Media', *Journalist*, October 1985, p. 2. So, 'despite [the fact that she has brittle-bone disease] and the fact that

she's broken one or other of her legs nine times, Sharon keeps smiling', or else she wouldn't have got into the *Radio Times*. ('Raising Hopes, Raising Laughs, and Raising Money', *Radio Times*, November 15–21, 1986.)

 9. Tony Macaulay, 'Disability and the Broadcasting Media' (The Volunteer Centre Media Project, December 1985).

10. Maggie Woolley, *et al.*, 'That Was Our Year Was It?', *The Times Health Supplement*, 22 January 1982, p. 9.

11. Diane Lattin, 'Telethons – A Remnant of America's Past', *Disabled USA*, 1: 4 (1977), p. 19.

12. Woolley, *et al.*, 'That Was Our Year Was It?'.

13. Nancy Banks-Smith, 'Just a 'Thon at Twilight', *Guardian*, 31 October 1985.

14. Quoted by Mark Patterson, 'Children in Need', *Media Project News*, September 1984, p. 11.

15. Diane Lattin, 'United Cerebral Palsy: Communicating a Better Image', *Disabled USA*, 2: 7 (1979), p. 5, which also describes some innovative UCP TV ads featuring a married couple with cerebral palsy.

16. Armstrong and Moore, 'Shut Out by the Media', p. 2.

17. B. D. Leonard, 'Impaired View: Television Portrayal of Handicapped People' (unpubl. doctoral thesis, Boston, Mass., Boston University, 1978), quoted in Timothy R. Elliott and E. Keith Byrd, 'Media and Disability', *Rehabilitation Literature*, 43: 11–12 (November–December 1982).

18. Joy Donaldson, 'The Visibility and Image of Handicapped People on Television', *Exceptional Children*, 47: 6 (March 1981). 'A Man Called Ironside' (1967–72) about a cop who happened to be a paraplegic was a rare exception.

19. Allan T. Sutherland and Steve Dwoskin, *Carry on Cripple* (National Film Theatre booklet, February 1981), p. 21.

20. Sutherland and Dwoskin, *Carry on Cripple*, p. 19.

21. Woolley interviewed by Dickey, 'Deafness and the Media'.

22. Raphael Samuel ('The Elephant Man as a Fable of Class', *New Society*, 19 November 1981) suggests that the film is an evangelical fable, resembling Sunday School moral stories, with Merrick the incarnation of the deserving poor, grateful to his benefactors and displaying inner grace.

23. Donaldson, 'Visibility and Image'.

24. The cinematographer Haskell Wexler, to avoid conveying a sense of diminishment by photographing the 'vets' from above, devised a special camera dolly to put the camera at the same height as the men in wheelchairs (Martin F. Norden, 'The Disabled Vietnam Veteran in Hollywood films', *Journal of Popular Film and Television*, 13: 1 (Spring 1985)).

25. The deaf actress Marlee Matlin may have helped: she used sign language when accepting an Oscar for her performance in *Children of a Lesser God*, and her speech was relayed across the world's television to millions.

26. The idea developed out of a meeting between the voluntary group Mencap and Central TV's Controller, himself father of a mentally handicapped child. Mencap was enthusiastic because

> we thought it was about time viewers were able to see a mentally handicapped person in a programme which was not a documentary. Confining them to documentaries seemed rather like confining them to institutions.... Secondly, it seemed likely that the audience of 'Crossroads' would include some of the people Mencap most wanted to reach with information about mental handicap: those who switch off when documentaries come on. It would also be an oppor-

tunity to air some of the common prejudices, fears, and misunderstandings about mental handicap, by allowing them to be expressed by characters in the series. (Brian Rix, 'Mencap at the Crossroads', *Media Project News*, January 1984, p. 28.)

Questions

1 What is your view of images of disabled people in mainstream media output? Is it tokenistic voyeurism in the interests of a new 'angle' or have they actually raised public consciousness about the causes and consequences of disability?
2 What about media representations of mental illness? Could the media be accused of 'sins of omission' here too? When does a condition like mental illness become of interest to programme-makers and newspaper editors? Who is given a voice by the media to speak about the mentally ill (in other words, do those suffering from mental illness speak for themselves in the media or do others speak on their behalf?)
3 How would you explain the overwhelming popularity of TV medical shows such as *Cardiac Arrest, Casualty, Jimmy's* and *E. R.?*

Further reading

Barnes, C. 1992: *Disabling imagery and the media: an exploration of the principles for media representation of disabled people*. British Council of Organisations of Disabled People. Halifax: Ryburn Publishing.

Gabe, J., Kelleher, D. and Williams, G. 1994: *Challenging medicine*. London: Routledge.

Gilman, S. L. 1988: *Disease and representation: images of illness from madness to AIDS*. Ithaca, NY: Cornell University Press.

Negrine, R. and Cumberbatch, G. 1992: *Images of disability on television*. London: Routledge.

Oliver, M. 1990: *The politics of disablement*. London: Macmillan.

Philo, G., Henderson, L. and McLaughlin, G. 1993: *Mass media representations of mental health/illness*. Glasgow: Glasgow University Media Group.

13

Moral Panics
Simon Watney

From *Policing desire: pornography, Aids and the media* (University of Minnesota Press 1989).

In this extract, based largely on the British and American experience, Watney argues that media coverage of Acquired Immune Deficiency Syndrome and public responses to the disease are illustrative of an overtly homophobic society and that the media has been largely responsible for fuelling public hysteria, even among the medical community who treat those with Aids. He introduces the long-established and widely known theory of moral panics first put forward by Cohen in his famous study *Folk devils and moral panics* (1972), but concludes, like other recent commentators (see, for example, McRobbie referenced in the 'Further Reading' section of this reading) that the concept of the moral panic is inadequate in explaining the long-term societal prejudice against those whom society has traditionally regarded as sexual 'deviants'.

He does not deny the existence of moral panics or even that the treatment of people with Aids *is* one, but claims that the theory used to expound them is limited, not least because of its inability to explain the operations of ideology within all representational systems. According to Watney, a moral panic merely marks the site of wider ideological struggles which are conducted right across society and within all its fields of public representation. The tone of hysteria that characterised the coverage of Aids through the late 1980s and early '90s cannot be described as an easily identifiable, individual moral panic, but is part of a long-term ongoing campaign waged by politicians and other 'opinion leaders' to safeguard the moral welfare of society and promote the institution of 'the family'.

Representations of homosexuality have traditionally only appeared in the media in densely coded forms, which has made the portrayal of an illness predominantly suffered by gay men doubly difficult for the media, and it has resorted to falling back on heavily moralistic discourses which presuppose common notions of 'human nature', 'normality' and 'decency'. As such, the reporting of Aids is part of the overtly sanctimonious discourse which has characterised the political and media agendas for many years.

In 1941 the English novelist Sylvia Townsend Warner wrote to an American friend comparing the German propaganda machine to 'a clown with homicidal mania – ludicrous and terrifying both at once'.[1] However we may personally respond to the general sleep of reason surrounding Aids, we are nonetheless obliged to try to make some wider sense of the social climate in which we find ourselves. Writing in *London Portrait* earlier this year, John Withington described the number of people with Aids in the United States as 'fairly small' (16,000), a figure which in itself offers a profound and significant underestimate. The 300 British cases were regarded as 'small beer' compared to the notorious influenza epidemic which killed some twenty million people worldwide after the First World War. Such judgements and comparisons are all the more odious for the casual, matter-of-fact way in which they are presented, as if Aids and the influenza epidemic of 1918 co-existed in some timeless dimension of abstract medical statistics, as well as mischievously conflating the very different issues of infection and contagion. Withington suggests that the HIV virus 'seems to behave completely differently' in Africa where, we learn, it 'seems to affect men and women equally', concluding that 'perhaps the virus just behaves differently in the tropics'.

It is nonsense such as this which makes up the greater part of Aids commentary in the West, with an ideological stethoscope stuffed firmly in its ears to block out any approach to Aids which does not conform in advance to the values and language of a homophobic science – a science, that is, which does not regard gay men as fully or properly human. Thus, according to Peter Seitzman, a Manhattan doctor, American

> hospital policies have more to do with other patients' fears than a concern for the health of Aids patients.[2]

Five years into the epidemic, the 'commonsense' of Aids commentary continues to register endless concern at the (non-existent) threat of infection by casual contact, to the complete disavowal of the real and constant threat which other sick people in hospitals present to people with Aids, whose damaged immune system render them so dreadfully vulnerable to other people's disease. Thus, commentary produces expectations, and expectations fan out into lived experience.

> An eighteen year-old Coventry man, who thought he had caught Aids after drinking from the same bottle as a gay man, punched and killed him, Warwick Crown Court heard on Friday.

The man received a three-months sentence in this 'wholly exceptional case'.[3] 'Theatre cleaners are threatening to boycott a group of gay actors because they are frightened of catching Aids.'[4] Such stories are invariably accompanied by denials that Aids can be contracted via casual contact, but their framing is always top heavy, focusing on fear rather than allaying it, dramatising anxiety rather than alleviating it.

The most widely favoured explanation amongst lesbian and gay commentators of the social climate surrounding Aids lies in the theory of moral panics. Drawing on the influential school of 'new' criminology from the 1960s, which tried to explain the social context of crime and 'deviance', Stanley Cohen described in 1972 how societies

> appear to be subject, every now and then, to periods of moral panic. A condition, episode, person or groups of persons emerges to become defined as a threat to societal values and interests; its nature is presented in a stylised and stereotypical fashion by the mass media; the moral barricades are manned by editors, bishops, politicians and other right-thinking people; ... Sometimes the panic passes over and is forgotten, except in folk-lore and collective memory; at other times it has more serious and long-lasting repercussions and might produce such changes as those in legal and social policy or even in the way that society perceives itself.[5]

For Cohen the mass media provides 'a main source of information about the normative contours of a society ... about the boundaries beyond which one should not venture and about the shapes the devil can assume'.[6] The mass media is understood to construct 'pseudo-events' according to the dictates of an unwritten moral agenda which constitutes newsworthiness. Thus 'rumour ... substitutes for news when institutional channels fail',[7] and in ambiguous situations 'rumours should be viewed not as forms of distorted or pathological communication: they make sociological sense as co-operative improvisations, attempts to reach a meaningful collective interpretation of what happened by pooling available resources'.[8]

Subsequent writers such as Stuart Hall have opened up this debate about the representational strategies behind different types of moral panic, arguing that they are indicative of how people are persuaded 'to experience and respond to contradictory developments in ways which make the operation of state power legitimate, credible and consensual. To put it crudely, the "moral panic" appears to us to be one of the principal forms of ideological consciousness by means of which a "silent majority" is won over to the support of increasingly coercive measures on the part of the state, and lends its legitimacy to a "more than usual" exercise of control."'[9] Hall's work on the historical structures of British racism has encouraged him to develop a 'stages' theory of moral panics, leading to ever increasing punitive state control (although he would be the first to admit that it is not only the state which is involved, however loosely we may define it). This is equally a problem for anyone trying to analyse the representation of homosexuality in terms of available theories of moral panic, since the entire subject is historically constituted as 'scandal', with subsequent calls for state intervention.

In an important essay on Aids, Jeffrey Weeks relies heavily on moral panic theory, explaining how its mechanisms

> are well known: the definition of a threat to a particular event (a youthful 'riot', a sexual scandal); the stereotyping of the main characters in the mass media as particular species of monsters (the prostitute as 'fallen woman', the paedophile as 'child molester'); a spiralling escalation of the perceived threat, leading to a taking up of absolutist positions and the manning of moral barricades; the emergence of an imaginary solution – in tougher laws, moral isolation, a symbolic court action; followed by the subsidence of the anxiety, with its victims left to endure the new proscription, social climate and legal penalties.[10]

Gayle Rubin also sees special 'political moments' in the history of sexuality, observing that,

> moral panics rarely alleviate any real problem, because they are aimed at chimeras ... They draw on the pre-existing discursive structure which invents victims in order to justify treating 'vices' as 'crimes' ... Even when activity is acknowledged to be harmless, it may be banned because it is alleged to 'lead' to something ostensibly worse ...[11]

Dennis Altman also discusses Aids in terms of moral panic, but modifies the notion against local and national factors. Thus, 'the Australian panic is not only a product of homophobia but is also tied to the ... belief that they can insulate themselves from the rest of the world through rigid immigration and quarantine laws' and 'a less sophisticated understanding and acceptance of homosexuality than exists in the United States'.[12] Calls for draconian legislation in such disparate societies as West Germany and even Sweden, lead him to conclude that 'the link between Aids and homosexuality has the potential for unleashing panic and persecution in almost every society'.[13]

Whilst such analyses offer a certain descriptive likeness to events, they also reveal many severe limitations, which suggest the inadequacy of the concept of moral panic to the overall ideological policing of sexuality, especially in matters of representation. To begin with, it may be employed to characterise *all* conflicts in the public domain where scape-goating takes place. It cannot, however, discriminate between either different orders or degrees of moral panic. Nor can it explain why certain types of events are especially privileged in this way. Above all, it lacks any capacity to explain the endless 'overhead' narrative of such phenomena, as one 'panic' gives way to another, or one anxiety is displaced across different 'panics'. Thus one moral panic may have a relatively limited frame of reference, whilst another is heavily over-determined, just as a whole range of panics may share a single core meaning whilst others operate in tandem to construct a larger overall meaning which is only partially present in any one of its individual 'motifs'. Clearly there is not (yet) a moral panic in British or American government circles, compared to their public profiles over, for example, immigration, pornography or abortion. But this is only to say that the theory of moral panics makes it extremely difficult to compare press hysteria and government inaction, which may well turn out to be closely related. In both instances we are facing symptoms – symptoms of sexual repression which manifest themselves across a spectrum which ranges from stammering embarrassment to prurience, hysterical modesty, voyeurism and a wide variety of phobic responses. In other words, the theory of moral panics is unable to conceptualise the mass media as an industry which is intrinsically involved with *excess*, with a voracious appetite and capacity for substitutions, displacements, repetitions and signifying absences. Moral panic theory is always obliged in the final instance to refer and contrast 'representation' to the arbitration of 'the real', and is hence unable to develop a full theory concerning the operations of ideology within all representational systems. Moral panics seem to appear and disappear, as if representation were not the site of *permanent* ideological struggle over the meaning of signs. A particular 'moral panic' merely marks the site of the current frontline in such struggles. We do not in fact witness the unfolding of discontinuous and discrete 'moral panics', but rather the mobility of ideological confrontation across the entire field of public representations, and in particular those handling and evaluating the meanings of the human body, where rival and incompatible forces and values are involved in a ceaseless struggle to define supposedly universal 'human' truths.

What we are dealing with in such phenomena is the public forum in which modern societies and individuals make sense of themselves. Together with the increasing industrialisation of this forum, we should note its centrality for political debates where interest groups attempt to bypass the traditional structures of democratic process in order to force the enactment of laws in the name of the 'good' of a population which is never actually consulted. This is precisely what the mass media were invented to do, since they have evidently never responded to the actual diversity of the societies which they purport to service. We are looking at the circulation of symbols, of the basic raw materials from which human subjectivity is constructed. It is not in the least surprising that those attempting to manipulate conscious attitudes should play on themes which possess deeper, unconscious resonances. Hence the danger of thinking of newspapers or television as being primarily concerned with 'news' values, as distinct from entertainment, or drama, or sports coverage, or advertising, or whatever. For all these categories of production share an identical presumption about their audience, which is projected across them in different genres as a unified 'general public' over and above the divisions of class, age and gender. This subject audience is massively worked on to think of itself in the terms which familiarity has established through repetition. The very existence of homosexual desire, let alone gay identities, are only admitted to the frame of mass media representations in densely coded forms, which protect the 'general public' from any threat of potential destabilisation. This is the context in which we should think about the crisis of representation with which Aids threatens the mass media, understood above all else as an agency of collective fantasy. Aids commentary does not 'make' gay men into monsters, for homosexuality is, and always has been, constructed as intrinsically monstrous within the entire system of heavily over-determined images inside which notions of 'decency', 'human nature' and so on are mobilised and relayed throughout the internal circuitry of the mass media marketplace.

It is the central ideological business of the communications industry to retail ready-made pictures of 'human' identity, and thus recruit individual consumers to identify with them in a fantasy of collective mutual complementarity. Whole sections of society, however, cannot be contained within this project, since they refuse to dissolve into the larger mutualities required of them. Hence the position, in particular, though in different ways, of both blacks and gay men, who are made to stand outside the 'general public', inevitably appearing as threats to its internal cohesion. This cohesion is not 'natural', but the result of the media industry's modes of address – targeting an imaginary national family unit which is both white and heterosexual. All apparent threats to this key object of individual identification will be subject to the kinds of treatment which Cohen and his followers describe as moral panics. What matters is to be able to understand which specific groups emerge as threats to which 'societal values and interests'. Moral panics do not speak to a 'silent majority' which is simply 'out there', waiting to listen. Rather, they provide the raw materials, in the form of words and images, of those moral constituencies with which individual subjects are encouraged to identify their deepest interests and their very core of being. But in so far as these categories are primarily defensive, in so far as they work to protect the individual from a partially perceived threat of diversity and conflict, they are also themselves vulnerable. Hence the repetition of moral panics, their fundamentally *serial* nature, the infinite variety of tone and posture which they can assume. The successful policing of desire requires that we think of 'the enemy' everywhere, and at all times. This is why there is such a marked conflict throughout the entire dimension of Aids commentary between the actual situation of people with Aids, and the model of contagion which they are made to embody.

We are not, in fact, living through a distinct, coherent and progressing 'moral panic' about Aids. Rather, we are witnessing the latest variation in the spectacle of the defensive ideological rearguard action which has been mounted on behalf of 'the family' for more than a century. The very categorisation of sexuality ... is part of this same action. How we respond to it is therefore of the greatest importance, since at this point in time our liberties and very lives are being put increasingly at risk. We need precisely to be able to *relate* phenomena which present themselves, in terms of the theory of moral panics, as discrete and unconnected. Thus we may draw a significant parallel, for example, between local American state decisions to enact laws which refuse confidentiality to those who have tested positive to HIV infection (despite the clear advice and recommendation of the Centers for Disease Control that confidentiality should be a priority), and the recent decision of British police to arrest the singer Boy George at the clinic where he was being treated for heroin addiction. In both instances a 'moral' agenda has permitted punitive actions which are positively counter-productive, both to limiting the spread of Aids and helping drug addicts. On the one hand, few if any gay men are likely to undertake a test which might immediately render them liable to the loss of civil liberties if the results are not kept confidential and, on the other hand – as George's doctor pointed out – retroactive charges for the past possession of drugs are unlikely to encourage addicts to come forward for treatment.[14] The *Village Voice* reported in May, 1986, that since the state of Colarado introduced identification record requirements for people wanting HIV tests, applications at gay men's health clinics have dropped by 600 per cent in only three months. In both cases actual practice at local state and police levels flies in the face of clearly stated medical and governmental policies. Both cases also illustrate the danger of identifying individual 'moral panics' in a simple one-to-one relation to their ostensible targets. This is why I prefer to think in terms of Aids commentary, rather than assuming the existence of a unified and univocal 'moral panic' over Aids.

A similar problem occurs if we try to explain away all the variations and nuances of Aids commentary as epiphenomena deriving from a single source. This, however, is very frequently the case, and the source most readily identified by lesbians and gay men is 'homophobia'. This is hardly surprising when *The New York Times* feels sufficiently at liberty to print a long article by the American darling of the New Right, William F. Buckley, which concludes, after acres of drifting around, that,

> everyone detected with AIDS should be tatooed in the upper fore-arm, to protect common-needle users, and on the buttocks, to prevent the victimisation of other homosexuals.[15]

The last time people were forcibly tattooed was under Nazi rule, when millions were slaughtered because their politics or race or sexuality, or combinations of these, did not conform to the master plan of a totalitarian state. Such prescriptions remain unthinkable in relation to any other category of American citizen. But Buckley clearly regards gay men as so far 'outside' the body politic that no measure is too extreme to contemplate. What is so very remarkable about such pronouncements, however, is that they are announced *on behalf* of gay men and, at the same time, are 'balanced' on the same page of the newspaper in question by another article which eloquently insists that 'those who have a stake in using AIDS to prove the morality or immorality of any particular lifestyle, should be deemed disqualified from the scientific debate'.[16] This may, in some respects, be naive, since presumably all scientists subscribe to some system of moral judgement or another; nonetheless, as the writer points out, 'the flow of solid data should not be polluted by personal moralism'.

In Britain last June (1985), the *Times* gave its editorial space over to one Digby Anderson whose headline blazened 'No moral panic – that's the problem'.[17] Anderson begins where he intends to end, with an inflammatory invitation. 'Excuse me, may I have the pleasure, would you care to panic?' Aids, he notes,

> is causing considerable consternation among sexually and politically progressive persons, as well it might. But the prime cause of concern is not the threat of incurable illness and death of persons progressive or otherwise. The major matter for concern is that the consternation of non-progressive persons about Aids may inconvenience 'the gay community' and damage progressive efforts to 'liberalise' public attitudes. The unenlightened populace might succumb to a 'moral panic' which increases their latent 'homophobia'.

He then proceeds to dismiss the efforts of moral panic theorists to turn attention to the ways in which the media construct particular kinds of events, such as 'mugging' in the 1970s, showing that street violence is by no means a modern phenomenon, and that its victims are in fact mostly blacks and Asians – members of the very groups which the press 'blames' for muggings in the first place. He is particularly critical and disparaging of groups like the London Gay Teenage Group, and seems extremely upset at the exposure of 'heterosexism in the school curriculum', though he displaces his own impatience with such attitudes back on to the sociologists who have studied them.

Irony is heaped on irony in order to belittle medical and sociological supporters of gay teenagers and gay identity as such. His aim is to show evidence of a deafening chorus of encouragement for the situation of lesbians and gay men in contemporary Britain.

> In fact, [he concludes] there has not been a moral panic about Aids – headlines of course, but only sociologists take headlines that seriously ... What there have been are various attempts by political activists, academics and assorted unappointed spokespersons for 'the gay community' to politicise homosexuality, relativise moral standards, make homosexuality not only tolerated but regarded as just as normal as heterosexuality, to remove obstacles to it and thus, inevitably, extend the incidence of homosexual practice.

This is the nub of the matter. Like the author of the 1960s sex education handbook quoted earlier, Anderson clearly dreads what he regards as the possible 'extension' of homosexuality. He dreads the actual sexual diversity of his own readership, which he addresses in a compact of presumed collective heterosexual scorn for positively identified gay men. He can cope 'at a personal level' with 'homosexuals among my friends'; what he recognises is precisely the distance between the cowed subservient identity of the 'homosexual' and the scandalously affirmative presence of the gay man.

> Should not those within Judaism, and Christian churches, Islam and among half-churched but traditionally inclined parents, and the many homosexuals who do not approve of homosexual proselytisation, start to be concerned? In short, what we need is a little *more* moral panic?

So the piece moves full circle, from a blanket dismissal of those who have drawn attention to the problems of contemporary Aids commentary, to a blanket injunction against gay culture. Aids does not concern him in the least, save as a platform from which to launch an anti-gay invective.

Whilst Buckley's calls for tattooing and 'more drastic segregation measures' are based on totally spurious and dishonest notions of risk from infection by casual contact, which *The New York Times* had itself dismissed earlier in the year,[18] Anderson's moralising speaks from an older position which stands against sexual diversity as such, in the name of 'relativism'. Both voices lock together in the knowingly world-weary tone affected by those who feel it their painful but necessary duty to enforce 'standards' which should – in their vision of a 'decent' society – be beyond debate.

Notes

1. *The Letters of Sylvia Townsend Warner*, (ed.) W. Maxwell (London, Chatto & Windus, 1982), p. 73.
2. Peg Byron, 'No Room at the Ward: City Hospitals Hide from Aids', *Village Voice*, 20 May 1986, p. 27.
3. *Capital Gay*, 203 (2 August 1985).
4. *Daily Mirror*, 19 February 1985.
5. Stanley Cohen, *Folk Devils and Moral Panics: The Creation of the Mods and Rockers (1972)* (London, Martin Robertson, 1980), p. 9.
6. Cohen, *Folk Devils and Moral Panics*, p. 17.
7. Cohen, *Folk Devils and Moral Panics*, p. 154.
8. Cohen, *Folk Devils and Moral Panics*, p. 154.
9. Stuart Hall, *et al.* (eds.), *Policing the Crisis* (London, Macmillan, 1978), p. 221.
10. Jeffrey Weeks, *Sexuality and Its Discontents: Meanings, Myths, and Modern Sexualities* (London, Routledge & Kegan Paul, 1985), p. 45.
11. Gayle Rubin, 'Thinking Sex: Notes for a Radical Theory of the Politics of Sexuality', in Carole S. Vance, (ed.), *Pleasure and Danger: Exploring Female Sexuality* (London, Routledge & Kegan Paul, 1984), p. 297.
12. Dennis Altman, *Aids and the New Puritanism* (London, Pluto, 1986), p. 186.
13. Altman, *Aids and the New Puritanism*, p. 187.

14. *Guardian*, 16 July 1986.
15. William F. Buckley, 'Identify All the Carriers', London, *New York Times*, 18 March 1986, p. A27.
16. Alan M. Dershowitz, 'Emphasize Scientific Information', *New York Times*, 18 March 1986, p. A27.
17. Digby Anderson, 'No Moral Panic – That's the Problem', *The Times*, 18 March 1985.
18. Eric Eckholm, 'Study of Aids Victims Families Doubts Disease Is Transmitted Casually', *New York Times*, 6 February 1986, p. 87.

Questions

1   Summarise Simon Watney's main objections to the use of 'moral panic' theory. In what ways does he feel that it has limitations with regard to responses to the disease Aids?

2   To what extent has the representation of gays and lesbians improved in mainstream media in the ten years since this book was first published? Do you detect any difference in attitudes towards sexuality between the press, TV or film?

Further reading

Cohen, S. and Young, J. 1973: *The manufacture of news: social problems, deviance and the mass media*. London: Constable.

Dines, G. and Humez, J. (eds.) 1994: *Gender, race and class in media*. London: Sage.

Dyer, R. 1993: *The matter of images*. London: Routledge.

Gilman, S. L. 1988: *Disease and representation: images of illness from madness to AIDS*. Ithaca, NY: Cornell University Press.

Karpf, A. 1988: *Doctoring the media: the reporting of health and medicine*. London: Routledge. (See previous reading.)

McRobbie, A. 1994: *Postmodernism and popular culture*. London: Routledge.

Murray, J. 1991: Bad press: representations of AIDS in the media. *Cultural Studies from Birmingham* 1. University of Birmingham.

Patton, C. 1990: *Inventing AIDS*. London: Routledge.

Redman, P. 1991: Invasion of the monstrous others: identity, genre and HIV. *Cultural Studies from Birmingham* 1. University of Birmingham.

Watney, S. and Carter, E. (eds.) 1989: *Taking liberties: AIDS and cultural politics*. London: Serpents Tail.

14

The Most Repeated, Most Read Messages of the Cult: 1949–74
Marjorie Ferguson

From *Forever feminine: women's magazines and the cult of femininity* (Heinemann Educational Books 1983)

This extract is concerned with stereotypical representations of gender: specifically the extent to which women's magazines shape the roles and values to which women aspire. Underpinning these representations are crucially different assumptions about the respective positions of men and women in society and the appropriate behaviour and collective attributes that such magazines should foster among their female readership.

Ferguson charts the history of what she calls the 'cult of femininity' which, she argues, was perpetuated in popular women's magazines between 1949 and 1974. Earlier on in the book she establishes that at the very heart of the cult is the notion that women share a common bond which separates them from men and transcends the differences amongst their own gender. In other words, the belief system preserved by women's magazines reinforces their differences from men, and at the same time makes them feel that their weekly journal is a 'surrogate sister' and that through collective veneration they belong to an exclusive female 'club'.

The cult of femininity is revealed in a detailed, although not comprehensive, content analysis of the three most popular women's magazines of the period (advertising, although presumably an important element in the perpetuation of the cult, is only briefly mentioned in relation to the quest for beauty). Ferguson concludes that two overall themes dominate the representations of women: 'love and marriage' and 'self-identity', the sense of self derived primarily from husband and children. Indeed at a later stage in her discussion, she argues that the three female roles most frequently featured are wife, marriage-fixated single woman, and mother. Yet, perhaps unsurprisingly, the representations of men are *not* explicitly aligned to status as husband/father, but rather by personal achievements related to work, money and success.

The content analysis of *Woman, Woman's Own* and *Woman's Weekly*, 1949–74

These three weeklies were chosen for analysis because they consistently had the largest sales of any women's magazines in Britain between 1949 and 1974, and although the size of a magazine's audience is not necessarily related to its influence, there is clearly some correlation.

[...]

Why analyse features?

The term 'features' refers here to articles produced by the general features department (as distinct from other specialist departments such as cookery or fashion). This subject category was chosen because it covers a wide range of material – from entertainers' life stories to 'real reader' dramas; from case studies of emotional and sexual problems to general wisdom about coping with life.

Since the early 1970s it has been the area of general features in which new topics relevant to social and economic change have usually made their first appearance in the pages of women's magazines. This area of discourse has widened out of all recognition, as subjects formerly taboo such as abortion, lesbianism and 'living together' have taken their place alongside old standbys like 'life at home with the stars' or 'triumph over tragedy in everyday life'. From among the several general features in a given issue of a magazine, one was chosen for detailed analysis. Two criteria guided this selection: which article was most relevant to female roles and goals, and which was most indicative of social change or continuity.

Why analyse the problem page?

Three principal reasons recommended this subject category for analysis. The problem pages are the area of women's magazine discourse which consistently strive to strike the most intimate tone of voice. Their message content is also the most intensely prescriptive; and their correspondence and readership levels remain consistently high. They also present an ideal–typical example of the multiple purposes that women's magazine journalists believe themselves and their products serve: they entertain the audience at the same time as they provide a form of psychological and social support. This is based on a bracing mixture of warmth, understanding, and practical information and advice about sexual and familial anxieties and 'worries' generally. Readers are invited to write to named persona – long-standing magazine pen names for many years, but now more commonly the writer's own – and their letters provide a prized form, albeit a self-selecting one, of audience feedback.

Until the early 1970s, the range of problems that women wrote to women's magazines about was readily classified. These included sex ('too little' or 'too much'), courtship ('he just ignores me'), and infidelity (the 'other' woman, the 'man in the office', the 'man next door'). Those letters that were printed often reflected the very subjective definitions of permissible behaviour upheld by the editors of these pages. During the 1960s, for example, the problem page formula on one of these weeklies was the 'something for everybody' mix of 'young letter', 'old letter', 'sex letter' and 'mystery letter', i.e. '"Frantic" of Tunbridge Wells, send a self-addressed envelope for a fully confidential reply'.

The 1970s brought changes both in the range of questions asked (or at least those printed) and the frankness of the replies, with the highest growth area that of correspondence concerning social services and welfare rights.

Why analyse beauty?

This subject category was chosen primarily because it has received remarkably little attention from social scientists compared with, for example, food (cf. Douglas and Gross, 1981; Deckard, 1975), and because of the very considerable attention it is given by women's magazine editors and advertisement directors.[1]

In society, as in these journals, the subject of female beauty is significant, and this significance in both arenas reflects the extent to which a woman's worth is defined in terms of her appearance. The status bestowed by the wider culture is reinforced through the cult's beliefs and practices: systematic content analysis reveals layers of manifest and latent meaning in the offerings that women's magazine beauty writers present before a high altar of female fantasy.

The goddess worshipped there is the Self, and there are prescriptive elements in the narcissistic rituals that accompany these genuflections to a mirror: there is the *duty* to beauty. But physical beauty is more than a goal in its own right; it also symbolises a separate power structure within female society. Among women, the difference lies between those who hold the scarce resource of beauty and those who do not, between the 'haves' and the 'have nots'. Within the world of women's magazines, however, all followers of the cult of femininity are *potentially* beautiful, sharing both the rights and obligations of that state.

There is a further and less metaphysical reason which makes Beauty a significant category. In the economics of women's periodical publishing, advertisement revenue from cosmetics, hair care and slimming products account for a high percentage of income. In 1981 the 'toiletries and cosmetics' category accounted for approximately one-fifth of the total advertisement revenue on *Woman*, for example....[2]

Why analyse fiction?

Fiction manifestly has aspiration and fantasy-inspiring potential (cf. Hoggart, 1957; Mann, 1974; Fowler, 1979). But there are other reasons for choosing fiction for analysis. These include the editorial importance attached to serials and short stories, the audience response that they are believed to evoke, the sameness of many fiction plots and the tight conceptual corset placed upon writers briefed 'to order'.

The importance that editors attach to fiction, the care with which they accordingly frame their requirements, and in particular the extent to which editors act as 'gatekeepers' of the feminine agenda is strikingly illustrated by the detailed brief used by a British weekly magazine in the mid-1970s:

Fiction specification. A British woman's weekly magazine, 1974[a]

Serials	Contemporary background.
	Romantic central theme, involving, especially in serials, some central conflict that is not resolved until the end.

	Sympathetic main characters for whom the reader can feel involvement, liking and recognition.

Age group   Central characters, especially in serials, within the 20–35 age group (in other words, the generally acknowledged 'Courtship' age).
In short stories the characters' ages are not so circumscribed.

Status   Characters may be married, single or widowed.

Taboos   *Divorce*, as a central theme is not acceptable, though it can be a factor in the past that has brought about an existing state of affairs (e.g. heroine hasn't met one parent for a number of years; heroine or hero has had an unhappy childhood).
We avoid *Political* or *Racial* plots, feeling that such controversy is out of place in our fiction, and is better dealt with in other non-fiction media.
Plots are not based on *Class Conflict*.
We try to uphold traditional moral standards, i.e. *No Sex before Marriage; No Drug-taking; No Violence.*

Promote good causes   We try to give indirect publicity to good causes through our fiction (e.g. characters rarely smoke; characters are intellectually compatible, giving greater hope for a lasting happy relationship).
Women's Lib. is given a boost by our endeavouring to give heroines an interesting, worthwhile occupation.

a Copy document, personal communication (emphasis original)

The dominant themes of the three most widely read British women's weeklies, 1949–74

When the content analysis framework was applied to these four subject categories, it was found that dominant and sub-themes were often interchangeable; often some that had seemed minor emerged as of major significance. It was found possible to identify one dominant theme for each beauty, fiction, problem page or feature item analysed, although the number of sub-themes varied.
[...]
Only two themes emerged as consistently dominant. First, there was the overwhelming star billing given to *love and marriage* – and the family – as the peaks of female experience and satisfaction. Second, there was the heavy emphasis placed upon *the Self*, and the responsibility ethic laid upon every woman to be the self-starting, self-finishing producer of herself.

The theme of themes: 'getting and keeping your man'

This represented between one-half and three-quarters of all non-beauty themes (i.e. all features, problem and fiction themes) analysed in these three weeklies – some 59 per cent overall – between 1949 and 1974. The primacy and constancy of Man as goal in the cult's messages has never been so conclusively demonstrated as in this single aggregated finding. The extent to which romantic love leading to marriage is emphasised within western societies as a particularly powerful goal for females, has attracted the attention of sociologists, anthropologists, and literary and feminist critics alike. But hitherto, we have had only limited evidence of the extent to which women's magazines define and reinforce that goal – and often that evidence has been more impressionistic or polemical than systematic.[3]

The message that romantic love was both a necessary and sufficient condition for marriage rang out loud and clear during the 1950s and 1960s. It spelled out both the condition and institution as basic entry requirements for female group membership. What was never spelled out was the competitive nature of achieving these twin goals: all women were eligible for the race, but only some would win the prize. Love as a norm was a state of existence to be sought out and welcomed, just as its absence was to be avoided and feared. The woman who loved and was loved, either en route to, or within marriage, was the proto-female. The woman who was alone or unloved was not a candidate for the cult. Throughout the twenty-five years covered by this sample, there were only four instances of women who were not in the before or during marriage category: two spinsters (in the sense that they had neither hope nor scheme), one widow and one divorcee.

What forms did 'Getting and Keeping Your Man' take between the 1950s and the 1970s? Highly polemic, totally prescriptive was 'Feed the Brute' in which dutiful wives were urged to value domestic skills above book learning, and warned against straying from first duties to Him and Home:

> Girls' schools don't teach nearly enough domestic science. If a few Latin lessons had to go by the board for it, what will the girl care five or ten years later when she's stirring soup, with a yelling baby under one arm, the iron burning a hole in the ironing board, the sitting room fire smoking to high heaven and her husband clamouring for his supper....

As for the alternative of combining home and work tasks, there was the dreadful cautionary tale of the bride who:

> ... of course, went back to work after the honeymoon and she and her husband feed mostly out of cans or in restaurants and he can never find a pair of socks without a hole in them. (*Woman's Own*, 25 February 1949)

The nature of 'true' love, as opposed to other forms, was – and is – a frequent theme of the fiction and problem pages. With her besotted daughter in mind, Mrs Marryat advised a mother to 'Tread warily':

> It is easy for you to judge these two suitors objectively since you are not influenced, as your daughter is, by that emotion which draws her towards one of them, in spite of his faults of character.
>
> You see, unfortunately, she only 'likes' the one you favour, whereas whatever

she feels, or thinks she feels, towards the other is something far more thrilling than mere liking.... But try not to be too disappointed if you find she is willing to risk the ups and downs of life with a not too satisfactory partner. (*Woman's Weekly*, 14 September 1957)

Occasionally, a less romantic, more 'down-to-earth' note was sounded – somewhat defensively – on other possible consequences of 'true love'. Ruth Martin of *Woman's Own* 'Woman to Woman Service' spoke of the chanciness of 'For Better or for Worse':

Whenever a couple marry, *the odds are against it being entirely successful* and it is only by realising this, that success can be achieved.... I shall be severely criticised for saying this, but just think for a moment, and see if I *am* so wrong after all.

and on sex:

The physical side of marriage is at the same time the most *important* and the most *unimportant* factor. It *must* be both. If it is one, or the other, it is fatal. (*Woman's Own*, 17 February 1952, emphasis original)

Throughout the 1950s, 1960s and into the early 1970s, pre-marital sex was strictly taboo. The rewards of repression and the punishments of promiscuity were messages relentlessly reinforced by these weeklies. Virginity and monogamy were two cultural ideals slow to vanish from the 'getting and keeping your man' scenario. Overtly and covertly marriage and family life were set as primary goals for men as well as women. Although unselfish love and sacrifice for the loved one was a concept hammered home to females, there were occasional hints that men could give up 'all' for another:

There are many men who have built their lives around the women they love, for it is not only the wives who can make sacrifices for their partners.

Men can love as truly, tenderly, as faithfully, as women. And husbands have as much need of a loving partner, the stability and joys of family life, that inner, warm love of existence, which gives all their works purpose and makes them as worthwhile as for women.... (*Woman's Weekly*, 25 February 1967)

What of romance with a capital 'R' – and the fantasy delights suggested by glittering scenarios of privileged places and people? What was their part in raising expectations of 'happy ever after'? Were the idealisations of the early 1970s markedly more 'true to life' or conducive to 'reader identification' than those of the 1950s? Not always is the short answer, and particularly not in the fictional world of *Woman's Weekly* serials. In 1974, the heroine of 'The Swallow of San Fedora' muses:

I studied that slender young man, with a profile like the head of some ancient Greek coin as he bowed low over the Australian bride's hand. Then he did the same with Kim's and then mine. A gentleman, who above all else revered women, you might have said to describe him. All sorts of romantic ideas flitted through my brain ... as his bold dark eyes looked deep, first into Kim's and then into mine. Searching for something, I thought, romantically again. Someone, perhaps, to love him for himself, not for the title or his castle. (*Woman's Weekly*, 28 September 1974)

However, by 1974, the possibility, nay probability, of marriage and romance turning out to be rather less of a rose-petalled bower, more of a thorny thicket, was being explored elsewhere. In a six-page special, *Woman's Own* opted for openness, mutual responsibility and reciprocity:

> For the many thousands of couples bewildered by the problems they face as man and wife ... CAN THIS MARRIAGE BE SAVED?
>
> One remark which I hear over and over again from wives in my work for the Marriage Guidance Council is: 'It's his fault. He did it. How can I be expected to forgive and forget?' Husbands tend to say the same sort of thing: 'She doesn't understand'. But is there only one person at fault in a marriage crisis? (*Woman's Own*, 11 May 1974)

Here the turning away from sharply segregated to shared roles including mutual – not wifely alone – responsibility for marriage 'success' or 'failure' *was* a new development.

... And next comes 'The Happy Family'

The emergence of 'The Happy Family' as a dominant theme in its own right reflects the cultural and structural significance of the family as a sacred institution in this and other societies. It also reflects the profound social and economic implications that the family holds for females. Until the feminist movement clamoured for a re-think of sex roles in society and a change of gender emphasis within sociology itself, the family was seen as the primary location of female participation.[4] Children were the expected outcome, not only of imperfect contraception, but also of the perfect union – providing emotional and sexual fulfilment within marriage.

Within these weeklies, heavy emphasis was placed on the centrality of family life to the world of women. Implicitly and explicitly the message was clear: the satisfaction that derived from wifehood and motherhood was quintessential to the cult itself. For this reason a high normative value was placed on family solidarity and for long the message was preservation of the marital and familial status quo, at any cost – with responsibility placed particularly on the wife to maintain stability. The appearance of 'the happy family' – 8 per cent – as a theme in its own right is particularly significant when taken in conjunction with 'getting and keeping your man'. It completes a logical progression, or cultural constellation, of female aspirations and expectations, giving a combined love–marriage–family score which amounts to two-thirds – 67 per cent – of all dominant themes found outside the beauty pages.

The idealised, iconographic role model for 'the happy family' was, and still is, the royal family. The majority of British women's magazines, and especially the weeklies, have helped to create, develop and perpetuate this regal myth. No article remotely critical of the royal family appeared in any of the issues analysed. The image of royalty consistently portrayed throughout the period 1949–74 was that of the royal *family*. Year in, year out, the royals are presented as simple homebodies at heart, sharing the joys and cares of 'normal' family life – 'just like you', the female audience, 'and me', the women's magazine journalist: see, for example – 'Their Happy Marriage' (*Woman*, 22 *November 1952*); 'The Family At the Palace' (Woman's Own, 29 July 1972); 'My Perfect Granny' (by Prince Charles, *Woman*, 2 August 1980).

For less wealthy and aristocratic happy families, the guidelines for wifely and motherly performance were quite specific. In the 1950s, polemical columnists laid down the law on 'It's the Woman Who Makes the Home':

> The woman of the house is the most important person in it. Her husband may be stronger and cleverer than she is. He may be a business tycoon, or a genius or a famous personality. His wife may seem inferior to him in the more obvious ways, but there is one subtle way she can outdo him every time, and that is in her influence in the home....
>
> 'What is a home without a mother?' asks the text that used to hang against the florid paper of Victorian walls. What indeed? Widowers have been known to make homes for their children, but seldom very successfully. They usually have to rely on a sister, or an aunt or a housekeeper – some woman – to fill, at least in part, the gap left by the mother. (*Woman's Own*, 11 April 1957)

'Self-help: Overcoming Misfortune' and 'Self-help: Achieving Perfection'

The second most striking finding of this study was the extent to which the weeklies' messages stress individual achievement and self-determination for women. This underground value system stemming from Victorian England flowered and flourished throughout the 1949–74 period.[5] There are two versions of directives aimed at women pulling themselves up by their own suspender belts. One emphasises individual improvements, ever striving towards a more perfect presentation and performance of self. The other holds out the carrot of hope that one's material, physical or emotional disasters can be overcome through the application of sufficient effort, courage and true grit.

If these two individualistic themes are added together, they total 13 per cent of all dominant themes. When their pre-eminence as a sub-theme is taken into account – some 28 per cent – the total strength of 'self-help' within this universe of discourse is made clear. Both versions suggest that self – not other – determination is desirable, feasible, and obtainable through the exercise of just that much more control and effort on a woman's part. Both imply free choice rather than fated 'determinism', imply active doing rather than passive acceptance, and stress a distinctly anti-collectivist, highly individualist ethic. Here, too, a competitive theory of female 'achievement' is postulated: all women are capable of 'helping themselves', but only those who try harder win through.

The first, 'Self-help: Overcoming Misfortune', demonstrates the discipline and effort required of women if they are to transcend their personal difficulties, from the trivial to the tragic. The second, 'Self-help: Achieving Perfection', concerns a highly gender-specific form of achievement motivation. Here a woman is directed not only to try harder in the labour market, because of her historical disadvantages there; she must also strive industriously to achieve high performance standards on the homefront as well. Here the messages and advertisements directed at women set the standards of perfection; whether it's the never-fail soufflé or the perfect hair style.[6]

The recurrent melody of helping oneself to *overcome* is a classic theme. Known in 'the trade' as a T.O.T., or 'triumph over tragedy', this theme frequently takes the form of first person accounts. Journalistic drama and immediacy is invoked by a whole range of individuals who overcome a variety of physical and emotional problems – from disease to bereavement, from alcoholism to acne.

Other variations on this theme of overcoming fate include stern stuff from problem page editors or columnists: 'Do something, don't just sit down and passively accept the blows of misfortune.'

An early example came from 'The Man Who Sees':

> I think it is much better, as the poet said, to 'toughen the fibre' than to harden the skin. It is better to be firm-hearted than to be thick-skinned. And that is a matter of one's faith.... In the manger at Bethlehem there was no sect; just the centre. And the centre is more important than the sect.... Make that centre firm, and keep your sensitiveness, and, whatever the world brings you, you will find a share of happiness. (*Woman's Weekly*, 24 December 1949)

In counselling those disturbed by changes such as moving or early retirement which threaten comforting familiarities, women are urged to find security in sameness, reassurance in ritual:

> In the face of impending change, it may often seem pointless to carry on with the daily routine. Yet this may be the most effective way of fighting those unsettled feelings.... To occupy oneself with the familiar round even if one must live from day to day, is tranquilising and strengthening. (*Woman's Weekly*, 19 August 1972)

Outside the columns of philosopher–kings such as 'The Man Who Sees', it is in the beauty and problem pages that the emphasis on self-help is strongest. Implicit and explicit within all problem page replies is the admonition: 'Do something about it.' This was so even when 'doing something about it' in the 1950s and 1960s meant accepting what would be unacceptable by today's standards to preserve a marriage. This theme continued in the 1970s, when Mrs Marryat advised on how to learn to live with a marital problem:

> Don't try to conquer the problem [jealousy] by calling yourself names ... say to yourself ... 'Now I expect I shall feel jealous soon because Jim is dancing with that pretty girl. I am not going to give way to it. I'm going to smile and talk to the person next to me, and not say a single word of complaint afterwards.' (*Woman's Weekly*, 28 September 1974)

These examples demonstrate another aspect of self-help, the link between personal responsibility and individual achievement. 'Just make up your mind to do something, try hard enough, and it can be done', is the positive message pounded home on their pages.

This setting of performance standards – of the practices that define the cult of femininity – emerged in this study as one of the most visible and constant purposes served by women's magazines. The perfection-achieving variant of the self-help theme shows how women are directed towards an ever more perfect production and presentation of self. From child-care to hair-care, from cooking to conversation, the parameters of female excellence portrayed as normative – in terms of their desirability and achievability – are universally high. This conclusion contrasts to the feminist view that women are presented with low-level reference groups by comparing themselves with other women rather than men.[7] Until recently this was true of the paid work occupational categories suggested to women as possible or desirable in these journals. It was never true of the primary occupational category – the business of being a woman. Writ large in all these messages of the cult of femininity is the exhortation to improve and excel.

Which categories of perfectability should a female strive for? Multiple forms of excellence are promulgated: *be* a better mother, *be* a better lover, *be* a better cook, *be* better dressed and *be* better looking. The urge to achieve is ever evident in women's magazine problem-solving and fact-giving – through all the editorial 'service' areas from how to paper the bathroom ceiling, to how to teach Him to be better in bed.

In counselling about marriage and the proper performance of the wifely role, attainable perfection is inclusive of 'Him':

> Do you Agree that the Average Man is Less Given to Fault Finding Than the Average Woman? If We Try to Put Our Own Failings Right, Perhaps We May Set a Good Example to Our Men Folk. (*Woman's Weekly*, 24 May 1952, capitals in original)

Learning, and especially learning by doing, is seen as important to achieving a more perfect standard of house-care, child-minding, beautifying or friendship. In 1962 a male columnist suggested flat-sharing as preparation for matrimony, as a form of apprenticeship.

> SHARING HAS PITFALLS
>
> Two girls sharing a flat may learn to be tolerant in many ways – but not when their boy-friends are involved.... It helps to rub off some of her sharp corners almost without realising it and teaches her a practical daily tolerance of irritating little habits ... this could stand her in good stead in the early years of marriage. (*Woman*, 24 February 1962)

'Heart Versus Head'

This theme captures the conflicts of the female condition and attributes which have acquired the status of secondary sex characteristics, and which reflect forms of 'cultural labelling' whereby 'emotional' or 'rational' modes of thought or behaviour become 'female' or 'male' respectively.[8] This process begins with nursery rhyme socialisation and expands to encompass philosophical and psychological distinctions between emotion and reason. It is linked to the legacy of the Enlightenment whereby the western European 'rationality' model takes precedence over other ways of experiencing and ordering the world, and incorporates a hierarchy of understanding which elevates reason (male) over and above emotion (unreason, female) which provides a legitimating logic for male domination in the process.

The tension implied by this emotion–reason dichotomy rests on more than the positing of oppositional 'His' and 'Hers' categories. It rests upon a deeper division between two incompatible sets of values. One assigns to females the role of expressive nurturers. The other locates females within the mechanics of bureaucratic and industrial processes that require logic, consistency and conformity to rules. This juxtaposing of 'thinking' and 'feeling' norms poses more acute problems for women than for men. It creates anxiety about how to conform to definitions of femininity which require that 'bright girls pretend to men that they are not' (see e.g. Komarovsky, 1946, 1973).

Within these weeklies, 'Heart Versus Head' was most often related to decisions affecting the course of love in fiction stories or in celebrities' 'own true-life' dramas. This accounts in part for the high incidence of this theme within *Woman's Weekly*, given its romantic fiction emphasis. For example, in 'The White Oleander', the heroine, Laurie, visits an exotic island to care for her wicked older sister's child. There her bad sister insists that she pretend to be the nanny, and warns her against the fascinating nobleman she meets. Laurie struggles to control her feelings:

> She had allowed herself to become bewitched by his comradeliness into completely forgetting the implications of her promise to Stella. In those minutes, while Felipe stood obliterating the light from the doorway, his face dark and withdrawn, she saw the utter folly of permitting freedom to her emotions. (*Woman's Weekly*, 6 December 1952)

Here, as elsewhere within the value structure laid down for women, individual responsibility is defined in terms of self-control. The cultural ideal is one of womanly rectitude. Typically warnings about the dangers of 'giving way' to emotions and feelings were strongest concerning sex. In the pre-pill era two groups were identified as most at risk: sexually dissatisfied wives and love-sick adolescent girls. The force with which the 'head must rule' message was delivered is shown by a dialogue between a 'real reader' and an editor. The prescription is clear – beware being tricked by passion and losing all control:

> MY MOTHER DOESN'T WANT ME TO BE IN LOVE
> a heartcry from a 17-year-old
> Q. What is she (the mother) afraid of?
> A. (*Woman's Own*) That strong emotion will break her daughter's self-control.
> Q. I want to keep my self-respect
> A. All that can be swept away by passion, etc. etc.
> (*Woman's Own*, 4 December 1957)

This shows the unequivocal nature of moral directives handed down to females during this period, designed to serve the twin ideals of virginity before and fidelity after marriage. Eternal vigilance was the only guard against fleshly temptation – and distinctly possible pregnancy.

A much starker interpretation of the reason–emotion conflict was given in the early 1970s, in discussing abortion five years after the 1967 Abortion Act:

NEVER QUITE THE SAME AGAIN

More than for any other operation, the reason behind the decision to have an abortion is the desire to return to normal – to things as they were. But is that really possible, or does an abortion leave an emotional scar for ever afterwards? Five single girls and a married woman talk about their experiences ... (*Woman's Own*, 16 September 1972)

'The Working Wife is a Bad Wife'

Pilot analysis showed the early strength of this theme, especially during the 1950s. The sociological question arises, was conflict between home and work roles suggested, and how explicit was the normative direction? Historically, the extent to which the messages of the cult directed or reflected any such conflict has not been systematically explored in relation to the contribution of the women's press to the re-socialisation of the wartime female labour force towards domesticity. The virtual invisibility of this theme, 3 per cent, raises questions about the limits placed on topics put before the female audience during the 1950s and 1960s – limits created as much by exclusion as by inclusion. Which role models and reference groups were offered to the mass of the cult's followers? For the growing numbers of wives and mothers experiencing the personal, social and economic consequences of dual commitments and rewards, which satisfactions or dissatisfactions were suggested or acknowledged, withheld or ignored?

Until the early 1970s such questions were either avoided altogether or answered negatively. Female priorities were clear: a woman's world was finite, bounded by the traditional task division which assigns child and home-care exclusively to her. Editorial recognition of non-domestic female occupations within these weeklies was confined largely to 'first job' features, or glossy accounts of the successful careers of models and actresses (cf. Hatch and Hatch, 1968). One recognised females working before marriage, on the assumption that this would cease at latest with the birth of the first child. The other presented readers of all ages with idealised role models and 'success' scenarios for day-dreaming or identification.[9]

Marginally present in the 1950s, absent altogether in the 1960s, this theme reappeared in the 1970s, especially within the innovatory *Woman's Own*. There, stood on its head, altered beyond recognition it became 'The Working Wife is a Good Wife'. The extent to which Him and Home-centredness persisted as a dominant image of British womanhood within these weeklies is illustrated below. Two examples from *Woman's Weekly*, the most traditional of the three weeklies, demonstrate a slight shift, the slow filtering of social change, whereby the impossible of the fifties – a paid job for any woman who valued the quality and durability of her marriage – was redefined by the 1970s to permit some questioning of the 'captive housewife' situation. In the 1950s women were warned about 'Knowing When to Call a Halt':

> The establishing of marriage values may be postponed along with that notice to the office. A young wife doing two jobs just may not have enough time, nervous strength and thought to give to this difficult business of marital adjusting.
>
> Doing two jobs saps strength and vitality and often there is an inner conflict, which is tiring in itself, because she is occupied with one job when she knows the other is going wrong because she cannot give it her fullest attention and energy at the moment needed for it. (*Woman's Weekly*, 14 September 1957)

Seventeen years later Mrs. Marryat advised a restless housebound young mother that she was 'Not Just a Housewife' and how initiative and sharing the problem might help:

> ... as you have a young child, what about offering to help in a local play-group or starting one yourself? Information from ... (*Woman's Weekly*, 1 June 1974)

At this stage, the mid-1970s, no such tentative noises came from the pace-setting weekly, *Woman's Own*. The paid work vs. home duty conflict was resolved, and a five-page 'special' announced 'How to Get the Right Job at the Right Time':

> At 16, 23, 35, 45 plus there's the right job for you. Whether you are just about to leave school in your mid-twenties and need a change, or in your thirties or forties and want to be trained for something entirely new, we've planned this supplement to help you make the right choice. Begin by consulting your Careerscope chart below. (*Woman's Own*, 23 March 1974)

The 'Female State Mysterious'

Pilot analysis showed the presence of this theme, especially in the 1950s. It portrays the female condition as complex, unpredictable or incomprehensible on masculine and/or rational criteria where the terms 'masculine' and 'rational' frequently are being used interchangeably, or as logically connected. It also defines female characteristics in relation to male ones. In the event it was statistically insignificant at 2 per cent. Has this cliché stereotype of female emotionality and impetuosity disappeared? Or is it covertly held by members of both sexes, one with which women themselves have colluded?

For a woman to define herself as irrational and impulsive is to write herself a blank cheque in interpersonal relations. To state 'I am by definition changeable and unpredictable, therefore logically I cannot be held accountable for my actions' is to apply a powerful lever to the balance of power within family or interpersonal relations. As such, it offers partial redress within the conventional power structure of this period, which allocated material or psychological dependence to women. Unpredictability, when not used so frequently that it becomes the norm, can be a powerful counter to reasoned argument or choice. The conscious or unconscious adoption of such attitudes offers some support for the view of women as informal power holders. Oakley (1974) refers to the power that gossip control invests in women. Here, female 'unpredictability' may serve similar ends.

A second side to the 'mysterious female' stereotype is the echo that it provides of primitive fears of the female as unknowably threatening: the carrier of some powerful magic adhering to her menstruating and child-bearing functions. Anthropologists and psychoanalysts have explored such beliefs and behaviours and their implications for the psyches and social roles of both sexes.[10] A third variant of feminine mystery much favoured by women's magazines involves a woman's choice of a particular female typification or 'style' as her own. These alternative images help to perpetuate a cultivated climate of delightful or disconcerting uncertainty:

> WHAT KIND OF GIRL ARE YOU REALLY?
> Romantic? Practical? Selfish? Generous? What are you really like? And how do others, especially your boy friend or husband, see you? Answer the ten questions below to discover your true personality – and see yourself as you really are. (*Woman's Own*, 10 June 1967)

Contiguous or overlapping with the 'Female State Mysterious' is the 'Natural Order' sub-theme. It contrasts to the uncertainties or alternatives of the former and sees the female world as but one-half of a divinely ordained, because unquestionable, sexual division of society. Accordingly, men *are* this, women *are* that; men *do* this, women *do* that (cf. Fransella and Frost, 1977).

'Gilded Youth'

The western cultural emphasis on youth as 'the best years of your life' is not exclusive to females. It reflects a long, historical, aesthetic and philosophical tradition which has influenced both sexes. In the post-war and present media market place, glistening youth was and is the ruling visual concept employed by journalists and advertisers alike. British women's magazine publishers exploited the 'youth cult' through the development of a separate young women's sector. Thus 'teenagers' or 'sub-teens' female audiences are both the stimulus for, and cash register response to, the cosmetics, fashion and entertainment industries' discovery of adolescent spending power in the late 1950s and early 1960s.[11]

Given the commercial and cultural emphasis upon youthful appearance as an ideal for women of all ages, the relative invisibility of this theme, 2 per cent, is interesting. Where it did occur most frequently was in *Woman's Weekly*, the magazine with the oldest readership profile – reaching some 4 per cent of dominant and 14 per cent of sub-themes overall. This suggests some support for the thesis that fantasy elements are involved in the identification process – or that editors believe that older readers prefer youthful idealisations to elderly realisations.

'Success Equals Happiness'

On the face of it, this theme was unimportant, but in fact it was ever present below the surface. It was insignificant in terms of the achievement-orientated nature of industrial societies, at least in terms of women gaining 'success' through a career.[12] Within the messages of the cult that define femininity itself as a career, however, achievement norms exist in abundance. They specify a range of goals and performance standards that relate to herself – love, family, happiness and 'looking good'. Yet alongside these personal goals we see happiness equated with worldly success to a considerable extent.

The material and status rewards of fame and riches, which are used to spell out the meaning of success, raises the question: how does an achieving society define 'success' other than through media role models of status visibility or symbols of conspicuous consumption? The success icons of the cult's messages are celebrities and 'personalities'. They people the pages of these weeklies, proffering their 'shared' dreams and disasters, kudos and cash to the millions:

> HOSTAGES TO FORTUNE
> We all dream of hitting the pools jackpot one day and abandoning ourselves to a life of carefree luxury. But what is it like to be part of the family who became rich by giving vast sums of money away? At the end of the season in which more than ever has been won on the football pools, *Woman* talks to the brothers who share in the Littlewoods millions. Each has a different kind of life and his own way of coping with the joys and problems of enormous wealth. (*Woman*, 13 May 1972)

'Be More Beautiful'

The female duty to beautify was soon evident as this study progressed. The characteristics and internal consistency of this theme less so. Unquestionably 'Be More Beautiful' offers an archetypal example of women's magazine messages presenting the desirable as though it were the possible – just as they present the possible as though it were desirable. This particular form of the message heightens aspirations, allies them with rituals of self-discipline, and encourages every female to 'make the most of herself'. (For this reason, 'self-help: achieving perfection' was occasionally the dominant theme; otherwise 'be more beautiful' was self-selecting on the beauty pages.)

Beauty is 'taken for granted' as both means and end within the female world, and physical appearance is a highly normative cult message. Injunctions to improve the perfect – the *duty* to beautify – are proclaimed from billboard and television advertisements and are not confined to the women's press. There are latent as well as manifest meanings in these messages. Covetable and pleasurable rewards accrue to the possessor of gleaming hair, sparkling eyes and a satiny complexion – transfixed on a moonlit balcony, lolling by a palm-fringed surf and always with an adoring male attendant as the perfect prop in the luxurious backdrop.

The esteem conferred by ownership of these desirable physical attributes suggests an alternative power structure within female society, a hierarchy based upon possession of certain physical qualities – albeit changing from time to time, the relative importance of hair and eyes, or legs and bust. It is a social, cultural and economic fact that for some women their facial contours or body shape can determine their income and status more than their life chance situation, enabling us to posit 'tit' and 'cheekbone' determinism. This is possible because it concerns the distribution of a scarce resource. To be born beautiful is to be born a rarity, yet female beauty is a generalised cultural ideal.

The single-minded dedication required to 'be more beautiful' is reiterated through the same limited range of goals, values and roles. This produces a tight prescriptive package, but one packed with positive reinforcement: 'you *should* look like this', and 'you *can* look like this'. No allowance is made for day-dreaming or wishful thinking in these firm, sometimes stern idealisations that a woman should toil to emulate. 'Soft and pretty' or 'bright and sophisticated'? Simply choose this type, follow the required rituals, and the desired end is assured. Thus, second only to messages of female obligation to maximise physical attractiveness, are promises of its attainability. Achievement of better looks is the logical outcome of personal effort. Comfort and inspiration are combined: any flaws in genetic make-up can always be camouflaged by the cosmetic kind, by sufficient effort – and glitter eye shadow.

Several complex and overlapping processes are at work here – social, psychological and editorial. There is goal-setting: physical beauty is presented less as an aspirational ideal, more as a holy commandment. There is reassurance: salvation can be achieved from a state of non-beauty. Then lest these aspects seem over-deterministic, an element of free will is introduced: individual group members may choose their preferred ideal or image. Finally, once choices are resolved, detailed prescriptions follow, often requiring a greater sacrifice of time, effort and dedication than of money spent on cosmetics or consumer goods. The ritual aspects of the perfecting process are demonstrated by the 'step-by-step' instructions, the day-to-day diets, leading the initiates towards physical images and ideals which are as culturally and commercially determined as ever they are biologically given.

Finally, for whom and for what ends are these active, achieving beauty rituals performed? Technical advice about beautification can only relate to the female, yet surprisingly there were hardly any references to the benefits of women beautifying themselves to attract or hold a male's attention. The beauty messages largely ignored the existence of, or impact upon, men – thereby producing the 'Invisible Male' role category discussed below.

The significance of these absent males is twofold. Firstly, it emphasises the extent to which physical appearance is made integral to a woman's self concept and her femininity as such – narcissism is an explicit norm within these pages. Secondly, it confirms the extent to which the totemic object of female society is Woman, not Man. The absence of his overt presence should not be interpreted as a signal of the male's unimportance. Rather it suggests an implicit and latent meaning so powerful that it does not require explicit and manifest statement: men are the goals, not the gods.

How duty and discipline, possibility and perfection, routine and ritual form a constellation of physical prescriptions is well illustrated in the 'good-to-be-alive GIRL':

'There's more to true beauty than meets the eye' and even if you were not 'pretty really' ... someone with verve, vitality and spring in their step is always a joy to meet....

This positive thinking starts with getting up earlier to exercise, eating more fresh fruit, keeping a dry pair of shoes in the office, because:

When you feel fine, your looks improve, your work, your life: when that happens you feel even better and more pleased with life.

With a gay step and shining eyes, you can look around you and take in all the interesting facets of daily life.... That's the secret of a vital outlook. Look ahead to the day before you with zest and enthusiasm, and you'll look better, feel better and get much more out of life than ever before. (*Woman*, 16 March 1957)

Another example shows the helpful, problem solving of the editorial tone. Here effort is untypically and explicitly directed at Him:

MISS WONDERFUL, THAT'S YOU
... it's certainly true that for a girl to score a real romantic rating in a man's eye her looks have got to be just a little special. *She* doesn't have to have a pin-up profile either ... but she won't get far without polishing up her good points and disguising her bad ones so that he's completely befogged by glamour! It's at this stage that the romantic compliments are paid and the diamond engagement rings get shopped for! (*Woman's Own*, 18 September 1951)

The element of hope implicit in the beauty fantasy, the urge to transform what is into what can be, is illustrated by 'New Fitness Starts Here'. The promise of resurrection goes hand in hand with reassurance where:

Almost every woman is concerned about her figure ... The fact is, perfect bodies are pretty rare. Even model girls have their problems ... there's no figure fault that's worth despairing over! All the help-ways in this book work and they work for everybody ... everyone – yes really everyone – can look younger, lighter, fitter ... and feel it too. Start now on the new you! (*Woman*, 21 October 1967)

These examples also illustrate how the emphasis placed on individual effort and self-help, as the most rational means to the end of beauty, are persistent and powerful themes within women's magazine content as a whole.

The themes discussed above incorporate normative pictures of roles, goals and values. Any answer to the question 'What do women's magazines tell women about the sorts of women they are, can be, or should be?' involves knowledge of the roles that they specify and the aspirations that they set. Few social scientists, journalists or advertisers could examine the pages of women's magazines and disclaim that one of their most potent purposes is that of secondary socialisation: the recipes for, and values of, the female gender role.

Notes

1. As Oakley (1982) comments on the narcissistic nature of such beauty rituals: 'the careful watching of one's body and its fabrication as a public viewing object, is one of the aspects of feminity Freud referred to when he identified women as narcissistic' (p. 82).

2. Source: IPC, BRAD, 1980. This compares with the lower revenues which *Woman's Weekly* attracts in the toiletries and cosmetics category – 10.1 per cent 1981 – which in part reflects its older readership profile compared with its sister weeklies.

3. Commentators and critics on the theme of romantic love in popular culture, and fiction in particular, point to 'escapism' and 'vicarious living' as gratifications assumed to derive from reading the latter (e.g. Hoggart, 1957; Hall and Whannel, 1964). Feminist writers who have analysed the pervasiveness of romantic love in the mythology of womanhood, or women's magazine fiction in particular, include Bailey (1969); Cornillon (1972); Dwayne-Smith and Matre (1975); Fowler (1979); and Winship (1978).

4. The two 'classical' sociological statements are those of Engels (1902) and Parsons and Bales (1955). The former assigns woman to an under-class within the family until she is freed of child minding and joins the labour force; the latter examine the evidence before permanently assigning her to the role of 'expressive' nurturer (a conclusion which was effectively challenged by the cross-cultural research of Crano and Aranoff, 1978). Both positions drew the wrath of feminists, for example Rowbotham (1972); Mitchell (1971).

5. For an enlightening account of the great popular impact which Samuel Smiles' *Self-Help*, first published in 1859, made upon the Victorian public – male and female – see Asa Briggs' introduction to the centenary edition (Smiles, 1958).

6. International agencies have directed their attention to the question of stereotyping of female images in the media in general and advertisements in particular. UNESCO (1974) found in a survey of 28 countries that advertisement rather than editorial content was more culpable in this regard. Reporting to the European Social Development Programme, Marsden (1977) concluded that media sex-role stereotyping should be 'monitored and countered' (p. 82). More recently, the Equal Opportunities Commission (1982) has reported in *Adman and Eve* on some transformation of advertisement images of women which pointed to the sales success of products using non-traditional, 'modern' women in their sales approach.

7. Questions concerning the degree of female competitiveness in terms of achieving the high standards set for the rites, duties and obligations of female membership by primary and secondary sources of socialisation has been under-researched and examined. Oakley (1979, 1981) has written about this in relation to child bearing: 'They [children] symbolise achievement in a world where under-achievement is the rule' (1982, p. 228). The findings of this study suggest that similar symbolic achievements are to be found in other areas definitional of femininity: principally those associated with the 'creative' rites of fashion, beauty and cookery.

8. For an examination of the oppositional categories assigned to males and females, including the emotion–reason dichotomy, from a feminist perspective, see Janeway (1972); see also Maccoby and Jacklin (1974) for the classic psychological evidence on this question.

9. Social psychology offers clarification on the notion of 'identification': individuals can be seen to respond to other individuals – or objects – by imitating their behaviour literally or symbolically (Kagan, 1958); but principally this concept derives from Freud (1959, pp. 37–42).

10. Bettleheim (1968) commenting on the 'menstrual taboo' observes that 'if men had not envied menstruation *per se* they would have grown envious because it was tabooed' (p. 137). In July 1981, British *Cosmopolitan* initiated some taboo-breaking of its own when it exhorted on the front cover: 'Lift the curse, and make it *the most sensual time* of the month' (emphasis in original).

11. The classic account of the post-war discovery of teenage spending power is Abrams (1959); see also White (1977) and Braithwaite and Barrell (1979) for a discussion of the growth of young women's magazines.
12. The notion of industrial societies being 'achievement orientated' belongs to an earlier era of economic growth, full employment, and rising expectations (e.g. Bell, 1974). It no longer seems so plausible for theorists to make such assertions in a period of falling expectations, or what Inglehart (1982) terms 'post-materialism'.

References

Abrams, M. 1959: *The teenage consumer*. London: The London Press Exchange.

Bailey, M. 1969: The women's magazine short-story heroine in 1957 and 1967. *Journalism Quarterly* 46.

Bell, D. 1974: *The coming of post-industrial society*. London: Heinemann.

Bettelheim, B. 1968: *Symbolic wounds*. New York: Collier.

Braithwaite, B. and Barrell, J. 1979: *The business of women's magazines*. London: Associated Business Press.

Cornillon Koppelman, S. (ed.) 1972: *Images of women in fiction*. Ohio: Bowling Green University Press.

Crano, W. and Aranoff, J. 1978: A cross cultural study of expressive and instrumental role complimentarity in the family. *American Sociological Review* 43(4), 463–71.

Deckard, B. 1975: *The women's movement: political, socioeconomic and psychological issues*. New York: Harper & Row.

Douglas, M. and Gross, J. 1981: Food and culture: measuring the intricacy of rule systems. *Social Science Information*. London: Sage, 1–35.

Dwayne-Smith, M. and Matre, M. 1975: Social norms and sex roles in romance and adventure magazines. *Journalism Quarterly* 52.

Engels, F. 1902: *The origins of the family, private property and the state*. Chicago: Charles. H. Kerr & Co.

Equal Opportunities Commission 1982: *Adman and Eve: a study of the portrayal of women in advertising*. Manchester: EOC.

Fowler, B. 1979: 'True to me always': an analysis of women's magazine fiction. *British Journal of Sociology* 30(1).

Fransella, F. and Frost, K. 1977: *How women see themselves*. London: Tavistock.

Freud, S. 1959: *Group psychology and the analysis of the ego*. London: The Hogarth Press and the Institute of Psychoanalysis.

Hall, S. and Whannel, P. 1964: *The popular arts*. London: Hutchinson.

Hatch, M. G. and Hatch, D. L. 1968: Problems of married working women as presented by three popular women's magazines. *Social Forces* 37.

Hoggart, R. 1957: *The uses of literacy*. London: Chatto & Windus.

Inglehart, R. 1982: Post-materialism in an environment of security. *American Political Science Review* 75(4).

Janeway, E. 1972: *Man's world, woman's place*. Harmondsworth: Penguin.

Kagan, J. 1958: The concept of identification. *Psychological Review* 65(5).

Komarovsky, M. 1946: Cultural contradictions and sex roles. *American Journal of Sociology* 52, 184–9.

Komarovsky, M. 1973: Cultural contradictions and sex roles: the masculine case. In Huber, J. (ed.), *Changing women in a changing society*. Chicago: University of Chicago Press.

Maccoby, E. E. and Jacklin, C. N. 1974: *The psychology of sex differences*. Stanford, Calif.: Stanford University Press.

Mann, P. H. 1974: *A new survey – the facts about romantic fiction*. London: Mills & Boon.

Mitchell, J. 1971: *Women's estate*. Harmonsworth: Penguin.

Oakley, A. 1974: *The sociology of housework*. London: Martin Robertson.

Oakley, A. 1982: *Subject woman*. London: Fontana.

Parsons, T. and Bales, R. F. 1955: *Family, socialisation and interaction process*. Glencoe, Ill.: Free Press.

Rowbotham, S. 1972: *Women, resistance and revolution*. London: Allen Lane.

Smiles, S. 1958: *Self-Help*. London: John Murray (originally published 1859).

White, C. 1977: The women's periodical press in Britain 1946–76. Royal Commission on the Press, Working Paper no. 4. London: HMSO.

Winship, J. 1978: A woman's world. In Women's Studies Group, *Women take issue*. Birmingham: Centre for Contemporary Cultural Studies.

Questions

1   Collect a range of magazines aimed at women of different ages (*Just Seventeen, More, Company, Cosmopolitan, Marie-Claire, Woman* etc.) Do these magazines still promote a repertoire of desirable female assets and, if so, what are they and do they differ substantially from magazine to magazine? What changes or continuities in the maintenance of the cult of femininity can you detect in women's magazines in the postwar period? With the plurality of titles now available, do women's magazines still make women feel that they belong to a kind of exclusive 'sisterhood'?

2   Could it be said that other media texts (for example, soap operas and daytime TV and radio shows) perpetuate a cult of femininity in the same way as women's magazines? What examples can you think of which would support or challenge this view? Can the 'ideal' female roles that women's magazines promote be traced even further back to comics for young children?

3   Do you think that stereotypical images of women in magazines, and in the media at large, have any impact on society's attitudes towards women and on women's perceptions of themselves?

4   What about magazines aimed at men? The last decade has seen something of a revolution in the men's magazine market with the launch of many titles in the 1990s following the success of predecessors such as *GQ, Arena* and *The Face* (*Loaded, Maxim, Men's Health* and *Attitude* being some of the more recent titles). Is there any evidence that men's magazines promote desirable roles and assets for males and, if so, what are they and how have they changed since the market started to fragment and expand in the mid-1980s?

Further reading

Beetham, M. 1996: *A magazine of her own? Domesticity and desire in the woman's magazine, 1800–1914*. London: Routledge.

Fowler, B. 1991: *The alienated reader*. Hemel Hempstead: Harvester Wheatsheaf.

Frazer, E. 1987: Teenage girls reading *Jackie*. *Media, Culture and Society* 9(4).

Hermes, J. 1995: *Reading women's magazines*. Cambridge: Polity Press.

Macdonald, M. 1995: *Representing women: myths of femininity in the popular media*. London: Edward Arnold.

McRobbie, A. 1991: *Feminism and youth culture: from Jackie to Just Seventeen*. London: Macmillan.

McRobbie, A. 1996: *More!* New sexualities in girls' and womens' magazines. In Curran, J., Morley, D. and Walkerdine, V. (eds.), *Cultural studies and communications*. London: Edward Arnold.

Mort, F. 1996: *Cultures of consumption: masculinities and social space in late twentieth century Britain*. London: Routledge.

Nixon, S. 1993: Looking for the holy grail: publishing and advertising strategies and contemporary men's magazines. *Cultural Studies* 7(3).

Tinkler, P. 1995: *Constructing girlhood: popular magazines for girls growing up in England, 1920–1950*. Washington D.C.: Taylor & Francis.

Winship, J. 1987: *Inside women's magazines*. London: Pandora.

Winship, J. 1992: The impossibility of *Best*: enterprise meets domesticity in the practical women's magazines of the 1980s. In Strinati, D. and Wagg, S., *Come on down? Popular media culture in post-war Britain*. London: Routledge.

15

The Social Role of Advertising
T. H. Qualter

From *Advertising and Democracy in the Mass Age* (Macmillan 1991)

This extract draws together many of the themes of this section in its analysis of stereotypical representations of class, race and gender in advertising.

Advertising has traditionally relied on the use of stereotypes to put across information in a format that is quick and easy for the viewer or reader to understand. The success of a 30-second television commercial, for example, depends on immediate recognition and identification on the part of large numbers of the audience, and stereotypical representations convey messages in a shorthand and easily decoded form. But in order to achieve some sort of consensual understanding, the images that advertisements present are, according to Qualter, conservative, limited and rarely innovatory. As Barker argues in an earlier extract (reading 8), the images are 'safe' because they will gain immediate audience recognition, they are 'known', but they are not necessarily typical or representative.

Qualter's focus is on the stereotypical representations found in advertisements from the 1980s, although it is demonstrated that ads since the 1920s have avoided the controversial and perpetuated a number of myths concerning representations of class, race and gender. Class is most often linked to occupation, and work has commonly been romanticised in the advertisements of the entire period. Just as commercials fail to reflect the harsh realities of working life, they are also guilty of 'sins of omission', to use Karpf's phrase (reading 12), when it comes to portrayals of unemployment, homelessness and the underclass. Qualter suggests that this should not come as any surprise, as the industry is one which emphasises and reinforces the structures and ideologies of conservatism, capitalism and consumerism. In the few representations of race seen in advertisements, black people have been largely portrayed as part of the mainstream middle class, which does not accurately reflect the lives of many blacks who find themselves excluded from such a life in advanced capitalist societies (see Lewis, reading 9), while images of women perpetuate many of the stereotypical representations associated with the 'cult of femininity' that Ferguson analyses in women's magazines (reading 14).

In the six years since this extract was first published, some of its premises have been challenged and there are now arguably many more adverts on screen which represent people in a less stereotypical manner; in fact many contemporary advertisements 'play' with stereotypes or use them ironically. Despite that, however, innovative, ground-breaking representations are still few and far between and, as Qualter points out, there have been superficial improvements in the ways that women and 'minority' groups are represented, but few changes can be regarded as in any sense fundamental.

Advertising is, overall, a reluctant and largely ineffective initiator of social change beyond the trivia of fashion. Even as it introduces an endless array of new products, and new models of the old, it is an overwhelmingly conservative social force, powerful in defining and preserving the *status quo*. Advertisers seldom question the attitudes that lie behind a purchasing philosophy. They do not encourage reflection on the underlying character or motivation of a consumer society, or of the social attitudes that sustain it. On the contrary, almost all the images in advertising contribute to the preservation of the existing order. Advertisers prosper through the perpetuation of traditional stereotypes of class, race and sex. As a predominantly conservative force, they prefer a romanticised past to an uncertain future. Resisting social change, advertising responds only slowly to unfolding circumstances, tending to lag behind the general course of events reflecting innovation, seldom initiating it. Change, when it does come, is usually precipitated by other social movements which cannot be denied.

Stereotyped images are important sources of knowledge about our society, and about our personal roles in it. People's actual behaviour owes much to the symbolic role models set before them in films, books, the entertainment media and, of course, advertisements. As long as media stereotypes are mainly conservative, therefore, they will have a conservative impact on behaviour, limiting the variety of ways in which people can choose to react to each other, and to themselves. Advertising demands economy of communication. In a brief television commercial there is not time to say much, certainly no time for detailed explanation. The commercial therefore depends on instant recognition, calling upon familiar, sharply-defined stereotypes to set the stage for the message. Advertisers take it for granted that, because most of the audience share a common frame of reference, and a common set of symbols, they will understand most of what is being said. Like pre-war British movies, modern television commercials use stock characters to establish class, occupation, role and mood – bib-overalls mean farmer, indicating down-home earthiness, traditional values; white coats mean scientific, and therefore authoritative or professional; computer terminals mean high technology, implying modern, and so on.

Earlier advertising stereotypes were unashamedly class biased. Roland Marchand examined what he claimed were 'hundreds of thousands' of magazine advertisements in the 1920s and 1930s. In these, he said, husbands were invariably portrayed as businessmen.

> Even doctors and dentists appeared only in their functional roles – not as typical husbands.... as truckers, delivery men, house painters, or mechanics, they joined the tableaux to demonstrate the product's manufacture or use. But working-class men never appeared as consumers; an unspoken law decreed that the protagonist ... in every ad must be depicted as middle class. Not one motorist in a thousand, for instance, ever appeared in anything but a suit, tie, and hat or elite sporting togs.[1]

Advertising in the 1920s relied heavily on 'snob appeal', frequently featuring the aristocracy, the rich, and the famous as role models – appealing to the masses through the good example of their 'betters'. Change followed as sellers began to wake up to the huge market of a more affluent working class. But even now, working-class stereotypes are at odds with the complexity or monotony of working life. Work is still a romanticised, noble, individualistic activity – truck driving or tree felling – never the deadening routine of the assembly line or typing pool. There is certainly little inclination to use the advertising image to depict a harsher reality. Advertising deals with the problems of unemployment, homelessness, urban blight, racial violence or crime, by ignoring them. Adaptation of the stereotype, when it does occur, is the result of external pressures, not of inner desire to give a more accurate picture of society.

Race and sex in advertising illustrate the point. In early advertisements, blacks and other racial minorities, if they appeared at all, were shown only in servile, supporting parts. The common role conformed to a long-standing American cultural tradition of the black slave and servant – simple-minded, happy and devoted. The alternative role was as entertainer. But the gradual realisation of the enormous economic potential of the black consumer market, combined with a much more militant, and effective, black political pressure, brought about change. Blacks now appear quite often in commercials, although not in the same proportion as in the total population. Class discrimination, however, has proved a stronger barrier than race by itself. Blacks in commercials 'are usually shown as part of a group of typical, happily consuming, middle-class Americans in some salubrious environment'.[2] Advertising's general response to minority movements has been to present advertisements in which minorities are integrated into the mainstream of middle-class status seekers. This gives rise to a new dilemma, for the more often blacks are introduced into middle-class prosperity in both commercials and regular television programming, the more obvious it is that the vast majority of the black populations of all advanced capitalist societies are excluded from just such a life.

In many respects, women in modern society face the same kind of problems as blacks – a stereotyped portrayal of a subordinate role giving legitimacy to the actuality of that role, and serving as a barrier to any role redefinition. There are, however, important differences. The accelerating political and social emancipation of black Americans, the result of sustained political activism, has been reflected in their slightly more accurate representation in the media. Blacks in advertisements now sometimes appear as doctors, police, farmers, and shoppers, still mostly safely respectable and middle-class. For women, however, change in traditional advertising presentation has proceeded more slowly.

One reason lies in the 'real life' social tensions outside the world of advertising. The black populations of America, as also in the United Kingdom, have all experienced racial discrimination. Few therefore opposed greater racial equality. Apart from those who feared the insecurity of any change in the established order, most welcomed new economic opportunities, and their expression in advertisements, and this despite the fact that prosperity has benefited mainly middle-class blacks, and that poor blacks, especially black women, are the principal victims of the economic inequalities of the 1980s. Few, even among the poorest blacks, however, have any wish to return to the older order. By contrast, there are still women who willingly, joyfully, accept that woman's place is in the home, caring for a husband and raising children. They believe this to be the appropriate, perhaps even divinely sanctioned, role of women. They are therefore not sympathetic to those women who seek a new future outside the home, in what they perceive to be a man's world. Many women remain content, or have been socialised into contentment, with domestic service and, especially, the unpaid domestic service of wife and mother.

All this complicates the problem of the full emancipation of women in advertising. There is no consensus among women themselves about the need for such emancipation, or what it means. Even those who want change are not agreed on what the ideal future might be like. While most of those active in women's movements condemn the limited depiction of women's lives, not only in commercials, but in the mass media generally, others are equally offended by what they see as attempts to subvert women from their 'natural' function. They view with alarm, even anger, suggestions of equality, or of success in careers outside the traditional. Their attitudes, reflecting a more generalised fear of the new and the unknown, are manifested in an aggressive conservatism, hostile to any change in the status of women. Some women's organisations newly active in the 1980s openly repudiated the feminist movements of the 1960s and 1970s.

The dilemma of the advertising industry, therefore, is that it must reconcile two contradictory versions of woman's place in the world. The industry sets up, on the one hand, the traditional wife and mother role model, and on the other, the career woman model which all too readily shades off into the woman as sex symbol model. Rosemary Scott's study of sex roles in advertisements, for example, categorised advertisements under two major headings, each with several sub-themes. The first major theme was that women are ultimately and naturally housewives and mothers. This implied that: '(a) Women do not work outside the home. (b) When women work outside the home, they are not successful; they do not do "male" jobs. (c) Women are happy doing housework: it is satisfying. (d) Men and Women have strictly delineated sex roles and household duties. (c) Little girls grow up to be housewives, wives and mothers.'

The second major, and contrary, theme was that a woman's goal in life is to attract and keep a man. This in turn implied: '(a) Woman are always attractive; they are sexual objects. (b) Women operate alone; they do not relate with other women, only to men. (c) Men are intelligent, women are not. Men do not like intelligent women (who are "unfeminine"). Women have inferior ability.'[3] The author added substantial detail and illustration to each of these headings.

The most persistent theme in advertising is that a woman's domain is the household, where her primary task is to maintain a home that is a credit to her husband. This is the concept most congenial to the prevailing sentiments within what is still a male-dominated industry. Although the situation is improving, in the world of advertising there remains a clear distinction between what is regarded as man's or woman's work. From the time they leave school women are subjected to a continual propaganda bombardment reinforcing the rightness, the normality, of this traditional arrangement. This, wrote Dorothy Aaron, is where the stereotype affects reality.

> If no alternatives to traditional roles are presented, it makes it all the more difficult for women to break away from these roles and try something new. More than that, the fact that many women are doing precisely that, is virtually ignored in most advertising, for women are rarely shown involved in activities or occupations outside the home, or if they are, these are almost invariably traditionally female jobs such as secretary, teacher, or nurse.[4]

Advertising images today still almost totally ignore the economic reality which compels many women to work outside the home while often also continuing to perform their traditional roles. There is little room in the safe, comfortable, middle-class world of the commercials for working-class women or single parents. The contribution of women to the labour force is barely acknowledged, while the women who populate the beer, soft drink, and sports car advertisements are all young, carefree hedonists who never, apparently, need to work for their living. Even when women do begin to play non-traditional roles, there remains a tendency to treat women as subordinates, under the protection of men. The social situations in tableaux advertisements, especially in magazines, present many ritualistic examples of this subordination. 'Women frequently, men very infrequently, are posed in a display of the "bashful knee bend".'[5] Women are more likely to be cast in supportive or 'background' roles – secretary, maid, nurse, assisting the male protagonist. Often they more closely resemble a 'prop', a piece of furniture, or an ornament, than a functioning human being. Males are seldom cast in a similar support role to a female central character, except, perhaps, in an attempt at humour. Women are still widely portrayed as simple-minded, even stupid, requiring a man to explain to them the operation of household appliances – including those in practice mostly used by women. However, while men are often pictured instructing women, the reverse situation is seldom seen. As one sign of a gradual change of attitudes, in the 1980s one began more often to see commercials with men using such things as washing machines. Generally, however, the implicit suggestion is that men are being required to do what is properly women's work.

Many women are distressed by the fact that after years of objections there are still a great many offensive advertisements. Particularly when dealing with cleansers and household products, women are patronised, frequently depicted as 'feather-brained', incapable of thought or concerns deeper than the shine of their kitchen floors, ecstatic over whiter socks, and with mental horizons limited by the walls of the home. It is true that, since the women's movement gained strength in the 1970s, there have been changes. More housewives are prepared to admit that they do not find inspiration in a cleaner toilet bowl, and that they are fed up with being urged to try a new and improved way of doing something they would rather not be doing in the first place. Older conventions are more frequently challenged, although they are still not all overcome. Increasingly in magazine advertisements and television commercials women are presented in 'non-typical' occupations.[6] But although they may appear as professional workers, or handling machinery, as yet not many are shown as authority figures. Few changes are in any way fundamental. The more grossly offensive advertisements have been moderated, and the semi-clad 'bimbo' as an accessory in an advertisement for automobile parts has largely disappeared. However, despite protest, and some significant revision of attitudes, overt sexuality survives in advertising. Sexual imagery, veiled eroticism, innuendo and semi-nudity are still common features of display advertising, especially in 'up-market' magazines. Advertising has always relied heavily on the 'sexual sell', often seeking to attract the audience's attention with sexual stimuli, even when quite unrelated to the product. Advertisers use provocative female models, and sexually suggestive situations even in messages directed to women, because they believe they sell products.

Changes, when they have come, have not always had the intended effect. 'Advertising's liberated woman incorporates everything the women's movement has fought against.'[7] Advertising's original conception of women's liberation was to make the liberated woman a more efficient, independent consumer. The 'modern' woman knew how to operate complicated household gadgets and labour-saving devices, 'liberating' her from older, heavier, household chores. She was still not liberated from the household itself. Modernity was translated to imply the more competent handling of a wider variety of consumer goods. Some early advertisements depicted women as 'GPA' – General Purchasing Agent – drawing an analogy between the home and a business, with the wife as manager. But the husbands did not lose their traditional role. 'If his wife was the home's purchasing agent – and thus analogous to a business executive of modest power – the husband was more elegantly defined, either implicitly or explicitly, as the home's "treasurer" or its "president".'[8] Modern women might acquire new managerial skills, but they were to be exercised only in the home. Freedom meant more independence in pursuing traditional goals. It did not mean freedom to pursue different goals.

'Liberation' could also be expressed in social attitudes and behaviour. The purchase of a bicycle, and a costume appropriate for riding it, was promoted as an early manifestation of women's escape from stifling older conventions. In some advertisements in the 1920s and 1930s women expressed their new freedom by overcoming old taboos about smoking cigarettes in public. Christopher Lasch referred to the advertising industry's 'pseudo-emancipation' of women, 'flattering them with the insinuating reminder, "You've come a long way, baby", and disguising the freedom to consume as genuine autonomy'.[9] In the 1980s the 'liberated woman' was often presented as sexually available. 'Advertising ... seems to interpret the movement towards female equality largely as a moderate sexual liberation whose function is to legitimize pre- and possibly extra-marital affairs.'[10] For this is another side of advertising's portrayal of women – the sex object who can be, and longs to be, 'possessed' by the man with the advertised mouth-wash or imported car. Women, in the advertisements, seldom play the initiating role, but are confronted with the fear of sexual inadequacy, of not being desired by a male, unless they use the advertised product.[11] Advertising's conception of feminine attractiveness makes few concessions to nature. Sex appeal is obtained only from commercial products – hair shampoos, beauty aids, skin conditioners, perfumes, and so on, which make women glamorous, and therefore attractive. Men are not expected to be glamorous. Even as executives, women are supposed to be 'alluring' and to spend money on artificial aids to that purpose. They must be tall, slim and elegant. Male executives can succeed looking just like themselves, and can be any shape.

Stereotypes, while active and powerful guides to behaviour, and normally a conservative force, inhibiting reform, can and do change, usually in response to external events. But they do not spring from nothing. They are learned responses that can be developed to the point where they lose all contact with, and relevance to, the world around them.[12] Advertisers have a vested interest in protecting old stereotypes for as long as possible. Yet social norms and practices are dramatically changing the role of women in modern urban society. More women than ever before are independent income earners, and more are entering a wider range of occupations previously the preserve of males. And advertisers will lose credibility if their stereotypes are too far removed from reality. Women, as they currently appear in many advertisements, seem to resemble some idealised, perfect consumer, unrelated to the actual women one sees every day as next-door neighbours or as co-workers in office or factory.

> Sex stereotyped advertising no longer reflects the roles of the majority of men and women in North American society, it creates consumer irritation and dissatisfaction, and it is increasingly less effective as a communications tool. It is therefore surprising that so little in advertising has changed and that, for the most part, the changes that have taken place result from pressures coming from outside the advertising industry itself.[13]

Leaders of the advertising industry are to some extent justified in claiming that their depiction of women corresponds to reality, but it is a very limited reality, only now beginning to acknowledge the woman who is neither wife nor sex object. The advertisers themselves often concede that their messages concentrate on women who are wives, mothers and housekeepers. But, they assert, as this is the real chosen world for most women, there is no distortion, nor do many women feel insulted. If significantly large numbers of women indicated their dissatisfaction with advertising practices by not buying the products, they would change those practices.[14] They have not yet felt called upon to do this because, they argue, the majority of 'sensible' women are not offended by advertising's stereotypes. Protestors are dismissed as unrepresentative malcontents. This is a self-serving argument. Often there are no convenient alternative products. The industry sees no benefit in establishing empirically how many women feel slighted by their customary portrayal. Because it believes that the established is safer than the innovative, it offers little encouragement to new expressions of women's part in society. Advertising therefore remains a major force, consistently strengthening the image of a traditional place for women, and offering few inspirational role models for alternative life-styles. Here, of course, the stereotypical woman is not vastly more distorted than advertising's stereotype of the world in general. Stereotypes, seldom dependent on verifiable empirical evidence, are not usually shaken by such evidence.

The modern woman may be permitted a wider range of occupations, and she may sometimes be pictured with a life outside the home, but in the world of advertisers she is still above all a consumer. The educated woman today is regularly expected to exercise her mind by acting as an intelligent shopper. The very structure of modern capitalism compels this emphasis on consumption-management as a major focus of women's concerns.

> It is a prime tenet of modern economic belief ... powerfully reinforced by advertising and salesmanship – that happiness is a function of the supply of goods and services consumed.... how better can a woman contribute to her own happiness and that of the family she loves than by devoting herself to the efficient and energetic administration of the family consumption? ... [Society] celebrates as uniquely moral the woman who *devotes* herself to the well-being of her family; is a gracious helpmate; is a good manager; or who, at lesser levels of

elegance, is a good housekeeper or real home-body. By comparison, mere beauty, intellectual or artistic achievement or sexual competence is in far lower repute. And qualities that are inconsistent with good and acquiescent household administration – personal aggressiveness, preoccupation with personal interests to the neglect of husband and family and, worst of all, indifferent housekeeping – are strongly deplored.[15]

All this is crucially important to a capitalist economy. 'Without the willingness of women to stay at home and administer consumption, the present economic order would be severely hampered in its ability to expand.'[16] As long as we live in a mass consumer society, some segment of the population must take responsibility for the management of domestic consumption, and unless other forces lead to a massive transformation of social relationships, that responsibility will inevitably be assigned to women. There is an enormous economic benefit in persuading women to accept the status of an unpaid semi-servant class. This has become especially necessary as other economic forces led to the virtual disappearance of a separate domestic work force. In the latter half of this century middle-class women have been conditioned to do for love and virtue what servants were once paid, albeit very badly paid, to do for them.

The reluctance of advertising to become involved in the social controversies of race, class and sex reflects the uniqueness of its ideology. Advertising, as a conscious persuasive activity, is an important element in market capitalism, which also has an identifiable, unifying ideological basis of its own. A central tenet of that ideology is that there are no ideologies, for advertising manifests its political position by being ostensibly non-political. It is not any indifference to, or any deliberate withdrawal from politics, but an awareness that the political cause is not advanced by frenzied demagoguery. The implicit political doctrine of advertising is that there are no political doctrines to discuss. The corporate sponsors of most mass media advertising like to present their world view as the established, non-arguable world view of all intelligent people of good will. There is no call to debate what everyone knows to be true. For this reason only a small percentage of mass media advertisements contain explicit political indoctrination. Most advertisers are more interested in selling goods and services than in promoting ideologies. But, of course, we must bear in mind that selling goods and services *is* the ideology of capitalism. The ideological function of advertising reflects its economic function. The commercial message, the exhortation to buy, is the political message, which declares that, as all is right in the world, it is safe to acquire, possess, and accumulate.

Economic and political stability are the necessary conditions for a culture which defines progress as the capacity of more and more people to buy more and more things. That stability, in turn, requires a climate of calm assurance and confident security, something best achieved by keeping disturbing thoughts off the public agenda. Because it is difficult to take sides on any issue without offending someone, and because the offended may be lost as customers, advertising deals with controversial issues, not by strident partisanship, or by shouted dogmas, but by ignoring the controversy. Advertisers try to steer clear of the controversial, to defuse tensions, and to portray a world of familiar, untroubled certainty. In the entertainment media, corporate advertisers prefer to avoid association with programmes dealing with contentious matters.

> Burning controversy looks good in press releases and TV reviews. It looks awful in ratings, sales, comments from aggrieved affiliate stations and nasty letters from offended viewers. Constant, warm, bright reassurance is the emotional climate in which American business, including the television business, feels most at home, and television executives instinctively work to maintain that climate.[17]

Bland is safer than controversy and is more conducive to maximum sales. Large-scale business and industry flourish in a climate of stability and certainty – not only in the market itself, but in the surrounding political and social environment. Put in the simplest terms, capitalism knows that social unrest is bad for business.

Notes

1. Roland Marchand, *Advertising the American Dream* (1985), p. 189.
2. D. L. Paletz and R. M. Entman, *Media–Power–Politics* (1981), p. 179.
3. Rosemary Scott, *The Female Consumer* (1976), p. 224. Note also Alladi Venkatesh, *The Significance of the Women's Movement to Marketing* (1985).
4. Dorothy Aaron, *About Face: Towards a Positive Image of Women in Advertising* (1975), p. 8.
5. Erving Goffman, *Gender Advertisements* (1979), p. 45.
6. See Rena Bartos, *The Moving Target: What Every Marketeer Should Know About Women* (1982), pp. 228*ff*.
7. Denise Warren, 'Commercial Liberation', *Journal of Communication*, 28:1 (1978), p. 169.
8. Marchand, *Advertising the American Dream*, pp. 169–70.
9. Christopher Lasch, *The Culture of Narcissism* (1978), p. 74. See also Paletz and Entman, *Media–Power–Politics*, pp. 178–9.
10. Torben Vestergaard and Kim Schroeder, *The Language of Advertising* (1985), p. 108.
11. See A. E. Courtney and T. W. Whipple, *Sex Stereotyping in Advertising* (1983), pp. 10–12.
12. See, for example, Mark Snyder, 'On the Self-Perpetuating Nature of Social Stereotypes', in D. L. Hamilton, (ed.), *Cognitive Processes in Stereotyping and Intergroup Behavior* (1981), p. 204.
13. Courtney and Whipple, *Sex Stereotyping in Advertising*, p. 191.
14. See Cyndy Scheibe, 'Sex Roles in TV Commercials', *Journal of Advertising Research*, 9:1 (1979), p. 23.
15. J. K. Galbraith, *Economics and the Public Purpose* (1974), p. 37.
16. David Reisman, *Galbraith and Market Capitalism* (1980), p. 78.
17. Robert MacNeil, *The People Machine* (1968), pp. 79–80.

Questions

1 Summarise the arguments put forward in this extract. What are the dominant themes in the representation of class, race and gender, and what, for Qualter, are the greatest sins of omission?

2 Undertake your own content analysis of advertisements across a range of media. Do your findings back up those of Qualter, or do you detect any substantial changes or improvements in present advertising culture?

3 What about other groups? Do you find limited and stereotypical representations of, for example, young people, the family or the elderly in advertisements? How do you think that advertisers would defend the allegation that they promote narrow and often misleading images of people?

Further reading

Cumberbatch, G. 1990: *Television advertising and sex role stereotyping*. London: Broadcasting Standards Council.

Davidson, M. 1991: *The consumerist manifesto: advertising in postmodern times*. London: Routledge.

Dyer, G. 1982: *Advertising as communication*. London: Methuen.

Goffman, E. 1979: *Gender advertisements*. London: Macmillan.

Goldman, R. 1992: *Reading ads socially*. London: Routledge.

Leiss, W., Kline, S. and Jhally, S. 1986: *Social communication in advertising*. London: Routledge.

Williams, R. 1980: Advertising the magic system. In *Problems in materialism and culture*. London: Verso.

Williamson, J. 1978: *Decoding advertisements: ideology and meaning in advertising*. London: Marion Boyars.

Willis, S. 1995: I want the black one: is there a place for Afro-American culture in commodity culture? In Carter, E., Donald, J. and Squires, J. (eds), *Cultural remix: theories of politics and the popular*. London: Lawrence & Wishart.

16

Television's 'Personality System'
John Langer

From *Media, Culture and Society* 4, 351–65 (1981)

It has long been recognised by those in Media and Cultural Studies that film stars have played a significant and highly visible role in the twentieth century as cultural symbols or icons: embodiments of particular kinds of values, objects for widespread forms of identification by modern audiences. The final extract in this section takes this as a starting point, but then shifts our attention from the realms of cinema and film to that of television and to popular culture more generally. The reading therefore recognises that film stars are now part of a more general social and cultural phenomenon of public visibility and mediation, involving not only the sphere of television, but also popular music, sport, the press, magazines and other areas of the mediated 'personality'.

Langer begins his discussion by contrasting the conditions and forms which give rise to film stars and television personalities, discussing the ways in which the two systems compare and interrelate, and the extent to which the regime of television is simply a modern form of that established when cinema was the dominant mode of moving image medium. As you will note, he suggests that there are some key differences between the appeal to audiences maintained by film stars and that of the relations established by television personalities and their respective audiences or fan communities. For Langer, writing in the early 1980s, these differences crystallise fundamental contrasts in the nature and the reception of each medium, and these correspond with very different types of ideological appeal and function. In the changing circumstances of the 1990s, when current television has developed a growing obsession with so-called 'reality programming' and with revealing the private and public lives of 'real people' (see Section 4, readings 30 and 31), Langer's assessment provides an important and provocative focus for renewed attention and study.

I begin with a question: What is the significance of the fact that whereas the cinema established a 'star system', television has not? There are stars of stage screen *and* television, but no stars of television alone. Instead we encounter what television calls its 'personalities' – those individuals constituted more or less exclusively for and by television, who make regular appearances as news readers, moderators, hosts, compères or characters, and those individuals who exist outside of television in their own right, but are recruited *into* television at various strategic junctures as resource material – politicians, celebrities, experts or 'ordinary people ... made strangely important' (Monaco, 1978: 7).

[...]

Star system and personality system as paradigms

In order to locate and define the personality system as it is coded into television it may be useful to look at what might be seen as its paradigmatic counterpart and historical antecedent in the cinema – the star system. It has been argued that the star system experienced and finally fell victim to the 'embourgeoisement of the cinematic imagination', which eventually saw the transformation of stars from 'gods and goddesses, heroes, models – embodiments of ideal ways of behaving' to 'identification figures, embodiment of typical ways of behaving' (Dyer, 1979: 24). According to Morin, this process was inextricably bound up with cinema's 'search for realism', which was marked by certain technical innovations (the introduction of sound, colour, deep focus), the growth of social themes in Hollywood films during the 1930s, the psychologization of cinema's protagonists and paradoxically, the 'dogma' of the happy ending. 'Realism, psychologism, the "happy ending" ... reveal precisely the bourgeois transformation of this imagination' (Morin, in Dyer, 1979: 25)

> Chance and occult possession are replaced by psychological motivation. Bourgeois individualism cannot take the death of the hero, hence the insistence on the happy ending. So stars become more usual in appearance, more 'psychologically' credible in personality, more individuated in image (Dyer, 1979: 25).

Stars became less directly the filmic representatives of particular 'virtues' or 'essences'. The cinematic archetype – the vamp, the good girl, the gentleman, the clown, the innocent, the landlord – gave way to more individuated social types. Psychological realism and the motivational credibility of screen characters were accompanied by the desire of audiences to know the stars that played these characters 'as people', to have access to their 'real' lives, to what they were 'really' like; in short, to know their 'personalities' – hence the proliferation of the fan magazines and the publicity machine which became crucial to the star system as an image maker. Lowenthal traces a similar process at work during the first half of the century in the expansion of biographical stories in popular magazines, where he finds a significant shift away from what he calls the 'idols of production' who serve primarily as 'educational models' to be 'looked upon as examples of success which can be imitated' (Lowenthal, 1961: 113) toward the 'idols of consumption' who provide a 'readily grasped empire', merely confirming 'identification with normalcy' (ibid.: 135). Analyzing the stories over time, he discovers that 'while it once was rather contemptible to give much room to the private affairs and habits of public figures, the topic is now the focus of interest' (ibid.: 119). Parentage, personal relationships, friendships, domesticity, sociability, hobbies and culinary proclivities abound as the thematic structures through which the heroes and celebrities of magazine biography are revealed in their 'private lives', not so very different a format, so it seems, from that used in the fan magazine for the star system.

This 'intimate vision' with its attendant 'obsession with persons' – one of the most pervasive conditions characterizing social life under modern capitalism (Sennett, 1974) – seriously eroded the 'divine' status of the star system, but it did not succeed in doing this completely. As Morin points out, the star does not cease to be special, but now combines 'the exceptional with the ordinary, the ideal with the everyday' (Morin, in Dyer, 1979: 25). The 'magic' of the silver screen still lingers, even if this is only in terms of a collective but very powerful folk memory of Hollywood 'as it used to be'. It is left to television's personality system to take up this process of embourgeoisement and move it forward, considerably advancing the 'intimate vision' to the point where what is presented on television is precisely that which is 'the ordinary', where 'the everyday' has superseded and supplanted 'the exceptional', where 'the exceptional' is the exception rather than the rule.

In some respects what might be termed the classical paradigm of the star system, before its subjugation to the 'reign of intimacy', can be situated in direct opposition to the personality system manifest in television. It is this opposition which begins to articulate some of the terms of each system. Whereas the star system operates from the realms of the spectacular, the inaccessible, the imaginary, presenting the cinematic universe as 'larger than life', the personality system is cultivated almost exclusively as 'part of life'; whereas the star system always has the ability to place distance between itself and its audiences through its insistence on 'the exceptional', the personality system works directly to construct and foreground intimacy and immediacy; whereas contact with stars is unrelentingly sporadic and uncertain, contact with television personalities has regularity and predictability; whereas stars are always playing 'parts' emphasizing their identity as 'stars' as much – perhaps even more than – the characters they play, television personalities 'play' themselves; whereas stars emanate as idealizations or archetypal expressions, to be contemplated, revered, desired and even blatantly imitated, stubbornly standing outside the realms of the familiar and the routinized, personalities are distinguished for their representativeness, their typicality, their 'will to ordinariness', to be accepted, normalized, experienced as *familiar*.

Media contexts

If television is indeed an apparatus for the production of symbolic goods which are made intelligible by a process of encoding, how then is the personality system 'arranged' within the television discourse, and what operations are at work which preclude the formation of a star system? To begin with what at first glance seems most obvious: watching television by and large, as a socially constructed act, takes place, to use a phrase adopted frequently and fondly by television's practitioners, 'in the comfort of one's own home', very much embedded within the intimate setting that circumscribes the routines of everyday life; watching film, however, except of course those on television, leads away from the home, elsewhere into an unfamiliar 'exceptional' setting not directly connected with the network of intimacies which make up everyday life. Television is always 'there', routinely encountered and ready for use whenever the television experience is required. Cinema watching, on the other hand, needs to be pre-arranged, calculated and attended to. The intimacy of domestic life has to be set aside in order to participate in the 'special' experience of the cinema. In fact this is one of the major ways in which film as a leisure activity is promoted in advertising – 'give yourself a break, go to a movie', 'go for a night out and be entertained'. The television image is 'close', occupying a relatively restricted space within the field of vision (Heath and Skirrow, 1977: 54), in a sense positioning the spectator to take a 'closer look'. It can be acted on and manipulated in the moment of transmission – turned on, off, fine tuned or switched for alternative images. Because of its proximity to the ebb and flow of everyday life it can be received casually, with the potential to become the focus for social participation during the viewing situation itself. The film screen image, in contrast, hovers over and above the spectator massively imposing itself upon the visual field. By not being subject to control or modification at the time of its reception, it remains 'distant, inaccessible and fascinatingly fixed' (Heath and Skirrow, 1977: 54). Once the film begins, even if one goes with a group of people to the theatre, the conditions of viewing are constituted by anonymity – the nexus of screen image and spectator alone, silent and in the dark, the possibility of social participation ruled out until the film is over.

Like the world, television never stops, is more or less continuous (Heath and Skirrow, 1977: 54). Its reality runs a parallel course to the reality of everyday life itself, can be tuned in or out at will, and can be 'met' virtually at any one point in time. Television's 'flow' is contemporaneous with the flow of life. So, not only is television 'always already available', there will always be something to watch immediately, as soon as the set warms up. Television's 'communicationality' is not constrained by time or scheduling. Certainly there are programmes organized around particular time slots within the continuous flow, but if one programme is missed, there will always be another one to take its place. As Heath and Skirrow explain, 'the role of the image is to be present' (ibid.: 56). Cinema, on the other hand, is more institutionally grounded within temporal operations – it requires active attention to its delineation in time. Unlike just sitting down to 'watch television', 'going to the movies' generally means going on time, 'getting there for the credits', 'not wanting to miss the beginning', 'staying to the end'.

At this point it becomes clear that those apparently 'natural' taken-for-granted arrangements which differentially structure viewing in relation to film and television are also working to inscribe and reproduce an entire cluster of terms – distance/intimacy, ordinary/extraordinary, familiar/exceptional, immediate/remote – as they pertain to the star/personality systems, and this occurs even before the set is switched on or the film is rolling through the projector gate. The act of television watching is found in the intimate and familiar terrain of everyday life where we receive television's own 'intimacies' and 'familiarities' brought to us through its personalities. This correspondence between the intimacy structure of television watching and the way in which intimacy is structured through the personality system forms one of the major conditions through which television negotiates effectively to win the consent of audiences and to render invisible its ideological work.

The regular and the episodic

If one of television's central characteristics is the 'experience of flow', another is its ritual regularity, its tendency 'toward an idea that it is capable of reproduction' (Alvarado and Buscombe, in Eaton, 1978/79: 68). Within the sequential flow of television there are moments carved out and arranged into particular cyclical, repeatable televisual occurrences which give the flow its shape and substance. Television programming, in the main, operates in terms of 'seasons' – the series, for example, if initiated, usually runs for a number of consecutive episodes normally scheduled at the same time on the same day each week, although these schedules may be altered in response to poor ratings. If a series is deemed successful – winning ratings, capturing audiences and landing sponsors – there is every chance that it will re-appear for the next season. On this basis a series can be sustained for several years in a row. This has, in fact, been common practice with genres like the police drama, the situation comedy, or the late-night talk show. Other programmes are not necessarily subject to seasonality – the news cycle, for example, is one which recurs each day, and possibly several times a day on a single channel all through the year. These cycles of repetition provide a forum for the regular appearance of the personality – the newsreader, the talk show host, the lead actor in a cop show – around which the programme is organized. As a result, these cyclical repetitions tend to play a part in television's structure of intimacy and immediacy. Each repeated appearance, even though it may not elicit 'personal data' – as in the case of the very formal demeanor of the newsreader – nonetheless tends to build what is perceived to be a knowable and known 'television self'. This television self, increasingly authenticated with each regular appearance, coheres into the form of a 'genuine' personality. Finally, the very appearance itself becomes a mark of knowledge about that personality.

This, of course, is quite different from the appearance of a star in a film, which occurs perhaps twice in a year at best. The star's appearance occurs as an eventful arrival, often heralded ahead of time in press and industry releases, not to be repeated in that same context again, except perhaps in a sequel. Even there, however, the event is discrete and unique. It needs to be caught in its singularity, and if it is repeated, it always emerges full blown in its originally fixed form. Access to stars through their films must be deferred over long periods of time: it is episodic and ephemeral, coming only once in a while. In between appearances, time can be spent re-viewing their earlier films or reading fan magazines in an attempt to rekindle the 'aura', or other stars can be taken up and appreciated. There is none of this capriciousness or uncertainty where the television personality is concerned. He or she reliably appears over and over again, week after week, even year after year, providing the coherent fixed point of regularity within the overall flow of television. By never becoming overly routinized and familiar the star system can maintain its remoteness and unattainability, whereas the personality system crucially embedded within television's cyclical rituals can much more readily facilitate a sense of familiarity and accessibility.

Identity

Television personalities also become anchoring points within the internal world that each programme uniquely establishes in and for itself. They exist as more or less stable 'identities' within the flow of events, situations or narratives which are presented in a particular programme at any given point in its cycle of repetition. For example, despite the panoramic flow of news stories which constitute any single early evening news broadcast, it is always the newsreader who remains the constant, unfaltering and coherent indentity, who 'carries on regardless'. The world changes, but the television personality stays the same. In the case of the news, one of the conventionalized marks of this coherent stable identity which persists despite a world of flux and change, is the way the news reader is framed by the camera. The head and shoulders dominate, appearing balanced and central in glistening, unwavering focus – like the authoritative carriage of a portrait – which looks at us with calm deliberation. The 'real' world, where stories come from, is, in contrast, often skewed, off balance, with shaky camera work done in the heat of the newsworthy moment. The 'real' world may be unstable and unbalanced, but the world of the television news personality who *explains* that world to us is not.

The establishment of the television personality as a coherent identity is also the occasion for coherence to be imparted to what is potentially a diverse and seemingly chaotic universe of events. Newsreaders, then, not only function as coherent identities in the flow of events, but they act as the principal instrument for classifying and unifying these events into some kind of acknowledged order. The newsreader is responsible for giving events meaning, placing them in referential contexts and providing appropriate clues to their significance in 'the scheme of things', functioning as 'a very definite ethical figure (giving) unity to what is essentially a very disjointed format' (Mills, 1980). Similar encoding procedures work to build the personality system across a whole range of non-fiction/ actuality forms of television – essentially the same principles appear to be at work in current affairs, talk shows, variety shows, documentaries and so on.

References

Dyer, R. 1979: *Stars*. London: BFI.

Eaton, M. 1978/9: Television situation comedy. *Screen* 19(4).

Heath, S. and Skirrow, G. 1977: Television: a world in action. *Screen* 18(2).

Lowenthal, L. 1961: *Literature, popular culture and society*. Palo Alto, Calif.: Pacific Books.

Mills, I. 1980: Pulpit drama, the mythic form of TV news programmes. In Edgar, P. (ed.), *The news in focus*. London: Macmillan.

Monaco, J. 1978: *Celebrity: the media as image makers*. New York: Delta Books.

Sennett, R. 1974: *The fall of public man*. New York: Vintage Books.

Questions

1 Summarise the main arguments concerning the differences between the film star and the television personality. Select some examples of each and research their particular appeal and significance as well as their respective differences.
2 Assess the role of the popular press in the construction and mediation of film stars and TV personalities.
3 How do other modern stars, e.g. those in the fields of sport or pop music, relate to the ideas and arguments discussed in this extract?

Further reading

Buxton, D. 1990: Rock music, the star system and the rise of consumerism. In Frith, S. and Goodwin, A. (eds.), *On record: rock, pop and the written word*. London: Routledge.

Connell, I. 1992: Personalities in the popular media. In Dahlgren, P. and Sparks, C. (eds.), *Journalism and popular culture*. London: Sage.

Corner, J. 1995: *Television form and public address*. London: Edward Arnold.

Ellis, J. 1982: *Visible fictions: cinema, television, video*. London: Routledge.

Geraghty, C. and Lusted, D. (eds.) 1997: *The television studies book*. London: Arnold.

Lewis, L. (ed.) 1992: *The adoring audience: fan culture and popular media*. London: Routledge.

Livingstone, S. and Lunt, P. 1994: *Talk on television: audience participation and public debate*. London: Routledge.

Lusted, D. 1984: The glut of the personality. In Masterman, L. (ed.), *Television mythologies*. London: Comedia/MK Media Press.

Tolson, A. 1996: *Mediations: text and discourse in media studies*. London: Arnold.

Audiences and Reception

The various extracts in the previous section tended to assume that media representations are implicated in the ways in which we make sense of the social world and construct a sense of identity within it. This section shifts attention to the relationships between audiences and various forms of media output and use. The study of audience reception of media forms has been an especially productive focus for recent mass communication research, although much of this work needs to be contextualised against an historical tendency to assume the *direct effects* of media imagery on behaviour. In fact, the history of audience research can be understood as a dialogue and debate between two largely opposed positions: one stressing the effects that the media cause in their audiences, the other countering with an emphasis on the various and diverse uses which different audiences in their respective social contexts may make of given forms of media output. One way of summarising this division has been to contrast the idea of *what the media do to people* against *what people do with the media*.

The readings in this section encompass and analyse both of these dominant premises. Reading 17, by **Andrew Tudor**, is an historical overview of the developments in audience research and it provides an entry into a discussion undertaken in the following two readings about the power of the media to persuade, influence and corrupt. **Graham Murdock** and **Robin McCron** critically assess the perspectives and methods which have dominated effects research since the 1930s, while **Julian Petley** focuses on two recent cases where the media was blamed for influencing the perpetrators of specific violent and much publicised crimes.

Readings 20 to 22 are characteristic of a type of research which has assumed prominance throughout the 1980s. They are loosely characterised as ethnographic studies and although they differ from the tradition of ethnography established in anthropology, they are united in that they draw on observation, informal interview techniques and naturalistic research settings. While much of this research has centred on television consumption, **Mark Pursehouse's** study is significant in that it focuses on readers of a tabloid newspaper, **Ann Gray's** is an analysis of women's relationship with video technology, and **Shaun Moores'** is a study of satellite television viewers. Together, these readings help us to build up a picture of media usage in Britain in the 1990s. The section ends with an extract from a useful summary of audience studies by **Nick Stevenson**, in which he outlines the key debates and dilemmas facing contemporary audience researchers.

17

On Alcohol and the Mystique of Media Effects
Andrew Tudor

From J. Cook and M. Lewington (eds.), *Images of alcoholism* (BFI/Alcohol Education Centre 1979)

In this first short extract, which introduces the section, Tudor provides what he calls a 'potted history' of research into media audiences. He identifies four key periods which, he argues, have been characterised by particular forms of research, concern and distinctive ways of conceptualising media audiences. As he suggests, the study of media audiences has historically been dominated from its earliest stages by a number of ingrained and publicly recurrent assumptions and ideas concerning the negative, anti-social effects of exposure to diverse forms of media output. The historical map which he sketches in what follows indicates a general shift from perspectives which asked 'what do the media do to people?' to those which by contrast have reversed the question and ask 'what do people do to/with the media?' In the study of media audiences, their social and cultural contexts, and their consumption of the increasing ranges of media forms and output available to them, this is a pivotal move of great significance. The reading thus provides a useful historical foundation and overview from which to approach and work through the rest of this section on audiences and reception.

It has long been claimed that the media can encourage people into acts that they would otherwise not consider and into beliefs that they would otherwise not espouse.

[...]

[I]t is still widely claimed that the mass media are responsible for much ... that is wrong in our society, a belief given constant currency by the media themselves. Thus we periodically find ourselves embroiled in what Stan Cohen has called 'moral panics': times at which the news-media, in particular, amplify certain topics into issues of apparently enormous public concern.[1] When such 'panics' focus on the role of the media themselves (where violence and sex are the favourite topics) they presuppose the truth of the view that the media effect us simply and directly, whatever our individual commitments and characters.

I find that hard to accept. Although the media are certainly not guiltless, they do not cause us to act in specific ways or to believe in certain things simply by virtue of the fact of their media presentation. The influence that the media can exert over social behaviour cannot be understood in such simple terms. Yet, in public discussion we persist in talking about media effects as if they are well understood, although remarkably few effects studies could be said to have conclusively demonstrated anything at all. To understand how that has come to be so, and to consider the alternatives ..., it is necessary to know something of the history of media research. It is a large topic, and there are a number of useful summaries available; here I shall limit myself to something of a potted history.[2] For convenience I divide it into four periods: 1925–1940; 1940–1960; 1960–1970; and 1970 onward.

On media research

(i) 1925–1940

It was in this period that the mass audience for cinema and radio expanded beyond all expectations, a development which in consequence occasioned a good deal of public discussion. Much argument revolved around the adverse effects movies were presumed to be having upon children and upon certain classes of adult who, it was implied, were less discriminating than more distanced observers of the cultural scene. Often that concern found highly moralistic expression (the Legion of Decency were responsible for the 1934 Production Code) taking for granted that the movies did indeed have unfortunate effects. In that respect, of course, the pattern remains the same today. Organisations like the National Viewers and Listeners Association still start by assuming media effects, even though the accumulated evidence of half-a-century of research hardly permits such simple generalisations.

In the thirties, however, there was no accumulation of research, and it was as a result of concern about the effects of motion pictures upon children and adolescents that there emerged the first major systematic attempt to assess the impact of the movies. These researches were collectively known as the Payne Fund Studies, and ultimately reported in a dozen volumes covering topics as varied as attitude change, emotional responses, effects on sleep patterns, and juvenile delinquency. Some were based on experiments, some on survey work, yet others on extended interviews. Not surprisingly, given their assumptions, they came down on the side of those who believed that the cinema was having serious effects (*Our Movie Made Children* ran the title of the popular summary volume) and they generally emphasised adverse effects rather than beneficial ones.[3]

Of course their conclusions now need serious qualification. Several of the studies are methodologically suspect, and most of them suffered from their emphasis on individual effects at the cost of neglecting the social contexts in which the movies featured. In that, however, they followed the characteristic thinking of the period. These years saw the beginning of a development of a view of modern society – later to be christened Mass Society – in which the mass media were conceived to be undermining, even replacing, traditional patterns of social relations. People in mass society, it was suggested, were becoming isolated anonymous automatons – reflex products of the media. It was an image of social life that dovetailed neatly with the idea that the media affected people directly, regardless of the socio-cultural world in which they lived, and it was this account that was to dominate thinking about the media for almost thirty years.

(ii) 1940–1960

By the mid-fifties the Mass Society theory was at its most influential, an unquestionable and unquestioned framework. The essence of the view is well expressed in this passage from C. Wright Mills:

> (1) the media tell the man in the mass who he is – they give him identity; (2) they tell him what he wants to be – they give him aspirations; (3) they tell him how to get that way – they give him technique; and (4) they tell him how to feel that way even when he is not – they give him escape.[4]

To all intents and purposes society was now Mass Society, and the process of communication a one-way hypodermic injection into the vein of the body politic. Whoever they were, wherever they were, the media of mass communication affected all its uncritical consumers equally.

Yet even in this, the finest hour of the Mass Society researches, there was work in progress which would ultimately render the master image suspect. The war had generated considerable interest in propaganda and, especially in America, there were attempts to assess the effects of different sorts of propaganda material.[5] The net result was increasing recognition that the 'effect' of a particular item was not a simple linear consequence of the content of the item itself. Selective perception (perception conditioned by the predispositions of audience members) proved far more important than Mass Society theory suggested. Researchers found people perversely able to interpret what they saw or heard in line with their own already established beliefs; they were rarely passive recipients of media messages. Nor were they the social isolates, the anonymous 'faces in the crowd' of the fifties. Mass society had not replaced localised group structure with a world of isolated individuals – easy game for the carnivorous media. Social life had changed, certainly, but groups still existed, people still interacted. The media reached them, if at all, via a network of social relations; it may have been different to traditional patterns, but it wasn't necessarily inferior.[6]

By the end of the fifties such deviations from the orthodoxy were demanding more and more attention. Though the dominant perspective still emphasised direct effects on individual subjects, there was now a growing body of research which, at the very least, was inconclusive about media effects.

(iii) 1960–1970

It was during these ten years that media researchers recognised that their failure to arrive at convincing findings was a result of the way in which they had conceptualised 'effects' rather than a failing in research technique. In 1960 a major review of the current state of effects research could put it no stronger than this: 'mass communication does not ordinarily serve as a necessary and sufficient cause of audience effects, but rather functions through a nexus of mediating factors'.[7] The problem now was to establish the mediating factors and so generate a new and less restrictive model of the process of mass communication. All the time and money invested in traditional effects research had produced only confusion.

Recognising the need to rethink the problem, however, was not the same as rethinking it. A new understanding of the relation between media and society was not immediately forthcoming; understandably, researchers first tried modifications of existing approaches. The so-called 'laissez-faire' view became popular (particularly among those working in the media) in which the media were no longer seen to play the manipulative role allocated to them in the Mass Society theories. Instead, they were said to provide a wide range of cultural materials from which people chose what best suited them. In a real sense the people were 'given what they want'. The school of research most closely related to this rationalisation was dubbed the 'uses and gratifications' approach. Audiences were studied from the point of view of the *use* they made of media products to gratify particular needs: the emphasis being on the active audience which avoided the traditional passivity and isolation assumptions. Descendants of that style of research still thrive, and have indeed arrived at a richer understanding of the social-psychological functions of the media. But in recent years yet another model of media effects has begun to emerge, this time asking a different set of questions and in more general social terms.

(iv) 1970 onward

Perhaps the easiest way to appreciate the change is to contrast the traditional 'effects' emphasis with some of the common features of more recent perspectives. The old effects studies focused on specified effects on individuals who, if not in experimentally simulated isolation, were selected so as to minimise the impact of their individuality and social background. In its crudest versions this approach produced almost no serious evidence of media effects. In the hands of more imaginative researchers it did produce some evidence, but even then the effects thus isolated were highly mediated and barely identifiable within the conventional before/after methodology. Even on the most extensively researched topic, screen violence, the modest results of effects studies could hardly be generalised beyond laboratory restrictions.[8]

To this day researchers can rarely agree on the precise significance of television and movie violence. Yet common sense urges that all those violent battles and chases must be of some significance; if traditional effects studies can tell us little about it, then what can? It is in answer to that sort of question that some recent work has emphasised what I shall call the 'cultural effect'. On screen violence, for instance, this leads to two key assertions. First, that what is at issue is not simply the incidence of violence, but also the various contexts in which it features. Thus, in analysing representations of violence in the media we would need to ask *detailed* questions about the kinds of narrative in which it features, about the stereotypes and character typifications to which it relates, and about the media-constructed 'worlds' in which it appears. This, in combination with systematic audience analysis, would lead us to a much better understanding of the meaning media violence has for those who see it. Secondly, that it is not the single before/after effect which is significant, but the more general consequences of patterned repetition. Hence the well known 'desensitisation' argument: the claim that constant exposure to media violence desensitises us to the real thing. Behind that lies the more general claim that repeated patterns of action, familiar narratives or typical images can be significant in ways not immediately discernable to those concerned with effects at an individual level.

I have called this the 'cultural effects' approach because it leads us to ask how the world-views and stereotypes found in the media affect the cultural frameworks we use to understand our everyday world. The media provide us with a sort of 'cultural reservoir' which, directly and indirectly, influences what is taken for granted in our society. By providing us with the terms within which we comprehend the world around us, the media tend along with other agencies actually to constitute that world. It's a very different emphasis to that found in the traditional concept of 'effects', and it leads to very different styles of research. Such analysis would, for instance, require a far more comprehensive and systematic understanding of media representations themselves (and the 'languages' in which they are cast) as well as demanding that we conceive the media as articulators of our cultures rather than as sources of individual effects. Four decades of effects research have not delivered the goods. That does not mean – as some have suggested – that the media have no effects. It means that the effects that they do have are not those which researchers have traditionally sought. The virtue of the cultural effects approaches (and there are many different variants currently available) is that they take this failing of media research seriously, and try to develop a new analysis which will overcome it.

On cultural effects

What sorts of questions, then, should one be asking? In general I think there are two major areas to which we must pay attention: they might be termed 'world construction' and 'world maintenance'.[9]

(i) World construction
Here we are dealing primarily with learning or socialisation and hence particularly with the impact of the media on children and adolescents. To them the media offer an almost infinitely expandable peer group, a formidable addition to family, school, and friends, through which ways of understanding the world and of mapping its features are provided along with dramatic models of what will count as appropriate behaviour. Note that this isn't necessarily a consciously articulated process; these are aspects of our lives that, in the very

social nature of things, we come to take for granted. Such socialisation involves first learning how to act in society, and then unlearning the fact that this was a lesson in the first place. So it is not the most obvious questions I am proposing here – what effects will the violence in this movie have on an audience of 14 year olds? – but rather: if coercive forms of social interaction are repeatedly shown to be the norm and to be functional for the individual 'hero', will resort to coercion become an established part of our culture and hence naturalised, made an unquestionable feature of 'human nature'? Over time we do learn frameworks from the media, ways of seeing. And when we have learned them we conveniently forget that they are learned. They come to be seen as 'common sense' or 'what everybody knows'. They are no longer recognised for what they are: partial, learned frameworks which relate to particular interests and generate particular points of view. Instead, they become the constants of our cognitive processes, the fundamental assumptions on which we rest our sense of an ordered social life. In that way they become part of the very constitution of the world as we see it.

(ii) World maintenance

For adults, whose basic frameworks are already established, the problem is to legitimate or maintain the world as they see it. Accordingly, what we choose to watch or read – itself limited severely by what is made available to us – helps to define a tacit range of consensus, setting the boundaries of our toleration by labelling as deviant certain roles, attitudes, and activities. It isn't necessarily a matter of conspiracy, though it may be. In large part those who control the media are as much captives of past learning as we are; they can, in all honesty, maintain their own claims to integrity and independence while still maintaining us in our basic conceptions of the world. Indeed, they are almost obliged to do so. If they are to be intelligible to so many of us they cannot step too far beyond the bounds of what we will accept. Their trade lies in articulating a common culture, and we select that which best fits our conceptions and requirements. But, and it must be emphasised, we can only select from what is there. It is in this respect that the media act as a cultural reservoir. Their limitations are also our limitations, and there is a real sense in which something not provided for in a culture becomes unthinkable. Thus, in research, as well as establishing what the media *do* say, we must also ask about what they don't say, about what is simply absent from the reservoir of conceptions they provide. For instance, a great deal can be learned about media representations of women by asking about the many ways in which they are *not* portrayed, itself a reflection of the restrictions on how they actually are portrayed.

Notes

1. Stan Cohen, *Folk Devils and Moral Panics* (London, 1972). The moral panic that interests Cohen here is that surrounding the confrontations between mods and rockers in the mid-sixties.

2. See, for example, J. T. Klapper, *The Effects of Mass Communication* (New York, 1960); Roger L. Brown, 'Approaches to the Historical Development of Mass Media Studies', in Jeremy Tunstall, (ed.), *Media Sociology* (London, 1970); Denis McQuail, 'The Influence and Effects of Mass Media', in James Curran, Michael Gurevitch and Janet Woollacott, (eds.), *Mass Communication and Society* (London, 1977). And many others.

3. Many volumes of the Payne Fund Studies have now been reprinted by the Arno Press of New York. Perhaps the most interesting is the volume by Herbert Blumer, *Movies and Conduct* (New York, 1935).

4. C. Wright Mills, *The Power Elite* (New York, 1959), p. 314.

5. The best known of the work on propaganda was probably that conducted in the American Soldier researches and reported in Carl Hovland, Arthur Lumsdaine and Fred D. Sheffield, *Experiments in Mass Communications* (New York, 1949). But there was also a great deal of less well known work.

6. The responsibility for this 'rediscovery of the primary group' is usually attributed to Elihu Katz and Paul F. Lazarsfeld in their study *Personal Influence* (Glencoe, Ill., 1955).

7. Klapper, *The Effects of Mass Communication*.

8. For an excellent short summary of work in this area see André Glucksmann, *Violence on the Screen* (London, 1971).

9. These terms owe something to the work of Peter Berger. Especially Peter Berger and Thomas Luckman, *The Social Construction of Reality* (Harmondsworth, 1967), and Peter Berger, *The Sacred Canopy* (New York, 1967). However, I do not intend them to carry the whole apparatus of Berger's style of work.

Questions

1　Summarise the principal characteristics and distinctive features of the four historical periods which Tudor outlines in the extract. Can you think of any examples taken from recent debates concerning the media in contemporary settings which are relevant to his discussion?

2　Research and draw up an historical map of the growth and development of media audiences, from the medieval period to the present. How and in what major ways have audiences and forms of media consumption changed?

3　Compare and contrast the characteristic forms of audience relationships established by people with any two different media, for instance newspapers and films, or videos and radio.

Further reading

Curran, J. and Gurevitch, M. (eds.) 1991: *Mass media and society*. London: Edward Arnold.

Jensen, K.B. and Rosengren, K.E. 1990: Five traditions in search of the audience. *European Journal of Communication* 5, 207–38.

Lury, C. 1992: Popular culture and the mass media. In Bocock, R. and Thompson, K. (eds.), *Social and cultural forms of modernity*. Cambridge: Polity Press.

McQuail, D. 1994: *Mass communication theory: an introduction*. London: Sage.

Morley, D. 1992: *Television, audiences and cultural studies.* London: Routledge. (See Section 5, reading 34.)

O'Sullivan, T., Dutton, B. and Rayner, P. 1994: *Studying the media: an introduction.* London: Arnold.

18

The Television and Delinquency Debate
Graham Murdock and Robin McCron

From *Screen Education* 30, 51–67 (Spring 1979)

One of the most fiercely debated areas in media research has been that of 'effects', and in particular the potentially *harmful* effects that various media might have on audiences. This debate has been brought dramatically into the public domain on a number of occasions, and has gained a particular intensity in recent years following the murder of the toddler James Bulger in February 1993 and renewed calls for government legislation to ban so-called 'video nasties'.

As we saw in Section 1, the media have long been credited with having a powerful influence on people, and early research – coinciding with political propaganda movements – stressed the potential of the media for persuading and manipulating audiences. But despite the fact that more recent research has moved away from a notion of passive audiences susceptible to media messages, to a more sophisticated view of audiences as active *users* of media material who cannot be viewed in the isolation of their social contexts, the notion of all-powerful media that can persuade, manipulate and corrupt remains strong. Thus, the media has persistently been held responsible for declining moral standards generally (particularly among young people) and blamed for a number of specific 'copy-cat' crimes.

As this reading emphasises, worries about rising crime and violence in society have a long history, with a marked inclination to blame popular entertainment. Public outrage tends to become even more focused with the introduction of each new media innovation, and one can chart this history from the popularity of 'Penny Dreadful' comics in the nineteenth century to current fears about unregulated information and images on satellite or cable TV and the Internet. Such anxieties frequently reflect deeper concerns about social change, and declining standards of behaviour among children have been a recurrent focus of attention.

The reading notes that two broad perspectives have dominated this area of study: the *psychologistic* approach, which assumes a direct link between exposure to deviant images and imitative behaviour; and the sociological or *relational* approach, which emphasises the social and cultural contexts within which deviant activities are embedded. The former presents media output as the principal cause of aggressive and deviant behaviour and its methods are primarily those of the controlled laboratory experiment, while the latter sees the media as peripheral and relies largely on ethnographic techniques (interview, observation etc.) to consider the subject in relation to, and in the context of, his or her social background and class position.

Murdock and McCron criticise both perspectives for their rather narrow and mutually exclusive approaches. While acknowledging that the sociological perspective has produced some of the best empirical work on causes of deviance in Britain in the postwar period, they are nonetheless critical of ethnographers such as Paul Willis for failing to address explicitly the possible impact of media on behaviour: specifically, that of television viewing on criminal activity among juveniles. But they are far more condemnatory of the opposing perspective – as represented by the work of Belson and of Eysenck and Nias (see the 'Further Reading' section of this reading) – which, it is argued, is inadequate in explaining delinquency because the researchers tend to start out with the premise that there *is* a direct causal link between television viewing and violent behaviour, and set out to prove it, rather than researching possible causes of juvenile crime and asking how television *might* fit into the overall picture. The insistence on removing television (or any other medium) from the social and cultural context of the viewer and analysing its impact in isolation from other important variables is one of the major criticisms that has been levelled at psychologistic and laboratory-based effects research over the last 20 years.

Despite the criticism of such methods, which is part of a more widespread rejection of early research into 'cause and effects', these types of study continue to have credence in a number of quarters. Thus, while Media Studies academics in the UK maintain that there is no substantial evidence for a link between screen violence and real-life violence, and that this is not the most important starting point for any research into why some types of violence are on the increase in society, popular opinion – fuelled by insistence from many psychologists and public figures in the UK and America that there *is* an indisputable link – continues to uphold the view that it is a matter of 'common sense' that society has become more violent since the advent of television and video, and therefore the two phenomena are 'naturally' connected. Belson, and Eysenck and Nias were widely quoted in press reports following the publication of *Video violence and the protection of children* by child psychologist Elizabeth Newson in 1994, which itself was a response to the killing of James Bulger. For further discussion of this case see reading 19.

Roots of reaction

> What shall we do with our juvenile delinquents? is a question often asked, but as yet most unsatisfactorily and variously answered ... prisons multiply and are better regulated; Juvenile Offenders Acts are passed and boys whipped by the hundred. The schoolmaster walks abroad enlightening our youth on Geography, History, the Steam Engine and Social Science ... And still, in spite of all, the vexing fact of a large amount of juvenile delinquency remains – and the young offender gains ground upon us, the plague of the policeman, the difficulty of the magistrate, a problem to the statesman, and a sorrow to the philanthropist.[1]

This passage comes at the beginning of an article on delinquency which appeared in the *Edinburgh Review* for 1851. Apart from a few dated phrases, it could easily be a recent editorial in the *Daily Telegraph* or *Daily Mail*. Over a hundred years on, commentators are still asking why, in spite of all the reforms and changes, 'a large amount of juvenile delinquency remains', and they are still coming up with the same answers. Then, as now, many observers saw a strong and direct connection between the rising adolescent crime rate and the growth of popular entertainment featuring scenes of sex and violence. Back in 1851, concern was focused on the cheap theatres which were springing up in the working class areas of the large towns and attracting a sizeable adolescent audience. The *Edinburgh Review* was in no doubt that these shows, with their suggestive sketches and vignettes of violent crimes, were making a major contribution to the increase in immorality and deviance they saw among working class youth.

> One powerful agent for the depraving of the boyish classes of our towns and cities is to be found in the cheap shows and theatres, which are so specially opened and arranged for the attraction and ensnaring of the young. When for three-pence a boy can procure some hours of vivid enjoyment from exciting scenery, music and acting ... it is not to be wondered at that the boy who is led on to haunt them becomes rapidly corrupted and demoralised, and seeks to be the doer of the infamies which have interested him as a spectator.[2]

This style of argument rests in three basic propositions: (1) that deviant imagery in popular entertainment is a powerful contributory cause of delinquency, (2) that there is a direct relationship between exposure to deviant images and involvement in delinquency – the higher the exposure, the more the involvement, and (3) that since imagery is connected to action through psychological processes such as imitation, explaining subsequent delinquency is primarily a problem for psychology and can be adequately tackled without looking at the social and cultural contexts within which delinquency is embedded. This psychologistic approach has tended to find its professional academic expression in controlled laboratory experiments which deliberately isolate subjects from their social life. As we shall see, it has been enormously influential and continues to dominate the current debate on the detrimental effects of television.

From the outset, this approach has been vigorously and consistently challenged by sociological perspectives which place delinquency firmly in the context of social relations and class structure. In the same year as the article just quoted came out, 1851, Mary Carpenter published her influential book on juvenile offenders, in which she stressed the need 'to view the child, *not only in his individual position, but in his relation to the class among which he is placed*'.[3] Versions of this relational perspective have underpinned a long tradition of ethnographic studies in which researchers have tried to unpack the dynamics of delinquency using a combination of informal interviews and direct observations. This approach was pioneered by the great Victorian investigative journalists like Henry Mayhew and Clarence Rook, and later taken up and developed by academic sociologists. These studies provide a very different slant on the influence of the mass media. In the first place they present the media as peripheral rather than central, as a minor contributory cause at most. Secondly, they reject the notion of direct influence and see adolescents as actively selecting and interpreting media material in line with their pre-existing patterns of social and cultural involvement.

The opposition between these two perspectives – the psychologistic and the relational – was finally cemented during the debate on the impact of the movies in the 1920s and 1930s, when for the first time opinion on both sides was backed with evidence gleaned from academic research. On the one side stood the psychologists, including the formidable figure of Sir Cyril Burt, influential advocate of intelligence testing and one of the founding fathers of academic psychology in Britain. He weighed in with *The Young Delinquent*, which concluded that as causes of delinquency, 'psychological factors are supreme both in number and strength over all the rest'.[4] Drawing on six hundred odd pages of research results, he ranked the various contributory causes in order of importance. 'Specific instincts', 'emotional instability' and 'intellectual disabilities' all came in the top six, closely followed by 'detrimental interests such as a passion for the cinema' at number seven. 'Poverty and its concomitants' came next to last at number fourteen.[5] Meanwhile across the Atlantic in Chicago, home of Al Capone and one of the capitals of violent crime, a team of sociologists from the university were developing a relational perspective in a series of twelve studies of the movies' impact on youth. For them, differences in response mainly resulted not from individual differences in intelligence or personality, but from variations in 'the social background of viewers' which provided 'the basis for selection and interpretation'. The same motion picture, they argued, 'may exert influence in diametrically opposed directions' depending on 'the social milieu, the attitudes and interests of the observer'.[6]

As the locus of debate has shifted from cinema to television, so the gap between the two major perspectives has widened. The arrival of television as a mass entertainment medium in the mid-fifties coincided with a marked rise in the juvenile crime rate, particularly for violent crime, on both sides of the Atlantic. This conjuncture generated two very different research responses. Sociologists of deviance more or less ignored the possible impact of television and continued to look for the social and cultural roots of teenage deviance and their relation to patterns of deprivation and disadvantage. Following Albert Cohen's path-breaking book *Delinquent Boys* in 1955, a great deal of this work has concentrated on observing groups of teenage boys in school and out on the streets. The response of psychologists on the other hand was almost the complete opposite. They took the possible link between television and delinquency as a central research topic and pursued it through controlled laboratory experiments which deliberately detached subjects from their everyday social interactions.

The observational approach has produced some of the best British empirical sociology of the last two decades, from the work of David Downes and David

Hargreaves in the sixties to the recent studies of Howard Parker, Paul Willis and others. Although this material offers an implicit account of the impact of television it does not address the question directly. The relationship between the mass media and deviance has become a prominent topic of sociological research, but in the context of labelling and amplification studies which focus on the way in which media presentations of deviance structure the responses of control agencies and the population at large. This work has been immensely valuable in opening up the debate and in raising important questions about the relationship between coercive and ideological control. At the same time it has meant that the possible links between television viewing and initial deviance have been more or less totally ignored or dismissed as a pseudo-problem, a figment of media publicity. This, together with the general lack of interest in the question shown by ethnographers, has left a sizeable gap in the sociological literature – a gap that is currently being occupied by the opposing perspective. Recent months have seen the publication of two important books on television's impact on social violence: *Sex, Violence and the Media* by Hans Eysenck and D. K. Nias, and William Belson's *Television Violence and the Adolescent Boy*.[7] Both of them received a lot of publicity and the psychologistic perspective they promote increasingly commands a central place in academic and official thinking. It is symptomatic that they both ignore the sociology of deviance, Eysenck by design, Belson by default. They can do this because sociologists have themselves dismissed the question of television and violence by slipping around it or displacing the debate elsewhere. If you take a broad theoretical view of delinquency then the possible impact of television is not a particularly important issue. But equally, given their centrality to current debates, the evidence and arguments by Belson and Eysenck should be taken seriously and confronted head-on.

Decontextualising delinquency

Eysenck and Nias begin by claiming that 'the problem in question, and the methods of empirical enquiry, are psychological'.[8] This definition of the field has several advantages for them. It enables them to dismiss more or less the entire corpus of research in criminology and sociology as inadequate and irrelevant. It also bolsters their general professional claim that since psychologists are the only people with the relevant competence and expertise they are the only ones entitled to scarce research funds in a period of cut-backs. For most of the book this streak of blatant self-interest is concealed behind a façade of disinterested scientificity, but it occasionally becomes explicit:

> Non-psychologists may have a supportive role to play in research, particularly when there is concern about institutional problems and policies, but without the necessary training in statistics, methodology and especially psychological theory *they should never be asked to design or control the research projects.*[9]

The book, then, is rather less than the comprehensive review of relevant literature it claims to be and rather more of a promotion job for psychology in general and the trends favoured by Eysenck and Nias in particular. The more adventurous research in social psychology and symbolic interactionism hardly gets a look in. The emphasis is very firmly on laboratory experimentation and on the brand of personality theory that has made Eysenck's professional name.

Laboratory experiments have been very widely used in research on television and violence and most follow the same basic design. You take a group of people and divide them into two (sometimes three) sub-groups, either by assigning them at random so that everyone has an equal chance of ending up in either group, or by trying to match them so that both groups have the same basic composition. You might, for example, want to ensure that both groups had an equal number of men and women, middle and working class subjects, introverts and extroverts, or whatever factors you felt were pertinent. Both groups are then shown a piece of film. The so-called 'experimental' group is shown a sequence featuring violence (almost always inter-personal) while the 'control' group watch a piece showing 'neutral' or co-operative behaviour. The responses of both groups are then measured. A variety of techniques have been tried from charting physiological changes during viewing (blood pressure, sweating and so on) to observing social behaviour directly afterwards to see if subjects behave more aggressively. Since other relevant factors affecting response have supposedly been controlled or equalised, any differences between the groups are attributed to differences in the experimental stimulus – the film they have just seen. If the people in the group which has watched the violent sequence are more aggressive than the 'controls' afterwards, this difference is put down to the effect of the film. With a few notable exceptions, the experimental studies have tended to produce evidence of direct and powerful effects. However, they are open to criticism on several counts.

First, there are questions to be asked about the procedures employed. For example, how far are the differences in response attributable to the films and how far are they due to the subjects' willingness to please the experimenters by fulfilling their expectations? How far do the sorting procedures really control the influence of 'external' factors? Matching people by age, sex and social background, for example, in no way equalises the impact of these factors on their consciousness and behaviour. In addition, there is often a very considerable jump from the stimulus shown on the film to the response that is being measured. Take the well-known experiment by Mussen and Rutherford for example.[10] In this, some children saw a cartoon of a weed trying to choke a flower while others watched a film of a frog and a duck playing co-operatively. Afterwards members of both groups were asked if they would like to play with a balloon or burst it. The first group were more likely to express a desire to burst the balloon. Given that this response is only very tenuously related to the behaviour depicted in the film it is difficult to accept the results as firm evidence for a direct connection between the two. Certainly several alternative explanations suggest themselves. It is even more difficult to take it as evidence for a relationship between television and social violence. Yet Eysenck and Nias are prepared to add this study to their list of 'good' evidence without commenting or raising queries. How then do they get from Mussen's marauding weed to street fights and muggings? Their answer is that wanting to burst a balloon and knocking down old ladies both stem from the same basic psychological processes. For them,

> There seems no reason why mild forms of aggression should not be subject to the same laws as more extreme forms. We do not have one set of theories of mild aggression and another set for serious.[11]

This approach conveniently ignores the fact that violent behaviour is always embedded in wider patterns of social and cultural relations, ranging from the brief encounters between experimenters and their subjects to the continuing relations of everyday life. This does not mean that psychological processes and individual differences are irrelevant or unimportant. But it does mean that since they work in and through social relations they cannot be adequately studied in isolation from them. Yet this is precisely what laboratory experiments are designed to do.

Notes

1. 'Juvenile Delinquency', *Edinburgh Review* (1851), pp. 403–4.
2. 'Juvenile Delinquency', p. 409.
3. Mary Carpenter, *Reformatory Schools for the Children of the Dangerous and Perishing Classes and Juvenile Offenders* (facsimile edn) (Ilford, The Woburn Press, 1968), p. 77 (our emphasis).
4. Sir Cyril Burt, *The Young Delinquent* (London, University of London Press, 1925), p. 607.
5. Burt, *The Young Delinquent*, p. 606.
6. Herbert Blumer and Philip M. Hauser, *Movies, Delinquency and Crime* (New York, Macmillan, 1933), pp. 201–2.
7. H. J. Eysenck and D. K. Nias, *Sex, Violence and the Media* (London, Maurice Temple Smith, 1978); William A. Belson, *Television Violence and the Adolescent Boy* (Farnborough, Saxon House, 1978).
8. Eysenck and Nias, *Sex, Violence and the Media*, p. 10.
9. Eysenck and Nias, *Sex, Violence and the Media*, pp. 265–6 (our emphasis).
10. P. Mussen and E. Rutherford, 'Effects of Aggressive Cartoons on Children's Aggressive Play', *Journal of Abnormal and Social Psychology*, 62 (1961), pp. 461–4.
11. Eysenck and Nias, *Sex, Violence and the Media*, pp. 74–5.

Questions

1 Summarise Murdock and McCron's main criticisms of psychologistic studies. Given that much of our understanding of the media has been dominated by American psychological 'effects' models, what would you define as the main

problems with the tradition and how can we best understand this dominance?

2   A common view among many effects researchers is that concerns over new media frequently reflect or crystallise deeper anxieties in periods of social change. For example, some reactions to radio and cinema in the 1930s reflected fears of change associated with growing industrialisation and mass production techniques, increasing urbanisation, the rise of extremist political movements etc. How could this argument be applied to *contemporary* concerns about the effects of the media?

3   The media is blamed for causing almost exclusively *negative* effects, not just desensitisation to violence, but also, for example, the greed and dissatisfaction with one's consumer power which game shows might illicit. But can media content also be said to have *positive* effects?

Further reading

Bandura, A. and Walters, R. 1963: *Social learning and personality development*. New York: Holt, Rinehart & Winston.

Belson, W. 1978: *Television violence and the adolescent boy*. Farnborough: Saxon House.

Cumberbatch, G., *et al.* 1987: *The portrayal of violence on British television: a content analysis*. London: BBC Data Publications.

Eysenck, H. and Nias, B. 1978: *Sex, violence and the media*. London: Paladin.

Gauntlett, D. 1995: *Moving experiences: understanding television's influences and effects*. Luton: John Libbey.

Hodge, B. and Tripp, D. 1986: *Children and television*. Cambridge: Polity Press.

Klapper, J. 1960: *The effects of mass communication*. New York: Free Press.

Noble, G. 1975: *Children in front of the small screen*. London: Constable.

Pearson, G. 1983: *Hooligan: a history of respectable fears*. London: Macmillan.

Willis, P. 1978: *Learning to labour*. Farnborough: Saxon House.

19

In Defence of 'Video Nasties'
Julian Petley

From *British Journalism Review* 5(3), 52–7 (1994).

The previous extract was written in an age when *television content* was under scrutiny and 'cop shows' such as *The Sweeney* and *Target* were being blamed for declining moral standards and a general desensitisation to violence by groups such as the National Viewers and Listeners Association (of which Mary Whitehouse was vociferous chairperson). Julian Petley's article, written 15 years later, is concerned with two specific cases – the murders of toddler James Bulger and teenager Suzanne Capper in 1993. Much of the reporting on these cases was characterised by attributing blame to violent *videos* (especially *Child's Play 3*).

In particular, the trial of the two children 'caught on camera' and subsequently convicted of killing James Bulger, became a catalyst for widespread and powerfully expressed anxieties about the presumed effects of violent media content on the young, and there were a number of calls for greater controls in the form of more stringent censorship. These included a proposal by Liberal Democrat MP David Alton to amend the Criminal Justice Bill to enact a ban on the sale and rental of 'video nasties' (already, in fact, legislated for under the Video Recordings Act of 1984). Within this climate a number of films which had been successful at the cinema were denied video certification, while others had their cinema release delayed for several months.

One of the stories given greatest prominence by the media in the aftermath of the Bulger case was the publication of the 'Newson Report' signed by 33 'leading experts', which supported, and indeed purported to provide evidence for, the assumed, common sense view, that there is a direct causal link between screen violence and violence in real life. Petley takes issue with Newson and the newspapers which, in his view, uncritically reported her findings, accusing them of perpetuating a moral panic which they had started in the mid-eighties and trying to find a convenient scapegoat for an incident which could not *easily* be explained away by other means. Once again, at the heart of the fear and indignation expressed by most reporters was the myth of childhood innocence and its corruption by persistent and prolonged exposure to violent video content.

According to most newspapers, Britain is awash with 'video nasties' which are openly available to young children; there is a direct causal link between the video *Child's Play 3* and the murders of James Bulger and Suzanne Capper; academics have at long last recognised the 'obvious' link between screen violence and real-life crime; and the British Board of Film Classification is irresponsibly liberal in its decisions.

In fact, 'video nasties' were outlawed by police action under the Obscene Publications Act even before the Video Recordings Act was passed in 1984; there are no causal links whatsoever between *Child's Play 3* and the Bulger and Capper murders, as the police involved in both cases readily testify; there has been no wholesale U-turn by academics on the vexed question of 'media effects'; and Britain has one of the strictest regimes of film and video censorship in the western world.

So what lies (and that is indeed the operative word) behind the latest example of the 'video nasty' panic, which the press was instrumental in igniting in the early eighties and which with its help has periodically flared into life ever since? The initial impetus clearly lay in attempts to find some sort of explanation for the seemingly inexplicable murder of James Bulger in February 1993. Examine the brutalising, impoverishing and destructive effects of policies carried out in the spirit of the dogma that 'there is no such thing as society'? Not on your life! So step forward the scapegoats: sixties 'permissiveness', 'trendy' teachers, single mothers, the 'underclass' and, of course, the ever-reliable 'video nasty', this last helped into the spotlight by the Bulger trial judge's exceedingly ill-informed and uncalled-for remark that 'it is not for me to pass judgement on their [Jon Venables' and Robert Thompson's] upbringing but I suspect that exposure to violent films may be in part an explanation'.

But there's more to it than that. First of all, there's pure and simple hypocrisy. Our inimitable papers have long excelled at revelling in what they purport to condemn, and their lip-smacking descriptions (or, rather, distortions) of various supposed 'nasties' in the wake of the Bulger and Capper murders were the epitome of this kind of journalism, which has now reached such depths that it's almost impossible to parody. Almost, but not quite, as *Private Eye* demonstrated:

> Once again the Daily Gnome has forced a major change in Government policy and made the powers that be see sense. Our week-long series of pieces on the top 100 disgusting videos currently available was a masterpiece of campaigning journalism. Only the Daily Gnome gave a full plot summary and detailed description of each obscene and depraved action on every one of these revolting videos. Only the Daily Gnome published graphic stills of the sort of corrupting filth that is getting into our homes every day. And only the Daily Gnome is offering a cut-price video compilation of all the most twisted and most vile moments of the videos that we have now successfully curbed.

Circulation wars also played their part here too. The *Mirror*, the *Telegraph* and *The Independent*, then, as now, fighting off predatory pricing by the Murdoch papers, all had cause to add to the attack on *Child's Play 3*, since it had been shown twice by Murdoch's BSkyB during the Bulger murder trial in November 1993. (A third screening, which would have been broadcast after the trial, was cancelled – thereby, of course, only adding to the myth that the film had played a role in the murder.) Thus a sarcastic Diary entry in *The Independent* of 26 November under the headline 'Outraged of Wapping', a *Telegraph* article on the same day headed 'Sky drops film James's killers may have seen' (even though Sky's actions take up only two of the story's 17 paragraphs), and an editorial in the same day's *Mirror* which argued that 'such violence is not only available from the local video shop. It is pumped into millions of homes virtually every night on satellite television. The rules which govern BBC and ITV do not apply to satellite. They can show what they like, how they like, when they like. And they do. Failure to control their output has been due to Government cowardice. It does not want to upset powerful friends.'

Thirdly, this latest twist in the 'nasty' saga gave the press a marvellous chance to attack another of its favourite targets: 'intellectuals'. This came about because, on 31 March 1994 under the front page headline 'U-Turn Over Video Nasties', the *Evening Standard* purported to reveal that 'Britain's top psychologists today confess that they had got it wrong in denying a link between video nasties and real life violence'. This was meat and drink to the populist press. The next day's *Mirror* branded them as 'Vidiots' for taking so long to reach the 'obvious', 'common sense' conclusion, the *Daily Mail* complained of a 'tardy conversion' and the ever reliable Peter McKay in *The*

Sunday Times claimed that 'the idea that we possess 25 "top" psychologists is black comedy. You might as well talk about 25 top three-card trick operators.' Meanwhile, the *Telegraph* accused those academics who remained sceptical about the link of being guilty of a *'trahison de clercs'*.

In fact, there was both more and less to this story than the papers realised, or cared to admit. Firstly, the document to which the *Standard*, followed by other papers, referred had been signed not simply by psychologists but by psychiatrists and paediatricians as well. However, of the total of 33 signatories (not 25 as the *Standard* claimed) only three had ever spoken publicly on the topic before. The story was thus seriously misleading on at least two counts: certainly no 'U-turn' had taken place. But not only did the papers fail to point out that not one media specialist had signed the document (thereby rather vitiating the papers' claims that it represented 'expert' opinion) but, worse still, no-one noted (or cared, perhaps) that the document has been written by Professor Elizabeth Newson of Nottingham University at the specific invitation of the MP David Alton, to be used as evidence to support his Criminal Justice Bill amendment to tighten up film and video censorship! Only Richard Boston in his video column in *The Guardian* went into this crucial matter of the document's genesis and *raison d'être* in any significant detail.

Lobby

Even more seriously, at the time of writing not one paper has thought it worth revealing that the Alton amendment was the result of a highly organised religious lobby. Tucked away in a couple of *Daily Telegraph* and *Sunday Telegraph* pieces about Alton I came across references to something called the Movement for Christian Democracy and its newspaper *The Christian Democrat*. As I could find neither in the London phone directory I rang the SPCK bookshop and got a number; this I then rang, and asked them to send me details of the Movement and a copy of *The Christian Democrat*. Hardly a feat of investigative journalism, but the literature which I was sent revealed, *inter alia*, that the Movement had raised £13,000 to support its video campaign, that it had instructed a parliamentary draughtsman to draft the amendment to the Criminal Justice Bill, and that it was responsible for gathering the 100,000 signatories on the much-publicised petition supporting the amendment. *The Christian Democrat* for June 1994 trumpets that 'with this, the MCD can be seen as coming of age politically – and can look forward to more successful campaigns', and Alton is quoted as saying that 'this has shown how the MCD really can affect events if it wants to, if it picks its issues, attaches them to Government bills that are going through parliament, campaigns around them'. Some idea of what we can expect is contained in the statement that 'we will now direct our campaign to the anomalies this amendment will create between what may be shown on video and what is shown on satellite, cable and terrestrial TV'. Well, don't say you haven't been warned, but why not by the mainstream press, especially given the rising level of concern about parliamentary lobbying? I suspect it would be a very different story if the MCP turned its undoubted energies to lobbying for a Privacy Bill.

The highly selective nature of press interest in academic research was nicely illustrated a few days after the revelation of the Newson document when the Policy Studies Institute published its long-awaited report into the viewing habits of young offenders. This was funded by the BBFC, BBC, Independent Television Commission and Broadcasting Standards Council. Disappointingly for large sections of the press, the report showed that young offenders do not have significantly different viewing habits from non-offending children of the same age. (One might also note in passing that amongst those offenders who read newspapers, the *Sun* came out as favourite.) The report was totally ignored by most papers – the *Sun* included. Still, it got more coverage than a document signed by 23 media academics (myself included) which questioned the whole basis of Newson's discussion paper and forcefully stated that her conclusions were completely out of kilter with most recent academic research on the media. This was sent to all the same places as the Newson document – and *totally* ignored. Never let the facts get in the way of a good story.

Unable to get over the rather awkward fact that the police officers leading the Bulger and Capper cases had consistently denied that videos, and specifically *Child's Play 3*, had caused the killings, most of the press simply fell back on repeating ad nauseam that there *must* be a link because 'common sense' demands it. There are all sorts of variations of this one basic 'argument' (or, rather, assumption), and from the truly vast number of examples one could cite, two will have to suffice. In *The Times* of 26 November 1993 we get the would-be sophisticated version, dressed up in fancy language: 'To claim that only some indisputable proof of causal link could justify the curtailing of "freedom of expression" is an evasion of an obvious truth: a society that accepts vividly enacted brutality is *ipso facto* making such acts conceivable, and even encouraging the belief that they are commonplace. This is not a matter for proof; it is self-evident.' To which the simple answer is: rubbish. The more populist version is nicely illustrated by Anne Diamond (who else?) in the *Mirror* of 1 December 1993: 'Our gut tells us they *must* have seen the evil doll Chucky. They *must* have loved the film. And they *must* have seen it over and over again, because some of the things they did are almost exact copies of the screenplay.' To which the answer is: no amount of wishful thinking or petulant foot-stamping will alter the fact that there is not a shred of evidence that the Bulger killers watched *Child's Play 3*.

However, we do know that they watched cartoons in their local video shop and that Jon Venables' favourite film was *The Goonies* (this courtesy of the consultant forensic psychiatrist Dr Susan Bailey, who interviewed Venables before his trial). There are no parallels of any significance between the film and the murder of James Bulger; Diamond must have been reading the incredibly distorted press descriptions of the film which tried desperately to draw such parallels. Still, Diamond obviously knows much more about the media than I do; as she puts it: 'God protect us from the "ologists" – because their hackneyed perception is dangerous. I sometimes think that a degree in some sort of "ology" blinds you to common sense. We all know that violence begets violence.' So that's it – now we know. Of course, once upon a time 'everybody knew' that the earth was flat and that the sun revolved around it, that illnesses were caused by 'evil humours' and cured by bleeding, and that misfortunes were the result of witchcraft. But, of course, we're much more intelligent now, and we've got *The Times* and the *Mirror* to prove it.

The problem with 'common sense' assumptions, particularly in such a bleakly anti-intellectual culture as our own, is that, being deeply ingrained into 'folk wisdom' and held particularly dear by the populist press, they're very difficult to challenge effectively. The problem is all the more tricky when those 'common sense' assumptions concern the media. This is because of the commonly held view that since everybody consumes the media then everyone is an 'expert' on it. Thus during the aftermath of the Capper and Bulger trials we had to put up with the likes of Dillie Keane, Roy Hattersley, Lynda Lee Potter and other assorted pundits giving us their 'common sense' views about the alleged effects of the media, and doing so with a totally unwarranted air of expertise and authority to boot. It is simply not the case that because people watch television they are expert on it – although, of course, they're obviously entitled to hold views about it. *Mutatis mutandis*, we all use language but we're not all experts in phonetics, phonology and morphology, or able to debate the finer points of transformational grammar.

Finally, and this is perhaps the most disturbing aspect of the whole affair, it's interesting to note the worrying prevalence of attempts to hitch the 'nasty' bandwagon to now-fashionable ideas about the 'underclass', or the 'undeserving poor' as they used to be called in Victorian times. Unsurprisingly this attempt to de-legitimise the welfare system by blaming the poor for their wretched state had its roots in Reagan's America, but thanks to sustained campaigns by the *Mail*, *The Times* and *Sunday Times* it now has followers on the Tory Right. The link was first made by Bryan Appleyard (who used to work for *The Sunday Times*) in a lengthy piece in *The Independent* on 1 December 1993 in which he asked rhetorically 'would you allow an ill-educated, culturally deprived, unemployable underclass unlimited access to violent pornography?' Then, in a conscious echo of the famous remark about servants in the 1960 Lady Chatterley trial, he goes on to argue that if you do away with censorship 'you don't just get Mapplethorpe for the connoisseur, you also get vicious drivel for the masses. More painfully, you also get unarguably fine films such as *Taxi Driver* and *Goodfellas*, which, if you are honest, you would rather were not watched by certain types of people.' *Reservoir Dogs* is also singled out as a 'brilliant, bloody film that I would prefer not to be seen by the criminal classes (sic) or the mentally unstable or by inadequately supervised children with little else in their lives'. I suppose this is what Thatcherite pundits would proudly call 'thinking the unthinkable'. Personally I prefer the word snobbery. The *Mail* of 18 December, in the wake of the just-concluded Capper trial, was even more 'unthinkable'. Noting that the police had commented on the murderers' 'ordinariness' the *Mail* proclaimed that 'they are the product of a society which tolerates petty crime, the break-up of families and feckless spending. It subsidises and, in many cases, encourages them. It is interesting to note that most of Suzanne's tormentors were on social security. But then those in society who are genuinely out of work but who have savings, do not receive income support. Thus are the prudent penalised while the negligent are nurtured. All this reflects a society showing reckless disregard for the survival of its own decency. An underclass is being created today which is a grave threat to Britain's future. If it is not countered, then we will continue a decline towards lawlessness and degeneracy.' Ah, *now* I understand – it's not video nasties which create sadistic killers, it's the welfare state (or what's left of it).

This kind of 'thinking' re-emerged in April 1994 around the time of the Alton amendment. Thus in *The Sunday Times* of 3 April we find Margaret Driscoll arguing that 'the children most likely to be damaged are those being brought up in sink estates where family values no longer hold sway – the products of the "anything goes" society', whilst a *Times* editorial of 11 April held forth that 'horror-video addiction is part of a socially-disadvantaged sink culture in which lack of parental supervision is endemic'. Meanwhile in the *Mail* two days later the inevitable Lynda Lee Potter shrieked that 'there are thousands of children in this country with fathers they never see and mothers who are lazy sluts. They are allowed to do what they want, when they want. They sniff glue on building sites, scavenge for food and, until now, they were free to watch increasingly horrific videos. By 16 they are disturbed and dangerous.'

Given the way in which the press have consistently demonised horror videos in the wake of the Capper and Bulger murders it's hardly surprising that so many MPs should have lined up behind David Alton. Of course, these are the very last people who should be allowed to legislate about the media: given the ludicrous hours they choose to work they rarely watch TV; and I suspect that most of them have never seen, or probably even heard of, *Psycho* or *Peeping Tom* let alone more recent horror movies. Still, it's altogether fitting that the amendment is to the Criminal Justice Bill, undoubtedly one of the most shameful pieces of legislation ever to be contemplated in Britain. Its intended criminalisation of squatters, travellers, ravers and other Tory hate-objects has been massively facilitated by exactly the same kind of vicious, distorted, hysterical reporting of their activities in the press that has characterised the papers' scapegoating of video in the wake of the Bulger and Capper murders. The recommendations of the recent Royal Commission on

Criminal Justice have been not simply ignored but stood on their heads: clearly when it comes to law-making in Britain today, whether we're talking about videos or anything else that can be hitched up to the Law 'n' Order juggernaut, it is not reason that prevails but the saloon bar pundits of the populist press and the braying mob on the floor of annual Tory Party conferences.

Questions

1   What are the predominant elements in 'common sense' accounts of media effects? How would you challenge the common sense view which has dominated the censorship lobby, that we have become a more violent society since the advent of television and that therefore the two are linked?

2   One of the problems with the way that this debate is carried out seems to be with the definition of violence and what constitutes a 'violent act'. How would *you* define 'violence'? Are there some kinds of violence which are deemed more acceptable for portrayal by the media than others?

3   Carry out your own monitoring of an evening's TV. How many acts of violence and what *kinds* of violence are portrayed, and how would you analyse them in the light of your understanding of the above readings?

4   One of the most common arguments put forward by those who support the causal links thesis is that the media *must* have an effect or advertising would not work. How would you assess the adequacy of this argument?

Further reading

Barker, M. 1984: *The video nasties: freedom and censorship in the media*. London: Pluto Press.

Barker, M. and Petley, J. 1997: *Ill effects: the media violence debate*. London: Routledge.

Barwise, P. and Ehrenberg, A. 1989: *Television and its audience*. London: Sage.

Buckingham, D. 1993: *Children talking television: the making of television literacy*. London: Falmer Press.

Buckingham, D. (ed.) 1993: *Reading audiences: young people and the media*. Manchester: Manchester University Press.

Cumberbatch, G., Maguire, A. and Woods, S. 1993: *Children and video games: an exploratory study*. Aston University. Birmingham: Communications Research Group.

Gunter, B. and McAleer, J. 1990: *Children and television: the one-eyed monster?* London: Routledge.

Liebert, R., Neale, J. and Davidson, E. 1982: *The early window: effects of television on children and youth*. Oxford: Pergamon Press.

Postman, N. 1982: *The disappearance of childhood*. New York: Dell.

20

Looking at *The Sun*: Into the Nineties with a Tabloid and its Readers
Mark Pursehouse

From *Cultural Studies from Birmingham* (Department of Cultural Studies, University of Birmingham 1991)

The following extract has been chosen for two principal reasons. First, it deals with questions about the 'influence' that a particular *newspaper* format – the popular tabloid – might be said to exert over and among its readership. In so doing, it shifts our attention away from screen-based media – film, television, video and recently computer – to consider the *relationships* between other, different media, forms of popular culture and their readers. More specifically, the extract calls into question the extent to which we can think about direct and simple 'effects' resulting from all forms of media exposure or use. We have become used to debates and assumptions about the effects or power of the media in the context of films, videos or television programmes. The preceding readings in this section have served to outline some of the major lines of contending debate, argument and evidence in this respect. We are perhaps less used to arguments about the 'effects' of the popular press. They are less often accused of causing direct effects. However, their coverage of controversial issues and their involvement at the cutting edge of the 'manufacture of news' has guaranteed them a special place in public, private and political debate.

The study is interesting because, rather than analysing the text of *The Sun* and then inferring particular 'effects' on its readers, it focuses on the readers themselves and their uses and views of the newspaper they read and buy. Unfortunately we do not have the space to incorporate the full study with its lengthy ethnographic data, but we have included the conclusion which encapsulates many of the findings and makes reference to some of the views expressed in interviews, including those of one of *The Sun's* most famous adversaries, the Labour MP Clare Short. If you wish to follow up your reading of this extract by turning to the original text and studying the interview material in its entirety, you may find it useful, as you are reading, to make notes about firstly the *method* used, secondly the *responses* of interviewees and finally, how they are *interpreted* and made sense of by the author.

Introduction

'Well, folks, this is the big moment you have all been waiting for' – claimed *The Sun* front page of 12 July 1991. The phrase was used to describe the exclusive uncovering of an old photograph showing 'Prince Andrew as you have never seen him before'. It was a typically direct appeal to *The Sun's* loyal readers, complete with over-the-top hype of a perfect tabloid story depicting naked royalty. Perhaps nothing has changed.

Yet questions are being asked about a decline in tabloid sales (Leapman, 17 April 1991; Greenslade, 1 July 1991). *The Sun* itself hit a circulation height of 4.3 million in 1988, with the audited daily sale for May 1991 being just over 3.6 million. Economic recession may account for much of the fall, but there may be other reasons for the drop in public demand.

The main focus for this paper is a small-scale, qualitative piece of research on the relationship between *The Sun*, and its regular readers, carried out when *The Sun* was at its brightest in 1988. It is primarily a study of how *The Sun* seemed to fit into the real lives of many young people in the late eighties. The additional question is whether the decline of *The Sun* since can be attached to political changes. Was the relationship between *The Sun* and Thatcherism so intense that *The Sun* has lost its shine in the nineties?

Certainly the tabloid environment has changed. The press has supposedly been watching its own standards since the Calcutt Report of June 1990 focussed on the excesses of tabloid behaviour. Conservative-led legislation against the press, arguably affecting *The Sun* more than most, would in some ways be ironic proof of changing times. The media philosophy of Murdoch and Thatcher only accounted for regulation by the free market, but now older Conservative principles of surface-level respectability and public morality threaten to re-emerge. Calcutt articulated concerns about tastes and standards which have forced the tabloids into some form of self-censorship. It is possible to detect *The Sun* being less vicious in its personal attacks, slightly less brazen in its opinions and attempting to show more of its gentler, human face. Coinciding with this pressure has been the dilemma of *The Sun* in facing the demise of its idol: Margaret Thatcher and her political practice. The gradual sense that the Thatcherite programme was losing public favour, followed by the hastiness of her removal from office must have taken some confidence from *The Sun*, after its years of forceful support.

Readers, too, have had numerous causes for thought over recent years. Most infamously, the vile reporting of the deaths of ninety people at Hillsborough stadium in April 1989, precipitated an effective boycott of *The Sun* on Merseyside. Simply too many 'ordinary' people have been victims of the paper's offensiveness, spreading its reputation as a 'bad' newspaper beyond celebrity targets, intellectuals and left-wing politicians.[1]

The public mood towards *The Sun* might indeed have changed. The Gulf War coverage of January 1991 was another tabloid loser as readers demanded harder information than *The Sun's* appeal to 'Support Our Boys And Put This Flag In Your Window' (with a Union Jack and anonymous 'Tommy' taking up the front page of 16 January 1991). Perhaps the genuine anxiety and sense of the multinational scope of the conflict made *The Sun's* blazing jingoism feel misplaced. It perhaps missed the mark even further with the following ludicrous appeal of 1 November 1990: 'At the stroke of noon tomorrow, we invite all true Brits to France and yell "Up Yours Delors"' (the phrase selected for the front page headline). Debates about European financial strategy are simply not *The Sun's* strengths!

Prior to Robert Maxwell's demise, the rival *Daily Mirror* was proclaiming itself: 'Newspaper for the Nineties.' Quite apart from the outcome of the battle for ownership of the *Daily Mirror*, there is an intriguing struggle ahead within the newspaper market, around the type of press Britain will have, as the nineties develop, and which of the tabloids will best capture the climate of the times.[2] It is a battle related to a bigger question, about the type of political climate and agenda which is going to emerge post-Thatcher.

Ways of looking

Theoretical positions

The Sun seems to be identified in widely divergent ways, posing difficulties for attempts at 'academic' analysis. The so-called 'liberal' intellectual response seems to be one of wondering what there could possibly be to analyse about *The Sun*. Such popular taste can either be ignored, allowed as 'fine for someone else', in the name of cultural relativism, or dismissed as 'rubbish', not worthy of consideration.

From a left political perspective the paper seems almost too easy to describe in terms of its racism, nationalism, sexism, homophobia, consumerism and Conservatism. It is tempting to conclude that this is critical analysis enough! The danger here is two-fold. On the one hand is the problem of sheer complacency – failing to consider the endless ways *The Sun* can cause real offence to a variety of groups, cultures and beliefs, simply because all 'right on' people know they should expect nothing else from the right-wing press.[3] On the other hand is the problem of writing off the whole constituency of tabloid readers as misguided victims of a mass deception, as passive, duped dopes.

Media and cultural studies suffered for some time with this problem of acknowledging genuine cultural reasons for the appeal of the popular, while remaining critical. A closer look at the 'popular' audience, the realities of their media-use, and the recognition of the audience by critics shifted the focus of the debate from the complexities of the 'text' to the complexities of daily life (Bennett, 1983: 214–227, 1986: 6–21; Buckingham, 1987; Hall, 1980: 128–138; Hobson, 1982; Morley, 1980, 1981, 1986; Radway, 1984, 1986: 93–123, 1988: 359–376; Walkerdine, 1987: 167–199; Williamson, 1986: 14–15).

The closer exploration of how the popular medium are enjoyed by the audience disturbs the idea that they carry unified, coherent ideologies. In the case of *The Sun*, consideration of different positions from which it can be read presents a series of conflicts and contradictions within *The Sun's* view of the world. The 'fun' of endless, unproblematic heterosexual 'bonking' sometimes clashes with a sterner moral code and traditional views of the family. The hedonistic 'cheeky' rebellion of *The Sun* has to fit with some vicious authoritarianism. Snubs and criticisms of authority figures, including royalty, peers,

MPs, judges and the police never stretch to questioning that the British system is best. The flashing pound signs of instant consumerism sit with derision for 'yuppies' and praise for the values of thrift and hard work.

In order to observe these conflicts a vital analytical step is necessary and on which James Curran and Colin Sparks have recently argued:

> When people write about British newspapers, they usually comment only on their overtly political content. Thus, most historians and social scientists have ignored the entertainment features of the popular press... This view is based on the elitist assumption that most of what people read most of the time does not warrant critical study (Curran and Sparks, 1991: 215).

The need is to view *The Sun* as a media product in relation to its regular readers.[4] This requires moving away from the notion that an 'academic' researcher can ideologically interpret 'a text' and 'read' it on behalf of everybody else. Such a practice, with its peculiar version of what it is 'to read', avoids all the important questions about how such a paper enters into very real areas of lived culture. After all, market research can show that despite the offence often recognised, many black people and many women do buy and enjoy *The Sun*. Trying to find something of the investments these readers find in taking the paper is getting closer to the ways everyday ideological conflicts are actually experienced. If something can be discovered about the aspects of their identity which are positively responding to the paper this could be a valuable resource for left politics.

Getting closer to the social relations in which popular culture is involved does not necessarily mean throwing away ideological critique. Rather, the critique can be formulated from more clearly defined positions.

Put another way, readers become less of a 'problem' in need of explanation (trapped as ideological victims, in a rather Althusserian way) and become more active participants in the meaning contest.

Politically, there are urgent questions for the left about its images and its culture from which the example of the relations between *The Sun* and its readers may even prove useful. Somewhat ironically, I am suggesting there may be more valuable political insights by getting away from the more overt, direct style of ideological analysis.

[...]

Conclusions

Living The Sun

The sheer enthusiasm with which people spoke about their uses and opinions of the tabloids confirmed the sense of a lively, active engagement with such papers. 'Readings' cannot only be explained in relation to 'deep' ideological bases (identities around race, nation, class, gender, age) because the tabloids become a resource amongst all sorts of everyday experiences. In particular, the way *The Sun* seemed to offer relaxation, both at work and at home, positions the paper as a site of 'private' leisure space – perhaps in an attempt to smooth over some of the daily aspects of identity conflict. *The Sun* offers a temporary respite from some more serious social relations and instead fits into patterns of leisure interests.[5]

In addition, the evidence from these interviews would suggest that *The Sun* is recognised as containing some important ingredients for appearing to know and get close to its readers. *The Sun*'s humour, 'street credible' sociability and simplifying 'commonsense' are important aspects to its appeal. It gains credibility, almost becomes friends with readers, through appearing to 'talk the same language'.

However, it seems important to emphasise that there are many elements of everyday experience, many ways of talking, which *The Sun* cannot satisfy. Even the most avid readers had conflicts and doubts in their relationship with *The Sun*. There was a strong knowledge of what could be expected from the tabloid genre. They criticised factual inaccuracies, identified many over-the-top opinions and did not appreciate some of the gross exaggerations of character descriptions. They expect to laugh 'at' as well as 'with' *The Sun*. Paul openly criticised the one-dimensional critique of *The Sun* which fails to account for either the scepticism or the frustration provoked in regular readers:

> All these people who go round slagging off *The Sun* – saying "Oh you buy *The Sun*, ha-ha-ha" and laughin', erm – well they ought to think twice about why they're laughin'. I mean, yes laugh if they – if I was buying it because I thought it was a good paper but keep your mouth shut if er, you don't really know why I'm buying it.

The 'private' enjoyment of *The Sun* does not directly produce more 'public' approval of its apparent values. While people spoke of their personal investments in looking at the paper, they were aware other people could be reading it differently. The relationship between *The Sun* and its readers operates in this sometimes conflicting space between 'private' uses and investments in the paper and the simultaneous knowledge of other positions and considerations from a wider 'public' perspective. The relationship with the paper consequently lives and changes in relation to particular identity priorities, depending upon a variety of personal experiences, responsibilities and investments. Questions of 'influence' depend upon how readers are seeking to resolve the fragmented priorities of identity in which they have to operate in their own lives. It may well be that the only way to predict likely responses to material physically in *The Sun* is to look at the way the identity investments of people are offered as socially active outside the reading moment.

This at least offers some optimism for alternative constructions to the tabloid world of *The Sun*. There are limits to the capabilities of *The Sun*. Readers know how much there is to gain from reading a tabloid newspaper. They do not expect to find answers to life's real anxieties or features which align with many real experiences. The main site which seemed strongly relevant in real life but barely present in negotiating *The Sun* was the importance of a sense of the social, as opposed to the isolated individual. The only real group *The Sun* acknowledges is the community of *Sun* readers. In its crude classifications *The Sun* may ignore that people live by helping each other out and leaving each other room to live. Readers did not seem to recognise *The Sun* with any sense of warmth or honesty, but with an ironic distance, realising the phoney nature of much supposedly spontaneous wit and accepting stories could not always be taken as they seemed. This at least leaves room for alternative constructions to find a more relevant language – reaching the same readers with a more accurate version of everyday language, humour and people's real considerations.

While *The Sun* gets close to some aspects of how real culture is lived, there are other possibilities which it does not reach. The central focus of attention needs to be the dimensions of everyday life which contribute towards various possible relations with such 'popular' texts. *The Sun*'s ability to work from multiple positions and pay close attention to cultural movements offers lessons for those involved in disseminating a very different set of values. The important point is that *Sun* readers are not simply mistaken or wrong but that they have a variety of genuine social factors and positions giving them particular investments in what the 'text' contains. Indeed the supposed 'text' is a multiple, shifting body, existing only in relation to these other social factors and positions. It is the real social practices in which 'texts' and 'readers' are involved which need further study rather than any notion that they can be separated and held in an isolated relationship.

There is clearly a difference between truly 'living *The Sun*' and the tendency of my own style of analysis of *The Sun*, from the perspective of a left recognition of reactionary elements of social concern. The Left has had to revive the importance of the 'politics of identity' in an era when increasing social fragmentation and division necessarily means people occupying a more multiple range of identity locations (Brunt, 1988: 20–23 and Hall, 1988: 24–29). A look at the full, varied ways readers meet *The Sun* is perhaps proof enough of a complex, lively struggle in this era of the 'politics of identity'.

In truth, so far, *The Sun* may illustrate, rather better than the Left, the possibilities gained by addressing multiple identities.[6] *The Sun* does not constantly bombard a single identity position or expect to always gain everybody's approval, but it does work to different aspects of identity (at different times, to variable degrees). The Left has to get used to ways of relating to that constituency of people who lead largely apolitical and often conflicting lives. These are the people who chiefly read *The Sun* because it is convenient, relaxing and might offer an enlightening moment, the chance for something to do, a conversational item or a touch of humour.[7]

Politcal and tabloid futures

Looking at the relationship between *The Sun*, its readers and Thatcherism offers some relevant lines of thought for the unclear political future ahead for

Britain in the nineties. To begin with, the idea that I could look at *The Sun* in 1987–88 to find a coherent popular expression of Thatcherism, and then speak to readers who were picking up these values, soon looked inappropriately simplistic. Both the media product and the readers were involved in more conflicting and fluid relations than could be reduced to the dominant tenets of a political, hegemonic movement. However, this is not to argue that these complex relations never do align. *The Sun* put forward certain Thatcherite voices, on occasions very loudly, and must have reached through to many readers, at various times, just by putting forward such values as part of the stock of possibilities. Paul found a useful metaphor when he said he may use the paper for 'ammunition' to bolster his opinions.

The Sun is unlikely to change an opinion against a conflicting view constructed by more primary relations and experiences. *The Sun* might have the 'influence' of providing material to an argument when there is already an investment in taking such a stance. Perhaps, unfortunately, this conclusion that heart-felt attitudes and values will not change, however hard a newspaper tries, if other experiences are not served by this change, need not apply to the practice of switching voting intentions. The political apathy of many readers means there is not really an important investment in holding a political identity as a priority when reading the paper. This sheer lack of interest leaves a gap where the instant headlines, images and arguments of *The Sun* might cause a change in the casting of a vote, which is itself seen as of little relevance to the routines of everyday life.[8] The other important argument in relation to political 'influences' is that ideas or arguments initially hardly noticed or registered as relevant can be recollected or returned to in conversation later. The 'stock of possibilities' can be activated if personally relevant circumstances arise. For example, I should not expect to find one coherent response to the whole of Thatcherism or *The Sun*'s ideology from one person, but in a situation such as the opportunity to buy privatised shares or a disagreement with a Labour council this real, practical situation may bring to the fore a point or an attitude encountered in *The Sun*. Just as the paper need never be read in a 'total', unified way the experience of Thatcherism for many people was probably not one of either all 'for' or all 'against', but one of encountering particular aspects of policy when they had to be lived.

Undoubtedly *The Sun* fitted best with its readers when it was not engaged in obviously representing Thatcherism. Yet in some ways the horoscopes, crosswords, cartoons, sports pages and television chat say the most about *The Sun*'s politics. It is a world of 'entertainment', consumerism, easy self-pleasure, rather than social concerns or active, productive contributions to society. The very rejection of 'politics' in favour of 'entertainment' perhaps illustrates the changes to the political climate during the eighties. *The Sun* was able to turn far-reaching 'public', ideological values into accessible personal stories and its confident personality suited the individualised spirit of Thatcherism. Above all, *The Sun* was involved in the apparent depoliticising of politics itself and public life, turning all into individual issues, personalities and choices, creating a connection with the increasingly 'private' forms of social identity people experienced as larger senses of social groups were denied or fragmented.

However, just as *The Sun* supporters I spoke to at the height of its success felt doubts, absences and ambiguities about the paper, it seems many people felt conflicts and antagonisms about the Thatcherite direction. As ordinary people began to question the Thatcherite programme some of the certainty and boldness faded from *The Sun*. At the end of the eighties people who had gained from tax cuts were seeing they had not been part of an 'economic miracle' and many services, like health and education became more appreciated as the onslaught on public spending deepened. People did not seem to like the look of a society based on ruthless economic individualism and as splits developed at the level of overt politics a number of old values found an opportunity to be rearticulated. Even advertising agencies were proclaiming a softer image of 'the caring nineties' before the final fall of Thatcher in November 1990.

It was 'the men in grey suits' and an older version of paternalistic, pragmatic Conservatism which stopped the 'radical' Thatcherite steamroller. Unfortunately for *The Sun*, other than an interest in large profits, this represents very different ground on which to work. It certainly is not clear yet exactly what John Major led post-Thatcher Conservatism contains, but any kind of return to 'consensus' politics (even if only a gloss of style) provides difficulties for Right-wing tabloids after their zealous, crusading years. This gap in the political-cultural climate, on top of doubts about what tabloid excesses will be tolerated post-Calcutt, leaves *The Sun* without a refreshingly bright vision or purpose.

The relative fightback from the *Daily Mirror* perhaps aligns with the fact that many non-Thatcherite values never did really go away. The *Daily Mirror* has picked up its own more confident identity based on a more 'human' face, following some years of trying to out-*Sun The Sun*. The tackiness has been reduced and the news content increased. Talking to a small group of tabloid readers, as I did, highlighted a simple truth: social concerns, sharing, helpful communities, knowledges of injustice and senses of inequalities never disappeared. As part of my research I sought the views of Clare Short on *The Sun*, and its particular relationship with its readers and her own perceptions of the target of her campaign. In September 1988, she expressed frustration that the above values were remaining politically untapped:

> *The Sun's* success is, sort of, another side of the coin of some of Labour's problems.... We've got to the point where people's sense of why they're voting Labour – what values that represents – that should be a natural part of their life – have been so eroded that they're not surprised or offended by it [*The Sun*]. It's a complex thing the Thatcher success. It isn't true that she's created a new consensus – it's partly with an idea of opposition that just electorally explains things and partly the eroded values that belong to us that we've [the Labour Party]

failed, erm, made to live in people's lives. And I think *The Sun* belongs to such an era.

Some of the successful attachments of *The Sun* to its readership provide useful lessons for visions of the democratic Left. A key feature, from the evidence of this research, is the need to use a language recognisable to the ways by which people really live. The politics of the nineties will have to pay close attention to how groups of people identify themselves and the terms by which they articulate their lives. Clare Short provided a clear example:

> People who are objectively 'working class' don't all call themselves 'working class' ... It doesn't mean that class doesn't exist and all the issues of class don't exist, but it's no good using a language that people aren't talking ... So if you have ranting speeches about 'working class means stand together' then nobody's going to be listening to that kind of thing.

It can be argued that *The Sun* has played a part in moving the Left away from the everyday language of people by using a largely depoliticised language to represent its own preferred interests and promoting a light-hearted entertainment which seeks to laugh at all opposition, leaving Left counter-arguments with the appearance of 'serious' political rhetoric. *The Sun* holds a form of influence simply by recognising the importance of everyday conversation. Amongst my interviews Dave summarised the significance of this point: 'Even politics they [*The Sun*] make simple ... and people think they know about politics so they can argue about it at the bar.'

Another opportunity for the Left that *The Sun* clearly illuminates is the need to put forward a positive vision of a future society. *The Sun* gained appeal from its up-beat, bright, lively attitude and images, leaving the Left with a somewhat grey, dowdy contrast. The dismantling of oppressive communist bureaucracies might help, but there is still a vacuum the Labour Party's red rose hardly fills. Again, by working at the cutting edge of popular culture the tabloids have a part to play in offering hopeful visions. I asked Clare Short about her own 'spoilsport' image (at best!) in *The Sun* and she was rather amused at the idea that 'Fun and freedom and happiness' could possibly belong more to the Tory MPs who 'look like little old men when they're thirty' than the Labour movement's more 'irreverent', 'libertarian' traditions. Again, the Left has lost ground in an advantageous area, possibly because of its recent struggle in the field of popular culture.

It is tempting to conclude that Left politics is in need of a revival with regard to popular culture. Stuart Hall has asked, 'Can a socialism of the 21st century revive, or even survive, which is wholly cut off from the landscapes of popular pleasures, however contradictory a terrain they are?' (1988: 28). My argument, from this research, must be that, however contradictory the ground worked on by the tabloids, the kind of appeals they work on have to be tackled if the Left is to reach significantly wider than the already converted. There may be a high price to pay for condemning tabloids with the type of critique which only focusses on the level of (admittedly awful) ideological representations. The danger is of entirely missing the levels at which such tabloids are recognised (the identities and investments they serve) and thereby abandoning the popular ground. A closer look at the politics of 'entertainment', leisure and pleasure needs to be part of the vision of the democratic Left just as much as the consumerism of the Right. To this end, talking to *Sun* readers provided an interesting resource for studying changing times.

Notes

1. Clare Short's campaign and Bill against the display of sexually provocative naked women in newspapers provides an example. She has received thousands of letters of support, culminating in the publication of selected letters: Short, 1991.
2. Michael Leapman makes this point: 'Historically ... individual titles have forfeited market supremacy by failing to adapt quickly enough to changes in public preferences; for instance, the *Daily Herald* and *Sunday Dispatch* in the fifties, the *Daily Express* and *Daily Mirror* in the seventies ... The first tabloid editor to capture the true mood of the nineties could move well ahead of the field', *The Independent*, 17 April 1991.
3. Racism has been identified with *The Sun* so frequently the Institute for Race Relations have published work on the subject; see Searle, 1989.
4. There are a number of books viewing *The Sun* 'from the inside' shedding some light on the production and construction of *The Sun*'s world: see Chippindale and Horrie, 1990; Lamb, 1989; Grose, 1989.
5. Janice Radway (1988), has noted the importance leisure pursuits can play in perceptions of self-identity; 'For many individuals and subgroups, in fact, the conceptually subordinated leisure world is the primary site for the elaboration of what is taken to be meaningful identity.'
6. Frank Mort and Nicholas Green (1988), have made a similar point in relation to the multiple complexities advertisers put to work: 'Advertisers seem to know instinctively what political activists have been slow to understand. Most of us do not have one fixed political identity. We are not in any simple sense "black" or "gay" or "upwardly mobile".'
7. These reasons for reading the paper offer a contrast to some of the 'old', alienating language of politics: Brunt (1988), 'It is not, after all, obvious why anyone, particularly in such an apolitical culture as Britain, should ever choose to define themselves as political. For the commonsense opinion of politics is that, like religion, it spells trouble. It is what you do not discuss at high points of social togetherness, like family weddings or Christmas, or even just having a drink.'
8. Recent research from William Miller at Glasgow University argues the Tory tabloids can indeed change voting patterns. This research has been published (*How Voters Change* from Clarendon Press) though the argument is outlined by Ivor Crewe's article 'Revenge of the Mind Benders', in *The Guardian*, 19 November 1990.

References

Bennett, T. 1983: Text, readers, reading formations. *Literature and History* 9(2)

Bennett, T. 1986: The politics of 'the popular' and popular culture. In Bennett, T., Mercer, C. and Woolacott, J. (eds.), *Popular culture and social relations*. Milton Keynes: Open University Press.

Brunt, R. 1988: Bones in the corset. *Marxism Today*, October.

Buckingham, D. 1987: *Public secrets: EastEnders and its audience*. London: British Film Institute.

Chippindale, P. and Horrie, C. 1990: *Stick it up your punter – the rise and fall of The Sun*. London: Heinemann.

Curran, J. and Sparks, C. 1991: Press and popular culture. *Media, Culture and Society* 13.

Grose, R. 1989: *The Sun-sation – behind the scenes of Britain's bestselling daily newspaper*. London: Angus & Robertson.

Hall, S. 1980: Encoding/decoding. In Hall, S., Hobson, D., Lowe, A. and Willis, P. (eds.), *Culture, media, language*. London: Hutchinson.

Hall, S. 1988: Brave new world. *Marxism Today*, October.

Hobson, D. 1982: *Crossroads: the drama of a soap opera*. London: Methuen.

Lamb, L. 1989: *Sunrise – the remarkable rise and rise of the best-selling Soaraway Sun*. London: Macmillan.

Morley, D. 1980: *The 'nationwide' audience: structure and decoding*. London: British Film Institute.

Morley, D. 1981: The nationwide audience – a critical postscript. *Screen Education* 39.

Morley, D. 1986: *Family television: cultural power and domestic leisure*. London: Comedia.

Mort, F. and Green, N. 1988: You've never had it so good again. *Marxism Today*, May.

Radway, J. 1984: *Reading the romance: women, patriarchy and popular literature*. Chapel Hill: University of North Carolina Press.

Radway, J. 1986: Identifying ideological seams: mass culture, analytical method and political practice. *Communication*, 9.

Radway, J. 1988: Reception study: ethnography and the problems of dispersed audiences and nomadic subjects. *Cultural Studies* 2(3).

Searle, C. 1989: Your daily dose: racism and *The Sun*. In Murray, N. and Searle, C., *Racism and the press in Thatcher's Britain*. London: Institute of Race Relations.

Short, C. 1991: *Dear Clare ... this is what women feel about Page 3*. Radius.

Walkerdine, V. 1987: Video replay: families, films and fantasy. In Burgin V., Donald, J. and Kaplan, C. (eds.), *Formations of fantasy*. London: Methuen.

Williamson, J. 1986: The problems of being popular. *New Socialist*, September.

Questions

1 From your reading of this short extract, what would you surmise might be the main questions and problems concerning method of analysis and the conclusions drawn?

2 The study was based on interviews carried out with readers of *The Sun* in 1988 ('when *The Sun* was at its brightest'). What has happened to the style of *The Sun* and its tabloid market since 1988, especially with regard to its shifts of support prior to the 1997 general election?

3   Carry out one or two interviews of your own with readers of a current popular tabloid daily newspaper. On the basis of these interviews, how would you summarise their relationship with the paper in question?

Further reading

Chippindale, P. and Horrie, C. 1988: *Disaster! The rise and fall of News on Sunday.* London: Sphere.

Chippindale, P. and Horrie, C. 1990: *Stick it up your punter – the rise and fall of The Sun.* London: Heinemann.

Dahlgren, P. and Sparks, C. (eds.) 1992: *Journalism and popular culture.* London: Sage.

Fiske, J. 1989: *Reading the popular,* London: Unwin Hyman.

Fiske, J. 1989: *Understanding popular culture.* London: Unwin Hyman.

McGuigan, J. 1992: *Cultural populism.* London: Routledge.

McNair, B. 1995: *An introduction to political communication.* London: Routledge.

21

Technology in the Domestic Environment
Ann Gray

From *Video playtime: the gendering of a leisure technology* (Routledge 1992)

Like the previous extract, this reading demonstrates by means of detailed interview the relationship between a specific medium – in this case, video – and its users. But as with the previous extract, limitations of space prevent us from including the detailed interview transcripts in their entirety and, as before, we would recommend that if you wish to follow up your reading with more detailed information about the ethnographic research methods employed and the responses of interviewees, you should refer to the original text.

The overall aim of the research was to understand how, and on what terms, the video cassette recorder (VCR) was domesticated in British homes in the 1980s. This was the decade when the VCR rapidly became a widely accepted part of the technological and cultural landscape of many homes, a taken-for-granted attachment for the television screen. In particular, Gray was concerned to investigate how women related to and used the VCR, and to explore the types of impact it made upon their lives and the household cultures in which they lived. The central focus for the study lies, then, in its analysis of the significance of gender in structuring women's and men's relationships with domestic media and communications technologies. Earlier in the study, Gray investigates the extent to which social class, education and generation play a part in women's relationships with video technology, but she concludes that while such variables raise some important issues relating to gender, in terms of different kinds of viewing contexts, confidence in one's ability to operate the VCR etc., gender itself is the key determinate in the use of, and expertise in, video technology in the home. The reading begins by exploring the reasons behind the acquisition of the VCR in the home.

Winning consent

The purchase of the VCR was often the subject of negotiation, largely, but not always, instigated by men, with a variety of 'carrots' offered. Beth's husband, for example, had a work-related reason for the purchase of the VCR, but, as she pointed out, her house is full of 'gadgets'.

> We've got several tape recorders, we've got an early Sinclair computer and a later Sinclair computer, certainly a wireless for each room ... it's just that we've always had video recorders before anybody else had video recorders ... the only thing we haven't got is a compact disc player ... but that's just because we'd just bought a whole new stereo system. But we bought a video recorder. We were working for the Open University at the time and he made this great case that we really needed a video recorder so we could watch our programmes, and we did-n't watch many OU programmes. (Beth)

At another point in the interview I asked her why they had got the video, and she replied,

> Because George loves gadgets. He bought it, I wouldn't have bought it, but then he buys all those things. I buy silly things. (Beth)

For three of the women, the reasons for the decision to purchase the VCR had resulted in the women being marginal to its use. Sheila and Kay were 'not interested' in getting a video, although their husbands and family were very keen. Kay felt that her husband and family were already watching too much television.

> *Were you in favour of getting the video?*
> No. I was dead against it until the Royal Wedding. That's where I slipped up you see. I said I would love that, you know, for posterity, to have ... and he said, right ... I'll go and get a video recorder and you shall have it [laugh] and that's what he did. (Kay)

Kay hardly ever recorded things – 'I don't even know how to work the thing properly' – and whilst her husband's case for getting the video was that he would be able to record things and therefore go out more with her, this hadn't actually happened. In effect, he had ended up watching more.

> Well, because he records ... there's always something on the other side he wants to watch, so he'll watch one channel, record the other side, and then he has a backlog of things that he's got to sit and watch, so even when ... like Monday night is very bad on television, there's nothing really on, but he's got a backlog of stuff that he wants to watch, so ... (Kay)

Similarly, Sheila, whose teenage children were the main instigators of the purchase, rarely used the video recorder and was not interested in its use.

The prime motivation in Shirley's household for the purchase of a video recorder was the desire for a video camera to record their children.

> Roger had been toying with the idea of getting a camera for some while and eventually we bought it to coincide with the second daughter ... so ... that was the incidental reason for it, although I suppose we do use the video for recording. (Shirley)

Whilst they did use the video, as we have seen in the previous chapter, Shirley did not feel it was 'her territory'; her husband operated the camera and tended to dominate the use of the video recorder.

Rene was very keen to get a video and its purchase was part of a bargain.

> We needed a new television and my husband said, right, we'll have one with Teletext. I said, well, if you're having your Teletext, I'm having a video.

Why did you want a video?

> Well, because of the things he used to watch. Say, for instance, *Match of the Day* on a Saturday night, well, there could be, as I recall, *Tales of the Unexpected* on the other side which I enjoyed, but because I got my own way so much during the week, I thought, well it's only fair to let him watch *Match of the Day* in colour. Now, I would either take the television up to bed in the winter, or I'd go in the kitchen and watch ... and it's damned uncomfortable in the kitchen and I don't always particularly want to be in bed. You know, watching television, particularly because I fall asleep, you know, if I take the television to bed I've really ... it's got to be really something special that keeps me awake to watch it, so that's the reason I wanted a video. (Rene)

Rene is a keen video user and so is her husband, although he was not in favour of having a VCR; his reaction to her wanting a video was 'you watch enough rubbish already', associating the VCR with entertainment as against 'his' Teletext, the provider of information.

Another important bargaining position was the argument that the video was 'for the children' and this often came into play at Christmas. A number of working-class women reported that the VCR was rented at Christmas 'for the children' because of the good films on then, which they could record.

> It was my husband really wanted it in the first place. I honestly didn't think we'd watch it. I mean we do. But all the time I thought, oh we don't really need one. Then it got to Christmas time and he said it would be nice for the kiddies ... so ... (Betty)

For those households on low incomes with young children, it is not surprising that economic factors and lack of freedom to go out were motivating elements.

> He bought a video because we couldn't afford to go to the pictures. It was expensive when there's five of us going. (Alison)

The other factor for two of the women was the fact that they worked in the evening and it meant that they didn't miss their favourite programmes (soap opera).

He decided he wanted a video, he's wanted one since a couple of years ago and I said no ... I'm not interested. But then when I started on in the evenings ... he says 'Well, we can get one now because then I can tape *Coronation Street* for when I'm at work' ... so I wouldn't be without it now. (Cathy)

There is no doubt here whose decision it was to have a video and here is a very clear example of this kind of negotiation. Brenda reported that they wanted a VCR mainly for recording.

The Olympics were coming on and I was working in the evening, and my husband would tape things we could watch together when I came home.

Can you remember whose idea it was to get the video?

Well, my husband had seen one and we talked about it and said ... when they first came out we said, no ... because what was the point if you wanted to watch something, if you were out you'd stop in and watch it, if you really wanted to watch it ... but then I started working evenings and he found out what it was like looking after three kids [laugh]; that clinched it. (Brenda)

Everybody's got one

The acquisition of VCRs by friends and colleagues was an important additional factor behind the decisions for lower-income groups. VCR-related talk becomes a feature at work, in the neighbourhood and at social gatherings and in this way information about the advantages of the VCR is shared and non-owners can rapidly be persuaded to become owners.

Well, they were all getting them where he works, and he thought it would be a good idea. (Alison)

I think Megan was the first to get one round here and, you know ... well that persuaded us really. Most people have got 'em now. (Janet)

Two of the women declared that it had been a joint decision to purchase the machine. These were Susan and Michelle – full-time workers, married but with no children.

There's nothing else to do

Two of the women were under 21 and living with their parents. Although one had a job, working in a supermarket, and the other was unemployed, they both had a very limited amount of money to spend on going out and lived in an area which, as far as they were concerned, offered very little in the way of entertainment. Christine, the one in employment, said,

There's nothing to do ... I think it's with not many of us having much money and it costing so much to go out, I think that's the reason. I don't go out during the week, unless it's a special occasion, I mean there's not much going off, except pubs that are open ... it's a shame though because we're only 21 and we've no life, really. (Christine)

Sandra, unemployed, was also short of cash and both these women went to the cinema very infrequently.

I think I've been once so far this year. I went about twice last year. It's only if there's a film that I really want to watch and usually my sister goes with me because we both like the same kind of films, but normally we can get a video and watch it at home, all the family can watch it together. (Sandra)

Sometimes, on Monday nights we'll go 'cos it's only a pound in for any age, and if there's a decent film on we'll go, but there haven't been many films. We go see cartoons and weepies, that's all we do. I sometimes take my sister, or sometimes go with people from work if they want to go see it as well. (Christine)

The main reason given by Christine for renting a VCR was that there was nothing good on television during the week when she had to stay in.

My life's more or less come home, have my tea, watch television and go to bed about nine o'clock and I was just getting fed up and all my friends, well some of my friends at work, have got videos and they were saying, 'Oh I watched so and so video this week, and it was really good' and I thought, well, if they're watching all them films and there's nothing on television, I might get one. (Christine)

Again this is evidence, as seen earlier, of peer group pressure to acquire a VCR. However, she found hiring films from the video library often beyond her means.

I haven't watched one for a while, it's just a matter of going down and getting one, I'm a bit skint you see ... they cost a pound to one pound fifty; it isn't much, but with me going out on Saturday and Sunday and spending more money than what I intended ... I haven't been able to afford one and my dinners at work has cost me a bit more, and I've got some new things, new clothes; there are a few new films, but not many that interest me, so I think that's the reason. (Christine)

Unlike Christine, Sandra found that there were lots of programmes on television that interested her and that she wanted to record. Her married sister and brother both had a VCR and she found she was constantly asking them to record things for her. She therefore managed to persuade her father to rent a machine.

Well, my brother had his video for about a year and a half, and my sister had had hers for nearly a year and I had some tapes at her house, you see, and I used to ring her up and say ... oh quick, you know, put the tape in, I want this taping and ... I don't know, I think my Dad got fed up with the 'phone bill and I kept saying, you know, it's wonderful, you'll be able to sit here with all your cowboy films on a Saturday ... so I kind of persuaded my Dad to get it. (Sandra)

Both these women were the dominant users in the household and both claimed to use it more for hiring films than recording off air.

Summary

It would seem that class and education are not significant variables in attitudes towards technology in the home. Gender is the key determinant in the use of and expertise in specific pieces of domestic equipment. This in turn can be seen to relate to the gendered division of labour within the home and its associated technology. Recent research into the acquisition of radio and television has identified very similar patterns of use and decision-making across gender (Moores 1988; O'Sullivan 1991). In the light of the women's attitudes to older forms of entertainment technology such as radio and cassette recorders, we can perhaps see their resistance to video technology as a passing phase. This would certainly find support in Sherry Turkle's (1984) arguments in relation to 'computerphobia', which she argues is transitional. However, we can see from this study that there is more at stake for many of the women. One point to make is that it seems that the women will always be 'lagging behind' in mastery of entertainment and information technology. However, the crucial point to be drawn from this analysis is that the domestic context and the social relations within it have quite powerful consequences in relation to women and new technology.

Jonathan Gershuny has created an index showing the extent to which different pieces of domestic technology are used by women and men (Gershuny 1982). Using time-budget survey data he found that the men in his study mainly used equipment like electric drills and electric saws to perform one-off jobs with a highly visible end product. The women used technology for the execution of day-to-day chores, the end products of which are usually immediately consumed, technology such as the cooker, the washing machine, the iron, and so on. Also, Gershuny notes that the more 'hi-tech' a device is, the more likely it is to be male-dominated in its use. His study indicates that entertainment technology falls within a neutral cluster, being neither female nor male specific. Unfortunately, he does not include the VCR amongst this equipment, but we can see that most of the women in the study do not feel proficient in the operation of the VCR, and in particular with the time switch for pre-setting recordings.

Advertisements for domestic and entertainment technology often imply a male or female operative through both visual and textual codes. Early advertisements for the VCR stressed its 'hi-tech' nature, were very rarely seen in a domestic setting, and emphasized technical complexity in its use and operation. In an interview during August 1987 with Mastercare Ltd., a follow-up service agency for VCRs, I discovered that a very high percentage of call-outs for engineers resulted from malfunctions of timer mechanisms, largely owing to user error. This led to design changes and a number of campaigns stressing the simplicity rather than the complexity of time-switch mechanisms and, significantly, women were often represented as operatives in these advertisements. Conversely, micro-wave cookers have been marketed on their simplicity, but here the operatives are male: 'so simple even men can use it!' (Hitachi advertisment, 1987).

The ways in which consumers are addressed through advertisements on television, in the press, and in magazines would seem to have an effect in terms of the assumed knowledge and use of specific pieces of equipment in the home. This places women at a disadvantage with regard to use of the VCR, and those members of the household who have time to become VCR-competent tend to dominate its use.

The majority of the women were persuaded into the purchase or rental of the VCR by their partners. This makes sense given gender specific concepts of 'spare time' in the home and the targeting of advertising campaigns. The men were looking towards further home entertainment and leisure provision for which the women themselves could see no need. Their spare time is limited, and the VCR is conceived as needing time for its use. It is interesting, however, that some of the men managed to persuade their reluctant partners by convincing them that they *did* have a need for the VCR. Consent was also often won by virtue of an 'event'. Christmas was the most common, but public events such as a royal wedding and the Olympics were also cited as key factors in the eventual decision.

There is also evidence, particularly in the lower-income groups, of access to a VCR becoming the norm in social and work groups and an important part of conversational currency. In the higher-income group this dimension was not explicitly stated. However, the fact that available disposable income is spent on the VCR, rather than on any other product or service, indicates their awareness of the product. Simon Frith has plotted the middle-class consumer's gradual approach to this moment of acquisition:

> We read of new devices that cost huge amounts of money and seem to have no immediate purpose; we follow reports of the prices coming down and domestic value going up; we see or hear the machines at work for richer or more foolish friends; we find ourselves thinking one day 'if only *I* could do that', and then the price or rental costs suddenly seem right, we get the equipment for ourselves and soon can't live without it. (Frith 1988: 91)

It is the case, however, that for some of the households the VCR was seen as a necessity, mainly because of lack of disposable income for trips to the cinema, or because of the presence of children. There is thus a marked distinction between households: between those where the VCR was thought of as an indulgence or impulse buy, the purchase of which was made possible by available extra cash, and those where the purchase or rent of a VCR was a major expense to be carefully considered and planned.

References

Frith, S. 1988: Fast forward. *Screen* 29(2).

Gershuny, J. 1982: Household tasks and the use of time. In Walman, S. *et al.* (eds), *Living in South London*. London: Gower.

Moores, S. 1988: The box on the dresser: memories of early radio and everyday life. *Media, Culture and Society* 10(1).

O'Sullivan, T. 1991: Television memories and cultures of viewing 1950–65. In Corner, J. (ed.), *Popular television in Britain: studies in cultural history*. London: BFI.

Turkle, S. 1984: *The second self: computers and the human spirit*. London: Granada.

Questions

1   How would you assess the strengths and weaknesses of the ethnographic methods employed in this kind of research (i.e. based on in-depth interviews, detailed discussion and observation)? What are the key issues at stake in evaluating this kind of data and evidence?

2   Carry out some of your own interviews with both males and females and summarise their relationships with video and other 'new' technologies. To what extent – and how –do the responses of women differ from those of men?

3   Carry out a content analysis of advertisements for various media or other technologies. To what extent is it still appropriate to say that 'the more hi-tech a device is, the more likely it is to be male-dominated in its use' and how far, and in what ways, does advertising perpetuate and promote such ideologies?

Further reading

Baehr, H. and Gray, A. 1995: *Turning it on: a reader in women and media*, London: Arnold.

Cockburn, C. and Furst-Dilic, R. 1994: *Bringing technology home: gender and technology in a changing Europe*. Buckingham: Open University Press.

Hammersley, M. and Atkinson, P. 1983: *Ethnography: principles in practice*. London: Tavistock.

Livingstone, S. 1992: The meaning of domestic technologies: a personal construct analysis of familial gender relations. In Silverstone, R. and Hirsch, E., *Consuming technologies: media and information in domestic spaces*. London: Routledge.

Lull, J. 1990: *Inside family viewing: ethnographic research on television's audiences*. London: Routledge.

Moores, S. 1993: *Interpreting audiences: the ethnography of media consumption*. London: Sage. (See reading 22.)

Morley, D. 1986: *Family television: cultural power and domestic leisure*. London: Comedia.

Morley, D. 1992: *Television, audiences and cultural studies*. London: Routledge. (See Section 5, reading 34).

Van Zoonen, L. 1994: *Feminist media studies*. London: Sage.

22

Satellite TV as Cultural Sign
Shaun Moores

From 'Media, Technology and Domestic Life', in *Interpreting audiences: the ethnography of media consumption* (Sage 1993)

In this extract Moores, like Gray in the previous reading, is concerned to explore and to understand the cultural contexts and conditions which surround the entry and reception of new media technologies in the home. Whereas Gray focused on the VCR and women's attitudes to and relations with television and video, in this extract Moores writes about the recent purchase and reception of satellite television in Britain. As in the previous two readings, his method of research is ethnographic in that it uses extended informal interviews, discussions and observations based upon a relatively small number of cases. His discussion foregrounds the picture which emerges from two particular households in one suburban residential area in a large city in South Wales. His long-term aim is to report on a range of households from varying types of residential neighbourhood.

In approaching the reading, you will find it useful to spend some time initially on the discussion of three central concepts – consumption, embedding and articulation – which form the theoretical framework for the study. This provides the foundation from which to work through and assess the detailed accounts provided in the latter half of the reading. You may find that these accounts of the 'micro-worlds' of the domestic and familial interiors of others invites comparison with your own settings or those known to you.

Satellite TV as cultural sign

My current research ... rather like the work I did a few years ago on early radio's arrival in the private sphere (Moores, 1988), is concerned with the place of a new media technology in everyday life. It is an investigation of satellite TV's cultural significance as an object of domestic consumption. Through an analysis of conversational interviews recorded at the homes of consumers living in a South Wales city, I am mapping out various meanings which have come to be invested in the technology at the point of its entry into specific social contexts and situations. The method of inquiry, then, can broadly be described as ethnographic – and my purpose has been to chart the conditions of satellite TV's 'multi-accentuality' within and across different household and neighbourhood cultures. This [extract] offers a series of reflections on the study, addressing some of the general theoretical issues that underpin the project and identifying particular themes which have emerged in the course of the fieldwork.

I begin by discussing three terms, or keywords, that help to provide a conceptual framework for the research. The first of these, 'consumption', is evidently undergoing something of a rehabilitation in media and cultural studies at present. If, in the past, it has often been placed alongside production in a binary opposition – with passive consumption as the poor relation to an active production – then a number of theorists have now begun to redress the imbalance by referring to consumption itself as 'productive'. It is a moment at which objects and texts are actively appropriated and interpreted as they come into contact with the everyday practices of social subjects. Of course, there can be dangers associated with this kind of approach. In focussing on the meanings that consumers create when they 'read' satellite TV, we should be careful not to lose sight altogether of the technology's design and marketing or the sounds and images that are broadcast. Satellite TV's significance is partly determined by its positioning within the home and residential area, but the moments of manufacture and promotion also exert considerable pressure on reception activity. So technologies are not completely open to be used and made sense of in any way one chooses. A degree of closure has already been imposed elsewhere in the cultural circuit (Johnson, 1986).

Another, related danger is the populist celebration of consumer freedoms. Despite his good political intentions, John Fiske (1989) presents us with a model of cultural consumption which is guilty of such a mistake. Following Michel De Certeau (1984), he has emphasized the 'tactical resistances' of subordinate groups in their constant daily struggle against the power of the dominant. For Fiske, 'the popular' is a site where the weak frequently succeed in putting one over on the strong – 'poaching' on the commodities of a capitalist system, and asserting their own meanings and pleasures in the process. Although it is undoubtedly the case that culture is a contested sphere, his writings unfortunately suffer from an overly optimistic and rather romantic perception of everyday life in the postmodern world. Fiske tends to overestimate the progressive potential of consumption practices and fails to acknowledge any of the profoundly reactionary elements at play in popular culture.

Somebody else who might be accused of straightforwardly celebrating the 'symbolic creativities' of consumers is Paul Willis in *Common Culture* (1990). However, Willis's recent book has important advantages over Fiske's. He grounds his commentary in an extensive empirical study of young people's cultural experiences, and he is keen to stress the material and social constraints that bear down on those research subjects. In the strand of British cultural studies which is represented by his continuing work (see also Willis, 1977, 1978) – and by Morley's audience inquiries too (Morley, 1980, 1986) – detailed attention to questions of interpretation, use and context has always been accompanied by a genuine sociological concern with the patterning of culture and communication. I would want my own investigation to be considered part of this same analytical strand, because it opens up a convenient pathway between De Certeau's interest in imaginative ways of 'making do' and Pierre Bourdieu's preoccupation with the structured distinctions of consumer behaviour (Bourdieu, 1984). What we require is a theory and method that recognizes both creativity and constraint in quotidian life.

The second term in my conceptual vocabulary is 'embedding'. I employ it in an effort to stress the situated nature of consumption practices and cultural objects. Studying satellite TV's position in the day-to-day lives of social audiences necessarily involves an understanding of the technology as embedded at several, interconnected levels or instances (Silverstone, 1990: 174). Primarily, there is the level of households and families – the immediate physical and human contexts of reception. This includes spatial divisions inside the home, the temporal routines of its inhabitants, and the interpersonal ties and tensions that have formed between household members. Any new commodity that arrives will inevitably become enmeshed within the existing dynamics of power in the domestic realm. It therefore has to be analysed in conjunction with the range of artefacts and activities that are already in place. Once again, though, potential problems arise when the notion of embedding is taken up in ethnographies of media use, just as there were certain dangers associated with ideas about the productivity of consumption. We run the risk of assuming domestic cultures to be fixed entities into which goods are inserted and incorporated without any resulting impact on the pre-given structure. Instead, as I have found in my conversations with consumers, the family is best seen as a 'system in process'. To a limited extent, practices and dynamics may change over time, and the entry of a new technology can occasionally serve as the signal for a renegotiation of internal boundaries and relationships in the home.

Communication technologies can also be implicated in the redrawing of boundaries and relationships between the private sphere of the household and various public worlds beyond. This actually goes for 'communications' in its most general sense, and would apply just as well to a machine like the motor car as it does to the medium of television. Both these objects are in the business of transportation – albeit of slightly different sorts – and each facilitates what Giddens (1984) has called a 'time-space convergence'. They have brought individuals and families into the presence of places and events that were previously distant or unknown, enabling them to identify with dispersed yet knowable communities and to imagine themselves as embedded in regional, national and even transnational collectivities. It is worth remembering here how Williams (1974: 26), in his book on television as technology and cultural form, lists broadcasting side by side with the car when discussing the tendency in twentieth-century living which he refers to as 'mobile privatization'. So, in researching the domestic consumption of satellite TV, I am interested in asking about the kinds of mobility that the object and its texts offer viewers – to what new destinations is it promising transport and who chooses to make the journey?

At an intermediate level, between the micro-context of the home and the large-scale 'imagined communities' to which the media provide access, there is the artefact's embedding in particular residential neighbourhoods and urban cultures. Few household technologies are visible from the street – they are usually hidden out of sight behind closed doors and drawn curtains – but satellite TV's dish aerial is an extremely public symbol of possession. Displayed on exterior walls or rooftops, dishes openly announce the technology's arrival. They give outsiders a fair indication of the types of sounds and images that are being consumed in private. We could pursue the comparison with automobiles a little further now, because just as the car parked at the front of the house says something about the lifestyle of its driver, so the satellite aerial is a sign to be read by neighbours and passers-by. How it is valued will depend, of course, on the person making the judgement and the geographical area in which it is sited. For onlookers, the dish can either be a focus of disgust or a matter of indifference. Similarly, for owners, it may be a source of pride or else a cause of embarrassment. The task is to match these varied decodings and dispositions to social patterns of taste in contemporary culture.

This leads us neatly on to questions of 'articulation', the last of my key-words. As Hall (1986: 53) has pointed out, the term can have a dual significance. On the one hand, it refers to the act of speaking – to the production of linguistic utterances – and on the other it implies a linking together, a connection that is forged between two separate things. For example, in his writings on the British New Right, Hall (1988) employs the word to account for a linkage of ideological elements in the political discourse of Thatcherism. I make use of the term rather differently here, whilst retaining its double-edged meaning. My own concern is with the ways in which a new media technology gets 'hitched up' to lived cultures of consumption, and thereby enables social subjects to actively 'voice' senses of identity and distinction. As satellite TV is embedded at each of the levels or instances outlined above – articulating with relations in and between the private and public spheres – it gives consumers an opportunity to articulate their subjectivities.

In these simultaneous practices of connection and expression, the technology becomes – to borrow Valentin Volosinov's remarks on the spoken word – 'a little arena for the clash and criss-crossing of differently oriented social accents' (Volosinov, 1973: 41). The continual dialogue between artefact and everyday contexts is what transforms satellite TV into a multi-accentual sign and what allows it to function, quite literally, as a 'medium' for cultural forces of identification or differentiation. Hall (1986) reminds us that articulations are always contingent and non-necessary. There is nothing inevitable, he suggests, about the coupling together of discursive elements. This applies to the embedding of media technologies as well. We cannot predict, simply from the development of a new means of broadcasting, how it will eventually come to have significance for audience groupings. It is certainly the case, as I noted earlier, that designers and advertisers play an important part in encoding the object prior to consumption. Programming policies are also formulated with specific viewing publics and market segments in mind. However, the linkages made with local settings demand detailed empirical investigation. My commitment, therefore, has been to qualitative research carried out at homes in selected neighbourhood areas where satellite dishes have recently been erected. Households in my study are distributed across three different areas of the same city (the basic idea for such a geographical segmentation is borrowed from models now being employed in commercial market research – for example, see CACI Market Analysis, 1985). By talking to family members about their newly acquired commodities, and by observing the domestic and residential environments, I believe it is possible to construct suitably 'thick' descriptions (Geertz, 1973) of situated consumer activity.

For the purposes of the present discussion, I intend to concentrate on data from one of my three neighbourhoods (a more complete account of all the households appears in Moores, 1996). This particular district is made up of privately owned properties that were originally built just after the turn of the century – a collection of large bay-fronted Edwardian terraces and detached houses. Situated in it is a small park with trees and a stream, surrounded by ornate antique railings. Estate agents refer to its 'authentic' historical qualities, and while some of the road names echo those of English stately homes, others recall famous military battles overseas. Lying approximately five kilometres from the city centre, the area has a mixed population of skilled manual work-ers and middle-class professionals. In some ways, then, it is comparable with a community in the north-west of England that was studied by Derek Wynne (1990). He sought to contrast the lifestyles and leisure patterns of housing estate residents who had very different sorts of 'cultural capital' at their dis-posal – and his fieldwork highlighted the frictions between them over matters of taste. Similar clashes of interpretation and disposition in my own district give rise to certain anxieties about satellite TV which are frequently expressed in the conversational interviews.

A distinguishing feature of the neighbourhood I have chosen to analyse here is its age. Wynne's ethnography was conducted out of town on a modern estate. The households discussed below are located in a city suburb which, for various reasons outlined in the previous paragraph, has strong connotations of 'her-itage'. In these circumstances, the arrival of a new communications technology – with its futuristic dish on open display – results in a curious collision of aesthetic and cultural codes (early promotional material for satellite TV made interesting use of science fiction imagery – with advertisements for the popular 'Amstrad Fidelity' system picturing the dish and receiver unit together on a cratered moonscape). Brunsdon (1991), in her review of newspaper reports on contro-versies over the siting of aerials, notes that tensions tend to surface when the objects are installed on old buildings considered to have architectural merit. Discourses of innovation and conservation confront each other, exerting pres-sure in opposite directions, and it is precisely this contradiction between senses of 'the modern' and 'the traditional' which runs through much of the following commentary. Such a conflict, I will argue, is not confined to antagonisms at the level of the residential area. It can get 'gridded', in complex and shifting ways, on to social divisions of gender or generation within domestic life – and may also help to constitute our broader feelings of collective identity.

Let me start to unpack these remarks now by looking in more detail at some of the homes in my neighbourhood (names of the families have been changed). For instance, the Gibsons – who have a 'Cambridge' dish – live in an old house which once belonged to a well known family of solicitors in the city. There is a striking divergence of tastes and competences between Mr Gibson and his nineteen-year-old son. The father takes great pleasure in the 'character' and heritage value of the building they own. He is currently restor-ing one of the original antique fireplaces, which he discovered hidden behind a plasterboard wall, and has plans to strip and varnish a wooden dresser in the back dining room. As we shall see, he is extremely anxious about the dish's appearance on their housefront. It was the son, Tony, who wanted a satellite receiver. Since he left school three years ago and gained his own independent source of income as a shiftworker in a bakery, Tony has chosen to buy a range of the latest media technologies. These commodities adorn his attic bedroom, described to me by Mr Gibson as 'a conglomeration of electronics'. To understand the position that satellite TV occupies in this particular family's intergenerational and time-space relations, it is necessary for us to explore the dynamic structure of identifications and distinctions which is in play.

At the top of the house, separated from the main living area by a narrow staircase and landing, is Tony's room. He is intensely proud of this space and the objects that are arranged inside, regarding it as a place into which he can retreat and as a symbol of independence from the rest of his family: 'I'm the only one who really knows how to use any of my electrical equipment. Nobody else comes in my room – I think of it as my space ... up here, I can watch anything I want, read, sleep, think about life, listen to music.' Around the television set there is a remarkable 'entourage' (Leal, 1990:21) of technological hardware and software, as well as an array of decorative images and artefacts. Two video recorders, a hi-fi system and the satellite receiver are all stacked on shelves underneath the TV. They have been wired together, too, so that the sound comes out of four 'Dolby Surround' speakers mounted on brackets in each corner of the room. According to Mr Gibson, 'it's like a disco in there ... if he turned the volume up any more, it'd blow the whole roof off'. Tony has moved his bed to a central point between these sources of sound, and five different remote control devices rest on top of the 'Bart Simpson' duvet cover (*The Simpsons* is an American cartoon show broadcast on Sky). On a bedside table there is a Simpsons alarm clock which wakes him in time for the shiftwork. The walls are covered with posters of sports cars, whilst neat piles of video tapes and CDs lie on the floor. His viewing preferences are for science fiction and horror – recording several films off the Sky Movies channel – and he also collects tapes about the making of films, especially those concerned with stunts and special effects.

It is possible, I believe, to read these assembled goods as signs of a struggle to fashion some limited degree of autonomy in the face of parental authority. The bakery job has not earned him enough to get a home of his own, enforcing a reliance on parents for accommodation, but he is able to save up and purchase things – items that are treasured precisely because they provide a statement of personal identity. Of course, that identity takes shape under conditions not entirely of his own choosing. He is, as the poststructuralists would say, constituted as a subject only as a consequence of being 'subject-ed' to and positioned within the symbolic order of culture. Tony inhabits a specifically masculine world of gadgets, fast cars and sci-fi fantasies (a world which he shares, incidentally, with his friends and fellow workers). However, in the spirit of current developments in audience studies, I want to insist on a more situated theory of subjectivity and discourse that recognizes a measure of human agency and understands meaning as negotiable. For this teenager in this immediate context, then, satellite TV is part of a constellation of technologies and practices which provides the cultural material to express difference and establish competence. Tellingly, his father confesses complete incompetence when it comes to operating the machinery in Tony's bedroom: 'He knows where everything is, but I don't ... I remember glancing over at it – the electronics and wiring – and just one look was enough for me.'

Mr. Gibson's interest in restoring antique furnishings and fittings has, it should be stated, grown considerably over the period since satellite TV entered their home. This heightened investment in the traditional is a direct response to his son's passion for the modern. As I argued earlier, the introduction of a technology into the family system occasionally coincides with a redrawing of domestic boundaries and relationships, and it certainly appears to be the case here. Tony makes a partial bid for independence. His father, meanwhile, defines a clearly contrasting field of knowledge and skills. The intergenerational pattern is clear – although there remains a single exception to the general rule. Mrs. Gibson's taste for sixties pop music has been inherited by Tony, who started borrowing her scratched LPs when he was still at school. Those same recordings have now been bought on CD, forming a large part of his musical library. Perhaps the raiding of styles from a previous era is not so surprising – considering the contemporary trend in youth cultures which Dick Hebdige (1988) has termed 'retro-chic' – but it adds a further twist to the oppositions between 'old' and 'new' in the Gibson household.

The story of how their external dish was selected and then positioned on the front wall is a revealing account of conflict and compromise. In this instance, installing the satellite aerial was very much a public enactment of private tensions. It was also going to be a potential cause of embarrassment for Mr. Gibson, given the 'tone' of the neighbourhood they live in. Realizing the technical impracticalities of siting at the rear of the house, Tony had to enter into a debate with his father over the aesthetics of display. Mr. Gibson's comments on the circular Amstrad dishes – the most commonly seen aerials – are decidedly uncomplimentary. He calls them 'frying pans with handles on', and says:

> They look completely out of place on houses like this, old houses with character ... I didn't want an unsightly thing hovering up there. If it was just a prefabricated sort of house, then sure, I wouldn't mind – but as we've got bay windows and all the stonework at the front, I wasn't going to have something that wouldn't blend in ... wouldn't retain the character of the area.

After consulting one of the consumer guide magazines which have recently come on to the market, Tony eventually managed to convince his father of the 'Cambridge' system's unobtrusive qualities. The name itself suggests a higher-status commodity, with distant associations of education and heritage, and its aerial is a rectangular stone-coloured block rather than the usual white sphere. Even Mr. Gibson admits that 'it's compact and looks neater on the side of houses ... there's many a person'll pass and not notice you've got it' (I return to the theme of 'invisibility' later).

This tentative agreement between father and son is not quite the end of the story, though. When a workman came to fix the dish at the front, there were reception difficulties caused by a tall tree which stands across the way from their home. A snow-like effect was created on the screen, and the interference problem could only have been solved by using an extension pole stretching out a metre or so above the bay. Predictably, Mr. Gibson refused to accept such a solution – 'it's be stuck out like a lollipop' – so the aerial went up in an alcove of the bay window despite the rather poor picture quality. Thereafter, Tony had a constant visual reminder as he watched of the intriguing compromise that was struck. It took the launch of a second 'Astra' satellite, and another visit from the installation engineer to realign his dish, for the situation finally to be rectified.

My closing comment on the Gibsons – one which provides a convenient link with the next household I discuss – concerns their identifications, through television, with larger national or transnational communities. Some might protest that small-scale ethnographic research of the sort I have been doing is an inappropriate means of investigating the cultural construction of collective identities. The best existing work on this theme has taken public representations and narratives as a starting point for analysis (e.g. Formations Collective, 1984; Bhabha, 1990), rather than trying to explore the sentiments of actual social subjects in the private domain. However, a recently published book by Michael Billig – *Talking of the Royal Family* (1992) – demonstrates the relevance of conversational interviews with families for examining discourses of nationhood. Getting them to speak about the British royals, he points to powerful 'common sense' articulations of monarchy, domesticity and nationality. Talking about TV, in both its terrestrial and satellite varieties, can deliver similar insights into processes of identification. As Morley (1991:12) puts it, 'the sitting room is exactly where we need to start from if we finally want to understand the constitutive dynamics of abstractions such as "the community" or "the nation"'. Although Morley overstates the argument a little, broadcasting does connect the space of the home with electronic 'image spaces', and in the case of the Gibsons an interesting distinction is made between different territories of transmission. Tony's positive feelings about the Astra broadcasts (he tunes in to continental stations like RTL Plus or Pro 7 as well as the Sky channels and MTV Europe) are intimately related to his dismissal of established terrestrial programming as traditional and old fashioned. In fact, he labels it negatively as 'British' TV. Mr. and Mrs. Gibson use precisely the same label themselves, but here its value is completely reversed. They prefer to watch BBC or ITV in the living room downstairs.

For the Harveys, a family living nearby, there are further interesting connections being forged between everyday experience and the new 'spaces of identity' made available by satellite TV. Dave and Liz Harvey are in their late twenties and have three young children aged five, four and six months. They moved to the city four years ago from the Midlands region of England, where he had studied for a polytechnic degree in electronic engineering. She works as a housewife and Mr. Harvey is now self-employed, having given up a salaried job to start his own small business designing and manufacturing computer robotics equipment for export. This married couple perceive the satellite technology to be offering them an expanded range of viewing choices – although Dave gets to exercise that choice more than Liz – and, significantly, he speaks about the 'larger feel' created by a type of television transmission which transcends the boundaries of narrowly British broadcasting.

Whilst the first of these perceptions is what we might reasonably expect to hear from satellite TV consumers, since the technology has been marketed as offering increased freedom of choice for its viewers, the second set of feelings is far less predictable. Mr. Harvey explains that:

> When I'm watching Sky – because it's from a European satellite – and when I'm looking at some of the other continental stations that are available, I very much get the sense of being a European. A lot of the channels are an hour ahead, they're on European time. If you're just channel-hopping, which is a bit of a sport for me – buzzing round eight or nine stations to see what's going on – you do get the feeling of not being restricted in the good old British way. It's quite something when you can sit down in your own front room and watch what's on in another country.

Willis (1980:90) has written about the potential that ethnography has for 'surprising' us – for throwing up empirical data and conceptual issues not prefigured in the researcher's starting paradigm – and in this early interview, I was genuinely surprised by Dave's statement of identification. The opposition he constructs here between restriction and mobility is mapped on to another distinction in which 'Britishness' and 'Europeanness' are contrasted ('not being restricted in the good old British way'). Even if his viewing pleasures take the form of a 'touristic grazing', it remains the case that satellite TV is helping him travel to new places and to reimagine the boundaries of community. Of course, the image spaces produced by a communications technology cannot reshape national subjectivities on their own. Only when those audio-visual territories are articulated with existing situations and discourses can a fiction like Europe be 'realized' by certain groups of people.

So Mr. Harvey, who manufactures hi-tech goods for the export market, already identifies strongly with a transnational business community. The fact that his parents have bought a retirement home on the continent also contributes to Dave's recognition of himself as 'a European'. Their villa is now a regular destination for family holidays abroad. Mrs. Harvey, too, finds that the idea of Europe has a certain limited salience. When her younger sister – an arts student at university – came to visit with a boyfriend from France, they were able to show them French-language programmes on satellite TV. Some of these circumstances are obviously unique to the Harvey household – while others, such as the commercial and cultural significance of a single European market, have much wider currency. What we need to specify, though, are precisely those interdiscursive moments at which private lives and public worlds meet and mesh together. Any transformation of collective identities will inevitably be uneven in its development and will necessarily be grounded in quotidian practices.

The theme of 'modern versus traditional' runs just as powerfully through pursuits and disputes in the Harveys' home as it did through the Gibsons'. In this family, it is the father who is a self-confessed gadgeteer. From the time he began playing around with lightbulbs and circuits as a teenager, Dave has always been enthusiastic about electronics. He can be located within what Haddon (1988) has called 'hobbyist' culture – a predominantly masculine sphere of social activity where consumers are concerned to experiment with all the latest innovations in information and communication technology. Their house currently contains three computers (one of which he assembled himself out of IBM parts), two VCRs and two televisions, in addition to the satellite system and a compact disc player. An interest in electronic music has also resulted in plans to buy a synthesizer. Liz, however, is extremely conscious of the fact that 'people do take the mickey out of us ... we're constantly tripping over monitors and things'. Her feelings towards these gadgets are distinctly more ambivalent than those of her husband. Indeed, she is clearly frustrated by the fact that money spent on his 'toys' is money which goes unspent on her preferred pastime of collecting antique furniture (there is a growing body of work on family resource distribution and the control of money within marriage which serves to illuminate these sorts of situations – see Brannen & Wilson, 1987; Pahl, 1989).

If the household dynamics and differences of taste appear to be organized chiefly along gendered lines, they are best highlighted by focussing on interpersonal relations across three generations – by looking first at the ties that Mr. and Mrs. Harvey have with their children, and then at the tensions which arise when her parents come from the Midlands to visit. Although the youngsters are denied access to certain areas of domestic space, including the front living room where satellite TV is watched, this does not mean that they are kept away from media technologies altogether. On the contrary, the older video recorder was 'given to the kids' and Dave's micro-computer from college days has now been handed down to the five-year-old, Phil. These are very good illustrations of the 'cultural biography' of objects (see Kopytoff, 1986; Silverstone et al., 1992), where a technology's position and function within the home environment has shifted, and its 'career' can be traced against the changing biographies of family members. Goods and competences here are passing through a gradual process of inheritance. Mr. Harvey reports proudly on his son's progress with the micro: 'he knows how to put discs in, knows what disc drives are, and can operate them ... which is great because I'd like him to get into computing'. Understandably, Liz is less sure about the acquisition of his father's enthusiasm for electronic gadgetry. She readily acknowledges the educational advantages of a technological literacy – yet describes Phil with some regret as 'a child of the nineties'. Her own recent efforts to hand on nostalgic pleasures to the children ended in bitter disappointment. Mrs. Harvey purchased a video recording of the BBC's original *Watch with Mother* broadcasts as a gift for them, only to discover that they found it slow and boring in comparison with modern American cartoon shows like, for example, *Teenage Mutant Hero Turtles*.

Meanwhile, Mrs. Harvey's mother and father have taken exception to the satellite aerial which is mounted on the house exterior. It has been the source of arguments between parents and daughter when they come to stay. 'My mum thinks it's rather vulgar,' Liz explains. 'She says to me, "You really shouldn't have that thing on the front of such a lovely Edwardian home".' There could be no more emphatic statement of the innovation/conservation conflict. Comparing the perceived ugliness of an Amstrad dish with the assumed beauty of period architecture, the grandmother forms a critical judgement on the basis of certain moral and aesthetic values that privilege past over present. We have seen how this juxtaposition of traditional and modern codes is at the root of numerous frictions in the Harvey family. Liz's desire for pieces of antique furniture is opposed to Dave's fascination with electronic gadgets. Similarly, the uncertain feelings she has about Phil learning to use a micro-computer contrasts with Dave's evident pride in his son's achievements. As for the disagreement between Mrs. Harvey and her parents over the dish on the front wall, she chooses temporarily to side with her husband – reluctantly identifying with 'modernity' because she is forced on to the defensive by their unfavourable comments. In these different situations, Liz has to negotiate the contradictions of her gendered and generational subject positions as they are related to particular senses of 'old' and 'new'.

Both Mr. and Mrs. Harvey are amused by her parents' remarks on the satellite dish, and yet there are strong indications that they too are anxious over its appearance. So Dave sees it, in part, as a symbol of technological progress – a sign of being ahead of the times – but worries about the connotations it may have for others in view of the 'character' of the neighbourhood. He admits that if they were to put their property on the market in the near future, he would seriously consider taking the aerial down – 'if it proved detrimental to the sale of the house'. Liz confesses that 'most of the people we know do actually think it's a bit vulgar'. Also, a local councillor has been distributing leaflets to residents in the district, asking for opinions on the spread of dishes. The following extract from my interview with the Harveys clearly demonstrates the anxieties they have about the positioning and visual impact of the aerial, which Dave installed himself, on the front wall:

> *Liz*: We did try to put the dish round the back, didn't we? ... Still, I don't think it's as bad – as noticeable – on our house as it is on some where there's just a straight row of houses in a line. Then it can look awful.

Dave: Yes. If it was out at the end of the bay, it'd be apparently obvious from all directions. Whereas at the moment you can actually come down the road and not realize it's there.

It is interesting to compare the sentiments being expressed here with the opinions that were voiced by Mr. Gibson. He perceived aerials on modern 'prefabricated' buildings as less of an eyesore than those on traditional Edwardian houses. Mrs. Harvey disagrees – but only because she believes bay fronts help to hide them better. What Liz and Dave share with Mr. Gibson is a desire for the object to be made 'invisible'. On this point, Mr. Harvey announces his intention to site their next dish in the loft. One of the specialist magazines for satellite TV consumers ran a feature recently on the possibilities of receiving a signal through acrylic glass rooftiles, and he is willing to try the idea out for himself. In fact, there are regular advertisements in these magazines for pigments that promise to stain the aerial in colours which blend neatly into any residential background – adding the tactic of camouflage to existing methods of seclusion.

Listening to the accounts given by other families in the same neighbourhood, we can hear a whole range of 'resonances' with those processes of consumption, embedding and articulation that are at work in the Gibson and Harvey households. In my two portraits, I have opened up and explored a number of important issues. Close attention has been paid to the ways in which media technologies get stitched into the fabric of domestic cultures – and, in particular, to the ways in which social divisions of gender or generation produce differential dispositions towards a technology like satellite TV. The part played by this new medium in helping to construct senses of collective identity and transnational community was also discussed. I anticipate objections to using conversational interviews for such an inquiry, but continue to argue that field research provides us with valuable material on the interrelations of private and public in everyday life. Finally, my analysis has sought to understand the contested meanings of satellite dishes in a specific residential setting – including the feelings of pride, disgust or embarrassment evoked by these objects. Pursuing each of the thematic strands developed above, I now want to cite some further examples from the interview data in order to amplify my ethnographic reading.

For instance, there is a definite pattern of satellite technology being desired and acquired by male consumers. Only in one family, the Clarks, have I come across a situation in which the woman was responsible for the decision to purchase a dish – and in this case, it was a mother buying her thirteen-year-old son a special gift at Christmas. The boy – a keen follower of the sports coverage on Astra – always used to be out watching at a friend's house before the Clarks got a receiver just over a year ago. His mother wanted him to spend more time at home in the evenings, and saw satellite TV as a means to that end. Programmes on the Eurosport and Screensport channels have been the main attraction to male viewers from other households in the neighbourhood too. So, against their wives' wishes, Mr. Morgan and Mr. Lloyd bought aerials which enable them to see soccer and boxing matches that are not shown on the terrestrial stations:

> *Mr. M.*: I was the one who wanted to have it. She didn't want me to have it at all. I was watching sport all the time and she didn't like it. It cost us two hundred pounds. That was the other thing she didn't like – the money it cost – but I won in the end, I always do.
>
> *Mrs. L.*: He got it for the sports channels.
>
> *Mr. L.*: The boxing ... they've got a lot on there which you don't get on the ordinary television. It's on nearly every night.
>
> *Mrs. L.*: I didn't want to have it. I was very much against it, but I had to get used to it.

There is also another instance of a young gadgeteer in his bedroom – echoing the experiences of Tony Gibson. Steve Price, a merchant sailor in his early twenties, still lives in an upstairs flat at the parental home for several months of the year when he is not at sea. With the money he earns, Steve has put together a high-quality hi-fi system and owns two video machines in addition to the satellite TV equipment. By contrast, and in common with Mr. and Mrs. Gibson, the mother and father 'never watch it ... they're not interested – they get the ordinary channels on their set downstairs'.

This young man, much like Dave Harvey or Tony, talks about feeling 'limited' by the four stations which are available from terrestrial broadcasting services. His work in the merchant navy occasionally takes him to the USA, where he has witnessed multi-channel cable systems first hand. Steve's acquisition of satellite television on returning to the UK was an attempt to recreate that experience: 'I've watched quite a bit of TV over there, and thought "the more the merrier", you know – a wider variety – which is why I bought it.' The sign of 'America' is prominent here, rather than the idea of 'Europe', but the principles of travel and mobility (both actual and imaginary) are present again. There has, of course, been a long history of debates concerning the export of American styles to Britain (Hebdige, 1982) – with some social groups branding US culture as vulgar and others choosing to celebrate it. What we have to do, as ethnographers of media reception, is seek out those interdiscursive moments of connection I spoke about earlier in this chapter – where identifications with new image spaces are made. One such moment can be found in my interview with the Sharmas, a middle-class Asian family. For the father, Astra's 'non-Britishness' is of particular significance. Comparing the modes of address employed by announcers on BBC1 and Sky News, he comments that:

> With the BBC, you always feel as though the structure of society is there – the authority. Their newsreaders speak just like schoolmasters. They're telling you, like schoolmasters telling the kids. I think Sky News has more of a North American approach. It's more relaxed. They treat you like equals and don't take the audience for a bunch of small kids.

Mr. Sharma's assessment is the consequence of a broader hostility towards establishment values in white British society – and towards the BBC as an institution which, from his perspective, embodies them.

Anxiety over the public display of dishes, clearly evident in my family portraits, is widely expressed by consumers elsewhere in the neighbourhood. Mrs. Clark, the woman who purchased a satellite receiver to please her son, found that she worried about the aerial's appearance when it was fitted to the front of the house: 'I wanted it to go on the back ... they're a bit unsightly, and nobody else in the street has got one.' Similarly, Steve Price admits to second thoughts after installing a dish by himself. 'I do wonder if it looks a bit out of place,' he says, 'because the local council have painted the old railings and made the park nice – I suppose that's why.' It is the now familiar opposition between innovation and conservation which provokes his doubts, and this conflict of cultural tastes functions in the Morgans' home as well. While the husband usually gets his way in disputes over the acquisition and use of media technologies, the wife controls decisions in the domain of interior decoration. Mrs. Morgan has created an antique look in the lounge with traditional ornaments and furnishings, alongside a fireplace which she had specially restored for the room. Her general opinion of satellite TV, as I have previously noted, is low – and there are concerns about how the aerial is interpreted by people living in their street. Mr. Morgan, a lorry driver, refers to the views of a teacher's wife across the road: 'She thinks it lowers the tone of the area with a dish out the front ... there's a lot of doctors and teachers round here, and I don't think they're keen on them.' As for his own perception, Mr. Morgan is less anxious than most interviewees in the district. 'Why worry?' he asks. 'Life's too short, isn't it?' In fact, his expression of indifference has more in common with responses recorded in my working-class neighbourhood. There, the erection of dishes seems to be relatively unproblematic.

On a final note, I would like to stress the considerable divergences in emphasis and method between my own current work and existing academic writings on satellite broadcasting. In the main, published essays and monographs (Negrine, 1988; Collins, 1990; Critcher & McCann, 1990) have focussed on institutional and policy issues. They outline patterns of ownership, draw from the available quantitative data on audience size, and make speculative forecasts about the future take-up and economic viability of the technology. What remains totally absent from this literature is any understanding of the significance that satellite TV has for consumers in everyday social contexts. Of course, all types of research (mine included) will have their 'opportunity costs' – those lines of inquiry which are sacrificed in favour of others – and I am certainly not suggesting that the matters dealt with by these authors are unimportant. However, I am insisting on the need for an analysis which engages with the fine-grained detail of situated consumption practices. My investigation can therefore be seen as contributing to what Klaus Bruhn Jensen (1991) calls 'the qualitative turn' in mass communications research – and it forms part of an emerging tradition of work in cultural studies that is addressing the domestic uses and meanings of media technologies.

References

Bhabha, Homi (ed.) 1990: *Nation and narration*. London: Routledge.

Billig, Michael 1992: *Talking of the royal family*. London: Routledge.

Bourdieu, Pierre 1984: *Distinction: a social critique of the judgement of taste*. London: Routledge & Kegan Paul.

Brannen, Julia and Wilson, Gail (eds.) 1987: *Give and take in families: studies in resource distribution*. London: Allen & Unwin.

Brunsdon, Charlotte 1991: Satellite dishes and the landscapes of taste. *New Formations* 15, 23–42.

CACI Market Analysis 1985: *A classification of residential neighbourhoods*. London: CACI Inc.-International.

Collins, Richard 1990: *Satellite television in Western Europe*. London: John Libbey.

Critcher, Chas and McCann, Paul 1990: Satellite television: pie in the sky? In Williams, Noel and Hartley, Peter (eds.), *Technology in human communication*. London: Pinter.

De Certeau, Michel 1984: *The practice of everyday life*. Berkeley Calif.: University of California Press.

Fiske, John 1989: *Understanding popular culture*. Boston, Mass.: Unwin Hyman.

Formations Collective (eds.) 1984: *Formations of nation and people*. London: Routledge & Kegan Paul.

Geertz, Clifford 1973: *The interpretation of cultures: selected essays*. New York: Basic Books.

Giddens, Anthony 1984: *The constitution of society: outline of the theory of structuration*. Cambridge: Polity Press.

Haddon, Leslie 1988: The home computer: the making of a consumer electronic. *Science as Culture* 2, 7–51.

Hall, Stuart 1986: On postmodernism and articulation: an interview with Stuart Hall. *Journal of Communication Inquiry* 10(2), 45–60.

Hall, Stuart 1988: *The hard road to renewal: Thatcherism and the crisis of the left*. London: Verso.

Hebdige, Dick 1982: Towards a cartography of taste, 1935–1962. In Waites, Bernard, Bennett, Tony and Martin, Graham (eds.), *Popular culture: past and present*. London: Croom Helm.

Hebdige, Dick 1988: *Hiding in the light: on images and things*. London: Routledge.

Jensen, Klaus Bruhn 1991: Introduction: the qualitative turn. In Jensen, Klaus Bruhn and Jankowski, Nicholas (eds.), *A handbook of qualitative methodologies for mass communication research*. London: Routledge.

Johnson, Richard 1986: The story so far: and further transformations? In Punter, David (ed.), *Introduction to contemporary cultural studies*. London: Longman.

Kopytoff, Igor 1986: The cultural biography of things: commoditisation as process. In Appadurai, Arjun (ed.), *The social life of things: commodities in cultural perspective*. Cambridge: Cambridge University Press.

Leal, Ondina Fachel 1990: Popular taste and erudite repertoire: the place and space of television in Brazil. *Cultural Studies* 4(1), 19–29.

Moores, Shaun 1988: 'The box on the dresser': memories of early radio and everyday life. *Media, Culture and Society* 10(1), 23–40.

Moores, Shaun 1996: *Satellite television and everyday life: articulating technology.* Acamedia Research Monograph 18. Luton: John Libbey Media.

Morley, David 1980: *The 'nationwide' audience: structure and decoding.* London: BFI.

Morley, David 1986: *Family television: cultural power and domestic leisure.* London: Comedia.

Morley, David 1991: Where the global meets the local: notes from the sitting room. *Screen* 32(1), 1–15.

Negrine, Ralph (ed.) 1988: *Satellite broadcasting: the politics and implications of the new media.* London: Routledge.

Pahl, Jan 1989: *Money and marriage.* London: Macmillan.

Silverstone, Roger 1990: 'Television and everyday life: towards an anthropology of the television audience'. In Marjorie Ferguson (ed.), *Public communication: the new imperatives.* London: Sage.

Silverstone, Roger, Hirsch, Eric and Morley, David 1992: Information and communication technologies and the moral economy of the household. In Silverstone, Roger and Hirsch, Eric (eds.), *Consuming technologies: media and information in domestic spaces.* London: Routledge.

Volosinov, Valentin 1973: *Marxism and the philosophy of language.* New York: Seminar Press.

Williams, Raymond 1974: *Television: technology and cultural form.* London: Fontana.

Willis, Paul 1977: *Learning to labour: how working class kids get working class jobs.* Aldershot: Saxon House.

Willis, Paul 1978: *Profane culture.* London: Routledge & Kegan Paul.

Willis, Paul 1980: Notes on method. In Hall, Stuart, Hobson, Dorothy, Lowe, Andrew and Willis, Paul (eds.), *Culture, media, language: working papers in cultural studies 1972–79.* London: Hutchinson.

Willis, Paul 1990: *Common culture: symbolic work at play in the everyday cultures of the young.* Milton Keynes: Open University Press.

Wynne, Derek 1990: Leisure, lifestyle and the construction of social position. *Leisure Studies* 9(1), 21–34.

Questions

1 What do you take to be the key ideas in the extract associated with consumption, embedding, mobile privatisation and articulation? How are they helpful in studying forms of media reception?

2 Analyse a range of advertising material for new media technologies – satellite TV, compact discs and players, domestic multi-media systems etc. What techniques do these adverts use in attempting to promote the appeal of their product and how do they do it?

3 Using Moores' approach as a model, carry out at least one detailed household-based study of media technologies – established as well as new – and their use and cultural significance for various members of the household. As well as recording matters of relevant detail you should consider any issues which might arise concerning the method of enquiry itself and your role as investigator/researcher.

Further reading

Alasuutari, P. 1995: *Researching culture: qualitative method and cultural studies.* London: Sage.

Jensen, K.B. and Janowski, N. W. (eds.) 1991: *A handbook of qualitative methodologies for mass communication research.* London: Routledge.

Lull, J. 1990: *Inside family viewing: ethnographic research on television's audiences.* London: Routledge.

McGuigan, J. 1992: *Cultural populism.* London: Routledge.

Moores, Shaun 1996: *Satellite television and everyday life: articulating technology.* Acamedia Research Monograph 18. Luton: John Libbey Media.

Silverstone, R. 1994: *Television and everyday life.* London: Routledge.

Silverstone, R. and Hirsch, E. (eds.) 1992: *Consuming technologies: media and information in domestic spaces.* London: Routledge.

23

Critical Perspectives within Audience Research
Nick Stevenson

From *Understanding media cultures: social theory and mass communication* (Sage, 1995)

In the final reading in this section on audiences and the reception of media output, Stevenson provides a very useful overview and commentary on the key issues at stake in audience research in its current phase. Initially, he begins by noting the intensifying competition for audiences and consumers in the 1980s and 1990s and the complications posed by the development of new technologies – VCRs, remote control units and cable networks for instance – and their cultural and market impacts in the same period. The extract then 'maps' and provides a critical survey of key areas of research and debate associated with recent audience studies. In its original format, Stevenson's discussion is quite lengthy and we have only been able to include his assessment of the work of John Fiske and his particular approaches to the study of popular culture and modern forms of cultural reception. This forms the final part of the extract and includes a series of arguments about the possibilities for diverse forms of cultural creativity and resistance to be understood as part and parcel of the ways in which people actively use and relate to popular culture in everyday life. The commentary that Stevenson provides assumes a fairly advanced degree of familiarity with the historical as well as the contemporary contours of sociological and cultural theories concerning media audiences. One of the strengths of the extract, however, is its ability to summarise cogently different or contending positions of research and theory, and to provide useful signposts for further reading and study, as well as posing the key questions to think about. Throughout your reading of the extract, you will find it useful to make notes on both conceptual and methodological issues for discussion.

The emergence of critical audience studies

Basically two kinds of audience research are currently being undertaken. The first and most widely circulated form of knowledge about the audience is gathered by large-scale communication institutions. This form of investigation is made necessary as television, radio, cinema and print production need to attract viewers, listeners and readers. In order to capture an audience modern institutions require knowledge about the 'public's' habits, tastes and dispositions. This enables media corporations to target certain audience segments with a programme or textual strategy. The desire to know who is in the audience at any one time provides useful knowledge that attracts advertisers, and gives broadcasters certain impressions of who they are addressing.

Some critics have suggested that the new cable technology that will allow television transmissions to be transferred down phone wires will be able to calculate how many people in a particular area of the city watched last night's Hollywood blockbuster. This increasingly individualised knowledge base dispenses with the problem of existing networks of communication where the majority of advertisements might be watched by an underclass too poor to purchase the goods on offer. Yet the belief that new technology will deliver a streamlined consumer-hungry audience to advertisers sounds like an advanced form of capitalist wish fulfilment. This might be the strategy behind a number of investments in new communications technologies, but its realisation is a different matter. Audiences have devised ways of avoiding semiotic capitalism's attempts to make them sit through obligatory periods of advertising. This is achieved by watching another channel, making a cup of tea during the commercial break, or pressing the fast-forward button on the video. In response, commercial culture has sought to integrate advertising into the programmes themselves. Although this makes some form of engagement with consumer products unavoidable, the audience has not been rendered passive. During the 1994 World Cup, American viewers keen to avoid a variety of commercial strategies that had been integrated into the commentary switched to Spanish-language cable television stations. These provided better coverage, as the advertising was not as intrusive, although it is unlikely that the vast majority of the viewers would have understood the linguistic framing of the event. This example points to a situation where the capitalisation and proliferation of different networks make it easier for the audience to escape 'particular' media strategies for their attention. The channel-hopping viewing patterns fostered by these conditions will again make it more difficult to calculate audience share.

But, as Ien Ang (1991) has argued, the practice of making the audience statistically knowable has the consequence of reifying its actual social practices. We may know that 20 per cent of women health workers watched last night's episode of *thirtysomething*, but this actually tells us very little about their viewing context, or indeed the meaning that was constructed from the programme by the women. The form of quantifiable knowledge required by commercial and state institutions is continually disrupted by the everyday practice of the audience. For Ang, and others, the members of the audience remain slightly anarchistic. Our health worker settling down to watch *thirtysomething* might also be zapping over to another channel to watch the new Prince video, or indeed she could be interrupted by a work-related telephone call. In such a context it would be difficult to decide what actually counts as 'watching'. It is the so-called ordinary practices and pleasures of viewing, listening and reading that constitute the second paradigm of mass communication research. This strand of audience watching has been developed by interpretative approaches to sociology and media studies. Against the more instrumental concerns of commercial organisations these studies have sought to address the life-world contexts of media audiences. Here the concerns of audience research are focused on offered interpretations and the social relations of reception.

Contemporary interest in the interpretative activity of the audience usually contains a strong critique of the cultural pessimism of certain members of the early Frankfurt school, and an indebtedness to the so-called uses and gratifications approach.... [C]ertain members of the Frankfurt school tended to view popular culture through a specific attachment to high forms of modernist art. This particular cultural disposition meant that they did not problematise the reading activities of a socially situated audience. It is a disposition evident in literary approaches to the media, like that of Raymond Williams, and Fredric Jameson, whose readings of culture are intended to both mirror and replace those of absent social subjects. Uses and gratifications research, on the other hand, has sought to substitute the idea of what measurable 'effects' the media have on the audience with an analysis of the ways in which people use the media. This research, mostly pioneered by postwar social psychology, brought to the fore the notion that the audience's perceptions of messages could be radically different from the meanings intended by their producer(s). While there remains some dispute as to the debt current audience research owes to this perspective, it is not our concern here (Curran, 1990; Morley, 1992). Instead, a word or two needs to be said, by way of an introduction, on the intellectual roots of the renewed concern with the audience. The strands of cultural theory I want to address have all grown out of the questioning of the assumption that the meaning of an action can simply be taken for granted. That is, the subjectivity of the audience is constructed through its interaction with certain material conditions of existence and a variety of symbolic forms. These concerns are usually connected with a symbolic conception of culture.

The writing of the anthropologist Clifford Geertz (1973) has been particularly vital in helping shape a *symbolic* approach to cultural studies. Geertz argues that what we call culture is the web of signification that has been spun by meaningful actions, objects and expressions. In this sense, culture is neither objective nor subjective. The empiricist claim that the production of hard objective data (such as that produced by viewing figures) can provide a secure anchoring for the social sciences is dismissed by this approach. Such objectivistic claims seem to hold out the possibility of breaking out of the circle of interpretation altogether. Geertz's stress on the symbolic nature of culture retains an openness to further interpretations by the lay actors themselves or the investigative sociologists. Here there is a need to distinguish between first- and second-order interpretations: a separation needs to be made between the intersubjective meanings produced by the agents themselves, and the sense social scientists make of these interpretations. Cultural expressions are meaningful for social agents as well as for the researchers that study them. Further, if we can agree that meaning is a public and intersubjective property, this entails that it is not somehow held inside people's heads. In short, a good interpretation of a particular linguistic community is not governed by the author's cleverness, but by his or her ability to take the reader to the 'heart' of the symbolically produced common meanings.

James Carey (1989), commenting on the recent 'interpretative turn' within media sociology, argues that there has been a corresponding move away from functional approaches. By functional analysis he means research that concentrates upon whether or not the mass media confirm or disrupt the status quo. A more symbolic approach to cultural forms, he suggests, would seek to examine the interaction of symbolic meanings within communication. And yet while this is a legitimate area of inquiry, there remains a fundamental difficulty with this kind of approach to mass communication studies. To put it bluntly, some of the studies that have utilised this particular understanding of culture remain under-appreciative of the operation of power and social structure in the production and reception of symbolic forms.... I shall argue that the production of meaning should be related to the operation of institutions and power. Further, that the symbolic celebration of the interpretative capacity of the audience, in certain instances, has been allowed to replace a more critical and normative social theory.

[...]

John Fiske and the pleasure of popular culture

John Fiske ... has sought to articulate a theory of popular culture that builds upon Hall's original encoding/decoding essay. Running through most of his writing on popular culture is the distinction between instrumental streamlined forms of production that characterise capitalism, and the creative meanings invested in these products by the consumers. There is a radical break between the interests of the economic institutions that produce cultural forms and the interpretative concerns of the audience. Fiske expresses this distinction as an opposition between the 'power bloc' (the dominant cultural, political and social order) and the 'people' (sets of felt social allegiances cut across by class, gender, race, age, etc.). The 'power bloc' produces uniform mass-produced products which are then transformed into practices of resistance by the 'people'. As Fiske argues, 'popular culture is made by the people, not produced by the culture industry' (Fiske, 1989a: 24). To be considered popular, therefore, commodities have to be able to be mass produced for economic return, and be potentially open to the subversive readings of the people. For Fiske, once I have purchased the new Madonna compact disc from the local music store, the product has become detached from the strategies of capitalism. The music of Madonna is not simply a standardised product that can be purchased through the institutions of global capitalism, but is a cultural resource of everyday life. The act of consumption always entails the production of meaning.

The circulation of meaning requires us to study three levels of textuality while teasing out the specific relations between them. First there are the cultural forms that are produced along with the new Madonna album to create the idea of a media event. These can include concerts, books, posters and videos. At the next level, there is a variety of media talk in popular magazines and newspapers, television pop programmes and radio shows all offering a variety of critical commentary upon Madonna. The final level of textuality, the one that Fiske claims to be most attentive to, involves the ways in which Madonna becomes part of our everyday life. According to Fiske (1987a, 1989b), Madonna's career was launched by a rock video of an early song called 'Lucky Star'. She became established in 1985 as a cultural icon through a series of successful LPs and singles, the film *Desperately Seeking Susan*, nude shots that appeared in *Penthouse* and *Playboy*, as well as the successful marketing of a certain 'look'. Fiske argues that Madonna symbolically plays with traditional male-dominated stereotypes of the virgin and the whore in order to subtly subvert patriarchal meanings. That is, the textuality of Madonna ideologically destabilises traditional representations of women. Fiske accounts for Madonna's success by arguing that she is an open or writerly text rather than a closed readerly one. In this way, Madonna is able to challenge her fans to reinvent their own sexual identities out of the cultural resources that she and patriarchal capitalism provides. Hence Madonna as a text is polysemic, patriarchal and sceptical. In the final analysis, Madonna is not popular because she is promoted by the culture industry, but because her attempts to forge her own identity within a male-defined culture have a certain relevance for her fans.

While Fiske draws from a range of cultural theory, most notably semiotics and post-structuralism, the work of Michel De Certeau (1984) has a particular resonance for his approach. For De Certeau, popular culture is best defined as the operations performed upon texts, rather than the actual domains of the texts themselves. Everyday life has to operate within the instrumental spaces that have been carved out by the powerful. To read a fashion magazine, listen to a punk album, put on a soccer supporter's scarf, or pin up a picture of Bruce Springsteen, is to discover a way of using common culture that is not strictly proscribed by its makers. The act of consumption is part of the 'tactics' of the weak that while occupying the spaces of the strong converts disciplinary and instrumental time into that which is free and creative. The specific tactics that evade instrumental modes of domination, or what De Certeau sometimes calls cultural poaching, in practice never become reified as they are constantly shifting and thereby evade detection. In this vein, De Certeau describes as 'la perruque' those artful practices that are able to trick order. For instance, the practice of writing a love letter while at work is a means of stealing time from an instrumental activity and diverting it into a more sensuous pursuit. Thus while the practices of the powerful dominate the production of cultural forms and regulate the spaces of their reception, the reading processes of the weak elude strategies of direct control. To take another example derived from De Certeau; while Spanish colonisers were 'successful' in imposing their own culture on indigenous Indians, the dominated were able to make of this imposed culture something different from that which the conquerors intended. This was not achieved through revolutionary struggle, but by accepting the culture of the Spanish and subtly transforming it for their own ends.

Following De Certeau, Fiske dispenses with the notion of the 'preferred reading' evident within the original encoding/decoding model. Both Fiske and De Certeau are keen to distance themselves from cultural theories, like those proposed by the early Frankfurt school, which assume that the consumer becomes more like the product, rather than the notion that consumers make the product more like themselves. More conservative cultural accounts, for De Certeau, stem from the Enlightenment belief that certain authorised forms of knowledge were capable of transforming the habits of the people. This particular disposition establishes a definite hierarchy between those professional intellectuals who construct the text and those who are meant to passively assimilate it. The 'power bloc', in this reading, attempts to close down the potential meanings of the text by hierarchically fixing certain interpretations over others. The modern world, however, has witnessed a decline in the power of tradition in general, and intellectuals in particular, to prescribe meanings in this way. De Certeau writes:

> Just as the aeroplane makes possible a growing independence with respect to the constraints imposed by geographical organisation, the techniques of speed reading obtain, through the rarefaction of the eye's stopping points, an acceleration of its movements across the page, an autonomy in relation to the determinants of the text and a multiplication of the spaces covered. Emancipated from places, the reading body is freer in its movements. (De Certeau, 1984: 176)

Indeed, for De Certeau, the need to write flows from a psychic desire to master and order the world. The emergence of the novel, therefore, was an attempt to recapture some of the cosmological language that had previously defined one's place in the world within traditional society. In the modern age of atomised individualism there has been a further decline in the commitment to certain beliefs. Further, as those institutions, such as religious and political organisations lose their capacity to engender belief, the people take refuge in media and leisure activities. We now live in a 'recited' society that constantly circulates narratives and stories through the medium of mass communication.

In the post-truth world, the people are saturated by a plurality of discourses that are struggling for the consent of the audience, the difference being that the explosion of messages that characterises modernity is no longer stamped with the 'authority' of their authors. De Certeau aptly describes the way in which old religious forms of authority have been supplanted by a plurality of narratives that empower the reader, rather than the writer. Similarly, Fiske argues that the shift from national to global capitalism has meant that the system of production has become more 'distant', leaving the necessary space for oppositional tactics. The central paradox of modernity identified by Fiske and De Certeau is that the more information that is produced by the power bloc, the less it is able to govern the various interpretations made of it by socially situated subjects. To illustrate this point, Fiske (1987b) often draws upon the seminal research of Hodge and Tripp (1986) into children's relationship with television.

Hodge and Tripp aim to refute the joint myths that television is necessarily educationally bad for children and that parents and children read television in the same way. This concern is particularly evident in their attempt to unravel the reasons for the popularity of the soap opera *Prisoner Cell Block H* amongst Australian schoolchildren. Hodge and Tripp found that the schoolchildren psychically identified with the women prisoners of the television series. The authors explain this phenomenon through the structural similarities of the position of the children within the school and those of the fictional prisoners. Schoolchildren and the prisoners live under a single authority, are treated alike in a tightly scheduled order imposed from above, and have their activities co-ordinated by the rational planning of the institution. The schoolchildren also articulated a number of points of similarity, between the school and the prison, in terms of the way they are often shut in, separated from friends, have no rights, wouldn't be there unless they had to be, and are made to suffer rules they see little point in keeping. The pupils' own self-perceptions resembled those represented by the prisoners, who were also reduced to 'childlike' roles within the programmes. Similarly, the teachers and the prison warders, as figures of authority, were often positioned together. Hence the popularity of *Prisoner Cell Block H* is the result of the children's understanding that schools are like prisons. To return to Fiske's arguments, as Hodge and Tripp amply demonstrate, the 'popular' is an open, fluid and shifting culture that is realised through the symbolic tactics of the weak. The symbolic practices of the schoolchildren can only be made sense of if their various interpretations are understood in terms of the asymmetrical relations of power that exist between adults and children. If Fiske's conclusions are accepted, although I admit I am not totally convinced, then research into children and television should be concerned less with the ideological corrupting influences of television than with the way it is used as a form of resistance.

Life's more fun with the popular press

In a reprinted interview, Fiske describes his own theoretical output as being concerned to articulate 'a socialist theory of pleasure' (Fiske, 1989b). These irreverent forms of *jouissance* that erupt from below are opposed to the disciplinary techniques utilised by the power bloc. Here there is a double pleasure involved in the audience's reading of popular texts. The first is the enjoyment involved in the symbolic production of meanings that oppose those of the power bloc, and the second concerns the actual activity of being productive. These practices are particularly important within modern settings, as not unlike his colleague John Hartley (1992), Fiske argues that modern bureaucratic politics is controlled by a small, powerful minority. The 'distance' of parliamentary democracy from the fabric of people's everyday lives means that participation in the political comes through the creative use of popular products. In this scenario, the market, unlike the declining high culture of the powerful, brings certain cultural products within the critical horizons of the people. The problem with much of the cultural production of the power bloc is that it remains insufficiently polysemic and too concerned with the discovery of objective truth. The search for a final universal truth, which this position implies, is totalitarian rather than democratic. The result is the closing down of the plurality of truths that should be allowed expression under a democratic order. Arguments that the news should be more accurate and objective are actually supportive of the discursive practices of the power bloc. A more democratic form of electronic journalism would seek to ironise truth claims by seeking to reveal the ways in which they are socially and historically produced. To claim that there is one truth, therefore, is to capitulate to the dominant regime of truth, and deny the potentially liberatory pleasure of the text. But once the production of information has given up 'the tone of the author-god' (Fiske, 1989b: 193) this should encourage viewers to become more actively involved in making sense of the world. While citizens are excluded from direct forms of involvement in the decision-making processes of modern representative democracies, they could be allowed more micro forms of participation in a semiotic democracy.

Fiske (1992) has recently sought to make these theoretical points more concrete through a discussion of the press. Here he outlines three different forms of news production: quality, alternative and popular. As we saw above, the cultural production of the 'power bloc' ideologically disguises the interested nature of its production by appeals to universal values. In this way, the quality press, through the production of objective facts actually gears its output towards producing belief rather than scepticism amongst its readers. The eighteenth-century public sphere, defended in Habermas's (1989) account, was not so much about communicatively opening up certain repressed questions, as it was a strategy of domination. It was the power bloc rather than the citizens who decided to circulate certain forms of information that did not require the active engagement of the weak. Next, the transmission of more radical perspectives is sustained by the alternative press, which is dependent upon the practice of radical journalists and is mainly consumed by the educated middle class. This form of news is more critical of the practices of the dominant than the quality press, but its readers and writers are usually made up of more marginal representatives of the power bloc itself. The tabloid or popular press, unlike the quality or alternative press, deconstructs the opposition between news and entertainment. This is a necessary move as entertainment is just as much a discursive product as so called 'hard' news, and for the news to become more popular it needs to be able to pleasurably engage the audience. Fiske also claims that while the quality press produces a believing subject the tabloids encourage more critical forms of cultural production amongst their readers. Through the production of open texts the tabloid press produces:

> sceptical laughter which offers the pleasures of disbelief, the pleasures of not being taken in. This popular pleasure of 'seeing through' them (whoever constitutes the powerful them of the moment) is the historical result of centuries of subordination which the people have not allowed to develop into subjection. (Fiske, 1992: 49)

What is important about the tabloid press is not whether the articles and features it runs are actually true, but its oppositional stance to official regimes of truth. Fiske illustrates this argument by referring to a story concerning aliens landing from outer space, which he claims to be a recurrent one within tabloid journalism. The point about such stories is that they subversively blur the distinction between facts and fiction, thereby disrupting the dominant language game disseminated by the power bloc. Further, while official news attempts to ideologically mask the contradictions evident within its discourse, the tabloid press deliberately seeks to exaggerate certain norms, hereby *abnormalising* them. Fiske's argument here is that the sensationalised stories characteristic of the tabloids produce a writerly text in that they openly invite the interpretative participation of their readers. The tabloids, like other popular texts such as Madonna and soap operas, maintain their popularity by informing people about the world in a way that is open to the tactics of the weak. In this reading, the various forms of depoliticisation evident within Western democracies are attributable more to the quality than to the popular press. On the other hand, Fiske claims to be aware that the popular press is rarely orchestrated towards politically progressive ends. But the cultural and stylistic form of the popular press could, according to Fiske, be turned against the interests of the powerful. A Left political strategy should steer clear of 'preachiness' (Fiske, 1989a: 178) and advocate pleasurable texts that refuse the temptation of imposing certain socially correct meanings. This would hold open the possibility of a genuinely left-wing paper that did not seek rigidly to control the meanings produced by its readers.

Pointless populism or resistant pleasures?

The main strength of John Fiske's approach to the study of media and culture is the emphasis he places upon the creative work undertaken by the audience in the production of negotiated and oppositional readings. The study of popular culture is not about the macro issues of political economy, ideology or the public sphere, but about the evasive tactics of the weak. This view offers an important corrective to those who continue to ignore the capacity of the audience to involve themselves in semiotic insurgence. But I want to argue that the writing of John Fiske is irredeemably flawed. Here I shall offer five main reasons for this claim: (1) his account pays insufficient attention to the institutions that structurate the reception of symbolic forms; (2) his arguments foreclose the possibility of a theory of ideology; (3) his view of the popular press excludes any concrete investigation of its actual content; (4) he lacks a critical conception of the political importance of the fragmentation of the public sphere; and (5) he consistently substitutes his own reading of popular forms for those of the audience.

1. Fiske's socialist theory of pleasure is dependent on a view of the market democratising the people's access to cultural goods. This assumption can only be maintained if mass forms of culture are compared with so-called 'high culture'. As Bourdieu (1984) has argued, access to the relevant cultural disposition for the enjoyment of the 'official arts' is dependent upon the subject's family and educational background. This disposition, or what Bourdieu refers to as the dominant aesthetic, is a learnt bodily sense that emphasises the primacy of detachment and contemplation over active forms of involvement. The habitus of the dominant class can be discerned in the ideology of natural charisma, as well as the notion that 'taste' is a gift from nature. The dominant lifestyle is historically born out of a division within the dominant class between the industrial bourgeoisie and the intelligentsia. The intelligentsia's separation from material necessity has meant that they have traditionally misrecognised their own cultural production as disinterested. Bourdieu's aim is to treat apparently neutral practices, such as those involved in cultural production, as a strategic means of gaining money and power. The intelligentsia's aesthetic disposition naturalises their specific production and reception of certain types of symbolic goods. In opposition, the popular aesthetic, the product of the cultural disposition of the working class, expresses a desire for participation and immediate forms of gratification. This would explain the popularity of soccer as a spectator sport amongst working-class males, given the opportunities for participation through fashion, chanting and singing. The range of cultural practices that are embodied in the popular aesthetic are distinct from those generated by the dominant aesthetic. Hence the social space generated for audience participation within the dominant aesthetic is more tightly regulated. To gain pleasure from the less spontaneous atmosphere

of an art gallery or museum, according to Bourdieu, presupposes that one has access to the appropriate social codes and dispositions.

To return to Fiske, we can see that his and Bourdieu's accounts retain a similarity in relation to the popular need for a strong sense of involvement in cultural practices. Whether these practices are the result of the excess of the tabloids, the writerly texts of soap operas or the more immediate pleasures of soccer spectatorship, they can be defined in opposition to both the instrumental production of the power bloc and the aesthetic disposition of the bourgeoisie. There does indeed seem to be some justification in the argument that the popular culture of the market-place is more inclusive than that of the educated bourgeoisie or the power bloc. But neither Fiske, nor Bourdieu, in their admittedly distinct analyses, pay any sustained attention to the institutions of the culture industry (Garnham, 1986). For instance, the commercial institutions of late capitalism are geared towards targeting certain audience segments. Dick Hebdige has described the post-Fordist move away from mass to more flexible forms of production as the 'sociology of aspiration' (Hebdige, 1989: 53). By this he means that commercial forms of culture are symbolically arranged to connect with the lifestyles and the future desires of consumer groups. What is not clear is that the oppositional readings of target groups actually constitute forms of resistance that subvert the economic structures of late capitalism, or that commercial forms of culture are as materially accessible as Fiske implies.

Computer games, for example, are sold to a young teenage audience through television advertising, trade magazines, television programmes, radio shows and the popular press. Fiske could argue that some game formats constitute relatively open texts, which leaves them open to semiotic forms of resistance. The problem with this argument is that it is difficult to see how the structures of late capitalism are threatened by this activity. Indeed, as with other cultural forms, computer games are likely to have a certain semiotic openness deliberately built into them. ... [S]tructures of domination are just as likely to be maintained through social atomism as by ideological consensus. A society whose imaginary is constituted through difference and diversity rather than sameness provides a plurality of markets for capitalist accumulation strategies. Of course this does not mean, as Fiske demonstrates, that certain readings critical of the dominant social order cannot be opened up through an engagement with the popular. What I am arguing instead is that a fragmented culture may undermine the social cohesion necessary to produce relations of solidarity with those not immediately present in time and space. This situation is likely to destabilise political attempts to symbolically create alliances amongst the weak against the power bloc. Indeed, one could argue that the culturally fractured nature of the audience works in the interests of the culture industry, as it provides new markets and promotes an individualistic culture.

If this argument is followed, then a more effective means of resisting the capitalist computer game industry would be by the use of decommodification strategies. Such practices could include the setting up of public lending libraries in computer games and the production of new games by co-operatives. That such projects are unlikely to occur is surely due to the fact that investment is controlled by large transnational corporations, which in turn are progressively privatising public forms of culture. This problem is completely bypassed by Fiske. In fact, he even suggests, at one point, that new forms of solidarity evident on the dance floor, in fan culture and other popular practices could provide the basis for a more socially just society (Fiske, 1989a: 176). A more institutional frame of reference could have more adequately contextualised the creative responses of the audience by linking them to socially reproducible structures of domination. In this interpretation semiotic playfulness and the dominance of the status quo could be more closely related than Fiske is aware.

Similarly, the absence of an institutional perspective blinds Fiske to material rather than symbolic distinctions amongst the audience. As Peter Golding (1990) has argued, the Western capitalist nations exhibit massive inequalities in terms of their access to cultural goods. This situation is mainly determined by the much publicised ever-widening gap between rich and poor. Fiske seems to assume that the capitalist market has a democratising effect in that it makes widely available a whole range of pleasurable texts. This argument, as we have seen, has some validity, if one compares genuinely popular cultural forms to those that require the application of scarce symbolic resources. Yet if we return to the analysis of computer games presented above, what should be obvious is that it neglects to mention the unequal distribution of the necessary computer technology. In 1986, 32.1 per cent of those whose household income was over £550 a week owned a home computer, compared to 1.3 per cent of those surviving on £45 or less (Golding, 1990). Class structure then erects certain material, in addition to symbolic, barriers to cultural forms of participation, that are neglected by Fiske's concern with signs and symbols.

2. A critical theory of ideology is dependent upon the notion that certain linguistic signs symbolically reinforce or leave unquestioned material relations of domination. Fiske, I would argue, forecloses the possibility of a theory of ideology by always reading the popular as a form of resistance. Returning to Bourdieu, it is apparent that Fiske lacks a theory of cultural domination as such. Bourdieu refers to the dominant aesthetic as arbitrary, since there is no intrinsic reason why certain upper-class accents and tastes should be indicative of a high culture. Culture is a tool of class domination. The bourgeoisie misrecognise their lifestyle and cultural forms of production as being ahistorical and disinterested. The education system, for example, reproduces the dominance of the bourgeoisie through the recognised superiority of the dominant aesthetic. Bourdieu and Passeron

(1977) argue that education institutions impose the dominant form of life on the working classes. The dominant habitus does not socialise subjects into the cultural patterns required by the education system, but results in the self-exclusion of the dominated classes. Through a process that Bourdieu calls symbolic violence, the working class recognises that the dominant habitus is superior to its own. For Bourdieu (1991) language does not serve as a pure instrument of communication but expresses the social position of the speaker. It is not, in other words, the complexity of the bourgeoisie's vocabulary that ensures its superiority. Instead the symbolic dominance of the bourgeoisie is maintained by its ability to censor the legitimacy of other modes of expression. Working-class lifestyles, on this reading, are culturally dominated and evaluated from the perspective of the dominant cultural style. Thus even those who enjoy the robust activities of supporting a soccer team are likely to view higher forms of cultural practice (such as visiting the opera) as having greater worth. Alternatively, Fiske views the popular as the site of resistance rather than domination. He discounts the possibility, which admittedly Bourdieu overstates, that the people would view their own cultural practices as being less important than those of the power bloc. What Bourdieu's analysis reveals is that certain cultural styles and dispositions are able to impress themselves upon others due to relations of authority that exist outside of language.

On a different subject, Michael Schudson (1993) shares Fiske's doubts concerning the extent to which advertising directly affects consumer choices. This is because advertising competes with other forms of information (press reviews, peer assessment, brand loyalty) and is also the subject of popular disbelief. In some respects, however, advertising can be a powerful medium for persuading more *vulnerable* consumers of the merits of a particular product. One such group are young children, who necessarily have access to more restricted sources of information when compared to adults. While they are able to make sense of television advertisements, they are unable to decipher much of the output of the print media and are relatively inexperienced cultural consumers. Fiske, in response, would undoubtedly object that Hodge and Tripp's study argues that children and adults read television in very different ways. While this may be true, Fiske is unable to account for the reasons why children seem to be such easy prey for advertisers. Jim McGuigan (1992) adds that not only are advertisements geared towards creating material desires amongst a young audience, but television programmes and films are often specifically produced in order to sell a range of products from expensive toys to T-shirts. That is, children may decode symbolic forms differently from the ways the producers of the image intended, while becoming convinced of the desirability of a particular product. Thus, in so far as Fiske is hostile to a critical concept of ideology, it would seem that he is able to appreciate only a narrow range of cultural practices.

3. What immediately strikes the reader of Fiske's analysis of popular culture is the inadequacy of his perceptions of its content. Although Fiske's (1982) background in semiotics means that he was fully equipped to probe the internal structures of popular texts, he gives them a decidedly one-dimensional reading. There are, in fact, few sustained analyses of popular texts in his work. This leads one to doubt some of the claims he makes on behalf of popular culture. At the heart of his view of the popular press is the assumption that discursive modes of exaggeration produce a certain scepticism within the reading subject. For Fiske, stories about aliens landing from outer space subvert the language game of the power bloc. One of the problems with this argument is that Fiske offers very little by the way of evidence to support his argument concerning the widespread nature of such stories. Indeed, much more evidence is available for arguing that the actual content of the tabloid press is overtly ideological. For instance, the systematic content studies of Van Dijk (1991) have demonstrated the racist nature of much of press content. In a study of the British and Dutch press during the 1980s he uncovers the extent to which press coverage ideologically reproduces a system that sustains white group dominance. While these issues cannot be explored here, it could be argued, in terms of actual content, that the popular press is more readily characterised by the racist nature of its content, than by the sort of bizarre stories Fiske discovers. Rather than abnormalising commonly held norms, the popular press is more often involved in symbolically creating certain out-groups. The white national press consistently ignores those subjects that are of most concern to ethnic minorities (housing, work, health) while representing them as a social problem (riots, crime, immigration). There is a case for arguing – and this point is forcibly made by Van Dijk – that by representing ethnic minorities in such a way the press is helping to sustain white dominance. This is not to argue that such stories would necessarily be uncritically accepted by their readers, but I would want to at least hold open such a possibility. That Fiske largely ignores such arguments irredeemably compromises his more impressionistic view of the content of popular culture.

4. In dealing with the alternative press, Fiske argues that it has a tendency to be authoritarian and overly prescriptive. Similarly, in his view the culture of the power bloc concentrates upon the 'official' activities of the rich and powerful in a way that is distant from the lives of so-called ordinary people. These very practices constitute the major reason, offered by Fiske, for the 'culture gap' that has opened up within Western democracies between elected politicians and the populace. In place of the quality and alternative press, Fiske advocates a more politically diverse range of popular texts. This argument contrasts with the perspectives of Williams and Habermas who suggest that modernity has witnessed the growing differentiation of high- and low-quality forms of information. This and

other processes, including the privatisation of knowledge, social atomism, economic stagnation and the restricted nature of democracy, has contributed to the progressive depoliticisation of the public sphere. In turn, this has created a social vacuum which the tabloids fill with their particular brand of scandal and sensation. Fiske, on the other hand, uncovers some of the discursive strategies that have been incorporated by popular news, and reminds us that the audience is capable of making plural meanings. However, Fiske's argument that a pluralist, participatory culture can only be sustained once the quality press has become more like the tabloids is totally mistaken. Colin Sparks (1992) has argued that the popular press tends to represent the world in terms of an individualised conflict between good and evil. The quality press, regardless of its political content, is much more concerned with relating 'events' to the public context of social and political relations. Sparks justifiably argues that an informed public debate necessarily rests on the discussion of institutional processes and practices opened up by the quality press. I would add that Fiske misunderstands the original notion of the public sphere that has been developed by Williams and Habermas. Despite the limitations of their approaches, both writers stress the need for a communicative sphere protected from the operation of money and power. Thus the culture of the power bloc should be less about producing belief, and more concerned with the process of rational argument and discussion. That the actually existing public sphere often employs ideological strategies to legitimise the dominance of ruling elites is undeniable. But, as Williams and Habermas argue, a more democratic society and culture can be ensured only by the production of diverse forms of knowledge, and the social and political structures that encourage democratic forms of participation. John Keane (1991) argues in this vein that informed debate amongst the citizens of modern democracies, especially within globalised settings, is dependent upon high-quality forms of information. In his terms, and similar to Sparks, good investigative journalism depends upon the patient processes of investigation that seek to keep a watchful eye over those in power. My suspicion is that Fiske's vision of a more participatory culture is more likely to revolve around a diet of hype and scandal. This view is reinforced by his misrepresentation of certain democratic traditions and his populist belief in tabloid fictions.

5. Fiske's central claim is that the fluid practices of consumers constitute a form of resistance against the dominant instrumental society. While I have questioned some of his assumptions concerning the notion of semiotic resistance, Fiske has been accredited with opening up the theoretical space for the investigation of the audience. The problem here is that, similar to De Certeau, Fiske often substitutes his own experience of the text for that of the audience. John Frow (1991) argues that De Certeau's semiotic categories lead him to implant his own voice, where we should expect to find

those of the users of popular culture. Fiske offers very little by way of empirical evidence to support his claims concerning the vibrant activities of the audience. This is due to his own enthusiasm for popular texts and his intellectual background in semiotic forms of content analysis. His analysis of the intertextual nature of Madonna is largely based on his own skilful reading, and only briefly engages with the perspectives of her 'fans' through the letters page of a teenage magazine. Similarly, Fiske's argument that the tabloid press is open to the subversive tactics of the weak remains at the level of the text. He is unable to offer any empirical support for his argument. Admittedly, while television and film studies are beginning to open up perspectives on the audience, there has, as yet, been little research of a comparable quality on magazine and newspaper culture.

One of the few examples of such research is offered by Mark Pursehouse (1987) in an ethnographic account of the reading practices of tabloid consumers. Pursehouse accurately describes the mode of address of the *Sun* newspaper as 'heterosexual, male, white, conservative, capitalist, nationalist' (1987: 2). His study represents the interview subjects as artfully negotiating with the way in which the newspaper is symbolically constructed. This was particularly evident amongst the women readers who viewed the page three pin-ups and the sports sections as off limits. Pursehouse also reveals that many of the readers viewed the paper as a source of fun and relaxation to be enjoyed as a 'break' from work routines. Yet the newspaper is commonly interpreted as a working-class paper, unlike the qualities, which are presumed to have a more middle-class readership. The *Sun*, for these readers, is defined by the personal use it has in ordinary contexts. We can interpret this reading as a form of ideological masking or dissimulation. As J. B. Thompson (1990) has put it, dissimulation is established when certain social relations are linguistically concealed. When the newspaper is read as a form of private entertainment it becomes detached from the axes of power and politics. The identification of the newspaper as working-class, I would suggest, denies its political and institutional location. As is well known, the *Sun* is owned by the global media empire of Rupert Murdoch, and throughout the 1980s it helped construct the authoritarian populist politics of the far Right. That Pursehouse's readers are unable to give the newspaper a more political reading is probably the result of its being seen as a means of private pleasure rather than public concern. Fiske's lack of hermeneutic sensitivity to the horizons of the audience, despite his claims to the contrary, slides his own reading of tabloid newspapers into that of the audience. More interpretatively sensitive investigations should both open out the space for the responses of the audience, while positioning them within unequal social relations. This is precisely what Fiske fails to do.

References

Ang, I. 1991: *Desperately seeking the audience*. London: Routledge.

Bourdieu, P. 1984: *Distinction*. London: Routledge.

Bourdieu, P. 1991: *Language and symbolic power*, ed. and introduction by John B. Thompson. Cambridge: Polity Press.

Bourdieu, P. and Passeron, C. P. 1977: *Reproduction in education, society and culture*. London: Sage.

Carey, J.W. 1989: *Communication as culture: essays on media and society*. London: Unwin Hyman.

Curran, J. 1990: The 'new revisionism' in mass communications research. *European Journal of Communications* 5(2–3), 135–64.

De Certeau, M. 1984: *The practice of everyday life*. Berkeley, Calif: University of California Press.

Fiske, J. 1982: *Introduction to communication studies*. London: Routledge.

Fiske, J. 1987a: British cultural studies and television. In R. Allen (ed.), *Channels of Discourse*. London: Methuen

Fiske, J. 1987b: *Television culture*. London: Methuen.

Fiske, J. 1989a: *Understanding popular culture*. London: Unwin Hyman.

Fiske, J. 1989b: *Reading the popular*. London: Unwin Hyman.

Fiske, J. 1992: Popularity and the politics of information. In Dahlgren, P. and C. Sparks (eds.), *Journalism and popular culture*. London: Sage.

Frow, J. 1991: Michel de Certeau and the practice of representation. *Cultural Studies* 5(1), 52–60.

Garnham, N. 1986: Extended review: Bourdieu's distinction. *Sociological Review* 34.

Geertz, C. 1973: *The interpretation of cultures: selected essays*. New York: Basic Books.

Golding, P. 1990: Political communication and citizenship: the media and democracy in an inegalitarian social order. In Ferguson, M. (ed.), *Public communication: the new imperatives*. London: Sage.

Habermas, J. 1989: *The structural transformation of the public sphere*, trans. Thomas MacCarthy. Cambridge: Polity Press.

Hartley, J. 1992: *The politics of pictures: the creation of the public in the age of popular media*. London: Routledge.

Hebdige, D. 1989: After the masses. *Marxism Today*, January.

Hodge, B. and Tripp, D. 1986: *Children and television*. Cambridge: Polity Press.

Keane, J. 1991: *The media and democracy*. Cambridge: Polity Press.

McGuigan, J. 1992: *Cultural populism*. London: Routledge.

Morley, D. 1992: *Television, audiences and cultural studies*. London: Routledge.

Pursehouse, M. 1987: *Life's more fun with your number one 'Sun' – interviews with some 'Sun' readers*. CCCS Occasional Paper, no. 85, Birmingham.

Schudson, M. 1993: *Advertising, the uneasy persuasion: its dubious impact on American society*. London: Routledge.

Sparks, C. 1992: Popular journalism: theories and practice. In Dahlgren, P. and Sparks, C. (eds.), *Journalism and popular culture*. London: Sage.

Thompson, J. B. 1990: *Ideology and modern culture: critical social theory in the era of mass communication*. Cambridge: Polity Press.

Van Dijk, T. A. 1991: *Racism and the press: critical studies in racism and migration*. London: Routledge.

Williams, R. 1979: *Marxism and literature*. Oxford: Oxford University Press.

Questions

1 Stevenson suggests that there are a number of key dilemmas facing contemporary studies of media audiences. How would you summarise his main arguments?

2 Choose an example of media output and discuss issues concerning its reception and cultural impact. Use your example to work through the issues that Stevenson develops in his critique of Fiske's work.

3 What methods of investigation might be used for researching and studying audiences and their varied forms of media consumption? Discuss the strengths and weaknesses of selected methods.

Further reading

Abercrombie, N. 1996: *Television and society*. Cambridge: Polity Press.

Alasuutari, P. 1995: *Researching culture*. London: Sage.

Ang, I. 1996: *Living room wars: rethinking media audiences for a postmodern world*. London: Routledge.

Boyd-Barrett, O. and Newbold, C. (eds.) 1995: *Approaches to media: a reader*. London: Edward Arnold.

Buckingham, D. 1993: *Children talking television: the making of television literacy*. London: The Falmer Press.

Fiske, J. 1989a: *Understanding popular culture*. London: Unwin Hyman.

Fiske, J. 1989b: *Reading the popular*. London: Unwin Hyman.

McGuigan, J. 1992: *Cultural populism*. London: Routledge.

Moores, S. 1993: *Interpreting audiences: the ethnography of media consumption*. London: Sage. (See reading 22.)

Morley, D. 1992: *Television, audiences and cultural studies*. London: Routledge.

Silverstone, R. 1994: *Television and everyday life*. London: Routledge.

Van Zoonen, L. 1994: *Feminist media studies*. London: Sage.

Section 4

Producers and Production

Section 4 turns from issues concerning the reception of media output to matters of production, and in readings encompassing a wide range of media – television news and drama, the press, radio, pop and rock music, cinema and video technology – we hope to show the economic, political and cultural determinants which influence the production of all media texts and which in turn shape their distribution, reception and consumption.

The common thread running through all these readings is that media texts are commodities just like any other products of industry, and their production shares many of the routines and characteristics of assembly line manufacture, such as that of cars or computers. In the first two readings, **Peter Golding** and **Roger Bolton** analyse the 'manufacture' of broadcast news and current affairs respectively, demonstrating that both have certain ideological functions, operate within various constraints, and serve particular vested interests. **Stephen Barnard** extends this focus to consider the restrictions which radio producers and programme-makers face, and he draws our attention to the role of 'gatekeepers', a theme which is picked up and developed by **Keith Negus** in his analysis of the practices of key personnel in the record industry. **Richard Kilborn**, in reading 28, taken from his study of the making of soap operas, continues the theme of the constraints which guide production practices and also refers back to some of the issues raised in the previous section about the sense that audiences make of this enduring genre.

The final three readings in this section introduce the theme of new media technologies and consider their implications for cultural forms. In reading 2, **Janet Wasko** looks at film production, specifically the use of special effects in Hollywood movies, while in readings 30 and 31 **Peter Keighron** and **Andrew Goodwin** consider the rather different production issues and problems raised by so-called 'reality programming' or 'people TV'.

Common to all the readings in this section, then, is a consideration of the technical, structural and financial pressures which face media producers. Although many adopt a more optimistic stance and argue that in an increasingly fragmented market the media cater for all tastes, interests and opinions, most of the writers here are rather more pessimistic and broadly support the view that such pressures frequently result in takeover, merger and integration. It is argued that these forces can in turn lead to standard professional routines and institutional practices which limit the parameters of power and freedom, undermine professional autonomy and encourage consensus among the audience by repetition and imitation of successful tried-and-tested formulae.

24

The Missing Dimensions – News Media and the Management of Change
Peter Golding

From E. Katz and T. Szecsko (eds.), *Mass media and social change* (Sage 1981)

In this reading, Golding considers the processes and structures of news production and the extent to which news can be said to be 'manufactured'. In other words, he argues that far from being spontaneous reactions to random events, news is selected, shaped and structured according to a range of ideological conventions, institutional practices and assumptions about the audience, as well as the more obvious practical considerations.

Golding argues that there are many requirements and regulations governing broadcast news (as distinct from news in the more partisan press) and outlines in detail the sequential processes of planning, gathering, selecting and presenting news for television broadcast. He goes on to highlight what he sees as the missing dimensions of television news (social process and power) which result in the promotion of a particular 'world view'. Finally, the extent to which this world view can be considered a coherent ideology is discussed. The ideological nature of broadcast news cannot, according to Golding, be put down to a deliberate intent to deceive on the part of those who work in news organisations, but must be attributed largely to the occupational routines and practices of journalists, and he concludes that reporters and editors play a vital role in consensus formation which they perpetuate by means of a structure of professionally defined *news values*. In doing this, the news media reproduce the very definitions of a situation which favour those in power and legitimate existing structures, reinforce scepticism towards those who dissent or deviate in some way from the perceived consensus, and portray a view of a world where change is unnecessary and undesirable.

What then are the routine practices which define news production? Our research was conducted in the newsrooms of the main television stations in three highly contrasted societies: Nigeria, Sweden and Ireland. Broadly, our research found production falling roughly into a cycle of four sequences: planning, gathering, selection, and presentation. We can describe each of these briefly.

(a) Planning
Central among journalistic beliefs is the idea of news as random and unpredictable events tracked down by the skills of journalistic anticipation and circumspection. In fact much time is spent in the newsroom reducing the uncertainty of the task by plotting events in advance and determining which are to become news. Long-term planning considers general themes and

policies to be included in news coverage and often its relationship to other broadcasting. More important, because closer to and more a determinant of daily news production, is short-term planning. Two mechanisms achieve this: the diary and the editorial conference.

The diary is a key document in any news office. It records predictable events that automatically merit coverage by their unquestionable public importance. It is also a register of less significant events vying for inclusion in the 'automatic' category. In a sense production of the diary is news production in advance, except that it is based on the mere knowledge that events will occur not in observation of them unfolding. The diary is the implicit script of news.

The diary is written from the press releases and invitations which flow into the newsroom, and from the past record of routine coverage. It is a newspaper practice much scorned for the 'soft' nature of the news it promotes, and because it stifles initiative, inventiveness and journalistic enterprise.

On the other hand there's something about the special nature of broadcasting, its monopoly situation and quasi-official status, that makes the recording of such events a matter of duty. Television news becomes a broadcast 'journalism of record'. Many Nigerian journalists took pride in the diary as evidence of the professionalism with which their work was conducted, and took it as a sign of the improved status of the occupation that they were invited to such events. However, many were sceptical of its value, and voiced the conventional dislike of diary stories as dull, repetitive, and undemanding. This distaste for diary stories is universal, suggesting that their persistence is due to organisational imperatives more powerful than the taste or choice of journalists. These imperatives are the unchanging definitions of newsworthy events and the need for pre-planning in an essentially cumbersome operation.

The daily routine of planning is conducted at editorial conferences: gatherings of variable formality which ritually celebrate the limited discretion involved in news selection. Editorial conferences signify on the one hand the degree to which news is arranged and selected a priori, while on the other hand their repetitiveness from day to day and limited outcome point up the unchanging nature of these a priori choices.

(b) Gathering

If news is about the unpredictable, its production is about prediction. Both the diary and the editorial conference are aimed at plotting the flow of events in the world and marking them for manufacture into 'stories'.

Among the most common of sentiments in the newspaper world is the 'pride in being a reporter', a pride often advanced in deliberate reaction to the lowly status of the news-gatherer by the side of the leader-writer or by-lined correspondent. The sentiment lives on in broadcasting, but is stunted by the limited opportunities for active foot-in-the-door sleuth journalism offered by the medium. First, broadcast journalism actually produces far fewer stories per day than newspaper journalism; there is just not the space for a large volume of reportage. Secondly, the demand for film or tape accessories to a story puts a premium on swift, individual reporting, and at its most cumbersome involves a full team of reporter, cameraman, sound-man, lighting man and associated equipment which cannot possibly be as mobile or flexible as one man and a note pad. Third, broadcast journalism is inherently passive because of the labour and resources required for processing, as opposed to gathering news. Only a minority of stories can be covered by newsroom-based reporters or correspondents.

News gathering, then, taps some of the core elements of journalism's occupational ideology: the journalist as news hound, the outward orientation of journalism as an active collector of information, the independence of journalist from source. In practice broadcast journalism is relatively limited in the gathering it can do, and the production of television news is in large part about the passive processing of news the newsroom cannot avoid. Gathering is possible in proportion to resources available, but the threshold is very high so that news gathering remains the icing on the cake. Even in highly equipped and financed news organizations there is enormous reliance on the news gathering of agencies and on a few defined institutional sources, most notably government.

(c) Selection

The sifting and moulding of material coming into the newsroom is the process of converting observed events into stories. The skills involved are largely those of 'sub-editing'; that is editing, but with less power of discretion than a newspaper editor. In practice these skills range from the correction of style and grammar to conform with standard practice, to complete responsibility for the final product.

First among eligible stories for selection are those produced by reporters and correspondents working for the newsroom. The fact that these are normally produced in response to a desk request adds to the likelihood that they will be used.

Traditionally reporters and sub-editors are in permanent conflict. To the reporter the sub is an unfeeling butcher hacking the finest prose for unworthy ends. To the sub the reporter is callow and undisciplined, unaware of the overall needs of the programme. Like many mythologies created in the newspaper world this image carried over into broadcasting but is much muted. The opportunities for conflict are few; there is little chance for extensive writing on which to wield the axe, most stories prepared are used, and many other restraints apart from the sub-editor are apparent to the reporter, including technical ones.

The second source of material for selection is the news agencies. These are a prime example of a supply which creates and shapes its own demand. There are three significant aspects of the use of the wire agencies in news compilation. First, despite reservations about the suitability of their material, the agencies are essential sources of foreign news. Indeed, they are quite literally irreplaceable. Thus the most fervent opponent of agency style or approach has the choice of agency foreign news or no foreign news. The cost of foreign correspondents is infinitely greater than agency subscriptions. For less well-off organizations support of foreign correspondents is beyond their budgets. For them the regionalized services of the agencies, often at scaled-down subscription rates, are the only feasible source of foreign news.

The second aspect of agency use is the global uniformity of news definitions their use imposes on newsrooms. Selections can only be made from the material available, and clear guidance is given as to the importance and relative significance of news items. 'Nightleads', mid-day summaries, 'splashes', 'flashes' are provided as cues for copy- and sub-editors. In remoter stories for which the newsroom cannot supply its own expertise agency interpretation is not lacking.

This leads to the third aspect of agency significance. Although newsrooms clearly have an autonomy, to a greater or lesser extent, in their choice and treatment of foreign stories, these choices tend to be influenced by the sheer authority of the agencies. One agency may be despised for providing Hollywood gossip and baseball scores, but the subscription continues. Another is derided for its lingering British imperial undertones, but again it remains. Agency coverage alerts the newsrooms to world news events, and it is around this knowledge that newsrooms build their own coverage. So even those newsrooms able to send out teams to foreign stories will depend on agency selection for notice of which stories to consider. The agencies are thus an early warning service for newsrooms whose actions are determined by the observations in agency wires.

(d) Presentation

Simply stated, news gathering is most concerned with news sources, news processing with the audience. This is an oversimplification, but the presentation of news is, of all the production processes, the most hedged around with trade lore about what audiences will and will not accept, comprehend or enjoy.

Concern about audiences involves social values. But day to day production has no time to consider social values and relies on news values to guide selection and presentation. Presentation is the skill of turning taken-for-granted news values into rules of production. In assessing audience response journalists have to rely on accepted definitions of news, what makes a good or a not so good story. Journalistic notions of what is and is not news have been forged in the workshops of a commercial press serving historically particular needs and interests. It is in this process that news values are created.

News values are used in two ways. They are criteria of selection from material available to the newsroom of those items worthy of inclusion in the final product. Second, they are guidelines for the presentation of items suggesting what to emphasise, what to omit, and where to give priority in the preparation of the items for presentation to the audience. News values are thus working rules, comprising a corpus of occupational lore which implicitly and often expressly explains and guides newsrooms practice. News values derive from unstated or implicit assumptions or judgements about three things:

(a) The audience. Is this important to the audience or will it hold their attention? Is it of known interest, will it be understood, enjoyed, registered, perceived as relevant?

(b) Accessibility – in two senses, prominence and ease of capture. Prominence: to what extent is the event known to the news organization, how obvious is it, has it made itself apparent? Ease of capture: how available to journalists is the event, is it physically accessible, manageable technically, in a form amenable to journalism, is it ready-prepared for easy coverage, will it require great resources to obtain?

(c) Fit. Is the item consonant with the pragmatics of production routines, is it commensurate with technical and organizational possibilities, is it homologous with the exigencies and constraints in programme making and the limitations of the medium? Does it make sense in terms of what is already known about the subject?

In other words, news values themselves derive from the two prime determinants of news-making, perceptions of the audience and the availability of material. Historically news values come to imbue the necessities of journalism with the lustre of good practice. They represent a classic case of making a virtue of necessity.

There is no need here to describe at length the major values used to evaluate and present news. The most obvious are drama (news stories are, after all, stories as well as news); visual attractiveness; importance (begging the large question of significance); size (of its kind); proximity (both cultural and geographical); brevity [...]; 'negativity (news is about interruptions in the smooth flow of social process, a historically derived definition); and recency. News is about elites, and about personalities.

This list may not exhaust all news values but it includes the main ones. Their obviousness can be illustrated by compiling a list of antonyms. It is hard to imagine broadcast journalists anywhere seeking news which dealt with small events, the long term, dull, distant, visually boring, unimportant people, and so on. Yet many of these labels describe events and processes which may well have significance for news audiences, but which are not news. The application of news values is part of the process by which this labelling occurs.

These four sequential processes in television news production each have characteristics with important consequences for the final product. In sum, the production of television news is passive, routine, limited and selective. This is not a criticism of journalists but an inevitable consequence of the working routines and occupational lore which shape their professional lives. I want briefly to turn to some of the consequences of these patterns for the content of television news.

Television news: the missing dimensions

Our research included a detailed statistical analysis of television news in the three countries. Rather than struggle here through the quagmire of statistics produced, I want to highlight one or two areas. I want to suggest that television news lacks two crucial dimensions as an account of the world around us. These are power and process. By making social power and social process invisible, television news creates a particular view of the world which is incomplete, not by design or intent, but by its very nature.

Power is invisible in three ways. First geograpically, the picture television news gives us of international relations reflects the distribution of agency and organization correspondents rather than world power structures. Roughly 60 percent of these correspondents are in Western Europe and North America. For many European audiences, Latin America is virtually invisible, while Africa and Asia emerge as occasional locations of unrest, war, disaster, or as exotic locales for inspection by Western leaders. Especially for audiences in the Third World their fellows in three continents are invisible, and communality of interests cannot emerge. Thus it is not the *effect* of rich and powerful nations on the Third World which is seen, but their attractiveness as models and benevolence as aid givers and diplomatic mediators.

While foreign news is geographically distorted in this systematic way, it is still only a part of news bulletins. The more obvious geographical imbalance is the heavy concentration on domestic affairs and events. Home news represented from 30 percent of the stories on RTE (this excludes Northern Ireland stories which accounted for another 36 percent) to over 50 percent on Rapport in Sweden. The Irish concern with Ulster of course influences the figures there, while in Nigeria the relative simplicity of dealing with foreign news contrasts with the difficulties of local news gathering, particularly in television, where foreign news is two-thirds of the total. But generally the world news is first and foremost a domestic affair.

The second way in which power is evacuated is in the simplification of the dramatis personae of news. The further away, both geographically and culturally, the more a country's affairs are likely to be portrayed in the activities of one or two senior political figures, until in remoter countries only the head of state is visible. News is about the actions of individuals, not corporate entities, thus individual authority rather than the exertion of entrenched power is seen to be the mover of events. Journalism, and especially television news, is the last refuge of the great man theory of history. Yet faces change, power-holders are replaced, and such changes take pride of place in the circumspection of news. The continuing and consistent power of the position is masked by emphasising the recurrent changes of office-holder and their significance.

Thirdly, power disappears in the process of institutional definition the news creates, the agenda of issues and arenas to which attention is directed. In particular politics is separated from power. Politics is seen in the public display of formality, gesture and speech by major political actors. It is defined by reference to the state and central institutions of political negotiation. Thus power is reduced to areas of negotiable compromise, and politics to a recurrent series of decisions, debates and personalities. It is removed from the institutions of production; thus news bears witness to the institutional separation of economics and politics, a precondition for the evacuation of power from its account of the world.

Social process is the other dimension largely absent from news. News is about the present, or the immediate past. It is an account of today's events. In the words of Ortega y Gassett, the journalist 'reduces the present to the momentary, and the momentary to the sensational'. The world of broadcast news is a display of single events, making history indeed 'one damn thing after another'. Yet in this whirl of innumerable events the lingering impression is of stasis. Events are interchangeable, a succession rather than an unfolding. What is provided is a topping up of the known range of events in the world with more of the same. A reassuring sameness assimilates each succession of events to ready-made patterns in a timeless mosaic.

This fragmentation of social process, evacuating history, has been described as 'a kind of consecration to collective amnesia'. In a real sense reason disappears as actors flit across the journalistic stage, perform and hurriedly disappear. Thus industrial relations appear not as an evolving conflict of interest but as a sporadic eruption of inexplicable anger and revolt. Similarly the political affairs of foreign lands appear as spasmodic convulsions of a more or less violent turn, while international relations can sometimes appear to be no more than the occasional urge for travel and conversation indulged in by the diplomatic jet-set. Simplifications to be sure, but no more so than in the product they describe.

These are, of course, broad generalizations. But I believe they are a fair summation of the statistical analyses of news broadcasting which have been produced by numerous researchers in the last few years. They are no more a criticism of television journalists than the limitations of production noted earlier. They are a commentary on the intrinsic characteristics of the cultural artefact we have come to accept as television news.

Bias, objectivity, and ideology

The notion of bias is often contrasted with objectivity, and for clarity's sake two distinctions should be made. First, impartiality and objectivity are distinct.

Impartiality implies a disinterested approach to news, lacking in motivation to shape or select material according to a particular view or opinion. Objectivity, however defined, is clearly a broader demand than this. A journalist may well be impartial towards the material on which he works, yet fail to achieve objectivity – a complete and unrefracted capture of the world – due to the inherent limitations in news gathering and processing. Second, the bias of an individual reporter dealing with a single event may be reduced or even eliminated by, for example, the deliberate application of self-discipline and professional standards of reportorial fairness and accuracy, or by the use of several reporters of known and differing views. This form of bias must be distinguished from bias inherent in the practice of journalism per se. The former is conscious or at least detectable in individual reports, the latter is accumulative and results from news collection and production as a total process. In other words we should distinguish bias as the deliberate aim of journalism, which is rare, from bias as the inevitable but unintended consequence of organization.

There are, then, three possible views of journalistic objectivity and impartiality. First, there is the professional view that it is possible to be both, based in the idea that objectivity and impartiality are attitudes of mind. Second is the view that objectivity may well be a nebulous and unattainable goal, but that impartiality is still desirable and possible.

The third view, that neither objectivity nor impartiality are in any serious sense possible in journalism, comes from a change of analytical perspective, from the short-term and deliberate production of news stories to the long-term and routine, unreflective practices of journalism as I have analyzed them in this paper. Objectivity and impartiality remain the aims of most day to day journalism. But we should understand these terms as labels applied by journalists to the rules which govern their working routines. Objectivity is achieved by subscribing to and observing these sets of rules, which are themselves the object of our analysis. We have seen how these rules, both the explicit regulations of organizational charters and newsroom manuals, and the implicit understandings of news values, are derived from the currents of supply and demand which eddy round the newsroom. The assumed needs and interests of audiences on the one hand, and the truncated supply of information into the newsroom on the other, both exert pressures to which the organization of news production responds. What are the consequences of these pressures?

When we come to assess news as a coherent view of the world, that is to step up from news values to social values, we enter an altogether more complex and tangled argument. News is ideology to the extent that it provides an integrated picture of reality. But an ideology is more than this; it is also the world view of particular social groups, and especially of social classes. The claim that news is ideology implies that it provides a world view both consistent in itself, and supportive of the interests of powerful social groupings. This can come about in two ways.

First, news is structured by the exigencies of organized production which are the main concern of this study. These allow only a partial view of the reported world which may or may not coincide with a ruling ideology. The historical process by which this coincidence occurs is more than accidental, and is rooted in the development of news as a service to elite groups. Thus most of the basic goals and values which surround journalism refer to the needs and interests of these groups. Second, in attempting to reach widespread, anonymous audiences, news draws on the most broadly held common social values and assumptions, in other words the prevailing consensus, in establishing common ground for communication with its audiences. In the case of broadcast journalism the complex relationship with the state exaggerates this need to cling to the central and least challenged social values which provide implicit definitions of actions and events as acceptable or unacceptable, usual or unusual, legitimate or illegitimate.

I have suggested that there are two key elements to the world of broadcast news: the invisibility of social process, and the invisibility of power in society. With these two missing dimensions – social process or history, and power – news indeed provides a world view. The question remains to what extent this is a coherent ideology. Analyses which see news as necessarily a product of powerful groups in society, designed to provide a view of the world consonant with the interests of those groups, simplify the situation too far to be helpful. The occupational routines and beliefs of journalists do not allow a simple conduit between the ruling ideas of the powerful and their distribution via the air-waves. Yet the absence of power and process clearly precludes the development of views which might question the prevailing distribution and control. A world which appears fundamentally unchanging, subject to the genius or caprice of myriad powerful individuals, is not a world which appears susceptible to radical change or challenge.

There are three ways, then, in which broadcast news is ideological. First it focuses our attention on those institutions and events in which social conflict is managed and resolved. It is precisely the arenas of consensus formation which provide both access and appropriate material for making the news. Second, broadcast news, in studiously following statutory demands to eschew partiality or controversy, and professional demands for objectivity and neutrality, is left to draw on the value and beliefs of the broadest social consensus. It is this process which Stuart Hall describes as 'the steady and unexamined play of attitudes which, via the mediating structure of professionally defined news values, inclines all the media toward the status quo' (Hall, 1970: 1056). The prevailing beliefs in any society will rarely be those which question existing social organization or values. News will itself merely reinforce scepticism about such divergent, dissident, or deviant beliefs. Thirdly, as we have seen, broadcast news is, for historical and organizational reasons, inherently incapable of providing a portrayal of social change or of displaying the operation of power in and between societies. It thus portrays a world which is unchanging and unchangeable.

The key elements of any ruling ideology are the undesirability of change, and its impossibility; all is for the best and change would do more harm than good, even if it were possible. Broadcast news substantiates this philosophy because of the interplay of the three processes we have just described.

Conclusion: news and the containment of social change

Legitimation is the process by which a social order is made to appear inevitable and just. The extent to which any social order appears unjust will depend on the structural location and experiences of those who, objectively, might seem most likely to wish to challenge that social order. I cannot, in this paper, review the various approaches which have been made to this problem by sociologists and historians. Most such attempts are concerned with the production of a value system which is able to accommodate the existence of inequalities, either by masking their extent or by justifying the social processes which generate them.

In this paper I have suggested that one of the sources of such a value system may be broadcast news. For large numbers of people television news in particular has become a dominant source of explanations and imagery by which they make sense of their own lives and the society around them. I have suggested that television news provides a picture of the world which renders radical social changes invisible, undesirable, and unnecessary. In the complex interplay of mediated and situational culture the crucial contribution of television news is to contain social change by failing to provide the values and symbols which would provoke or sustain it.

Reference
Hall, S. 1970: A world at one with itself. *New Society*, 18 June, 1056–8.

Questions

1   At the beginning of this extract, Golding outlines some of the tensions between sociologists' and journalists' perspectives of news. How would you summarise these differing approaches and objectives?

2   Analyse a news bulletin on radio or television. What are the news values underlying the reporting and how might the treatment of the same story vary as a result of different news values on other stations/channels or programmes? Which stories conform to the stages of planning, gathering, selection and presentation to which Golding refers?

3   How do the news values underpinning news content reflect the concerns and preoccupations of the media industry, and indeed the society of which it is a part?

Further Reading

Bell, A. 1991: *The language of news media*. Oxford: Basil Blackwell.

Cohen, S. and Young, J. (eds.) 1973: *The manufacture of news: deviance, social problems and the mass media*. London: Constable.

Golding, P. and Elliott, P. 1979: *Making the news*. London: Longman.

Hall, S., Critcher, C., Jefferson, T., Clarke, J. and Roberts, B. 1978: *Policing the crisis: mugging the state of law and order*. London: Macmillan.

Halloran, J., Murdock, G. and Elliott, P. 1970: *Demonstrations and communication: a case study*. Harmondsworth: Penguin.

Hartley, J. 1982: *Understanding news*. London: Methuen.

Negrine, R. 1994: *Politics and the mass media in Britain*, 2nd edn. London: Routledge.

Philo, G. (ed.) 1995: *The Glasgow media group reader*, vols. I and II. London: Routledge.

Schlesinger, P. 1987: *Putting reality together*. London: Methuen.

Tunstall, J. 1971: *Journalists at work*. London: Constable.

25

The Problems of Making Political Television: A Practitioner's Perspective
Roger Bolton

From P. Golding, G. Murdock and P. Schlesinger (eds.), *Communicating politics* (Leicester University Press 1986)

This extract further illustrates the point made in the previous reading that news and media output is ideological, not by virtue of an overt intent to deceive or manipulate, but because those who work in the media are socialised into its ethics and processes and meet the routine demands of the job in ways which uphold the procedures and conventions of media institutions and the economy which supports them. In both extracts, the different – and in many ways complementary – approaches of social scientists and journalists are highlighted and Bolton, who is a former editor of BBC's *Panorama*, concurs with Golding's view that TV news and current affairs reflect and reproduce a consensual view which frequently renders invisible those who hold genuinely original or radical viewpoints; as Bolton puts it, the debate is often 'deprived of the richness of the unorthodox'. He also alludes to the news values which he and his colleagues almost unwittingly adhere to and which, in his view, lead to an over-dramatised, simplified and largely superficial view of events.

Throughout this reading Bolton draws our attention to the pressures on reporters to make news and current affairs programmes which entertain as well as inform within the almost overwhelming constraints – technical, structural and financial – which face them. And although he concentrates on the ways in which those who work in the media can be manipulated by politicians and civil servants, which, he argues, limits informed debate and reduces accountability, he also states that broadcasters and journalists must take *their* share of the blame. Finally, he concludes that it is incumbent upon media academics and practitioners to work together for a greater understanding of the processes and structures which underlie the production of broadcast news and documentary.

Political television is getting better, as are media studies of broadcasting. That point must be made first as any study of the problems of political programme-making will make the whole enterprise seem impossible. The problems range from the internal and external constraints a journalist faces to the problems of his own limited experience and understanding, the technical demands of his medium, the limited attention span of his audience and their different levels of knowledge and intelligence.

Then there are the manifold temptations along the way: money, ambition, self-publicity. Occasionally there is a test of courage and, without glamorizing the business or mistaking careless rashness for bravery, there are moments when the individual is tested in a way that rarely happens in other parts of television. However, despite all the problems it's getting better all the time and there is tonight's programme to get on the air. Broadcasters are eternal optimists, always believing that yesterday's disaster will be wiped out by today's success.

The internal constraints

Most practitioners are aware of the limitations of the medium and the internal constraints faced by broadcasters and in particular by makers of political television programmes. Television is a 'mass' medium, its audience has a wide range of intelligence and knowledge. Despite the widespread belief that most of the viewers for serious current affairs programmes must be of more than average income and education, audience research studies show that the majority of the audience for the BBC's flagship current affairs programme *Panorama* comes from the lower reaches of the class structure. Broadcasters cannot assume too much but if they assume ignorance it severely limits what they can get across in what is a very limited period, the ordinary attention span. The eternal compromise begins, and it is compounded by the need to keep a frequently tired audience attentive. Nobody *has* to watch, and most people wish to be entertained as well as informed. I plead guilty to forgetting that on many occasions.

As one cannot re-read a television paragraph the programme-maker must signpost with particular care, summarizing at frequent intervals. It is hard to avoid simplifying and there are sirens to be heard calling the producer away from the difficult and the complex.

'Television can't cope with ideas, it's for story-telling, for facts not issues.' I have heard this siren song from the mouths of most distinguished broadcasting figures. It has to be admitted that the argument has some force. For every *Civilisation* and *Ascent of Man* there are many failures, but those two series stand as beacons and surely demand of all practitioners of political journalism an answer to the question, Why hasn't there been a series about political ideas of equal distinction? *The Sea of Faith* provides a further example, presented by Don Cupitt, Dean of Emmanuel College, Cambridge, a leading theologian who some believe can no longer be considered a Christian. It had its difficult moments, but it demonstrated that television and complex ideas need not be incompatible, and can be watched with enjoyment by significant numbers. Another siren voice sings, 'You've got to have a villain, it's got to be us against them.' Investigative and consumer journalists are particularly prone to the overwhelming compulsion to nail a villain in the last frame. Narrow chauvinism is often present; if in doubt blame the Frogs. Other voices: 'Forget the issues, it's the personalities that matter.' 'Make the facts fit the story the public want to hear.' 'Oh God that's boring.'

'Yield not to temptation'

In some ways television can encourage a superficial approach to political television. A 'scandal' is more attractive than a complex and difficult argument. For example, it is much easier to make a moving short film about the closure of a hospital (usually attributed to 'grey unfeeling bureaucrats') with understandably angry and emotional parents and moving pictures of child patients, than to explain the conflict of priorities in a declining economy. This is not to argue that such films are bad, simply that they are not sufficient. The situations they portray must be placed in context.

A programme which is on the side of the suffering and which focuses the public's anger on a target is often thought successful. It has brought an 'evil' out into the open and the 'guilty' persons have been identified. This 'accusatory' form of television gives the viewer and the makers a glow of satisfaction but I fear it is often close to the satisfaction given by unscrupulous politicians to a bewildered public. The need to blame rather than to understand is shared among politicians and broadcasters. It leads to a quieter mind, and a more straightforward film, if only the prosecution's case is heard – and the defence doesn't get a word in edgeways.

I do not mean to suggest that investigative programmes that champion consumer rights, like BBC I's *Watchdog* or Radio 4's *Checkpoint*, do a disservice: far from it. They do a genuinely good job on behalf of the public, for they deal with areas where the truth and the facts can often be established. This product *is* dangerous, that man *did* defraud his company, this unemployed person *was* cheated by a loan shark. Nor do I argue that broadcasters should be afraid to put conclusions at the end of their programmes. All I wish to do is to point out the tendency of the medium to push one into black-and-white programme-making. One should not go with the tide unless the necessary thought, research and open-minded consideration of alternative arguments has been carried out. In addition, this 'black and white' approach usually draws one away from the major issues to the more dramatic and visible ones. This does democracy a disservice, makes sensible political decision-making more difficult and plays into the hands of those who wish to see us frolic on the surface while they carry on unobserved in the depths.

Consider. You are a young programme-maker. You are faced with the choice between making a film about Dr. Armand Hammer, friend of Lenin, Brezhnev, American presidents, the Chinese, Prince Charles, patron of the arts, oil tycoon, etc., etc., with a PR Company pushing glamorous material, free jet flights around the world and an 'exclusive' interview, or trying to explain the coming crisis in the funding of pensions. One way lies pleasure, the applause of audience and editors, and good ratings. And the other? I sometimes think Mephistopheles sits in the cutting rooms. It is to the credit of many programme-makers that they do resist the temptation.

An expensive business

The economics of the medium are a further, obvious constraint, as is what I often regard as an obsession with overmanning and productivity. People are expensive, cameras don't charge overtime or eat, so there is an understandable tendency to hold down numbers of those elements of production upon which one cannot charge capital depreciation.

The BBC is particularly bothered about this, especially at licence fee time. Some newspapers seem to positively enjoy taunting the Corporation over the numbers of people it employs, as if a number, say 30,000, were a good or bad thing in itself. At Party Conference time there are always articles about BBC overmanning. However, they often fail to relate the numbers to the range of broadcasting the BBC does on the External Services, four national radio networks, two national television networks, regional television and local radio. The same person cannot service *Breakfast Time* and *Newsnight* and sleep as well. Nor do [the articles] take into account the complex technical facilities required. A television producer has to take more than a typewriter to get his programme on the air; in effect he has to take his whole printing press.

So there is considerable pressure to restrict the number of production staff, and the expansion of daily programming makes it even more difficult for departmental heads to husband their human resources and give broadcast journalists the time to do original research. One can end up simply reprocessing someone else's 'facts'. Increasingly too the complex technical requirements of television mean that more and more time has to be spent on mastering the 'television typewriter', using the complex graphics, and so on, rather than on the subject material itself. In such circumstances it is not necessarily the best journalists who rise to the top. Sadly this problem is often compounded by Luddite political journalists who sometimes refuse to learn initial production techniques, though, to be fair, there is little training to help them do so. It is usually sink or swim in television, even today. The late entry from Fleet Street, or elsewhere, is rarely able to catch up on the techniques required. His political knowledge, insights and enthusiasms may then go to waste.

The mote in the eye

There is a further potential internal constraint on broadcasters and indeed all journalists, the difficulty of reporting the affairs of our own workplace and of acknowledging the pressures upon us. One has to acknowledge that the journalistic integrity of an organization does sometimes come into conflict with what is perceived as its institutional interest. Or put another way, do media organizations report themselves as freely as they report other groups? I have my doubts. Or put a third way, does the BBC in the licence fee application period act with greater caution than at other times? The answer is yes. Such damage can be limited by a more honest approach to the audience, acknowledging the conflict. And, to be fair, many 'difficult' programmes are transmitted and some only temporarily postponed. One ought not to be surprised: we would be angels or possibly masochists if we gladly scored what in the business is known as 'own goals', and no one is objective about themselves or their own organization.

I have to admit that I felt betrayed by my BBC News colleagues when they published a factual statement about my involvement in a particular controversy. The statement was accurate but necessarily brief and therefore the context was not supplied. 'But you don't understand, you're giving a misleading impression.' I found myself mouthing the words my 'victims' must have used about investigative programmes I've made. It's a salutary experience. When we know something about a subject we become aware of how superficial the reporting of this is. Hence our anger. None the less, the news report had been accurate.

In the case of the broadcasting institutions such sensitivity is often heightened by a mistrust of the fairness of the reporting of certain newspapers who are thought to be opposed to the Broadcasting duopoly and the licence fee and to have a financial interest in its dismemberment. Can it be coincidence that the Rupert Murdoch-owned *Times* published so many leaders critical of the BBC during the 1985 licence fee campaign? This tends to make management defensive and wary of public debate. Still the BBC management has a decent record of going on to the air to be 'clobbered' over an issue, although the producers of review programmes like BBC 2's *Did you see ...?* and BBC radio 4's *Feedback* must be aware of the limits of their critical independence. I admire the way they explore the cliff edges. There is another problem hindering open discussion. Far too many of us making programmes are both too proud and too scared to admit mistakes. Our apparent arrogance irritates the public but we fear an admission will be exploited by our enemies, and the press.

[...]

The outside world

Reporting is often not the problem, it is analysis that poses the difficulty. The facts can often be established, the causes may be matters of opinion. But simply to state the facts, 'two people were shot in Northern Ireland today', isn't enough. Why were *they* shot, why is anyone shot in Northern Ireland? The question 'why?' is arguably the most important one.

So have the opinions, the various analyses, been given air time? It is here that we must acknowledge that the range of voices, of opinions, is too narrow. The desire, sometimes encouraged by the main political parties, to ensure that discussions are representative of percentages and power groups means that the radical, minority, or new opinion is less well represented. The debate is therefore often too narrow, deprived of the richness of the unorthodox. Conservative maverick Enoch Powell on the nuclear deterrent or on the Russians is seldom heard. The distinguished historian and anti-nuclear polemicist E. P. Thompson struggles in relative silence until the Campaign for Nuclear Disarmament flourishes. Too often ideas wait upon political backing before reaching the airways.

The BBC does keep a list of appearances by MPs in its journalistic programmes and it does try to keep a balance between them. It is perhaps inevitable that news and current affairs programmes tend to feature representatives of groups that decide whether ideas will be put into effect, rather than those with simply fresh or interesting ideas. The difficulty of access can be explained by a lack of intellectual curiosity by producers as well as by external pressures, but the BBC Community Programme Unit and Channel 4 are ensuring that many more voices are heard.

Facts? – what facts?

Let us turn to the 'missing' facts then. The laws of libel, 'D-Notices' and the Official Secrets Act keep some matters from the public, and an expensively lost libel case is a powerful incentive to adopt a much more cautious approach in giving legal advice. In April 1985 the BBC settled a libel case brought against one of its programmes, *That's Life*, by a Dr. Gee. The BBC's costs were reported to be over £1 million. It gave many pause for thought, and it would not be surprising if some journalists decided to take a break from 'investigations' in the consumer area leaving many stories untouched.

A further problem is our sources of information. They are limited, and government and most institutional bodies, from the trade unions to Whitehall, want to keep it that way. Information is to be released on *their* terms. J. Downing writes elsewhere ... about government secrecy and the media, and the legislation in operation. However, ministers break some of these Acts continually with 'leaks' and with impunity. The price of the 'leak' for journalists is often the inability to check it against the facts. The reward for politicians is either setting the agenda and dictating the terms of the argument, or testing an idea before publicly backing it; or, of course, the cowardly dissociation of a Cabinet member from his Cabinet without the inconvenience of leaving it, a technique pushed to its limits and beyond in the Thatcher Cabinet in early

1986. So journalists are well advised to treat *all* sources of information with suspicion. I hope we are as energetic in discovering information as we are in receiving it.

Those who give us information are increasingly aware of the mechanics of broadcasting and are therefore in a much improved position to manipulate it. And of course Whitehall is full of people who are paid to release information only in the interests of governments. Even prime ministers' press secretaries ('sources close to the Prime Minister') have been known to tell terminological inexactitudes. Harold Wilson 'let it be known' how he had 'read the Riot Act' to the Parliamentary Labour Party on many occasions. On one famous day he was reported as threatening to take their 'dog licences' away, that is, withdraw the whip. These accounts were often read with amazement by MPs who were present and remembered things very differently.

Harold Wilson was also extremely well informed about newspaper deadlines and frequently captured headlines with a last-minute story. Nowadays most politicians play that game. Get your retaliation in first, said the late Bill Shankley, Manager of Liverpool Football Club. Most inhabitants of governments don't need to be told that.

There are various other tricks which can be used in the PR offensive. Ring up a television programme and offer an 'exclusive' interview. The producers rarely say no if they think they will beat a rival. Go on current affairs programmes like *Weekend World* or *The World This Weekend* on Sunday as Monday morning's newspaper headlines are the easiest ones to capture. Issue a very long and complicated White Paper to journalists only on the day of publication, and hold a press conference close to the news deadline. The journalists will not have time to absorb it all, they will have to accept the summary given by the politicians and a day or so later when the difficult questions are beginning to be formed in the broadcaster's mind, who cares? The headlines have been won, the terms of the argument established in favour of the politician concerned.

If a difficult television discussion is proposed – refuse to take part, say you were misled about the nature of the programme, and if it goes ahead say it is obviously biased. If you are a Cabinet minister refuse to participate in a discussion with anyone less senior than yourself. It limits the field. The other trick in this area is to demand a separate interview. Programme makers can be so desperate to get the minister that they agree. I have buckled to such pressures, I'm afraid.

Another technique is to do only a 'live' interview on the news. That way you can't be edited and in the two or three minutes available it is unlikely that the questioner will be able to put you on the spot. During the Falklands War, television was sometimes taking the Ministry of Defence pressman Ian MacDonald's statements 'live', thus frustrating any attempt to put the remarks into context. The dangers of such 'live' interviews are well understood by the broadcasting authorities who have tried to ensure that they do not recur.

A significant blow to informed political discussion and debate was struck by the emergence of Mr. (later Sir Gordon) Reece and the Saatchi Brothers at Conservative Central Office. While they were amateurs compared with Ronald Reagan's entourage, they signalled a concentration on image rather than content. They were concerned with winning elections not arguments.

Attention was switched from the quality press in Fleet Street to the mass circulation newspapers. Knighthoods and ennoblements followed. In broadcasting, Jimmy Young on Radio 2 was favoured rather more than *Panorama*, chat shows rather than Robin Day. Mr. Young frequently asked difficult questions and occasionally Sir Robin or Sir Alastair *was* allowed in but, this aside, the overall result was a gentler ride in more relaxed surroundings for a larger audience. Eminently sensible if you are Mrs. Thatcher, extremely frustrating if you are a political journalist. And 'tough' interviews are getting tougher – for the interviewer. For example, Mrs. Thatcher has invented her own way of dealing with questions. Don't take a breath, or halt, at the end of sentences. This means that the interviewer either can't get his question in or seems to be rudely interrupting if he is. If the programme is live the time soon runs out, and accountability is evaded.

What politics does television cover?

So the problems of making political television are considerable. What sort of political television do we make? How successful has news management, image-making and pressure groups' lobbying been? Of course, those who are employed in making political television have a vested interest in proclaiming its success. Perhaps it is successful only in the short term, and in the margins. The pendulum swings and governments are ejected from office as the signs of their failure become apparent, or through simple boredom on the voters' part. Eventually the truth may come out but a lot of damage can be done in the short term, a lot of decisions taken and a lot of time and energy spent on isolating the PR and pressures, time and energy which ought to have been spent addressing the issues and informing the public. Yesterday is, well, yesterday, say the PR men. Today's headlines are what matters.

It all acts as a sort of camouflage to hide the real political debate which should be taking place. Harold Wilson is reported as saying that the Labour Party was rather like a stage-coach. The important thing was to keep it going. If you did that then the passengers inside would talk to each other and leave the driver to get on with it. However, if the stage-coach stopped at the crossroads then the passengers would get out, argue about which direction to go and never get back in again. I would suggest that while it is the politicians' job to drive the coach, it is the journalists' responsibility to ensure that the passengers have seen the signpost.

All of this leads to two tiers of political debate, the public and the private. The public debate usually starts when the decision has been taken; sometimes it may never happen at all. On the surface statements are made, images created, poses struck, insults exchanged. Underneath the reality is often the opposite. One of my main frustrations as a political journalist and editor has been my frequent failure to help the public get into the real debate while it is going on, while it is undecided in Cabinet, party and Parliament.

At the time of writing there is a real debate to be had about the forthcoming defence crises where once more our commitments exceed our capacities. It is also clear that unemployment is unlikely to go down significantly in the long term, let alone the short term, but where is the debate about how society should adjust to that fact? The Conservative and Labour Parties, for differing reasons, find it difficult to accept this publicly, although they must know it to be true. The real problems of managing economic decline cannot be addressed without acknowledging this decline, but this is hardly the best prescription for re-election. Anyway it has to be admitted that much of the public is just not interested. Does this suggest that the media provide a platform for the sound and the fury, while elsewhere 'real politics' goes on?

That would be unfair to many parts of the media. It would be wrong to lump the *Financial Times* in with the *Sun*, or *Newsnight* with *TV-am*. Somewhere in the media most of the important issues are dealt with at one time or another. The problem is one of priority, not presence. Getting the important issues to the forefront of the debate, ahead of the peripheral and transient, is the problem.

Political television should be about the way countries are governed, or could be governed, their political systems and the important decisions which are being taken, or which need to be taken. Many argue that political coverage is too much about personalities rather than politics. Others argue that television's political coverage is too Westminster- or Whitehall-dominated, not enough of the 'real' world and people's ordinary experience. I believe political television should be, and is, about all these things. It is the proportions we should argue about and which are wrong.

Our domestic political coverage is obviously hampered by the fact that none of us is objective about our own country. We must try to become more so but we must first acknowledge the subjective impulses. As I have mentioned earlier, the BBC acknowledges a bias – towards parliamentary democracy, a bias which I welcome. But we must acknowledge, if we are to begin from that standpoint, that voices outside that form of democracy must be heard.

However, some people believe that broadcast journalism has taken a knock to its collective confidence because it is now being said that there is no such thing as objectivity. The trained observer is now being told that all his judgements are subjective, and he is still recovering from the shock. The Glasgow University Media Group has perhaps had the greatest influence here although *its* own subjectivity and lack of broadcasting experience has limited its effects upon many practitioners.

[...]

What can the broadcaster do?

Faced with these problems of internal and external restraint and with the inadequacy of much that we do, broadcast journalists should be asking themselves some very hard questions. How much better can we do, even given these problems?

We broadcasters should blame ourselves as well as the politicians for the state of political broadcasting. Their responsibility is to manage change not ensure a good debate and one should accept that there are many issues where it would be politically irresponsible to be frank in public, although governments frequently do use the cover of 'the national interest' simply to conceal mistakes and cover embarrassment. Arms limitations talks and discussions over Zimbabwe or Ireland are examples where political discretion is vital in order to achieve the end result. However, if we recognize the need for such discretion by politicans, yet also recognize the need for the public to be properly informed about these issues, while they are current, then I believe it must fall to journalists to place these items on the public agenda.

A former Director-General of the BBC disagreed. In his view it was the duty of Parliament, as an elected body, to decide the agenda. It was not an issue, in his view, if there was no real debate about it in the Commons. Thus the unification of Ireland was not an issue because the front benches of both major parties had agreed that it was not, despite the views of a very large minority recorded in public opinion polls, not to mention many people in Ireland, north and south.

I disagree with him. Broadcasters have no right to place the issues they regard as important before everything else but they do have a duty to put them on the list. This duty derives from the knowledge they have of the real political debate that goes on outside the Chamber or the studio, and the facts they unearth in their reports. The broadcasters' responsibility to the audience is to speak the truth as they see it, to be more open about their procedures and limitations, to be more aware of their own subjectivity. The broadcaster is privileged with information and he must share it.

In the light of all these formidable problems and duties, how qualified are television's producers to produce political journalism? Well, they are mostly white, middle-class and relatively young, and they are almost as likely to be female as male. A large number will have gone to Oxbridge, they will be instinctively suspicious of authority, liberal on social issues, uncertain on economic ones. They will be independent, ambitious and intelligent. They will probably have arts or politics degrees. They are not representative, but they are often highly skilled, and the vast majority try not to wield private prejudices and do strive for the truth. And of course they are not alone. They have editors above them (who will probably be 35–45, almost exclusively male) who are well advanced on the road to cynicism! And they work with presenters and reporters who are often highly qualified and rather older.

What they do require is far more time to think and far more training. In my view young producers should be shipped to Party Conferences and made to listen to every debate, and go to evening meetings. Such attendance is an essential part of political education regardless of what the *Sun* or the *Mail* or the *Daily Telegraph* will say. Producers should frequently attend the House of Commons and also get out of London. Above all, television management should arrange that the best authorities in different fields should be brought to them, a wide variety of political thought and analysis placed before them. In short, we must ensure that a continuing political education is built into a producer's career, to supplement his practical experience. Those political specialists in broadcasting must also share their knowledge, not just with their audience, but also with their colleagues.

It is a tragedy that Philip Elliott is no longer here to make his always pertinent contribution. I found his writing full of sympathy, understanding and good sense, even when it hurt. He eschewed the easy gibe and the easy answer and he was never deflected from the central questions. He underlined our limitations without self-righteousness. He knew that broadcasters and media academics have a responsibility to educate each other, as well as to educate themselves. And it is here that media academics can play a part. They must reach the parts of the BBC they haven't reached so far, the daily and weekly practitioners, as well as managers like myself. They will meet some prejudice and antagonism within the Corporation and they will have to make sacrifices! They must write in simple, direct English. They must acknowledge their lack of practical knowledge and attempt to remedy it. They must look for the cock-up rather than the conspiracy. Perhaps the result of this dialogue will be a temporary loss of confidence by both parties in old certainties, but it is an essential prelude to our being able to discharge our joint duty, to pursue the truth more rigorously and to inform our democracy more fully.

Questions

1 What are the predominant 'news values' which current affairs programmes such as *Panorama* and *World in Action* adhere to? How and in what ways do they differ from the underlying values in TV and radio news broadcasts?

2 If, as both Golding (in the previous reading) and Bolton suggest, news is produced by, and aimed at, a political and cultural elite, what are the implications for those who are not part of that elite, or who are in some way marginalised from the mainstream? Who might those groups include?

3 Bolton refers to Margaret Thatcher's urge to starve terrorists of the 'oxygen of publicity'. What are the cases for and against imposing a broadcasting ban on interviews with opponents of the government, including terrorist organisations?

Further reading

Barnouw, E. 1992: *Documentary: a history of the non-fiction film*, 2nd revised edn. Oxford: Oxford University Press.

Elliott, P. 1972: Media organisations and occupations: an overview. In Curran, J., Gurevitch, M. and Woollacott, J. (eds.), *Mass communication and society*, London: Edward Arnold.

Gallagher, M. 1982: Negotiation of control in media organizations and occupations. In Gurevitch, M., Bennett, T., Curran, J. and Woollacott, J., *Culture, society and the media*, London: Routledge.

Hillyard, P. and Percy-Smith, J. 1988: *The coercive state: the decline of democracy in Britain*. London: Fontana.

Horrie, C. and Clarke, S. 1994: *Fuzzy monsters: fear and loathing at the BBC*. London: Heinemann.

Lorenz, A. L. and Vivian, J. 1996: *News reporting and writing*, Massachusetts: Allyn & Bacon.

Philo, G. (ed.) 1995: *The Glasgow media group reader*, vols I and II. London: Routledge.

Schlesinger, P., Murdock, G. and Elliott, P. 1983: *Televising terrorism: political violence in popular culture*. London: Comedia.

Tracey, M. 1977: *The production of political television*. London: Routledge & Kegan Paul.

Tunstall, J. 1993: *The television producers*. London: Routledge.

Winston, B. 1996: *Framing the real*. London: BFI.

26

Keepers of the Castle: Producers, Programmers and Music Selection   Stephen Barnard

From *On the radio: music radio in Britain* (Open University Press 1989)

This extract continues the emphasis on media producers and the constraints associated with particular contexts of production which is the dominant theme running throughout this section. Radio is a modern medium which has, by comparison with television and film for example, received relatively little analytical attention. It has been described as the 'Cinderella' of Media Studies. In what follows, Barnard provides a detailed account of the production contexts associated with popular music radio in Britain, in particular BBC Radio 1. In the initial stages of the extract, Barnard usefully summarises the idea of the producer as a *gatekeeper*, someone who makes key decisions and selections concerning the fate and the form of potential media output or content, in accordance with their role and position within a professionalised occupational culture and hierarchy. He provides a brief historical account of the development and key changes within BBC music policy in the post-war period and then focuses on questions concerning the playlist – a weekly list of records which have guaranteed regular airtime – and its function for Radio 1 in the 1980s. At the heart of his discussion are a number of issues concerning the relationships between the music industry, the charts and radio airtime given to particular types and formats of popular music.

It is important to approach Barnard's study with a view of its own history. It was published first in 1989 and based very much on research undertaken in the 1980s. Since then a number of significant changes have overtaken the empirical detail of the research, perhaps most notably changes in the compilation and organisation of the weekly music charts and some major and much reported changes of personnel and policy at 1 FM, as it now prefers to call itself, as well as key changes across the radio sector in the United Kingdom as a whole. However, the style and focus of the analysis provide a useful basis from which to think about questions concerning the formats of the radio 'soundscapes' – musical and otherwise – of the late 1990s. Barnard usefully summarizes some of these issues in the postscript which he wrote especially for this volume.

> I don't mind when people say we play wallpaper music. A lot of people spend a
> lot of time and money choosing the right wallpaper for their homes.
> Bob Snyder, former Programme Controller, Radio Trent[1]

... I have touched upon the general principles guiding the use and selection of popular music by radio stations in Britain: the tendency to concentrate on the most musically familiar, the unwillingness to deviate from a selection of records based on chart placings or potential chart placings, the isolation of non-mainstream music to peripheral programmes outside the peak-time hours, the preference shown for commercially produced records over live or specially recorded music during those peak hours. These tendencies need to be examined more closely in the context of the decisions taken by those who, to use sociological terminology, are the 'gatekeepers' of radio: the programme controllers and programme producers who oversee not only what is played on the radio but the environment in which it is heard, the frequency of its playing and its positioning within programmes. They, far more than presenters, are the source of power in music radio, but the intention here ... is not simply to equate their apparent control of radio output with a necessarily major influence over the fate of record-industry product, nor is it to pin 'responsibility' on them for the blandness and predictability of so much music programming. Rather, it is to explore how gatekeepers both represent and patrol the twin ideologies of consensus and consumer sovereignty, and to assess the end result – a pattern of programming and a style of presentation which, during the daytime hours at least, uses popular music as a barrier against tension, conflict and disruption.

First of all, we must clarify what 'gatekeeping' entails. Gatekeepers, of course, can be found in all media, and the source of the concept (and the term) is David Manning White's study of editorial practices in mid-west newspapers, *The 'Gatekeeper': A Case Study in the Selection of News.*[2] White found that editors chose which stories to follow up, which to headline and which to relegate to shorter items, according to a number of different criteria: the particular editorial line (political and otherwise) of the newspaper concerned, whether the story had a local angle, qualities of 'human interest' and so on. Media gatekeepers, in White's analysis, determine not only what is mediated by technological means but the *manner*, the nuances of its communication. Later research work has concentrated on exploring the value systems and organizational constraints under which gatekeepers work, and how these are communicated and reinforced down a chain of command. Certain researchers, for example, have paid particular regard to the inculcation of notions of professionalism from seniors to juniors (most obviously, editors to reporters) and the maintenance of an editorial line – an encapsulation of a certain ideology – not so much through direct enforcement or threats of the sack as through encouraging a kind of notional independence based on self-censorship, the skill of *knowing* without having to be told which stories are acceptable and which are not.[3] This is all relevant to understanding the 'editorial' practices of music radio, because programme producers, too, are continually called upon to put their own tastes and preferences behind them in favour of a professional assessment of which music will most fit the editorial profile of their station. However, the fact that the radio gatekeeper is dependent on a commercial source – the record manufacturers – for much of his material complicates the issue, as he then becomes a mediator in their marketing strategies as well as an enactor of his own. The radio gatekeeper may appear to mediate between manufacturer and consumer, in the same way that record reviewers in newspapers do, but his *responsibilities* ultimately lie elsewhere. Radio gatekeepers have a responsibility to the public only in the vaguest sense: their primary concern is to serve the *particular* publics that the stations' managers or owners have delineated.

Precisely who, then, are the gatekeepers who make the decisions as to which music is played on British radio, and how has their role evolved? In the case of Radio 1 and Radio 2, the responsibility for music selection lies with individual programme producers, though in the former case the producer draws on a playlist predetermined by committee; within independent local radio (ILR), the responsibility generally lies with a single person, usually the station's programme controller or a specially appointed head of music. Differences in personnel levels mainly reflect different economies of scale, but they also reflect different traditions and priorities. For one thing, there is a strong bureaucratic tradition within the BBC which ILR stations, because of the perpetual concentration on commercial returns and cost-effective, self-sufficient operation, have largely avoided emulating. Also, the commercial imperative in ILR is to maintain a consistent musical identity throughout the prime-time hours; the emphasis is on continuity, flow, a consistent voice, to encourage listeners to stay tuned. That kind of consistency can be threatened when presenters either indulge their own musical tastes or play the same record too often, so there is a particular need in ILR for music formats to be both predetermined and policed by an individual who has the complete day-to-day output of the station in mind. Radios 1 and 2 have tended to be much 'freer' in comparison, the key difference being that, despite the sequential nature of much of their output, both networks were run until late 1987 (when policy changes, discussed later in this chapter, were introduced) as collections of connected but individually executed programmes. In traditional BBC thinking, separate programme production is a sign of quality and attention to detail, a mark of professionalism; as Radio 1 controller Johnny Beerling says, 'the most successful thing you could do on the surface of it is just play Top Forty music all day with disc jockeys like Tony Blackburn and put the thing on a format and just rotate it. We don't do that by any means. I think we try to treat the audience intelligently'.[4] Most important of all, Radios 1 and 2, unlike ILR stations, see themselves as personality stations first and foremost, their success hinging on the appeal of the disc jockeys. Producers act as stage managers to the presenters and may even choose records on the basis of whether they are 'right' for that presenter's public image. In local radio, with a few exceptions, presenters have a much more low-key role and their personalities are generally (and quite deliberately) subservient to the image of the station.

Given all this, the music choices made by gatekeepers in both national and local BBC and commercial radio nevertheless follow a remarkably similar pattern, which self-imitation and continual aping of competitors cannot alone explain. That they share similar perceptions, a similar sense of professionalism, even a common ideology, is obvious, and I have already commented on the mobility of labour between the two systems and the degree to which ILR stations deliberately drew on BBC experience in fashioning their music policies. Historically, musical gatekeeping in British radio has been paternalistically motivated, and the legacy of this lives on.

Producers and programming

...[T]he gatekeeper role evolved at the BBC with particular reference to popular music, initially through dance-band leaders who learnt the degree of acceptability of certain songs or types of music by trial and error, then via the BBC's two directors of dance music, Jack Payne and Henry Hall, who sought to lead by example. Although directly responsible to senior management for the decisions they made, both men were to some extent their own masters, interpreting a vague brief to provide tasteful, acceptable dance music in a manner calculated not to incur the displeasure of their employers – operating what was in effect a kind of self-censorship, creating music that not only matched the BBC perception of popular music as light, relaxing and 'domestic' but helped institutionalize it. Beginning in the war years, the gatekeeping function became more diffuse, less open to individualistic interpretation, as policy-making came under the jurisdiction of committees and producers assumed an almost clerical role, continually referring back any songs or records thought likely to be contentious. Out of the ensuing bureaucracy grew the two centres of popular music output, the Gramophone Department and the Popular Music Department, and a dual supply system that only outlived its usefulness once Radios 1 and 2 started and the need for programmes with a consistent network identity was established. Radio 1 in particular was not just a departure in programming terms but also in administration, as the producer's prime accountabilities shifted from supply departments to the network itself, thereby facilitating the development of a Radio 1 'house style' in presentation and a corporate policy on music selection. That policy has changed in ways both subtle and obvious over the years, but a certain Radio 1 'ideology' has been maintained throughout, to which the attitudes and working practices of its present-day gatekeepers – the network management team and, most crucially, the producers who report to them – give clues.

As Light Programme offshoots, both Radios 1 and 2 retain the vestiges of Light Programme values. Like its parent network, Radio 1 categorizes popular music as *either* easy-listening background music *or* as a culturally valid, quasi-classical music requiring isolation to the periphery of the schedules, both in deference to its assumed superiority to standard pop fare and to prevent it disrupting mainstream programming. (That the Radio 1 version of background music is different from Radio 2's interpretation of it is simply a factor of the former's dependence, for reasons we shall examine, on the record sales chart as a source of material.) The pervasiveness of Light Programme values – its populism, its domestic ambience, its commitment to the entertainment ethic – can be attributed to two factors in particular, both to do with the personnel involved. First, there has been a continuity at management level: Radio 1 has been successively headed by Robin Scott, Derek Chinnery and Johnny Beerling, all of them Light Programme trained and the latter two with technical backgrounds, having come to the BBC after service in the armed forces as technical operators. One of the most telling features of BBC radio's pre-1967 popular music output was that it was trusted to those on the technical rather than editorial side of BBC operations, in contrast to the academic editorial bias among producers on the Third Programme. A Third Programme producer, because of his 'cultural' responsibilities, was recruited on the basis of his musical know-how; Light Programme producers on the other hand might well have been musically literate (several during the 1950s and 1960s were ex-musicians with dance-bands), but they were primarily recruited on the basis of their technical expertise, administrative ability and/or their experience in radio overseas. Both the British Forces Broadcasting Service (BFBS) and the radio services of the old Commonwealth were regarded as good training grounds. While the criteria for recruiting producers have changed in the twenty years since the 1967 upheaval, the internal management structure of the two networks remains much as it was in the Light Programme days, with the respective Controllers presiding over a two-tier hierarchy of executive producers and programme producers.

The other key to Radio 1's maintenance of essentially populist values lies in the general area of producer professionalism – the way in which programme producers, working to those in executive positions, absorb and replicate those values in their daily decision-making. A good starting-point here is to develop the parallel made earlier between the selection of records for broadcasting and the selection of news items for dissemination: the process of selection in both cases calls upon the producer/journalist to exercise judgement on questions of priority, topicality and audience interest. *Professional* judgement overrides personal taste or personal politics: in newspapers, for instance, news value may be determined by requirements for sensationalism, beating the opposition in a circulation war, a certain political line, an internationalism or parochialism in outlook, the consumer orientation of the readership. Likewise in music radio, professional judgement on the acceptability of certain records to the audience overrides personal likes or dislikes, and 'entertainment value' will be similarly evaluated according to questions of how the records match the tone and ambience of the station. As John Downing writes in *The Media Machine*, 'ingraining a definition of professional excellence is the only effective mechanism for ensuring the *spontaneous* [his italics] production of acceptable items';[5] in other words, the process of selecting or discarding items, prioritizing some and underplaying others, becomes internalized to the point that no reference back to one's superiors is necessary – the house style, the editorial policy, is absorbed and justified by the individual on professional grounds. On a practical level, the news journalist is continually faced by a number of control mechanisms that have some parallels in radio: recruitment itself, whereby potential staff are judged by their past work according to how well they fit in with the editorial posture of the newspaper; short-term contracts, the insecurity engendered by which fosters a spirit of acquiescence rather than challenge; subordination of individual style to that of a house style; and of course the submission of work to editors or sub-editors.

In television and radio news there is the additional requirement, set down in the BBC Charter and the IBA Act, to 'balance' every item: the news reporter or newsreader is, in theory, a passive relater of events, neutral in his opinions and impartial in his coverage. That the notion of 'neutrality' is disingenuous probably needs little elaboration here, as there is plenty of empirical evidence to suggest that impartiality becomes synonymous with an insidious *partiality* for the notion of political 'moderation', but it is important to record that journalistic professionalism within the BBC, ITN and IRN is equated with an adherence to the neutrality ethic. And as in journalism, so in other editorial broadcasting matters: nowhere does the concept of professional neutrality – of acting as what Simon Frith calls an 'honest broker' between the record industry and the radio audience[6] die harder than in the corridors of Radio 1's Egton House. Radio 1 depends so heavily on the sales chart – and invests a considerable sum in its compilation – because the chart is itself supposedly a neutral, dispassionate, accurate record of currently popular preferences.

Picking the playlist

BBC radio producers are co-ordinators and administrators, taking responsibility for budgeting, for mediating between presenters and management, for compiling Performing Right Society (PRS) and Phonographic Performance Ltd (PPL) logging sheets, for ensuring that the programme meets the required technical standards, and for the auditioning and hiring of bands for studio sessions. Most of all, however, producers have a degree of editorial control over output that the BBC tends to publicly underplay:

> It's BBC policy generally that if you employ a freelance [a presenter] whose interest is in exploiting his own talent, he is not and shouldn't need to be concerned with BBC policies. In the case of someone like Mike Read who rolls on day after day, he knows the content is going to be largely Top 40 and he's very happy to leave it to a producer to choose the running order or to listen to the hundred or so singles released during a week. The job of sifting and sorting, deciding what is good entertainment value for our market, is something the producers do. Someone has to take the responsibility.[7]

The key phrases here are 'responsibility' and 'deciding what is good entertainment value for our market' (*sic*): professionalism and the sustainment of the BBC's ideology of public service (which, since the war, has meant serving up what the public is assumed to want, not what Reith and his colleagues once deemed it to be in need of) go hand in hand. Yet in seeking to define what constitutes 'good entertainment value' in popular music, BBC producers tend to absolve themselves of responsibility by taking the Top Forty chart as their frame of reference: the thinking is that the chart is a reflection of what people are buying, therefore of what is most currently popular, therefore it is the function of a radio station with a brief to *be* popular and provide an up-to-date, pop-based service to take heed of what the chart indicates. Just as a news reporter claims to do no more than report facts, so a music radio producer claims to do no more than reflect public taste.

Many writers have pointed up the circularity of this argument, that a record is only likely to reach the sales chart after it is heard on Radio 1; frequently, the station is only playing those records that its own producers have *pre-selected* as potential chart hits, so the Top Forty is to a great extent self-fulfilling. Radio 1's own spokespeople continually contradict themselves when explaining the importance of a Top-Forty-based music policy. This is Chinnery again:

> We're a popular service. Why do people listen? They want to hear their favourite music and that is represented by the charts, the one yardstick you have of the popularity of the material.... Those listeners who don't buy records don't know what they want to listen to until they hear it; the fact that enough people buy a record to put it into the chart, that makes it even more important that Radio 1 plays it. By playing it you are increasing its familiarity and hopefully its popularity, and people will grow to recognise it.[8]

What this amounts to is a belief in consumer sovereignty – a doctrine that of course has its own pitfalls, as consumers can only make preferences as to one product over another on the basis not only of what is available but what is promoted as *being* available. The choice of what to promote rests with the producers and the Radio 1 playlist is a weekly expression of their gatekeeping role.

Playlisting has a curious history at Radio 1. It was originally introduced in 1973, in anticipation of the launch of ILR, when it became clear that producers were being *too* selective in what they played from the Top Forty chart, to the point that certain chart discs were being heard too infrequently during the peak daytime hours. The playlist was brought in as a means of encouraging a uniform station identity and of ensuring that 'people who switched on at random knew exactly what sort of music they were going to hear, that is some of the top ten hits of the day at some time within the coming hour'.[9] The playlist was limited to fifty records, three of which would be played in any half-hour, the remaining discs being the producer's own choices of either new releases or oldies; the list was arrived at in 'democratic' fashion, with producers recommending particular new releases and stating their case in open discussion at a weekly playlist meeting headed by executive producer Doreen Davies.[10] It gave Radio 1 a more cohesive sound while formalizing the station's dependence on the Top Forty, and what was remarkable about the decision to drop the list in 1979 was that it had actually become unnecessary; producers were automatically making their choices from the stance of an unstated yet assimilated corporate policy, though a number of guidelines remained, including the amount of times that the Number 1 record could be played in a week (twenty). Although portrayed in the press as a move that would give producers and presenters greater freedom of choice, it made only a marginal difference – as both Chinnery and his successor, Johnny Beerling, later admitted – to what was played. Ironically, Beerling's decision to reintroduce the playlist during 1986 was actually to *encourage* a greater diversity in Radio 1 music rather than restrict it further, the feeling being that Radio 1's sound had once again become too narrow for a national, well-patronized station. Whereas in 1973 the playlist had been introduced to ensure that the biggest selling records were regularly played, the new playlist system was mounted to prevent the *over*playing of the biggest selling records. The playlist came back after an informal series of meetings, designed to give an opportunity for evening show presenters and producers to suggest records for daytime play by marginally more left-field artists and groups, failed to achieve the desired result.[11] A formal system at least ensured that a record recommended in this way would receive a number of set plays rather than anything from one to twenty plays willy-nilly.

Radio 1's new, revised version of the playlist consisted initially of a 'front page' of fifty records guaranteed at least a dozen plays per week, comprising in the main the Top Forty 'climbers' and non-movers, a few singles 'bubbling under' the chart and likely to enter it in time, and selected new releases. In late 1987, following the appointment of Roger Lewis to the new post of Head of Music, this was modified to an 'A' list of forty priority records (grouped in fives and rotated in 30-minute blocks) and a 'B' list of twenty records played with less frequency.[12] In the United States, where playlist broadcasting was first introduced, playlists are traditionally very narrow, even at demographically defined 'specialist' stations (country music or Latin music stations in urban areas, for example), because of the intensity of the competition: the theory is that listeners will automatically switch stations once they hear a record they dislike, and that narrowing down the list of records to be played to apparent popular favourites (i.e. those that are currently selling well) limits this likelihood. By comparison, the Radio 1 playlist is bigger and broader, partly because the switch-over factor is not so important – listener loyalty to radio stations is continually highlighted in both BBC and IBA research – and partly because people listen for longer, often tuning in to complete programmes at a stretch. But the broadness is to some extent illusory, as it does not necessarily extend to any great catholicism in music selection; at its worst, a playlist of the size operated by Radio 1 may simply result in much more of the same mixture. Everything depends, inevitably, on the input of the producers who compile the playlist (and it is compiled 'fairly democratically', in Beerling's words, by a committee of producers), and one of the early problems facing Beerling's much-publicized updating of the station in 1985–6 was that the process of inculcating Radio 1 values into the practices and thinking of its producers had been almost too successful: after years of relative safety in music choices, producers were disinclined to change. Beerling tackled the problem at its root, dispensing with some of the more established producers and taking on a number of newcomers, all on a freelance basis rather than as permanent members of staff:

> Now they're not all staff producers who play it safe, we have a number of contract producers who are on a similar contract to the deejays, if slightly longer term. So they do tend to be a bit more adventurous and a bit more freewheeling with their programmes.[13]

To date, these new producers have come from both ILR and, with splendid irony, Radio 2: at the time of Beerling's appointment, the average age of Radio 1's producers was actually older than that of Radio 2's production team, while the latter's reshaping into a traditional middle-of-the-road network during 1986 left several of its producers seeking more challenging work elsewhere. In 1987 Beerling took the still more radical step (by Radio 1's standards) of reshaping the management structure of the network and moving producers from control of individual programmes to responsibility for complete programme *sequences*, which were designated as weekday mornings, weekday afternoons, evenings and weekends.

Turning to an analysis of the playlist itself, the first and most obvious point is that Radio 1's use of the Top Forty, whatever the belief in consumer sovereignty, is selective: records are not given an equal number of plays, chart positions do not automatically merit a certain ratio of airplay. Not every Top Forty record will even figure in the playlist, and the list of banned records includes those deemed salacious (Max Romeo's 'Wet Dream', Frankie Goes to Hollywood's 'Relax'), politically contentious (Paul McCartney's 'Give Ireland Back to the Irish') or offensive (the Sex Pistols' 'God Save the Queen'). These are relatively clear-cut cases, and there have been occasions when Radio 1 has been caught up in a prevailing moral panic about certain issues, notably in July 1986, when the Jesus and Mary Chain (a group treated very gingerly by radio producers anyway, by virtue of their name) issued 'Some Candy Talking' at a time when tabloid headlines were focusing on the heroin addiction and arrest on possession charges of Boy George of Culture Club. Mike Smith, at that time presenting the new release programme *Singled Out*, took the record off in mid-play and announced he would not play it on his breakfast time show because of supposed references in the song to cocaine (the 'candy' of the title). As it happened, Smith's comments split opinion within Radio 1's producers and presenters, and Johnny Beerling took the unusual step of consulting John Peel, one of the group's early champions, before finally deciding not to ban the record. The significance of the episode, however, lay in Radio 1's nervousness at the prospect of public censure if it was not at least *seen* to have considered the issue seriously; it followed hard on the heels of a Radio 1 'social action' campaign against drug addiction. (One should note, too, that suggesting the occasional record for banning is something of a convention for breakfast time disc jockeys on Radio 1: Smith's predecessor, Mike Read, was behind the ban on 'Relax'.[14])

Such episodes are, nevertheless, of only peripheral importance to Radio 1's overall airplay policy and particularly its treatment of 'disruptive' musical styles or fashions. Radio 1's management is acutely aware that banning a disc can cause more problems than it solves, in that a record's very notoriety can encourage sales; and of course there have been examples of records on highly dubious themes (Lou Reed's 'Walk on the Wild Side', for example, which contained references to transvestitism and 'giving head') being deemed acceptable simply because the playlist committee made no sense of the lyrics. Both in choosing records from the Top Forty and in selecting from each weekly batch of new single releases, producers exercise judgement based on their own perceptions of what the audience will find acceptable. There are points to be made about this selection process, both of which reflect directly on the professional backgrounds and attitudes of producers: their choices reflect a continuing, nostalgic preoccupation with the 1960s, and they work (whatever formal attempts Beerling may make to change it) to a narrow definition of what constitutes good daytime Radio 1 music, narrow both musically and in terms of its sources – the Top Forty, the 3-minute single, new releases by established chart 'names'. There is nothing laid down, no written guidelines by which a producer will assess a disc's suitability for daytime play, and only the most intensive, sustained monitoring of the records played and the frequency of playing (a monitoring which would require pre-categorization of records into musical styles or types – a dangerous kind of pigeon-holing) would provide concrete empirical evidence of these tendencies. Rather, general observations can be made, and Radio 1's approach to the punk and new-wave music of the 1977–8 period – an important one in pop music history, if not quite the turning-point that some critics have claimed for it – proves an excellent case in point.

The case of punk

Punk music was by nature deliberately disruptive, in the sense that it *sounded* noisy, calamitous and violent (the typical early sounds of punk were the buzz-saw drone of guitars, the relentless reworking of three chords), and in its ideology, which valued amateurism over professionalism, emotion and energy over technical perfection, anarchy over order, and maintaining closeness to 'the street' in the face of the distancing, corrupting effects of pop stardom. It was not 'entertaining' in the conventional Radio 1 sense: Johnny Beerling, speaking in 1986, explained its relative exclusion from the airwaves in exactly these terms: 'It wasn't very entertaining on the radio, it was like a lot of disco music, just not very entertaining because it was so repetitive'.[15] Punk broke the unwritten Radio 1 (and ILR) rules of good record-making, in that the music itself was too raucous for daytime listening, too dubious in the content of its lyrics, and also too 'unprofessional' in its production to stand alongside the standard pop fare of the time – Abba, Electric Light Orchestra, Dr Hook, Queen. Indeed, the reason most regularly proffered for the exclusion of punk records from daytime Radio 1 was their poor 'technical quality'. (Even John Peel's espousal of punk on his late evening shows was criticized internally because he was held by some to be wasting the station's limited VHF facility on technically appalling record productions.)

Punk posed a particular problem to Radio 1 because it was subversive, and not just in the sense of carrying anarchic lyrics. It subverted Radio 1's own criteria for playlist inclusion. While it fitted uncomfortably into the daytime shows on musical grounds, it nevertheless demanded representation there if the doctrine of consumer sovereignty was to be respected: punk was, after all, essentially a 3-minute singles form and was well represented in the Top Forty chart. It was a problematic music, but in a much different sense to that other problem form, progressive rock, in the late 1960s, when there were ready-made *technical* reasons for that music's separation from daytime output – the length of typical progressive tracks, its availability on stereophonic albums (and therefore best appreciated on VHF, which was available to Radio 1 only in the evenings and at weekends). Additionally, there were disc jockeys available (John Peel, Bob Harris, Alan Black, Pete Drummond) ready and willing to oversee the music's treatment. Progressive rock was *manageable*, in addition to which it had an intensely conservative streak, reflecting not political concerns but religious dilettantism, Tolkien-like mystical quests, astrology, the lure of the East, all the trappings of a middle-class pursuit of personal fulfilment. Progressive rock had artistic pretensions, while one of the critical poses adopted by punk supporters (including Peel) was that punk musicians, by returning to a deliberately primitivist approach, were actively rebelling against the progressive, élitist values that Radio 1 implicitly endorsed.

How, then, did Radio 1 come to terms with punk? Certain records could be banned outright, on the grounds of offensiveness; the Sex Pistols' 'God Save the Queen' was the obvious example, particularly because its release was deliberately timed to coincide with British royalty's Silver Jubilee celebrations. Most commonly, records with less contentious lyrics were played but distanced by the presenter, who would preface playing a punk disc with jokes about safety pins or gobbing or – in something of a 'rebel' Radio 1 tradition started by Tony Blackburn with his comments about Black Sabbath and heavy metal and continued by Johnnie Walker's remarks about the Bay City Rollers and David Cassidy – would priggishly announce that they had to play the records because they were popular but that didn't mean they necessarily had to like it. In *One Chord Wonders*, Dave Laing contrasts punk with disco music, which was of strictly more commercial importance during the 1977–8 period, and as a general observation it is certainly true that disco was more favoured, but the process of excluding punk by various means was not static.[16] By mid-1977 it was clear that punk was not a passing craze but the catalyst for important structural changes within the record industry itself, precipitating the growth of independent companies and recording studios and encouraging the proliferation of bands on a country-wide basis. With this acknowledgement came a steady *incorporation* – hesitant, selective – of punk into the Radio 1 playlist. The process by which 'punk' as a style and a movement mellowed into 'new wave', a more malleable and less subversive form with which the record industry could operate, has been told on several occasions and is in some respects simply a paradigm of a regular process in rock music, by which increasingly predominant, threatening styles (like rock 'n' roll itself in the United States in the mid-1950s) become tamed by record company exploitation. The media play their own crucial role in this, both by responding to record companies' own tendencies in this direction (for example, *Top of the Pops* would not agree to have the Sex Pistols in the studio for fear of a repetition of the events of their notorious appearance with Bill Grundy on the ITV programme *Today*, but Virgin's provision of a video film enabled the programme to feature 'Pretty Vacant'), and by a more general incorporation, such as by national newspapers running stories on 'my son, the punk', rendering threatening 'extremes' harmless by stressing the ordinariness of punks or their love of animals. Dick Hebdige's *Subculture: The Meaning of Style* shows how this happened in the case of punk, though one of the omissions of that book is any account of the role that radio played in the incorporation of punk into the mainstream, arguably a considerably greater role than that played either by the national press or by television.[17]

Hebdige's argument echoes that of Raymond Williams in his essay 'The Growth and Role of the Mass Media', which pointed out how media select and transform particular facets of working-class culture and offer them back to working-class audiences in neutralized form.[18] Hebdige shows how, in the case of punk, the process took a commodity form (subcultural signs converted into mass-produced objects) and an ideological form, by which deviant behaviour is labelled and redefined, transforming difference into sameness and the dangerous into a comic spectacle. To this one can add a third form, that of relegation to a quasi-artistic, quasi-élitist periphery, typified as John Peel territory, by which punk is defined as a 'meaningful' cult, with its own claims to cultish 'relevance' but irrelevant to the mass audience. One can see these three forms in action at key points in pop music history: the presentation of teenage music as a comic spectacle (typified by the *Oh Boy!* programme on ITV) in the late 1950s, the transformation of difference into sameness (for example, the emergence of Elvis Presley clones, especially Cliff Richard, who were revealed in the press as home-loving boys who sent their Mums flowers every Mother's Day), then the invention of a cultural category (progressive rock) towards the end of the 1960s. The spread of all-day music radio since that time simply accelerated these processes: punk's true heyday was very short-lived, not so much because of industry exploitation (and the willingness of certain punk groups to submit to it) but because of the intensity of (usually distortative) media coverage. Punk became 'new wave' as Johnny Rotten of the Sex Pistols' comic sense became noticed by the press and punk fashions spread to the department stores, and the very fact of its assimilation by other media – particularly television – made a similar assimilation of it by Radio 1 not only inevitable but necessary if the network was to maintain a degree of credibility with a young listenership.

Credibility is an important concept here, as perhaps the most important legacy of punk was *attitudinal*: it undermined pop music's love affair with technology for its own sake by presenting a new set of values, re-establishing rock 'n' roll virtues and returning pop to its (albeit romanticized) roots as a subversive, rebel music with teen appeal and racial/class connotations. It readjusted the critical perspective on pop to a profound degree: the post-punk consensus automatically favoured the independent over the mainstream, the small label over the major company, the 'new, young' band over the ageing dinosaur, the primitive over the cultured, do-it-yourself over passive acceptance. Similarly, acceptance or rejection of the punk ethos (if not of punk music itself) became a yardstick by which the credibility of Radio 1's disc jockeys and producers was judged, if only by the music press. 1977 in particular was a vital year for the network, when its disc jockeys began either pinning their credibility to the mast by picking the latest independent releases as Records of the Week or setting themselves against punk altogether. It was the year in which several of the older presenters took the opportunity to move from Radio 1 (including Noel Edmonds, Tony Blackburn, and Rosko) and some of the others, notably Simon Bates and Andy Peebles, declared their new faith. This did not mean any overnight change in Radio 1's musical identity and certainly no sudden accommodation of Peel-proselytized records, but in a small yet significant way, punk had the indirect effect of refocusing Radio 1's attention on the *music*. The post-punk period saw a subtle change in the disc jockey stereotype, from the egotistical supermarket opener of tradition to figures, perhaps equally self-obsessed, who made a virtue of their interests in the music *as* music. Post-1977 Radio 1 personnel prided themselves on their awareness; they wore their hipness on their sleeves. What undermined their sense of awareness – the eagerness with which they sought to persuade their listeners that they were themselves part of the scene – was that their use of the music, their championing of post-punk pop, was ultimately as unthinking and as uncritical in its own way as Tony Blackburn's automatic championing of Tamla Motown output had been in the early 1970s. Perhaps more importantly, the enthusiasm of presenters such as Simon Bates and Peter Powell for independent label releases was not necessarily matched by their producers, whose sense of conservatism was informed both by a more traditional view of pop and by the requirement of the network, as defined by the management team, to deliberately centre on mainstream tastes at times of peak listening.

Radio 1 lived far more comfortably with the aftermath of punk – the transition from punk to 'new wave' mentioned earlier – than with punk itself. There was a certain irony in this, as one of the characteristics of post-punk pop was a far greater, far more vocal and visible politicization of the music than punk had witnessed. This extended to chart music; the polemical records of mixed black and white groups like the Specials AKA ('Too Much Too Young', 'Ghost Town'), Selecter ('Too much Pressure'), the Beat ('Stand Down Margaret') and UB40 ('One in Ten') were aimed quite deliberately at the musical mainstream represented by Radio 1 and the Top Forty, to spread the anti-unemployment, anti-racist, anti-Thatcher message to as wide an audience as possible. As Jim Brown, drummer with UB40, put it, 'a dance band is a package with which to sell your politics':[19] if punk was openly confrontational, post-punk music (of the 1978 to 1981 period at least) was more insidiously challenging, offering subtle, usually non-specific but often barbed political comment clothed in innocuous pop-ska colours. That Radio 1's playlist compilers rarely saw fit to actively exclude such records showed the success of the strategy, though this was arguably one of the few times in British pop history when non-broadcasting factors had the most direct bearing on sales and opinion, particularly the music press (which universally endorsed the 2 Tone stance) and the crucial impact that the groups had on audiences on several intensive tours of British pop venues. Post-punk music did not *appear* to disrupt standard Radio 1 notions of pop as listenable dance music, it even carried musical connotations of those 1960s pop styles (Motown, soul, ska, beat music) so beloved of the pirates; but it followed what Elvis Costello once defined as 'the golden rule of subversive pop ... don't say it's subversive'. The other distinctive feature of post-punk music was its source on independent labels: Radio 1 found itself dealing with a succession of mostly completely new companies, some (like 2 Tone, whose roster included the Specials and Selecter) run by musicians themselves, who actively sought airplay (as earlier album-based independents like Virgin and Charisma had generally not done) on daytime radio. That a large amount of the output of independent labels very quickly became characterized by radio (ILR as well as Radio 1) as 'indie music' was arguably one of the failures of the post-punk years, typical of a standard process by which any music which does not fit the criteria for non-disruptive daytime fare becomes confined to the élitist margins of the airwaves. At least in part because of Radio 1 policy on seeing daytime and evening audiences as diametrically different, 'indie music' became invested with post-1967 progressive values, a negation of what punk initially represented.

Postscript (written as an update for this book, December 1996)

No radio station exists in isolation, and the challenge for Radio 1 in the 1990s has been to counter the threat to its status arising from deregulation of the airwaves. Overseen by a new Radio Authority with far less power and influence than the old IBA, deregulation has made possible not only a proliferation of new radio operators at national, local and regional levels but also the sanctioning of programme sponsorship; the splitting of frequencies to allow existing operators to run separate services on AM and FM; and the transformation of ILR through merger and takeover from a collection of locally controlled stations to a string of regional networks in all but name.

In the years since the above extract was written, Radio 1 has changed significantly in image, style, sound and ethos. The main catalyst for that change has been the advent of a national rival in Virgin, though the arrival of services with no direct competitive content – Talk Radio or Classic FM, for example – also gave listeners new choices and helped encourage a new volatility in radio listening. External pressures, too, prompted crucial changes in BBC administration, including the opening up of programme-making to independent producers and a comprehensive restructuring that culminated in the appointment of Radio 1 controller Matthew Bannister as overall head of BBC radio and Trevor Dann as head of the pop music output of BBC radio *and* television. The changes at Radio 1 should therefore be seen as part of a corporate response to a new and evolving broadcasting environment in which nothing – least of all funding via the licence fee – is guaranteed.

Some kind of shake-up at Radio 1 was to be expected after Johnny Beerling's retirement, but its scope and scale were surprisingly far-reaching. Assuming that Virgin's 'adult contemporary' music programming would rob the station of a large number of older (25 years plus) listeners, Radio 1's new management team took the strategic decision to re-position the station towards a target audience much younger in age and numerically smaller than its established multi-age listenership. Beerling had long wrestled with the conundrum that, because Radio 1's core listeners were pop fans who stayed with the station as they grew older, its music policy was too all-embracing to be cohesive. Bannister's solution was to alter Radio 1's remit as a pop music station with cross-generation appeal: the station would be reinvented as a service aimed squarely at under 25s, with the inevitable drop in listeners seen as a necessary, acceptable and even welcome price to pay in return for a sharper image and enhanced loyalty from the listeners who remained. Radio 1 effectively conceded ground to Virgin even before the two stations had had a chance to properly compete for listeners.

The strategy dictated a radical overhaul of the music played by Radio 1, and of the presenters who represented its public face and voice. Gatekeeping processes were reviewed, with playlisting based on a more selective use of the Top 40 and the individual preferences of producers and presenters – or rather, their 'professional' skill in selecting material (from albums as well as singles) likely to keep a young and aware audience listening. Radio 1's new music policy found virtually no room for anything produced before the mid-1980s; actively excluded were records by such artists as Status Quo (who took the matter to litigation), Paul McCartney, and Robson and Jerome, and even, during the Christmas season, pop records of traditional seasonal appeal.

The other key weapon in Radio 1's makeover was the fast and loose, in-your-face presentation of Chris Evans, recruited from Channel 4's 'The Big Breakfast'. Established presenters were eased out – Dave Lee Travis resigned on air, while Steve Wright departed and eventually re-appeared on Radio 2. John Peel (a lone survivor from Radio 1's launch in 1967) was shifted from weekday evenings to weekends, and a clever advertising campaign portrayed the young inheritors of Peel's mantle – Mark Radcliffe, Steve Lamacq, Jo Wiley – as the lifeblood and conscience of the station. Cool, hip and street-wise, Radio 1 attempted to re-locate itself at the cutting edge of contemporary music, for example by wholeheartedly espousing 'Britpop' of Oasis, Blur, Pulp and others in 1995–96 (including a week devoted to British pop music and exclusive live coverage of Oasis' record-breaking Knebworth concert).

At the time of writing, the process of policy overhaul at Radio 1 is far from complete – the projected appointment of a head of music policy at the station will refine its direction still further. But for some the new Radio 1 has an arrogance every bit as galling as that which once dictated airplay choices according to chart positions and dubious notions of 'acceptability' to mass audiences. It depends, still, on programme-makers making music choices in line with the self-image of presenters and the 'professional' assessment of producers as to what its target listeners will find acceptable, while John Peel for one has expressed unease at founding a music policy on basically ageist lines.

Perhaps the real test of Radio 1's new-found hipness will come when the station is faced, as it once was by punk, by a new style or movement which in attitude as well as sound opposes the easy assumptions of those who control the station's output.

One final, general point should be made. Radio 1's makeover offers a prime example of one of the recurring features of radio broadcasting in Britain – what I would define as an *engineered complementarity* between services. This goes back a long way. When the BBC was the sole provider of radio services, the concept of complementary programming informed its whole structure – for example, the splitting up of BBC services in 1945 into three distinct networks for three distinct audiences, the Light Programme, Third Programme and Home Service, and the changes of 1967 that saw a renaming of these networks as Radios 2, 3 and 4 respectively and the introduction of Radio 1 itself. Even the Conservative Government of 1970–74 was careful to introduce commercial radio on a local basis and therefore complementary to the BBC's national services. Complementarity dies hardest within local radio: when ILR stations were obliged by the old IBA to split their AM and FM frequencies, most seized it as an opportunity to provide complementary services – a pop-based service on FM and a 'gold' station (playing '60s and '70s hits) aimed at older listeners on AM. Similarly, BBC local stations no longer compete directly with ILR counterparts: most have switched to all-talk formats in the 1990s, freeing ILRs to concentrate on music programming. Radio 1 now offers programming that complements not only the BBC's other services – notably Radio 2, whose considerable policy upheavals have been informed by the assumption that ex-Radio 1 listeners would turn to it in droves – but also those provided by commercial operators, especially at a national level.

The deregulatory era has *not* seen a rash of competitive services: it has given us a plurality of services that dovetail in a haphazard way, in keeping with the Radio Authority's policy of awarding franchises according to both financial viability and the distinctiveness of the projected programming. While this reflects an ideological commitment to expanding consumer choice, it also reflects economic realities: radio's slice of the advertising cake is too small and the availability of frequencies too limited to support a radio industry based on competition for the same mass market. It is still too early to predict the survival of those stations whose communities of taste or interest do not command great advertising income: the many programming swings experienced by Jazz FM, for example, from diehard, specialist-appeal jazz through to jazz-*influenced* sounds (jazz-funk, acid-jazz, R&B) designed to attract a broader listenership, underline how difficult it is to maintain a station's original remit in the face of falling profits. The real winners of the deregulatory era have not been the new operators at all but the existing ILR owners, who have been allowed to expand, merge, take over their neighbours in many cases and remould their programming almost at will.

Notes

1. Quoted in an interview by the author published as 'Trent: Bridging the Gap', *Gongster*, University of Nottingham Students Union (8 March 1977).
2. D. M. White, 'The "Gatekeeper": A Case Study in the Selection of News', *Journalism Quarterly*, 27 (1950), pp. 283–90.
3. For a brief critical discussion of the gatekeeper concept, see Margaret Gallagher, 'Negotiations of Control in Media Organizations and Occupations', in *Culture, Society and the Media* (London, Methuen, 1982). For an application of the concept to American radio, see 'The Gatekeepers of Radio', in R. Serge Denisoff, *Solid Gold: The Popular Record Industry* (New Brunswick, Transaction, 1975).
4. Johnny Beerling, from an unpublished interview with the author, 17 November 1986.
5. John Downing, *The Media Machine* (London, Pluto Press, 1980), p. 175.
6. Simon Frith, *The Sociology of Rock* (London, Constable, 1978), p. 91.
7. Derek Chinnery, from an unpublished interview with the author, 24 January 1985.
8. Chinnery interview.
9. Chinnery interview.
10. For a fuller account of the playlisting procedure as it existed at Radio 1 at this time, see Simon Frith, 'Playing Records', in Simon Frith and Charlie Gillett, eds., *Rock File 3* (St Albans, Granada, 1975), pp. 38–43.
11. For the background to the relaunch of the playlist, see Colin Shearman, 'Why Radio 1 Has Changed Its Tunes', *Guardian*, 5 May 1986.
12. See Nick Higham, 'Plugging the Radio 1 Disc Promo Gap', *Broadcast*, 9 October 1987.
13. Beerling interview.
14. For an account of the Jesus and Mary Chain 'ban', see Mark Cooper, 'The Blasphemy of Stardom', *Guardian*, 21 July 1986. See also Mike Smith's riposte on the letters page of the *Guardian*, 29 July 1986.
15. Beerling interview.
16. Dave Laing, *One-Chord Wonders: Power and Meaning in Punk-Rock* (Milton Keynes, Open University Press, 1985).
17. Dick Hebdige, *Subculture: The Meaning of Style* (London, Methuen, 1979).
18. Raymond Williams, 'The Growth and Role of the Mass Media', in Carl Gardner, ed., *Media, Politics and Culture* (London, Macmillan, 1971).
19. Quoted in Mark Williams, 'Signing Off', in Ashley Brown, ed., *The History of Rock* (London, Orbis, 1984), p. 2215.

Questions

1 Summarise what you take to be the central point made by Barnard in this extract.

2 Research and outline some of the key changes which have taken place since the original extract was published – i.e. since 1989/90. In a later part of his discussion, Barnard indicates that what he calls 'the old homogeneity' between radio and popular music had begun to break down in the 1980s. What has happened to the charts, to musical forms and styles, to Radio 1, to independent local radio (ILR) and to new national radio stations in recent years? Refer to the discussion outlined in the postscript.

3   Research either a local, regional or national music radio station in terms of its particular music policy and relationship to the mainstream music charts. In terms of musical selection, who is addressed, how and at what points in the broadcast day? Does popular music radio have any function other than the promotion of the music industry?

Further reading

Burnett, R. 1996: *The global jukebox*. London: Routledge.

Chambers, I. 1985: *Urban rhythms: pop music and popular culture*. London: Macmillan.

Chapman, R. 1992: *Selling the sixties*. London: Routledge.

Crisell, A. 1994: *Understanding radio*, 2nd revised edn. London: Routledge.

Frith, S. 1988: *Music for pleasure*. Cambridge: Polity Press.

Frith, S. and Goodwin, A. (eds.) 1990: *On record: rock, pop and the written word*. London: Routledge.

Lewis, P. and Booth, J. 1988: *The invisible medium*. London: Macmillan.

Thornton, S. 1995: *Club cultures: music, media and subcultural capital*. Cambridge: Polity Press.

Wilby, P. and Conroy, A. 1994: *The radio handbook*. London: Routledge.

27

Priorities and Prejudice: 'Artist and Repertoire' and the Acquisition of Artists

Keith Negus

From *Producing pop: culture and conflict in the popular music industry* (Edward Arnold 1994)

In this extract, Negus looks at the work of Artist & Repertoire (A & R) staff in their acquisition and signing of bands for record companies, both large and small. Once more, it is demonstrated that a balance has to be found between financial priorities and encouraging creativity – in this case, translating the business requirements of the record company into a workable artistic policy.

Negus establishes that A & R can be a lucrative profession, but that its practices are shaped by certain priorities and prejudices, inevitable in an industry dominated by middle-class grammar school and college educated white men who favour the rock music tradition which was predominant in the late 1960s and early '70s when they were students. Negus highlights the conservative and rather insular nature of the music industry and states that the well-established mainstream record companies have tended to recruit A & R staff with similar professional experience, cultural values and musical tastes. However, it is not only backgrounds and personal preferences which dictate the kinds of bands signed by A & R men. The business of launching a new musician or band is costly, and although they are clearly shrewd enough to cover every potential market (provided it will recoup enough money to cover the initial outlay), the tendency is to play safe and sign acts which conform to a tried-and-tested formula. Similarly, aspiring musicians may be tempted to shape what they do to suit the demands of the recording industry. This tendency to discourage originality and encourage replication can be seen in the rise of the 'boy band' in Britain in the 1990s – all-male pop groups principally aimed at attracting a very young female audience (contemporary examples being Take That, Let Loose, Boyzone and Upside Down). The rather artificial construction of many of these pop groups, with the emphasis as much on the individual group members' looks and appeal to teenage girls as on musical talent or song-writing ability, underlines Negus' point about the significance of marketing personnel in record companies and his further arguments about the power and authority of managers.

Artist and repertoire (A & R) staff are formally responsible for acquiring artists, and have usually been described as 'talent spotters' – continually engaged in seeking new acts and material. However, this is only a small part of what they do. Most of their time is devoted to working with acts who are already under contract. An A & R person can be involved in every aspect of an artist's relationship with a record company: from the initial negotiations and signing of the contract through to the rehearsal, arrangement and recording of songs, to liaising with staff employed in marketing, video production and promotion.

In the past A & R staff have often signed artists without reference to the opinions of other personnel within their record companies. However, as the costs of producing and marketing popular music have increased, and as record companies have been re-orienting themselves towards entertainment rather than just music, other divisions within the corporations have begun exerting a greater influence over the type of artists which are acquired. This [article] has been written at a time when some of these tensions – particularly between A & R and marketing – are becoming more sharply defined. However, as A & R staff have, historically, had the first say in proposing the type of artists and music acquired by record companies, this chapter is about the distinctive activities and beliefs which guide the work of artist and repertoire departments.

Formal divisions and business affairs

All record labels, regardless of their size, identity and specific history, divide their departments or staff into the following occupations: artist and repertoire; marketing; public relations; publicity and press; radio and television promotion; sales; business affairs/finance and legal; manufacture and distribution; administration and secretarial. The organisation is coordinated by the directors of the company, with the managing director or president responsible for day-to-day policies and practices.

The work of record company departments is carried out within the general business plan of the company. ... The business affairs division (incorporating both accounting and legal staff) is involved in setting parameters to the deals that can be offered to prospective acts, and the company lawyer will often negotiate the details of a contract directly with an artist's lawyer. As Simon Frith has noted, all decisions about who to sign and record 'are basically financial and calculations have to be precisely made' (1983, p 102). However, this does not simply mean that the accounting and business affairs departments 'outweigh all the creative divisions in wielding company power' (Denisoff, 1986, p 158). Company power is not something that is exerted by an identifiable faction, such as accountants or lawyers. Record company power arises out of and is exercised through the internal and external relationships which are stretched throughout the production, mediation and consumption of popular music. Senior executives establish general policies and accountants and lawyers advocate certain business strategies, but this does not 'determine' who is signed or what is recorded. In day-to-day practice it means that staff are involved in constantly negotiating these demands as they translate the business requirements of the record company into an artistic policy.

The Artist and Repertoire department

Unless it is a very small company the A & R department tends to be divided hierarchically and staff accorded such titles as A & R director, senior A & R manager, A & R manager and talent scout. These titles denote seniority and experience, and the work-load is often divided so that the more senior staff are responsible for the most established artists. However, the roster of artists for which individual A & R staff are responsible is often built up in an ad-hoc way. The person who 'finds' and has the initial enthusiasm for an act will tend to form a relationship with the artist and initiate the process of negotiation for them to sign to the record company. Once the artist has been signed, this person will be responsible for overseeing the development and 'career' of that act for the A & R department. The less experienced members of staff will usually draw on the knowledge and informal guidance or be under the explicit supervision of more senior members of staff.

Successful artist and repertoire staff are some of the most highly paid personnel in the recording industry. In 1990, one A & R director quoted me the following figures as an indication of what A & R staff were earning: the 'cheapest talent scout', a school or college leaver would earn about £10,000 per annum and additionally be provided with a car and have all their expenses paid. A 'reasonably successful' A & R manager who had worked with acts for two to three years would earn approximately £40,000, and a senior A & R manager with over five years of success could earn about £100,000. The A & R director would, needless to say, earn considerably more.

In addition to these basic earnings, senior A & R staff receive cash bonuses when the recordings of their artists achieve high chart positions, and a percentage of the sales of the recordings of their artists – usually one per cent, although a small number of 'name' A & R directors are reputed to receive between two and three per cent. Not only do these figures indicate the importance placed on A & R staff, and on commercial sales, they also act as an incentive for staff to achieve success in an area in which there is considerable risk and uncertainty.

Investment, risk and uncertainty

Record company staff assess potential acts with a working knowledge that approximately one in eight of the artists that they sign and record will achieve the level of success required to recoup their initial investment and start to earn money for both themselves and the company. The response of the recording industry to this economic risk and commercial uncertainty has often been explained in terms of a strategy of overproduction combined with differential promotion, in which record companies attempt to cover every potential market possibility (Hirsch, 1972; Frith, 1983). A similar, but more cynical version of this is the 'mud-against-the-wall' model in which record companies rather aimlessly throw out as much product as possible in the hope that some of it will stick. Although record companies have undoubtedly employed these techniques, they were more appropriate at a time when the unit costs of producing recordings was lower and the marketing involved less sophisticated. Throughout the 1980s greater levels of investment have been required to record, market and promote artists. At the beginning of the 1990s a major record company in Britain anticipated having to spend between £250,000–£330,000 over the first 12–18 months of an average deal for a new act; roughly broken down into £100,000 for advances to the artists, £150,000 for recording costs and £80,000 for basic promotional expenses.

In addition to the economic risk involved, a record company must decide whether they have enough staff with the relevant experience to accommodate a potential act. Most record labels have clearly defined the number of acts that they can accommodate at any one time. The acquisition of a new act will inevitably require the re-arrangement of rosters and re-assessment of the contracts of existing artists. It is easier for a record company to assess the economic and personal investment necessary if an act has already demonstrated its potential in some way.

Hence, the established record labels have become reluctant to seek 'raw' talent in dingy dance halls, smoky pubs or amongst the continuous stream of unsolicited recordings (demonstration tapes – 'demos') that they daily receive. The major record companies have been increasingly looking for acts which have already undertaken a significant process of development, or who are able to provide a clear indication of their commercial potential. As a result of this an early 'discovery and development' role has been devolved to publishers, production companies, managers and small record companies; and these different parties actively mediate the boundaries between corporations and aspiring artists.

The unrecorded musicians

Very little attention has been paid to the vast number of amateur and semi-professional bands, performers and singers making music in Britain. Research by Finnegan in Milton Keynes (1989) and Cohen in Liverpool (1991) suggested that there was approximately one band for every thousand members of the population in the cities they studied. But such estimates only include those who are sporadically visible at a local level, and do not take account of numerous singers and musicians who are creating music alone or with others in the home using cheap instruments and portable recording equipment.

Accounts of these 'hidden musicians' have tended to concentrate on the pragmatics of composing, rehearsing and performing and the degree of personal investment involved; emphasizing the way music making provides opportunities for individual and social expression and learning experiences (Bennett, 1980; Bayton, 1989; Finnegan, 1989; Fornäs, 1989). Whilst many of these musicians are playing purely for the intrinsic satisfaction derived from the experience, a vast number are composing, rehearsing, recording and performing in the hope that they will secure a recording contract. Yet, Cohen (1991), in her study of rock bands in Liverpool, is the only writer who has devoted detailed attention to the way in which 'unknown' musicians are attempting to shape what they do to suit the demands of the recording industry, and the way in which the logic of 'making it' informs local music making.

The experiences of these potential stars of tomorrow goes largely unrecorded, unless they are successful – in which case their story is retrospectively accommodated to the ascending tale of struggles, discovery and success found in popular biographies. These narratives, as Simon Frith once observed, are the 'dominant source of pop information', and provide an enduring source of inspiration to tens of thousands of aspiring recording artists, sustaining them in the belief that at some point in the near future they will be recognised by, and then signed to a major record company. Such recognition is rarely as dramatic as many biographies imply and various interested parties may become involved with an unknown act prior to the signing of a recording contract. Often a local manager is the first person to begin acting on behalf of an unknown artist.

Managers

From Larry Parnes who worked with Tommy Steele and Billy Fury in the 1950s, to Tom Watkins who managed Bros, and Maurice Starr who worked in shaping New Kids On The Block in the 1980s, managers have often been portrayed as 'starmakers and svengalis' – moulding and manipulating the music and image of their artists (Rogan, 1988). However, the majority of managers tend to operate as representatives and advisers, guiding rather than manipulating artists. The manager plans the overall career strategy of an act, defining objectives and setting standards. She, but more frequently he, attempts to motivate both the artist and the record company, and intervenes to resolve any disputes. Record companies have a number of artists on their books and the manager works behind the scenes, spending considerable time ensuring that staff in the record company are working for an act, and ironing out any potential problems. The manager is, in the words of Simon Napier-Bell who managed Marc Bolan, Wham! and Japan, 'the balance in the middle' who sways both artist and record company to see the other's point of view (Rogan, 1988)

An unsigned act who are attempting to obtain a recording contract may or may not have a manager. But most acts will usually find it necessary, or be required by record companies, to find management soon after signing. Artists without a recording contract will often sign a management agreement which contains a clause stipulating that the manager must obtain a deal within a specified time period or the agreement is terminated. As the manager usually receives between 15 to 25 per cent of the artist's earnings, this provides an incentive – if the artist does not obtain a recording contract then the manager is not going to make any money.

An experienced manager who can draw on a network of contacts can undoubtedly assist an act to obtain a contract. But, equally, there have been instances where a record company have turned down a potential signing because the manager was considered to be an unreliable or untrustworthy operator with whom senior staff did not wish to do business. Many unsigned acts who approach record companies have a manager who is often little more than an enthusiastic, hustling friend. In such a case the manager is often learning how the industry operates at the same time as the artists. One partner in a management company who had achieved commercial success with a number of artists could look back and with a smile reflect on some 'horrendous mistakes' that he had made on the way. Others, however, may not recover from a lack of knowledge or errors of judgment....

The deal: recording contracts

Although recording contracts became more complicated and highly specific throughout the 1980s as major record companies increasingly dealt with artists through the mediation of third parties, there is a basic character to the artist–company relationship embodied in a recording contract, upon which particular variations are inscribed.

A record company agrees to advance an artist a specified amount of money and to pay certain royalty percentage 'points' on the sales of that artist's recordings once the advanced sum (and all expenses involved in producing that artist's material) have been recouped by the company out of the artist's earnings. In many respects the company are advancing an artist a tax free loan which must be paid back if they are successful. For this the artist must deliver to the record company a specified amount of recorded material, usually albums, during the period of the contract. The contract will usually cover a period of 5 to 7 years, but will contain an 'option' clause every 12–18 months (or per album, whichever is longer). This gives the record company the right to retain or release an artist from a contract. If the company decides to retain an artist they will usually be required to pay a further advance.

A newly signed act will probably receive a royalty of between 10–14 points, and most contracts are structured in such a way that the advances and percentage royalty points payable to the artist increase each year; the implication being that the record company must have achieved a degree of success to make it commercially viable to retain an artist and pay out further advances. In principle this is to safeguard the artist against a company which might sign and retain them on an exclusive contract without investing in them. The company are placed in a position where they are financially committed to an act, so they either work to establish that artist and generate a return on investment, or they save their money and free the artist from the contract to go elsewhere.

The days in which naive acts signed exploitative contracts have been well documented (Garfield, 1986; Rogan, 1988) and are by no means over. However, they have become less widespread as the music industry has consciously attempted to cultivate a more professional image. It has become standard practice for contracts to stipulate that the artists must have received professional legal advice before signing. As was the case with small jazz and rhythm and blues labels earlier this century some of the most exploitative contracts are offered by small, inexperienced, or just incompetent companies involved in signing poorly advised acts (Gray, 1988). Artists are now accredited with being more commercially minded and aware of what the contractual relationship with a record company entails. Artists are also surrounded by business advisers, lawyers and accountants who may engage in some quite sophisticated signing strategies. They may attempt to play the record companies off against each other by initiating the routine practice of 'bidding wars'. In addition they may attempt to withhold signing a publishing (songwriting) contract until the artist has secured a record deal.

Whilst a recording contract pays royalties on the discs and tapes sold (to put it simply), a publishing contract pays a much higher royalty rate (on less average income per song) on the rights of the material composed by the songwriter (which is often collectively a band). A separate royalty is collected every time a particular song is performed or broadcast in public. As a song will not usually be played until an artist/songwriter has a recording released, an artist with a recording contract is in a position to attract large advances and higher royalty rates from the major publishers.

The contract between record companies and artists is, therefore, one with legal obligations on both sides, in which a balance of power is negotiated between artists, who are dependent upon record companies to reach potential audiences, and record companies who are dependent upon artists for images and musical material.

Publishers and production companies

A number of management companies simultaneously operate as production companies, signing artists and financing the development of their music to a point where it is in a form suitable for public consumption (Lambert, 1980). This can then be released through a 'production and distribution' deal with a record label. Many managers have taken this step because they could not get an artist signed purely on the basis of presenting 'demo' recordings. The production company is therefore formed to develop the artist a stage further. This may be taken a step further again, and the company may develop into a hybrid management/production/record label, publishing the material themselves and operating through various licensing, production and marketing arrangements with larger companies.

Until the 1960s the work of music publishers involved signing songwriters and then placing their songs with singers who would use them for commercial recordings or public performances. The publisher would then receive an income from sales of the recordings and sheet music, and revenue from performance rights.

The emergence of rock music changed the relationship of publishers to popular music production. In the Tin Pan Alley tradition there was a clear cut distinction between writers and publishers on one side, and performers and record companies on the other. The success of artists such as The Beatles and Bob Dylan and the emergence of the rock aesthetic which placed great emphasis on individual expression resulted in performers increasingly writing their own songs. A considerable body of material now published is simultaneously composed and recorded by artists and bands, rather than the work of an independent songwriter.

In the past it was standard practice for songwriters to enter into agreements with 'publishing houses' based on a 50/50 split. Every royalty earned would be divided equally between the publisher and songwriter. In return, the publisher was performing an entrepreneurial role in placing songs with different singers and furthering that writer's career. However, as more and more performers began writing and recording their own material the publishers were able to 'publish' a song without having to place it with a singer or invest much energy in getting it commercially recorded and performed. Music publishers reached a point where they could derive a substantial income from publishing prerecorded material and had to do very little work, merely administering music through agencies collecting copyright revenue.

As artists and their managers realised that publishers were doing less for their money, they either began forming their own publishing companies and thus retained the rights to the material and the bulk of income or artists began demanding that publishers reduce their cut. It became common practice for acts, particularly if they were in a strong bargaining position with recordings released and being purchased, to request publishing agreements split 85/15 in the artist's favour. As publishers operating costs and overheads can sometimes be as much as 12 per cent, this left a very small margin on which the publisher could make a profit. Hence it favoured both the successful acts who could generate a guaranteed return on investment that would cover these costs and the large corporations who could afford to acquire them.

One of the ways in which a small company can work alongside and compete with a large company is to gamble with artists at an earlier stage of their development: get them under contract when they have not clearly demonstrated their commercial potential and when they will settle for a modest advance and lower royalty rates in return for the work that the minor company is going to do on their behalf. This is what smaller publishers, production companies and record labels increasingly attempted to do during the 1980s. The minor company can then be a third party taking an active interest in an act's progress, and intervening between the artist and the major corporation; establishing contact, presenting the act, making a deal and earning a cut, and perhaps establishing a reputation in the process.

[...]

Artist and repertoire and information networks

The artist and repertoire department is the repository of knowledge about past, present and future musical trends and stylistic developments. Staff in the A & R department constantly monitor changes among established artists, the new acts that are being acquired by other companies, and attempt to follow developments amongst various audiences and subcultures. In order to deal with the fast-changing musical styles and fashions which are a particularly important characteristic of popular music in Britain, A & R staff regularly utilise a contact network covering a range of production companies, minor record labels, publishers, managers and lawyers. A complex web of information networks is employed so that what is happening across the country can be communicated to and assessed by the corporation.

A & R departments in the United States operate in a similar way. The main difference between Britain and the USA in this respect is one of geography. As a senior A & R manager who was based in America, but who had previously worked in London explained:

> In England you can sit behind your desk and do bugger all if you know a few people. If there's a hot act out there, within two to three weeks you've got to be an idiot if you don't know about it. It's such a small community. Glasgow's an hour's plane ride. Dublin's an hour's plane ride. Whereas here, it's a case of

finding the real talent, out there in the great divide between New York and Los Angeles.

Despite this difference the basic method of acquiring information through networks of contacts, rather than unsolicited approaches or random searching in clubs, is very similar.

Within these networks there is a regular exchange of information, communicated by telephone and in person. The A & R staff ask these various third parties what they are doing: who are they signing, recording and developing? What trends have they identified or heard about? In turn these smaller set-ups present what they are doing to A & R staff. They might enthusiastically 'talk-up' certain artists. They may informally play recordings to staff at a major company in order to gain feedback or in an effort to generate interest in a particular act. They will probe the large company for information about the type of acts and material being sought. Minor labels continually attempt to find out which staff and artists are joining or leaving a major company, and generally glean any gossip that will enable them to assess the situation within the major corporations.

These smaller companies also have their own networks of regional contacts. These might include DJs and mixers who are responsive to trends on the dance floor and adept at identifying imports that might be worth acquiring. Studio producers and engineers working with unsigned artists might pass on information, as will people in rehearsal rooms and local clubs, magazines, fanzines and regional radio stations.

People at all points in this ever-changing web are constantly cultivating new contacts and consolidating existing relationships, and it is within these networks that interest in a particular act or recording is usually initiated. Rarely do staff from major record companies approach potential artists 'cold'. For the studio-quality tape they are about to hear, the video they are about to view or the showcase performance they are about to witness, the A & R staff have usually been prepared with prior knowledge which has been disseminated and acquired through these networks.

Talent scouts

Record companies also recruit young staff who are receptive to immediate changes and emerging trends amongst various youth groups or within specific musical genres. This is a practice which can be traced back to the reorganisation of the music business in the 1950s when the industry began to restructure in order to deal with younger consumers in a less arbitrary manner (Gillett, 1983). In the late 1960s record companies employed house hippies to establish contact with the counter culture and underground musical community (Dilello, 1983). In the 1970s punk fanzine writers were enticed into record companies, and disc jockeys were recruited from night clubs during the dance music boom of the 1980s.

The young personnel employed by record companies often have a dual role of bringing material into the company and promoting the company's recordings in clubs or amongst particular audiences. The employment of these staff can enhance a company's image by presenting a 'hip' and knowledgeable face to prospective artists, and if working part-time as a disc jockey or journalist these staff may bring a further network of contacts within the orbit of the company. In the course of their work talent scouts become acquainted with the junior A & R staff at other companies and hence they are able to provide useful information about what is going on elsewhere.

Talent scouts spend their time visiting two or three gigs or clubs per night, and continually listening to 'demo' tapes. They tend to have very little responsibility within A & R departments, although they may occasionally be involved in bringing an artist to a record company and might look after minor aspects of that artist's career. Talent scouts are primarily employed to keep the company in touch with musical changes and up to date with developments amongst other companies. Despite their job title they tend to bring information to the company rather than 'talent'; this they will do if they manage to stay at the company long enough to become an A & R manager.

[...]

British A & R culture and the rock tradition

In an account of record company A & R departments based on research conducted in the middle of the 1970s, Simon Frith (1976) described how staff were drawn from a variety of backgrounds, including music writers, disc jockeys, musicians, promoters and sales staff. Between 1989 and 1992, when my own research was carried out, A & R staff were still drawn from similar backgrounds. However, the range of occupations that A & R staff are recruited from belies the characteristics and cultural values that they share in common. The majority of staff involved in acquiring artists for major record companies are white, male and have entered the industry from what might loosely be called the college-rock tradition. The director of a small management company that represented rock, pop and dance acts was one of a few people to remark on this bias:

> You can get a third division rock act a serious amount of money. If you're dealing with black dance, and I use the racial thing significantly, then quite often you're hard pushed to get any kind of treatment of the same order.... In the record companies individuals come from the rock tradition. Hardly ever do they come strictly from a soul, r'n'b, dance tradition. Very, very rarely. You know, they've been social secs at college. What do social secs at college deal with? They deal with bands, and they get used to that, and they come through the system and they go on. Or, they come out of bands themselves. Quite a lot of the staff in record companies were in bands. Very rarely in anything but a rock band. Now and again producers, but generally they're producing white acts, who, by and large, will be in the rock tradition. And there is a belief, a kind of belief that is really hard to break down.

These comments about the background of staff were echoed in an industry trade magazine profile which appeared following the appointment of Paul Conroy to President of The Chrysalis Group in 1989:

> Getting back to Conroy's roots in the business and some clues as to why he is so universally liked, he is one of a long line of college social secs of similar age (Conroy is just 40) who now man the middle and upper echelons of the UK music industry. For those unfamiliar with the British education system, social secretaries are a breed of students most prevalent in the Sixties and Seventies heyday of the live college circuit who devoted more time to booking bands than to their studies. Chrysalis founders Chris Wright and Terry Ellis, as well as Conroy's WEA boss Rob Dickins, got hooked on the music business in just such that way. (Dalton, 1989, p. 10)

During the 1960s there was an expansion in British higher education, and a change in the composition of the audience for commercial popular music. Whereas the music of the rock'n'roll era had been associated with working class teenagers, during the 1960s various elements of pop were 'appropriated' and re-christened 'rock' by a recently enfranchised grammar school student and 'hip' middle class audience (Chambers, 1985). Rock was not only a source of pleasure for these consumers, but it was imbued with libertarian and artistic allusions as the emergent middle class audience (and artists) drew on an aesthetic vocabulary inherited from an appreciation of European high culture. The 'increased legitimation of rock music' during the 1960s directly accompanied a shift in the social class background of the audiences and performers (Vulliamy, 1977).

The relationship between rock and the newly educated middle class frequently found expression in events associated with the student counter-culture, in which music was often central. One consequence of this was that a number of educated, middle class, mildly bohemian young people were attracted into and actively recruited by the music industry. In a business which has a high turnover of staff, reputations are established but are easily lost; executive careers follow artists into obscurity. Historically, those who entered the British recording industry during the late 1960s and early 1970s, and who had remained, were in higher corporate management, running an A & R department or managing a label by the 1990s. Throughout this period a 25 year tradition had been established during which staff were recruited into A & R departments from similar backgrounds or with similar working experiences, musical tastes and preferences.

[...]

In touch with the street, man

In 1990, Dave Massey, who was working for Chrysalis Music, compared getting into A & R to 'joining the masons, difficult for everyone, nearly impossible for women'. In the course of the research for this book I spoke to one woman who had worked in artist and repertoire in Britain. At the time of our meeting she was working in the United States. Reflecting on the lack of women in A & R she said:

> I'll tell you why I think there are not many women in it. Because, number one, it's a very chauvinistic industry, it really is. Number two, the A & R lifestyle does not suit the majority of women at all. The fact of going out every night to clubs, being up all night in sleazy, dodgy clubs or whatever.

Although a number of younger staff who had entered the recording industry during the 1980s, and who were mainly involved in dance, pop and soul music, had begun to question the usefulness of seeking artists in pubs and clubs, A & R departments still tend to be dominated by staff drawn from rock culture with its emphasis on performing live in front of an audience in a 'natural' setting. In addition, and clichéd as it might sound, a number of people in record companies espouse a belief of 'being in touch with the street' and 'the kids'. These terms were used quite seriously by a number of artist and repertoire staff and senior executives who described their work to me. As this female A & R manager herself replied when I asked whether this type of approach, and the lifestyle it implied, was still necessary: 'Oh I think so. You have to be out there, in touch with the street. It's all about those kids out there.'

This emphasis on the street – no matter how romanticised, and whether it really is where most artists are found – further reinforces the male culture of artist and repertoire. Because most of 'the kids', out there, on the street and in the sleazy clubs are male. As Angela McRobbie has pointed out, with its negative moral connotations for women and the very real threat of violence 'street visibility ... both proclaims the publicization of the group and at the same time ensures its male dominance ... the street remains in some ways taboo for women' (1980, p 47). Hence, this approach militates against finding artists who might be 'in the home' and is part of a working practice which operates to exclude women from this area of the recording industry.

In discussing what she enjoyed about her work the A & R manager quoted above emphasised a more personal approach to the job than the male A & R staff I spoke to. Her work involved:

> dealing with people, and their lives as well; their personal problems, their fuck ups, their mental whatever, their little quirks. And my A & R forte is understanding those people and respecting that and trying to work with that and being supportive to them. Supporting their musicality, and believing in them, and being there to hold their hands when it gets rough. That's what I'm about. They'll bring me in when there's problems with artists. I'm good at understanding them ... I do think that record companies would save themselves a bloody fortune if they had an in-house psychiatrist.

Many A & R men have been in bands themselves and give the impression of living out the rock lifestyle by proxy, through the artists they are working with. They tend to stress the 'buzz' and excitement from the music and are often most animated when discussing the possibility of finding the 'next-big-thing'. Although just as involved in 'nurturing' artists, this was usually discussed in terms of the pragmatics of songwriting, studio production and arranging. In contrast this female A & R manager emphasised the supportive, caring and understanding side of the work, and the way in which this aspect was actively utilised by the company who 'brought her in' if there was a problem with artists. At the same time she was just as involved in criticising her act's songs, negotiating with producers and overseeing studio production.

Priorities and prejudice

During a decisive phase in the formation of the modern popular music industry, the dominant practices within the artist and repertoire departments of the major record companies in Britain have been established by staff drawn from backgrounds within the rock tradition. These staff have been predominantly white, male and college educated. Unlike the United States, where record companies have employed specialist, predominantly black, staff to acquire and promote artists in the areas of rap, dance, soul and rhythm and blues, there has been a conspicuous absence of black people in the major labels in Britain. One of the few notable exceptions to this has been Island Records where the distinctive character of the company has developed under the influence of its founder Chris Blackwell and through a steady tradition of working with artists from the Caribbean. In most of the record labels in Britain there is only the occasional black messenger, talent scout or accountant; the vast majority of staff are white.

However, it is not simply that there have been hardly any women or black people in key decision-making positions; it is that there have been few people from a popular music tradition other than rock. This has resulted in a taken-for-granted way of working in which staff view artists that can be accommodated to the naturalistic organic conventions of the rock tradition as long term career acts, and pop, soul and dance acts as short term, fashion dependent artists. These are viewed as artists who might attain longevity or produce a career, but by chance or accident, rather than through strategic planning. As Ian Hoare (1975) once pointed out, the naturalistic ideology of rock has tended to promote a very simplified and restrictive attitude which regards much soul as a 'cheapened' and 'diluted' version of more authentic forms of music. There has been an uncritical and selective acceptance of the enduring dominance of the rock tradition over other musical styles, and the application of the taste preferences, aesthetic values and preferred working practices of this loosely aligned dominant group have set the priorities for the acquisition and future development policies of the major record companies.

This has been reproduced and maintained by existing staff and through recruitment policies. Staff tend to be selected to fit into the existing A & R culture, where there is peer group pressure to conform, which is reinforced by constant contact with other A & R staff at gigs, in studios and at music business events. There is also the risk of failing and making a mistake, which results in a tendency to sign acts which can be easily accommodated to existing conventions and routes which have proved successful in the past.

Will the naturalistic rock aesthetic break down throughout the 1990s? At the beginning of the decade some commentators were claiming that dance music had 'broken the mould' and that the emphasis on the live rock act was diminishing. However, not many British dance acts were established beyond a few records. Soul II Soul were one of the rare exceptions, which both excited and confused various recording industry personnel depending on their musical taste and their assumptions about which types of artists could achieve widespread success with albums. It is clear that considerable investment is still being poured into conventional rock bands in an attempt to emulate the worldwide commercial success of U2, Simple Minds, Dire Straits, REM and Guns'n'Roses – and there has been, conspicuously, no British equivalent to Madonna, Prince or Michael Jackson. As Cynthia Cherry from the Eternal record label, part of Warner Music, remarked in 1991: 'I find that for black music, a lot of companies still don't understand it. The record companies are still not behind dance in the way they are behind the big live act. If they gave dance acts the push that rock acts get, it could really break through.'

References

Bayton, M. 1989: *How women become rock musicians*. Ph.D. Thesis, Warwick University.

Bennett, H. 1980: *On becoming a rock musician*. University of Massachusetts Press.

Chambers, I. 1985: *Urban rhythms*. Macmillan.

Cohen, S. 1991: *Rock culture in Liverpool: popular music in the making*. Clarendon Press.

Dalton, D. 1989: The marketing miracle worker. *Europe Etc*, Music Week Publication (September 1989), 10.

Denisoff, R. 1975: *Solid gold: the popular record industry*. Transaction Books.

Denisoff, R. 1986: *Tarnished gold: the record industry revisited*. Transaction Books.

Dilello, R. 1983: *The longest cocktail party*. Pierian Press.

Finnegan, R. 1989: *The hidden musicians: music making in an English town*. Cambridge University Press.

Fornäs, J. 1989: *Papers on pop and youth culture*. Working paper 1, Centre for Mass Communication Research, University of Stockholm.

Frith, S. 1976: The A & R Men. In Gillet, C. and Frith, S. (eds.), *Rock file 4*. Panther.

Frith, S. 1983: *Sound effects: youth, leisure and the politics of rock'n'roll*. Constable.

Garfield, S. 1986: *Expensive habits: the dark side of the music industry*. Faber & Faber.

Gillett, C. 1983: *The sound of the city*. Souvenir Press.

Gray, H. 1988: *Producing jazz*. Temple University Press.

Hirsch, P. 1972: Processing fads and fashions: an organizational set analysis of cultural industry systems. *American Journal of Sociology* 77(4), 639–59.

Hoare, I. 1975: Introduction. In Hoare, I., Anderson, C., Cummings, T. and Frith, S., *The soul book*. Methuen.

Lambert, D. 1980: *Producing hit records*. Schirmer/Macmillan.

McRobbie, A. 1980: Settling accounts with subcultures: a feminist critique. *Screen Education* 34, 37–49.

Rogan, J. 1988: *Starmakers and Svengalis*. Futura.

Vulliamy, G. 1977: Music and the mass culture debate. In Shepherd, J., Virden, P., Vulliamy, G. and Wishart, T. (eds.), *Whose music? A sociology of musical languages*. Latimer New Directions.

Questions

1   What are the main responsibilities of Artist & Repertoire staff, according to this extract? What is their relation to other departments within a record company, e.g. the marketing department and the distribution team? How do their roles change according to whether they work for large or small record companies?

2   According to Negus, what are the limitations of the 'gatekeeping' model when applied to those who work in the music industry?

3   As far as Negus is concerned, A & R men will frequently seek to replicate success with similar formulae, and groups may be 'artificially' created and marketed to this end (the Monkees being one of the first bands contrived to imitate and cash in on the success of another – the Beatles – in the 1960s). Yet music fans – particularly young fans – will often show strong allegiance to a band because of their perceived uniqueness and originality, their 'authenticity', and strongly reject or ridicule bands which may fall into the same musical style. In your opinion, to what extent are fans expressing real choice in following a particular group and to what extent are they manipulated by the marketing departments of the major record labels?

Further reading

Cohen, S. 1991: Rock culture in Liverpool: popular music in the making. Oxford: Clarendon Press.

Finnegan, R. 1989: *The hidden musicians: music making in an English town*. Cambridge: Cambridge University Press.

Frith, S. 1983: *Sound effects: youth, leisure and the politics of rock 'n' roll*. London: Constable.

Frith, S. and Goodwin, A. (eds.) 1990: *On record, rock, pop and the written word*. London: Routledge.

Hesmondhalgh, D. 1996: Rethinking popular music after rock and soul. In Curran, J., Morley, D. and Walkerdine, V., *Cultural studies and communications*. London: Edward Arnold.

Lewis, L. (ed.) 1992: *The adoring audience: fan culture and popular media*. London: Routledge.

Lull, J. (ed.) 1991: *Popular music and communication*, 2nd edn. London: Sage.

Street, J. 1992: Shock waves: the authoritative response to popular music. In Strinati, D. and Wagg, S., *Come on down? Popular media culture in post war Britain*. London: Routledge.

28

How Are Television Soaps Produced?
Richard Kilborn

From *Television soaps* (Batsford 1992)

Many media researchers have written about soap opera in recent years, but by and large the focus has been on the *reception* rather than the *production* of soaps. In this extract, taken from a study which looks at both processes, Kilborn extends the focus of interest to a number of production issues, including technical concerns, financial restrictions and the roles of scriptwriters and actors, and demonstrates, like previous writers included in this section, that producers are not entirely independent or autonomous but are subject to a range of institutional constraints and influences. He also notes that the viewers of soaps are equally *active* participants in the production process, often negotiating or producing meanings other than those intended by the writers, directors and producers.

For Kilborn, many soaps in Britain and America play a vital role in the overall programme schedules and policy decisions of the institutions which broadcast them, being shown at peak times and delivering large audiences to advertisers and TV executives. The BBC is not exempt from such 'commercial' pressures, and soaps – or continuous drama serials as they prefer to call them – play an important role in enabling the BBC to justify the continuation and cost of the annual licence fee. The great appeal of producing soaps, then, as opposed to, for example, one-off period costume dramas, is the relatively low investment costs coupled with high returns in terms of audience figures and, in the case of the commercial channels, advertising revenue.

The main problem for the producers of soap, however, lies in the task of maintaining high production standards (the days of wobbly sets and fluffed lines are long gone in British soaps) in the face of rigorous time schedules and strict deadlines – a problem made all the more acute as many soaps contemplate increasing the number of episodes to four or even five per week. The necessity to adhere to strict deadlines has resulted in producers of soap adopting an industrial mode of production, with all the connotations of routine, discipline and hierarchy which that implies. Nowhere is that more evident than in scriptwriting and direction, which, according to Kilborn, rank fairly low in the production hierarchy. Usually employed in large numbers and on fixed-term contracts, no writer or director has real autonomy or influence because, in the interests of historical continuity and consistency from episode to episode, a text cannot be stamped with any individual writer's distinctive character or a particular director's creative flair, and scripts must preserve the illusion of originating from an unauthored source.

Finally, Kilborn addresses the role of actors in TV soaps, discussing the pros and cons of appearing in a long-running regular TV series. He notes that the 'killing off' of a popular soap character can elicit storms of protest from viewers, underlining his earlier comments about audiences being active producers of meaning, and he concludes that the unpredictability of audience tastes means that there is no such thing as a guaranteed success, even in the overwhelmingly popular and competitive world of soap.

In this chapter we shall be exploring a number of issues relating to the making of television soaps, principally the *contexts* in which the production takes place and the main *processes* involved in the putting together of a TV drama serial. Restrictions of space mean that we will only be able to cover the broader aspects of production, although, where appropriate, readers will be directed to accounts which give a far more detailed description of how individual soap operas reach our screens.

A further objective of the chapter will be to correct certain popular, but mistaken, notions of how soaps are actually produced. This is not to suggest that many viewers are of the belief that soap actors and actresses are making it up as they go along, but there is a distinct danger – particularly given the style of reporting in some of the tabloid journals – that some phases or aspects of production will be given a much higher profile than others. The constant stream of tabloid stories about the lives and loves of leading players in soaps may, for instance, give a very exaggerated impression of their importance within the larger production cycle and obscure the role of others in the production hierarchy. A more accurate idea of how soaps are made is provided by the occasional behind-the-scenes television documentaries and the chapters in those 'official companion' volumes which address production issues. Here again the picture that readers or viewers get may well be somewhat partial, since the works in question are generally conceived as part of a promotional drive to sustain interest in the soap in question, so any major problems which have been encountered in, say, financing the serial, tend not to be given particular prominence.

Who produces what?

A somewhat different approach to the issue of production is to start by asking questions about what is actually being produced. The common-sense response to such an enquiry is that the combined evidence of tens of thousands of TV soap episodes all emanating from the same source should leave one in little doubt as to who is producing what. Adopting only a slightly different perspective, however, it is just as feasible to conclude that the audience itself is crucially involved in the business of production. Viewers are not so much passive recipients of what television offers, but rather are active participants in the production process – in the sense that they do not simply read off the meanings implanted there by a producer-author but produce their own meanings through a more active process, which can be thought of as one of negotiation.[1] The claim that meanings are generated principally in the minds of viewers or readers is one which can be applied to a wide variety of both literary and visual texts, but it seems especially applicable in the case of soap opera.... [s]oaps encourage a very active form of response for audiences. It is out of this constant exchange of views and speculation that the 'meanings' of soap opera are produced. As Taylor and Mullan observe in their discussion of audience viewing habits, largely based on a study of soaps: 'it seems that television drama has only properly occurred, been thoroughly realised, when the plots and the moral messages they contain have been discussed and interpreted and re-dramatised in the company of friends or mere acquaintances' (1987, p. 206).

As well as asking questions about *how* meanings are produced, one can also legitimately begin to ask questions about *what* is being produced in soap opera. Again the obvious response is to observe that the evidence, say in the form of 30 years of *Coronation Street*, is plainly there for all to see. An alternative view, however, is to say that it is not a regular supply of television entertainment that is being produced, but a large and loyal contingent of viewers. As one critic of the soap genre put it most succinctly: 'One does not have to be a cynic to hold the view that television transforms viewers into units of economic exchange' (Allen, 1985, p. 45). Since one of the highest priorities of commercial television has been to deliver viewers into the hands of advertisers (TV advertising rates are measured in terms of what it costs to 'reach' a thousand viewers), it is not difficult to see why such reliable audience-producing programmes as soaps should always have featured prominently in commercial schedules.[2]

Whilst it may be appropriate to talk of audiences being produced for advertisers within a television system largely financed out of advertising, how is one to understand the economics of soap opera production within the non-commercial sphere? As we have already had occasion to comment, over the years the BBC has had something less than a thorough-going commitment to soap opera production, believing that pandering too much to popular taste might undermine its other important aim of providing a measure of cultural enlightenment. On the other hand the corporation has at times turned to the continuous drama serial (preferred BBC terminology) when it felt it needed to compete with ITV for the television audience. Many observers, for instance, have seen the arrival of *EastEnders* in the mid-1980s as directly resulting from the BBC's urgent need to produce a big ratings success at a time when the corporation was being made to feel that it was vulnerable to various forms of attack (Buckingham, 1987, pp. 117–18).

The high ratings obtained by *EastEnders* have therefore, in the opinion of many observers, proved a valuable asset in the corporation's continuing quest to obtain adequate levels of funding through the government-supervised licence fee system. The programme has also proved to have economic potential in its own right. It has sold well abroad ... and has also provided the BBC with many opportunities for commercial exploitation. This can take the form of direct spin-offs from the programme itself (home-videos, books based on the lives of earlier generations of 'East Enders') or can be one of various types of merchandising (sales of T-shirts, mugs and other desirable commodities).

Taking the lid off TV soap production

Various factors have to be taken into account when talking about the production of TV soaps. One major consideration is that they are made for the most part by or for large broadcasting institutions or companies and will, for this reason, be subject to a whole series of institutional constraints and influences. These range from what funds are initially made available to start a project, to what niche it is envisaged the programme will occupy in a particular broadcasting schedule, or what production resources – in the form of studio and technical facilities – can be allocated on a fairly long-term basis. All this means that whilst at any one time creative minds are spawning many new ideas or scenarios for new soaps, only a small proportion of them stand a chance of ever getting beyond the 'initial outline' stage. As to who determines what programmes actually go into production, this decision usually lies with a small group of individuals at the head of some organizational hierarchy, whether this be the management staff of Procter and Gamble Productions Inc. or top executives at the BBC.

Whilst it is not always possible to account for all the forces – institutional and otherwise – which have affected the production of a particular soap opera, one cannot underestimate the importance of budgetary matters. The glossiness of the American soaps, especially supersoaps like *Dallas* and *Dynasty*, has much to do with the generous budgets which are made available (though the phenomenal international success of these products more than justifies the high production costs). On the other hand, where production teams are working within much tighter budgets, modes of production will have to be employed which will balance the demand for a quality product with the financial limitations under which they are operating. In Europe, for instance, we are now seeing a growing number of examples of soap operas made by much smaller production teams on relatively low budgets.[3]

Though budgets have an important determining influence on the sort of soaps that are produced, there are also other factors which have to be taken into account. Developments in the structures of broadcasting can in themselves often lead to changes in techniques or modes of production. In Britain, for instance, we have witnessed over the last few years a significant increase in the number of small or medium-sized television companies, as demand for out-of-house programme making has grown (partly as a result of the arrival of Channel 4 and partly as a consequence of government encouragement of the independent production sector). These companies have not only been responsible for various types of new-look programming, they have also on occasions devised certain innovatory production techniques. The company which makes the Channel 4 soap *Brookside*, Phil Redmond's Liverpool-based Mersey Television, is a good example of the successful introduction of new – and Redmond would argue more effective – procedures for putting together a tri-weekly serial.

In the case of *Brookside* this has involved acquiring a number of houses on a small private estate and fitting them out in such a way that they could form a permanent set. This has not only brought benefits in the shape of reduced costs, it also has enabled recording to take place in a situation far removed from the 'artificiality' of the large studio-based television factories; the claim being that one is better able to capture a live atmosphere in this way and thus convey a greater sense of realism.

Cost advantages of soaps

The examples cited above give some indication of the different modes which can be employed in the production of TV drama serials. At one end of the scale there are the American supersoaps which are for the most part not only recorded on film but use many of the techniques we associate with Hollywood-style film making. At the other end of the scale we have relatively modest, small-scale productions where the emphasis is on cost efficiency and quite a short production cycle. In the following section we shall confine ourselves mainly to looking at what goes into the production of the more traditional type of bi-or tri-weekly soap, such as *EastEnders* or *Coronation Street*, since these are the programmes with which readers will probably be most familiar.

From the point of view of broadcasters, soaps always have the advantage of being much less costly than other forms of TV drama, especially if the very large audiences which a soap can usually be relied on to generate are included in the calculations. The reasons for soaps' relative cost-effectiveness are not difficult to fathom. Whereas in the case of series drama each new self-contained episode will normally require substantial investment in new sets or costumes, soaps – with their restricted number of recurring settings and their traditional emphasis on the everyday world of domestic interiors – make far fewer material demands. Soaps are in this respect extremely economical, even though there has been something of a tendency in recent years to include a larger number of scenes shot on location which can in some circumstances cause a substantial increase to the overall cost.

The initial start-up costs for a programme can of course involve substantial investment, so with all new soap projects much time and thought is devoted to 'product development'. With American soaps this will often entail the pre-testing of the product on selected groups of viewers and then introducing whatever changes are thought necessary in the light of subsequent comments. In addition, with all new ventures into soap opera the most careful consideration is given to how the new product can be made sufficiently distinctive and attractive to compete with long-established programmes on rival channels, while retaining many or all of those features which audiences expect to find in standard soap entertainment.

Once a new soap has been successfully launched, however, the benefits from the broadcasters' point of view may well be incremental. In other words, the longer a particular soap runs, the more economical it can appear to be. In contrast to other types of programme production, an established soap opera is an item which can be easily and regularly accounted for. In these cost-conscious times the knowledge that expensive equipment and studio resources are being utilized on this regular and intensive basis can represent a powerful economic argument to those who decide what programmes are produced. An additional factor which helps keep down the cost of soap opera production is that the salaries paid can be lower than for other types of television production. Actors appearing in traditional soaps, even though they may become household names, are only paid a fraction of the amount which the prima donnas of the supersoaps demand and receive. Other members of the production team, directors, producers and writers, have also been known to voice their dissatisfaction on occasions that the level of remuneration they receive does not always reflect the range of skills they are called on to deploy.

One should perhaps hasten to add, however, that complaints about soaps being under-resourced are heard less frequently nowadays than they once were. Yet there was a time not so long ago when soaps were viewed as being virtually beyond the pale in terms of production standards. Soaps became almost synonymous with the type of programme which had been thrown together on a shoe-string budget and which showed up all manner of deficiencies, whether of acting, scripting or technical management. In the early years of television serials, for instance, parts of the flimsy studio sets always appeared to be on the verge of collapsing and the whole soap opera 'world' seemed to be characterized by a distinct lack of solidity. Given the conditions under which soaps were produced and the absence of many of the technical aids now available, it is small wonder that a certain lack of polish showed through. What is far more regrettable is that the myth about soaps' generally shoddy production standards should have persisted for so long and that this label should have been applied so indiscriminately.[4] On occasions one feels that it has been used by critics as a general tactic for devaluing or ridiculing what they see as a highly dubious and addictive form of entertainment.

Producing the goods

The major problem, or rather challenge, that all makers of TV serial drama face is the task of maintaining a high level of productivity in the face of a deadline pressure that is greater than with most other forms of broadcast drama. The necessary output can only be achieved by adopting a broadly industrial mode of production. The production process is accordingly broken down into a chain of separate operations, and individuals or groups are given responsibility for carrying out specific tasks. In this way the making of TV soaps can be likened to other manufacturing processes where each phase of production is routinized to the greatest possible degree.

A considerable number of skills is being mobilized in the course of making a soap opera, but the success of the operation depends on how well all these skills are coordinated. In other words, though certain individuals may be more conspicuous than others, every successful soap remains essentially a team effort. Responsibility for ensuring that all cogs in the production machine function satisfactorily lies with the producer. One person with experience of producing soaps once likened the work to that of a quantity surveyor, in that the producer's main task is that of translating, with a set number of resources, the blueprint which the programme's architects have prepared into a series of finished units: the recorded episodes (Redmond, 1985, p. 39).

The precise powers of the producer will differ according to how the particular company is organized and how the chain of command operates. In the United States, the more one peers into the labyrinthine structure of companies which control soap opera production, the more limited the role of the individual producer seems to be. In Britain producers of TV drama serials appear to have more of a say in the way things are organized and managed, but even so their powers are ultimately constrained by those who have superior positions in the hierarchy: the directors of programmes for the company or the TV drama section chiefs.

The first that a television audience sees or hears about a new soap tends to be in press items or in various forms of publicity put out by the channel itself just prior to the launch of the new programme. As readers will probably be aware, however, this final pre-launch phase is preceded by a long gestation period, often several years in duration, during which a team of workers will have been busily engaged in the many types of planning and preparation which this type of production demands.

Scriptwriting

As might have been anticipated, given the huge popularity of soaps, television companies are constantly being approached – by both established scriptwriters and by non-professionals – with new ideas for soaps. Only a small number of these ideas or outlines is considered viable however, and even those which are acquired with a view to further development will in all probability have been first offered to several other potential buyers. Phil Redmond, for instance, tells the story of how in 1973 he first came up with the idea for a drama serial to be centred on the lives of residents on a new housing estate. He duly submitted this outline to the five major ITV companies and the BBC, all of whom judged there to be no mileage in the idea. It was not until Channel 4 was set up in 1981 that Redmond found an organization willing to support the project.

In the course of the initial gestation period of a new soap, a number of pilot scripts will have been produced, often by just one or two writers. When the programme moves into full production, however, it is standard practice for a team of writers to be employed, in order to be able to cope with the demands that continuous serial production makes. This is in contrast to the early days of radio soaps where in many cases just one writer handled the script requirements for a daily fifteen-minute show. Scriptwriters, like all other workers involved in the production process, occupy a set position in the organizational hierarchy. One critic with personal experience of producing scripts for soaps, provides the following sobering assessment of scriptwriters' relative importance: 'The writer ... comes below the script editor or the continuity department, who answer to the associate producer, who is junior to the producer, whose boss is the executive producer, who is employed by the production company, which is owned or controlled or funded by the network or sponsor' (Buckman, 1984, p. 94).

Within the ranks of the writers themselves there is also a hierarchy. There are those who are mainly responsible for determining the general direction which present or future story-lines will take, and those whose principal function it is to translate these broad outlines into scripts for individual episodes. As always, there will be certain company-determined variations as to how different scriptwriting tasks are divided up between those concerned, but in most production teams there is a distinction between those whom we might call the strategic planners with the longer view and those whose job it is to flesh out these basic outlines.

To illustrate how the logistics of scriptwriting are handled in a specific case, one might cite the example of the longest-running soap in existence: *The Guiding Light*. In common with most of the American daytime soaps *The Guiding Light* is broadcast five times a week and has sixty-minute episodes. There are three 'head writers' attached to the programme whose task it is to come up with what is known as the 'long story'. The story-lines and plot developments covered by the 'long story' are sufficient to carry the programme through the next six months. The head writers also have to supply a 'story calendar' which in the words of one of the show's producers 'gives us a week-by-week listing of emotional and physical events, so that we know where we are by story – not necessarily by individual character, but by story – each week' (Barrett, 1985, p. 37). The next stage in the operation is to pass on the 'long story' to 'breakdown writers' who carve up the narrative in such a way as will conveniently fit into a five-day sequence of episodes. One particular concern is to produce an outline which will accommodate all the commercial breaks (seven per hour!) and end on a tense or intriguing cliff-hanging note to ensure that the audience returns for more on the following Monday.

Once agreement has been reached on these breakdowns (which is usually achieved in collaboration with the show's producers), the outlines are sent to the dialogue writers, who have between a week and ten days to produce their completed scripts. *The Guiding Light* carries a team of five such writers and as the production staff readily admit, the task of turning out this amount of dialogue on such a regular basis can often lead to premature burn-out. With so many writers working on the scripts of different episodes, there are also inevitably certain problems with continuity. In order therefore to ensure that characters continue to use the same sort of language throughout and to avoid any narrative inconsistency, a story editor is employed to pick up all such lapses. Depending on the nature of the changes to be made, one or more of the head writers may again be consulted at this stage and the producer will also have to give his/her seal of approval.

Viewed in this light, working as a dialogue scriptwriter on one of the more popular soaps is a heavily constrained activity. Story contours are clearly marked and much of the landscape detail along the route has already been pencilled in. To some observers this might be – indeed has been – regarded as something of a betrayal of what some claim to be the writer's prerogative, namely to be an inspired begetter of texts. As far as scripting soap opera is concerned, however, it is important that each member of the scriptwriting team resists any temptation to mark the text with the stamp of their own individuality. This not only preserves a sense of continuity, but also maintains the illusion that the whole soap narrative is emanating from an unauthored source.

Directing soaps

What the above description of scriptwriting for soaps makes clear is that the making of a television serial demands a particular discipline from all those involved in the production process. This is no less true of the director, who, like scriptwriters, is usually employed on a fixed-term contract basis when working on a TV soap. In other forms of 'moving image' production, especially in certain types of film-making, the director's contribution will be measured in part by the degree to which the finished product bears the marks of that individual's creative flair. The primary requirement of a TV soap director on the other hand is that such individualistic aspirations are constantly kept in check. It is more a question of discovering and then falling in line with the presentational style and tone which has been developed in the course of the programme's short or long history. As one critic put it: 'Consistency of tone is all-important, even if the tone has to be low' (Buckman, 1984, p. 141).

The main task of the director is to translate the scripts – as produced in the manner outlined above – into the form of episodes ready for transmission. The director's role is thus one which carries with it major responsibility and calls for a range of skills, not the least of which is the ability to extract the best performance out of both actors and technical personnel in situations where rehearsal time is always going to be short. What all directors have to bear in mind is that the majority of the studio staff and the actors they are working with have had in all probability a much longer association with the serial than they have had themselves. Tact, charm, enthusiasm, a fund of relevant experience on which to draw and above all a steady nerve when disaster threatens are all vital prerequisites of being a successful director of soap opera.

With most bi- or tri-weekly soaps the productivity levels which have to be maintained mean that several directors have to be employed simultaneously and given responsibility for a set number of episodes. A typical production schedule for a bi-weekly soap will be geared to a three-week cycle, with, say, three directors in harness, each at a different stage in the cycle. The first two weeks are taken up with final preparations: working through the script and discussing with set designers any special needs for the time spent in the studio. As already noted, recent years have also seen a larger number of scenes shot on location, so one or more location shoots will have to be incorporated into the plan of campaign. The director also has to find time during this fortnight to prepare a *camera script*, which maps out in some detail the shots and camera moves which are best suited to capturing that section of the narrative. The director will also mark on the camera script what movements, actions and gestures are going to be required of the players.

More than perhaps any other form of television drama production, the directing of soaps necessitates various types of compromise, since there is simply not the time to indulge in lengthy experimentation with what shots work best or to test whether a change in the lighting set-up would bring slightly better results. The consequence of this is that most directors tend to fall back on tried and tested formulae, rather than risk a complicated shot sequence which might add something to the dramatic impact of the scene, but only at the cost of involving everybody in a mad scramble to complete the rest of the episode in the time allotted.

Rehearse and record

The third week of the production cycle is given over to rehearsing and recording. As much as one whole day in this week can be set aside for the outside location scenes. There are then normally two full days of rehearsals. These frequently take place in specially hired rehearsal rooms, where tape markings on the floor indicate the position of certain items to be found on the studio set. This preparative phase is quite important, because in the tightly organized space of the studio it is just as imperative that actors remember their positions as it is they remember their lines. These final rehearsals also give the director the opportunity to make further adjustments to the camera script, since what sometimes appears feasible when plotting things in the mind's eye can often prove to be unworkable when enacted in front of a camera. It is also worth mentioning that actors themselves may have suggestions to make at this stage. It can be the case that certain lines are difficult to deliver, or the actor may pick up on some narrative or character inconsistency which no one else had spotted before that moment.

The latter part of this week – usually at least two full days – is given over to the recording of the rehearsed episodes. Before the final move into the studio, there normally will be a so-called technical run-through, again in the rehearsal room, this time, however, with key members of the studio personnel present.

The purpose of this run-through is to check that the rehearsed episodes are viable from the technical point of view and that each episode does not significantly exceed or undercut the prescribed length.

As already suggested, the success of any soap opera depends on the most careful planning and on the well-coordinated efforts of a large number of production workers. The importance of teamwork is at no time more apparent than during studio days when a wide range of professional skills (acting, technical and production) are being deployed. It is vital therefore that on studio days a good working atmosphere is created in order to achieve maximum efficiency. This calls for considerable managerial as well as diplomatic skills on the part of both director and producer, especially as it involves bringing together what one critic has described as 'two different work cultures in television production' (Hobson, 1982, p. 77): the technical staff who are for the most part studio-bound and the performers who divide their time between rehearsals, location work and studio recording sessions.

Regularly having to set up a studio to record the required number of soap episodes is not only logistically demanding, it is also quite time-consuming. This partly explains why some of the more recent soaps have acquired or had built for them a permanent set. In a conventional TV studio, dressing and lighting the required sets will sometimes take as much as half a day, which means in turns less studio time for performers and crew.

Working practices in the studio vary slightly from soap to soap, depending on how tight the schedule is, but most TV serial productions nowadays adopt the 'rehearse and record' procedure. This simply means that, after some preliminary camera tests, each scene in an episode is rehearsed before being recorded on video tape. It is worth noting, however, that with this approach the scenes are not usually recorded in the order they will eventually occur in the transmitted episode. The reason is the fairly obvious one that it is more efficient to shoot all the scenes scripted for each set one after the other rather than constantly having to switch between different parts of the studio.

Once the studio recordings have been made, the production enters the final editing phase. Though everything possible will have been done to get the timing of individual episodes right at the rehearse/record stage, a certain amount of fine tuning can be done by means of careful editing. An episode which marginally over-runs its allotted time can, for instance, be trimmed to size with comparative ease. More difficult problems arise, however, if the episode under-runs, for it is now too late to take any type of remedial action.

Acting in soaps

From the television public's point of view, the most conspicuous participants in the whole production process are the actors. Because they are so conspicuous – they are literally so often in the public eye – they are especially subject to the kind of sensationalist exposure they frequently get in the popular press.

One result is that the distinction between their personal identity as an actor or actress and that of the character they are playing tends to become progressively more blurred. One might have predicted that – as a result of this blurring – some actors might well develop distinctly schizoid traits. As far as one can judge, however, most actors seem to cope surprisingly well with the pressures that appearing in a long-running soap imposes. Any possible disadvantages (about which more in a moment) tend to be outweighed by the not inconsiderable benefits that being a soap actor can bring. For one thing, acting is a very uncertain profession where at any one time more actors are out of work than are gainfully employed, so getting a part on even a half-way successful soap can mean relative job security. Most soap actors are also able to gain additional income from various forms of promotional activity, made possible by their enhanced status as soap opera personalities. There are of course those who will wish to exploit their 'soap star' status as a way of launching out into another branch of show business entirely (this has recently been a favoured option with several teenage stars who have appeared in Australian soaps).

The kudos that regularly appearing in a TV soap brings should not be allowed to obscure some of the less well-publicized, and possibly more problematical aspects of soap acting. Most performers are, for instance, hired initially on short (often 13-week) contracts, which do not exactly represent secure employment conditions. A long-term involvement with a particular soap can, by contrast, bring problems of a different kind in that the actor concerned becomes so identified with their fictional character that he or she gets virtually straitjacketed within that role. It is for this reason that some actors decide it is in their best interests to sever their connections with the serial in question in order to be able to extend their repertoire of acting roles. It is sometimes possible for soap actors, especially those with minor roles, to take on other forms of TV or film work whilst still being contracted to a particular soap. The pressures of production, however, are such that this type of moonlighting is not all that frequent.

An actor's desire to 'move on' will mean that their character has to be written out of the script, though occasionally it will be decided simply to use another actor in the vacated role. Being written out of a script does not always happen at an actor's request, however. As we have seen, it is the head writers or production chiefs who determine in what way the plot and the various story-lines will develop. If it is decided that the future course of the soap narrative makes certain roles redundant, those characters will be duly jettisoned, using one of the time-honoured devices which writers have fashioned for this purpose: road accident; contracting a terminal illness; emigration; murder or madness. On other occasions it will have been the individual actor who – for a variety of reasons – will have incurred the displeasure of the production chiefs and will be subsequently written out of the script. Almost invariably the 'killing off' of a character will lead to complaints from viewers.

If it is a central character who is being forced to depart, there can be a veritable storm of protest. One of the best-known and most highly publicized departures of a character in British soaps was that of Meg Mortimer of *Crossroads*. Meg, played by actress Noelle Gordon, had been the central character in this long-running serial from 1964 until 1981 and for many viewers it was beyond belief that she should be abandoned in this way. For the programme planners on the other hand the future format of the programme counted for more than the audience's long-standing attachment to a character, and in spite of a long campaign to have the character 'saved', the planners eventually had their way.

Meg's departure – like most things in soaps – was not irrevocable, as she made a brief return visit to the programme two years later, but it does point up a general feature of all TV drama serials. This is that no one character (and therefore actor) is absolutely indispensable for the survival of any soap (even though some readers might consider that *Dallas* without JR is practically inconceivable). This has partly to do with one of the distinctive design features of soaps, that – given the constant interweaving of story-lines – audience interest is distributed amongst quite a large number of characters. The other reason is that characters in traditional TV soaps are not, as with certain other forms of drama, created with the physical or temperamental attributes of a particular actor in mind. Characters are developed according to strictly dramatic criteria. This is not to say that actors – especially those in a long-running serial – will not in the course of time to some extent make the character their own by inflecting him or her with some of their own personal idiosyncracies.

Concluding remarks

There is clearly much more that goes into the making of a TV soap opera than it has been possible to include in the above sections. There are, for instance, elaborate promotional campaigns that precede the launch of any new soap and the continuing efforts to maintain a high profile for the programme in the eyes of the viewing public. Television companies – especially in view of the very competitive environment in which they find themselves today – will be continually on the look out for new programme material. Developing a programme from scratch can be a very time-consuming business and the success of the product is by no means guaranteed. The history of soap opera is therefore full of cases where successful manifestations of the genre have been copied or cloned, in an attempt to secure further mileage from a winning formula. Predictably enough – given the fortunes that can be made from a successful soap opera in the United States – some of the best known examples of cloning occur with the American supersoaps.

As television executives and producers continue to seek new ideas, they will be constantly considering how the standard ingredients of soap opera can be freshly blended into a new programme mix. Assessing what is likely to go down well with the current generation of viewers is never an easy task, since audience tastes are notoriously difficult to predict (even with such a popular genre as soaps).

Notes

1. For more on this idea of the 'active reader' see in particular the work of Roland Barthes, especially his essay 'The Death of the Author' in *Image-Music-Text* (1977), pp. 142–8.
2. One has only to look at the daytime schedules of American television to see the extent to which soap operas are indeed 'commodifying' the television audience.
3. In 1984 Swiss German-language television (DRS) in Zurich started broadcasting a weekly TV drama serial *Motel* (was it inspired by *Crossorads*?) which was put together by a small production team working within the constraints of a very tight budget and operating with late production deadlines (Bichsel, 1984, pp. 13–15).
4. One of of the favourite targets for this sort of attack was the now-defunct British soap *Crossroads*. For years *Crossroads* was a frequent butt of popular jibes about all manner of supposed shortcomings, to the point where it was sometimes felt that if a stand-up comedian could not raise a laugh by any other means, then cracking a joke at *Crossroads'* expense might.

References

Allen, Robert C. 1985: *Speaking of soap operas*. Chapel Hill, N.C., and London: The University of North Carolina Press.

Barrett, Ellen 1985: Daytime soap in America. In *European Broadcasting Union Review* (Programmes, Administration, Law) 36(6) (November), 37–8.

Bichsel, Hannes 1984: *Motel* – a low-budget series. *European Broadcasting Union Review* (Programmes, Administration, Law) 35(6) (November), 13–15.

Buckingham, David 1987: *Public secrets:* EastEnders *and its audience*, London: BFI Publishing.

Buckman, Peter 1984: *All for love*, London: Secker & Warburg.

Hobson, Dorothy 1982: Crossroads: *the drama of a soap opera*. London: Methuen.

Redmond, Phil 1985: *Brookside* – a socially realistic twice-weekly drama. *European Broadcasting Union Review* (Programmes, Administration, Law) 36(6) (November), 39–42.

Taylor, Laurie and Mullan, Bob 1987: *Uninvited guests*. London: Hodder & Stoughton.

Questions

1 Not all soaps have enjoyed the long-standing success of *Coronation Street*, *EastEnders* and *Brookside*, and some of the casualties you may remember are *Eldorado*, *Empire Road* and *Castles* (all on BBC1). Based on your understanding of the production routines outlined above, how would you explain the success of some soaps and the failure of others? Choose a soap new to British television and assess its chances of success.

2   Given Kilborn's assessment that soaps are increasingly being produced in an industrial 'assembly-line' context, with all the constraints and conformity which that implies, do you feel that soaps are becoming 'safer' and more predictable or do you think that there is still evidence of experimentation? What story-lines (recent or otherwise) from contemporary soaps would you regard as genuinely innovative or risk-taking? Is there evidence that the more successful a soap is, the more formulaic it becomes?

3   Are there any discernible differences in production values and routines between British, American and Australian soaps? What bearing might these production issues have on the narrative structure, characterisation and ideologies of different soaps?

4   Soap operas are not confined to TV, and Britain's most enduring soap is *The Archers* on Radio 4. Based on your understanding of the production issues outlined in the extract, think of a scenario for a new radio soap.

Further reading

Allen, R. 1994: *To be continued ... soap opera around the world.* London: Routledge.

Ang, I. 1985: *Watching* Dallas: *soap opera and the melodramatic imagination.* London: Methuen.

Buckingham, David 1987: Public Secrets: EastEnders and its audience. London: BFI Publishing.

Dyer, R., Geraghty, C., Jordan, M., Lovell, T., Patterson, R. and Stewart, J. 1981: *Coronation Street*, BFI Monograph no. 13. London: BFI.

Fiske, J. 1987: *Television culture.* London: Routledge.

Geraghty, C. 1991 *Women and soap opera.* Cambridge: Polity Press.

Hobson, D. 1989: Soap operas at work. In Seiter, E., Borcher, H., Kreutzner, G. and Warth, E-M. (eds.), *Remote control: television audiences and cultural power.* London: Routledge.

Horrie, C. and Clarke, S. 1994: Soft soap, flywheels and the poisoned chalice. In *Fuzzy monsters: fear and loathing at the BBC.* London: Heinemann.

29

Film Production in the Information Age
Janet Wasko

From *Hollywood in the information age* (Polity Press 1994)

Film production has many facets and the book from which this extract has been chosen is about the American movie industry and the production and distribution of films in the 'information age'. As particularly illustrative of the dramatic changes which new technologies have allowed in film-making, we have chosen an extract on *special effects* in Hollywood movies.

Special effects have been used since the earliest days of cinema (perhaps most famously in *King Kong* in 1933), but it is the computer-generated images of the last 15 years which have radically extended the techniques that film-makers can employ. In fact, the pace of development is astounding and this decade has seen many ground-breaking innovations, from the 'morphing' sequences in *Terminator 2* (1991) to the computer-generated dinosaurs in *Jurassic Park* (1993). Other recent landmarks in film production have been the images of Brandon Lee generated by computer after the actor's death during the filming of *The Crow* in 1993 which were used to complete the film, and the first entirely computer-animated feature film, *Toy Story*, released in 1996.

Wasko emphasises that, like all forms of technical transformation, film production is grounded in economics and labour, and the downside of new developments such as these is that they are costly and they threaten jobs. When actors can literally be brought back from the dead, and when films can be made entirely using computer-generated characters, or when old films can be given a new lease of life through 'colourisation' techniques, what are the prospects for the budding actors of tomorrow? She also poses questions about the career prospects of many others in the film industry, including musicians, sound technicians and editors, all of whom face competition from technology. Furthermore, despite the success of some relatively low-budget, technically unsophisticated films, Hollywood's appetite for big-budget, high-tech movies seems to remain unsatiated, and the view among some film producers in the 1990s is that they have to make movies with ever more breath-taking special effects, in order to gain the audience's attention (and win the coveted industry awards) in an increasingly competitive marketplace. However, special effects do not necessarily guarantee the success of a film and there have been some notable failures in recent years (e.g. Kevin Reynolds' 1995 blockbuster *Waterworld*, starring Kevin Costner, where stunning effects were not sufficient to bring critical acclaim).

Special effects

Perhaps the most obvious use of new technology, at least for the audience, is in the area of special effects. With their bag of technological tricks, special effects experts now can create new worlds, alien creatures and previously dangerous or impossible actions on film. One visual effects supervisor has noted that 'now virtually anything can be done visually. If you can describe it, you can do it.'[1]

The aim of special effects has been to create things that do not actually exist. Some of the techniques used by the earliest filmmakers, such as double exposures and miniaturized models, are still employed. *King Kong* (originally released in 1933) represented a landmark in special effects and incorporated many of the same techniques used by today's special effects teams: models, matte paintings for foreground and backgrounds, rear projections, miniature or enlarged props and miniaturized sets, combined with live action.

However, the use of computers, robotics and digital technologies over the last 20 years has added to the sophistication of the effects process, and also enhanced the filmmaker's ability to create nearly anything imaginable on film.

There is a wide variety of optical or special effects, which are constantly changing as every film has its own set of unique requirements which inspire effects masters to create new techniques. Only a few of these techniques can be discussed here.

First, the use of computerized cameras has made stop-motion techniques smoother and more believable, while image compositing has become more complex.[2] Examples include everything from the flying sequences in *E.T.* to undersea shots in *The Hunt for Red October* and aerial combat footage in *Flight of the Intruder*. A more obvious recent example, however, is *Who Framed Roger Rabbit?*, in which computer-driven camera methods were used extensively to allow cartoons to interact with live actors.

Meanwhile, computers have been used not only to assist in manipulating images, but to create new ones. Computer Generated Imaging (CGI) has reached a new level of sophistication, as characters, objects and settings can be created and then composited with real images (or live-action). The spectacular results were apparent in the top-grossing film for 1991, *Terminator 2*, which perfected techniques called 'morphing' (short for metamorphosis) to meld film and computer-generated images through digital compositing, and 'making sticky' to graft the characteristics of one image onto another.[3]

With the 1993 film, *Jurassic Park*, new heights in special effects were reached with the creation of computerized images of ancient creatures. In addition to full-size models, the film includes about six and a half minutes of digitized dinosaur footage, which required 18 months of work by 50 people using $15 million worth of equipment.[4]

Other types of effect can be achieved through digital image processing, including manipulation of color, contrast, saturation, sharpness and shape of images. Certain elements of images can be removed, making it possible to repair damaged film, or eliminate unwanted parts of scenes. Examples are the flying sequences in *Hook*, which utilized heavy cable guides which could be electronically 'painted' out of each shot.[5] One prediction is that stunt people will be unnecessary when 'real' actors are (seemingly) able to accomplish these difficult feats.[6]

Another possibility is to create situations that seem real, but are actually computer enhanced. Rearranging scenes from famous films or newsreels is not only a possibility, but a reality, as illustrated in films such as *Zelig* and *Dead Men Don't Wear Plaid*, as well as the 1991 Coca-Cola commercial, featuring images of Humphrey Bogart and Louis Armstrong in the same scene with Elton John and other contemporary players. Some have predicted that these manipulations will become games of the future. A photo accompanying a *Discover* article features Clark Gable and Cher in *Casablanca*, stating that 'in 2001 we'll be toying with old movies on personal computers, changing actors and story lines to fit our own cinematic taste.'[7]

For some films, the number of effects can be staggering. For example, the underwater setting and alien creatures in *The Abyss* generated 290 effects shots covering 21 minutes of film, while one shot in *Back to the Future II* required compositing nearly 100 effect elements.[8]

Yet, some of these techniques and technologies actually save time, as effects can be done quicker and involve fewer people. One software program, Quicktime, uses digital and video compression to produce an inexpensive version of an effects sequence or edit.[9]

Computerized human images also have been integrated into films, for example, the villain in *RoboCop 2*, the skeleton images in *Total Recall*, and various images in *The Lawnmower Man*. The possibility of synthetic actors has attracted the attention of many filmmakers. George Lucas predicted in the late eighties that 'more advanced technology will be able to replace actors with "fresher faces" or alter dialog and change the movement of the actor's lips to match.' While these possibilities may raise serious ethical questions, the problem may not be an immediate one for the acting profession. One of the drawbacks of computer-generated images has been the high costs involved. And, even though the price was falling rapidly and progress was being made at the beginning of the nineties, it was still impossible for synthetic actors to be mistaken for humans. In other words, morphed cyborgs may be one thing, but most experts agree that a fully computer-generated, 'normal' human is somewhere in the future.[10]

The special effects boom has led to the creation of a few new companies. An example is Apogee Productions, which was formed in 1977 by a group led by John Dykstra, who had worked on the special effects for *Star Wars*. Its first project was the television series, *Battlestar Galactica*, but it went on to produce 'spectacular images, models, mechanized props, and/or optical composites for over 50 feature films and television programs.'[11]

Apogee also serves the varied interests of the entertainment business, designing and manufacturing a wide array of special effects devices and theme park attractions, as well as producing commercials, feature films and television movies.

However, one company seems to dominate the special effects scene. Industrial Light and Magic (ILM), formed by George Lucas while producing *Star Wars*, claims to do more business in the special effects field than its five major competitors combined.[12] The company has worked on six of the top ten box office hits in history and has created some of the most spectacular effects in the industry, including those in *Jurassic Park*, *Terminator 2*, *The Abyss*, *Back to the Future(s)* and *Star Trek(s)*. ILM must be doing well: they reportedly spent $3.5 million on new equipment for work on *Terminator 2* and used $15 million worth of equipment for *Jurassic Park*, as noted previously.[13]

Sound

Sound editors also are assisted through the use of computerized storage of sound effects, as well as the manipulation of sound via computers. New developments in sound reproduction have been introduced during the last two decades, in particular Dolby Audio Recording and various digital sound systems.

In the late eighties, 70 mm prints of *Dick Tracy* were distributed with a six-track system called Cinema Digital Sound. The company responsible for the new system is partially owned by Eastman Kodak and promises digital sound for 35 mm prints (thus suitable for screening in most theaters) in the next ten years.[14]

Music composition and performance also has been influenced by computerization. Just as scriptwriters are able to employ computers to assist in their work, music composers are also using software to aid in the composition of screen scores. In addition, there is the possibility of the electronic origination of music, via sophisticated synthesizers.

Other production/post-production activities

Animation renaissance

Computers have been integrated into animation work, making it possible to complete drawings more efficiently and clean up animated frames, but also to create scenes from new perspectives based on original drawings.

Because of these technical developments and marketing factors, there has been a renaissance in animation.[15] A good deal of animated programming is completed by lower-paid workers in Europe and Southeast Asian countries. Not only can animated features be accomplished more quickly, efficiently and cheaply, the films tend to be popular with a wide range of audiences, making them particularly suited for international markets. As a recent *New York Times* article concluded, 'Like so much else in Hollywood, the renewed interest in animated films after decades of general neglect stems largely from a hunger to duplicate some very impressive box office numbers.'[16]

From 1986 through 1990, it was estimated that animated films grossed more than $400 million domestically.[17] Some of the really successful animated films (and their box office revenues) that have whet Hollywood appetites have included: *Who Framed Roger Rabbit?* ($154 million), *The Little Mermaid* ($84 million), *Oliver and Company* ($52 million) and *An American Tail* ($47 million). Meanwhile, *Beauty and the Beast* set a record by selling more than 14 million videocassettes, while *Aladdin* provided even more treasures for the Disney company. The goal is to attract young and old audiences over and over again through perpetual re-releases and video distribution, and to capitalize on merchandising possibilities. In other words, other companies are trying to emulate the Disney model.

Color me richer

While special effects and other new processes have received little but raptured awe from the popular press and Hollywood fans, another process has attracted nothing but controversy. A computer software system developed in the eighties can differentiate between shades of gray in black and white images, making it possible to select appropriate colors and thus colorize previously black and white films.[18] While the technique apparently had been available for a few years, it wasn't until the mid-eighties that a company called Color Systems Technology was able to find anyone interested in the process.

Even though films have been altered in numerous ways for television since the fifties, colorization immediately drew the wrath of Hollywood's creative community, legislators, and critics. The debate became especially heated after 1986, when Ted Turner purchased the libraries of MGM, RKO and pre-1950s Warner Brothers films and television programs. Turner immediately arranged for 100 films (including *Casablanca, Father of the Bride* and *The Maltese Falcon*) to be colorized by Color Systems Technology. The Hal Roach Studios also started colorizing films in the public domain (including *It's a Wonderful Life* and *Topper*) at its (partially-owned) Toronto-based company, Colorization Inc.[19]

For the most part, the Hollywood community was outraged. The strongest complaints came from directors, who wanted to draw a strict line between art and commerce. Fred Zinneman cried that it was 'a cultural crime of the first order.'[20] Martin Scorsese called colorization a 'desecration,' explaining that '*Casablanca* is art. You don't mess around with it.'[21] In addition to directors (and the Directors Guild of America) and film stars, other groups opposed to the process included the American Film Institute, the Writers Guild of America West, and the American Society of Cinematographers. During congressional hearings on the issue, the AFI stressed the cultural role of film, while the 'moral rights' of artists – the right to approve *any* changes made in completed films – eventually became the issue.[22]

Those who colorize, however, saw the issue differently. A film can be changed from black and white to color for as little as $1,500 a minute, although $2,000–3,000 is probably more common.[23] A colorized film can then be sold to syndicated television and cable channels and released on videocassettes for a tidy profit. Color Systems is said to have attracted contracts worth more than $20 million around 1985.[24] As one colorizer explained, 'We're talking about making them viable in today's television and cassette market.'[25]

And, indeed, the market did seem to respond: *It's a Wonderful Life* sold a total of around 10,000 copies in the original black and white version in 1985–6, but between 55,000 and 75,000 copies had been sold of the colorized version by November 1986.[26] As Ted Turner finally concluded, 'The vast majority of people really don't give a hoot whether you colorize movies or not. It's a handful of elitists in Hollywood that don't like it.'

While the head of the Directors Guild claimed that classic films were 'bastardized by people intent on squeezing the last possible penny out of marketing those pictures,' others pointed out that Hollywood film companies were making the deals.[27] Turner not only insisted on his right to do anything he wanted with the films he owned, he also stressed the business side of filmmaking that the directors wanted to ignore: 'Movies were made to be profitable. They were not made as art, they were made to make money, and any moviemaker who did make movies for art's sake is out of business. Anything that could make more money has always been considered to be OK.'[28]

Crude, perhaps, but ultimately ownership rights and business sensibilities ruled. *Casablanca* appeared in its colorized form in November 1989, and around the same time, *Citizen Kane* was on its way to the computerized paintbrush.

Reflections on the production process and new technologies

Labor issues

The question of new technological development ultimately involves a wide range of questions concerning the future of film workers.

Many of the developments discussed in this chapter have the potential for eliminating jobs in the film industry. Will workers be replaced by new technological developments or will their jobs become easier and more efficient? As noted previously, some editing positions are threatened by video editing techniques. In addition, musicians also may be replaced by increased use of synthesized music and computers also may threaten the craft of cinematographers. And, it is even possible that computerized actors or robots may one day replace real-life actors and actresses.

Other problems relate to the rivalries between workers and unions over jurisdictional problems. Film editors replaced by video technicians have resulted in skirmishes between the two technical unions in the industry, the National Association of Broadcast Employees and Technicians (NABET), which typically organized video technicians, and the International Alliance of Theatrical and Stage Employees (IATSE), which generally organized film technicians. Another example cited by Michael Nielsen is the controversy between sound technicians and film editors using electronic editing, which allows sound and picture editing simultaneously.[29]

Another question has to do with education and reskilling. Who should be responsible for training film workers to use the newest technologies? Production companies, trade unions, equipment companies, universities, the government, or employees themselves? Nielsen cites an example of a state-sponsored job retraining program to prepare film editors for electronic editing techniques.

Other issues pertain to creative decisions, as the potential for shifting control of a film's creative elements is influenced by many of these new processes. For example, with electronic editing systems, there is the potential for less influence by film editors, even on the first cut of a film.

While unions and guilds should be able to protect jobs and the control of the work process, the labor organizations in the film industry generally have not represented a united front against technological change. As Nielsen concludes, 'The net result of this dissension among the craft unions involved in broadcasting and film is that the producers have continued to have the upper hand in all negotiations. The unions seem too concerned with their immediate organizational needs to recognize fully the potential impact of new technologies.'[30]

Independents/competition

With the addition of new technologies in production, the ability of independents to produce the slick, sophisticated look of the major production companies becomes more difficult. To compete, independents must locate the capital needed to use these new (and often expensive) techniques and equipment. Otherwise, they are relegated to making lower-budget films or cheaper versions (or, perhaps, satires) of the more expensive, blockbuster films.[31]

Yet the rhetoric from the Hollywood crowd is still that you do not really need the technology to make a successful film. We are told over and over that despite computer storyboards, shiny new editing machines and elaborate special effects, movie making still demands storytellers, and the industry is in need of imagination and talent.[32]

Technological genres

It might be argued that these technological developments also influence the types of film produced by Hollywood companies. Certainly, the number of science fiction or space epics have increased with the evolution of sophisticated special effects techniques. Indeed, seven of the top ten hits of the eighties were 'effects' movies.[33]

The box office successes of action films incorporating special effects and spectacular stunts entice filmmakers to not only continue using such techniques, but to reach even further into their special effects bag with each film. It may even be possible that many audience members may reject films without such high-tech adventures and action, finding them slow, uninteresting and even boring.

Notes

1. Kirk Honeycutt, 'Pushing the Envelope with Visual Effects', *Los Angeles Times*, 19 March 1990, p. F1.
2. See '2001 Entertainment: Personal FX', *Discover*, November 1988; Richard Wolkomir, 'High Tech Hokum is Changing the Way Movies Are Made', *The Smithsonian*, October 1990; Richard Zoglin, 'Lights! Camera! Special Effects!', *Time*, 16 June 1986, pp. 92–3.
3. Similar computer graphic techniques were used by Industrial Light & Magic for the film *Willow*. See Ron Magid, 'ILM Gets a Piece of the Action', *American Cinematographer*, January 1992; 'Make Sticky, Morph!', *Time*, 8 July 1991, p. 56. Morphing also was used in *The Abyss* to create the undulating sea creature called the Pseudopod. See 'Lights! Action! Disk Drives!', *Newsweek*, 22 July 1991, p. 54; Bob Fisher, 'The Dawning of the Digital Age', *American Cinematographer*, April 1992, pp. 71–2; Janet Maslin, 'Movie Wizards Tell Cyborgs' Secrets', *New York Times*, 21 February 1992; David Hutchinson, 'Digital Dawn', *SFX*, 3, pp. 48–58; 'Technology in the Movie Industry: Special Report', *Wall Street Journal*, 16 September 1985.

4. See David A. Kaplan, 'Believe in Magic', *Newsweek*, 14 June 1993, pp. 60–1.

5. Bob Fisher, 'The Dawning of the Digital Age'; see also Alfred D. Harrell, 'AFI/Apple Alliance Bears Fruit', *American Cinematographer*, April 1992.

6. 'Lights! Action! Disk Drives!'.

7. '2001 Entertainment'.

8. Honeycutt, 'Pushing the Envelope'.

9. Harrell, 'AFI/Apple Alliance', p. 92.

10. One film during the late eighties entitled *Lookers* dealt with the idea of computerized actors. Also see Kathleen K. Wiegner and Julie Schlax, 'But Can She Act?', *Forbes*, 10 December 1990; Edith Myers, 'Behind the Scenes', *Datamation*, March 1982, pp. 36–42; Harrell, 'AFI/Apple Alliance', p. 92.

11. Mimeographed material from Apogee Productions.

12. Wolkomir, 'High Tech Hokum'. Also, see Magid, 'ILM Gets a Piece of the Action'.

13. 'Lights! Action! Disk Drives!'; Kaplan, 'Believe'. See Thomas G. Smith, *Industrial Light and Magic: The Art of Special Effects* (New York, Ballantine Books, 1986) (excerpt in 'Reel Illusions', *Omni*, June 1987, pp. 71–6). For more on Lucasfilm, see Dale Pollock, *Skywalking: The Life and Films of George Lucas* (New York, Harmony Books, 1983); Charles Champlin, *George Lucas: The Creative Impulse* (New York, Harry N. Abrams, 1992).

14. Chris Willman, '"Dick Tracy" Brings in Arresting New Cinema Sound System', *Los Angeles Times*, 30 May 1990. Also see Martha Groves, '"Star Wars" Scores Go Digital at Lucas' Skywalker Ranch', *Los Angeles Times*, 24 March 1990, p. F10.

15. Several special sections of trade magazines have focused on the animation revival: *Variety*, March 1992; *The Hollywood Reporter*, 26 January 1993, pp. S1–S76; Ray Bennett, 'Animation Draws Winning Hand', *Daily Variety*, 5 February 1993. Also see Aljean Harmetz, 'Video Alters Economics of Movie Animation', *New York Times*, 1 May 1985; Charles Solomon, 'That Won't Be All, Folks, as Cartoons Make a Comeback', *Los Angeles Times*, 25 March 1990, p. F1.

16. Larry Rohter, 'The Feature-Length Cartoon Returns', *New York Times*, 16 May 1991, p. c17.

17. Solomon, 'That Won't Be All'.

18. David Wilson, 'Colour Box: New Films for Old', *Sight and Sound*, Summer 1985, p. 147.

19. Susan Linfield, 'The Color of Money', *American Film*, January/February 1987.

20. Wilson, 'Colour Box'.

21. Linfield, 'The Color of Money', p. 30.

22. See Jack Mathews, 'Colorization Debate Takes on a New Hue', *Los Angeles Times*, 16 March 1989; Don Shannon, 'Panel Weighs "Moral Rights" of Film Alteration', *Los Angeles Times*, 25 October 1989.

23 Robert S. Birchard, 'My Hair Is Red, My Eyes Are Blue', *American Cinematographer*, October 1985, p. 76; Linfield, 'The Color of Money', p. 30.

24. Wilson, 'Colour Box'.

25. Birchard, 'My Hair Is Red', pp. 75–7.

26. Linfield, 'The Color of Money', p. 30.

27. Wilson, 'Colour Box'.

28. Greg Dawson, 'Into the 90s: Ted Turner', *American Film*, January/February 1989, p. 39.

29. See Nielsen, 'Labor's Stake'.

30. Nielsen, 'Labor's Stake', p. 83.

31. *Spaceballs* is an example of a film which satirizes the sci-fi genre which is rich in

special effects, yet the film still had to incorporate some of the same special effects techniques in the process.

32. This sentiment is repeated consistently in discussions with Hollywood 'insiders', and is a common theme of those interviewed by Tom Brokaw for NBC's documentary on 'The New Hollywood', aired in March 1990.

33. Wolkomir, 'High Tech Hokum', p. 124.

Questions

1   Think about the films that you have seen over the last 12 months which use special effects. In which did you feel that the effects were detrimental to the film (in the sense of being distracting or trying to compensate for a weak plot, for example)?

2   Wasko suggests that some of the larger media conglomerates have the power to squeeze out smaller independent film companies because of their ability to use dramatic and spectacular effects, yet some notable successes of recent years have included the relatively low-budget and technologically unsophisticated *Four Weddings and a Funeral*, *Trainspotting* and *Secrets and Lies*. How would you account for these successes in an industry which, as Wasko points out, is dominated by producers who feel the need to 'reach even further into their special effects bag with each film'.

3   In view of current innovations in computer-based film technology, what future developments do you expect to see in film and other media (e.g. television advertising, where many film directors learn their craft)?

Further reading

Coe, B. 1981: *The history of movie photography*. New Jersey: Eastview Editions.

Hayward, P. and Wollen, T. 1993: *Future visions: new technologies of the screen*. London: BFI.

Mealing, S. 1992: *The art and science of computer animation*. Oxford: Intelect.

Smith, T. G. 1991: *Industrial light and magic: the art of special effects*. London: Virgin.

Webster, C. 1996: Film: the place where art and technology meet. In Nelmes, J. (ed.), *An introduction to film studies*. London: Routledge.

30

Video Diaries: What's Up Doc?
Peter Keighron

From *Sight and Sound* 3(10), 24–5 (October 1993)

'Real life' television shows have increased in number and popularity over the last decade and the final two extracts in this section explore the range of programmes encompassed by the term 'reality programming'. Most reality television relies on the audience's fascination with other people's lives and, in this reading, Keighron concentrates on those programmes which exploit a relatively new innovation in media technology and capitalise on its widespread use and popularity, the video camcorder.

Fly-on-the-wall documentaries have been popular for more than 20 years and continue to provide entertaining and relatively inexpensive TV (BBC 2's *The Village* is a recent example) but although more 'natural' and often more revealing than traditional forms of documentary, these stories of people's lives are subject to considerable professional intervention and are 'packaged' for television with, for example, a presenter/narrator, accompanying music, careful editing and even a cliff-hanger on which to end every programme. Keighron's focus of study, the BBC's *Video Diaries* series, takes the production process one stage further, blurring the distinction between producers and consumers of television output, and giving ordinary people the opportunity to make personal and often very intimate documentaries about themselves or an aspect of their lives on a video camcorder.

Far from being seen as a weakness, the amateur quality of these programmes is viewed by Keighron, and many others, as lending the series an integrity and authenticity which is absent from more traditional documentaries. Although new video technology has, in the past, been treated with hostility by some members of the broadcasting establishment, it seems that, on the whole, mainstream television has now enthusiastically embraced the camcorder aesthetic, to the extent that the video diary format has now been appropriated in a number of other genres, including advertisements (e.g. for *Radion, Pot Noodle* and *Ryvita*), travel programmes (like Channel 4's *The Real Holiday Show*) and light entertainment shows (such as *Beadle's Hot Shots* on ITV). Indeed Keighron suggests that these programmes are shaping and responding to the tastes of the audience who, he argues, are becoming increasingly cynical about slick, highly edited programmes, and view series like *Video Diaries* and *Video Nation* as raw, credible and offering a 'truth' which is absent elsewhere in news and documentary.

Video is in the vanguard of a technological revolution in television. But exactly what sort of revolution, and who's got the upper hand, is not clear. Opinions are divided: either power flows from the barrel of a camcorder, and Dixons is the people's armoury, or our every move is being surveyed and controlled by the video police in league with a cabal of media moguls.

It would be easier just to say that technology is winning. But technology is only ever created, developed and deployed within particular social, political and cultural frameworks. Technology enables certain forms of social, political and cultural manipulation but determines none. And what's interesting about video technology is that it is enabling revolutionary changes not just within the television industry but outside it, not just among professionals but among amateurs.

Video is enabling us to think about the way we define these categories and how broadcasting divides its producers from its consumers. In other words, it enables us to think about television and democracy, to reflect upon the fact that television is a source of (unelected) power for those who work in and control the industry – researchers, directors, programme-makers, producers, schedulers, broadcasters. Video is enabling us to think again about who should have that power, what they are doing with it, and why.

Such questions are being raised by the whole 'reality television' genre, so popular in the US and most successfully imitated in the UK in BBC1's *999*. They are also pertinent to 'people' shows such as *You've Been Framed!* and *Caught in the Act*. But the *political* nature of the question is most clearly brought into focus by *Video Diaries*, not least because of the way the series is affecting professional documentary-makers.

When *The Man Who Loves Gary Lineker* won the Flaherty award at this year's BAFTAs, it was the clearest indication yet that *Video Diaries* had moved out of the ghetto of worthiness in which access programming is invariably dumped and was now residing in the vicinity of documentary proper. While some professional film-makers may view this as a case of 'there goes the neighbourhood', for most it poses an exciting challenge.

'Without any question at all I think *Video Diaries* is the most important development in television probably since the hand-held camera itself,' says documentary-maker Roger Graef. 'At the cutting edge of all factual programme-making,' says Channel 4's Controller of Factual Programmes Peter Salmon. 'Absolutely brilliant ... when they work they make people like me redundant,' says documentarist Molly Dineen. And so on. If the gist of all this is that we could be living through revolutionary times in documentary-making, the question is how, exactly, will that revolution be televised?

Already professionals are attempting to integrate, some would say appropriate, the Video Diary format in different and controversial ways. In the recent series of BBC2's *40 Minutes* – the first under series editor Paul Watson – two of the documentaries use camcorders. *Will They Ring Tomorrow/A Change of Heart* uses Hi-8 cameras to follow four heart patients waiting for a transplant, while somewhat more controversially, *Away the Lads* integrates video footage taken by some Geordie 'lads' on holiday in Benidorm with professional 16mm footage.

'It absolutely stank,' says *Video Diaries* editor Jeremy Gibson of *Away the Lads*. 'That's what gets it a bad name.' Gibson was calling foul on the way the programme exploited the 'lads' by using their footage but not giving them any editorial control. The diarist's right to editorial control is an essential part of the *Video Diaries* project. But Watson denies any misuse of the format. 'I don't think it's been prescribed that nobody else should use it,' he says. 'It's rather like somebody inventing an engine and saying it can't be used for anything other than a car.'

What Gibson is defending (though Watson would deny that is what he is attacking, since Gibson is talking about an ethic whereas Watson is talking about a product) is integrity. 'There is a kind of appropriation going on and it's not just an appropriation of a technique, it's an appropriation of an integrity,' says *Video Diaries* series producer Bob Long. In part, that integrity is an aesthetic. In much the same way as the shaky black-and-white images of *cinéma vérité* claimed to be somehow closer to reality than Hollywood technicolour, so the video aesthetic can promise the closest shave yet. The wobble of the image, the lurch of the autofocus, the bleeding reds all add up to a new authenticity which, claims Long, is a very tangible quality. 'I think that integrity comes through not just in a kind of discussion among media people. I think that it is felt in watching a diary by the audience,' he explains. 'That's one of the reasons we're liked, people do believe that it's real, that it's honest. I think people have a deep sense of seeing honesty ... it's such a subtle thing, just the way someone looks at the camera, the way they're talking.'

The whole 'what you are about to see is the work of an amateur' aspect of the series is no longer merely a negative apology for poor technical quality, but a positive advertisement for the integrity of the amateur. As viewers become increasingly televisually literate, ever more aware of the tricks of the trade and the constructed nature of documentary objectivity and balance, the amateur retains the power to cut through the layers of scepticism and cynicism with which we have learned to protect ourselves from the professional media, the great manipulator.

But *Video Diaries* entails not so much a replacement of the professional by the amateur, as a changing relationship between those terms. In some ways this *is* technologically led. The far higher ratios made possible by the economics of video (it is rare for documentary-makers to exceed a ratio of 30:1 when using film, whereas a typical *Video Diary* will use a ratio of at least 150:1) can change the whole nature of production, since much of the research and preparation can in effect be done 'in camera'. In *Video Diaries* the diarist is at different times, and often at the same time, researcher, director, producer, camera operator, sound person and editor (not to mention subject) and the role of the professional producer is in the process not so much removed as renegotiated.

The real driving force of *Video Diaries*, though, is not technology but control. The ultimate editorial control of the diarist – the amateur – is, says Bob Long, 'the only thing that's set in stone.' But while diarists make the final editing decisions, the *Video Diaries* professionals make the first and in some ways most important ones. They select (edit) the half dozen or so diarists in each series from the thousands of applicants and choose the political and ethical structure of the series. So if the professionals are still in control at this stage, by what authority, and on the basis of what ideologies do they wield that power?

The theory and practice of editorial control and the different ways it can be mediated have developed over the last 20 years at the BBC's Community Programme Unit (CPU). Influenced by the theory and practice of access television in the US in the late '60s and a leftist reading of Reithian public service broadcasting ideals, the CPU was set up at the BBC in the early '70s following the success of the first *Open Door* programmes. As much as any politics dares speak its name at the BBC, the CPU is, then, liberal and of the left.

These politics clearly shape not just the selection of the diarists, but the whole production process, and in particular the editing stage, during which Gibson, Long and the *Video Diaries* producers make no pretence to be disinterested technical assistants. One of their roles is to dissuade the diarist from what Gibson calls 'ethically worrying' tendencies. 'You're in control of your own diary and it's a great chance to be able to push yourself,' says Gibson. 'Your ego, and your attitude and approach, can come across from the rushes in a very offputting way that an outsider wouldn't like. It's our job to identify that and try to turn the diarist to take a less egocentric approach to something and less pushing of aspects of their personality which are difficult or confrontational. The other thing is they may be very much in love with a very contrived material, terribly in love with some parts that we know are a total contrivance.'

As Bob Long explains: 'It often happens that you say, "I believe that you felt this at the time but what I'm seeing I don't believe." It's not just a question of we've seen through it and the gaff is blown. There are times when [the diarists] do mean what they're saying but the way they're saying it ... as a viewer you just sit there saying: I don't believe you.'

Again it comes back to integrity, which, as Gibson admits, is 'very hard to define'. But definable or not, it can be tested in at least two ways. First, by the diarists themselves ('All the diarists. I can say without exception,' says Long, 'have been delighted with them in the end, though through the process very often they're not'). And second, of course, by the television viewer.

If *Video Diaries* is asking essentially political questions, the programme itself is an essentially personal format, almost by definition. And the critical and popular acclaim recently accorded to more 'authored' forms of documentary-making – Molly Dineen and Nick Broomfield being, in different ways, the most obvious examples – could be taken as another sign of a response to political pressures within documentary and current affairs.

Certainly the intense subjectivity of *Video Diaries* has eluded pressures to provide 'balance', either within particular programmes or within the series as a whole. Jeremy Gibson says that over two series of *Video Diaries* and one of *Teenage Diaries* there has never been any pressure from above. The third series, including as it does the diary of a miner's wife and the diary of a Spanish Civil War veteran International Brigadier, may test that immunity further.

The potential for more overtly political, perhaps more collective, diaries (which would not necessarily be less personal) is obvious. The recent *LA Stories* (produced by an independent American production company in conjunction with *Video Diaries*), which combined nine diarists' accounts of the year following the Rodney King riots, showed one possible future. The forthcoming *Video Nation* (in which some 60 people throughout Britain will collectively produce a video diary of the nation) shows another.

Gibson sees the most promising aspect of *Video Diaries* as coming from the way it can lead diarists or would-be diarists to think beyond the diary form.

'The diary format will go on because it is a very valid way of story-telling,' says Gibson, 'but the next development, and one which in my mind has been remarkably slow in coming forward, will be [people thinking]: "well, we have these cameras, we can use them ourselves, why do we need to make a diary? Why can't I go and make a documentary about anything I want?"'

It is in fact over a quarter of a century since the new technology of video enabled us to raise many of the issues of access that are only now coming to the fore (so much for the white heat of technology). One reason for this slowness is the industry's fear of the new. Television is, essentially, a very conservative medium. It is a medium whose incessant churn demands an unbroken input of new ideas, new programmes, new people, but it's precisely because those (old) broadcasters who control the medium are so dependent on the new that they distrust it and fear the uncertainty and unpredictability it entails.

Perhaps another reason is that new technology in broadcasting cuts both ways. While S-VHS and Hi-8 appear to be opening the doors of broadcasting to more of its previous passive consumers, new barriers of entry are being raised by the manufacturers' attempts to establish HDTV as the definition of broadcast quality for the future.

The most important debates to emerge around *Video Diaries* and the future of new technology in television documentary are those which raise questions about social power. Who should have access to precious broadcasting time? Who is to be allowed to document their stories, their understanding of the world we live in through the medium of television? Who should be the manipulators? One need only consider the HDTV camera in relation to the Hi-8 camcorder, or *Video Diaries* in relation to *You've Been Framed!*, to realise that, as Raymond Williams said, 'the moment of any new technology is a moment of choice.'

Less than 10 things you didn't know about '*Video Diaries*'

- '*Video Diaries*' are cheap, but not that cheap. If produced outside the BBC, it's estimated that they would cost an average of between £60,000 and £70,000 an hour, around two-thirds the cost of, say, a typical Channel 4 documentary.
- Diarists do not get any fee from the BBC.
- Most diaries are shot on Panasonic MSS4 (S-VHS) camcorders, which cost £1,400. A few are done on the smaller Hi-8 format. S-VHS and Hi-8 are not yet up to the 'broadcast quality' of Betacam SP, but broadcast news is increasingly augmented by S-VHS and Hi-8 footage.
- The Community Programme Unit receives an average of about eight applications a day from would-be diarists, far more when the series is being transmitted.
- Only about 1 in 50 applications gets beyond the waste bin of the Community Programme Unit.

- Recording may take up to 12 months and diarists sometimes have up to 400 hours (with an average of around 150 hours) of material to be whittled down to one hour at the end of shooting.
- Diarists, or the BBC, can withdraw from the project at any time. Diarists have control over the final edit and all footage is joint 'property' of the diarist and the BBC; neither can use it – for example re-edit it or sell the programme to other broadcasters – without the other's agreement.

Questions

1 Keighron describes television as a 'source of (unelected) power' but suggests that the use of camcorder footage in TV programmes represents the nearest that television has come to handing power to its consumers; indeed series like *Video Diaries* and *Video Nation* are widely known as 'access' television. What are the particular qualities of video as a medium which result in it being seen as inherently 'democratic'?

2 Given the significance of the entertainment imperative highlighted by Roger Bolton in an earlier extract (reading 25), how and to what extent is even reality TV 'packaged' for a mainstream television audience? What effect might this have on such programmes' claims to be authentic and democratic?

3 How do you think that reality TV might develop in the future? In your view should it be regulated?

Further reading

Bondebjerg, I. 1996: Public discourse/private fascination: hybridisation in 'true-life story' genres. *Media, Culture and Society* 18.

British Film Institute 1994: *Watching ourselves: real people on television*. Conference transcript. London: BFI.

Corner, J. 1995: *Television form and public address*. London: Edward Arnold.

Dovey, J. 1993: Old dogs and new tricks: access television in the UK. In Dowmunt, T. (ed.), *Channels of resistance*. London: BFI.

Dovey, J. 1996: The revelation of unguessed worlds. In *Fractal dreams: new media in social context*. London: Lawrence & Wishart.

Kilborn, R. 1994: How real can you get? Recent developments in 'reality' television. *European Journal of Communication*. 9, 421–39.

Vale, J. 1993: Captured on videotape: camcorders and the personalisation of television. In Corner, J. and Hawthorn, J. (eds.), *Communication studies: an introductory reader*, 4th edn. London: Edward Arnold.

31

Riding with Ambulances: Television and Its Uses
Andrew Goodwin

From *Sight and Sound* 3(1), 26–8 (1993)

Continuing the theme of reality TV, Goodwin considers the place in the American television schedules of two types of reality programming, both of which have their British counterparts: those whose content relies on viewers' home videos (for which Jeremy Beadle is famous in this country following the precedent set by *America's Funniest Home Videos*) and those which purport to offer the viewer a glimpse into the working lives of the police and emergency services, either through the use of camcorders or surveillance cameras (such as *Police, Camera, Action!* in the UK and *Cops* in the USA) or through dramatic reconstructions of real events (e.g. *Crimewatch UK, 999* and their American equivalents *America's Most Wanted* and *Rescue 911*).

Reality programming is, of course, cheap television but it is also enormously popular with audiences and frequently warrants prime-time scheduling. One of the reasons seems to be that reality TV is undeniably voyeuristic, giving us an insight into the lives, crimes and personal tragedies of other people. However, this rather morbid fascination is underscored by a message which is ultimately optimistic. Programmes like *999* rarely reconstruct stories which don't have happy endings, and why have nightmares when viewers of *Crimewatch UK* have helped to solve hundreds of crimes and given information leading to countless arrests? Even *Police, Camera, Action!*, by placing the viewer in the position of the police officers, reinforces the authority of the forces of law and order and the legitimacy of their actions. But despite being about heroism, and indeed despite the public service role that many of these reality programmes purport to have (Goodwin tells of how a child in the US knew to call 911 in an emergency after watching the programme and BBC 1's *999* has claimed to have improved *this* nation's emergency first-aid skills), Goodwin states that these programmes undermine the professionalism of broadcast journalism. He believes that in their quest to be entertaining as well as informative, many reporters and producers have 'broken the rules' of traditional journalism and deliberately misled the audience. Furthermore, he rejects the popular view that reality TV empowers the audience: far from empowering us, he believes that it is turning us into spies and voyeurs. Indeed, his tongue-in-cheek replies to the question 'what next?' have already been borne out, in part, by the enforced resignation in January 1996 of ten police officers in Sydney, Australia after surveillance footage of them accepting bribes, taking drugs and having sex while on duty was shown repeatedly (and to huge audience ratings) on mainstream TV.

One other frequent criticism which Goodwin does not address, but which is related to the issue of empowerment, is that surveillance cameras and video camcorders have reduced the need for 'real' people to be vigilant and police their own communities. So while cameras may help to catch criminals after the event, they can do nothing to prevent it from happening or intervene to stop it. Two examples mentioned in earlier sections – the beating of Rodney King by the Los Angeles police and the abduction of toddler James Bulger from a Liverpool shopping centre – are forceful testament to the powerlessness of the video and those of us who rely on it.

Television in America has routinely been disparaged and subjected to moral panics about its effects and impact. Written off as the 'boob tube', the 'Great Mother' (the metaphors are significantly gendered), as 'a vast wasteland' (by Newton Minow, Federal Communications Commission chief, in 1961) and, more recently, as 'a toaster with pictures' (by Mark Fowler, Ronald Reagan's FCC chairman), television is rarely taken seriously by cultural commentators. But judged even by these lowered expectations, the tabloid television shows and 'real-life' programming that first hit our screens in the mid-80s represent a new low, according to the medium's critics.

In the new formats of shows like *Cops, America's Most Wanted* and *Rescue 911*, 'factual' output is subjected to all the razzamatazz of a prime-time game show. Meanwhile, amateur video is increasingly prominent (CNN recruits would-be newsgatherers or so-called 'CNN News-hounds', from the video-taped beating of Rodney King to the domestic pratfalls of *America's Funniest Home Videos*. This material is increasingly packaged like a commercial or an MTV video clip, with all notions of 'keeping faith with the viewer' (is it 'fact' or 'fiction'?) subsumed under the need to generate excitement. Documentary and camcorder images are electronically manipulated and spiced up with music and dramatic and/or comic voiceover. Reporters are chromakeyed into dramatic reconstructions. And tabloid news values increasingly cross over into television's factual output, through sensationalised 'human-interest' shows like *Hard Copy, A Current Affair* and *Inside Edition*.

'Reality programming' is, of course, one of television's least expensive forms, and this has led some to argue that it is, in both senses, its cheapest. Many of these criticisms are well placed. But there is also much more going on in the new 'reality' shows: a move towards a utilitarian view of television, and an undermining of the ideology of naturalism.

Post-naturalism

Until a few years ago, you might confidently have asserted that the dominant ideology in television in Britain and the US was naturalism – a commitment to an impartial, objective portrayal of the world via the veracity of the camera. And as Richard Collins points out in an essay about the work of Roger Graef (in his book *Television: Policy and Culture*), the ideology of the neutral camera gells perfectly with the philosophy of 'balance'. The radicals who critiqued this view demanded an actively engaged television – the media as a form of social advocacy. Instead, what we have (in the US at least) is a break with objectivity that promotes a point of view, but one which is pro-television, pro-law and order and committed to a populist agenda of technological determinism that sees the spread of the camcorder as a sign of a vibrant, participatory democracy.

Many of these shows began in the late '80s. And yet the new post-naturalist television shows that are now coming out in the wake of *Cops, America's Funniest Home Videos* and *America's Most Wanted* also reveal a contradictory political impulse, if only because they take the challenge to dominant notions of the camera-observer even further.

After the success of three special episodes last season, *I Witness Video* started its first run as a regular NBC series. Like *Rescue 911* (imitated by the BBC as *999*), *I Witness Video* presents television and video as unmitigated blessings for humankind. Written off as 'snuff video' by *TV Guide*, this new show clearly sees itself as the socially redeeming version of *America's Funniest Home Videos*: 'Most of us use our camcorders to record parties, vacations, the happy times', says host Patrick VanHorn. 'But video is also used for much greater purposes. To help us see things in ways we never thought possible. To influence our behaviour, alter our opinions and even change our lives. Tonight, video that has made a difference.' When one of these instances is the use of a micro-cam in the helmet of a football player to give us a skull's-eye view of the game, that rhetoric sounds comic. And when a camera is taken aboard a helicopter on a last-minute search for a kidney-transplant patient on vacation in the desert, the ambulance-chasing factor does bring the snuff-video accusation to the fore.

Rescue 911, on the other hand, never chases ambulances, because it rides with them. Where *I Witness Video* gives us live recordings of real events, *Rescue 911* engages in harrowing reconstructions of real-life accidents and dramas featuring many of the original participants. The show's fourth season opener is an extended sixty-minute boast which begins unashamedly with the slogan: '100 lives saved'. 'A television programme's success can be measured in many different ways – ratings, awards, reviews. For us, the important measure has been in lives', says host William Shatner. In all his years as *Star Trek's* Captain James T. Kirk, Shatner has hardly uttered more preposterous words. But if you believe that popular culture cannot be understood unless you go beyond cynicism, then it is worth considering this statement not only from the point of view of NBC (as a lie) but also from the perspective of the audience (as a promise). We might not believe Captain Kirk (cynicism is necessary, albeit not sufficient), but he has a point. What is the critic, trained in the art of analysing 'texts', to do when television moves so swiftly from reflection to action?

Tabloid television

When television's appeal shifts so dramatically from truth to use, it places itself centrally as the new authority figure in a frightened, atomised society. 'I realised at that point that I was talking to a child and I realised that he was there by himself. I knew that he had not called his mom at work, he had not called his grandparents. He had immediately called 911, and that was crucial.' The point being made here, by a fire dispatcher dealing with a 911 call, is that the young boy called that number because he had seen the television show. *Rescue 911* is interested in effects, not in myth; although that leaves plenty of room to create the myth of its own effects. Some of which are truly bizarre: a woman unknowingly suffering from carbon-monoxide poisoning generated by a faulty gas heater is taken to hospital by her husband. *Rescue 911* comes on the television in the emergency room, featuring a story about a woman who has exactly the same symptoms, as a consequence of inhaling fumes from a gas heater in the home. The couple diagnose the problem on the basis of what they have just seen, and rush home to rescue their children from the brink of death.

'For most of us our homes seem so safe, we could never imagine them posing a threat to our lives', Shatner tells us. Of course, the media critic wants to take this as a metaphor. In paranoid, post-imperial America, the family has retreated to the home, where it nests comfortably in front of the television set ... only to find that here, too, there are dark threats in every nook and cranny. When the big bad world becomes a place where Americans fear to tread, the home, too, becomes a haven of insecurity. If Saddam doesn't gas you, your cooker will. But, as so often with metaphors, what does this explain? If *Rescue 911* is actually saving lives, and if, as a text, it offers a life-affirming promise that television will make the world a safer place, then why reduce social use to an allegorical figure?

Rescue 911 is thus a benign version of *America's Most Wanted*, the show that re-enacts crimes in order to set the general public on the heels of real-life felons. Similarly, the CBS series *Top Cops* (now in its third season) focuses not on hunting down bad guys (as in Fox's *Cops*) but on dramatising the personal stories of individual police officers. When an unlikely hero by the name of Dick Tracy foils a suicide bid by a young woman who plans to throw herself from a bridge on to the freeway, the dramatisation looks like standard stuff. But when the real cop (yes, his name is Dick Tracy) is reunited years later with the woman, who thanks him for saving her, the emotional pull is undeniable. How can you not choke up as the young woman comes on all emotional and Dick stands there looking all sheepish?

Each of these programmes (*I Witness Video, Rescue 911, Top Cops*) develops the earlier model of tabloid television, circa 1988–89, by placing the viewer even more firmly on the side of, and often physically in the position of, law-enforcement officers and fire and rescue workers. The camera sits there with the 911 operators and witnesses their anguish as a child almost dies from a drowning accident. It takes us through the shooting of a cop from the point of view of the police officer herself, reconstructing the ghastly moment when the villain turns the gun on me – I mean, her.

Of course, from the point of view of the television industry, this is a brilliant coup. Even as they garner respectable ratings shares from the trashiest and most manipulative televisual forms yet invented, the networks can also lay claim to a sense of social responsibility. These programmes are among the most violent on television, and yet they are also television's answer to the critics who claim the medium exploits the lowest common denominator for anti-social ends.

But what's in it for the audience? William Shatner's promise (message: 'we care') might echo the empty gestures of President Bush in some respects, but it also answers a need. Two needs, actually. First, there is the craving to be released from the guilty burdens of voyeurism. Like the good Samaritans who stop their cars and pull off the freeway to save the life of a young girl trapped under her overturned vehicle, we want to be involved. Shows like *Rescue 911* and *America's Most Wanted* rescue us from the epistemology of the couch potato (naturalism). We don't want to sit there any longer, ogling all those wars and famines with nothing to be done. Americans are constructed as a people who adhere to the admirable belief that there are no problems, only solutions. Traditional news is disliked precisely for its failure to pay lip service to that credo.

Second, there is the desire for what *USA Today* calls the 'journalism of hope'. Here, at last, is broadcast journalism which delivers solutions. In both areas, the new infotainment offers a utopian appeal: first, to a sense of community, and second, to a pragmatism which rejects the idea that the world is hopelessly out of control and which abhors television's usual implication that nothing can be done.

Is this a new populist aesthetic purging the bourgeois professionalism of network television in the name of a post-modern videocracy? Or is it simply a new urban idiocy, another turn of the screw by the moguls of consumer surveillance? What isn't going to work here is a trendy, populist cultural-studies take that sees all this in terms of liberatory *empowerment*. If video is increasingly a device for stitching us into a digital *Gesellschaft* (only dis-con-nect?) that the television set had been accused of dismantling, then just look at the particular way so much of the new video tech addresses us – as spies and competitors.

When the Frankfurt School critics observed that the culture industries tend increasingly to invade our private lives in the name of capital, they were accused of pessimism. 'One could not avoid the suspicion that "free time" is tending toward its own opposite, and is becoming a parody of itself', wrote Theodor Adorno in an essay which is almost a review-before-the-fact of *America's Funniest Home Videos*. But not even the most committed Marxist party-pooper could have imagined a day when people would sell images of their children being injured in order to gain fame and riches on a show where the top prize is in the order of $100,000. If this isn't the commodification of everyday life, in which Kodak and Sony are not simply

essential to our evenings and weekends, but also now agents for the transformation of 'leisure' time into a potent source of freelance income, then
what is?

It is also difficult to avoid the conclusion that in a period of recession and
rising concern about crime, tabloid television has found a way to give viewers
a sense of real empowerment (the camcorder shoots – it is a weapon) while
doing something concrete about crime. In one *I Witness Video* segment, a
retail-store camcorder captures images of three burglars stealing the camera
itself, and this footage is run over and over, a digital mantra, as if it has some
special significance. Which it does. The videotape was shown on local TV
news in Des Moines, Iowa, which then led to arrests. The camera protected
itself. Maybe these magical powers will protect you, too? The video-thief even
gave the medium the ultimate soundbite-as-endorsement: 'As soon as I saw
that on TV I knew I was going to get caught'.

So if the new shows are to be welcomed to the extent that they help
chip away at His Majesty Objectivity (this is a matter of meaning), there
is no denying that their social uses contain disturbing possibilities, and
actualities. As networks and independents (the increasingly powerful un-
affiliated stations) parade their post-production techniques and their
video vigilantes with new cost-effective reality shows, what's next? America's
most hilarious therapy notes? America's most incriminating telephone records?
America's most embarrassing trash-can contents? America's strangest X-ray
slides? Somewhere out there, a child is waiting to capture parental substance
abuse on home videotape, which will then be handed over to the authorities.

But who are the authorities today? Television, or the police? Just watch out,
there's a camcorder about.

What you feel is what you get

If the new tabloid and home-video programmes are about policing, then there
is also the question of their interesting transgressions of conventional broadcast practice. The new programming undermines broadcast journalism in
three ways. First, through its advocacy, the fact that it takes a stand. Second,
through the emotional techniques of re-enactment, deployment of music,
post-production video effects, etc. And third, via the anti-professionalism of
its DIY camcorder images.

None of these developments is unprecedented. The journalist-as-advocate has
explicitly pushed a point of view on television for decades, from
60 Minutes to *Crimewatch*. The use of dramatic techniques has shadowed
the debate about television drama-documentary since the '40s. And the
'amateurism' of the wobbly *vérité* camera has been made famous by
documentarians such as Roger Graef and Fred Wiseman. What is new here is
the pervasiveness of these techniques in primetime, the extent to which they
have begun to leak into more traditional formats (the infamous ABC news

segment, aired in August 1989, which recreated FBI footage of alleged spy Felix Bloch), and the new zest with which they are edited. The explicit goal of making an emotional appeal is also much in evidence in new current-affairs shows like *Inside Edition, Hard Copy* and *A Current Affair*. Graef's naturalism was intended as a truth-telling machine. Post-naturalism is all about what you feel.

Fakery exposed

While there are earlier examples, such as Geraldo Rivera's primetime drug-busting show *American Vice*, screened in 1986, it was during the 1988–89 television season that the most elaborate breaks with broadcast-journalism techniques came to the fore. It was during that season also that television began to push at the boundaries of acceptable journalistic practices, when the short-lived NBC programme *Yesterday, Today and Tomorrow* went beyond re-enactments to chromakey its reporters into reconstructed scenarios. This is, in fact, a perfect example of an electronic device which exposes a more established practice. The superimposition of chromakey was a piece of fakery that merely amplified the more common practice of having a reporter in, say, Paris, stand in front of an image of the Eiffel Tower.

In autumn 1989, a fascinating *Times–Mirror* poll revealed widespread mistrust of news conventions. 'Americans confused by pseudo-news shows on TV' screamed the *San Francisco Chronicle*. In fact, this questionable conclusion was drawn from empirical data suggesting that viewers (quite correctly) refused to believe that 'news' and 'entertainment' programmes are distinct entities. So where's the confusion? Obviously in the heads of media critics and the concerned but hardly disinterested professionals in the industry, who are unable to comprehend the fact that the public no longer buys the self-serving rhetoric of journalism.

Traditionally, journalism likes to think of itself as a rational beast. Since it isn't (dozens of studies now adequately show that news is partial, subjective and shaped by the social and economic forces which govern its very definition), then the overt introduction of advocacy, affect and manipulation may be no bad thing. Critics of television's factual output (as opposed to ideologues working on behalf of Objective Journalism Inc.) should welcome the development of textual strategies which undermine its credibility and look forward to the day when it introduces canned laughter.

Questions

1 What is the attraction of reality programming for both producers and viewers?
2 Echoing Keighron's comments in the previous reading, Goodwin accuses the reality programming on American television of being self-interested, establishment-oriented and 'committed to a populist agenda of technological determin-

ism that sees the spread of the camcorder as a sign of a vibrant participatory democracy'. Based on your reading of this extract and your knowledge of reality TV (both the British version and the American shows which you might have seen on satellite or cable) how would you assess this assertion?

3   Stressing the role of reality TV as entertainment, Barry Irving, director of the Police Foundation, was quoted in the *Guardian* (3 September 1990) as saying: 'a show like *Crimewatch* ... has everything. It panders to the British taste for a modicum of violence and nefarious activity, it's cheap to make, it promotes a whizz-bang action view of the police and encourages viewer participation. And over it all is a halo, because it is so evidently A Good Thing.' To what extent do you think that items are chosen for reconstruction in programmes like *Crimewatch* and *999* for their entertainment value, and where does this leave the much-lauded public service benefit and journalistic integrity of such shows?

Further reading

See 'Further reading' section in reading 30, page 334.

Global Media and New Media

In many ways Section 5 brings us full circle in that we return to, and develop, some of the issues introduced in Section 1 and elsewhere. In readings 32 and 33 we set up a debate between **Michael Tracey** and **Herbert Schiller** who take as their topic of discussion the impacts and consequences of cultural and media imperialism. Although their approaches and analyses are very different, they are both essentially concerned with the phenomenon of globalisation or, more accurately perhaps, the Americanisation of cultures around the world. Underpinning this theme are concerns which echo earlier extracts (e.g. by Thompson and Murdock in Section 1), namely, the organisation of global media and cultural systems and their position in, and impact on, the political, economic and social world order.

In reading 34, **David Morley** recalls some of the issues raised by Meyrowitz in Section 1 and poses questions about the ways in which media define our social identities and relationships, and mediate our experiences, in the era of new technologies such as global satellite TV channels and the Internet. **David Lyon** extends this focus, arguing that our relationships with media technologies not only play an important role in the construction of our identities and our position in society but may actually be essential in allowing us to participate adequately in all areas of public and private life. As such, new media and communications technologies, according to Lyon, merely maintain and reproduce traditional power structures and inequalities, with some groups invariably having better access to information, greater control over the means of production and more consumption power and leisure time than others. **Howard Rheingold** then endorses the view that far from technologies democratising societies, they simply increase and intensify existing inequalities, and he draws on the ideas of some of the leading European philosophers and commentators of this century to illustrate his challenging forecast of the uses to which future media and communication technologies will be put.

Many recent assessments of the contemporary media and cultural situation have used the idea of *postmodernity* to characterise the current state of affairs. In reading 37, **Dominic Strinati** defines and analyses postmodernism, and in doing so he reinforces the importance of understanding global media and communications technologies in terms of their impact on the dynamics and power structures of the world today. Just as earlier readings have helped us to gain insight into the power bases and organisational structures of 'modern' societies, so Strinati enables us to comprehend the ever more central position of media and communications systems in debates over the *postmodern* order.

Finally, we turn our attention to a consideration of Media Studies itself and its position and condition as an academic subject in the 1990s. Much criticised as a subject of study, ironically often by those who work *in* the media, **Ian Connell** and **Geoff Hurd** in reading 38 and **John Corner** in reading 39 look at aspects of the origins and development of the subject area and consider some of the reasons why Media Studies has frequently been derided by journalists and politicians, in much the same way as Sociology was in the 1970s. In their assessments they outline some of the problems and dilemmas which Media Studies faces in its current phase, and also suggest some of the directions that it might take in the future.

As you approach the end of this book, you might wish to consider your own views on the study of the media in schools, colleges and universities; why you chose the course you are currently undertaking; what you hope to gain from studying the mass media and what the aims of media education in general, and Media Studies specifically, *should* be as we approach a new millennium.

32

The Poisoned Chalice? International Television and the Idea of Dominance
Michael Tracey

From *Daedalus* 114(4), 17–56 (Fall 1985)

In the first half of the twentieth century, media systems and institutions have played a vital part in the consolidation and mediation of distinctive national cultures. The respective roles and centrality of print, film and broadcast media in the construction of the 'imagined communities' of the nation state have been a key focus for much mass media and mass communication research. In the latter half of the century, however, writers and researchers have also had to recognise and respond to the growing importance of the media as players on the international, world-wide political and cultural stage. As a result, the significance of growing international and global patterns of media technologies, media ownership, media imagery and its consumption and reception has formed a key focus for debate and research. At the heart of such debates are a number of issues concerning the consequences of increasing global networks and systems, especially their impact upon the power structures and the dynamics of the world order. A particular theme at stake here has been associated with the idea of *cultural or media imperialism*. In brief, this implies that modern world media systems have provided an important and strategic means whereby dominant nations have attempted to extend and develop their economic, political and cultural forms of control and power in the global arena.

In this extract, taken from a longer and more detailed article, Tracey sets out to challenge some of the methods and assumptions which have characterised the approaches of some researchers in this area. He focuses on television and specifically on the international flows and markets for television programmes. The original article was first published in 1985. That was before the break-up of the former Soviet Union, and before subsequent developments in global satellite systems and their impacts upon local, regional, national and global cultures and identities. As Tracey forecasts in his discussion, the expansion of DBS (direct broadcasting by satellite) technologies of international television has been one significant part of the emerging world communications map since the mid-1980s.

In the last week of February 1985, 160 buyers from foreign television stations assembled in the Shakespeare Centre at Stratford upon Avon. They were attending the BBC's 'Showcase,' organized by BBC Enterprises to market the corporation's programs abroad. The popular purchases this year were a series based on the Agatha Christie figure Miss Marple; David Attenborough's *The Living Planet*; a drama based in Norway called *Maelstrom*; and the Shakespeare cycle. A popular comedy program about the British civil service,

Yes Minister, has been sold to thirty-seven countries including Sri Lanka, Saudi Arabia, Yugoslavia, and Libya. Sales of this program to the Eastern bloc were non-existent. East European countries did, however, like *Allo Allo,* a comedy set in Nazi-occupied France. The German buyers at Stratford declined to buy this on the grounds that 'it would not travel well,' even though they did buy the brilliant, if curious, *Fawlty Towers.* As any fan of this knows, one of the show's key figures is the Spanish waiter Manuel. The Spanish buyer was told that, in fact, Manuel was Mexican, and he duly obliged by buying the series.

Looked at from one angle, this gathering was no more than a way for the world's television channels to buy some rather good programs very cheaply. From another point of view, however, here begins the insidious influence of North Atlantic culture over the rest of the world. Along with Basil Fawlty and Manuel, Sir Humphrey and Jim Hacker of the ministry, the detective as dame (in a traditional English sense, not that imported sense), the dramas of a Norwegian fjord, the Bard and all his works, and the many other products of the BBC, flow values that first enter and then slowly influence cultures that would be better off without them.

What can we say about television as a process of international cultural domination? What can we say about the idea of dominance? What can we say about why American programs are so much more 'popular' than those of other countries? What specific influences can we pinpoint? What grasp do we have of the relationship between the international distribution of television programs and the shaping of individual lives and whole cultures? What can we say even about the distribution of television programs? The answer to all these questions is: not very much.

Let me begin with that very basic final question: what do we know about the 'surface' structure of the international distribution of television programs? To answer that, it is necessary to recapitulate the findings of the research organized on behalf of UNESCO by Tapio Varis.[1] This study, which covered some sixty-nine countries, was an update of a similar survey completed a decade before. Varis found few overall changes since 1973 in the pattern of program flow, but did indicate a trend toward greater regional exchanges along with the continued dominance of a few exporting countries.

[...]

Varis's analysis is, without doubt, the best guide we have to the general distribution of television around the world. Overall, imported programs average one-third or more of total programming. The United States imports little – only about 2 percent of its total television output, mainly from Great Britain, Mexico, and Latin America. In Canada, the vast percentage of the material imported is from the United States. In Latin America, entertainment dominated all the TV programming studied, accounting for about 50 percent of total transmission time. Most of these entertainment programs are imported: 75 percent from the U.S.; 12 percent from Latin America; a small percent from Europe.

In Western Europe, there are important differences among countries. Overall, 30 percent of television programming is imported. Forty-four percent of the material is imported from the U.S., with U.S. programs accounting for 10 percent of total transmission time in Europe; sixteen percent is imported from the United Kingdom; 5 to 10 percent from Germany and France; 3 percent from Eastern Europe and the Soviet Union.

In the USSR 14 percent of entertainment programs are imported. Eastern Europe imported programs from twenty-six countries, 43 percent from other Eastern European countries and 57 percent from outside that area. Twenty-one percent came from the Soviet Union.

In Asia and the Pacific, 36 percent of all television programs are imported, but the variations among countries are enormous, ranging from 75 percent for New Zealand's Channel 2, to 3 percent for a Calcutta station. The U.S. and U.K. are the main source of programs; followed by Japan, with children's programs, documentaries, and movies; and India, Hong Kong, and Taiwan, with films. China produces almost all its own TV, taking just a little educational and news material from the United Kingdom.

In the Arab countries, 42 percent of TV is imported: one-third comes from other Arab states; 32 percent of non-Arabic imported programs come from the United States. In Egypt, 54.5 percent of imported programs are from the United States. Of the rest of non-Arabic imported programs, France provides 13 percent; the U.K., Japan, and Germany 5 to 7 percent each; the USSR less than 3 percent; and other socialist countries about 1 percent. Of the Arab countries, the most important source of imports is the United Arab Emirates (10 percent of imported programs), followed by Egypt (6 percent), Saudi Arabia (4 percent), and Kuwait (4 percent).

In Africa, about 40 percent of programs are imported, although there are quite wide differences among countries: Zimbabwe, for example, imports about 61 percent of its television. Of the imported material, 50 percent comes from the U.S., 25 percent from Germany, and the rest from Western Europe. In South Africa, 30 percent of programs are imported: 54 percent from the U.S., 30 percent from the U.K., 9 percent from France, 5 percent from Austria, and 3 percent from Canada. Seventy percent of this programming is entertainment.

At a global level, most imported programs originate in the U.S. and, to a lesser extent, Western Europe and Japan. The flow is mainly of programs of a recreational kind – light entertainments, movies, and sports. In both Western and Eastern Europe, more than 40 percent of imported programs originate within other countries in the region. In both regions, the superpowers predominate: the U.S. provides 40 percent of West European imports while the USSR provides 20 percent of East European imports.

The most notable increase in regional exchange over the past ten years has occurred among the Arabs, with one-third of imports originating within the region, and among Latin American countries where the figure for regional exchange is 10 percent.

The very general picture of TV flows described by Varis is, however, not a one-way street; rather, there are a number of main thoroughfares, with a series of not unimportant smaller roads. In this sense, his description parallels that of the distribution of news. What is clear is that television as an international communication system is far more complex than is sometimes assumed. We must allow for flows within flows, patterns of distribution that do not fit into the familiar and simplistic model that shows total domination of international television by the United States. Even when we simply count which programs are going where, that idea does not hold true. There are alternative sets of influences and movement within Latin America, within Europe, within Asia, within the Gulf States, within the Pacific basin: one cannot pretend these do not exist.

In assessing the pattern of program distribution, one must also consider video, a technology that has been largely absent from the general debate about international television, and yet which is becoming more and more important. At the end of 1983, there were an estimated 40 million VCRs (videocassette recorders) in the world, with a growth rate much faster than that of TV.

The Gulf States, for example, are an important area for the use of videocassette recorders to watch television and films from other countries. The penetration rate of VCRs in Saudi Arabia is about 85 percent of homes with televisions. A 1981 study that surveyed 120 people showed that they *all* had VCRs; a survey conducted in the Red Sea city of Jidda showed that 19 percent of all homes had *two* machines.

There are basically two types of material available on videotape. The first includes large quantities of TV Westerns and feature films. At the time of Douglas Boyd's research, the latest episodes of *Hill Street Blues, St. Elsewhere, The A-Team*, as well as such movies as *E.T.* and *Terms of Endearment*, were readily available. All of these were pirated. Similarly, every evening's total BBC output is taped and flown to the Middle East the following morning in a private plane. Pornographic material is acquired from London, Paris, and Frankfurt. There are also Arab television programs and films, obtained mainly from Egypt. As one observer noted: 'In the tumultuous arena of Arab politics, the soaps are a soft-sell commercial for Egyptian values, and thereby a vehicle for Egyptian influence. They are a reminder to the Arabs that even when Egypt's political course is in disrepute, Egypt is still number one among the Arab states.'

The success and influence of Egyptian television follows in the wake of the success of its films, which 'paved the way ... by promoting the faces of its stars, the voices of its singers and the tales of its writers in every Arab city and town. Even more important, it spread a familiarity with Egypt's dialect. Thanks to the movies, the Arabic spoken by the Egyptians has come to dominate a language spoken in a hundred different ways in the Middle East. This dominance now virtually precludes any other Arab country from successfully establishing an entertainment industry of its own.' An Egyptian TV producer observed: 'The rich markets for state TV are in Saudi Arabia and the Gulf, and [Egyptian TV] will not produce anything that will alienate the Saudis. The Saudis only want things that could have been shown in the Middle Ages. Like all Arab governments, they want to promote the status quo. So that is what we give them.'

In many Asian societies, governments are becoming worried that the use of VCRs is undermining development goals. For example, in Malaysia 75 percent of the viewers of VCR tapes are the Malaysian Chinese population. The government is trying to weld together a number of cultures through the use of a national language, Bahasa Malaysia, but the Chinese prefer Chinese-language videotapes from Hong Kong to the Bahasa Malaysia–dominated TV service, a fact that is less than pleasing to the authorities. In 1982, the information minister, Adib Adam, expressed his fears that government messages were not reaching the people, and that the loss of the TV audience to video might 'hamper government efforts to disseminate national aspirations and values and channel information to the people.' In an article in the Malaysian *Star*, on June 21, 1983, he warned that videotapes could expose people to policies contrary to government policies and national culture, hurt television news and information, and hinder the government's efforts to foster racial harmony. The counter-accusation, however, was one universally used when an audience begins to drift away: TV is boring. There have recently been efforts to make television more appealing by importing more Western material – a solution that is itself out of step with the ambitions of the Malaysian government for development and nation building. In short, the situation was no more than one version of that global problem in which, when given free choices, populations *tend* (a word I here use carefully and deliberately) to reject marching to the heights of a glorious and enriched future nation, in favor of heading to the playground.

Similarly in Indonesia, the reaction to the TV service has been to turn more and more to watching television programs and films on VCR. In Islamic cultures, the VCR is playing havoc with traditional values and morals. Middle-class Indians are also using VCRs extensively, watching a good deal of U.S. material....

One final point needs to be addressed in this discussion of the parameters of TV as an international process: the use, and planned use, of satellites to distribute television around the world. In July of last year, the magazine *Asian Broadcasting* ran a cover picture of the cargo bay of the space shuttle; the story headline read, 'Satellites: Everybody Wants One.' The theory is that direct broadcast satellite (DBS) systems are ideal for countries that are eager to provide their people with television and telecommunications systems without going to the expense and effort of building land-based networks of cables, transmitters, and microwave links. Behind that thesis lies the dangerous notion that the application of such technologies can enhance ambitions of boosting industrial growth and socioeconomic development. The other immediate advantage of DBS in the eyes of developing societies is the ability to multiplex, or split, the sound signals to serve a nation that may be geopolitically a single entity, but which in linguistic and cultural terms is no more than an aggregate of different groups. India and China are obvious examples. In India, the main objective of the satellite program is to harness spacecraft technology for the transmission of TV broadcasts designed to aid the country's development program. India's involvement began with the launching of its Satellite Instructional Television Experiment in August 1975. After an initial failure in 1982, with a new satellite INSAT-1A, a successful satellite INSAT-1B was launched in August 1983. This now transmits TV programs directly to augmented sets, as well as via a network of ground-based receivers. India expected to reach 70 percent of its population by the middle of 1985. It was estimated that by the end of 1984 there would be eight thousand direct-reception sets. The Indian government also plans to build four rebroadcast transmitters. By the late 1980s, India will have its new proto-INSAT system, with a significant TV component.

Last year, China formed the China National Satellite Corporation under the Ministry of Radio and TV, the purpose of which was to design and develop a TV reception system using domestic and imported technology. China already has an agreement with the German firm MBB to acquire a DBS system. The reason is simple: only one-third of China's one billion population can currently receive TV coverage through ground systems. The government plans to install three thousand reception and rebroadcast stations when the DBS goes up in 1986. An additional thirty thousand receive-only stations will go on stream before 1990 to reach 90 percent of the population.

South Korea is slowly examining the possibility of establishing a DBS system that would provide three TV channels and four thousand telephone circuits. Indonesia was the first Asian country to develop its own domestic satellite system, Palapa, which went into operation in mid-1976 to provide telephone, telex, and TV links for three thousand islands scattered over five thousand kilometers of ocean. A second-generation Palapa system has now been developed, shared with Singapore, Malaysia, Thailand, and the Philippines. Thailand, mightily impressed by Palapa, has now decided to develop its own system.

In the Middle East, the development by the Arab League, a consortium of twenty-one countries, of the Arabsat, which is capable of eight TV channels for both community sets and direct-receivers, indicates that region's commitment to this particular form of TV transmission. Forty ground receiving stations are now being built at a cost of $150 million. Pakistan is examining the possibilities of establishing its own direct television and communications satellites by the end of the decade.

And so it goes. I have not even touched on the major developments by the industrial societies to establish DBS systems. Yet it is quite clear that if one were to write this article a decade hence, programs, video, and DBS would have to be at the very forefront of the description and analysis. These are probably the two technologies that will ultimately shape the future structure of international television.

Whatever the complexities, it would be ludicrous to deny that there are distortions in the distribution pattern of communications around the globe. On so much we can all agree. What is less evident is that these patterns necessarily imply structures of dominance. In other words, we cannot take as given the nature of the social experience which is implied by the distribution of, for example, American television around the world. We cannot take as unproblematic the idea of national culture nor its alleged transformation under the impact of imported programs. Writing from within the confines of Britain in 1985, I would find it difficult even to delineate the parameters of my own national culture. Whose culture is it: that of Mrs. Thatcher or the militant miners' leader, Arthur Scargill; the south or the north; the rioting football fan or the Sunday cricketer? If a culture is to be found in shared symbols, then what symbols hold sway in these islands anymore, if indeed they ever did? Precious few, I fear, and getting fewer by the day.

A 1953 UNESCO publication (*TV, A World Survey*) made the statement: 'International cooperation is beginning to open up new fields for television and it is increasingly recognized how effective it can be to bring about greater awareness about each other among nations differing in language and character.' The same report spoke of how television could make the 'treasures of man's civilization' available, and of TV as a means of 'global peace and understanding.' Bliss was it in that dawn. The view of global television now espoused within the chambers of UNESCO is that it is a distinctly poisoned chalice.

By 1972, the General Conference of UNESCO was suggesting that there was a danger that the mass media could become vehicles for 'the domination of world public opinion or a source of moral and cultural pollution,' and that the one-way flow of television from a small number of countries threatened 'the cultural values of most of the remaining countries.' In 1973, at the meeting of the heads of state of non-aligned countries, there were calls for the 'reorganization of existing communication channels which are the legacy of the colonial past, and which have hampered free, direct and fast communication between them.' It was added that 'cultural alienation and imported civilization, imposed imperialism and colonialism, should be countered by ... a constant and determined recourse to the social and cultural values of the population which define them as a sovereign people.'

And so on, as large parts of the international community have become anxious about the adverse effects of foreign television on their countries. This is not just true of the developing countries; many important and influential voices can be heard throughout Europe expressing concern over the implications of 'foreign' television. It is admittedly not an anxiety overly present in American society – which in terms of the penetration of anything foreign and visual remains in a state of *virgo intacto*. International television and cultural dominance have, however, become an important issue of international politics. On that agenda, it is taken as given by most societies that adverse effects do follow from their populations' cultural appetites, as expressed in the TV they watch.

Equally influential sections of the academic community have argued vociferously about the alleged powerful influences of international television. Cees Hamelink, for example, ... speaks of how in recent years the delicate process by which developing societies evolve and adapt is being increasingly threatened by the advanced industrial states' large-scale export of cultural systems to Third World countries. As a result, he suggests, the survival of autonomous cultural systems in many areas of the Third World is very much in question. He adds: 'It is the argument of this study that cultural autonomy is essential for a process of independent development. However, cultural autonomy is virtually impossible in a system which attempts to integrate the weak and poor countries in a global community that serves best the interests of only the rich and powerful. This autonomy has to be secured through the formulation and implementation of national policies based on international dissociation which encourage self-reliant development and the cooperation of developing countries among themselves.'

The general effect he suggests, however, is for cultural 'synchronization' – the eradication of diversity, and its replacement with 'a single global culture' in which the cultural traffic is overwhelmingly one way, with the result that the 'whole process of social inventiveness and cultural creativity is thrown into confusion or is definitely destroyed. Unique dimensions in the spectrum of human values, which have evolved over centuries, rapidly disappear.'

[...]

Herb Schiller has also become well known as a theorist of communication as cultural domination. In his first and most influential work, *Mass Communications an American Empire* (1969), he states: 'Mass communications are now a pillar of the emergent imperial society. Messages "made in America" radiate across the globe and serve as the ganglia of national power and expansionism. The ideological images of "have not" states are increasingly in the custody of American informational media. National authority over attitude creation and opinion formation in the developing world has weakened and is being relinquished to powerful external forces.... Everywhere local culture is facing submersion from the mass-produced outpourings of commercial broadcasting.'

Fourteen years later, the tune remained essentially the same. In a paper on 'Electronic Information Flows: New Basis for Global Domination,' Schiller develops, in a somewhat polemical manner, his analysis of the evolving political economy of the industrial societies and the enormous power of a small number of multinational corporations. Nothing wrong with all that, apart from the occasional touch of hyperbole (at one point he talks of the welfare state as 'already mostly a memory' – this, a set of institutions that take up a huge part of the gross domestic product!). Where I part from Schiller's analysis is when he slips into such phrases as 'a vast extension in cultural control and domination to say nothing of economic and political mastery' and 'saturating the cultural space of the nation.'[7] Let me ask again: what does that mean, and, at the risk of being accused of outrageous positivism, where's the evidence? Certainly, he provides none.

What, then, about the idea of *domination?* A whole library of works exists on cross-national influences, trans-border data flow, the economics of cultural imperialism, TV flows, and so on. Hamelink and Schiller are just two of the more prominent members of an extensive school of thought.[8] Each tends to be loaded with sets of assumptions about cultural influences, about meanings and the shaping of consciousness. Yet each equally tends to hold those views in the abstract, outside of any grasp of their place within the life of a society. As the late Ithiel de Sola Pool observed: 'There is, in fact, remarkably little research of any kind on international communication. There is a great deal of essay writing about it. But by research I mean studies in which data is collected to establish or refute some general proposition.... The two topics regarding international communication that have been most extensively studied, and very badly, I must say, are the balance in the flow of communication among countries, and the cultural biases in what flows. These are topics on which there have been a few empirical studies, though by far the great bulk of that literature consists of polemical essays unenlightened by facts.'

[...]

Since its first appearance on American television in 1978 and its subsequent export to many foreign countries, *Dallas* has become the exemplar of the global influence of American television, the apparent embodiment of the theory of cultural imperialism, a metaphor for an entire argument. Clearly, at one level *Dallas* fits the stereotype: it is available in many different countries and is always sold at a lower price than any home-produced equivalent. What has been almost totally ignored, however, is the relationship between the program and the various audiences that, for whatever reasons, in whatever circumstances, with whatever consequences, actually sit down and watch it. Any exploration at that level, no matter how cursory, provides some important qualifications to the imperialism thesis. For example, in most countries *Dallas* is not as popular as home-produced soaps, and it is completely ignored in countries as diverse as Brazil and Japan, which nevertheless have well-established and highly popular domestic dramas as part of their main TV offerings. In New Zealand, other kinds of shows from other countries are more popular than *Dallas* and its ilk. While a number of researchers *have* recognized the need to understand the different audience responses to programs such as *Dallas* – e.g., Elihu Katz and Tamar Liebes in Israel, Jean Bianchi in France, David Morley and Dorothy Hobson in Britain[10] – these efforts have, to date, unfortunately been inhibited by a lack of real resources.

It is, in fact, simply untrue to say that imported television programs, from the U.S. or other metropolitan countries, always have a dominant presence within an indigenous television culture. Certainly they do not always attract larger audiences than homemade programs, nor do they always threaten national production.

In Brazil, for example, which is the sixth biggest television market in the world, the level of imported television material *fell* by 32 percent between 1973 and 1982, largely due to the activities of TV Globo, which captures between 60 and 80 percent of the television audience. Between 5:30 PM and 11:00 PM, 84 percent of the programs offered are in-house productions. In August 1983, the top ten programs were all Globo productions, including three 'telenovellas.' As Richard Paterson points out, in Brazil one sees 'a television devoted to national culture. TV Globo has fully utilized the possibilities created by these circumstances to develop a different sort of television. The development of an indigenous television puts into question Schiller's thesis about the inevitability of traditional drama and folk music retreating before the likes of Peyton Place and Bonanza.'[11]

Dallas, by the way, in 1982 occupied 69th position in the Brazilian ratings and 109th in Mexico.[12] In the very different context of Britain, however, while successful, it has never seriously challenged the domestically produced dramas *Coronation Street*, *Crossroads*, and *Emmerdale Farm*. Another illustration of how indigenous populations do not respond to imported material in stereotypical ways can be seen in South Africa. There, TV1 carries such imports as *Dallas* and *The A-Team*, with vernacular services on TV2 and TV3. In December 1983, however, Bophuthatswana Television, broadcasting from the capital of Mmabatho, began to broadcast in English but with increasing amounts of material of a local nature in Setswana. More and more of the black population of South Africa turns to this channel. Indeed, the success has been so great that President Mpepha of the tiny republic of Venda has now announced that he wants his own television service, Radio Television Thohoyandau.[13]

In Singapore, where the government's Singapore Broadcasting Corporation runs three channels broadcasting in English, Mandarin, Tamil, and Malay, and where 60 percent of the programs are English-language (the bulk of which are imported), Chinese programs, particularly from Hong Kong, are consistently the most popular. In Ireland, which imports 65 percent of its total output and where the BBC and ITV are readily available to most of the population, the most popular programs for many years have been *The Late, Late Show* on Saturdays, hosted by Gay Byrne, followed by the home-produced drama series *The Riordans*, *Bracken*, and *Glenroe*. In countries such as New Zealand and Sweden, where the local broadcasting services face enormous problems that necessitate the importation of foreign television, home-grown programs nevertheless compete in popularity. In New Zealand, in fact, there is evidence that the bulk of the population actively dislikes the American shows they see on their screens. In Zimbabwe in 1982, locally produced programs such as *The Mukadda Family* had much higher ratings than the imported *Dallas*, *Dynasty*, and *Falcon Crest*. One author writing about television in Bangladesh observed: 'Imported programmes are popular, but do not dominate BTV. In the 1980s some would say that the *Incredible Hulk* does sit uneasily between *Shilpo-O-Shahilya* [a series on art and literature] and *Jalsa* [a programme on classical music]. *Dallas, Charlie's Angels* and *Chips* are cheaper for BTV to transmit than any local dramas – but local productions challenge them in a way few outsiders would believe possible.'[14]

One could go on. This is not to say that imported programs are *not* an important part of the total structure of many countries' broadcasting, nor, indeed, that in some cases they are not very popular. It is merely to observe that even a limited glance at the available evidence – such as it is – about the most simple facts of television viewing, indicates that the picture of the role of television in any society is far more complex than is often allowed for. As far as we can tell, audiences discriminate and tend to prefer home-produced television, rather than slavishly pursuing imported programs.

The point of this Cook's tour, then, is actually quite simple: it is to show that a rather more discrete, subtle, and empirical approach is necessary before we can begin to understand the actual experience of the flow of international television, and thus the notion of television dominance. The question this in turn raises is: what model can best explain cultural influences in the lives of a given society, and where can we find the methodology to test that model?

The problem with the old model is that it took a not very good inventory and pretended it was an analysis. One can say nothing of influences, of how those programs engage with a society simply on the basis of a surface description; and yet that is all we have tended to have so far. As a former colleague of mine quite rightly argued:

> The development of theories about the ill effects of the importation of American television programmes depends on the measuring devices of imports/exports and the income earned from such sales for their substantiation. Unfortunately these measures, although useful, do not focus on the size and responses of the audiences who eventually see such programmes. There is an assumption that American TV imports do have an impact wherever and whenever they are shown, but actual investigation (or verification) of this seldom occurs. Much of the evidence that is offered is merely anecdotal or circumstantial. Observations of New Guinean tribesmen clustered around a set in the sweltering jungle watching *Bonanza* or of Algerian nomads watching *Dallas* in the heat of the desert, are often offered as sufficient proof.[15]

On the basis of what we know – *really* know as opposed to imagine we know – what then can be said about the notion of dominance by international television? What is the argument? What is the problem? Let me begin not with some humble, underdeveloped, exploited nation, but with a huge, wealthy, powerful one: Canada. Canada apparently has one overwhelming problem when it comes to the culture of television, and that is its proximity to an even more powerful, wealthy, and huge society, the United States. In a recent account of the development of cable TV in Canada, Tim Hollins made the following point:

Over 80 percent of the Canadian population lives within one hundred miles of the American border, and the realities of this situation have had a greater impact than somewhat abstract cultural aspirations. Although regulation has been imposed to promote both Canadian broadcasting and production, the Canadians themselves have consistently demonstrated a strong interest, even a preference for material from the United States. Consequently, the Government has had to find a path between accepting the reality of the U.S. cultural imperialism and forcing a Canadian cultural chauvinism which appears antithetical to the rights and wishes of its own citizens.[16]

The first, and rather tricky, problem for government leaders, intellectuals, reformers, and political evangelists (who may also be academics) around the globe is that, as Hollins suggests about Canada, populations do have this unfortunate habit of choosing television programs that are not 'good' for them. Indeed, one might construct the first law of international communications: that which is bad for them, they *will* insist on watching.

I am, you will detect, a touch less worried than some about this situation – described in endless meetings of UNESCO and kindred bodies, and enough books and articles to threaten the existence of tropical rain forests – partly because I suspect that assumptions about the extent of exposure to 'foreign' material are overstated, and mainly because I believe that the assumptions about their 'effects' are certainly overstated, and devoid of decent evidence and good theory. It is difficult, for example, to take too seriously the assumptions behind a phrase such as 'the Dallas-drugged viewers,' which I saw used recently in the context of a discussion of Italian television. Nor the sentiment, however well meaning, in this observation: 'For the survival and development of important human values, the study of intercultural communication may be one of the critical areas of communication research. One has only to witness *Kojak* and *Starsky and Hutch* bouncing off satellites *into the intimacy of minds and homes* [my emphasis] in cultures of India and Thailand to realize this.'

Such, however, is the power of the orthodoxy on these matters that I write these words with a feeling of guilt, a certain trepidation in waiting for the howls of scorn that one can doubt something so self-evident. Indeed, it seems to me that the Western writer, from within the comfort of his wealth, faces a difficult problem in addressing objectively issues of dominance and cultural imperialism. On the one hand, he is in danger of either assuming uncritically the notions and sentiments uttered by Third World leaders and their Western acolytes out of a wish for them to be right. On the other hand, if he challenges those arguments, questions them, suggests that maybe they are not totally correct, that perhaps they are self-interested or just plain innocently wrong, he is immediately open to the accusation of having a mealy-mouthed, uncaring attitude towards the problems of developing societies. Yet, in all honesty, one has to say that it is possible that, within the realms of international communications, a poverty of thought has emerged to match the real poverty of resources that afflicts developing societies.

In seeking to understand international television, then, one has to ask: What evidence is there? What can we say? What do we know? In researching this article, I constantly returned to these questions and to the simple statement: 'It is claimed that this mass of material coming in from outside is both erasing traditional cultures and inhibiting the emergence of authentic cultural changes. There is no clear evidence that this is in fact happening, nor indeed any that it is not.'[17]

[...]

The question to pose is not what is the nature of cultural domination or imperialism, with all the assumptions of intellectual, psychological, and emotional influence. The real question is why such simple, impressionistic analyses have come to hold such sway in the debate about the character of communications in international as well as domestic life. Why have such analyses – paradoxically dripping with human concern – become so divorced from any human contact?

There is a marvelous little article by Irene Penacchioni about the viewing of popular television in poverty-ridden northeast Brazil.[18] It is a fine example of the view that the role and use of television ought to be viewed ethnographically from *within* a culture, rather than condescendingly from without. She pulls no punches: 'In my opinion ... the investigations into television which are carried out by sociology are informed by the amused condescensions of intellectuals towards mass culture and by their dark fear of the alleged power of images.... Intellectuals use the written word to protect themselves from television as though it were a cross to protect them from vampires.' She writes of the popularity of the telenovella with the local people:

> It is important to understand the pleasure of following a fiction from day to day over a long period of time; pleasures associated with the 'to be continued,' of curiosity and expectation about the unpredictable, which will make itself heard again. What next? What will happen to our hero? The genealogy of pleasure, this joy related to the telenovella, has to be sought in the occidental history of folk poetry.... Television seems to correspond to a cyclical and everyday representation of time as found in folk poetry.... The phenomenon of television cannot be comprehended here without a systematic investigation of the cultural context, and its different aspects, in the Northeast of Brazil.

One of the moments she describes is of a group of people sitting around a TV set in the town square, not just watching telenovellas, but laughing uproariously at the exploits of Charlie Chaplin. When I read this, another very familiar image came to my mind.

I was born in a working-class community called Oldham, in the north of England. Before the First World War, Oldham produced most of the world's spun cotton. It is a place of mills and chimneys, and I was born and raised in one of the areas of housing – called St. Mary's – built to serve those mills. I recently heard a record by a local group of folk singers called the Oldham Tinkers, and one track is about Charlie Chaplin. This song was apparently very popular with local children in the years immediately after the First World War. Was that early evidence of the cultural influences of Hollywood, a primeval moment of the imperialism of one culture, the subjugation of another? It seems almost boorish to think of it that way. Was the little man not a deep well of pleasure through laughter, a pleasure that was simply universal in appeal? Was it not Chaplin's real genius to strike some common chord, uniting the whole of humanity? Is that not, in fact, the real genius of American popular culture, to bind together, better than anything else, common humanity? This is all terribly heretical, and yet I am more and more tempted in this little excursion to propose that the cultural imperialism thesis be stood on its head, and to suggest instead an analysis, not of exploitation, but of service – of the proffering of cultural imagery that is absorbed by more deep-seated cultural strata. That leads me, not to ask about the thesis, but to pose questions about those who proffer it. There has to be an explanation why such an intellectually undernourished theory holds such sway.

I also ask why it is that the ubiquity of the likes of *Dallas* is held in such contempt, whereas the ubiquity of, say, the Beatles or Chaplin himself is, one senses, held in awe. Perhaps we need an alternative way of looking at the general popularity of much television around the globe... Is it possible that in order to understand, at least in part, the popularity of the television of the North Atlantic basin one has to understand the ways in which it successfully employs certain themes, situations, and figures, rather than just pricing-mechanisms, pace, glossy sets, exotic locations, or whatever? Is the interesting thing about television, in short, perhaps not what it *imposes* but what it *taps*?

[...]

Those who favor the idea of cultural dominance through television have tended to study company reports, rather than the realities of individual lives; to describe the flow of communication in the abstract, rather than the cultural meanings of those flows. This idea is hitched to a model of influences which, for two decades, has been known to be at best inadequate. It espouses a touching belief in the perfectability of man, illustrated by the apparent conviction that human flaws, inadequacies, and problems flow from the sociocultural, Anglo-Saxon-dominated infrastructure of the world economy, in which the indigenous population is no more than an innocent fly caught in a beguiling, sticky, and overpowering spider's web. Supporters of this theory have demonstrated a certain myopia: their gaze has focused on the inadequacies and awfulness of Western society, while remaining blind to one or two problems and difficulties the more objective eye might detect east of the Elbe, and indeed within the sociopolitical character of many developing societies. They have failed to develop a model that allows for resistance, for oppositional forces – and not opposition by a captive population to the alleged dominant power and its culture, because such a captive population never existed in the first place. They have offered a patronizing, pat-on-the-head pity for populations they feel are not capable of knowing their own mind. Finally, the dominance model has failed to recognize that a theory that cannot be translated into empirically apprehendable propositions is no theory at all, and tends to dissolve into the fevered imaginings of the subjective observer.

[...]

What I have been suggesting throughout this paper is that we have barely begun to scratch the surface of understanding the function and consequence of TV as an international cultural process. I have also been suggesting that it is not good enough merely to reiterate the details of ownership and control on a global scale and thereby impute a cultural meaning to them.

Notes

1. Tapio Varis, 'The International Flow of Television Programs', *Journal of Communication*, Winter 1984.
2. D.A. Boyd, 'VCRs in Developing Countries: An Arab Case Study', *Media Development*, I (1985).
3. M. Viorst, 'TV That Rules the Arab World', *Channels*, Jan.–Feb. 1984.
4. Viorst, 'TV That Rules'.
5. J.A. Lent, 'Video in Asia: Frivolity, Frustration, Futility', *Media Development*, I (1985).
6. Cees Hamelink, *Cultural Autonomy in Global Communications* (New York, Longman, 1983).
7. See Herbert Schiller's *Mass Communication and American Empire* (New York, Kelly, 1969); and his 'Electronic Information Flows: New Basis for Global Domination', paper given at conference at the Institute of Education, London, July 1984.
8. Colleen Roach, 'Annotated Bibliography on a New World Information and Communication Order', *Media and Development*, I (1985).
9. Ithiel de Sola Pool, 'The New Structure of International Communication: The Role of Research', in *New Structure of International Communication? The Role of Research*, papers from the 1980 conference in Caracas of the International Association for Mass Communication Research (IAMCR). Published by the IAMCR, 1982.
10. Elihu Katz and Tamar Liebes, 'Once Upon a Time in Dallas', *Intermedia* (London), May 1984. Jean Bianchi, 'Comment comprendre le succès international des séries de fiction à la télévision? Le cas Dallas', Ministère de l'industrie et de la Recherche: action concertée Communication Audiovisuelle, July 1984. David Morley, *The 'Nationwide' Audience: Structure and Decoding* (London, BFI Publishing, 1980). Dorothy Hobson, *Crossroads: The Drama of a Soap Opera* (London, Methuen, 1982).
11. Richard Paterson, *Brazilian Television in Context* (London, BFI Publishing, 1982).
12. G. Lealand, *American Television Programmes on British Screens* (London, Broadcasting Research Unit, 1984).
13. Richard Paterson, ed., *International TV and Video Guide (1985)* (London, Tantivy Press, 1985).
14. Paterson, *International TV and Video Guide*.
15. Lealand, *American Television Programmes*.
16. Timothy Hollins, *Beyond Broadcasting: Into the Cable Age* (London, Broadcasting Research Unit, 1984).
17. R. Hoggart, 'The Mass Media and One Way Flow', in *An English Temper* (London, Chatto & Windus, 1982).

18. Irene Penacchioni, 'The Reception of Popular Television in Northeast Brazil', *Media, Culture and Society*, Oct. 1984.

Questions

1 Summarise some of the main criticisms that Tracey makes of the cultural imperialism arguments and evidence. How far do you find his position convincing?

2 Choose some recent examples of popular American television programmes and series, and assess their impact on a world-wide basis. To what extent might they be said to embody and act as vehicles for American values and interests?

3 Carry out a series of interviews with British television viewers about their attitudes towards American or Australian programming. How does access to satellite or cable forms of distribution and reception change the ratio of imported to home-produced television?

Further reading

Ang, I. 1996: *Living room wars: rethinking media audiences for a postmodern world.* London: Routledge.

Dowmunt, T. (ed.) 1993: *Channels of resistance: global television and local empowerment.* London: BFI/Channel 4.

Downing, J., Mohammadi, A. and Sreberny-Mohammadi, A. (eds.) 1995: *Questioning the media: a critical introduction,* 2nd edn. London: Sage.

Drummond, P., Paterson, R. and Willis, J. (eds.) 1993: *National identity and Europe: the television revolution.* London: BFI.

Liebes, T. and Katz, E. 1993: *The export of meaning: cross cultural readings of* Dallas. Cambridge: Polity Press.

McQuail, D. 1994: *Mass communication theory: an introduction,* 3rd edn. London: Sage.

Morley, D. and Robins, K. 1995: *Spaces of identity: global media, electronic landscapes and cultural boundaries.* London: Routledge.

Reeves, G. 1993: *Communications and the 'third world'.* London: Routledge.

Tomlinson, J. 1991: *Cultural imperialism.* London: Pinter Publishers.

33

Not Yet the Post-Imperialist Era
Herbert Schiller

From *Critical Studies in Mass Communication* 8, 13–28 (1991)

This reading takes up the challenge issued in the previous one and provides a contrasting and critical account of global media systems in the recent period. Schiller first wrote about American world-wide cultural domination in the 1960s and in what follows he begins by recognising that certain key changes have taken place in the world geopolitical order since then. Nonetheless, he seeks to restate the fundamental case for cultural dominance by arguing that the changes which have occurred have not radically altered the overall dispositions and inequalities of economic and cultural power. In fact, as he suggests, American and related transnational systems of cultural production and distribution may be more total – integrating across whole cultural sectors and markets – in their impact and presence.

In his assessment, Schiller is especially critical of theorists who have failed to appreciate the underlying political and economic relations which have driven recent global tendencies. He is also scathing of ideas which, within this broader context, have emphasised 'active' or 'unpredictable' audiences, suggesting that there are a number of problems with this perspective as it has been applied to understanding the realities of the global reception of media products. The reading therefore offers an explicit challenge to some of the ideas outlined by Tracey.

Apart from the persistent explanatory and semantic efforts in recent years to minimize or discredit the idea of cultural domination (Ang, 1985; Liebes & Katz, 1990), changing conditions make it desirable to reassess the original thesis.

Two governing circumstances strongly influenced the early elaboration of the theory of cultural dominance in the mid-1960s. The first was the then-existing world balance of forces.

Twenty-five years ago, the international order could be divided into three major groups. The most powerful of these was the so-called First World, including essentially those countries that were grounded in private propertied relations and whose production was undertaken by capitalist enterprise. The Second World comprised those nations that were organized along state ownership of property lines and that called themselves socialist. The last category (in every sense) was the Third World, containing those countries that had just emerged from the collapsed European colonial empires. In the case of Latin America, these nations continued to suffer economic exploitation although they had been nominally independent for over a century. In most of the Third World states, national liberation movements still existed, and the social structures had not yet been completely captured by new, privileged elites.

In this general map, the United States was by far the most powerful individual state in the First World and in the other two categories as well. Although the Soviet Union, after the Second World, claimed superpower status on the basis of possessing nuclear weapons, its economic and technological position was decidedly subordinate.

The other determining feature of this period in the cultural realm was the rapid development of television and its capability for transmitting compelling imagery and messages to vast audiences.

These geopolitical and technological conditions provided the social landscape for the era's cultural domination perspective. The essential assumptions undergirding it were (and are) few and relatively straightforward: Media-cultural imperialism is a subset of the *general* system of imperialism. It is not freestanding; the media-cultural component in a developed, corporate economy supports the economic objectives of the decisive industrial-financial sectors (i.e., the creation and extension of the consumer society); the cultural and economic spheres are indivisible. Cultural, no less than automobile, production has its political economy. Consequently, what is regarded as cultural output also is ideological and profit-serving to the system at large. Finally, in its latest mode of operation, in the late twentieth century, the corporate economy is increasingly dependent on the media-cultural sector.

The thesis assumed that the state socialist (Second) World was, if not immune to Western cultural-informational pressure, at least to some degree insulated from it and would, under certain circumstances, support limits on its advance. The Third World, in contrast, was seen as an extremely vulnerable and deliberate target of American cultural exports. At the same time, it also was viewed as a potentially organizable force – not yet frozen in class relationships – that might give leadership to a comprehensive restructuring of the world information system. The movement for a new international information order was one vehicle for such a mobilization.

The charge that American-produced cultural commodities – television programs in particular – were overwhelming a good part of the world hardly needed documentation. But the data were there (Nordenstreng & Varis, 1974).

Changes in the international geopolitical arena

Twenty-five years later, some of this map has changed. Most importantly, the Second World (the socialist 'camp') has all but disappeared. With the (temporary?) exceptions of China, Albania, North Korea, Vietnam, and Cuba, there is no longer a state socialist sphere in the global arena.

The Eastern European states, along with the Soviet Union, are in varying stages of capitalist restoration. Rather than providing an oppositional pole to the First World, they are now eager adherents to that world, as well as its supplicants. They offer national space to the marketing and ideological message flows of their former adversaries.

In a material sense, the strength and influence of the First World, especially that of its most powerful members, are less restrained than they were in the preceding period. This is observable not only with regard to the erstwhile socialist bloc but even more so with respect to the people and nations of Africa, Asia, and Latin America.

Actually, the condition of the Third World vis-à-vis the North (Western Europe, Japan, and the United States) is one of near-desperation. Now under the control of elites that accept and benefit from the workings of the world market economy, the African, Asian, and Latin American nations are deeply in debt and stalled for the most part in efforts for improvement. Most of the

Third World nations seem more helpless than ever to resist the demands of their creditors and overseers. Despite some variability in this condition and occasional balking by a recalcitrant ruling group, the general situation reveals practically an abandonment of the challenging economic and cultural positions this group advanced not so long ago.

The role of television in the global arena of cultural domination has not diminished in the 1990s. Reinforced by new delivery systems – communication satellites and cable networks – the image flow is heavier than ever. Its source of origin also has not changed that much in the last quarter of a century. There is, however, one significant difference. Today, television is but one element, however influential, in an all-encompassing cultural package.

The corporate media-cultural industries have expanded remarkably in recent decades and now occupy most of the global social space. For this reason alone, cultural domination today cannot be measured by a simple index of exposure to American television programming. The cultural submersion now includes the English language itself, shopping in American-styled malls, going to theme parks (of which Disney is the foremost but not exclusive example), listening to the music of internationally publicized performers, following news agency reports or watching the Cable News Network in scores of foreign locales, reading translations of commercial best sellers, and eating in franchised fast-food restaurants around the world. Cultural domination means also adopting broadcasting systems that depend on advertising and accepting deregulatory practices that transform the public mails, the telephone system, and cable television into private profit centers (Engelhardt, 1990).

Alongside this all-service-supplying cultural-media environment, the relative economic and political power of the United States continues to diminish. This suggests that American cultural domination is not guaranteed in perpetuity. Yet irrefutably that domination has been preeminent for the last four decades and remains so to this date, though subsumed increasingly under transnational corporate capital and control. The cultural primacy that the ruling national power in the world economy historically exercised may now be changing.

The commanding position of American media products in the post-World War II era, the expertise derived from more than a century of successful marketing activity, and the now near-universal adoption of English as the international lingua franca still confer extraordinary influence on U.S.-produced cultural commodities. How long this influence can be sustained while American systemic power declines is an open question. But in any case, American national power no longer is an exclusive determinant of cultural domination.

The domination that exists today, though still bearing a marked American imprint, is better understood as transnational corporate cultural domination. Philips of the Netherlands, Lever Brothers of Britain, Daimler-Benz of Germany, Samsung of Korea, and Sony of Japan, along with some few thousand other companies, are now the major players in the international market.

The media, public relations, advertising, polling, cultural sponsorship, and consultants these industrial giants use and support hardly are distinguishable from the same services at the disposal of American-owned corporations. Still, a good fraction of these informational-cultural activities continue to be supplied by American enterprises.

These developments leave most of the peoples and nations in the world more vulnerable than ever to domination – cultural, military, and economic. Former oppositional forces have collapsed.

Cheerful surveyors of the current scene

Not all view the developments described above with skepticism or dismay. Indeed, some see the phenomena that now characterize daily life in a very large, and growing, part of the world as evidence that cultural domination no longer exists, or that what appears as domination actually fosters resistance to itself.

The idea of cultural diversity, for example, enjoys great popularity among many cultural observers. The central assumption – that many diverse cultural tendencies and movements operate, with no one element dominating – is the familiar pluralist argument, now applied to the cultural field. A more recent construct is the notion of 'globalization.' In this proposition, the world is moving, however haltingly, toward a genuinely global civilization. There is also the very widely accepted hypothesis of an 'active audience,' one in which viewers, readers, and listeners make their own meaning from the messages that come their way, often to the point of creating resistance to hegemonic meanings. Most comprehensive of all is the postmodern perspective. Whatever else this approach offers, it insists that systemic explanations of social phenomena are futile and wrong-headed. Mike Featherstone, editor of *Global Culture*, writes:

> Postmodernism is both a symptom and a powerful cultural image of the swing away from the conceptualization of global culture less in terms of alleged homogenizing processes (e.g. theories which present cultural imperialism, Americanization, and mass consumer culture as a proto-universal culture riding on the back of Western economic and political domination) and more in terms of the diversity, variety and richness of popular and local discourses, codes and practices which resist and play-back systemicity and order (Featherstone, 1990, p. 2).

Each of these presently prevailing ideas asserts that:

1. Imperialism no longer exists. (A variant is that U.S. imperialism, in particular, is a spent force.)
2. A new global community is now emerging – global civil society, so to speak – that is independent of the interstate system. It is busily constructing alternative linkages and networks that provide space for new cultural environments.

3. Finally, it is of little consequence if cultural outputs from one source occupy a preponderant share of an audience's attention, because individuals reshape the material to their own tastes and needs. In this schema, the individual receptor takes precedence over the cultural producer.

How do these propositions stand up when examined against the actual context of observable conditions?

[...]

U.S. media-cultural dominance

American films, TV programs, music, news, entertainment, theme parks, and shopping malls set the standard for worldwide export and imitation. How long this dominance can endure alongside a receding economic primary is uncertain. Already, many U.S. media enterprises have been acquired by Japanese (film and TV), German (publishing and music distribution), British (advertising), and other competing groups. Yet even when this occurs, the new owners, at least for the time being, usually are intent on keeping American creative and managerial media people in executive positions.

American cultural domination remains forceful in a rapidly changing international power scene. It is also undergoing transformation. This occurs by acquisition and, more importantly, by its practices being adopted by the rest of the transnational corporate system. What is emerging, therefore, is a world where alongside the American output of cultural product are the practically identical items marketed by competing national and transnational groups.

For some time, critics of media-imperialism theory have offered, as evidence of the doctrine's fatal flaw, the emergence of new centers of media production. Brazil, in particular, is hailed as a strikingly successful example of this development. Its achievement in television production and export is supposed to demolish the notion of a single center of cultural domination (Rogers & Antola, 1985; Straubhaar, 1989; Tracey, 1988).

In reality, according to the work of Brazilian researcher Omar Souki Oliveira (1990), Brazilian TV now broadcasts a minimum of U.S. programming. The biggest audiences watch and prefer Brazilian shows, which are widely exported abroad. Globo, the main Brazilian private TV network, currently exports shows to 128 countries. 'Its productions outnumber those of any other station [sic] in the world.' Oliveira writes that one American researcher (Straubhaar, 1989) has concluded that Brazilian television programs have been 'Brazilianized almost beyond (American) recognition.' Other U.S. researchers (Rogers & Antola, 1985) see Brazil's exports as 'reverse media imperialism.' A third observer (Tracey, 1988) writes that 'in Brazil one sees a television devoted to national culture.'

In Oliveira's reading of the same evidence, Brazilian programming is 'the creolization of U.S. cultural products. It is the spiced up Third World copy of

Western values, norms, patterns of behavior and models of social relations.' He states that 'the overwhelming majority of Brazilian soaps have the same purpose as their U.S. counterparts, i.e., to sell products' – and, it should be emphasized, to sell goods made by the same transnational corporations who advertise in Brazil as well as in the United States. The 'local' sponsors are Coca-Cola, Volkswagen, General Motors, Levi's, etc.

'In most Brazilian soaps,' Oliveira finds, 'the American lifestyle portrayed by Hollywood production reappears with a "brazilianized face." Now we don't see wealthy Anglos any more, but rich white Brazilians enjoying standards of living that would make any middle class American envious.' Oliveira concludes: 'Glamorous as they [TV series] are – even outshining Hollywood – their role within Brazilian society isn't different from that of U.S. imports. Unfortunately, the refinements applied to the genre were not to enhance diversity, but domination.'

Domination is precisely what cultural imperialism is all about. With that domination comes the definitional power, Nye's 'soft power,' that sets the boundaries for national discourse.

Meanwhile, despite the developments already noted, the global preeminence of American cultural product is being not only maintained but extended to new locales. U.S. media incursions into Eastern Europe and the Soviet Union are assuming the dimension of a full-scale takeover, albeit shared with German and British media conglomerates.

American-owned and -styled theme parks, with their comprehensive ideological assumptions literally built into the landscape and architecture, are being staked out across Europe and Japan. 'Euro-Disneyland will open its first park at Marne la Vallee in 1992, with a second possible in 1996. Anheuser-Busch [the second-largest theme park owner after Disney] has launched a theme park development in Spain, and other U.S. corporations are exploring projects elsewhere in Europe' (Sloan, 1990, p. D-3).

It must be emphasized that the corporate takeover of (popular) culture for marketing and ideological control is not a patented American practice, limited exclusively to U.S. companies. It is, however, carried to its fullest development in the United States. Cultural-recreational activity is now the very active site for spreading the transnational corporate message, especially in professional sports, where American practice again provides the basic model.

In the United States, practically no sports activity remains outside the interest and sponsorship of the big national advertisers. The irresistible lure of big sponsorship money has become the lubricant for a sport's national development. Accordingly, sports events and games have become multibillion-dollar businesses, underwritten by the major corporations who stake out huge TV audiences. The hunt for sports events that can be made available to advertisers now includes university and, in increasing instances, high-school games. Assuming the mantle of moral concern, *The New York Times* editorialized: 'College athletic departments have abandoned any pretense of representing cap and gown and now they roam the country in naked pursuit of hundreds of millions of television dollars' (Bright lights, big college money, 1990, p. A-22).

Unsurprisingly, the practice has become internationalized. A report from Italy describes the frenzied pursuit, by the largest Italian corporations, to own soccer and basketball franchises. 'A growing trend in Italy ... [is] the wholesale takeover of a sport by the captains of industry in search of new terrain from which to promote a corporate product or image' (Agnew, 1990, p. 14). The new patrons of Italian sports include the agro-chemicals giant Montedison, which also owns the widely read Rome daily *Il Mesaggero*; the Agnelli family, owners of the giant Fiat company, who also own the successful Juventus soccer club; and Silvio Berlusconi, the Italian TV and film mogul, who owns the AC Milan soccer club and other teams.

Recent developments in East Germany illustrate the extent to which sports have become a venue of corporate image promotion and an aggressive marketing instrument. *Business Week* ('Look Out' Wimbledon, 1990) reports that

> the women's Grand Prix tennis tournament scheduled for the final week of September [1990] is moving from Mahwah, New Jersey to Leipzig, East Germany.... the tournament [is] the first successful effort to lure big corporate sponsors into a major tourney behind the old Iron Curtain.... a number of heavyweight sponsors ... include Volkswagen, Isostar, Sudmilch, Kraft-General Foods and American Airlines.

Major sports are now transmitted by satellite to global audiences. The commercial messages accompanying the broadcast, ringing the stadia, and often worn on the uniforms of the athletes constitute a concerted assault of corporate marketing values on global consciousness.

The total cultural package and the 'active audience'

The envelopment of professional and amateur sports for transnational corporate marketing objectives and ideological pacification is a good point at which to return to another one of the arguments contradicting the cultural imperialist concept. This is the belief in the existence of an 'active audience,' a view supported by a good number of Anglo-U.S. communications researchers.

According to this view, the audience is supposed to make its own meaning of the messages and images that the media disseminate, thereby playing a relatively autonomous role that is often interpreted as *resistance* to these messages and meanings (see Budd, Entman, & Steinman, 1990; H. Schiller, 1989). Active-audience theorizing has been largely preoccupied with the analysis of individual cultural products – a program or a TV series, a movie, or a genre of fiction. The theory follows closely in the tradition of 'effects' research, though not necessarily coming to the same conclusions.

Leaving specific studies aside, it can be argued that one overarching condition invalidates, or at least severely circumscribes, the very idea of an active audience, to say nothing of one resisting a flow of messages. This is the current state – impossible to miss – of Western cultural enterprise. How can one propose to extract one TV show, film, book, or even a group, from the now nearly seamless media-cultural environment, and examine it (them) for specific effects? This is not to say there are no generalized effects – but these are not what the reception theorists seem to be concerned with.

Cultural/media production today has long left the cottage industry stage. Huge conglomerates like Time-Warner, with nearly $20 billion in assets, sit astride publishing, TV production, filmmaking, and music recording, as well as book publishing and public classroom education. Theme park construction and ownership, shopping malls, and urban architectural design also are the domain of the same or related interests.

In this totalizing cultural space, who is able to specify the individual source of an idea, value, perspective, or reaction? A person's response, for example, to the TV series *Dallas* may be the outcome of half-forgotten images from a dozen peripheral encounters in the cultural supermarket. Who is to say what are the specific sites from which individual behavior and emotions now derive?

In 1990, even actual war locales become the setting for the marketing message. *Business Week* ('Publicity?' 1990) announces: 'Welcome to the New World Order, Marketing Dept. where companies are using history-making events as occasions to promote their products.' The magazine explains: 'With U.S. troops digging in their heels in Saudi Arabia, companies all around the country are vying to supply them with everything from nonalcoholic beer to video cassettes ... if a soldier is going to be photographed sipping a cold drink or playing poker, most marketers agree that he or she might as well be using their product.' In this new world of pervasive corporate message making, the dispatch of over 450,000 troops provides an opportunity to cultivate this or that taste for consumption, along with a powerful patriotic backdrop for the company and the product. How does the audience engage this spectacle of democracy and consumption?

There is much to be said for the idea that people don't mindlessly absorb everything that passes before their eyes. Yet much of the current work on audience reception comes uncomfortably close to being apologetics for present-day structures of cultural control.

Meaningful resistance to the cultural industries

There is good reason to be skeptical about the resistance of an audience, active or not, to its menu of media offerings. Yet this does not mean that the cultural conglomerates and the social system they embody are without an opposition. It is a resistance, however, that differs enormously from the kind of opposition that is supposed to occur in reinterpreting the message of a TV sitcom.

Some may believe in the end of history and others may insist that the era of revolution is finally over and that social (class) conflict is obsolete. The daily newspaper headlines tell a different story (though of course they don't explain it). What *is* apparent is that aroused people, if not their leaderships, all around the world are protesting their existing living conditions.

In the United States itself, still the most influential single unit of the world market economy, numerous oppositional elements force at least minimal acknowledgment, and some limited accommodation, from the governing crowd. For example, the congressional fight over the national budget in the fall of 1990 was essentially a class conflict, however obscured this was in its media coverage. To be sure, the class most directly affected – the working people – was largely absent from the deliberations. But the main question at issue was which class would be compelled to shoulder the burden of America's deepening crisis. This debate, and others underway, reveal the fragile condition of the dominating power in the country.

Between 1980 and 1990, the wealthiest 1 percent saw their *incomes rise* by 75 percent, while the income of the bottom 20 percent actually declined. The richest 2½ million Americans' combined income nearly equaled that of the 100 million Americans at the bottom of the pyramid (Meisler, 1990).

It is the still growing disparities between the advantaged and the disadvantaged countries, as well as the widening gap *inside* the advantaged and disadvantaged societies, that constitute the fault line of the still seemingly secure world market economy. To this may be added the ecological disaster in the making, which is the inevitable accompaniment of the market forces that are roaring triumphantly across the continents.

A routine headline in the Western media reads: 'Indonesia: The Hottest Spot in Asia.' Elaborating, *Business Week* ('Indonesia: The Hottest Spot,' 1990) rhapsodizes: 'With a 7% growth rate, a population of 182 million – the world's fifth largest – and a wealth of natural resources, Indonesia is poised to be the region's new success story.' As the twentieth century winds down, success presumably is achieved by adopting the long-standing Western industrialization model, profligate with resource use and wastage, and exploiting the work force to satisfy foreign capital's search for the maximum return.

Indonesia, with an average wage of $1.25 *a day*, is an irresistible site. The chairman of the American Chamber of Commerce in Indonesia explains: 'Indonesia will have a cheap labor supply well into the 21st century.... Nobody else in Asia except China can offer that.' Not unexpectedly, 'The income gap between affluent business people and the millions of impoverished who eke out a living in the villages and Jakarta's teeming slums is widening' (p. 45).

The Indonesian 'success story,' and others like it, are hardly confirmation for the end-of-social-conflict perspective. Much more convincing is the expectation that the next century will be the truly revolutionary era, accomplishing what the twentieth began but could not finish. In any case, communication theory, tied to the assumptions of political or cultural pluralism, harmonization of interests between the privileged and the deprived, resistance to domination residing in individualized interpretation of TV or film shows, or, overall, the long-term viability of capitalist institutions, is and will be unable to explain the looming social turbulence.

Certainly, there are no grounds for complacency about the prospects of the First and Third Worlds (the latter now including the once-Second World states) in the years ahead. Yet Western communication researchers seem intent on holding on to these assumptions. James Curran, surveying the English and continental research scene over the last fifteen years, concludes that

> a major change has taken place. The most important and significant overall shift has been the steady advance of pluralist themes within the radical tradition, in particular, the repudiation of the totalizing, explanatory framework of Marxism, the reconceptualization of the audience as creative and active and the shift from the political to a popular aesthetic.... A sea change has occurred in the field, and this will reshape – for better or worse – the development of media and cultural studies in Europe. (1990, pp. 157–8)

The same tendencies are well advanced, if not dominant, in the United States, though they have not totally swept the field as they seem to have done in England. There is still more than a little life left in those who look at the material side of the economy in general and the cultural industries in particular. Expressing this perspective is David Harvey, in his comprehensive approach to *The Condition of Postmodernity* (1989). Reviewing the same years that Curran surveyed, from the 1970s on, and relying on many of the same basic sources (though not as focused on the field of communication research), Harvey also finds that 'there has been a sea-change in cultural as well as in political-economic practices since around 1972' (p. vii). He concludes that these changes, and the rise of postmodernist cultural forms, 'when set against the basic rules of capitalist accumulation, appear more as shifts in surface appearance rather than as signs of the emergence of some entirely new post-capitalist or even post-industrial society' (p. vii).

Yet these 'shifts in surface appearance' have contributed greatly to the capability of the corporate business system to maintain, and expand, its global reach. For this reason, the acknowledgment of and the struggle against cultural imperialism are more necessary than ever if the general system of domination is to be overcome.

References

Agnew, P. 1990: Italy's sport madness has a very business like basis. *International Herald Tribune*, 4 September, p. 14.

Ang, I. 1985: *Watching 'Dallas': soap opera and the melodramatic imagination*. London: Methuen.

Bright lights, big college money 1990: *The New York Times*, 13 September, p. A-22.

Budd, M., Entman, R. M. and Steinman, C. 1990: The affirmative character of U.S. cultural studies. *Critical Studies in Mass Communication* 7, 169–84.

Curran, J. 1990: The new revisionism in mass communication research. *European Journal of Communication* 5, 135–64.

Engelhardt, T. 1990: Bottom line dreams and the end of culture. *The Progressive* 54(10), 30–5.

Featherstone, M. (ed.) 1990: *Global culture*. London: Sage.

Harvey, D. 1989: *The condition of postmodernity*. Oxford: Basil Blackwell.

Indonesia: the hottest spot in Asia. 1990: *Business Week*, 27 August, pp. 44–5.

Liebes, T. and Katz, E. 1990: *The export of meaning: cross-cultural readings of 'Dallas'*. New York: Oxford University Press.

'Look out' Wimbledon, here comes Leipzig 1990: *Business Week*, 24 September, p. 54.

Meisler, S. 1990: Rich-poor gap held widest in 40 years. *Los Angeles Times*, 24 July, p. A-11.

Nordenstreng, K. and Varis, T. 1974: Television traffic – a one-way street. *Reports and papers on mass communication* 70. Paris: UNESCO.

Nye, J. S., Jr. 1990: No, the U.S. isn't in decline. *The New York Times*, 3 October, p. A-33.

Oliveira, O. S. 1990: *Brazilian soaps outshine Hollywood: is cultural imperialism fading out?* Paper presented at the meetings of the Deutsche Gesellschaft für semiotik, International Congress, University of Passau, 8–10 October.

Publicity? Why it never even occurred to us 1990: *Business Week*, 24 September, p. 46.

Rogers, E. and Antola, L. 1985: *Telenovelas:* a Latin American success story. *Journal of Communication* 35(4), 24–35.

Schiller, H. I. 1989: *Culture, Inc.: the corporate takeover of public expression*. New York: Oxford University Press.

Sloan, A. K. 1990: Europe is ripe for theme parks. *Los Angeles Times*, 22 August, p. D-3.

Straubhaar, J. 1989: *Change in assymetrical interdependence in culture: the Brazilianization of television in Brazil*. Paper presented at the International Communication Association, San Francisco, 25–29 May.

Tracey, M. 1988: Popular culture and the economics of global television. *Intermedia*, March, 19–25.

Questions

1　Summarise the main ways in which Schiller suggests that the world geopolitical order has changed since the 1960s. How does he relate the media to other forms of cultural production in this assessment?

2　Outline Schiller's principal objections to the idea of globalisation and world-wide diversity, and to the theory of 'active audiences' world-wide.

3　What kinds of research and evidence are needed to develop the key ideas and themes suggested in this extract? Suggest or design some particular research studies which might develop these ideas, themes and arguments.

Further reading

Ang, I. 1996: *Living room wars: rethinking media audiences for a postmodern world*. London: Routledge.

Dowmunt, T. 1993: *Channels of resistance: global television and local empowerment*. London: BFI/Channel 4.

Downing, J., Mohammadi, A. and Sreberny-Mohammadi, A. (eds.) 1995: *Questioning the media: a critical introduction*, 2nd edn. London: Sage.

Liebes, T. and Katz, E. 1990: *The export of meaning: Cross-cultural readings of 'Dallas'*. New York: Oxford University Press.

Reeves, G. 1993: *Communication and the 'Third World'*. London: Routledge.

Tomlinson, J. 1991: *Cultural imperialism*. London: Pinter Publishers.

34

Where the Global Meets the Local: Notes from the Sitting Room
David Morley

From *Television, Audiences and Cultural Studies* (Routledge, London, 1992)

In this extract Morley considers the extent to which new communications technologies can simultaneously have a fragmenting and homogenising effect on their users. Recalling Meyrowitz (Section 1, reading 4), he notes how media redefine *individual* notions of social identity and place and create new communities across time and space, taking otherwise disparate groups out of the immediate confines of their locality and *homogenising* them in a common cultural activity. Morley is particularly interested in the part that *television* plays in the process of cultural homogenisation, but of course new computer-mediated communications technologies such as the Internet are allowing this to happen in a much more direct and immediate way – provided that people can pay for it. The fact that communication and culture are now mediated by means of technologies such as the television screen and the computer terminal, and are therefore restricted to those who can pay for them, is a common theme in much recent literature which claims to provide evidence for a widening gap between the 'info-rich' and 'info-poor', and documents its implications for cultural knowledge and informed democratic participation (see Golding, 1989, and Murdock, 1990, referenced in the Further reading section of this reading; also Lyon and Rheingold in the following two readings). However, money is not the sole determinant of access to information or cultural capital and Morley's focus is on other discourses determining the use and application of media and communications technologies, not least that of gender (see also Gray, Section 3, reading 21).

Morley ends with a defence of those audience studies which focus on television viewing in the domestic sphere (among the best known being his own 1978 *Nationwide* study, referenced under 'Further reading') on the grounds that it is in the average sitting room that television allows the immediate location to coexist with the trans-national, blurring the distinction between the public sphere and private spaces and situations.

Communications technologies: scenarios of the future

In this section ... I want to try to make a number of arguments concerning (a) the question of the 'effects' of communications technologies; (b) the ways in which these technologies have been claimed to be responsible for *both* the 'fragmentation' and the 'homogenization' of contemporary culture; and (c) how abstract (and technologically determinist) futuristic scenarios of this kind need to be informed by the analysis of the economic, social and cultural determinations of technology's impact, 'take-up' and use.

Erni argues bluntly that 'in the context of the enormous changes in television technology' (such as the increasing use of video technology and the development of 'television-computer-telephone hybrids') audience research work focused on broadcast television 'becomes somewhat obsolete' (Erni 1989: 39). In a not dissimilar vein, Lindlof and Meyer (1987) argue that the 'interactive' capacities of recent technological developments fundamentally transform the position of the consumer. As they put it,

> with increasing adoption of technological add-ons for the basic media delivery systems, the messages can be edited, deleted, rescheduled or skipped past with complete disregard for their original form. The received notion of the mass communications audience has simply little relevance for the reality of mediated communication. (Lindlof and Meyer 1987: 2)

The technological advances are often seen to have transformative (if not utopian) consequences for the television audience. Thus, in the Italian context, RAI's (Italian public service channel) publicity claims:

> The new telematic services, video recorders and video discs ... will make a more personal use of the medium possible. The user will be able to decide what to watch when he [*sic*] wants. It will be possible, then, to move beyond that fixed mass audience which has been characteristic of TV's history: everybody will be able to do his [*sic*] own programming. (quoted in Connell and Curti 1985: 99)

The problem, of course, is that many of these arguments run the danger of abstracting these technologies' intrinsic 'capacities' from the social contexts of their actual use. In understanding such technological developments, we could usefully follow Bausinger in his concern with the question of how these technologies are integrated into the structure and routines of domestic life – into what he calls 'the specific semantics of the everyday'. His basic thesis is that technologies are increasingly 'absorbed' into the everyday ('everyone owns a number of machines, and has directly to handle technical products'), so that everyday routines themselves are constructed around technologies which then become effectively 'invisible' in their domestication. The end result, he argues, is the 'inconspicuous omnipresence of the technical' (Bausinger 1984: 346). The key point is to understand the processes through which communications and information technologies are 'domesticated' to the point where they become inconspicuous, if not 'invisible' within the home. The further point is then to focus on the culturally constructed meanings of these technologies, as they are 'produced' through located practices of consumption. I will return to these points later in the chapter. First, however, I want to point to the parallel between these arguments about the individualizing effects of these new communications technologies and those 'postmodern' scenarios which simultaneously point to their homogenizing effects.

Let us begin with the well-known postmodern theorist Marshall McLuhan, who, of course, argued that the effect of television and computer technology was to erase time-space differences and to herald a new audio-visual age of global *Gemeinschaft*. Thus, McLuhan and Fiore (1967) argued:

> Electric circuitry has overthrown the regime of 'time' and 'space' and pours upon us incessantly and continually the concerns of all other men ... Ours is a brand new world of 'allatonceness'. 'Time' has ceased, 'space' has vanished. We now live in a global village. (quoted in Ferguson 1989: 163).

In recent years, writers such as Carey (1989), drawing on, among other sources, the work of Innis (1951), have rightly drawn our attention to the historical role of communications systems, both physical and symbolic (cf. also de la Haye 1979) in transforming our senses of space and time. Thus, at one point, for example, Carey speaks of the

> United States [as] the product of literacy, cheap paper, rapid and inexpensive transportation and the mechanical reproduction of words – the capacity, in short, to transport not only people but a complex culture and civilisation from one place to another ... between places that were radically dissimilar in geography ... and ... climate ... the eclipsing of time and space. (Carey 1989: 2–3)

Carey is concerned with, among other things, the role of communications in the construction of empire and the administration of power. Thus, Carey notes, the economic influence not only of the coming of the railways but, more dramatically perhaps, of the coming of the telegraph, which 'permitted for the first time, the effective separation of communication from transportation ... allowing messages to be separated from the physical movement of objects' (ibid., 203), thus freeing communication from the constraints of geography, and to that extent 'making geography irrelevant' (217) and 'diminishing space as a differentiating criterion in human affairs' (222).

In order to make my task easier here, rather than attempting to deal with Carey's carefully nuanced historical work on the mutual influence of communications technologies and social development, I shall choose as an example of contemporary scenario-writing Meyrowitz's (1985) fascinating (if overblown) analysis of the impact of electronic media on social behaviour, in transforming the 'situational geography of human life'. Meyrowitz's concern is with the way in which electronic media have undermined the traditional relationship between physical setting and social situation, to the extent that we are 'no longer "in" places in quite the same way' (Meyrowitz 1989: 333), as these media 'make us ... audiences to performances that happen in other places and give us access to audiences who are not physically present' (Meyrowitz 1985: 7). Meyrowitz's central argument is that these new media re-define notions of social position and of 'place', divorcing experience from physical location.

He argues that the electronic media have transformed the relative significance of live and mediated encounters, bringing 'information and experience to everyplace from everyplace', as 'state funerals, wars ... and space flights are dramas that can be played on the stage of almost anyone's living room' (ibid., 118) and, in Horton and Wohl's (1956) terms, viewers develop forms of 'para-social interaction' with media figures and 'stars' they have never met. In this way, these media, according to Meyrowitz, create new 'communities' across their spaces of transmission, bringing together otherwise disparate groups around the 'common experience' of television, in a process of cultural 'homogenisation of here and there'. Thus, argues Meyrowitz, television acquires a similar status to that of the weather, as a basis of common experience and source of conversation, as a sort of 'metaphysical arena' (ibid., 146), so that 'to watch TV is to look into ... the [common] experience: ... to see what others are watching'. Thus, Meyrowitz argues,

> the millions who watched the assassination of JFK ... were in a 'place' that is no place at all ... the millions of Americans who watch TV every evening ... are in a 'location' that is not defined by walls, streets or neighbourhoods but by evanescent 'experience' ... more and more, people are living in a national (or international) information-system rather than [in] a local town or city. (Meyrowitz 1985: 145–7)

Postmodern geography and the 'generalized elsewhere'

It is in this sense, Meyrowitz argues, that the electronic media are destroying our sense of locality, so that 'places are increasingly like one another and ... the singularity ... and importance of ... locality is diminished' (Kirby 1989: 323). This may be to overstate the case, as Meyrowitz admits in his reply to Kirby, but, minimally, the function of these electronic media is certainly likely to 'relativize' our sense of place – so that 'locality is no longer necessarily seen as the centre stage of life's drama' (Meyrowitz 1989: 330). That centre stage is, then, according to Meyrowitz, taken by national television in the home, bringing us news of the 'generalized elsewhere' of other places and 'non-local' people and their simultaneous experiences – thus undermining any sense of the primary of 'locality', as the 'unifying rhetorical space of daily TV extends into the living rooms of everyone' (Berland 1988: 47).

As Meyrowitz notes, part of the point is that, for instance, access to non-local people (for instance, via the telephone) is often faster and simpler than access to physical neighbours. The 'community' is thus 'liberated from spatial locality' and many intimate ties are supported by the telephone rather than by face-to-face interaction (cf. the telephone advertisement: 'Long distance is the next best thing to being there'). Thus, it seems, we should no longer conceive of community so much in terms of a local clustering of relationships as in terms of types of social relationship, whether local or distant – a 'psychological neighbourhood' or a 'personal community' as a network of (often non-local) ties (Wellman 1979; quoted in Meyrowitz 1989). Thus, 'community' is transformed: living physically near to others is no longer necessarily to be tied into mutually dependent communication systems; conversely, living far from others is no longer, necessarily, to be communicationally distant. Thus, it seems, locality is not simply subsumed in a national or global sphere; rather, it is increasingly bypassed in both directions – experience is both unified beyond localities and fragmented within them.

Such fragmentation, however, is rarely random; nor is it a matter of merely individual differences or 'choices' (cf. Morley 1980). Rather, it is a question of the socially and culturally determined lines of division along which fragmentation occurs. Central among these lines is, of course, that of gender. Both in the (HICT) research described earlier and in that of others in the field, there is an increasing recognition of the 'gendering' of technologies such as the telephone, which is an effect of the socially organized positioning of gendered categories of persons across the public/private division. As Garmarnikow and Purvis (1983) note, the public/private split can, of course, itself be seen as a fundamental metaphor for the patterning of gender. 'Place' and 'placelessness' can certainly be seen to be (among other determinations) highly gendered experiences.

The vision of an 'emergent placelessness' (cf. Berland 1988: 147) offered (celebrated?) by a number of postmodern commentators can be criticized on a number of different counts. On the one hand, it offers little recognition of the particular operations of power, in so far as what emerges across this electronic ('placeless') network is what Mattelart *et al.* identify as the 'time of the exceptional and the spectacular, the product of an international industrial entertainment culture' (Mattelart *et al.* 1987: 97) – a heavily standardized televisual language which will tend to disqualify and displace all others. On the other hand, as Ferguson (1989) argues, the 'techno-orthodoxist' world view, which proclaims that satellite and other new (ICTs) have effectively reduced time/space differences to insignificance, is badly over-abstracted. Principally, this is because the argument has little empirical grounding and operates at a level of abstraction which does not permit us to answer questions about *how* these media shift our everyday understandings of time and space, or about *which* media-forms influence *which* people in *which* ways in their conceptualization of duration and distance (cf. Bryce 1987). What is needed, in this respect, is 'qualitative research into *how* electronic communications magnify [or otherwise – D.M.] time-space imperatives and *which* forms produce *which* kind of intended and unintended consequences' (Ferguson 1989: 171).

If the homogenization of space and time in contemporary culture has not yet abolished all differences, still we must attend to the need to construct a properly postmodern geography of the relations between communications and power and the contemporary transformations of the public and private spheres. As Ferguson notes, despite the grand claims of the techno-orthodox-ist 'homogenizers', it remains true that 'just as they have differential access to new and old communication media, so do different cultures, social groups and national sources of power perceive, categorise and prioritise temporal and spatial boundaries differently' (ibid., 153). To take a 'European' example, rather than speculating, in the abstract, as to whether or not we are seeing the emergence of a unified 'European culture' under the impact of pan-European media, it may be more instructive to ask to what extent, for which groups (e.g. teenage viewers of satellite-television music channels, Euro-businesspersons, etc.) such a 'European' perspective is emerging (cf. Collins 1990).

Rather than presuming a uniform effect in which, from a crudely technologically determinist perspective, new ICTs impose new sensibilities on peoples across the globe, it may be more realistic to conceive of them as overlaying the new upon the old (cf. Rogge and Jensen, in Lull 1988). Thus, a new technology such as the home computer may often be principally 'made sense of' via its integration into the very old 'technology' of the peer-gossip network. Rather than the new media promoting a 'boundless media-land of common understandings', a variety of senses of 'temporal elasticity and local indeterminacy' may be the more likely result, where 'formerly finite absolutes take on a notably relativist character ... and old certainties ... [are undermined, to some extent by] new ambiguities' (Ferguson 1989: 155). This seems both a more realistic (cf. Miller, 1992) and a richer perspective from which to analyse the interaction of local definitions and larger communications systems. As Miller (ibid.) argues in his analysis of the consumption of American soap opera in Trinidad, the 'local' is not to be considered as an indigenous source of cultural identity, which remains 'authentic' only in so far as it is unsullied by contact with the global. Rather, the local is often itself produced by means of the 'indigenization' (or 'domestication') of global or 'foreign' resources and imputs.

Massey makes the point eloquently, in her critique of the widespread tendency to counterpose a concept of the local (usually conflated with the concrete) with that of the global (usually conflated with the abstract). As she puts it,

> the ... world economy is no less concrete than a local one [it] is 'general' in the sense of being a geographically large-scale phenomenon, to which can be counterposed internal variations. But it is also, unequivocally, concrete as opposed to abstract ... Those who conflate the local with the concrete ... are confusing geographical scale with processes of abstraction in thought ... [and] those who make this mistake then frequently ... confuse the study of the local with description, which they oppose to theoretical work ... this argument ... [confuses] ... the dimensions concrete-abstract and local-general ... The 'local' ... is no less subject to, nor useful for theorisation than big, broad, general things. The counterposition of general and local is quite distinct from the distinction between abstract and concrete. (Massey 1991: 270–1)

If 'geography matters', and if place is important, this is not only because the character of a particular place is a product of its position in relation to wider forces, but also because that character, in turn, stamps its own imprint on those wider processes. Moreover, places are not static or fixed, easily defin-able, or bounded entities into which external forces somehow (improperly or problematically) intrude, as those working in the Heideggerian tradition would often seem to imply. This is simply the theoretical correlative of Marx's observation that people are not 'in' society as an object is in a box, and of Voloshinov's concept of the 'social individual'. As Massey argues, places are to be seen as themselves processes; they are frequently riven with internal con-flicts and divisions (they are not internally homogenous) and are perhaps best seen not as 'bounded areas' but as 'spaces of interaction' in which local identi-ties are constructed out of resources (both material and symbolic) which may well not be at all local in their origin. But then perhaps, as Miller (op. cit.) observes, we should define 'authenticity' *a posteriori*, rather than *a priori*, as a matter of local consequences, rather than of local origins. Similarly, to the extent that imported television programmes penetrate local meaning systems, rather than thereby 'homogenizing' diverse cultures, their principal effect may be a rather variable one – in so far as they introduce a relativizing perspective, as an 'uncertainty principle' which may work to undermine established and dominant frameworks of meaning in a variety of ways (cf. Hebdige 1988 and Worpole 1983, on the effects of 'foreign' cultural artefacts in undermining the hierarchies of national taste cultures; but cf. also Chen 1990, on the signifi-cance of the fact that the 'foreign' is so often represented by the 'American').

From the sitting-room to the (inter)nation(al)

In recent years, one line of criticism of researchers such as Lull, Silverstone and myself has been that, in our concern with the domestic context of television-viewing, we were busy conducting an ill-considered (if not hasty) 'retreat' into the private realm of the 'sitting-room' and away from the important 'public' issues of power, politics and policy which constitute the proper subjects of the study of communication. I shall argue that this critique is misguided, on a num-ber of counts. It is not only that the average sitting-room (in my experience) is the site of some very important political conflicts – it is, among other things, one of the principal sites of the politics of gender and age. It is also that, in my view, the sitting-room is exactly where we need to start from, if we finally want to understand the constitutive dynamics of abstractions such as 'the communi-ty' or 'the nation'. This is especially so if we are concerned with the role of communications in the continuous formation, sustenance, recreation and trans-formation of these entities. The central point precisely concerns television's role in connecting, for example, the 'familiar' or domestic, and the national and international spheres, and in sustaining both the image and the reality of the 'national family' and of various trans-national 'communities'.

From this perspective, one of the key functions of broadcasting is the cre-ation of a bridge between the public and the private, the sacred and the pro-fane, the extraordinary and the mundane. Thus, as Silverstone argues,

In Durkheimian terms, television provides a forum and a locus for the mobilisation of collective energy and enthusiasm, for example, in the presentation of national events, from coronations to great sporting fixtures, and it also marks a consistently defined but significant boundary in our culture between the domestic and taken-for-granted world and that of the unreachable and otherwise inaccessible world of ... show business, *Dallas* and the moon landings. (Silverstone 1988: 25)

In a similar vein, Chaney (1983) analyses the role of broadcasting in enabling the public to participate in the collective life of the nation. As Chaney points out, a 'nation' is a very abstract collectivity, in so far as it is too big to be experienced directly by the individual. To that extent, the 'we-feeling' of community has to be continually engendered by opportunities for identification, as the sense of 'nation' is manufactured. Chaney is particularly concerned with the role of mass media in relaying civic rituals (coronations, royal weddings, etc.). As he notes, if such rituals are 'dramatizations' of the nation as symbolic community, then the infinite reproduceability of media performance makes the 'audience' for them possible on a scale previously unimaginable (Chaney 1983: 121). Recalling Silverstone's definition of television's role in establishing 'the space intimate distance' (1988: 23), Chaney analyses the 'quasi-democracy of intimate access' (cf. Dayan and Katz 1987: 88 'TV is that which abolishes distance') created by the presence of the television camera, 'representing' the public in the most intimate moments of symbolic ritual. At the heart of the process is an ambivalence, in which public figures are simultaneously humanized through vicarious observation (and the camera often gives the audience at home a closer view than those physically present – D.M.) but also distanced through the dramatic conventions of media presentation (Chaney 1986: 121).

Chaney is concerned with the spectacular character of ceremonial occasions, arguing finally (in a curious reversal of Ellis' (1992) comments on broadcast television as the 'private life of the nation state') that 'spectacular forms of mass communication are the public life of a mass culture': (Chaney 1986: 132). Contrary to the established view that 'ritual' is less significant in secularized industrial societies than it was in earlier times, Chaney argues that, because of the scale and nature of these societies (where the entire citizenry simply cannot be personally acquainted and a sense of collective identity must be continually invented), ritual becomes more salient as a mode of dramatizing (indeed, constituting) 'community'. Thus, Chaney notes that 'collective ceremonies have patently not disappeared from the calendar of institutional identity and reproduction; indeed they have been made more accessible and less arcane through their dramatisation as media performances' (132). This is, in some part, a question of 'access' – thus, Chaney notes the significance of the radio broadcasting of George VI's coronation in 1937 in involving a huge proportion of the national public, who 'spent the day listening in and thus partaking in the central events' (Jennings and Madge 1987; quoted in Chaney 1986: 129). However, it is not only a question of access. Thus, in his earlier article, Chaney notes that, in the end, the media's role transforms these events, so that 'national festivals ... become ... media occasions, rather than occasions to which the media have access' (ibid., 134).

It is also a question, as Stam (1983) argues, of understanding the specific form of the pleasure offered to the viewer by television, and in particular by television 'news' in its most general sense. Stam is concerned with what he calls the 'metaphysics of presence' of television and the ways in which television news promotes 'the regime of the fictive ... "we"' ... (39) as a 'community'. Stam's argument is that 'epistemophilia' (the pleasure of knowing) can offer only a partial account of the motivation of news viewing. Beyond this, argues Stam, we must attend to the ways in which the pleasures offered are narcissistic and are 'designed to enhance the self-image of His or Her Majesty the Spectator' (27). The principal point, argues Stam, is that television transforms us into 'armchair imperialists' and 'audio-visual masters of the world' (25). In this respect, Stam argues, while 'live' television is only a small portion of all broadcast television, it 'sets the tone' for much of what television offers. As he puts it, television

> allows us to share the literal time of persons who are elsewhere. It grants us ... instantaneous ubiquity. The telespectator of a lunar landing becomes a vicarious astronaut ... The viewer of a live transmission, in fact, can in some respects see better than those immediately present on the scene. (ibid., 24)

It is this 'interfacing' of the public and the private that concerns us here. On the one hand, the audience for such national events is usually atomized, either attending individually or in small groups such as the family or peer group. On the other hand, each such group sits in front of a television set emitting the same representations of this 'central' event. The 'public' is thus experienced in the private (domestic) realm: it is 'domesticated'. But at the same time the 'private' itself is thus transformed or 'socialized'. The space (and experience) created is neither 'public' nor private in the traditional senses.

In unravelling these connections, the work of Dayan and Katz (1987) on the representation of the royal wedding of 1981 on British television may be of some help. Drawing on Austin's (1962) theory of 'performative' speech acts, Dayan and Katz are concerned to analyse television's role in constructing (literally 'performing') media events such as the royal wedding. In this connection, they argue, television should be seen not as 'representing' the event but as constructing the experience of it for the majority of the population. Television, they argue, is not so much reporting on the event as actively involved in 'performing' it. Television is not simply transmitting such an event (or commenting on it) but is bringing it into existence.

General de Gaulle's concept of television as the face of the government in the sitting-room can, of course, be argued to apply only to broadcasting under quite particular conditions, specifically where broadcasting is allowed very little autonomy from direct governmental control. However, if we take our lead from the work of Chaney and Dayan and Katz (see above), we can not only begin to see the crucial role of television in articulating 'governmental' (cf. Foucault 1980) or 'public' with domestic space; we can also pose the more fundamental question as to the extent to which it still makes sense to speak of broadcast media as 'reporting' on political developments. The problem is that to pose the question this way is to presume that there exists some separate realm of 'politics' on which television then, subsequently, reports. In an age when international sporting events are routinely arranged to suit the convenience of broadcasting schedules and acts of war are timed with reference not so much to military requirements as to maximizing PR advantage, this may seem obvious. The fundamental issue is of some long standing. As early as 1974, Pateman argued a similar point in relation to electoral politics. His point was that television can only 'cover' an election when the campaign has an existence independent of the presence of television, and that nowadays these campaigns no longer have any such existence, being principally designed and planned – in terms of 'photo-opportunities', 'sound-bites', etc. – with reference to their televisualization. Thus, Pateman argues, 'we do not have television coverage of an election, we have a television election' (1974). Pateman's point can be extended well beyond the specific field of 'elections' to cover 'politics' in a much more general sense: for the majority of the population, 'politics' is principally a 'media event', and their participation in this realm is a heavily mediated one.

We are back, once again, with the politics of 'being there'. This is, increasingly, a complex issue. The *Guardian's* South Africa correspondent. David Beresford, offered a telling account (*Guardian*, 17 April 1990) of his attempt to report Nelson Mandela's speech in Cape Town on his release from prison – where 'being there' physically unfortunately entailed being unable to see or hear Mr. Mandela. This Beresford accounts as an experience of 'being there and not being there' where being the 'man on the spot' has the perverse effect of being unable to witness the images available to the rest of the global village. In a similar vein, Dayan and Katz refer to the seemingly puzzling (but increasingly common) behaviour of those physically present at public events who, if they can, also take with them a portable television, so they too can see 'what is happening'. Physical contiguity does not, then, necessarily equate with effective participation; and, of course, vice versa.

From this angle we could also usefully reconsider the debates that arose concerning the television spectaculars of the 1980s – from 'Band Aid/Live Aid' onwards. Meyrowitz comments: 'Live Aid was an event that took place nowhere but on TV, the ultimate example of the freeing of communications experience from the "restraint of social and physical passage".' Many commentators have been critical of the ways in which such 'trans-national' broadcasts expressed a 'mythology' of international (if not universal) community. However, in a very important sense this was no 'mythical' achievement. If a sense of community was created, this may have had something to do with the fact that all over the world millions of people were (in reality) watching these 'simultaneous' broadcasts – and, to that extent, in Dayan and Katz's terms, participating quite effectively in a 'diasporic ceremony' which was anything but illusory.

The question that Dayan and Katz pose is what happens to public ceremonies when, instead of being attended in person, they are delivered to us at home. As they note, being physically distanced from the ceremonial forms and isolated from each other, television audiences do not form 'masses' or 'crowds' except in an abstract, statistical sense (cf. Ang 1991). The question they pose is that of whether we can still speak of a public event when it is celebrated at home – and whether we can speak of a collective celebration when the collectivity is scattered (cf. Siskind 1992). As they note, under these conditions:

> The very hugeness of the audiences had paradoxically transposed the celebration into an intimate register. Ceremonial space has been reconstituted, but in the home. Attendance takes place in small groups congregated around the television set, concentrating on the symbolic centre, keenly aware that myriads of other groups are doing likewise, in a similar manner, and at the same time. (Dayan and Katz 1987: 194)

The analogy which Dayan and Katz offer is that of the Jewish Passover 'Seder' ritual – a collective ceremony without a central 'cultic temple', which translates the public celebration into 'a multiplicity of simultaneous, similarly programmed, home-bound, micro-events' (ibid., 195). Thus, Dayan and Katz imply, the television audience, as a dispersed community, can usefully be seen as being regularly united (both by its occasional viewing of special events and by its regular viewing of the 'news' or favourite soap operas) through precisely this kind of 'diasporic ceremony'. While 'media events' such as a televised royal wedding clearly constitute a special case, in which this issue is brought into particular prominence, this model can clearly be extended to the quotidian level – so that the regular viewing of the nightly television news or of a long-running soap opera can be seen in the same light – as a discourse which constitutes collectivities through a sense of 'participation' and through the production of both a simultaneity of experience and a sense of a 'past in common' (cf. the debates on 'popular memory': Wright 1985).

References

Ang, I. 1991: *Desperately seeking the audience*, London: Routledge.
Austin, J. 1962: *How to do things with words*. Oxford: Oxford University Press.
Bausinger, H. 1984: Media, technology and everyday life. *Media, Culture and Society* 6(4).
Berland, J. 1988: Placing television. *New Formations* 4.
Bryce, J. 1987: Family time and television use. In Lindlof, T. (ed.), *Natural audiences*. Norwood, New Jersey: Ablex.
Carey, J. 1989: *Culture as communication*. London: Unwin Hyman.
Chaney, D. 1983: A symbolic mirror of ourselves: civic ritual in mass society. *Media, Culture and Society* 5(2).

Chaney, D. 1986: The symbolic form of ritual in mass communication. In Golding, P., *et al.* (eds.), *Communicating politics*. Leicester: Leicester University Press.

Chen, K. H. 1990: 'Postmarxism'. Taiwan: Institute of Literature, National Tsing-Hua University.

Collins, R. 1990: *Satellite television in Western Europe*. London: John Libbey Books.

Connell, I. and Curti, L. 1985: Popular broadcasting in Italy and Britain. In Drummond, P. and Paterson, R. (eds.), *Television in transition*. London: British Film Institute.

Dayan, D. and Katz, E. 1987: Performing media events. In Curran, J., *et al.* (eds.), *Impacts and influences*, London: Methuen.

de la Haye, Y. 1979: *Marx and Engels on the means of communication*. New York: International General.

Ellis, J. 1992: *Visible fictions*. London: Routledge.

Erni, J. 1989: Where is the audience? *Journal of Communication Enquiry* 13(2).

Ferguson, M. 1989: Electronic media and the redefining of time and space. In Ferguson, M. (ed.), *Public Communication*. London: Sage.

Foucault, M. 1980: The eye of power. In Gordon, C. (ed.), *M. Foucault: power/knowledge*. New York: Pantheon.

Garmarnikow, E. and Purvis, J. 1983: *The public and the private*. London: Heinemann Educational Books.

Hebdige, D. 1988: Towards a cartography of taste. In Hebdige, D., *Hiding in the light*. London: Comedia/Routledge.

Horton, D. and Wohl, R. 1956: 'Mass communications and para-social interaction'. *Psychiatry* 19.

Innis, H. 1951: *The bias of communication*. Toronto: University of Toronto Press.

Jennings, H. and Madge, C. (eds) 1987. *May the twelfth. Mass observation day survey, 1937*. London: Faber and Faber.

Kirby, A. 1989: A sense of place. *Critical Studies in Mass Communication* 6(3).

Lindlof, T. and Meyer, T. 1987: Mediated communication: the foundations of qualitative research. In Lindlof, T. (ed.), *Natural audiences*. Norwood, NJ: Ablex.

Lull, J. (ed.) 1988: *World families watch television*. Newbury Park and London: Sage.

McLuhan, M. and Fiore, Q. 1967: *War and peace in the global village*. New York: Bantam Books.

Massey, D. 1991: The political place of locality studies. *Environment and Planning (A)* 23(2).

Mattelart, A. *et al.* 1987: *International image market*. London: Comedia.

Meyrowitz, J. 1985: *No sense of place*. New York: Oxford University Press.

Meyrowitz, J. 1989. 'The generalised elsewhere'. *Critical Studies in Mass Communication* 6(3).

Miller, D. 1992: The young and the restless in Trinidad. In Silverstone, R. and Hirsch E. (eds.), *Consuming technologies*. London: Routledge.

Morley, D. 1980: *The 'nationwide' audience*. London: British Film Institute.

Pateman, T. 1974: *Television and the February 1974 general election*, London: British Film Institute.

Silverstone, R. 1988: Television, myth and culture. In Carey, J. (ed.), *Media, myths and narratives*. London: Sage.

Siskind, J. 1992: The invention of Thanksgiving: a ritual of American nationality. *Critique of Anthropology* 12(2).

Stam, R. 1983: Television news and its spectator. In Kaplan, E. (ed.), *Regarding television*, vol. 2. New York: American Film Institute.

Wellman, B. 1979: 'The community question'. *American Journal of Sociology* 84.
Worpole, K. 1983: *Dockers and detectives*, London: Verso.
Wright, P. 1985: *On living in an old country*. London: Verso.

Questions

1   Summarise the main ideas put forward in this reading. How do they relate to other extracts in this reader?
2   In the first section we asked how electronic media have had implications for the public sphere and for private spaces and situations. Have your opinions been reinforced or challenged as a result of your further reading?

Further reading

Cockburn, C. and Furst-Dilic, R. 1994: *Bringing technology home: gender and technology in a changing Europe*. Buckingham: Open University Press.
Golding, P. 1989: Political communication and citizenship. In Ferguson, M. (ed.), *Public communication*. London: Sage.
Morley, D. 1980: *The 'nationwide' audience*. London: British Film Institute
Murdock, G. 1990: Television and citizenship: in defence of public broadcasting. In Tomlinson, A. (ed.), *Consumption, identity and style*, London: Routledge.
Silverstone, R. and Hirsch, E. 1992: *Consuming technologies: media and information in domestic spaces*. London: Routledge.

35

The Roots of the Information Society Idea
David Lyon

From *The information society: issues and illusions* (Polity Press 1988)

This reading is from a book which investigates the many facets of the new information age and its primary premise is that success in almost every field is now reliant on the application of new communications technologies. In fact, Lyon goes so far as to suggest that a working knowledge of computer technology and what computers can do for us (as opposed to the determinist view of how we should adapt to them) may be essential to participate fully in the society of the future, radically altering the ways in which economic and social exchanges are created, the means by which we access information and obtain knowledge, and the character of work and leisure.

But Lyon's vision of the new communications revolution is somewhat bleak. He suggests that technology is not being used in innovatory, creative ways, but is simply reinforcing old structures, existing power relations and established ideologies in new ways. He rhetorically asks: 'Does IT bring about a new society without precedent, or does it rather help to intensify certain processes in today's society of which we are all too aware?' His further comments on industrial power relations, the opportunities offered to women by information technologies and issues concerning surveillance and protection go some way to answer this question.

So, far from heralding a new kind of society (and has there ever been a generation which hasn't felt that it was at the threshold of a new kind of society?), Lyon argues that the emerging technologies of information and communication shape social and cultural experience along familiar lines and reinforce the power of some individuals over others, not only in terms of the processes of production, but also in the spheres of leisure and consumption.

> People started getting together and exploring the idea that there was going to be a revolution in technology which was going to change society so drastically.
>
> Wozniak (1986)[1]

Suddenly, success in just about any field has become impossible without information technology. In farming, manufacture, education, policing, medicine, entertainment, banking or whatever, IT is apparently set to change everything that human beings do in advanced societies. Steve Wozniak, of Apple computers fame, sees the real revolution as putting personal computers into the home. Others see it in direct broadcasting by satellite, automated work opening up new vistas for freed time, or in the potential for push-button democracy. While differing over details, telecommunications spells the start of a new age.

It appears that this is the only way forward. Initiation in the processes of information handling, transmission, storage and retrieval is the key to future prosperity and to qualitatively different ways of life. Failure to proceed in this direction carries dire consequences. Punishment for national laggards, according to a British National Economic Development Office report, will be relegation to 'Third World' status.[2]

Not surprisingly, this 'one way forward' is greeted by others with some sense of foreboding. Cheerful book-titles such as *Silicon Civilization* and *The Mighty Micro* are answered in *Eletronic Nightmare* and *Electronic Illusions*.[3] And fears of being sucked into a new transnational empire or being technologically dependent upon the USA or Japan are greater, for some smaller countries, than the threat of impending 'Third World' status. Nevertheless, for better or for worse, the arrival of the information society is felt to be imminent.

Are we at the threshold of a new kind of society? Discussions of the 'wired society' or of the 'wealth of information' certainly imply this.[4] Alvin Toffler's well-known 'third wave' concept is perhaps the clearest example.[5] The first 'wave' is agricultural, the second industrial, and the third, information society. Sociological debate has not yet crystallized around this single concept – the information society – but it is in sufficiently popular and social scientific use to make it the focus of this study. It finds a ready home in accounts of the 'social impact of new technology', is frequently referred to in policy studies, and is strongly related to other emerging concepts such as that of the 'information worker'. But should it be used as a basic means of characterizing 'society' today?

[...]

From postindustrialism to information society

The roots of the information society idea are intertwined in a complex manner. It is hard to disentangle the diverse strands of attempted social prediction, government policy, futuristic speculation and empirical social analysis. For instance, a Canadian government report, *Planning Now for the Information Society*[6] is clearly geared to identifying a national technology strategy in microelectronics. But it depends upon social scientific concepts such as the 'information economy', indulges briefly in quoted 'predictions' (for instance that by the year 2000 'smart' highways for semi-automated driving will enter development), and refers to empirical studies of the impact of microelectronics on, among other things, women's work.

One readily identifiable strand, on which hopeful accounts of information society often rely, is the idea of postindustrialism, especially the version associated with Daniel Bell. This is the view that, just as agrarian was replaced by industrial society as the dominant economic emphasis shifted from the land to manufacturing, so postindustrial society develops as a result of the economic tilt towards the provision of services. The increased part played by science in the productive process, the rise to prominence of professional, scientific and technical groups, plus the introduction of what is now called information technology, all bear witness to a new 'axial principle' at the core of the economy and society. This axial principle, 'the energising principle that is the logic for all the others', is the centrality of 'theoretical knowledge'.[7]

Bell argues that the information society is developing in the context of postindustrialism. He forecasts the growth of a new social framework based on telecommunications which 'may be decisive for the way economic and social exchanges are conducted, the way knowledge is created and retrieved, and the character of work and occupations in which men [*sic*] are engaged'. The computer plays a pivotal role in this 'revolution'.[8]

Bell also sketches other significant features of the information society. IT, by shortening labour time and diminishing the production worker, actually replaces labour as the source of 'added value' in the national product. Knowledge and information supplant labour and capital as the 'central variables' of the economy. He comments on the way that information is being treated as a commodity, with a price-tag on it, and how the 'possession' of information increasingly confers power on its owner. Unlike some postindustrialists, Bell recognizes some of the ambiguities involved in identifying a 'service sector' and proposes that economic sectors be divided into 'extractive, fabrication and information activities'. This way, he claims, one may monitor the penetration of information activities into more traditional areas of agriculture, manufacturing and services.

Bell underlines ways in which these areas are expanding in the wake of IT development. He foresees major social changes resulting from the establishment of new telecommunications infrastructures. Such huge changes will occur as 'the merging technologies of telephone, computer, facsimile, cable television and video discs lead to a vast reorganization in the modes of communication between persons; the transmission of data; the reduction if not the elimination of paper in transactions and exchanges; new modes of transmitting news, entertainment and knowledge'[9] and so on. These in turn will intensify concern about population distribution, national planning, centralization, privacy and so on. For Bell, the 'fateful question', or, one might say, the consumerist question, is whether the promise will be realized that 'instrumental technology' will open 'the way to alternative modes of achieving individuality and variety within a vastly increased output of goods'.[10]

Without doubt, Bell asks many of the right questions, and indicates worthwhile lines of inquiry. This is why his work deserves to be taken seriously. But it also demands serious critique because, as I shall show, Bell's attempt to find a thoroughgoing alternative to Marxian class analysis underestimates both the resilience of some familiar features of modern societies, and the extent to which new conflicts and struggles could arise within this 'information society'.

Those 'familiar features' include military, commercial and government power. No small significance lies in the fact that it was military requirements which gave birth to modern computers. The massive mainframe, ENIAC, built in 1946 in the electrical engineering department of the University of Pennsylvania, was intended to assist the aiming of guns, and was soon involved in calculations for the atomic bomb. Neither is it irrelevant to note that huge forces of international capitalist commerce are today locked in mortal combat to capture markets and conquer opposition within the lucrative high technology field. Nor is it an accident that governments are so active in promoting IT and purchasing its products. IT is a powerful tool for monitoring and supervising people's activities. In other words, one does not have to look far before this question comes to mind: Does IT bring about a new society without precedent, or does it rather help to intensify certain processes in today's society of which we are all too aware?

What of 'new conflicts and struggles'? Are we entering an era, not of Bell's rather smoothly harmonious information society, but of new social frictions and power alignments within a divided and contradictory 'information society'? Around the same time as Bell's work on postindustrialism a European contribution appeared which took account of the same social and economic trends: Alain Touraine's *La Société post-industrielle.*[11]

Touraine's study took a quite different tack from Bell's. He challenged the bland postindustrial assumption that class struggle was a thing of the past, although he argued that many class images are too bound up with the 'era of capitalist industrialisation'. He invited readers to consider the 'fundamental importance of class situations, conflicts and movements in the programmed society'. In particular he had in mind a major cleavage between technocrats and a more disparate grouping whose livelihood and lifestyles are governed by them. Property ownership is less a bone of contention than the opposition brought about because 'the dominant classes dispose of knowledge and control information'.[12]

So do changing technologies and shifts in educational qualification and skill lead to novel class alignments? ... [T]his question still concentrates upon the workplace and on production. The analyses of Touraine and others hint at wider movements of power. The use of IT within governments, education, the media and the domestic sphere as well as in the workplace means that more and more social relationships are mediated by machines. What does this imply for power? Mark Poster suggests that because 'new forms of social interaction based on electronic communications devices are replacing older types of social relations',[13] we should speak of a new 'mode of information'. He too is questioning the relevance today of some Marxian assumptions but for very different reasons from Daniel Bell's.

Social forecasters and social planners

The roots of the information society idea are found not only in sociology. Futurists and 'social impact of technology' commentators also contribute. They tend to share the belief that technology 'shapes' social relationships. One of the many cheerful social forecasts comes from Tom Stonier. 'Living in a postindustrial world', he avers, 'means that not only are we more affluent, more resourceful and less likely to go to war, but also more likely to democratise'.[14] Increasing prosperity is a common information society theme. By 'more resourceful', Stonier means that IT will enable us to overcome the environmental and ecological problems associated with industrialism. Again he touches on a common theme. James Martin, in *The Wired Society*, also stresses the 'non-polluting, non-destructive' quality of IT as a major point in its favour.[15]

New communications technologies hold out the next promise – the demise of war ('as slavery disappeared in the industrial era', says Stonier[16]). Some even hold this out as a 'stage' beyond information society: 'communication society'.[17] Lastly, IT ushers in the world of computer democracy. More information availability, plus push-button referenda, open the door for the first time to genuinely responsive participatory government. This, along with the burden of administration being thoroughly automated, is the contented futurist's world of information society.

[...]

The information society as problematic

So what are the prospects for the information society concept? The answer is not straightforward. For one thing, more than one image of the information society is available. The popular image of a social transformation along 'Third Wave' lines is not the same as the fuzzier image produced within more careful social analysis of societies coming to terms with a range of more and less profound political, economic and cultural effects of information technology. In his 'information society' essay Daniel Bell himself has become silent about the affluence and leisure he once associated with postindustrialism. Another complicating factor is that both popular and serious versions of the information society thesis either rely upon or provoke genuine questions of tremendous importance.

The idea of an information society is more than recycled postindustrialism. To be sure, the two concepts do share a number of common features, not to mention several common flaws. Popular versions of information society forecasting, often giddy with the astonishing progress of microelectronics since the late 1970s, are infused with the same technological determinism that informed much postindustrialism. While strong currents of critical social investigation cause some ripples, much present-day research focuses on social adaptation to IT, rather than how IT may be designed to suit people, which betrays the extent to which technologically determinist views have been accepted.

... Several analyses start by outlining important features of one or another aspect of the information society idea which are then sifted in order to retain what *is* significant or contrasted with alternative interpretations.

I choose this method because I see little point in summarily discarding the information society as the rotten fruit of futurist fancy or as ideology in the guise of social analysis. Rather, the information society should be granted the status of 'problematic'. According to Philip Abrams, a problematic is a 'rudimentary organization of a field of phenomena which yields problems for investigation'.[18] Without succumbing to the sociological simplism which sees the information society as a 'Third Wave' of evolutionary progress, it is nevertheless true to say that some of the most significant changes in late twentieth-century society are those inherent in, related to, or consequent upon IT. The information society concept points to that cluster of issues and its better exponents already use it in this sense.

As a problematic its components refer to changes in the workplace and employment and also the political, cultural and global aspects of the diffusion of IT. Whether the sum of these changes amounts to a shift beyond industrial capitalism, militarism or male dominance is highly questionable. Important continuities, such as the chronic persistence of inequalities and the growth of state power using IT, seem to suggest that changes may be more of degree than kind. In important respects many supposed changes highlighted by information society theorists originated well before information technology!

At the same time the category of information is undoubtedly becoming vitally important as an economic factor in its own right. The phenomenon of insider dealing on international stock markets is an obvious illustration. While it may not be supplanting property as a key to the social structure of modern societies, information is proving to be a crucially important element in our understanding of social relationships. Certainly at present it lacks adequate definition, let alone incorporation within a coherent theory of contemporary social change. Yet the new technologies which handle and process information simultaneously influence diverse but significant aspects of social, cultural and political reality.

Let me note two other features of the information society problematic. One is that social analysis must grapple with the ramifications of the *fusion* of technologies which comprise IT. Conventional distinctions between communication and media studies, on the one hand, and studies of the social aspects of computing, on the other, are eroded. For example, implications of the decline in public service broadcasting now extend far beyond traditional concerns for broadcasting as such. In the USA, the dissemination of government data, once a public function, is under increasing pressure as private profit-seeking firms compete to sell repackaged data. Burgeoning communication between computers and the coming of the commercial database brings 'public service' questions into the heartland of computing.

The other noteworthy feature is that as social analysis exposes alternative options in the adoption of new technology that are in fact available to government, industry and the public, discussions of the strategy for shaping new technologies become more relevant. Do government-sponsored slogans such as 'automate or liquidate' represent genuine choices? Is it 'data' or 'persons' that ought to be protected by law? How does one decide what counts as an appropriate technology where microelectronics is concerned? Social analysis can serve to indicate the conditions under which ethical considerations and social hopes might be realized.

Information society: the major themes

The information society concept inherits several symptoms of the troubles that beset postindustrialism. The postindustrialists largely failed to justify the significance granted to trends such as the growth of theoretical knowledge and of services. A leisured society based on automated manufacture, a vast array of services and a culture of self-expression, political participation and an emphasis on the quality of life does not seem to have materialized – at least, not for the majority of the populations of the advanced societies.

Will this hereditary syndrome prove fatal for the information society? The answer depends upon careful investigation in the following areas.

Information workers in an information economy
It is clear from job advertisements at least that in the late 1980s one's chances of obtaining employment are enhanced by the possession of

qualifications in microelectronics, computing, systems analysis, telecommunications, operational research, software design, fibre optics, expert systems and so on. But what does this proliferation of new job descriptions mean? Those that Tom Stonier refers to as 'information operatives' seem to appear in all manner of workplaces. The big questions are: who are these 'operatives', and what contribution do their activities make to the pattern of social relationships?

Central to much information society discourse is the contention that 'information workers' are rising to a majority within the labour forces of the advanced societies. As early as 1967, claims Marc Porat, 50 per cent of American workers were engaged in the 'information sector', and they received just over 50 per cent of total employee remuneration. But just who are these information workers? Unfortunately, because he does not actually explain what 'information' is (he only defines it as 'data that have been organized and communicated') the categories are blurred. Judges and rent-collectors find themselves in this sector but doctors, for instance, have an 'ambiguous occupation', straddling 'service' and 'information' sectors![19]

Few studies of 'information work' comment on its purpose, function, or content. Without this, however, we cannot know who makes decisions, on what basis, or with what effect. Masses of computer-generated information confers no power whatsoever on those who use it, whereas at certain points within organizations it may be crucial to the maintenance of power. As it happens, postindustrialism also glossed over questions of information, knowledge and power, especially with regard to the social significance of research and development (R&D). The sheer amount of R&D in any given society tells us little. We learn nothing about the social role of scientific and technical knowledge, the price put on it, and the power of those who manipulate it. The fact that R&D is often financed for political rather than social reasons, and developed for military rather than economic purposes, pulls the rug from beneath the (Bell-inspired) idea that universities are crucibles of power in the modern world.[20] The current squeeze on university funding and the politicizing of technology policy makes the idea laughable.

That said, changes are occurring in the occupational structure of the advanced societies. While the relabelling process noted in Krishan Kumar's critique of postindustrialism still occurs – though today it is programmers becoming software architects rather than plumbers becoming heating engineers – there is expansion at managerial, professional and technical levels. There is, moreover, a strong link between innovation and economic growth; hence the frequently expressed British worries about the lack of domestic R&D funding relative to other countries.

Two major questions are raised by the 'discovery' of information work and an information sector in the economy. First, are the apparently new categories of work and occupation leading to shifts in power? Is there an emerging information 'technocracy' which is wresting power from previously dominant classes? What opportunities for women are opened by the spread of IT? What is the likely effect of IT on industrial relations? When British Rail computerized its freight system, for instance, many 'middle managers' found their positions were simply redundant, and personnel in subordinate positions actually discovered they had new powers of control over the work process.[21]

The other question is this: how accurate is the idea of an 'information sector', and is there an historical 'march through the sectors'[22] as agrarianism gives way to industrialism, and industrialism to information society? This point affects not only the advanced societies but also those to which the promise is alluringly held out that they may be able to jump straight from a non-industrial to an information society. Is this really possible, or does 'informatizing' depend upon an already 'advanced' situation?

[...]

Political and global aspects

Echoes of postindustrialism are again heard with respect to the political and global aspects of information society. A common feature of each is that opportunities for political choice and participation will increase. The difference, however, is that the means of implementing these is now visible, particularly in the possibilities of two-way, interactive electronic networks. The extreme case is that of an 'instant referendum' in which voters' views are canvassed via cable television which allows people to receive as well as transmit signals from their living rooms. More soberly, IT is seen as a means of enabling an electorate to be more informed, or for decision-making to be more decentralized.[23]

Those committed to ideals of democratic participation on both the right and the left of the political spectrum may advocate the harnessing of new technologies to such ends. Without adequate access to modern means of communication, any idea of a just political community is indeed a chimera. But a number of important questions are raised by this, not least how the necessary telecommunications infrastructure is to be set up. While France is establishing a national *télématique* system which could in principle serve such ends, Britain has experienced some difficulties persuading domestic subscribers to pay for a suitable cable television network, whereas in the USA only local experimental systems have been tried. In the absence of a coherent policy which is intended to ensure equal access of all to such a communications network it is difficult to imagine how dreams of electronic democracy could be translated into realities.

The prominent source of anxiety, however, is the threat of an Orwellian society. Does the widespread political and administrative use of extensive databases which allow for the easy storage, retrieval and transmission of personal information portend a future fraught with the dangers of electronic eavesdropping? On the one hand police, defence, social security and other personnel reassure the public that no innocent person need have any worries about improper prying into their private lives. On the other, cases of wrongful dismissal or arrest which are traced to erroneous computer files serve to fuel fears that in fact 'ordinary citizens' may well be at risk.

But are these computerized forms of surveillance an intrinsically new departure? Or do they rather represent an extension of state garnering of information on citizens which has been occurring for many decades? Is it merely the use of these databases by law-and-order agencies which creates potential perils for citizens? Or is a deeper process at work in which more generalized forces of social control achieve more power by computerization? And what exactly are the risks involved, against which 'data protection' laws and policies are directed? Is wrongful arrest the tip of an iceberg, the submerged portion of which conceals a fundamental issue of invaded privacy and impugned integrity?

This, of course, is only one aspect of the state-and-IT connection. As I have already mentioned, the connections between government activity and economic-technological developments are numerous and significant. Whereas postindustrialist Bell insisted upon the relatively independent operation of economic and political spheres, this position is exceedingly hard to justify. It is quite clear that polity and economy are interdependent, and that the relationship between the two is far from simple.

Bringing the global situation into focus, however, other connections between the political and the economic become clear. The IT industry, as others, is dominated by giant transnational corporations – IBM, Exxon, Mitsubishi, AT&T, Philips, Siemens and so on – which often call the political tune. Many countries find their national sovereignty, not to mention the position of their workers, threatened by the activities of these 'stateless' economic interests. Such companies increasingly rely upon the free flow of data across national boundaries for financial reporting and management, marketing, distribution, R&D, and order processing.

Labour unions may debate the future of plants in vain if the crucial decisions are made on another continent. National governments may find their attempts to change direction thwarted, as when in 1985 Australian prime minister Bob Hawke tried to stop Australian bases being used to monitor MX missile tests. Dismayed financial and transnational corporate interests withdrew capital, putting pressure on the economy and thus the government.[24] It would appear that Walter Wriston (who seems not to treat this as a matter for regret) is right to claim that 'the ancient and basic concept of sovereignty which has been discussed since the time of Plato is being profoundly changed by information technology'.[25]

Of course it is not only the national sovereignty of the larger and more powerful countries which is challenged by the power of transnational corporations. The phenomenon of 'deindustrialization', for example, often viewed in the northern hemisphere in terms of the shrinking proportion of the labour force involved in manufacturing, may be equally well understood as the partial relocation of workers to 'offshore' plants in the south. The information society is not inaccurately depicted as a global phenomenon. The current expansion and development of microelectronics-related industries require a world market.

There is no doubt that the technological potential for beneficial change – 'deserts that bloom' – is tremendous, and nothing [here] should be taken as denying or minimizing that fact. Tom Stonier, Alvin Toffler and Jacques Servan-Schreiber make a lot of this angle. Stonier reports great gains made in the Upper Volta village of Tangaye when a solar photovoltaic-powered grain mill and water pump were installed.[26] (This is an example of what he calls the 'second silicon revolution'.) Such advances, he states correctly, are dependent on technology and information transfer. That such changes will take place and that 'the postindustrial economy will produce the wealth of information to make it all happen' is rather more open to question.

At present, as a matter of fact, things are somewhat different. Despite dreams of poorer countries 'catching up' with richer ones, or 'leap-frogging' the industrial era, the situation is overwhelmingly not just one of interdependence, but of dependence. While the advanced societies produce silicon chips comprising hundreds of thousands of elements, in Africa only one person in eighteen has a radio. Far from narrowing the 'North-South' divide, the evidence suggests that IT helps to widen it. As Juan Rada sagely observes, 'Technological fixes of whatever nature are nothing but a drop of water in the sea of reality'.[27]

No treatment of the political and global aspects of IT can afford to ignore the connections between new technology and the continuing Cold War. Like earlier postindustrialists, Stonier's focus is on the 'wealth of information' that spells 'unprecedented affluence both at the private level and in the public sector'.[28] But as Krishan Kumar laconically notes, 'the science-based "welfare" state can be rapidly reclassified as the science-based "warfare" state, and with greater respect for the actual history of the last fifty years'.[29]

For example, the Japanese 'Fifth Generation' computer project, which aims to introduce the world to ordinary language-recognizing 'artificial intelligence' during the 1990s, is ostensibly civil and commercial. But American responses relate to military supremacy. As Feigenbaum and McCorduck put it, 'the Defense Department needs the ability to shape technology to conform to its needs in military systems. A Fujitsu or a Hirachi marches to a different drummer from a Rockwell or a Lockheed. Our defense industry must obtain and retain a strong position in the new advanced computer technologies.'[30] It goes without saying that these are not the kinds of 'needs' which those concerned for a 'welfare state' – or world welfare – have in mind.

An information culture?

The notion of a 'fifth generation' of computers raises another set of questions besides those of military prowess. Unlike previous technological artifacts which typically have augmented human energy with improved sources of power, those spawned by IT augment – and, according to some, transcend – the human capacity to think and to reason. Needless to say, some references to machine intelligence are no more sophisticated than those associated with Hal, the 'thinking' computer from the film *2001, A Space Odyssey*. Others, however, are pointers to a series of profound cultural issues whose analysis could have far-reaching implications.

It must be said, though, that while debate over the workplace and employment aspects of IT is widespread, and awareness of the political and global dimensions is beginning to make itself felt, the cultural questions have not as yet received the attention they deserve. In what follows, therefore, I can do no more than set the scene.

Once again, Bell's thoughts on postindustrial culture make a suitable starting point. For him, 'a new kind of modernity' has been created by the 'revolutions in transportation and communication that have banded together the world society into one great *Oikoumene*'. It represents a break with the past, thus replacing continuity with variety, tradition with syncretism. Its agent is technology which by 'introducing a new metric and enlarging our control over nature' has 'transformed our social relationships and our ways of looking at the world'.[31]

Bell maintains that technology has been the 'chief engine' of raised living standards and reduced inequalities, created a 'new class' of engineers and technicians who plan work-tasks rather than actually performing them, brought about a new functional and quantitative way of thinking, created 'new economic dependencies and new social interactions', and altered aesthetic perceptions of time and space. While he believes that cultural issues are of the utmost importance, he partially disconnects analysis of them from political or social life. Each sphere has a different 'axial principle'; that of contemporary culture being the desire for fulfilment and enhancement of the self.[32]

Of course, when writing of postindustrialism (in the 1960s) Bell could have had little clear idea of the rapidity with which the technologies of computing and telecommunications would move to centre stage (hence his later work on the information society). But other theorists have taken further these kinds of ideas about the relation of IT to culture. Where Bell limited himself to comments about concepts of 'speed' or the 'view from the air' unknown to pre-moderns, writers such as David Bolter have argued that the computer itself is the harbinger of novel cultural transformations including a new human sense of self.[33]

Bolter's argument is as follows. Just as the clock is the key symbol of the industrial era, as Lewis Mumford rightly held, so the computer is becoming the key symbol of the present. It is a 'defining technology' which by its impact on certain basic relationships – of knowledge to technical power, and mankind to the world of nature – occupies 'a special place in our cultural landscape'.[34] Thus humans begin to think of themselves as 'information processors' and nature as 'information to be processed'.[35]

Sceptical eyebrows may well be raised about such speculations. Are not those who define themselves as information processors likely to be only a tiny minority of a given population? By what process does the computer become a defining technology? Bolter's thesis is well worth attending to, though not, I shall argue, for the reasons he gives.

Three issues concerning the 'culture of information' are outlined here. First, I draw together questions about computing and telecommunications; the fact of technological 'convergence' is a significant one. While Bell's idea of the 'overflowing of all the world's traditions of art, music and literature into a new, universal container, accessible to all and obligatory upon all'[36] is somewhat inflated, it does flag an important phenomenon. A form of cultural 'synchronization' is indeed taking place, as new communications carrying essentially similar messages encircle the globe.[37] Who controls these messages, and what is their content? Does the ownership of the means of (increasingly computerized) communication lead to the cultural dominance of certain elite groups and societies over others?

Secondly, is the 'defining technology' idea an appropriate means of social and cultural analysis? Are the emerging technologies of information and communication indeed shaping the social and cultural experience of those societies affected by them? Do the new technologies not confer on those with access to them considerable power to control not only the processes of production, about which Marx was concerned, but also those of leisure and consumption? Is there more than passing significance in the rise of 'hackers' and computer gamesters, who get totally absorbed in their machines, or in the ways that computers may 'converse' with each other about human destinies (I am thinking of credit-worthiness or welfare-eligibility)?[38]

Thirdly, consideration of the so-called culture of information is incomplete without reference to its religious and ideological aspects. Do human beings remake themselves in the image of their technology? If so, then there are obvious implications for philosophical debates about the unique place of human beings in the cosmos. Furthermore, there is scope for critique along 'religious' lines, as evidenced by the denunciation of IT as 'silicon idolatry'.[39] It also brings us back, finally, to the over-riding question of this study: does IT usher us into a new kind of society? And at this point a further query is highlighted: what is the social *meaning* of the 'information society'? Is it better understood as a kind of 'myth' or 'utopia' than the social 'forecast' it is more frequently taken to be?

Critique of the information society

For the sake of clarity, and oversimplifying, let me make some distinctions. There are two kinds of information society thesis, each of which makes two kinds of claims. The view popularized in many media and policy accounts stresses the major social changes for the better that follow in the wake of IT.

This popular version may well be buttressed by the 'findings of social science'. The other use of the information society concept is more cautious and open-ended. Here it is a 'problematic' rather than a descriptive term. The two images of information society overlap.

The claims made are both analytical and evaluative, and the two kinds of claim are interrelated. Thus both kinds of information society thesis try to anticipate the *sorts of social change* which can be expected as IT is diffused through different economic, political and cultural spheres. And both also provide at least strong clues as to whether such social changes are *desirable*. This book draws together evidence from a wide range of sources in an attempt to assess both the analytical and evaluative claims of each information society thesis.

The information society idea has both utopian and ideological aspects. I discuss there in the final chapter, but to put things in focus I comment on some of the dangers associated with using the information society concept, that is, its ideological aspects. Three are prominent.

Firstly, it obscures vested interests that are involved in IT and that in fact do much to shape its overall direction. The concept yields no clues as to who wields power. Repeatedly, for instance, the popular rhetoric assures us that 'everyone can own information' or 'the real revolution is personal computer ownership'. But information is not steadily diffused in a general way through all social echelons. As Cees Hamelink points out, some information is specialist and thus restricted to a few.[40] Intellectual and managerial skills are required to exploit information economically, and these are unevenly distributed in society. Advanced hardware and software for information processing are expensive, and therefore the few who can afford them are scarcely challenged by others using inferior machines.

Such inequalities are felt globally between north and south in the theatre of transnational corporations and military interests, and locally, whether with the word-processor operator's lack of control over her work or the suspected criminal's difficulty in gaining access to information held about him. 'Information power' is only a reality when access exists to the means of collecting, storing, retrieving and communicating the information.

Secondly, the inequalities and conflicts discernible on the surface are often related to underlying contradictions. These too may be disguised by the information society concept. Within capitalism, private gain is constantly set against efforts to 'socialize' production. In the late twentieth century, the latent potential for trade in information – for this entity to become a commodity – is being realized. While many undoubtedly gain from this process, others lose. Public libraries and public service broadcasting are both time-honoured concepts whose 'public' status is under threat as information has a price put on it. Likewise, new integrated services digital networks (ISDNs) mean more efficient information services, but higher costs for ordinary telephone subscribers.

Another discordant element, which may not qualify as a 'contradiction' in the same sense, is the collusion of military with microelectronic interests in the modern world. The same technologies whose avowed purposes (and actual achievement in many cases) are to reduce drudgery, increase efficiency, conserve resources and promote mutual communication are also dedicated to hostile, destructive and lethal ends. Regardless of any justifications which may legitimately be presented for expanding electronically a nation's 'defence' capabilities, most discussions of the information society conceal in the background the huge military impetus to IT research and development.

Thirdly, the arrival of the information society appears as an entirely natural event, the outcome of progressive tendencies within Western industrial societies. It may be 'revolutionary' in its consequences, such that it represents a new era in human history. But it is simultaneously the obvious and logical way forward. Witness the postures struck against any who dare question the ways in which IT is implemented! The chairman of the British Manpower Services Commission provided a clear illustration in a 1986 speech which recommended 'embracing wholeheartedly the new technologies'. He complained that 'We still have latter-day Luddites around in all parts of our society. They threaten our future, and the attitudes they reflect must go.'[41]

Very extravagant claims are often made for IT – 'Athens without the slaves' and so on – which suggest that the aura surrounding new technology is not merely that of the 'gee-whiz' variety. Perhaps, as Jacques Ellul and others have suggested,[42] new technologies are invested with a 'sacred' quality. The awe and veneration once accorded to the gods who supposedly controlled human destinies now belong to the machine. This dimension – which Michael Shallis refers to as 'silicon idolatry' – would tend to reinforce views of the information society as the obvious scenario.

Against the backdrop of the well-established Western belief in social progress via unlimited economic accumulation, the information society does indeed appear as a natural development. Information technology is its sacred guarantor. But granting it this 'natural' status forecloses debate over and action towards any alternatives to that dominant tendency. As such, it invites critique.

By arguing that the information society has significant ideological aspects I do not for a moment want to suggest that it is some kind of 'dominant ideology', accepted by the 'masses' of any given population.[43] On the contrary, there is plenty of evidence of coolness, fear and resignation towards, as well as sober and realistic acceptance of, the new technologies. Likewise it should be stressed that using the term 'ideological' does not mean that there is a deliberate conspiracy to 'deceive the general public' by using the information society slogan. If the above analysis is correct, however, the *effect* of using it is to disguise the reality of powerful interests and beliefs at work within it.

On the other hand, it is clear that notions like the information society have become a working 'reality' for many. Educational institutions meekly fall in line with pleas for closer ties with industry. Businesses do computerize, some most successfully, some soon discovering they are encumbered with digital white elephants. As Jennifer Slack admits. 'We are buying computers to have fun and to "keep up". And our children who do not learn to operate computers are "falling behind". And information is being developed to be bought and sold and protected like any other kind of commodity. And it *does* make a certain amount of "good sense" to try to "get by" in that world.'[44] The point is not to deny that it is happening, but rather to examine how it is orchestrated and by whom, to what purpose, and with what methods and effects.

Beyond liberal and Luddite critique

Just as there are different images of the information society, so critique comes from different angles. What might be called 'liberal' critiques, while refusing to be seduced by the siren songs of high-tech hype, still assume that 'things could go either way'. They issue warnings about the anti-social potential of some IT applications, but maintain that as long as people are alert to them, effective choices can be made to ensure that IT development will be appropriate and socially beneficial. For them, the information society is the outcome of an informed democratic process.

The Luddite would retort quickly that the liberal seems to have swallowed the idea of technological neutrality. The new technologies already express particular values and priorities. Far from choices being relatively free, they are in fact tightly constrained by dominant interest groups, above all by the power of capital. As for being 'informed', this is a sick joke. By insisting on the neutrality of technology, those dominant interests ensure that its 'real' effects and biases are effectively obscured. Thus the exposure of those dominant interests is of prime importance, before any choices can be made.

In so far as it stresses the importance of choice, and therefore of value, priorities and democratic participation, the liberal critique makes a valid contribution. Such an emphasis is a vital antidote to any technological determinism that forecasts that future society will be shaped by new technologies or that ignores social factors in technical change. On the other hand, the Luddite is correct to temper this by drawing attention to the ways in which choice is limited, often severely and systematically, by social, political and economic definition. But the negative image of Luddism is hard to live down. Luddism can be as pessimistic as the popular information society pundits are optimistic.[45] Their future may be similarly foreclosed.

The kind of critique to which [I aspire] catches both the sense of potential for socially appropriate development of IT without pretending that it can occur without considerable struggle on several fronts, and the sober realism of the Luddite, without succumbing to sheer negativism or pessimism. I do not hide the fact that some alternatives with which I have sympathy – such as partnership between women and men from the design stage onwards, or innovations originating from users' needs rather than mere commercial potential – represents a radical departure from present practice. By placing them in the context of a normative and critical social analysis, however, I hope to show both the enormity of the obstacles to be overcome, and possible routes to their realization.

The yawning credibility gap between futuristic forecasts and fantasies and the hard realities of government, transnational and military involvement in IT demands a sense of urgency within the information society problematic. It also points up a vital role for serious social analysis within the policy-making process, analysis which is not simply shut up within either optimistic or pessimistic societies.

Notes

1. Steve Wozniak, *Equinox* (Channel 4 (TV), November 1986).
2. NEDO, *Crisis Facing Information Technology* (London, National Economic Development Office, August 1984).
3. Christopher Evans, *Mighty Micro: Impact of the Computer Revolution* (London, Gollancz, 1982); Geoffrey Simons, *Silicon Shock* (Oxford, Basil Blackwell, 1985); John Wicklein, *Electronic Nightmare: The Home Communications Set and Your Freedom* (Boston MA, Beacon Press, 1981); Ian Reinecke, *Electronic Illusions* (Harmondsworth, Penguin, 1984).
4. James Martin, *The Wired Society* (Harmondsworth, Penguin, 1978).
5. Alvin Toffler, *The Third Wave* (London, Pan, 1980).
6. Science Council of Canada, *Planning Now for the Information Society: Tomorrow Is Too Late* (Ottawa, Science Council, 1982).
7. Daniel Bell, *The Coming of Postindustrial Society: A Venture in Social Forecasting* (Harmondsworth, Penguin, 1974), p. 14.
8. Daniel Bell, 'The Social Framework of the Information Society', in Tom Forester, ed., *The Microelectronics Revolution* (Oxford, Basil Blackwell, 1980), and also in Michael Dertouzos and Joel Moses, eds., *The Computer Age: A Twenty Year View* (Cambridge MA, MIT Press, 1980).
9. Bell, 'Social Framework', p. 533.
10. Bell, 'Social Framework', p. 545.
11. Alain Touraine, *La Société post-industrielle* (Paris, Editions Denoïl, 1969); English translation, *The Postindustrial Society* (London, Wildwood House, 1974).
12. Touraine, *Postindustrial Society*, pp. 28, 61.
13. Mark Poster, *Foucault, Marxism and history* (Cambridge, Polity Press, 1984), p. 168.
14. Tom Stonier, *The Wealth of Information* (London, Thames-Methuen, 1983), p. 202.
15. Martin, *Wired Society*, p. 4.
16. Stonier, *Wealth of Information*, p. 202.
17. Jean Voge, 'The New Economic Information Order', in *International Information Economy Handbook* (Springfield VA, Transnational Data Reporting Service, 1985), pp. 39–40.
18. Philip Abrams, *Historical Sociology* (Shepton Mallet, Open Books, 1982), p. xv.
19. Marc Porat, *The Information Economy: Definition and Measurement* (Washington DC, US Government Printing Office, 1977).
20. Krishan Kumar, *Prophecy and Progress: The Sociology of Industrial and Postindustrial Society* (Harmondsworth, Penguin, 1978).
21. Patrick Dawson and Ian McLoughlin, 'Computer Technology and the Redefinition of Supervision: A Study of the Effects of Computers on Railway Freight Supervisors', *Journal of Management Studies*, 23 (1), 116–32.

22. This phrase comes from Ian Miles and Jonathan Gershuny, 'The Social Economics of Information Technology', in Marjorie Ferguson, ed., *New Communications Technologies and the Public Interest* (London and Beverly Hills, Sage, 1986).

23. See, for instance, Ben Barber, *Strong Democracy* (Berkeley CA: University of California Press, 1984).

24. This example comes from Herbert Schiller, 'The Erosion of National Sovereignty', in Michael Traber, ed., *The Myth of the Information Revolution* (London and Beverly Hills, Sage, 1986), p. 28.

25. Quoted in Schiller, 'Erosion of National Sovereignty', p. 23.

26. Stonier, *Wealth of Information*, p. 73. See also Toffler, *The Third Wave* and Jacques Servan-Schrieber, *Le Défi mondial* (Paris, Fayard, 1980).

27. Juan Rada, 'A Third World Perspective', in Günter Friedrichs and Adam Schaff, eds., *Microelectronics and Society: For Better or for Worse* (London, Pergamon, 1982), p. 216.

28. Stonier, *Wealth of Information*, p. 32.

29. Kumar, *Prophecy and Progress*, p. 229.

30. Edward Feigenbaum and Pamela McCorduck, *The Fifth Generation* (London, Pan, 1984), p. 289.

31. Bell, *Coming of Postindustrial Society*, p. 188.

32. Bell, *Coming of Postindustrial Society*, pp. 114–15.

33. David Bolte, *Turing's Man: Western Culture in the Computer Age* (London, Duckworth; Chapel Hill, University of North Carolina Press, 1984).

34. Bolter, *Turing's Man*, pp. 8–9.

35. Bolter, *Turing's Man*, p. 13.

36. Bell, *Coming of Postindustrial Society*, p. 188.

37. See Cees Hamelink, *Cultural Autonomy in Global Communications* (New York, Longman, 1983).

38. Such issues are raised by Mark Poster in *Foucault, Marxism and History*.

39. See Michael Shallis, *The Silicon Idol* (Oxford, Oxford University Press, 1984).

40. Cees Hamelink, 'Is There Life after the Information Revolution?', in Traber, *The Myth of the Information Revolution*.

41. Bryan Nicholson's speech, recorded in the *Guardian*, 16 September 1986.

42. Jacques Ellul, *The New Demons* (Londons, Mowbray, 1976) or Shallis, *The Silicon Idol*.

43. See Nicholas Abercrombie and John Urry, *The Dominant Ideology Thesis* (London, Allen & Unwin, 1980).

44. Jennifer Daryl Slack, 'The Information Revolution as Ideology', *Media, Culture and Society*, 6 (1984), p. 250.

45. Pessimistic statements of Luddism include David Noble, 'Present Tense Technology', *Democracy*, Spring (8–24), Summer (70–82) and Fall (71–93), and Shallis, *The Silicon Idol*.

Questions

1 In this extract, Lyon refers to Bolter's comment (see reference below) that the computer is a 'defining technology' which gives us a different sense of self in relation to each other, to information and to nature. What impact have new technologies had on our social relations? Do you think that a different kind of society

is emerging from the ones preceding it, as a result of communications and information technologies?

2   Lyon believes that 'public' institutions (e.g. public libraries, the public broadcasting system etc.) are in danger of losing their public status because information
has a price tag. To what extent do you think that we will have to buy our cultural
capital in the future (including information and entertainment resources) and
who, if anyone, is likely to be classed as culturally impoverished?

3   Central to the arguments put forward in this extract are the notions of 'knowledge' and 'information', and they are frequently used in conjunction or interchangeably. What do you consider to be the differences between the two terms,
and does an 'information rich' society necessarily guarantee that its individual
citizens are more knowledgeable?

Further reading

Bolter, D. 1984: *Turing's man: Western culture in the computer age*. London:
Duckworth.

Cockburn, C. and Furst-Dilic, R. 1994: *Bringing technology home: gender and technology in a changing Europe*. Buckingham: Open University Press.

Forester, T. 1980: *The microelectronics revolution*. Oxford: Basil Blackwell.

Heap, N., Thomas, R., Einon, G., Mason, R. and Mackay, H. 1994: *Information technology and society: a reader*. London: Sage.

Murdock, G. 1990: Television and citizenship: in defence of public broadcasting. In
Tomlinson, A. (ed.), *Consumption, identity and style*. London: Routledge.

36

Disinformocracy   Howard Rheingold

From *The virtual community: surfing the Internet* (Minerva 1994)

This extract was chosen for a number of reasons: it introduces two important, and in
many senses oppositional, philosophical ideas: one – public sphere – based on a belief
in openness, democracy and the public good; the other – the panopticon – founded on
notions of isolation, inequality and social control. Furthermore, in relating these concepts
to new information and communications technologies, Rheingold continues the discourses of democracy and power which were introduced by Keighron (Section 4, reading 30),
Goodwin (4, 31), Morley (5, 34) and Lyon (5, 35).

Like these authors, Rheingold challenges the notion of technology being intrinsically
democratic and an opportunity for widespread citizen involvement, and states that the
deterioration of the public sphere, brought about by the rise of the mass media and the
commodification of politics, privacy and knowledge, has had a dramatic impact on our
sense of equality and participation. For Rheingold, reasoned discussion and informed

debate have been subsumed by the omnipresence of television, and the growth in new media and communications technologies will further erode authentic discourse as the consumer society takes hold, public participation is replaced by commercial desire and life becomes one long media event.

Rheingold's pessimistic predictions for future democracy continue with his comments on privacy and surveillance. According to Rheingold, Bentham's plans for an architectural construction which he named the panopticon, and Foucault's subsequent appropriation of the structure as an ideological concept, further demonstrate the potential of new technologies as instruments of power and social control; as an idea, Bentham's prison tower was a blueprint for future surveillance technologies which would allow a small, unseen few to control the lives of large numbers of people. This gloomy scenario extends to computer databases and encryption technologies, and Rheingold raises a number of important points about who has access to this kind of information and for what purposes it is used. Like other writers in this section, Rheingold believes that the solution to the problems presented to us in this reading is to reject the technological determinism which has characterised so many of the debates about new media, and to take control of the technology to aid the democratic process and strengthen communities rather than fragment them.

The selling of democracy: commodification and the public sphere

There is an intimate connection between informal conversations, the kind that take place in communities and virtual communities, in the coffee shops and computer conferences, and the ability of large social groups to govern themselves without monarchs or dictators. This social-political connection shares a metaphor with the idea of cyberspace, for it takes place in a kind of virtual space that has come to be known by specialists as the public sphere.

Here is what the preeminent contemporary writer about the public sphere, social critic and philosopher Jurgen Habermas (1984), had to say about the meaning of this abstraction:

> By 'public sphere,' we mean first of all a domain of our social life in which such a thing as public opinion can be formed. Access to the public sphere is open in principle to all citizens. A portion of the public sphere is constituted in every conversation in which private persons come together to form a public. They are then acting neither as business or professional people conducting their private affairs, nor as legal consociates subject to the legal regulations of a state bureaucracy and obligated to obedience. Citizens act as a public when they deal with matters of general interest without being subject to coercion; thus with the guarantee that they may assemble and unite freely, and express and publicize their opinions freely.

In this definition, Habermas formalized what people in free societies mean when we say 'The public wouldn't stand for that' or 'It depends on public opinion.' And he drew attention to the intimate connection between this web of free, informal, personal communications and the foundations of democratic society. People can govern themselves only if they communicate widely, freely, and in groups – publicly. The First Amendment of the U.S. Constitution's Bill of Rights protects citizens from government interference in their communications – the rights of speech, press, and assembly are communication rights. Without those rights, there is no public sphere. Ask any citizen of Prague, Budapest, or Moscow.

Because the public sphere depends on free communication and discussion of ideas, as soon as your political entity grows larger than the number of citizens you can fit into a modest town hall, this vital marketplace for political ideas can be powerfully influenced by changes in communications technology. According to Habermas,

> When the public is large, this kind of communication requires certain means of dissemination and influence; today, newspapers and periodicals, radio and television are the media of the public sphere.... The term 'public opinion' refers to the functions of criticism and control or organized state authority that the public exercises informally, as well as formally during periodic elections. Regulations concerning the publicness (or publicity [Publizitat] in its original meaning) of state-related activities, as, for instance, the public accessibility required of legal proceedings, are also connected with this function of public opinion. To the public sphere as a sphere mediating between state and society, a sphere in which the public as the vehicle of publicness – the publicness that once had to win out against the secret politics of monarchs and that since then has permitted democratic control of state activity.

Ask anybody in China about the right to talk freely among friends and neighbors, to own a printing press, to call a meeting to protest government policy, or to run a BBS [Bulletin Board System]. But brute totalitarian seizure of communications technology is not the only way that political powers can neutralize the ability of citizens to talk freely. It is also possible to alter the nature of discourse by inventing a kind of paid fake discourse. If a few people have control of what goes into the daily reporting of the news, and those people are in the business of selling advertising, all kinds of things become possible for those who can afford to pay.

Habermas had this to say about the corrupting influence of ersatz public opinion:

> Whereas at one time publicness was intended to subject persons or things to the public use of reason and to make political decisions subject to revision before the tribunal of public opinion, today it has often enough already been enlisted in the aid of the secret policies of interest groups; in the form of 'publicity' it now acquires public prestige for persons or things and renders them capable of acclamation in a climate of nonpublic opinion. The term 'public relations' itself indicates how a public sphere that formerly emerged from the structure of society must now be produced circumstantially on a case-by-case basis.

The idea that public opinion can be manufactured and the fact that electronic spectacles can capture the attention of a majority of the citizenry damaged the foundations of democracy. According to Habermas,

It is no accident that these concepts of the public sphere and public opinion were not formed until the eighteenth century. They derive their specific meaning from a concrete historical situation. It was then that one learned to distinguish between opinion and public opinion.... Public opinion, in terms of its very idea, can be formed only if a public that engages in rational discussion exists. Public discussions that are institutionally protected and that take, with critical intent, the exercise of political authority as their theme have not existed since time immemorial.

The public sphere and democracy were born at the same time, from the same sources. Now that the public sphere, cut off from its roots, seems to be dying, democracy is in danger, too.

The concept of the public sphere as discussed by Habermas and others includes several requirements for authenticity that people who live in democratic societies would recognize: open access, voluntary participation, participation outside institutional roles, the generation of public opinion through assemblies of citizens who engage in rational argument, the freedom to express opinions, and the freedom to discuss matters of the state and criticize the way state power is organized. Acts of speech and publication that specifically discuss the state are perhaps the most important kind protected by the First Amendment to the U.S. Constitution and similar civil guarantees elsewhere in the world. Former Soviets and Eastern Europeans who regained it after decades of censorship offer testimony that the most important freedom of speech is the freedom to speak about freedoms.

In eighteenth-century America, the Committees of Correspondence were one of the most important loci of the public sphere in the years of revolution and constitution-building. If you look closely at the roots of the American Revolution, it becomes evident that a text-based, horseback-transported version of networking was an old American tradition. In their book *Networking*, Jessica Lipnack and Jeffrey Stamps (1982) describe these committees as

> a communications forum where homespun political and economic thinkers hammered out their ideological differences, sculpting the form of a separate and independent country in North America. Writing to one another and sharing letters with neighbors, this revolutionary generation nurtured its adolescent ideas into a mature politics. Both men and women participated in the debate over independence from England and the desirable shape of the American future ...

> During the years in which the American Revolution was percolating, letters, news-sheets, and pamphlets carried from one village to another were the means by which ideas about democracy were refined. Eventually, the correspondents agreed that the next step in their idea exchange was to hold a face-to-face meeting. The ideas of independence and government had been debated, discussed, discarded, and reformulated literally hundreds of times by the time people in the revolutionary network met in Philadelphia.

> Thus, a network of correspondence and printed broadsides led to the formation of an organization after the writers met in a series of conferences and worked out a statement of purpose – which they called a 'Declaration of Independence.' Little did our early networking grandparents realize that the

result of their youthful idealism, less than two centuries later, would be a global superpower with an unparalleled ability to influence the survival of life on the planet.

As the United States grew and technology changed, the ways in which these public discussions of 'matters of general interest,' as Habermas called them – slavery and the rights of the states versus the power of the federal government were two such matters that loomed large – began to change as well. The text-based media that served as the channel for discourse gained more and more power to reshape the nature of that discourse. The communications media of the nineteenth century were the newspapers, the penny press, the first genera-tion of what has come to be known as the mass media. At the same time, the birth of advertising and the beginnings of the public-relations industry began to undermine the public sphere by inventing a kind of buyable and sellable phony discourse that displaced the genuine kind.

The simulation (and therefore destruction) of authentic discourse, first in the United States, and then spreading to the rest of the world, is what Guy Debord (1992) would call the first quantum leap into the 'society of the spec-tacle' and what Jean Baudrillard (1988) would recognize as a milestone in the world's slide into hyper-reality. Mass media's colonization of civil society turned into a quasi-political campaign promoting technology itself when the image-making technology of television came along. ('Progress is our most important product,' said General Electric spokesman Ronald Reagan, in the early years of television.) And in the twentieth century, as the telephone, radio, and television became vehicles for public discourse, the nature of politi-cal discussion has mutated into something quite different from anything the framers of the Constitution could have foreseen.

A politician is now a commodity, citizens are consumers, and issues are decided via sound-bites and staged events. The television camera is the only spectator that counts at a political demonstration or convention. According to Habermas and others, the way the new media have been commoditized through this evolutionary process from hand-printed broadside to telegraph to penny press to mass media has led to the radical deterioration of the public sphere. The consumer society has become the accepted model both for indi-vidual behavior and political decision-making. Discourse degenerated into publicity, and publicity used the increasing power of electronic media to alter perceptions and shape beliefs.

The consumer society, the most powerful vehicle for generating short-term wealth ever invented, ensures economic growth by first promoting the idea that the way to be is to buy. The engines of wealth depend on a fresh stream of tabloids sold at convenience markets and television programs to tell us what we have to buy next in order to justify our existence. What used to be a channel for authentic communication has become a channel for the updating of commercial desire.

Money plus politics plus network television equals an effective system. It works. When the same packaging skills that were honed on automobile tail fins and fast foods are applied to political ideas, the highest bidder can influence public policy to great effect. What dies in the process is the rational discourse at the base of civil society. That death manifests itself in longings that aren't fulfilled by the right kind of shoes in this month's color or the hot new prime-time candidate everybody is talking about. Some media scholars are claiming a direct causal connection between the success of commercial television and the loss of citizen interest in the political process.

Another media critic, Neal Postman, in his book *Amusing Ourselves to Death* (1985), pointed out that Tom Paine's *Common Sense* sold three hundred thousand copies in five months in 1776. The most successful democratic revolution in history was made possible by a citizenry that read and debated widely among themselves. Postman pointed out that the mass media, and television in particular, had changed the mode of discourse itself, by substituting fast cuts, special effects, and sound-bites for reasoned discussion or even genuine argument.

The various hypotheses about commodification and mode of discourse focus on an area of apparent agreement among social observers who have a long history of heated disagreements.

When people who have become fascinated by BBSs or networks start spreading the idea that such networks are inherently democratic in some magical way, without specifying the hard work that must be done in real life to harvest the fruits of that democratizing power, they run the danger of becoming unwitting agents of commodification. First, it pays to understand how old the idea really is. Next, it is important to realize that the hopes of technophiles have often been used to sell technology for commercial gain. In this sense, CMC [computer-mediated communications] enthusiasts run the risk of becoming unpaid, unwitting advertisers for those who stand to gain financially from adoption of new technology.

The critics of the idea of electronic democracy have unearthed examples from a long tradition of utopian rhetoric that James Carey (1989) has called 'the rhetoric of the "technological sublime."' He put it this way:

> Despite the manifest failure of technology to resolve pressing social issues over the last century, contemporary intellectuals continue to see revolutionary potential in the latest technological gadgets that are pictured as a force outside history and politics.... In modern futurism, it is the machines that possess teleological insight. Despite the shortcomings of town meetings, newspaper, telegraph, wireless, and television to create the conditions of a new Athens, contemporary advocates of technological liberation regularly describe a new postmodern age of instantaneous daily plebiscitory democracy through a computerized system of electronic voting and opinion polling.

Carey was prophetic in at least one regard – he wrote this years before Ross Perot and William Clinton both started talking about their versions of electronic democracy during the 1992 U.S. presidential campaign. If the United States is on the road to a version of electronic democracy in which the president will have electronic town hall meetings, including instant voting-by-telephone to 'go directly to the people' (and perhaps bypass Congress?) on key issues, it is important for American citizens to understand the potential pitfalls of decision-making by plebiscite. Media-manipulated plebiscites as political tools go back to Joseph Goebbels, who used radio so effectively in the Third Reich. Previous experiments in instant home polling and voting had been carried out by Warners, with their Qube service, in the early 1980s. One critic, political scientist Jean Betheke Elshtain (1982), called the television-voting model an

> interactive shell game [that] cons us into believing that we are participating when we are really simply performing as the responding 'end' of a prefabricated system of external stimuli.... In a plebiscitary system, the views of the majority ... swamp minority or unpopular views. Plebiscitism is compatible with authoritarian politics carried out under the guise of, or with the connivance of, majority views. That opinion can be registered by easily manipulated, ritualistic plebiscites, so there is no need for debate on substantive questions.

What does it mean that the same hopes, described in the same words, for a decentralization of power, a deeper and more widespread citizen involvement in matters of state, a great equalizer for ordinary citizens to counter the forces of central control, have been voiced in the popular press for two centuries in reference to steam, electricity, and television? We've had enough time to live with steam, electricity, and television to recognize that they did indeed change the world, and to recognize that the utopia of technological millennarians has not yet materialized.

An entire worldview and sales job are packed into the word *progress*, which links the notion of improvement with the notion of innovation, highlights the benefits of innovation while hiding the toxic side-effects of extractive and lucrative technologies, and then sells more of it to people via television as a cure for the stress of living in a technology-dominated world. The hope that the next technology will solve the problems created by the way the last technology was used is a kind of millennial, even messianic, hope, apparently ever-latent in the breasts of the citizenry. The myth of technological progress emerged out of the same Age of Reason that gave us the myth of representative democracy, a new organizing vision that still works pretty well, despite the decline in vigor of the old democratic institutions. It's hard to give up on one Enlightenment ideal while clinging to another.

I believe it is too early to judge which set of claims will prove to be accurate. I also believe that those who would prefer the more democratic vision of the future have an opportunity to influence the outcome, which is precisely why online activists should delve into the criticisms that have been leveled against them. If electronic democracy advocates can address these critiques successfully, their claims might have a chance. If they cannot, perhaps it would be better not to raise people's hopes. Those who are not aware of the history of dead ends are doomed to replay them, hopes high, again and again.

The idea that putting powerful computers in the hands of citizens will shield the citizenry against totalitarian authorities echoes similar, older beliefs about citizen-empowering technology. As Langdon Winner (an author every computer revolutionary ought to read) put it in his essay 'Mythinformation,'

> Of all the computer enthusiasts' political ideas, there is none more poignant than the faith that the computer is destined to become a potent equalizer in modern society.... Presumably, ordinary citizens equipped with microcomputers will be able to counter the influence of large, computer-based organizations.
>
> Notions of this kind echo beliefs of eighteenth-century revolutionaries that placing fire arms in the hands of the people was crucial to overthrowing entrenched authority. In the American Revolution, French Revolution, Paris Commune, and Russian Revolution the role of 'the people armed' was central to the revolutionary program. As the military defeat of the Paris Commune made clear, however, the fact that the popular forces have guns may not be decisive. In a contest of force against force, the larger, more sophisticated, more ruthless, better equipped competitor often has the upper hand. Hence, the availability of low-cost computing power may move the baseline that defines electronic dimensions of social influence, but it does not necessarily alter the relative balance of power. Using a personal computer makes one no more powerful vis-à-vis, say, the National Security Agency than flying a hang glider establishes a person as a match for the U.S. Air Force. (1986)

The great power of the idea of electronic democracy is that technical trends in communications technologies can help citizens break the monopoly on their attention that has been enjoyed by the powers behind the broadcast paradigm – the owners of television networks, newspaper syndicates, and publishing conglomerates. The great weakness of the idea of electronic democracy is that it can be more easily commodified than explained. The commercialization and commoditization of public discourse is only one of the grave problems posed by the increasing sophistication of communications media. The Net that is a marvelous lateral network can also be used as a kind of invisible yet inescapable cage. The idea of malevolent political leaders with their hands on the controls of a Net raises fear of a more direct assault on liberties.

Caught in the Net: CMC and the ultimate prison

In 1791, Jeremy Bentham proposed, in *Panopticon; or the Inspection House,* that it was possible to build a mechanism for enforcing a system of social control into the physical structure of a building, which he called the Panopticon. His design for this building was intended to be very general, an architectural algorithm that could be used in prisons, schools, and factories. Individual cells are built into the circumference of a circular building, around a central well. An inspection tower atop the well, in conjunction with a method for lighting the cells and leaving the inspection tower dark, made it possible for one person to monitor the activity of many people, each of whom would know he or she was under surveillance, none of whom would know exactly when. And the inspectors are similarly watched by other unseen inspectors. It was precisely this mental state of being seen without being able to see the watcher that Bentham meant to induce. When you can induce that state of mind in a population, you don't need whips and chains to restrain them from rebelling.

Historian and political philosopher Michel Foucault (1977), in *Discipline and Punish*, examined the social institutions by which powerful people control the potentially rebellious masses. Foucault felt that the Panopticon as an idea as well as a specific architectural design was an important one, for it was a literal blueprint for the way future tyrants could use surveillance technologies to wield power. Just as the ability to read and write and freely communicate gives power to citizens that protects them from the powers of the state, the ability to surveil, to invade the citizens' privacy, gives the state the power to confuse, coerce, and control citizens. Uneducated populations cannot rule themselves, but tyrannies can control even educated populations, given sophisticated means of surveillance.

When you think of privacy, you probably think of your right to be undisturbed and possibly unembarrassed by intrusions into your personal affairs. It does not seem, on the surface, to be a politically significant phenomenon. Kevin Robins and Frank Webster (1988), in their article 'Cybernetic Capitalism: Information, Technology, Everyday Life,' made the connection between Bentham, Foucault, and the evolution of the telecommunications network:

> We believe that Foucault is right in seeing Bentham's Panopticon as a significant event in the history of the human mind. We want to suggest that the new communication and information technologies – particularly in the form of an integrated electronic grid – permit a massive extension and transformation of that same (relative, technological) mobilization to which Bentham's Panoptic principle aspired. What these technologies support, in fact, is the same dissemination of power and control, but freed from the architectural constraints of Bentham's stone and brick prototype. On the basis of the 'information revolution,' not just the prison or factory, but the social totality, comes to function as the hierarchical and disciplinary Panoptic machine.

The Panopticon, Foucault warned, comes in many guises. It is not a value-neutral technology. It is a technology that allows a small number of people to control a large number of others. J. Edgar Hoover used it. So did Mao tse-Tung. You don't need fiber optics to institute a surveillance state – but it sure makes surveillance easier when you invite the surveillance device into your home.

Critics of those who pin their hopes for social change on computer technology also point out that information and communications technologies have always been dominated by the military, and will continue to be dominated by the military, police, and intelligence agencies for the foreseeable future. A computer is, was, and will be a weapon. The tool can be used for other purposes, but to be promoted as an instrument of liberation, CMC technology should be seen within the contexts of its origins, and in full cognizance of the possibly horrific future applications by totalitarians who get their hands on it.

The first electronic digital computer was created by the U.S. Army to calculate ballistics equations for artillery. The military and intelligence communities, particularly in the United States, have always benefited from a ten- to twenty-year technological lead on civilian applications of the computer technology. The U.S. National Security Agency, the ultra-secret technosnoop headquarters that applies computers to signals intelligence and codebreaking, and the U.S. National Laboratories at Livermore and Los Alamos, where thermonuclear weapons and antimissile defenses are designed, have long been the owners of the most powerful collections of computing power in the world.

Computer and communications technologies outside the military sphere are applied with great effectiveness by public and private police agencies. One example that I saw with my own eyes is suggestive of the range of goodies available to police forces: at a laboratory outside Tokyo, I saw a video camera on a freeway zero in on the license plate of a speeder, use shape-recognition software to decode the license number, and transmit it to police computers, where a warrant search could be conducted. No human in the loop – the camera and computer determine that a crime has been committed and instantly identify the suspect. Just as grassroots citizens' networks have been interconnecting into a planetary Net, police information networks have been evolving as well. The problem there is that law enforcement officers have the authority to shoot you dead; if they shoot you on the basis of misinformation propagated on a Net (and it is far easier to broadcast bad information than to recall it), the Net helped kill you. Jacques Vallee, in the very beginning of his prophetic 1982 book *The Network Revolution*, told the true cautionary tale of the innocent Frenchmen who died under police gunfire as the result of a glitch in a poorly designed police computer network.

The more spectacularly overt images of a Panoptic society – the midnight knock on the door, the hidden microphones of the secret police – are genuine possibilities worth careful consideration. Now it isn't necessary to plant microphones when a remote and inaudible command can turn any telephone – while it is on the hook – into a microphone. The old scenarios aren't the only ones, now. Privacy has already been penetrated in more subtle, complex ways. This assault on privacy, invisible to most, takes place in the broad daylight of everyday life. The weapons are cash registers and credit cards. When Big Brother arrives, don't be surprised if he looks like a grocery clerk, because privacy has been turning into a commodity, courtesy of better and better information networks, for years.

Yesterday, you might have gone to the supermarket and watched someone total up the bill with a bar code reader. Perhaps you paid with an ATM card or credit card or used one as identification for a check. Last night, maybe the data describing what you bought and who you are were telecommunicated from the supermarket to a central collection point. This morning, detailed information about your buying habits could have been culled from one database and sold to a third party who could compile it tomorrow into another electronic dossier somewhere, one that knows what you buy and where you live and how much money you owe. Next week, a fourth party might purchase that dossier, combine it with a few tens of millions of others on an optical disk, and offer to sell the collection of information as a marketing tool.

All of the information on the hypothetical mass-dossier disk is available from public sources; it is in their compilation, the way that information is sorted into files linked to real citizens, that intrusion is accomplished. On each CD-ROM disk will be a file that knows a lot about your tastes, your brand preferences, your marital status, even your political opinions. If you contributed to a freewheeling Usenet newsgroup, all the better, for your political views, sexual preferences, even the way you think, can now be compiled and compared with the other information in your dossier.

The capabilities of information-gathering and sorting technologies that can harvest and sift mind-numbing quantities of individual trivial but collectively revealing pieces of information are formidable today. This Panoptic machinery shares some of the same communications infrastructure that enables one-room schoolhouses in Montana to communicate with MIT professors, and enables overseas Chinese dissidents to disseminate news and organize resistance. The power to compile highly specific dossiers on millions of people will become even more formidable over the next several years as the cost of computing power drops and the network of electronic transactions becomes more richly interconnected. The commodization of privacy is piggybacking on the same combination of computers and communications that has given birth to virtual communities. The power to snoop has become democratized.

When our individual information terminals become as powerful as supercomputers, and every home is capable of sending and receiving huge amounts of information, you won't need a dictatorship from above to spy on your neighbors and have them spy on you. Instead, you'll sell pieces of each other's individuality to one another. Entrepreneurs are already nibbling around the edges of the informational body politic, biting off small chunks of privacy and marketing it. Information about you and me is valuable to certain people, whether or not we actively choose to disclose that information. We've watched our names migrate from magazine subscription lists to junk mail assaults, but we haven't seen the hardware and software that has evolved for gathering and exploiting private information for profit.

The most insidious attack on our rights to a reasonable degree of privacy might come not from a political dictatorship but from the marketplace. The term 'Big Brother' brings to mind a scenario of a future dictatorship held together by constant electronic surveillance of the citizenry; but today's technologies allow for more subtlety than Orwell could have foreseen. There are better ways to build Panopticons than the heavy-handed Orwellian model. If totalitarian manipulators of populations and technologies actually do achieve dominance in the future, I predict that it will begin not by secret police kicking in your doors but by allowing you to sell yourself to your television and letting your supermarket sell information about your transactions, while outlawing measures you could use to protect yourself. Instead of just telephone taps, the weapons will include computer programs that link bar codes, credit cards, social security numbers, and all the other electronic tell-tales we leave in our paths through the information society. And the most potent weapon will be the laws or absence of laws that enable improper uses of information technology to erode what is left of citizens' rights to privacy.

'Marketplace,' a CD-ROM that contained the collected available information about you, your family, and 120 million other people, was announced in 1991 by Lotus. After public criticism, Lotus decided not to market the product. Interactive television systems are being installed now, systems that allow customers to download videos and upload information about their tastes, preferences, and opinions. With high-speed digital communication capabilities of future fiber-optic networks, there will be even more ways to move information about you from your home to the databases of others, with and without your consent.

Informational dossiers about individuals are marketing gold mines for those who know how to make money by knowing which magazines you subscribe to, what kind of yogurt you eat, and which political organizations you support. Invisible information – your name, address, other demographic information – is already encoded in certain promotional coupons you get in the mail. Ultimately, advertisers will be able to use new technologies to customize the television advertising for each individual household. Advertising agencies, direct mail marketers, and political consultants already know what to do with your zip code, your social security number, and a few other data. These professional privacy brokers have begun to realize that a significant portion of the population would freely allow someone else to collect and use and even sell personal information, in return for payment or subsidies.

Here is one obvious answer to the inequity of access to Net resources and the gap between information-rich and information-poor. Some people would be able to afford to pay for 'enhanced information services.' Others would be able to use those services in exchange for a little information-monitoring. For answering a few questions and allowing certain of your transactions to be monitored, for example, you would be granted a certain number of hours of service, or even paid for the information and the right to use it. Why should anybody go to the trouble of seizing our rights of privacy when so many of us would be happy to sell them?

Selling your privacy is your right, and I'm not suggesting that anyone stop you. In fact, it might be a viable solution to the problems of equity of access. There is, in medicine, the notion of informed consent, however, which obligates your physician to explain to you the risks and potential side effects of recommended medical procedures. I'd like people to know what it is they are giving away in exchange for convenience, rebates, or online hours on the latest MUD [Multi-User Dungeon]. Do people have a right to privacy? Where does that right begin and end? Without adequate protections, the same information that can flow laterally, from citizen to citizen, can be used by powerful central authorities as well as by grassroots groups.

The most important kind of protection for citizens against technology-assisted invasion of privacy is a set of principles that can help preserve individual autonomy in the digital age. Laws, policies, and norms are the various ways in which such principles, once articulated and agreed on, are enforced in a democratic society. But high technology is often very good at rendering laws moot. Another kind of protection for citizens is the subject of current intense scrutiny by cyberspace civil libertarians, a technical fix known as citizen encryption. A combination of principles, laws, policies, and technologies, if intelligently designed and equitably implemented, offer one more hopeful scenario in which citizens can continue to make use of the advantages of the Net without falling victim to its Panoptic potential.

Gary Marx, a professor of sociology at MIT, is an expert on technology and privacy. Marx (1990) suggests that

> an important example of the kind of principles needed is the Code of Fair Information developed in 1973 for the U.S. Department of Health, Education, and Welfare. The code involves five principles:
>
> There must be no personal-data record keeping whose very existence is secret.
>
> There must be a way for a person to find out what information about him is in a record and how it is being used.
>
> There must be a way for a person to prevent information that was obtained for one purpose from being used or made available for other purposes without his consent.
>
> There must be a way for a person to correct or amend a record of identifiable information about himself.
>
> Any organization creating, maintaining, using, or disseminating records of identifiable personal data must assure the reliability of the data for their intended use and must take precautions to prevent misuses of the data.

The highly interconnected, relatively insecure networks, with their millions and billions of bits per second, are a tough environment to enforce rules based on these suggested principles. Many of the nuances of public conferencing or private e-mail or hybrid entities such as e-mail lists will require changes in these principles, but this list is a good way to focus societal debate about values, risks, and liberties. If the profit or power derived from Net-snooping proves to be significant, and the technicalities of the Net make it difficult to track perpetrators, however, no laws will ever adequately protect citizens. That's why a subculture of computer software pioneers known as cypher-punks have been working to make citizen encryption possible.

Encryption is the science of encoding and decoding messages. Computers and codebreaking go back a long way. Alan Turing, one of the intellectual fathers of the computer, worked during World War II on using computational strategies to break the codes created by Germany's Enigma machine. Today, the largest assemblage of computer power in the world is widely acknowledged to be the property of the U.S. National Security Agency, the top-secret contemporary high-tech codebreakers. Computers and mathematical theories are today's most important weapons in the war between codemakers and codebreakers. Like computers themselves, and CMC, the mathematical complexities of encryption have begun to diffuse from the specialists to the citizens.

A tool known as public-key encryption is causing quite a stir these days, not just because it enables citizens to encode messages that their recipients can read but are not readable by even the most computationally powerful codebreakers, but also because citizen encryption makes possible two extremely powerful antipanoptic weapons known as digital cash and digital signature. With digital cash, it is possible to build an electronic economy where the seller can verify that the buyer's credit is good, and transfer the correct amount of money, without the seller knowing who the buyer is. With digital signature, it is possible in the identity-fluid online world to establish certainty about the sender of a message. This has important implications for intellectual property and online publishing, as well as personal security.

Key is a cryptographers' term for the codebook that unlocks a particular code. Until recently, code keys, whether made of metal or mathematical algorithms, were top secret. If someone steals your key, your messages are compromised. Public-key encryption makes use of recent mathematical discoveries that enable a person to keep one key private and distribute to everyone and anyone a public key. If anyone wants to use that person's public key, only the owner of the private key can read the message; both public and private keys are necessary, and the private key cannot be discovered by mathematical operations on the public key. Because encryption is based on precise mathematical principles, it is possible to demonstrate that a particular encryption scheme is inherently strong enough to survive brute-force mathematical assault by powerful supercomputers.

Public-key encryption as it exists today is unbreakable by all but the most powerful computers, such as those owned by the National Security Agency. Policy debate and legal challenges have revolved around citizens' rights to use mathematically unbreakable encryption. The National Security Agency sees this as a security nightmare, when it can no longer do its job of picking strategic signals out of the ether and inspecting them for content that threatens the security of the United States. Certain discoveries in the mathematical foundations of cryptography are automatically classified as soon as a mathematician happens upon them. John Gilmore, one of the founders of the Electronic Frontier Foundation (EFF), recently filed suit against the National Security Agency for its classification and suppression in the United States of fundamental cryptography texts that are undoubtedly known to America's enemies. A few days after Gilmore filed suit and informed the press, the agency astonished everybody by declassifying the documents.

Think of digital cash as a kind of credit card that allows you to spend whatever credit you legitimately have without leaving a personal identifier linked to the transaction. The same techniques could be used to render other aspects of personal information – medical and legal records – far less vulnerable to abuse. Different applications of encryption technology already are being considered as safeguards against different kinds of panoptic danger. But ubiquitous encryption poses important problems: will citizen encryption, by making it impossible for any individual or group to crack encrypted messages, give the upper hand to criminals and terrorists, or will it force law enforcement and intelligence agencies to shift resources away from signals intelligence (monitoring communications) and into other, possibly even more invasive surveillance techniques? The impact of citizen encryption, for good or ill, looms as one of those unexpected applications of higher mathematics – like nuclear fission – that has the potential to change everything. There's still time to talk about it.

The third school of criticism builds on the foundation of commodification of the public sphere but veers off into a somewhat surrealistic dimension. Highly abstruse works of contemporary philosophy, much of it originating in France, have been proposing certain ideas about the psychological and social effects of previous communications technologies that raise disturbing resonances with the nature of CMC technologies.

The hyper-realists

Hyper-realists see the use of communications technologies as a route to the total replacement of the natural world and the social order with a technologically mediated hyper-reality, a 'society of the spectacle' in which we are not even aware that we work all day to earn money to pay for entertainment media that tell us what to desire and which brand to consume and which politician to believe. We don't see our environment as an artificial construction that uses media to extract our money and power. We see it as 'reality' – the way things are. To hyper-realists, CMC, like other communications technologies of the past, is doomed to become another powerful conduit for disinfotainment. While a few people will get better information via high-bandwidth supernetworks, the majority of the population, if history is any guide, are likely to become more precisely befuddled, more exactly manipulated. Hyper-reality is what you get when a Panopticon evolves to the point where it can convince everyone that it doesn't exist; people continue to believe they are free, although their power has disappeared.

Televisions, telephones, radios, and computer networks are potent political tools because their function is not to manufacture or transport physical goods but to influence human beliefs and perceptions. As electronic entertainment has become increasingly 'realistic,' it has been used as an increasingly power-ful propaganda device. The most radical of the hyper-realist political critics charge that the wonders of communications technology skillfully camouflage the disappearance and subtle replacement of true democracy – and everything else that used to be authentic, from nature to human relationships – with a simulated, commercial version. The illusion of democracy offered by CMC utopians, according to these reality critiques, is just another distraction from the real power play behind the scenes of the new technologies – the replace-ment of democracy with a global mercantile state that exerts control through the media-assisted manipulation of desire rather than the more orthodox means of surveillance and control. Why torture people when you can get them to pay for access to electronic mind control?

During the events of May 1968, when students provoked a revolt in the streets of Paris against the Gaullist regime, a radical manifesto surfaced, writ-ten by Guy Debord. *The Society of the Spectacle* made a startling tangential leap from what McLuhan was saying at around the same time. Cinema, televi-sion, newspapers, Debord proclaimed, were all part of a worldwide hegemony of power in which the rich and powerful had learned to rule with minimal force by turning everything into a media event. The staged conventions of the political parties to anoint politicians who had already been selected behind closed doors were a prominent example, but they were only part of a web of headlines, advertisements, and managed events.

The replacement of old neighborhoods with modern malls, and cafés with fast-food franchises, was part of this 'society of the spectacle,' precisely because they help destroy the 'great good places' where the public sphere lives. More than twenty years later, Debord looked back and emphasized this aspect of his earlier forecasts:

> For the agora, the general community, has gone, along with communities restricted to intermediary bodies or to independent institutions, to salons or cafés, or to workers in a single company. There is no place left where people can discuss the realities which concern them, because they can never lastingly free themselves from the crushing presence of media discourse and of the various forces organized to relay it.... What is false creates taste, and reinforces itself by knowingly eliminating any possible reference to the authentic. And what is gen-uine is reconstructed as quickly as possible, to resemble the false.

Another French social critic, Jean Baudrillard, has been writing since the 1960s about the increasingly synthetic nature of technological civilization and a culture that has been irrevocably tainted by the corruption of our symbolic systems. This analysis goes deeper than the effects of media on our minds; Baudrillard claims to track the degeneration of meaning itself. In Baudrillard's historical analysis, human civilization has changed itself in three major stages, marked by the changes in meaning we invest in our symbol systems. More specifically, Baudrillard focused on the changing relationship between *signs* (such as alphabetical characters, graphic images) and *that which they signify*. The word *dog* is a sign, and English-speakers recognize that it refers to, signifies, a living creature in the material world that barks and has fleas. According to Baudrillard, during the first step of civilization, when speech and then writing were created, signs were invented *to point to reality*. During the second step of civilization, which took place over the past century, advertising, propaganda, and commodification set in, and the sign begins *to hide reality*. The third step includes our step into the hyper-real, for now we are in an age when signs begin *to hide the absence of reality*. Signs now help us pretend that they mean something.

Technology and industry, in Baudrillard's view, succeeded over the past century in satisfying basic human needs, and thus the profit-making apparatus that controlled technology-driven industry needed to fulfill desires instead of needs. The new media of radio and television made it possible to keep the desire level of entire populations high enough to keep a consumer society going. The way this occurs has to do with sign systems such as tobacco commercials that link the brand name of a cigarette to a beautiful photograph of a sylvan scene. The brand name of a cigarette is woven into a fabric of manufactured signifiers that can be changed at any time. The realm of the hyper-real. Virtual communities will fit very neatly into this cosmology, if it turns out that they offer the semblance of community but lack some fundamental requirement for true community.

Baudrillard's vision reminded me of another dystopian prophecy from the beginning of the twentieth century, E. M. Forster's chilling tale 'The Machine Stops.' The story is about a future world of billions of people, each of whom lives in a comfortable multimedia chamber that delivers necessities automatically, dispenses of wastes, and links everyone in the world into marvelously stimulating web of conversations. The only problem is that people long ago forgot that they were living in a machine. The title of the story describes the dramatic event that gives the plot momentum. Forster and Baudrillard took the shadow side of telecommunications and considered it in light of the human capacity for illusion. They are both good cautionary mythmakers, marking the borders of the pitfalls of global, high-bandwidth networks and multimedia virtual communities.

Virtual communitarians, because of the nature of our medium, must pay for our access to each other by forever questioning the reality of our online culture. The land of the hyper-real begins when people forget that a telephone only conveys the illusion of being within speaking distance of another person and a computer conference only conveys the illusion of a town hall meeting. It's when we forget about the illusion that the trouble begins. When the technology itself grows powerful enough to make the illusions increasingly realistic, as the Net promises to do within the next ten to twenty years, the necessity for continuing to question reality grows even more acute.

What should those of us who believe in the democratizing potential of virtual communities do about the technological critics? I believe we should invite them to the table and help them see the flaws in our dreams, the bugs in our designs. I believe we should study what the historians and social scientists have to say about the illusions and power shifts that accompanied the diffusion of previous technologies. CMC and technology in general has real limits; it's best to continue to listen to those who understand the limits, even as we continue to explore the technologies' positive capabilities. Failing to fall under the spell of the 'rhetoric of the technological sublime,' actively questioning and examining social assumptions about the effects of new technologies, reminding ourselves that electronic communication has powerful illusory capabilities, are all good steps to take to prevent disasters.

If electronic democracy is to succeed, however, in the face of all the obstacles, activists must do more than avoid mistakes. Those who would use computer networks as political tools must go forward and actively apply their theories to more and different kinds of communities. If there is a last good hope, a bulwark against the hyper-reality of Baudrillard or Forster, it will come from a new way of looking at technology. Instead of falling under the spell of a sales pitch, or rejecting new technologies as instruments of illusion, we need to look closely at new technologies and ask how they can help build stronger, more humane communities – and ask how they might be obstacles to that goal. The late 1990s may eventually be seen in retrospect as a narrow window of historical opportunity, when people either acted or failed to act effectively to regain control over communications technologies. Armed with knowledge, guided by a clear, human-centered vision, governed by a commitment to civil discourse, we the citizens hold the key levers at a pivotal time. What happens next is largely up to us.

References

Baudrillard, J. 1988: *Selected writings*, ed. Mark Poster. Stanford, Calif.: Stanford University Press.

Bentham, J. 1843: *Works*, vol. 4, ed. J. Bowring. Edinburgh: William Tait.

Carey, J. 1989: The mythos of the electronic revolution. In *Communication as culture: essays on media and society*. Winchester, Mass.: Unwin Hyman.

Debord, G. 1992: *Comments on the society of the spectacle*. London: Verso.

Elshtain, J. B. 1982: Interactive TV – democracy and the QUBE tube. *The Nation*, 7–14 August, p. 108.

Foucault, M. 1977: *Discipline and punish: the birth of the prison*. New York: Pantheon.

Habermas, J. 1984: *The theory of communicative action*, vol 1, *Reason and the rationalization of society*. Boston, Mass.: Beacon Press.

Lipnack, J. and Stamps, J. 1982: *Networking: the first report and directory*. New York: Doubleday.

Marx, G. 1990: Privacy and technology. *The World and I*, September.

Postman, N. 1985: *Amusing ourselves to death: public discourse in the age of show business*. New York: Viking Penguin.

Robins, K. and Webster, K. 1988 Cybernetic capitalism: information, technology, everyday life. In Mosco, V. and Wasko, J. (eds.), *The political economy of information*. Madison, Wis.: The University of Wisconsin Press.

Vallee, J. 1982: *The network revolution: confessions of a computer scientist*. Berkeley, Calif.: And/Or Press.

Winner, L. 1986: *The whale and the reactor*. Chicago, Ill.: University of Chicago Press.

Questions

1   Rheingold refers to Postman's comments (see 'Further reading' below) that television has replaced genuine argument and reasoned discussion in the public sphere with fast cuts, special effects and sound bites. To what degree do you feel that this accusation accurately reflects political broadcasts and campaigns in Britain and/or America?

2   To what extent do you think that Bentham's concept of a Panopticon can be applied to the new communication technology 'revolution'? What particular surveillance or monitoring techniques might be said to be extensions of the panopticon model?

3   In addition to Habermas' formalisation of the public sphere and Foucault's development of Bentham's panoptic model, Rheingold also introduces two other important concepts from two of the leading French social writers of recent times: Debord's 'society of the spectacle' and Baudrillard's notion of 'hyper-reality'. From your reading of this extract, what is your understanding of these two concepts and their relation to media and cultural institutions and processes of power and democracy?

4   Do you think that Rheingold's rather pessimistic view is justified? In your view, do new communications technologies (including surveillance technologies) liberate or restrain?

Further reading

Dahlgren, P. 1995: *Television and the public sphere: citizenship, democracy and the media*. London: Sage.

Dovey, J. (ed.) 1996: *Fractal dreams: new media in social context*. London: Lawrence & Wishart.

Gandy, O. 1993: *The panoptic sort*. Oxford: Westview Press.

Postman, N. 1985: *Amusing ourselves to death: public discourse in the age of show business*. New York: Viking Penguin.

Silverstone, R. and Hirsch, E. 1992: *Consuming technologies: media and information in domestic spaces*. London: Routledge.

Webster, F. 1995: *Theories of the information society*. London: Routledge.

37

Postmodernism and Popular Culture
Dominic Strinati

From *Sociology Review*, 1(4), 2–7 (April 1992)

In this reading Strinati provides a useful account of the ways in which the term 'postmod-ernism' has been used to describe and analyse central aspects of contemporary culture and social life. He believes that some academic disciplines have traditionally used the term in such a way as to make it confusing and abstruse to others, and his aim is to dispel some of the mystique surrounding it.

Having outlined some of the distinguishing features which characterise postmodernism, Strinati highlights some particular examples of the 'postmodern' from the fields of architec-ture, cinema, television, advertising and pop music, which serve to illustrate exactly what it is to be 'postmodern' and how it can be distinguished from that which went before, i.e. modernism. Finally, he considers some of the reasons for the emergence of post-modernism at this particular historical, political and cultural juncture. In doing so he under-lines a theme which runs throughout this article and indeed this entire section: that is, the involvement and centrality of media, global communications systems and technological change in the construction of the postmodern condition.

In September 1989 the London *Evening Standard's* colour magazine con-tained an article on the 'postmodernisation' of many of the high-rise tower blocks of council flats built in London in the 1960s. It even displayed a page of cut-outs of things like classically designed roofs and entrance halls, decora-tive façades and ornate balconies, conifers, and so on, to allow readers to make their own 'Po-Mo tower blocks'. The point of the article was to show how the streamlined and uniform high rises, built in part as a result of the inspiration of modernist architecture in the 1960s, are now being postmod-ernised by the addition of new entrance halls and so on, or merely by being repainted in striking primary colours. The criticisms made by Prince Charles of the modernist architectural models for the new extension to the National Gallery led to the brief being given to an American firm of self-consciously postmodern architects, architects who have indeed been leading lights in the emergence of postmodern architecture. More recently, a character in the radio soap opera *The Archers* described a work of art as being 'very postmodern', while an advertisement for an alcoholic drink caricatured an art critic on TV identifying a painting by a postmodern artist, the painting in question being really the stain of a drink accidently knocked onto a blank canvas.

The fact that examples like these can be found on a purely casual basis suggests that the idea of postmodernism may have some importance. But it has been academic disciplines like Cultural Studies, English, Philosophy and Sociology which have encouraged its use and discussion. Here, however, it has usually been assessed in an abstract rather than a concrete way, and in a language which seems to be designed to put off (and exclude?) all but the most initiated, obstinate or foolhardy. What I therefore want to do in this article is to present a clear account of what I think postmodernism is about. I will confine my discussion to popular culture, for it is here in my view that postmodernism has had most impact.

What is postmodernism?

The following list of distinguishing features is by no means exhaustive, though each of them nonetheless characterises postmodernism.

(1) **The breakdown of the distinction between culture and society** Post-modernism is said to refer to a condition in which this distinction no longer holds. The idea is that popular cultural signs and media images increasingly dominate our sense of reality, and the way we define ourselves and the world around us. Postmodernism tries to come to terms with, and understand, a media-saturated society. The mass media, for example, were once thought of as holding up a mirror to, and thereby reflecting, a wider social reality. Now that reality is only definable in terms of the surface reflections of that mirror. It is no longer even a question of distortion since the term implies that there is a reality, outside the surface simulations of the media, which can be distorted, and this is precisely what is at issue.

It is equally difficult to distinguish the economy from popular culture since consumption – what we buy and what determines what we buy – is increasingly influenced by popular culture. Consumption is increasingly about popular culture; it has a greater and greater part to play in deciding what we buy and why we buy it. For example, we watch more and more films because of the extended ownership of VCRs, and advertising, which makes increasing use of popular cultural references, plays a more important role in deciding what we will buy.

(2) **An emphasis on style at the expense of substance and content** It follows from the first point that in a postmodern world, surfaces and style must become more important and evoke in their turn a kind of 'designer ideology'. Neville Brody, a designer for, amongst other things, the magazines *The Face* and *Arena*, has said that when people shop in supermarkets they are as interested, if not more interested, in buying the packaging and design of the goods on sale as the goods themselves. We therefore increasingly consume *images* and *signs* for their own sake. This is evident in popular culture itself when it said that surface and style, what things look like,

the playfulness and the joke for-jokes-sake character of much TV and many films and records, are beginning to predominate at the expense of content, substance and meaning, such that quality like intrinsic and artistic merit, seriousness, authenticity, realism, intellectual depth and strong narratives tend to be undermined.

(3) **The breakdown of the distinction between high culture (art) and popular culture** It follows on from the last point that as far as postmodern culture is concerned everything is up for grabs to be included as a joke, reference or quotation in the eclectic play of styles, simulation and surfaces. If popular cultural signs and media images are taking over in defining our sense of reality, and if this means the style takes precedence over content, then any meaningful distinction between art and popular culture can no longer be maintained. There are no longer any criteria which can do the job properly.

The artist Andy Warhol's multi-imaged print of Leonardo Da Vinci's famous painting *The Mona Lisa*, echoing an argument of Walter Benjamin and an earlier jokey version of the same painting by Marcel Duchamp, is a case in point. The print shows that the uniqueness, the artistic aura, of the *Mona Lisa* is destroyed by its infinite reproducibility through the silk screen printing techniques employed by Warhol, and is turned instead into a joke – the print's title is 'Thirty are better than one'. This point is enhanced by the fact that Warhol was renowned for his prints of famous popular cultural icons like Marilyn Monroe and Elvis Presley as well as of everyday consumer items like tins of Campbell's soup, Coca-Cola bottles, and dollar bills.

One aspect of this process is that art becomes increasingly integrated into the economy both because it is used to encourage people to consume through the expanded role it plays in advertising and because it becomes a commercial good in its own right: in the postmodern world, art is about consumption. Another aspect is that postmodern popular culture refuses to respect the pretensions and distinctiveness of art anyway so that crossovers between the two, and the blurring of any difference between them, becomes more and more the norm.

(4) **Confusions over time and space** The title and the narratives of the *Back to the Future* films capture this point fairly well. It is argued that contemporary and future compressions and focusing of time and space have led to increasing confusions and incoherence in our sense of space and time, in our maps of the places where we live, and our ideas about the 'times' in terms of which we organise our lives. The growing immediacy of world space and time resulting from the dominance of the media – we know what is going on in the Middle East, in so far as we are permitted to know what is going on, more or less as it happens, and we can be present, via TV, at the release of Nelson Mandela or at a worldwide Band Aid con-

cert – means that our previously unified and coherent ideas about space and time begin to be undermined and subject to distortions and confusions. Rapid international flows of capital, money, information, communications, and so on, disrupt the linear unities of time and the established distances of geographical space. Because of the speed and scope of modern mass communications, because of the relative ease and rapidity with which people and information can travel, time and space become less stable and comprehensible, more confused, more incoherent, more disunified.

Postmodern popular culture is thus seen to encapsulate, accentuate and reflect these confusions and distortions; it is no longer so likely to embody coherent senses of space or time. Try to identify the locations used in some pop videos, the linear narratives of some recent films, the times and spaces crossed in a typical evening of TV viewing, and you will get some idea of what is being argued. Postmodern popular culture is a culture *sans frontières*, outside history.

(5) **The decline of the 'meta-narratives'**   This sense of a loss of history as a continuous, linear narrative gives some indication of the idea that in a postmodern world so-called 'meta-narratives' are in decline. Consider also how we usually think of history and then recount the plot of any *Back to the Future* film in the same terms, using the concept of linear time, and then compare this complexity with earlier science fiction accounts of time travel. Postmodernism is sceptical of any absolute, universal and all-embracing claim to knowledge and argues that theories or doctrines which make such claims are increasingly open to criticism, contestation and doubt. It is thus becoming increasingly difficult for people to organise and interpret their lives in the light of 'meta-narratives'. Postmodernism is particularly critical of the 'meta-narrative' of Marxism and the claims it makes to absolute truth, as it is of any theory which tries to read a pattern of progress into history, but other 'meta-narratives' which can be cited include religion and science, or what we might like to call 'Big Science'.

The consequence of the above points is that postmodernism rejects the claims of any theory to absolute knowledge or of any social practice to universal validity. So, for example, on the one hand, there are movements in the natural or hard sciences away from deterministic and absolute 'meta-narratives' towards more contingent and probabilistic claims to the truth, while on the other hand, people appear to be moving away from the 'meta-narrative' of life-long, monogamous marriage towards a series of discrete if still monogamous 'relationships'. Just as postmodernism is about the loss of a sense of the unity of space and time, so it is about the loss (which it does not really regret) of the unity and certainty of knowledge. This point is clearly less important at first glance to developments in popular culture, but the increasingly disparate, cross-referencing, and collage-like character of the latter does draw inspiration from the absence or decline of 'meta-narratives'.

Signs of postmodern popular culture

I now want to look more closely at some examples of popular culture in order to show how certain signs of the emergence of postmodernism may be detected.

Architecture

This is a very good example to refer to because during the 20th century it has been influenced by architects who have self-consciously defined themselves as 'modernist' or 'postmodernist', and these terms have been used explicitly about contemporary buildings. Modernism in architecture, which first emerged fully in the 1920s, based itself upon a radical rejection of all previous forms of architecture, and argued that buildings and architecture had to be created anew according to rational and scientific principles. Functionality and efficiency have become its hallmarks as have high rise, streamlined and glass and concrete structures, since it sought to reflect, celebrate and entrench the dynamism of industrial modernity through the rational, scientific and technical construction of built space. The modernist architect knew what was best for people and became another hero (yes, hero) of the industrial age.

Postmodernism in architecture rejects totally this 'meta-narrative'. Fictionality and playfulness are its hallmarks as are highly ornate, diversely structured and highly coloured buildings, which mix styles from different historical periods in almost random and eclectic fashions. Postmodernism turns buildings into celebrations of style and surface, using architecture to make jokes about built space, as with Philip Johnson's Grandfather Clock shaped building for AT&T in New York, Adolph Loos's roman column design for the *Chicago Tribune*, or Richard Rogers's Lloyd's building in the City of London where things like lifts and pipes which are usually inside are instead deliberately displayed on the outside of the building. Rather than build or design according to rational scientific principles, postmodern architecture is said to proceed according to the context in which the building is to be placed, and to mix together classical (e.g. ancient Rome or Greece) and vernacular (signs and icons drawn from popular culture) styles. It thus embraces cultural definitions and the superiority of style, bringing together ideas and forms from different times and places. It rejects both the privileged 'meta-narrative' of modernist architecture, and the distinction between classical and modernist architecture as art and vernacular architecture as popular culture. Las Vegas has therefore been seen as both an exemplar and an inspiration for postmodern architecture.

Cinema

The most obvious examples of postmodern films are those which emphasise style, visual look and appeal, at the expense of content, character, narrative and comment – films like *Dick Tracey* or *9½ Weeks*. But to concentrate only on those films which deliberately sell themselves on their surface qualities obscures the other things which are going on in contemporary cinema. The series of films directed and produced by Steven Spielberg and his associates like *Indiana Jones* and *Back to the Future* are also cited as examples of postmodern films since their major points of reference, and the sources they most frequently invoke, are earlier forms of popular culture like cartoons, science fiction and the 'Saturday morning movie house' adventure series that people of Spielberg's generation would have been brought up on. Critics likewise point to the fact that they appear to stress spectacle, especially their technical sophistication and wizardry, and the helter-skelter pursuit of action rather than the convolutions and nuances of clever plotting and character development. Sometimes it is argued that the narrative demands of classical realism or premodernism are being increasingly ignored by postmodern cinema. The *Back to the Future* series and other films like *Brazil* are equally postmodern because of the way they are based on confusions over, and distortions of, time and space. Others like *Roger Rabbit* are seen to be postmodern because of their deliberate use of distinct genres; in this case the genres are technically as well as culturally distinct – the cartoon strip and the detective story.

One very good example to think of is *Blade Runner*. The architectural style of this film, about Los Angeles in the early part of the 21st century, clearly mixes different periods – the buildings which house the major corporation have lighting characteristic of contemporary skyscrapers but the overall look of ancient temples, while 'street talk' consists of words and phrases taken from a whole range of distinct languages. These architectural and linguistic confusions add to a slippery sense of time since we appear to be in the past, the present and the future at the same time. It is a science fiction film which is not obviously futuristic in its style or look. This effect is accentuated in two ways. First, the 'non-human humans' in the film are not robots, mechanical and modernistically conceived machines, but almost perfect simulations of human beings which are called replicants. Second, the genre of the film is not clear. It has been defined as a science fiction film, but it is equally defined for us as a detective film: the hero has many of the character traits we associate with the 'tough-guy' policeman or private eye, and his voice-over which relates the plot draws upon the idioms and tone of *film noir*.

Television

It has been suggested that TV itself is a postmodern medium since, in its regular daily and night-time flows of images and information, it merely splices together bits and pieces from elsewhere, constructing itself on the basis of collage techniques and surface simulations. Equally, there are a number of instructive examples of TV programmes which we can look at. One interesting case is the series *Thirtysomething* which concerns the domestic and work problems confronting a group of middle-class Americans living in Philadelphia. The group is important in any case as far as postmodernism is concerned because it contains occupations, particularly advertising, which have been seen as key creators of postmodern popular culture. The series seems to be a more or less straightforward soap opera, although in a series format, about the trials and tribulations of being middle class and thirty-something.

But what distinguishes it, what makes it different, are the interjections of fantasy/nightmare sequences, sequences drawn from popular culture which are nothing at all to do with the conventions of narrative realism. One character, an advertising copywriter who wants to become a serious novelist, goes to an evening writing class and has his attempts to write seriously parodied in a sequence of imaginary situations drawn from popular culture. Another character has her anxieties about video-dating pilloried in a dream sequence in which her friends confirm her worst fears by haranguing her on a sadistic TV game show. In the series, popular culture becomes the form through which episodes unfold.

A favourite example, however, is the police/crime series *Miami Vice*. Its construction on the basis of style and surface is fairly clear: its executive producer, Michael Mann, when asked once about the main rule he worked to when making the programme replied, 'no earth tones'. As a police series it is carefully designed visually in terms of colour, locations and camera set-ups. When it first came out in America, one critical response was to say 'this doesn't look like Television', a reference to the way it seemed more in keeping with the grander and more stylistic and adventurous conventions of cinema rather than the more cosy and intimate routines of TV. It is also clearly distinguished from the grim and grit realism of series like *Hill Street Blues* by its very resistance to the visual and aural conventions of both TV and realism.

This visual appeal has been as crucial to the series as the designer clothes worn by the detectives Crockett and Tubbs, and the imaginative day and night-time look and feel of Miami. The visual pleasures derived from style and 'look' – locations, settings, people, clothes, interiors, the city – have been a crucial motivation in the making and appreciation of the series. The use of an obtrusive pop and rock music sound track adds to these pleasures, providing a commentary and counterpoint to the action, while also representing a radical departure for the cop show. More than this, it has not so much rejected narrative as such but rather has parodied the established conventions of the genre: situations which should give rise to suspense like the holding of hostages can be dealt with summarily while the bad guys, when shot, always jump at least two feet in the air. It is equally very self-conscious about popular culture more generally and incorporates it and quotes from it extensively, quite apart from the use it makes of music and famous guest stars. A TV director wanting to make a film about the work of the Miami Vice police says he'll give it a *film noir* look, a point often made about the series itself. One character is told not to forget her 'sub-text'. The Italian gangster film is sometimes parodied by over-exaggerated and excessively stylised references to things like the demands of family loyalty and the cooking of fettuccine in just the right way, which work precisely because they are exaggerated and stylised. And one episode is a virtual remake and update of the western *High Noon*.

Advertising

Once upon a time advertisements were supposed to be about telling us how good, useful and essential a product was. Now they say less and less about the product directly, and are more concerned with sending up or parodying advertising itself by citing other ads and by using references drawn from popular culture. And this is what the postmodernising of ads is about. Advertising has, of course, always been seen as a superficial and empty exercise, more involved with surface and style and other trivial things than anything else. But the point at issue here is the changing content and tone of advertising, the move away from the simple and direct selling of a product on the basis of its value, whatever the visual style and trick effects used. Now, though the intention is still to sell, the postmodern effect is achieved by seemingly overt efforts within advertising to undermine this purpose. Once Guinness was good for us. Now all we see is an actor drinking a glass without any positive suggestions as to why we should drink it too. Postmodern ads are more concerned with the cultural representations of the ad itself as opposed to any reference it may have to the qualities of the product outside the ad, a trend in keeping with the collapse of 'reality' into popular culture. An emphasis on style and surface, the look of the ad, its clever quotations from popular culture and art (the use of Pavarotti singing 'Nessun Dorma' as an advert, a signal, for the BBC's televising of the World Cup is in this sense no accident), its mini-sagas, its jokey quips at the expense of advertising itself, all become traits of postmodern advertising.

Pop music

The recent history of popular music has been marked by a trend towards the direct and explicit mixing, or 'infiltration', of styles and genres of music in very direct and self-conscious ways. These have ranged from the straightforward stitching together or remixing of already recorded songs or records from the same or different eras on the same record to the quoting and 'tasting' of distinct musics, sounds and instruments in order to create and recreate new sub- and pan-cultural identities. Jive Bunny and the Master Mixers with their eclectic succession of old swing and rock 'n' roll records are the best example of the former, while the mixing and collage-like constructions of reggae sound systems, rap, house, hip hop and so on, are one of the best examples of the latter, though it is necessary to also include in this category the so-called 'art rock' musical innovations and styles of groups like Talking Heads and performers like Laurie Anderson.

Whatever the respective musical and political merits of these new departures, they are seen to share postmodern concerns: with collage, pastiche and quotation, with the mixing of styles which remain musically distinctive, with the random and selective pasting together of different musics and styles, with the rejection of divisions between serious and fun music, and with the attack on the notion of rock as serious artistic music which merits the high cultural accolade of the respectful concert – a trend started by punk. Clearly, these judgements seem more applicable to some types of contemporary mixing of musics than others, and it certainly ignores the political importance of the collage of sounds and styles associated with the reconstructions of black music. Jive Bunny, in this respect, appear to personify more closely postmodernist arguments since their records, sequences of already recorded tracks, derive from an eclectic ransacking of the history of pop with no attempt to go beyond the simulations and dissimulations this involves. What we have is a series of old records held together only by the fact that they can be danced to, lacking any recognition of the need to develop new musical forms and styles, which again differentiates it from newer forms of black music and from 'art rock'.

This postmodern music is contrasted with 'modernist' popular music which did attempt to fashion new and distinct forms out of previous styles. So what was distinctive about rock 'n' roll, for example, was not the fact that it too borrowed from, and based itself upon, already existing musics, but that it used these musics to construct something new, something which had not been heard before. Rock 'n' roll, as is commonly accepted, arose out of the cross-cutting influences exerted by country and western, on the one hand, and urban rhythm 'n' blues, on the other. The result was not, it is argued, a postmodern amalgam in which country and rhythm 'n' blues stayed recognisably the same, but a novel and original fusion – rock 'n' roll. Similarly with soul music. This is said to have arisen out of the coming together of gospel and blues within black American culture. Yet again the consequence was something strikingly new and different, not a sound which maintained the relatively separate identities of gospel and blues. Put very simply and crudely, the transition between modernism and postmodernism in pop music can be seen to be associated with the movement from rock 'n' roll in the late 1950s, and the Beatles and Tamla Motown in the 1960s, to Jive Bunny, Music Mixing and 'art rock' in the late 1980s. The very notable differences amongst the latter in terms of their originality, nihilism, cynicism and politics should indicate to us how there is more than one politics of postmodernism.

The emergence of postmodernism

If, as I have tried to indicate, there are signs that a postmodern popular culture might be emerging, then why should this be the case? I will now look at some of the answers to this question.

The rise of a media-saturated society

Postmodernism as a term represents one attempt to come to terms with the predominance of the mass media in contemporary societies. The fact that postmodernism refers to the increasing importance of mass media definitions of reality – that reality is what the media say it is, namely a question of images and surfaces – is related quite simply to the rise of modern forms of mass communications and the associated proliferation of popular cultural signs. The fact that for whatever reason the mass media have become so central to communication and information flows within and between modern societies, and that consequently the popular culture broadcast and promoted has come increasingly to define and channel everyday life in these societies, has given rise to the characteristic features of postmodernism described above. The world has come to consist of media screens and cultural surfaces – TVs, VDUs, videos, computers, computer games, personal stereos, ads, theme parks, shopping malls, 'fictitious capital' or credit, money as a set of figures on a luminous display screen – and these have become part and parcel of the trends towards postmodern popular culture. Postmodernism in this perspective is therefore an argument about the mass media taking over – a cultural invasion of our senses which knows no boundaries, only surfaces.

New middle-class occupations and consumer markets

The increasing importance of consumption and of the media in modern societies has given rise to new occupations – or changed the role and character of older ones – associated with the need to encourage people to consume in more frequent, more constant and more varied ways. This has been called the 'symbolic work of producing needs', and 'the symbolic violence needed to create and sell new products'. These occupational groups are involved in both creating and manipulating or 'playing with' cultural symbols and media images so as to get consumers to buy things, even those which they don't necessarily need but feel they ought to have because this is integral to the consumer ethic.

In view of this argument we can not only account for the growing occupational importance of advertising, marketing, design, architecture and media professions like journalism and programme production more generally, but also those occupations like social work, therapists of one kind or another, teachers, lecturers, and so on, associated with wider definitions of psychological and personal need and fulfilment. For all these occupations are thought to be the most important groups involved in establishing the taste patterns for the rest of the society, in exercising some influence over other people's lifestyles and values or ideologies (while expressing their own as well) – over what they buy, watch, listen to, wear, eat, drink, furnish their houses and flats with, etc., and how they evaluate or make sense of these things to other people and to themselves. Thus these new middle-class occupations, catering for the variety of consumer markets which already exist or which are in the process of being formed, are crucial to the development of the postmodern popular culture which we have made available to us, that culture common to the society as a whole.

The erosion of collective and personal identities

The struggle to create and sustain an identity is also significant in this regard because it has been suggested that this is something which it is becoming more and more difficult to do: the postmodernists, for example, may try to forge new identities and new cultures, but because they end up with postmodernism their efforts are doomed to failure. This has been singled out as another reason for the emergence of postmodernism. It has sometimes been referred to as the 'de-centring of identity' or the 'de-centred subject', but this sounds painful, and I prefer the gentler notion of erosion. However, it has to be pointed out that we are not talking about a simple process of decline but the fragmentation of a limited but dependable set of coherent identities into a diverse and unstable series of competing identities. Also, there is obviously no clear dividing line between the two forms of identity, and the personal derives in some part from the collective anyway. But to use both terms perhaps gives some idea of what is at stake.

The first part of this argument points to what it sees as the gradual disappearance of the traditional, long-standing and once legitimate frames of reference in terms of which people could define themselves and their place in society, and so feel relatively secure in their personal and collective identities. These traditional sources of identity – social class, the extended and nuclear family, local communities, the 'neighbourhood', religion, trade unions, the nation state – are said to be in decline as a result of tendencies in modern capitalism towards increasingly rapid rates of economic, geographical, political and cultural change. 'Economic globalisation' (the tendency for the making, financing and selling of goods and services to take place without regard to, and above and beyond, the realities of the nation state and local communities), for example, is seen as an important reason for the gradual erosion of these traditional identities as well as contributing to the declining significance of social class and trade unionism. The growing disruption of time and space associated with the pace and scale of contemporary changes also leads to the disintegration of traditional institutional sources of personal and collective identity like the family and religion.

The second half of this argument points to the fact that nothing emerges to take the place of the traditional sources of personal and collective identity. No new forms or institutions, no new ideas or beliefs, can now serve to give people a secure and coherent sense of themselves, their place and time, nor are there any longer legitimate and acceptable ways by which they can define themselves to themselves and to others. Those features of contemporary societies which are novel, which appear to be original or which represent the prominence of previously secondary trends, like the insatiable demands of consumerism or the superficial surfaces of the TV screen, do not offer viable, satisfactory and worthwhile alternatives to the traditional bases of identity.

In fact, these new trends are part of the problem rather than the solution. They encourage superficiality rather than substance, cynicism rather than belief, the thirst for constant change rather than the security of stable traditions, the desires of the moment rather than the truths of history. Consumerism, moreover, by its very nature is seen to encourage an anarchic individualism which runs riot with the possibilities for solid and stable identities. Television, which makes us what we are, which brings the world rushing into our living rooms, has similar effects because it is, at one and the same time, individualistic and universal; it speaks to everyone and to no one in particular. And, like the increasing confusions over space and time, it prevents new collective bases for personal identity from being formed. People relate to TV as individuals watching everything, and TV relates back to people as individuals and/or as abstract parts of a universal order, in both instances ignoring, eroding and fragmenting any wider collectivities to which people might belong and any legitimate ideas in which they might believe. TV is a constant flow which switches back and forth between different surface images; it is not a genuine source of identity and belief. But, and this is the crux of the argument, since there is nothing else, nowhere else, but the TV screen, people have no alternative (except perhaps to go to the shops) but to succumb to the TV image, to lose themselves in the blankness of the screen and the hollowness of its icons.

Although this should sound familiar particularly to students of the media, it does link up with the very first defining feature of postmodernism I identified above. It is the consequence of the argument that the mass media and popular culture, cultural images and media surfaces, come to form the only frames of reference available for the construction of identities. But equally unlike the old disappearing traditional identities, they are not up to the task, and so the surfaces and playfulness, the anti-hierarchies, the 'end' of history, the collapse of the academy and art, the postmodern media-based popular culture, start to take over.

This theory of postmodernism is not without its problems, but they will have to be discussed at a future date.

Questions

1   In the readings of Section 1 (particularly Williams, reading 2) we identified that *modern* society has been characterised as one of mass production and mass consumption. In your view, how have these – and other key identifying features of modern society – been challenged and replaced by *postmodern* trends and influences?

> 2 Think of some of your own examples of the 'postmodern' under each of Strinati's
>   five categories (architecture, cinema, TV, advertising and pop music). Are there
>   any other examples of postmodernism which you can think of which fall outside
>   these categories?
> 3 In what ways might your local shopping mall or a theme park such as
>   Disneyland, for example, be said to be 'postmodern'?

Further reading

Connor, S. 1989: *Postmodernist culture*. Oxford: Basil Blackwell.

Featherstone, M. 1991: *Consumer culture and postmodernism*. London: Sage.

Fiske, J. 1991: Postmodernism and television. In Curran, J. and Gurevitch, M. (eds.), *Mass media and society*. London: Edward Arnold.

Harvey, D. 1990: *The postmodern condition*. Oxford: Basil Blackwell.

Hebdige, D. 1989: New times: after the masses. In *Marxism Today*, January 1989.

Jencks, C. 1986: *What is post-modernism?* London: Academy Editions.

Kellner, D. 1995: *Media culture*. London: Routledge.

McRobbie, A. 1994: *Postmodernism and popular culture*. London: Routledge.

A revised version of this article appears in Strinati, D. 1995: *An introduction to theories of popular culture*. London: Routledge.

38

Higher Education, Training and Cultural Industries: A Working Partnership
Ian Connell and Geoff Hurd

Paper presented to the 1988 International Television Studies Conference, London

In the final two readings in this book we have selected material which examines the state of Media Studies itself, its direction and 'health' in the late 1990s. In the extract which follows, a paper presented to a conference in 1988, Connell and Hurd argue a strong and provocative case for the realignment of the aims and orientation of Media Studies and related fields of cultural and communication research, teaching and enquiry. The paper – but not, alas, the debate which it stimulated at the conference – is reproduced here in its entirety, and it begins by advancing a critique of the formation and directions taken by Media and Cultural Studies from the 1970s onwards. Central to this reassessment is the argument that media education and cultural analysis have been disabled by a mythology of critique and a misdirection or misplacement of purpose. For Connell and Hurd, the rapid changes which have occurred in cultural markets since the 1980s have opened opportunities for what they see as a new relationship, a partnership between educators and the media and cultural industries. In part, such opportunities reside, it is argued, in the research and analysis of the new consumer and media markets themselves and their unfolding dynamics and openings. Furthermore, it is suggested that Media Studies and media education should also be geared to enabling more positive, enterprising and realistic forms of creative intervention in those markets and their development.

The paper issues a number of key challenges which strike at major tensions in the heart of contemporary Media and Cultural Studies. Central to these are the dilemmas associated with claims related to vocationalism and vocational training. In close and related formation are questions concerning the nature and purpose of Media Studies and its principal rationales in current and future climates of development.

1. Introduction

This paper makes a case for orienting educational and training in cultural, communication and media studies towards preparing students to work effectively and successfully within one or other branch of the cultural industries. It does so for a number of reasons. There are, first of all, a series of educational reasons. Critical studies of culture have been allowed to become too remote from both the changed and changing needs of students as well as those within mainstream cultural industries. They have remained critical and deconstructive too long and at the expense of developing constructive approaches. We find it difficult to see in what ways they equip students to become responsive and useful cultural practitioners. This remoteness is especially felt in the Polytechnics as they become increasingly distinct from the traditions of higher education evolved within the universities.

In the second place, we would argue that critical studies of culture and cultural industry have at their core a certain mythology which seriously misrepresents contemporary cultural affairs, and thus makes it unnecessarily difficult to devise a strategy for productive intervention in them. It is a mythology which exaggerates the powers of organised cultural industry to attract, hold and meet the needs of potential consumers. It erroneously proposes that as commercial enterprises, cultural firms are inherently conservative institutions. It mistakenly assumes, moreover, that in its paranational phase cultural industry is exploiting and using communication technologies to create increasingly homogenised and undemocratic cultural formations. It is a misrepresentative mythology in the final analysis because it typically presents cultural industries as only capable of negative socio-cultural effects, rarely, if ever, positive ones. Where positive potential is identified, it is regarded either as a product of the critical work enacted on the text or as a symptom of the cultural industries' occasional inability to secure their ideological, political, or cultural boundaries. There is no account of positive effects which proceeds from an understanding of the dynamic and logic of these industries as such.

2. Educational problems

It is our contention that this is due to the fact that much critical education within the area of cultural, communication or media studies has rarely had in its sight the everyday business of conceiving, producing, and distributing cultural products and services. There are still very few studies of cultural industries, and those that exist are mostly concerned with TV production departments. Critical education is generally disdainful of any approaches that adopt industry based perspectives and presents itself as standing apart from or above such pragmatic matters. In short, such education is not very informative about how cultural enterprises are run on a day-to-day basis, the problems involved, nor about how they are, or might be, solved. Perversely, we have devised ways of teaching about culture which ignore the defining features of the processes of production, distribution and consumption.

In place of a close familiarity, critical approaches have mythologised the affairs of cultural enterprises, and all but rendered themselves irrelevant, by sticking to a series of largely untested assumptions about their character, power and effects. Instead of preparing students to explore systematically and methodically the character and potential of organised cultural industry, critical cultural studies implicitly and explicitly attempts to warn them off with stories of commercial contamination and constraints, as well as of an inherent ideological and cultural conservatism. By and large, the education and training it provides qualifies students only for remote reflection and detached criticism. Instead of creating opportunities whereby they can be equipped to enter one or other branch of cultural industry and operate there in ways sensitive to the needs of consumers, it prepares them to become intellectual *emarginati* pursuing fanciful visions of lost cultural freedoms.

From around November 1983, when the National Advisory Board for Local Authority Education began to use 'graduate employment' as one of its criteria for assessing courses, and initiated a distinction between preferred and non-preferred areas of work in Public Sector Higher Education, this critical distantiation has been more and more difficult to sustain. Yet, there are still those courses which have remained rock solid in eschewing any move to vocationalism. They do not really perceive it as a problem that not many of 'their' graduates find employment in the mainstream sectors of cultural industry, which are after all 'ideological apparatuses' dedicated to perpetuating things as they are.

There have been some reluctant and therefore superficial attempts to come to terms with the 'new reality'. Courses that were once 'essentially theoretical' have gone some way to becoming vocational. But the shift to a more vocational orientation has been done opportunistically, often only because it appears necessary to provide cover for their critical concerns. To stress skilling and training is seen as something of a sell-out to Thatcherite views on education, an undermining of the ancient principles of disinterested inquiry or of a commitment to the socialist transformation of society. Even worse, as in the dismissal of technicism, skilling is sometimes perceived as beneath the critical intellectual's dignity – the sort of thing best confined to *sub-degree* level work.

There is in our view little point in debating whether or not we should accept vocationalism as opposed to alternative notions of liberal education. We would argue that liberal education was always vocational for those of the right class, gender and race positions, equipped with the appropriate cultural capitals. What is *positive* (and we do indeed think there is something positive) about current emphases on vocationalism is that they establish some of the conditions for designing courses that: increase and widen access to higher education; are sensitive to the cultural competences with which students are already possessed; are simultaneously responsive to their developing needs; and make available to those now beginning to enter higher education, genuinely useful intellectual skills.

To deal with these problems, we are proposing, and have committed our own institutions to developing, a new phase of curriculum innovation aimed at producing a range of courses which do not rest the study of culture and cultural industries on the assumptions of a critical base shaped by the intellectual projects of cultural theory. This would not involve abandoning theoretically informed, empirical study. On the contrary, and in distinction to the critical phase in which ethereal speculation ruled, this would be encouraged. The new phase would be enabling. It would provide for the methodical study of the cultural conditions of communication and of the potential of various technology-based media. In addition it would encourage the systematic study, without prejudice, of cultural industry and of its potential for producing goods and services which meet the needs of consumers.

3. The critical mythology of cultural industry

As we said at the outset, critical studies have fashioned a certain mythology which seriously misrepresents cultural industries and thus makes it difficult to devise a strategy for productive intervention in them. Instead the development of an independent, experimental sector has been proposed. Yet after many years and the investment of considerable public funds, such a sector remains at best embryonic. Younger groups coming to cultural production for the first time have chosen to pursue a very different course.

The picture the mythology paints of cultural industry can be quickly sketched. At the centre of cultural affairs stand the media of communication, TV most prominently. In the modern world, people seem not to have to hand the resources by which they can make coherent sense of their lives for themselves. This is done for them by the media products they consume and upon which they gradually come to depend. Of course, the coherence made available through these products is flawed and limiting. It is saturated with misrepresentations of every conceivable kind. This is presented as an inevitable consequence of the commercial organisation and imperatives of cultural production.

We would not wish to deny that there are problems with the ways in which cultural industry is organised and managed, nor that there are problems with the products and services they offer to consumers. We do not think, however, that these problems can be traced to the commercial character of much cultural activity.

4. An alternative view

We use the term 'cultural industries' to refer to those firms whose job it is to conceive cultural products and services, and in addition market and distribute them to consumers. Whatever the products and services, their use value cannot be considered as independent of their consumption under quite specific sets of circumstances. In other words the same cultural product or service can be put to several different uses, not all of which may have been anticipated in the production or provision of the service or product. In other words, they are position goods and services that are marketed in terms of added value. That added value may be present as information, education, entertainment, thoughts, emotions, identities, or even entire structures of feeling and thought. It can come in several (material) forms of varying degrees of complexity: TV programmes, leisure activities, more fleetingly, sometimes, as styles in clothing and music, in the design of publicity and information materials.

For us the term is charged with the recognition that 'culture' – the organised business of making sense, of communicating and educating – is indisputably just that: a business, a mature and dynamic capitalist enterprise, like any other in many important respects. Hardly an earth-shattering observation you might think. Nevertheless, the extent to which the business aspects of organised cultural production are overlooked or dismissed is noteworthy. It is not possible, nor for that matter desirable, to recreate some distant moment in the past that can now, because it is distant, be romanticised as a moment of commercially untrammalled cultural activity. The commercial cultural industries are here to stay!

We would also stress their dynamic character. Like any other capitalist enterprise, cultural industry is intrinsically revolutionary. It cannot stand still. The logic of economic necessity compels it to be innovatory or to cease to exist if it cannot be. Arguably, economic necessity has always operated more ruthlessly in this sphere than in any other. Certainly the existence of cultural enterprises seems more precarious than others.

The drive to renovation can ride roughshod over the needs of specific groups, that's for sure. There is the permanent danger that if groups do not have the economic wherewithal they are threatened with cultural disenfranchisement. The exploitation of newer communication technologies and the development of older ones has undoubtedly put the needs of transnational financial and business organisations before those of domestic consumers in particular nations. There are now bodies of consumers at the national and domestic levels who echo the complaints that Third World countries have long made about the uneven development of communication and, more generally, cultural industries. We would concede that much and more to the critics of the commercial sectors. What cannot be conceded, however, is the notion that the course of development cultural organisations have elected to follow is inevitable, irreversible or inexorable.

5. Developments within and the potential of cultural industry

Cultural marketing operates in an environment in which the identification of unfilled needs, and their translation into economically backed demand for specific goods and services, is a complex and unstable process. This has proved to be especially so in the volume, or so-called mass, market though there is also some evidence of instability in the more specialist sectors, targeted upon high income groups with considerable access to acceptable stocks of cultural capital. Nevertheless, in somewhat rough and ready terms, higher income consumers, whose lifestyle patterns closely resemble those of cultural producers, have been able to enjoy well-designed clothing, domestic and work environments, good quality education, information and entertainment services, while lower income groups (for most practical purposes lumped together as an undifferentiated mess), until recently, have had to make do with a limited range of choice, short-lived goods and poorer quality services.

The long-standing distinction between the 'mass' and 'quality' markets has been disrupted in the course of recent years, and a whole series of classifications of consumers and assumptions about their needs have had to be revised as a consequence. This has been largely overlooked by critical reseachers who have instead expressed concern that the increasing privatisation of cultural industries, and communication industries in particular, will simultaneously strengthen dominant social groups' control of subordinate ones and rob the latter of much-needed information, and to a lesser extent, entertainment services.

According to the critical case, political-economic logic of development within cultural industry is such that the already culturally deprived must become more so as attention is concentrated upon those with reasonable and available disposable income – in the main young professional families and 'empty-nesters'. The consequences for those already unemployed and those who will soon join them may well prove severe and prolonged. With incomes that barely permit survival, they will become as well, progressively, culturally impoverished. They will not be able to meet the first requirement of access to cultural goods and services. In short, they will not be able to buy outright, or acquire by means of credit, any of the items of technology upon which cultural interaction seems set to depend.

As the ability to pay becomes a primary requirement of access to cultural goods and services, the chasm between the 'haves' and 'have nots' will widen dramatically. The latter, it seems, will just be overlooked. Without employment, without anything but the meanest and most grudgingly given forms of welfare support, they will also be left to fend for themselves as best they can without even the cold and lumpy comforts of distraction that public sector broadcasting is up to providing. The best of critical writing on these matters will suggest that none of these outcomes need be regarded as the consequences of malevolent intent. Instead, it will therein be presented as the inevitable outcome of unbridling commercialism within cultural affairs.

Needless to say, this is not the vision promoted by the publicists of cultural industries. The critical case presents a picture in which the upper echelons, entrepreneurs and economic planners within cultural industries have a clear sense of direction and purpose. The clarity and certainty attributed to them is, however, not always immediately evident in their own attempts at forecasting.

If we take as an example the broadcasting and communications sectors, we find there that the development of certain alternatives to TV broadcasting has not been as rapid nor as dramatic in its impact as many were prepared to predict at the turn of the decade. The day when systems based upon cable, satellites, and/or a combination of the two are commonplace still seems remote. Certainly the progress of the existing cable stations has been halting and the date of the first Direct Broadcasting by Satellite (DBS) transmissions is constantly being put back. Nevertheless, there have been a number of developments that have shaken confidence in the capacity of traditional TV broadcasting to deliver effective services.

Throughout this decade there have been various reports from academic and advertising agency researchers of increasing disenchantment with the existing TV services. In essence several surveys have found there are many segments of the potential audience who no longer perceive TV to be the pleasurable entertainment service it once was. Certainly there appear not to be many who would without qualification report finding watching TV satisfying.

There is evidence also that despite increases in the hours of transmission, the average amount of time devoted to TV viewing has remained fairly constant in the UK since the early 1960s. There have been, in addition, at least two major scares since 1980 about significantly reduced peak-time ratings, and a continuing concern that the ready availability of remote pads has resulted in diminishing attendance to TV advertising. The increasing domestic availability and use of two or more sets, of VCRs and of home computers have contributed to making a stereotype of the notion that a family groups around the TV set of an evening and watches till it goes to bed.

We have taken TV here as an example of this tendency towards fragmentation and diversification. But, while developing unevenly across the various sectors of cultural industry, it is a general feature of the application of new technology on the supply side in combination with rising levels of disposable income for those in employment (but not low pay occupations), changes in patterns of employment, as well as other socio-cultural or 'lifestyle' patterns.

In shorthand, we are entering what has been dubbed a 'post-Fordist' era in which production, marketing and distribution is increasingly targeted on smaller market segments, in which techniques based upon new technologies and sub-contracting allow greater and cost-efficient flexibility. At the same time, consumer fragmentation throws into relief the uncertainties and volatilities surrounding cultural production and marketing. The shift towards market segmentation is not the outcome of a manipulative and evermore effective attempt to control and exploit consumers: on the contrary, it is a response by the industries to the problems they face in coming to terms with structural changes in the ways in which socio-economic groupings are being recomposed around new identities and needs. Just as the history of cultural theory can be written as a history of the deconstruction of monolithic concepts such as 'class' and 'the economic' in favour of complex and shifting articulations of social, economic, political, sexual, racial and psychological variables, so the history of marketing over the last ten years can be written in parallel terms: the move away from Economic and Social Group Classification towards segmentation, 'lifestyle' classification, psychodynamics and so on. And just as cultural theorists remind readers of the complexity and difficulty inherent in understanding the contemporary world, so do some – the best – market researchers today. This opens up a range of new opportunities.

The expansion of markets is not now achieved by attempting to increase the number of consumers for the same limited range of products and services. Instead, there is a move to increase the range of services and products and to clearly differentiate, and even in some instances, customise or individuate them. These products and services can in some instances be brought on to the market well below the price thresholds that would disbar many from lower income groups. (Patterns of consumption have anyway been quite complicated for some time. Those on lower incomes do not always go for the bargain basement products the mean spirited think they ought to go for.) Mass markets in future, contrary to what many have proposed about the course of cultural development, will not be homogeneous but rather differentiated aggregates of segments. That said, we would prefer to view such development as the continuation of a trend rather than an utterly new departure. Simple notions of massified, homogeneous markets have always been inadequate.

Against this background, there has been much talk at conferences and in the trade press and journals of a new ball game. The new ball game is seen to be about targeting and addressing smaller groups of consumers. It is also about coming to terms with and responding to consumers who are seen to have newly acquired powers. We would want to suggest these powers are not as new as those involved in cultural industry seem to think.

Returning to our example of television, running through their discussions of the future is the view that audiences will be given a choice. And in the exercise of that choice, they will assume an active role in the marketing scene because a growing proportion of disposable incomes will be spent directly on the choice itself, rather than indirectly through advertising or the payment of a compulsory licence fee. In other words, in the case of communication there will be a period where items of hardware will be acquired to enable choices to be made. This will be combined with payment for 'software' – programmes and services.

Gary Davey, writing a few years ago on the development of Sky Channel, observed that

> the economics of modern commercial television instill a discipline that in itself represents the ultimate media democracy. It is simple; if the viewer does not like what we offer, we go broke. We believe passionately in this discipline of viewer choice as the fundamental principle of commercial television. Whether it be through marketing costs in the supermarket, national taxes or licence fees, the money that pays for our various television systems comes out of the consumer's pocket ... The viewer casts a vote every day at the touch of a button, but in an environment where the consumer's response does not matter, it is a significant gesture that goes unnoticed, or worse, ignored.

At least so far as TV broadcasting is concerned, then, consumer choice is a significant gesture that can no longer be ignored.

Now of course the notion of the active consumer has long been an aspect of commercial rhetoric. Those commercially involved in cultural industry have often presented themselves as attempting to understand and respond to consumer needs and demands to an extent which has virtually obscured their attempts to create, stimulate and control them. Consumers have often been presented by cultural entrepreneurs as a fickle lot. Just when they thought they had them taped, their preferences changed and the product bombed. The history of most branches of cultural industry is littered with such examples. This perception has in recent years taken on a new force. There are not many in the industry who will now say that they can invariably predict the ways in which consumer demand will develop. To the entrepreneurs and the researchers they hire, a fair amount of fundamental re-thinking seems necessary. The environment in which they work is no longer stable, no longer as predictable as it once seemed to them.

In response to developments within the consumer electronics market, there is a feeling that 'significant gestures' were allowed to go unnoticed too long. After all, what did expressions of dissatisfaction really matter when for most people over the last quarter of a century all that was domestically available to them were the schedules of three or four channels. Consumers might say they would prefer to go out or do something else than watch TV. What else was there for them to do, however? What else could they do if they had families and all the additional domestic costs this entails? They might complain, in surveys of their attitudes, that there were too many repeats and/or too many imports from the States. Nevertheless all such material had healthy TV ratings (TVRs). Even when they began to say that watching TV was not very entertaining, what did it matter? The majority still had little else they could do.

The situation changed dramatically when the availability of peripherals, the expansion of other sectors of leisure outside the home, and not least ever-more ready access to credit gave more and more people, especially those with the most attractive disposable incomes, alternatives.

The sense one gets from the cultural industries' published views is that there is, as yet, little confidence across all the sectors that the significance of the gestures of the last few years have been fully understood. If, for example, as some have acknowledged, the most readily accessible and constant audience for traditional TV is drawn from the old, ageing and poor, what can be done to generate income from advertisers? Chase younger, more affluent viewers? Who and where are they? With what sort of programmes? Can cultural firms afford economically to ignore, in the longer term, those who will remain on low incomes?

At the same time, confidence in the intelligence provided by research agencies has also suffered a knock or two. There are those who wonder whether, despite all the sophisticated statistical manipulation of data, the quality of the results and of the surveys by which data are generated in the first instance is all that it should be. Some have argued that the established research procedures and the long-standing classificatory schemes and procedures are simply not up to the job of exploring how potential consumers of cultural goods and services go about selecting and using them. In fact, it does not seem unreasonable to suggest that through the early 1980s a crisis of confidence in the established research procedures emerged, a crisis which has not yet been resolved.

From the point of view of the entrepreneurs and planners of the cultural industries, then, the current situation feels like it has slipped out of their control. It has become confusing and challenging. Moreover, it feels to them as if there are no clear and unambiguous strategies available to re-establish that control. What has not yet fully registered with them is that they may now not re-establish the degree of control they once could. Cultural production and consumption has entered a new, and rather more socialised phase. Contrary to many of our colleagues we do not believe the future will see consumers' needs and wishes entirely subordinated to those pale reflections of them which the decision-makers of cultural industries choose to fulfil. Many more, and increasing numbers of consumers, will become involved in the process of conceiving and executing cultural projects. Between producers and consumers relations of dependency and of mutual determination will, of necessity, be recognised as such.

The alternative view of development has a number of consequences which can be summarised as follows:

(a) As potential markets further distinguish themselves, and it becomes palpably clear that the notion of a 'mass' market is erroneous and misleading, new kinds of market research will be required. This requirement has already been recognised, and it would be fair to say that the research industry is now in a state of flux as new research systems are tried and tested. For the foreseeable future, 'qualitative' research is likely to assume greater importance.

(b) There will be a growing demand within the cultural industries for certain areas of skill, and for those who can offer some combination of administrative, managerial, financial, research and communication skills. It is worth noting that demand for those with certain skills in the area of 'qualitative cultural' research is already showing signs of increasing.

(c) As the gradual disintegration of established markets progresses and the degree of socialisation of cultural production increases, cultural industry will present opportunities to develop new areas of cultural enterprise that are more aware of and responsive to consumers' needs and wishes.

6. Education, training and cultural industry

We should perhaps attempt to go even further in justifying our arguments for curriculum initiatives by tackling whether or not an attempt should be made to educate and train people to take on the challenges presented by the developments we have referred to and sketched above. Suffice it to say that these developments in our view have, in deconstructing established markets and approaches to them, opened up opportunities that cannot be ignored. If the course of future events within the sphere of cultural industry is to be democratically controlled, we simple cannot afford not to educate and train people to deliver constructive alternatives.

What is the measure of the problem that educationists face? We believe this is indicated by Jonathan Gershuny when commenting upon future prospects for employment and leisure in light of the availability of new items of technology. He has made the following pertinent observations:

> The basic technologies are all in existence, but they do not yet constitute a new technological paradigm. There is a crucial infrastructure missing. Most obvious is the lack of appropriate telecommunications infrastructure ... We are also short of the technical skills and, most important, the forms of organisational know-how, and the appropriate social institutions for such development. A new technological paradigm needs in addition to the material infrastructure, a new cultural infrastructure to support the new forms of production and consumption. (Jonathan Gershuny, 'The Leisure Principle', *New Society*, 13. 2. 1987)

If we are to develop a clear sense of what we wish these novel paradigms to be and if we are to realise their developments, there must be a rather different direction to the study of culture and communication from that which has held more or less unchallenged sway to the present.

In the UK there is, as yet, no significant educational and training initiative toward cultural industry from within this field. Though there has been in the technological area, it should be clear enough from quoting Gershuny that it is our view that they cannot go it alone. Some joint educational projects are required if the material and cultural infrastructures are to be jointly developed. On the 'cultural side', there are a growing number of uncoordinated courses aimed at specific aspects of specific industries – for example, in tourism or leisure and amenities management. Beyond this, on the one hand, there are a range of art and design courses, principally (though rather haphazardly) supplying production and technical staff, and on the other, various business study courses which may include some reference to particular aspects of cultural industry.

In general terms, what we think is required are courses motivated by the major socio-cultural opportunities and problems we have sketched above. Such courses would take the concept of cultural industry *in general* and provide opportunities to acquire that range of skills, competences, and knowledge appropriate to future employment and subsequent training in any specific job function within a given branch of that industry. There are common elements which should be grouped around the tasks that follow from our initial definition – the *conceiving of cultural products and services and the successful marketing of them to consumers* – and, in addition, from the need to come up with appropriate responses to those transformations of cultural industry that are currently being carried out.

We would not envisage any further, significant expansion of education and training in creative and production skills, though we are concerned that 'creative' courses should provide more opportunities to students to study methodically the cultural potential of their chosen media as well as to acquire a greater understanding of the business and market environment in which production occurs.

Other reasons for recommending such a direction have to do with the changing composition of entrants to further and higher education and the diversification there of educational provision. We note, first, the considerable demand for courses which appear to study one or more branches of cultural industry. There are no signs that this is falling off, or that it will do so in the coming years, among the youngest of those able to enter post-school education. There are, however, signs that among those who are older and/or unconventionally qualified entrants demand for such courses is growing. There is a steady growth of 'open access' routes, along which one can now find many courses dedicated to communication and cultural studies. Indeed the expansion of such courses there has been more rapid than on the GCSE and 'A' level route. However they arrive, in our experience, they come with developed expectations that whatever else courses do, they will be vocationally relevant and useful.

In such an environment, much changed since the early 1970s when the first wave of cultural and communication studies was being established, there is an opportunity, not just to conform to the 'new vocationalism', but to explore and extend its possibilities.

Questions

1 Summarise what you take to be the main criticism of Media, Cultural and Communication Studies courses advanced in the paper. How do they relate to aspects of your own educational career to date?

2 The paper argues for a new working partnership to exist between media educators and media industries. What is this argument based upon? What kinds of skills and education should be provided for what kinds of current and future occupational entry?

3 In the light of the issues posed in this reading, how would you make out a case for – or against – your current course of study?

Further reading

Agger, B. 1992: *Cultural Studies as Critical Theory* London: The Falmer Press.

Alvarado, M., Gutch, R. and Wollen, T. 1987: *Learning the Media*. London: Macmillan.

Buckingham, D., Grahame, J. and Sefton-Green, J. 1995: *Making Media: Practical Production in Media Education*. London: English and Media Centre.

Curran, J. 1990: The new revisionism in mass communication research: a reappraisal. *European Journal of Communication* 5, 135–64.

Ferguson, B. 1981: Practical work and pedagogy. *Screen Education* No. 38, Spring

Lusted, D. ed. 1991: *The Media Studies Book*. London: Comedia/Routledge.

Masterman, L. 1985: *Teaching the Media*. London: Comedia.

Orton, L. 1996: *Media Courses UK*. London: BFI.

O'Sullivan, T., Dutton, B. and Rayner, P. 1994: *Studying the Media: An Introduction*. London: Arnold.

Pungente, J.J. and Biernatzki, W.E. 1993: Media education. *Communication Research Trends* 13, No. 2 (part I).

SCCCMSHE (Standing Conference for Cultural Communication and Media Studies in Higher Education) 1996: Advisory brochure produced by Dr. Martin Barker, c/o University of West England, Bristol.

39

Media Studies and the 'Knowledge Problem'
John Corner

From *Screen* 36(2), 147–55 (Summer 1995)

One might look for a conclusion in this, the last reading in the book. This final extract sustains the focus on the current state of Media Studies, but it does so less by single-minded attention to the dilemmas of vocationalism central to the previous extract. Instead, Corner provides a broader evaluative overview of what he calls the 'knowledge problems' facing the field of Media Studies as a whole. In this valuable and timely analysis, he begins by contextualising the relatively recent formation and development of Media Studies. This is achieved by tracing the intellectual and educational currents and contexts which have been influential in the shaping of the field. In particular he notes the contradictions associated with the combination of literary forms of criticism with sociology, the impact and legacies of Marxism, of feminist research, ethnography and postmodernism. In this account, Corner does devote some consideration to the issue of vocationalism, but this is one of a number of rather intractable problems or challenges which, he suggests, face the field of Media Studies in its current trajectory. In the final stages of his analysis, Corner argues for the need to reassess and to debate the importance and viability of the concept of ideology in negotiating and developing future research in the field. As he suggests, Media Studies is perhaps best understood as a multidisciplinary field of enquiry and research which, in common with many other disciplines, needs to rethink its position in the 1990s. This process of rethinking has to match and keep up with the rapid developments in media industries and communication technologies themselves, which threaten to overtake and to leave Media Studies behind.

I want to suggest that both teaching and research in Media Studies have a 'knowledge problem' which has recently become more visible and troublesome as a result of uncertainties, tensions and regroupings in the area. All fields of study have knowledge problems of course, and although they vary in the amount of self-consciousness they display about them and their degree of engagement with them, there has been a broad shift towards paying them more attention and making such attention an explicit and central part of study discourse.

Knowledge problems concern what it is that academic inquiries seek to find out, and the kinds and quality of data and of explanatory relations which particular ideas and methods might be expected to produce. In response to them, disciplines not only engage more closely and innovatively with questions of conceptualization and technique, but also develop a reflexive, sceptical sense of their own knowledge production and its vulnerabilities. From some perspectives, this sense may be considered radical, in that those who have it are placed in the position of professional doubters rather than practitioners in relation to the disciplinary project. One effect of the sweep of postmodernist thinking in the humanities and social sciences has undoubtedly been to encourage this latter tendency.

The distinctive character of the problem – or better, the set of problems – which confronts Media Studies is due partly to the history of this field, partly to the very diverse nature of its object of study, and partly to the particularly ambitious form of interdisciplinarity to which this diversity tends to lead. I am talking primarily about upper case 'Media Studies', a singular noun designating an institutionalized, self-concious grouping, rather than lower case 'media studies' (studies of the media), a plural designation referencing a broader range of work distributed across humanities, social science and even technological fields.

Media Studies needs to engage with expressive form, social action and social structure. It needs to explore the political and psychological determinants and consequences of media processes, as well as their discursive and technological means. To do this, it necessarily either draws on directly, or else 'shadows' with varying degrees of explicitness, concepts and methods developed in the primary disciplines. How far does it thus constitute itself as a unified project of inquiry? Or how far does it become an *aggregation* of inquiries, which are placed into tighter or looser relationships of contiguity with each other and have greater or lesser levels of mutual awareness and tolerance? If the latter were the case, one would expect the knowledge problems themselves to be an aggregation of the problems confronted by the constitutive disciplines. They would not therefore be addressable at a general level since the field would have no general discourse of inquiry within whose terms it could consider itself. But without such a discourse, what constitutes 'core knowledge' in the area for the purposes of teaching and research training programmes? Such a question has become a very real one for many course planners and others active in institutionalizing (and, indeed, variously assessing) Media Studies.

The particular academic configuration of British Media Studies today is primarily the product of two things. First of all, a certain combination of arts and social science approaches to the analysis of the media, institutionalized in the design and teaching of the interdisciplinary Communication Studies courses of the 1970s. Secondly, the legacy of Structuralist Marxism. North American, Australian, other European and Scandinavian versions of Media Studies vary in the resemblance they bear to this formative mix, but the relationships and interconnections are never quite the same.

The arts and social science combination in Media Studies is essentially one which brings together 'criticism' and 'sociology' as modes of academic knowing. Criticism is a mode privileging *individual percipience*, in which knowledge is the product of sustained analytic attention and intellection. It has a direct, informing link with 'opinion' and, indeed, it is 'opinion' rather than 'theory' as such which is its main generator of ideas. That such opinion is, by definition, subjective (often deeply and self-declaredly so) is by no means a drawback to the larger project of intercritical activity (characterized as 'debate'). In literary studies, for instance, a powerfully rendered account of a major novelist may be prized for its 'originality', precisely for the way in which it differs from the interpretations made by other people. In order for it to be acclaimed thus, it is necessary for some assumptions to be made about what is 'there' to be the object of such 'insight', yet this does not mean that the new interpretation has then to be established as dominant in relation to others. Critical knowledge does not contain truth claims requiring supercession or even superordination of this kind.

Sociology, on the other hand, in its classic and defining empirical project, is essentially a mode privileging *method*. However cautiously it relates itself to (or distances itself from) natural science paradigms, the production of knowledge is normatively regulated by the use of procedures which are explicit, in line with intersubjective agreements on validity (even if these are only partial) and able to be replicated by those who wish to 'test' findings. What the procedures produce is, first of all, 'data', and then an analysis and explanation of this data. Both data and the analyses which are made of it (the two should not be confused) have a very different status from 'criticism'. It can be recognized, without thereby succumbing to positivism, that data carries claims to objectivity, however much these claims are qualified by recognition of both the imprecision of the research tools and the 'constructional' dimension of the research concepts themselves. Analytical constructs used in asking questions of data and in attempting to answer them have objectivity obligations as a consequence, however tentative and conditional the honouring of these may be. *Theories*, here, are mostly explanatory propositions, with considerable attention being paid to those which are open to forms of empirical testing and, then, to the bodies of analysed evidence which result.

It is part of the intellectual history of Media Studies in Britain that it was formed, not only out of an increasing recognition of the media's political and cultural significance, but out of a dissatisfaction with both the perceived inability of literary-style analyses of the media to go beyond their textualist boundaries, and the perceived inability of conventional social science to engage with the complexity of meaning-making forms. The most influential perspective for this formation was Cultural Studies, the history of which has recently received a good deal of attention, at the same time as the field of study which is covered by the term has become increasingly subject to institutional variation and plain opportunism.[1] Initially an attempt to push out English Studies (meaning and value) to the point where an interconnection with the Sociology of Culture (structure and practice) could be established, Cultural Studies was soon displaying increased autonomy as an academic (but, at this stage, exclusively research-related) project. The warrant for this autonomy came neither from literary analysis nor social science. It was taken primarily from Structuralist Marxism, with the Althusserian perspective on ideology and the social formation as its 'sociology', and semiotics (taken largely from Barthes and Eco) as its 'criticism'. In relation to this broad framing, a Film Studies continued to exist and develop, deriving much of its own identity from its earlier literary and art historical connections. In some institutions this was extended to become Film and Television Studies in a manner which usually (and not unproblematically) continued to privilege the Film Study agenda. The broadest, and perhaps earliest, grouping for undergraduate work was Communication Studies, which often had a strong Cultural Studies element and a core of media work, but which also tended to draw on a wider range of arts and social science perspectives on communication, including those from psychology. The rapid development of Communication Studies in the mid 1970s was in part prompted by the need for polytechnics to design attractive interdisciplinary courses which could draw on a considerable range of staff interests. Alongside these interrelated projects, there remained a Sociology of Mass Communications (updated as Media Sociology), which was still the dominant category by which the systematic study of the media had an *international* identity.[2] Moreover, despite the growth in Cultural Studies approaches, some of the best research work done in the 1970s was done from within one version or another of a sociological problematic, though very few of the researchers were at that time involved in the construction of a field at undergraduate level.[3]

If the most significant question for any academic venture concerns the kind of things it wants to find out, then the Media Studies produced within the framework of Cultural Studies worked with an exceptional directness of purpose. It wanted to find out how the media worked to achieve an effective level of ideological closure on contemporary consciousness in a situation of capitalist development where direct control at the point of production and/or consumption was admitted to be far from total. This was its defining problematic, and engagement with it (initially brilliantly suggestive but, one might argue, increasingly prone to repetition and self-confirmation) produced a strongly theoretical-critical discourse linked to a subtle, typologically elaborate scheme for investigating textuality.[4] The conventional body of social scientific analysis was often deemed to be unsuitable for the new task, being irredeemably flawed both in aims and methods. A conflation of 'empiricism' with 'empirical' too frequently provided the project with that *Other* against which it defined itself epistemologically and politically, reinforcing the tendency to circular reasoning. This did not stop substantial internal rifting on questions of theorization however, quite apart from sustained and cogent criticism from researchers whose own application of Marxism suggested the need for primary attention to be given to the 'political economy' of the media and who strongly contested the increasingly hermetic terms of Cultural Studies' attention to ideology.[5]

The knowledge problems affecting current Media Studies have therefore to be understood, first of all as ones relating to a non-unified field in which the very different modes of criticism and sociology have been brought together but, in general, *not integrated*. Indeed, it might be said that in many studies and on many syllabuses they have not yet fully come to terms with each other. Secondly, they have to be understood in relation to a formative period of development which was dominated by debates centred on a Marxist-structuralist paradigm, in which a comprehensive materialist account of media power, independent of non-Marxist modes of study, was seen not only to be in the offing but, indeed, to be already under refinement.

Perhaps more than any other area of institutionalized inquiry, this foundational version of Media Studies has, in effect, been left marooned within the new post-Marxist, post-Structuralist context for political and social debate. One has to be careful with the inflections of 'post' here. It is not useful to talk of 'the collapse of Marxism' in a way which primarily refers to the dissolution of Communist Eastern Europe but which then smuggles in assumptions about the 'collapse' of Marxist theory and analysis. Nevertheless, materialist theory itself has had to adapt (sometimes quite radically) to changed historical circumstances and to an intellectual context increasingly aggressive towards it. Even the terms of the Political Economy perspective, robustly historical and empirical though they were, have received adjustment and may well receive more.[6] Theories of ideology have virtually disappeared from the media research agenda altogether, though not from the undergraduate syllabus, where their gloomy diagnoses are sometimes to be found in bizarre combination with the cheerful populism which has become a more recent perspectival option.

An often ambivalent, running engagement with postmodernism has provided Media Studies with one avenue for the continuation, beyond Structuralist Marxism, of a semi-autonomous (and self-defining) critical discourse. However, there has been a discernible shift away from unifying high theory, a shift which has revealed more strongly the character of Media Studies as a divided field, running an art and social science project together in ways which are often uneasy. No longer able to afford itself the luxury of devising its problems to fit already available solutions, it has been returned to a re-engagement with those discipline-based knowledge problems from which it once aspired to autonomy. Nowhere is this more true than in the rise of ethnography (both productional and consumptional) as a mode of media inquiry. Although an element in early Cultural Studies, it was only in the mid-1980s that ethnography started to become a defining approach, displacing textual analysis in research if not in teaching. Ethnography initially promised a way of looking at ideological reproduction 'from the sharp end',[7] but it quite quickly modulated into being the methodological correlative of a more general shift from a primary concern with researching 'power' to either an emphasis on 'resistance' or an expanded, contextualizing interest in the way in which media meanings are articulated within the terms of the 'everyday', the multiple lifeworlds of society. As researchers soon became aware, whilst it could be innovatively applied to the researching of media meanings, ethnographic inquiry carried with it a long history of methodological debate, both in sociology and anthropology. Indeed, many of the inquiries into audience interpretation which have been undertaken in the last decade are radically *mis*described as 'ethnography', since their relationship to researched subjects and to data is often very different from that of the broader tradition.[8] These inquiries often (and justifiably) have a particularity of research focus around mediated meanings which makes them, by comparison, 'narrow' and even 'shallow' in their specifically ethnographical engagement.

Ethnographic work has typically run into two related kinds of problem as an academic project. It can slip into *descriptivism*, rendering even thicker accounts of process but being unable to make any clear connection upwards to explanation because of a gravitational commitment to ground-level phenomena. It can also suffer from an *empiricism* whereby this commitment makes it lose sight of its own constructed, authorial character. In recent work, a third problem can be discerned – largely a product of postmodernist influence. This is an over-correction of empiricism where the self-consciousness of the researcher is raised to the point at which interest in the researcher-method-subject relationship begins to displace interest in the researched subject itself. The first and the third of these tendencies are now discernible within the new media ethnography.

Put simply, then, a post-Marxist Media Studies has been substantially shorn of those intellectual features which gave the field a degree of unity. It has been returned to a multiple knowledge problematic which draws extensively on the problems of established disciplines and then adds to them issues of combination and adaptation. Its general theories of ideological function, and the contexts of social formation and historical trajectory within which these were set, have been exposed to radical doubt (the recent upsurge of interest in the ideas of Anthony Giddens, whose conceptualizations of structure and agency have been receiving intensive debate in Sociology for well over a decade, is just one sign of current theoretical reorientation).[9] The mode of textual analysis around which a large part of the field organized itself – semiotics – has received a general theoretical questioning as well as increasingly being seen to fail in generating significant and original substantive analyses. The push out to 'ethnography', while it has produced some excellent work, is in grave danger of running into the doldrums as theoretical uncertainties reduce the consequentiality of its data or it becomes obsessed with its own authorialism.

There is yet another factor, an 'opportunity' carrying the possibility of 'threat', currently determining the shape of work under the Media Studies heading. This is the pull of vocationalism.[10] It would be hard to deny the mutual benefits of establishing a connection between study of the media and the acquisition of practitioner/professional skills. Many institutions have put considerable effort into making these connections work at the level of student experience. But too often, despite the claims about integration and complementarity in course documents, there has emerged the strongly dualistic language of 'theory' and 'practice', a language in which the whole project of academic inquiry is radically misdescribed as 'theory' and thereby pre-packaged for *potential* marginalization as a form of 'complementary study'. For if invited to allocate priorities between 'theory' and 'practice' in an educational world of increasing competition and scarce resources, what manager would not find the eminent soundness of the latter more attractive than the ethereal, not to say self-indulgent, ring of the former? To put it this way is to caricature the present situation, but many Media Studies departments could testify to the way in which what looked to be a splendid partnership between academia and the 'real world' can, when aided by certain committee decisions and nervousness over revenue, quite quickly turn into a relationship of domination, affecting resources, appointments, course development and careers. The emerging recipes for the expedient combination of academic and vocational goals will clearly exert a considerable influence on the mid-1990s identity of the area.

Such a view of Media Studies, facing a new and risky future situated rather uncertainly on the fringes of the social sciences (unlike Film Studies, it cannot situate itself primarily as an 'arts' project without a potentially fatal degree of contraction) might provoke several objections. Among these, it might be argued that the shaping influence of feminism and postmodernism upon the post-Marxist character of the field needs more attention.

Feminism has contributed important new ideas to the study of media processes, particularly to an understanding of the relationships between textuality and subjectivity. It has also produced an impressive range of new knowledge about the media and has considerably raised awareness of gender inequalities at all levels of the mediation process.[11] It is arguable, however, whether it has introduced wholly new *ways* of conducting research. Its conceptual and methodological innovations (and its valuable critique of existing practice) do not, on their own, seem to provide the basis for an adequate, 'internal' reconstruction of the field.

Postmodernism has become a quite central factor within the terms of much recent media analysis, but its weirdly dual status as both a *condition* to be debated (present or not? good or bad?) and as a *perspective* for reflecting on and analysing conditions, has made its influence more a matter of climactic change than intellectual renewal. It is tempting to regard 'it' (the singular entity is presumptuous) as being as much a symptom of current cultural shifts and intellectual blockages as a means of engaging with them.

Do the scale and complexity of these knowledge problems suggest that it would be best for the area to disaggregate itself into separate discipline interests? No. As a collective grouping for teaching and research activity around one of the major defining components of modern life, the category of Media Studies continues to be a valuable one. There is also a great deal of good and interesting work being done under the heading (certainly as much as, if not more than, within any other academic grouping of equivalent size) though it is being done from a range of different disciplinary backgrounds, using different concepts and methods and applying sometimes entirely different criteria about permissible forms of argument, about what constitutes 'evidence' and about the conventions for connecting propositions to data. In these circumstances, we need fewer rhetorical attempts at unification and at separate intellectual identity and a wider recognition of the lack of perspectival and methodological autonomy from the mainstream of international social studies which a post-Marxist Media Studies can claim. This means, among other things, recognizing a wider range of productive contexts for researching those questions of power, representation and subjectivity/identity which were so high on the 'autonomous' agenda although not always satisfactorily investigated within its terms. It means a re-engagement with general social theory and also a re-engagement with social research method at every point where the project seeks to produce something other than a discourse of 'criticism' (which it should also continue to do, exploring questions of form, value and response, whilst being very aware of what it is doing). It is important to note that these are not in any way conservative recommendations, fitting study of the media back, after a period of eclectic adventures, into the traditional and worthy frameworks of the disciplines. For it is clear that these frameworks and their associated methods have been fundamentally challenged at a number of points (by feminist research and by concepts of cultural process among other factors) and that hardly any social studies field has remained free of introspection, debate and change. But the project of social studies inquiry has not, as some would have it, collapsed into futility or terminal self-doubt, nor has it become indistinguishable from the various perspectives and procedures of the arts and humanities. Research on media and ideas about media processes need to be centrally introduced into its remaking and into its critical engagement with contemporary modernity.

In any reassessment of Media Studies, the question of how to think beyond 'ideology' is worth a measure of separate consideration. On its pivotal importance to the field as initially constituted (and therefore on the size of the hole its waning now leaves), I am fully with Christopher Williams in his recent attempt at a critical stock-taking.[12]

Williams wonders if it is not 'the case that ideology has become a hopelessly unusable term?' and finds that, indeed, 'repeated wielding of the clumsy club' has had a widespread deleterious influence.[13] Offering a more positive view of the future, he notes that it needs to be 'replaced' and, with quite extraordinary optimism, that 'this replacement need not, I think, be too difficult'.[14] In fact, what Williams subsequently says shows the sense of brisk remedy to be deceptive. First of all, he suggests that the concept of 'ideology' can be broadly equated with the idea of the 'social', but this would seem to be true of only the most loose and totemic of usages and hardly offers adequate 'replacement'. More indicatively, he goes on to suggest a wide variety of different conceptual alternatives, each relevant to different areas of inquiry, thus abandoning his idea of 'replacement' altogether since it was precisely the job of 'ideology' to unify ideas about meaning and power across the full range of expressive forms. Is there not more which needs rescuing from the debates about 'ideology' than Williams suggests? What the term points to is the way in which the legitimation of economic and political interests interconnects with the making of public meanings, often by way of the naturalization of the contingent. The focus on the links between representation and power, between the aesthetics and logics of signification and the forcefields of value and disposition within which subjectivities are developed, seems well worth maintaining, albeit in rethought terms. No shift to 'opinion' or 'attitude' or, following Williams' concern with textual form, to 'diction', 'expression' or 'convention' will keep a tight enough hold on the factors which need to be addressed *in their interarticulation*. Open argument about these issues, particularly as they appear (or not!) in a range of current research contexts is now, I agree with Williams, one of the most pressing requirements.

Media Studies is still a new arrival within the institutionalized orders of academic inquiry. Its house-style of boldness and disrespect, its eclecticism and its conceptualizing zeal have brought dividends in the context of the older, often evaluatively conservative, disciplines. But as many of these disciplines rethink themselves in the 1990s, the same qualities could quite easily work against its possibilities for steady self-assessment and for theoretical and methodological reconstruction as, precisely, a *multi*-disciplinary field of social research. Since the variety, intensity and importance of the media industries and their activities continue to increase, this would be both an academic and a political loss.

Notes

1. The major surveys include Graeme Turner, *British Cultural Studies: An Introduction* (London; Unwin Hyman, 1990): Patrick Bratlinger, *Crusoe's Footprint* (London; Routledge, 1990): and Jim McGuigan, *Cultural Populism* (London; Routledge, 1992).

2. A history of interrelated institutional and research developments in the late 1970s, particularly those relating to the course validations of the Council for National Academic Awards, would be useful. I merely offer a background sketch here. See also Alan Durant, 'Noises offscreen: could crisis of confidence be good for media studies?', *Screen* vol. 32, no. 4 (1991), pp. 407–28.

3. Apart from the continuing work of an older generation of social scientists, including Jay Blumler, Denis McQuail, Jeremy Tunstall and James Halloran, there was the work, among others, of Philip Schlesinger, Michael Tracey, Philip Elliott, Peter Golding and Graham Murdock.

4. Here, Hall's stencilled papers from the Birmingham Centre for Contemporary Cultural Studies were the single most influential publications, and often more theoretically cautious than selective quotation of the key formulations might suggest.

5. Graham Murdock and Peter Golding at the Leicester Centre for Mass Communication Research were chiefly identified with this position, following their article 'For a political economy of mass communications' in R. Miliband and J. Saville (eds), *The Sociaist Register 1973* (London: Merlin, 1973). As the Cultural Studies perspective increased in influence through the mid-1970s, the terms of their critique became stronger.

6. The continuing case for 'Political Economy' is updated in Peter Golding and Graham Murdock, 'Culture, communications and political economy' in J. Curran and M. Gurevitch, (eds), *Mass Media and Society* (London: Arnold, 1991). See also Nicholas Gamham, *Capitalism and Communications* (London: Sage, 1990), particularly his introductory essay, which as well as reflecting on recent theoretical developments also argues against those tendencies which 'cut the field off from the main stream of social science' (p. 2).

7. David Morley seems to have been the first to use the idea of 'ethnography' as an indication of the *kind* of approach required, in his highly original CCCS stencilled paper 'Reconceptualising the media audience' (1974).

8. These issues have been brought out more fully in Virginia Nightingale, 'What's ethnographic about ethnographic audience research?'. *Australian Journal of Communication* no. 16, (1969), pp. 50–63.

9. Giddens' ideas figure strongly in Graham Murdock's recent and useful survey of the media and modernity in 'Communications and the constitution of modernity'. *Media, Culture and Society*, vol. 15, no.4 (1993), 521–39.

10. This is commented on in Durant. 'could a crisis of confidence be good for media studies?'. Durant's polemical discussion engages with many important points concerning the development of media education, doing so from a position often close to the one I am outlining here. His own answer to his title question is 'yes, it could'.

11. See, for instance, the excellent appraisals in Liesbet van Zoonen, *Feminist Media Studies* (London: Sage, 1994).
12. Christopher Williams, 'After the classic, the classical and ideology: the differences of realism', *Screen* vol. 35, no.3 (1994), pp. 275–92. Williams sets out by appearing to take issue with an earlier piece of mine, but his only substantial complaint seems to be that I do not go as far as he would wish in my questioning of 1970s theory. See John Corner, 'Presumption as theory: "realism" in television studies', *Screen* vol.33, no.1 (1992), pp. 7–102.
13. Williams, 'After the classic, the classical and ideology', p. 276.
14. Williams, 'After the classic, the classical and ideology', p. 287.

Questions

1 Media Studies and its related disciplines frequently come in for criticism and derision (former Education Secretary, John Patten, famously described Media Studies as a 'cultural Disneyland for the weaker minded'). What are your views on such judgements? From your reading of the above two extracts, what would you surmise are the underlying reasons for such hostility (predominantly by MPs and journalists) and what are the key aims and objectives for media educators as we enter the next millennium?

2 In the light of the issues raised in the last two readings, how would you make out a case for – or against – your own current course of study?

Further reading
See 'Further reading' section in reading 38.

Index